THE TEXTILE READER

The cover art is a detail of the embroidered and pieced textile *Lenguaje* [*Language*] (2020), above, by the Argentine poet and artist Florencia Walfisch. Image courtesy of the artist and Galería Van Riel. Photographer: Daniel Duhau.

THE TEXTILE READER

**EDITED BY
JESSICA HEMMINGS**

2ND EDITION

BLOOMSBURY VISUAL ARTS
LONDON • NEW YORK • OXFORD • NEW DELHI • SYDNEY

BLOOMSBURY VISUAL ARTS
Bloomsbury Publishing Plc
50 Bedford Square, London, WC1B 3DP, UK
1385 Broadway, New York, NY 10018, USA
29 Earlsfort Terrace, Dublin 2, Ireland

BLOOMSBURY, BLOOMSBURY VISUAL ARTS and the Diana logo are trademarks of Bloomsbury Publishing Plc

First published in Great Britain by Berg 2012

This edition published by Bloomsbury Visual Arts 2023

Editor © Jessica Hemmings, 2023

Jessica Hemmings has asserted her right under the Copyright, Designs and Patents Act, 1988, to be identified as Editor of this work.

Cover image © Florencia Walfisch. Photographer: Daniel Duhau.

A catalogue record for this book is available from the British Library.

A catalog record for this book is available from the Library of Congress.

ISBN: HB: 978-1-3502-3985-2
PB: 978-1-3502-3984-5

Typeset by Deanta Global Publishing Services, Chennai, India
Printed and bound in India

To find out more about our authors and books visit www.bloomsbury.com and sign up for our newsletters.

CONTENTS

INTRODUCTION

Over a decade ago, I introduced the first edition of the *Textile Reader* with the acknowledgement that the writing compiled for the book was as concerned with *how* we write about textiles as it was interested in *what* we write about textiles. Selected content was intended to be eclectic rather than authoritative, in part out of my own discomfort with the possibility that the *Reader* may inadvertently contribute to building a textile canon that over time simplified and reduced, rather than expanded, readers' curiosity.

Editing the second edition has proven daunting work. Textile scholarship can no longer be described as 'emerging' as I wrote in 2012 and the sheer number of publications in the past decade has only made the task harder. Textile design now appears in more of the writing, as does a greater variety of geographies, albeit far from comprehensive. A number of new entries for the second edition are published in English translation for the first time from German, Russian and Spanish. This is an area of work that deserves continued attention if the anglophone dominance of academic scholarship is to genuinely be addressed. My sincere thanks to Liudmila Aliabieva, Lorna Dillon and Paulina Ortiz in particular for their recommendations of texts to consider for translation.

In truth, the opportunity to reconsider aspects of the first edition and the chance to rectify small errors that haunted perhaps few others than myself have instead given way to a realization that the first edition was far more flawed than I understood a decade ago. The content included here now represents the outcome of a number of factors. Pertinence of texts to neighbouring material is an editorial style I have continued, where possible, to preserve. Similarly, I have continued to set excerpts from novels and short stories, as well as poetry alongside more conventional academic writing. Structurally, the final section of this book has been reconfigured as 'community'. Otherwise, I have continued the difficult editorial decision to include only one example of writing from each contributor, in an effort to include the greatest number of voices.

Along the way, some entries have found their place under different themes than their placement in the first edition. The disproportionate copyright costs of some key texts in the first edition mean they no longer appear in the second edition. These absences reflect my inability to countenance the vast disparities in copyright fees demanded by some publishers. Much like the content, the second edition's further reading lists include less-well-known material that has come across my path. Continuing my aspiration for the eclectic rather than canonical, it is my hope these lists will be taken as a starting point for readers to also search out their own less familiar points of reference.

Kay Byrne has with patient tenacity and good humour undertaken the enormous administrative task of copyright clearance. While my own efforts as editor undoubtedly remain incomplete, I hope the content selected here will be taken as a representation of some of the voices that exist and some of the voices that are emerging in textile writing. The final content unashamedly remains a reflection of many things, not least of all my personal taste.

Jessica Hemmings
Professor of Craft
HDK-Valand, University of Gothenburg

PART ONE

TOUCH

PART INTRODUCTION

Common throughout the writing included in the first section of *The Textile Reader* is the acknowledgement that within the hierarchy of the senses, touch has long struggled for respect. But, as the writing here reveals, the hierarchies that have long relegated touch no longer enjoy such a tenacious hold. In this section, the voices of academics, artists, a curator and a fiction writer observe – but also challenge – the undervalued place touch.

A conference paper by Victoria Mitchell opens the section with discussion of the relationship between writing about textiles and making textiles. Mitchell recalls E. B. White's children's story *Charlotte's Web* and uses the seemingly innocent construction of words within the spider's web to begin a broader debate about what the construction of text and the construction of textiles share. Mitchell offers, 'the formative relationship between words and textiles alerts us to what I would like to call the textility of both thought and matter, a neologism which may be formative in minimising the separateness of the spheres within which text, textiles and *techne* might otherwise operate.'

An excerpt from T'ai Smith's book-length study of Bauhaus weavers follows. While the photographic image may seem to be a counterintuitive way to celebrate touch, Smith credits Otti Berger, a less well-known contemporary of Anni Albers, for her understanding of the importance of communicating woven texture optically through close-up photography. Elaine Igoe's writing similarly works to balance the importance of both touch and sight with a specific focus on the qualities and needs of textile design. Where Mitchell coined textility, Igoe writes of the 'textiley' as a quality familiar to those who work with textile design.

Two pieces of writing first developed for exhibition catalogues follow. Pennina Barnett shares with Mitchell an interest in the poetic voice of cloth, but also shares with Smith and Igoe a reluctance to separate the tactile from the optical. Barnett takes up the thinking of Michel Serres call for 'soft logics' and Gilles Deleuze's writing on the fold and suggests an approach to textile thinking that moves beyond binary hierarchies.

Catherine Harper's catalogue writing similarly names an interest in the potential of the textile to subvert power hierarchies. Speaking of Reko Sudo, the director of the textile company NUNO, Harper writes: 'I believe, moreover, that she consciously mobilises the act of seduction to reveal the unspoken (unspeakable), the unauthorised (authoritatively), the uncensored (without censure) in her liaisons with cloth.' Harper's experimental writing style adopts a hybrid voice that is part confessional and part critical to evoke the feeling of textiles experienced against the skin.

Karen Blixen (1885–1962), writing under the pen name Isak Dinesen, offers an example of fiction that can contribute to critical thinking about the textile. Dinesen's short story suggests the intimate place the textile occupies, while also offering the idea that the story can be at its most creative when details are left to the imagination. Here the textile is cast as a storyteller, referring to stains quite different in nature from those Jenni Sorkin evokes in the opening writing for the next section on memory.

The final entry in the first section on touch is part of a dialogue I had with Birgitta Nordström about her *Infant Wrapping Cloth Project*. From the metaphors and symbols evoked by many of the texts in this section, Nordström's project moves into the very literal realm of applied research. In the edited dialogue she describes the hand- and machine-woven blankets the project donates to Swedish maternity wards where women receive medical care for late-term abortions and miscarriages. As a harrowing example of touch, these textiles provide families with the option to hold lives which end before they begin.

1

TEXTILES, TEXT AND TECHNE (1997)

Victoria Mitchell

EDITOR'S INTRODUCTION

Victoria Mitchell is a Research Fellow at Norwich University of the Arts, UK. Anthropology, history, philosophy and critical theory often inform her wide-ranging research and writing about textiles. The essay 'Textiles, Text and Techne' opens this *Reader* by offering a map of writing about textiles in relation to textile making. The etymological links between text, textile and *techne* (Greek for craftsmanship or making with intention), as well as the distinct differences in the two ways of working, are acknowledged. Mitchell's writing begins with a reflection about the overlooked status of the maker as weaver-spider in *Charlotte's Web*. She then considers the significance of German-born Anni Albers's writing on textiles, as well as Albers's artistic practice with both cloth and graphic design, before returning to the etymological links shared by text and textile.

Mitchell's reminder that the one thing the written word can never do is to physically touch, in the most literal sense, applies to all the textiles that are of central concern to the writing included in this book. Mitchell foregrounds the importance of our sense of touch, explaining 'the privileging of words and the ocularcentrism of western culture can mask some of the sensibilities conveyed through textile practice', before acknowledging 'that making sense through the tactility of textiles has implications for perception in a wider sense'. Mitchell's ideas about the 'textility of both thought and matter' have been credited as influential to the thinking of British anthropologist Tim Ingold. Among many others, her recent publications include *The Material Culture of Basketry: Practice, Skill and Embodied Knowledge* (2020), co-edited with Stephanie Bunn.

Mitchell's essay, reprinted in full here, was first published twenty-five years ago, in conference proceedings edited by Tanya Harrod for 'Obscure Objects of Desire: Reviewing the Crafts in the Twentieth Century' held in England in 1997. At the time, Mitchell recognized the popularity of 'ambiguous verbal play' by textile practitioners, observing that 'such writing and the making to which it refers have become manifest at a time of critical appraisal and disruption of the primacy of language and its privileged relationship in thought and power'. In the decades to follow, linguistic games have been replaced with new trends in practice, particularly collaborative and community-based projects that work to disrupt the primacy of a single authoritative voice by instead welcoming a greater breadth of perspectives. Touch, nonetheless, has continued to remain a largely underacknowledged form of textile knowledge.

Textiles, Text and Techne (1997)

Victoria Mitchell

In E.B. White's story for children, *Charlotte's Web*, the spider Charlotte weaves the word 'SOME PIG' into her web.[1] The farmer Mr. Zuckerman and his workman Lurvy are taken aback at the sight of 'the writing on the web' and Mr. Zuckerman immediately informs his wife: '"Edith," he said, trying to keep his voice steady, "I think you had best be told that we have a very unusual pig."' He explains how the words were woven right into the web and were '"actually part of the web . . . There can be no mistake about it. A miracle has happened and a sign occurred here on earth, right on our farm, and we have no ordinary pig"'. '"Well," said Mrs Zuckerman, "it seems to me you're a little off. It seems to me we have no ordinary *spider*."'

Despite Mrs Zuckerman's observation, it is not Charlotte's skill which becomes the centre of attention. Charlotte's ability to transform the instinctual web into a slogan of support for her friend the pig Wilbur achieves the desired result and Wilbur is spared from a chopping board death. She uses her ingenious skill to promote the specialness of the pig; going beyond her instinctual skills as a maker of orb webs for the purpose of mating and capturing prey, it might be said that the web is transformed from one kind of snare (for tricking flies) to another (tricking the reader).

The fact that the words are 'actually part of the web', and are therefore impressive on that account, reinforces the 'miracle' of their effect which causes the message to be divorced from the skill which produced it. Peter Dormer spoke of the making which begins with the production of the raw material, as 'below the line'— that which is hidden from sight and which the consumer takes for granted.[2] In the case of the spider this might be the secretion of silk from the abdominal glands, drawn out by spinnerets, or the highly developed muscular sense which enables it to detect changes in tension in the thread.[3] In *Charlotte's Web* these aspects are secondary to the function of the signifying power of words.

Charlotte's Web is of course a fiction. Spiders make webs throughout their lives but they don't get better at making them. Whilst their ability to send and receive signals through vibration is subtle and complex, this ability is understood in terms of the mechanics of the nervous system; it therefore falls short of the kind of language experience typically associated with the written word. The linguist D. McNeil says that: 'We tend to consider "linguistic" what we can write down, and "non-linguistic" everything else, but this division is a cultural artefact, an arbitrary limitation derived from historical evolution.'[4]

In this paper I consider transitions and boundaries between text, textiles and *techne*, many of which are implicit in E.B. White's fictional example. Text, textiles and *techne* are etymologically linked, reflecting an intimacy and a complexity for thought in its association with making. Etymological links are not, however, the only form in which evidence of such association is manifest, and indeed the manner in which words are formed, in their differences and similarities, is often supple, subtle and cunningly playful in a way which can mask or even contradict those cognitive functions which are directly evidenced in the actions of making through materials.

Relationships between text, textiles and *techne* are of critical interest not only for what they may reveal about textiles and language; there are implications in their association which may be relevant to an understanding of what it means to create forms through materials. Such implications may require a

---

Source: Victoria Mitchell, 'Textile, Text and Techne', *Obscure Objects of Desire: Reviewing the Crafts in the Twentieth Century* (Crafts Council, London, 1997), pp. 324–32. Reproduced with permission.

refiguring and disrupting of the boundaries which divide instinct from cognition and nature from culture. The effect of such disrupting might be to create an enhanced significance for those practices which, sometimes with derogatory overtones, are referred to as 'craft'.

I begin by considering the senses as a basis of a phylogenetic and ontogenetic *conjunction* between language and textile. I will then suggest an historical, cultural context for their *separation*. Examples are drawn from the writings of Anni Albers and Edward Johnson to illustrate ways in which these associations and disassociations have affected the making of textiles and the perception of craft within the twentieth century. Finally I will consider the theorising of textiles from a contemporary perspective. I will argue that the privileging of words and the ocularcentrism of western culture can mask some of the sensibilities conveyed through textile practice, and that making sense through the tactility of textiles has implications for perception in a wider sense. In particular, the formative relationship between words and textiles alerts us to what I would like to call the textility of both thought and matter, a neologism which may be formative in minimising the separateness of the spheres within which text, textiles and *techne* might otherwise operate. The textility of making suggests a practice which informs thought; unlike an architectonic framework for cognition, it provides evidence of a more supple fabrication.

Language and textile formation share pliability as well as an inherent capacity to form structural relations between components. In both there is a suggestion of the drawing forth of minute physical sensation, fibre or particle into a form which is versatile and adaptable. The etymological and metaphorical use of words gives indications of some common associations, thus, according to Cecilia Vicuña: 'In the Andes the language itself, Quechua, is a chord of twisted straw, two people making love, different fibres united,'[5] and in Hungarian, the word for fibres is the same as that for vocal chords. The word 'language' derives in Latin and in Sanskrit from that which makes it, namely the tongue, and on a spinning wheel the point at which the yarn emerges fully formed is called the orifice. Text and textile share common association through the Latin *texere*, to weave.

These fragile references suggest for textiles a kind of speaking and for language a form of making.

Making and speaking, beginning with gesture and utterance, are both primarily tactile and sensory, of the body. Through the senses, touch and utterance share common origins in the neural system and in the pattern of synaptic, electrochemical connections between neurons. It is the fibrous form of the neuron which is said to provide 'the key to its role in the nervous system', and the synapse, both morphological and physiological in origin, which creates continuity and articulates differences between nerve cells. From each neuron, the dendrites which snake and twist as an extension of the cell body act as antennae, receiving impulses through the large surface area of their arborised endings.[6] Recent neuroscientific reconstructions of individual neurons are described by Peter Coveney and Roger Highfield as 'neural architectures',[7] but the intricacy of these architectures is of a fibrous form for which the metaphor of textiles might be more appropriate. In the fibrous tissue of the sensory body both the gestures of action and the utterance of speech are finely connected.

The complicated organisation of the nervous system confirms the views of psychologists of perception such as J.J. Gibson that the senses are perceptual systems and are integral to the formation of cognition.[8] Studies of gesture in the formation of language have also drawn on neurological evidence to support the link between oral and manual gestures and cognition. Language is an articulatory gesture of movement and feeling rooted in the body through neural activity:

> language, whether planned or produced, is always realized in some physical medium. At the level of planning, this medium is neural; at the level of utterance, it is articulatory (gestural). There is no translation from mental to physical; there is only motor activity brought about by neural activity.[9]

Of the various forms in which the senses are said to operate, the sense of sight has been, historically, the most privileged, whilst touch, with its implication of earth and base matter, has been less well served. Both philosophy and science have constructed a privileged role for sight as a cognitive organ, indeed Aristotle considered sight to be noble precisely because of the immateriality of its knowing, and hence its apparent approximation to the intellect.[10] In his book *The Eyes of the Skin*, the Finnish architect and theorist Juhani Pallasmaa tries to redress this one sidedness, by arguing that 'all the senses, including vision, can be regarded as senses of touch'.[11] This argument is necessary because, he suggests, sight has become a privileged social sense, whereas touch is now considered an archaic sensory remnant 'with a merely private function'.[12] He suggests that this is not the case for traditional cultures in which haptic and muscular senses of the body guide construction 'in the same way that a bird shapes its nest by movements of its body'.[13] The spinner and historian Patricia Baines reflects this polarising of the senses when she says that: 'it is difficult to describe in words and still pictures something which is a continuous movement, a rhythm and coordination between hands, foot and fibre, and which also sharpens the sense of feel.'[14]

It is clear that textiles are *not* words and the differences between them benefit the conceptual apparatus of thought at the expense of its sensory equivalent. Thus when an activity is *labelled* as textiles it ceases to be a substance and becomes instead a 'material of thought', and as such enters into the internal logic of a system which tends to privilege the autonomy of the mind. The word becomes surrogate for the substance. Despite the evocative power of the word, its potential to embody a presence through memory and association, there is a gap between word and thing which grows apace as verbal becomes written and written becomes printed, as the context of the thing itself recedes from view.

Historically, the development of writing coincides with a shift away from the locus of making. According to the structuralist Jean-Pierre Vernant, for example, a distinction was made, at the birth of the city state in Greece, between the private domain of the family and the public polis of the citizen, a category which excluded artisans, women and slaves.[15] Vernant suggests that the development of writing occurs in the exclusive public domain of the polis. Those who did not enter the polis, who did not write, who did not engage in the activities of the public space of the agora, were thereby marginalised both visibly and verbally. In the context of

the polis, the deliberate and conscious construction of reflection was informed by the *Logos*, the authority of the word as instrument of exchange of ideas.

A similar shift, away from the sensibility that arises through making, occurs with the advent of technology. With the advent of technological progress, Baudrillard suggests that the integrity of objects no longer is contingent upon individual needs which can be satisfied by artisanal production but upon a system which is technological and economic and which coheres around signifiers (notably words) which have the ability to select and direct the functioning of needs.[16] Thus exchange value, located in the signifying power of 'some pig' comes to predominate over the use value of the web. Charlotte's words, the *Logos* of the Greek citizen and the signifiers of exchange value reflect the privileged status of language as associated with notions of authority, truth and thought.

The yielding, domestic, female, decorative and material associations for textiles have in general determined their absence from this cultural hegemony, but it is an absence which may also be or have been an expression of resistance. In writings by textile practitioners in the twentieth century (until recently there are noticeably few), there is evidence of a desire to resist too great an involvement with words as the material of thought because it might hinder the articulation of meaning through the handling of materials. This resistance is repeatedly conveyed in the writings of Anni Albers, whose book *On Designing* (published in 1959 but based on writings from the late Thirties onwards) is one of the most substantial, analytic and wide-ranging in interpretation to have emerged from a textile practitioner in the modern period.

In her writing there is a tone of resistance to words as instruments of thought and, paradoxically, a note of discouragement to would-be maker-writers. Making through materials is justified as almost a superior kind of thought. She says: 'The inarticulateness of the artistic person is interpreted easily as a lack of intelligence while it is rather an intelligence expressing itself in other means than words.'[17] It is as if, by resisting one branch of intelligence, another will present itself through receptivity to the materials, thus: 'Resistance is one of the factors necessary to make us realise the characteristics of our medium and make us question our work procedure.'[18]

Albers distances herself from the subjective, and from the belief that knowledge gained through intellectual skills can benefit the maker. She says, for example, that 'with expanding knowledge goes limitation in range', that 'information means intellectualisation . . . one sidedness, incompleteness', and that 'layer after layer of civilised life seems to have veiled our directness of seeing' whereas the '*direct* experience of a medium' is seen as preferable. It is therefore 'better that the material speaks than that we speak ourselves.'[19] This denial of the self and of emotional introspection conveys a canonically Modern sensibility towards function and away from the obfuscating potential of art, or the privileging of the ego. For Albers, 'crafts become problematic when they are hybrids of art and usefulness,'[20] and thus by 'losing ourselves in the task we . . . would arrive at a result that is not individualistically limited.'[21]

In her practice, Albers was both a weaver who believed in the primacy of what she called 'the most real thing that there is', namely material, but also a graphic designer, particularly at the end of her life.[22] Weaving, writing and drawing share a common denominator through the practice of *graphein*, the graphic, a practice which demonstrates a formative trait for both text and textiles. A number of her woven pieces are given titles and forms which suggest writing or graphic signs. She wanted, she said, 'to let the threads be articulate again'. Pieces such as *Ancient Writing* (1936), *Memo* (1958), *Jotting* (1959), *Haiku* (1961) and *Code* (1962), suggest that she was exploring and rediscovering a graphic potential in both text and textiles, a coincidence conveyed through a response to the material.[23] Her deep regard for ancient Peruvian textiles, which predate the written word, reinforced this. Speaking of their double, triple and quadruple weaves she comments: 'if a highly intelligent people with no written language, no graph paper, and no pencils could manage such invention, we should be able—easily I hope—to repeat these structures.'[24]

Despite her concern for material processes, much of her work was designed for contemplation rather than practical use, to be touched with the eyes rather

than the hand. Also, Albers increasingly gave titles to her works from the late Thirties onwards, again suggesting a relinquishing of the tactile as the agent of formation. The naming and visual contemplation of textiles mark a shift in perception from the physical to the mental, a shift which grows apace through the development and proliferation of exhibition and publication contexts for textile and other crafts. As a consequence, physical responses of use and touch cease to operate as primary entry points of understanding. Like words and pictures in books, exhibitions tend to marginalise the technical, artisanal aspects of practice, and they do not, in general, allow the involvement of touch. In a review of the 1954 Arts and Crafts Exhibition Society exhibition, Peter Collingwood drew attention to the problem of textiles as objects of contemplation, suggesting that they suffered by not being felt: 'because a piece of cloth is only half-experienced unless it is handled, the visitors find it impossible to keep their hands off.'[25]

It may be said that words are substitutes for use. For Albers the articulation of threads as a formation from within and through interaction with the material gives way to a reading in which the threads are represented by the words which are used to describe them.

The typographer Edward Johnson, a maker for whom articulacy through words is formed through a combination of making *and* reading, analysed some of the problems posed by the distancing of tactile involvement in the exhibition of crafts in an address given to members of the Arts and Crafts Exhibition Society in 1933:

There is something necessarily artificial about a formal Exhibition. The objects are *posed* in a gallery to be *looked at*, and the Percipient—i.e., the 'Public'—can only use *one* of his five senses in appreciating them. On his own family goods and chattels all five senses confer in daily judgement. *Here* he must be content with Sight alone.

But even the sense of sight is restricted to viewing *motionless material effects* often little more than one-sided views. The Exhibits cannot by action demonstrate their fitness for use. We may not touch, still less handle or try the use of Things meant to be daily used and handled. An exhibition is, in fact, apt to be a kind of *lying in state*—of Talent at rest.[26]

It is in this gap, between use and sight, that words can function as a form of closure, as a mediation which can effect a partial recovery of that which has been lost. Rather than considering words as a further loss to sensory embodiment of meaning, Johnson's proposed solution is to encourage *makers* to 'write *critical and explanatory* . . . labels to accompany their work'. Even though, he suggests, the work itself is a 'sort of special language' and 'the thing he makes not only speaks for him, but also speaks for itself ', through engagement in writing: 'we can give a partial *translation of our Works into Words* which will assist understanding.' He appeals to the poet in the maker and suggests that 'We are . . . *Makers* of word arrangements by which we exchange ideas'.

Whilst the main purpose of Johnson's address concerned the maker's written interpretation, he also went further in suggesting that exhibitions might show evidence and explanations of materials and processes. Johnson's overall aim is not only 'to help people to see what they are looking at', but also to assist the understanding of the maker, and to enable makers to communicate through words with one another. In other words, writing becomes a form of making— making words—*and* an aspect of seeing. The sense of touch functions vicariously through a combination of indirect agents. Writing establishes the involvement of the viewer in forming a relationship between seeing and making, potentially guiding the viewer away from the flatness of a static object to the activity and ideas which it embodies.

Both Albers and Johnson are, in interconnected ways, entering into a system which coheres around signifiers which select and direct the viewer's response to the work. Seen from a contemporary perspective, the exhibition may be encountered not as a space within which objects are contemplated from a physical distance through the immateriality of the eye but as a medium of making or an intertextuality of signs in which the viewer's response is formative. Nevertheless, the tactility of making, touching and using remain as secondary and are silenced.

Within recent literary and critical theory there is evidence of a desire to make sense of the gap between words and things. In this, metaphors referring to textiles have been formative and transformative. Thus Michel Foucault uses the metaphor of interweaving to describe the relationship between things and words, and Roland Barthes uses the analogy of braid to illustrate the multiplicity of intersecting codes that constitute what he calls textuality: 'each thread, each code, is a voice; these braided—or braiding—voices form the writing', and the feminist Gayatri Chakravorty Spivak speaks enticingly of the fraying of the edges of the language-textile as seen from the perspective of translation between one language and another.[27]

In transferring, perhaps appropriating, the articulacy of threads from material to textual practice, the metaphorical ambiguity of textile terminology has unleashed previously undisclosed meanings for textiles as well as for critical theory. In recent years textile practitioners have begun to participate in ambiguous verbal play, for example speaking of the 'language of textiles' and suggesting that textiles are a form of writing or speaking. Textiles as metaphor have assumed in recent writing the agency of a sensory idea, a material of thought, so that it becomes possible to speak of textile thought and tactile literacy. The haptic and the conceptual have moved closer together through the agency of textile experience as expressed through metaphor and through words. Such writing and the making to which it refers have become manifest at a time of critical appraisal and disruption of the primacy of language and its privileged relationship to thought and power, and it is significant that textiles, which the contemporary artist Pierrette Bloch suggests is a 'dark other side to writing', has entered into and contributed to the disruption of that primacy.[28]

Textile practice remains, however, rooted in material, and for textile practice which identifies with craft the role of making and of handling materials is only partly served by textile-theory word-play. In the catalogue of a recent textile art exhibition, *TextileArt*, curated by makers, Judith Duffey Harding asks: 'Can a practice that grows out of making, that thinks with its hands by making, evolve its own theory, in a way that doesn't intimidate or constrain the makers by imposing it?'[29]

Perhaps, in response to this, it may be helpful to return to the formation of the word textile, and reconsider its origin within the practice of making. Within literary criticism the etymological link between text and textile, from the Latin *texere*, to weave, has been central in developing notions of textuality and intertextuality. The etymology that links text and textile can, however, be traced further back, to Greek and Sanskrit associations which emphasise the activity of making and forming. The Sanskrit words *takman* meaning 'child' and *taks*, to make, and the Indo-European root *tek-* used of men, meaning to beget, and of women, to bring forth, have all been linked to the Latin texere. In these, the sense of physical formation is emphatic. Through *tek-* the formation of techne further demonstrates the association of skill and through the Latin *texere* the sense of joining or fitting together reinforces the association of textiles with materials and away from the metaphorical associations illustrated by reference to text.

The notion of textuality, with its associated reference to textiles, evades, I suggest, these earlier traditions of making, joining and putting together, of bodies and buildings. Textiles, whilst they lend themselves to associations of text, also mediate between the fibrous body and the fabric of architecture. They articulate subtle physical sensations between substance and surface, and are most closely known to us through their relationship to the skin and to the sense of touch, a sense which is actively encountered through the making of textiles by hand. In addition to the analogy with the textuality of language and the intertextuality of signs, textile practice may also acknowledge this contiguity with the physical forms of bodies and of things, a kind of textility operating through and in between forms in space. As suggested here by Pallasmaa, the architectonic may give way to the tactile:

With the loss of tactility and measures and details crafted for the human body—and particularly for the hand—architectural structures become flat, sharp edged, immaterial and unreal. The detachment of construction from the realities of matter and craft further turns architecture into stage sets for the eyes into a scenography devoid of the authenticity of matter and construction.[30]

In her reappraisal of the myth of Arachne and Athena, Nancy K. Miller reminds the reader of Virginia Woolf's awareness of the fragility but tenaciousness of fiction's relationship to the real:

Fiction is like a spider's web, attached ever so lightly perhaps, but still attached to life at all four corners . . . When the web is pulled askew . . . one remembers that these webs are not spun in mid-air by incorporeal creatures, but are the work of suffering human beings, and are attached to grossly material things, like health and money and the houses we live in.[31]

We realise of course that it was a good thing Charlotte could write words in her web: it saved Wilbur's life. Within contemporary textiles it is also true that issues of gender and class, for example, have been voiced and heard through textiles. The subtle nuance and fragile pliability of textiles as embodied metaphor have contributed actively to the disruption of the authority of language, and have been abundant in intonations of sensory experience, thus serving to enable senses other than sight to achieve an enhanced status. Nevertheless, the manipulation of textiles has implications for meanings which come about directly, if not instinctively, through making, and these are often least well served in a culture of sign consumption. The spider's web has recently been the subject of tensile structure research with reference to use in architecture, as if, at last, Mrs Zuckerman's voice is heard.[32]

Notes

1. E.B. White, *Charlotte's Web*, Hamish Hamilton, London, 1952; Puffin Books, London, 1963, p. 78.
2. Peter Dormer, *The Meanings of Modern Design*, Thames & Hudson, London, 1970. p.15ff. Peter Dormer highlights the way in which engineering is often hidden and divorced from style. I am extending his notion of engineering in this instance (with reference to the production of spider silk), to suggest that 'natural' processes might be hidden from cultural

products in a similar way. Dormer suggests that the hidden only comes to be questioned when the product (in this case the signifying power of words) fails in some way.

3. Theodore H. Savory, *The Spider's Web*, Frederick Warne & Co. Ltd., London and New York, 1952.

4. D. McNeill, 'So you think gestures are non-verbal', *Psychological Review* 92, 1985, p. 351. Cited by David F. Armstrong, William C. Stokoe, Sherman E. Wilcox, *Gesture and the Nature of Language*, Cambridge University Press, Cambridge, 1995, pp. 7–8.

5. Cecilia Vicuña and Rosa Acala, *Palabra e Hilo/ Word & Thread*, Morning Star Publications, Royal Botanic Gardens, Edinburgh, University Press, 1996.

6. Alan Peters, Sanford L. Paley, Henry de F. Webster, *The Fine Structure of the Nervous System*, 3rd edition, Oxford University Press, Oxford 1991.

7. Peter Coveney, Roger Highfield, *Frontiers of Complexity*, Faber & Faber, London, 1995, p. 290 (illustrated). From a conversation between the neurophysiologist Colin Blakemore in 1994 and Coveney and Highfield, Blakemore is quoted as saying, 'The interesting parts of the brain are driven by the senses, right through to language, which surely evolved from sensory categorisation' (p. 283).

8. J.J. Gibson, *The Senses Considered as Perceptual Systems*, Houghton Mifflin, Boston, 1966.

9. Armstrong, Stokoe and Wilcox, *op cit.*, p. 33.

10. On this subject, a clear overview in Martin Jay, *Downcast Eyes: The denigration of vision in twentieth-century French thought*, University of California Press, Berkeley and Los Angeles, 1994.

11. Juhani Pallasmaa, *The Eyes of the Skin: Architecture and the Senses*, Academy Editions, 1996, p. 29.

12. Ibid., p. 7.

13. Ibid., p. 16.

14. Patricia Baines, *Spinning Wheels, Spinners and Spinning*, Oxford University Press, Oxford, 1976, p. 13.

15. Jean-Pierre Vernant, *Myth and Thought Among the Greeks*. First published in French in 1965, in English by Routledge & Kegan Paul, London, 1983,

pp. 256 and 324. The four essays of Part Four, 'Work and Technological Thought', provide an excellent analysis of the way in which artisans were ostracized from the thought-forming polis.

16. Jean Baudrillard, *Selected Writings*, edited and introduced by Mark Poster, Polity Press, Cambridge, 1988, pp. 14–15.

17. Anni Albers, *On Designing*, Pelango Press, New Haven, 1959, p. 32.

18. Ibid., p. 33.

19. Ibid., pp. 5, 6, 45.

20. Ibid., p. 15.

21. Ibid., p. 26.

22. Ibid., p. 50.

23. These works are reproduced in *The Woven and Graphic Art of Anni Albers*, Smithsonian Institution Press, Washington D.C., 1985.

24. Anni Albers, *On Weaving*, Wesleyan University Press, Middletown, Conn., p. 50.

25. Peter Collingwood, 'Arts and Crafts Exhibition', *Quarterly Journal of the Guilds of Weavers, Spinners and Dyers*, no.14, June 1955, p. 451.

26. Edward Johnson, Four Papers, The Arts and Crafts Exhibition Society, 1935, pp. 5–8.

27. Michel Foucault, *The Order of Things,* Tavistock Publications, 1970; Routledge, 1989, p. 160. Roland Barthes, *S/Z*, Hill and Wang, New York, p. 160. Gayatri Chakravorty Spivak, 'The Politics of Translation', in Michèle Barrett & Anne Phillips, eds., *Destabilizing Theory*, Polity Press, Cambridge, 1992, pp. 178, 181.

28. Pierrette Bloch, *Textile and Contemporary Art*, 16e Biennale Internationale de Lausanne, Benteli, Lausanne, 1996.

29. Judith Duffey Harding, 'Textile Thinking, Continuity and Craft', *Art Textiles*, Bury St Edmunds Art Gallery, 1996, p. 13.

30. Ibid., p. 20.

31. Virginia Woolf, *A Room of One's Own*, pp. 43–4, cited by Nancy K. Miller, *Subject to Change*, Columbia University Press, New York, 1988, p. 83.

32. Lorraine Lin, 'Studying spider webs: a new approach to structures', *The Arup Journal*, Jan. 1994, p. 23.

2

THE HAPTICS OF OPTICS
Weaving and Photography (excerpt) (2014)

T'ai Smith

EDITOR'S INTRODUCTION

T'ai Smith is Associate Professor of Art History at the University of British Columbia in Vancouver, Canada. Smith's research interests include the politics of mediation, gender, labour and economy. She is currently writing her second book: *Fashion after Capital: Frock Coats and Philosophy from Marx to Duchamp* (2024). Reprinted here is an excerpt from Smith's first book, *Bauhaus Weaving Theory: From Feminine Craft to Mode of Design* (2014), based on her PhD research.

The Bauhaus opened in the German city of Weimar in 1919, before moving to Dessau and later Berlin, closing its doors under Nazi party pressure in 1933. Today the Bauhaus continues to enjoy considerable critical attention as an exemplar of arts education. In 2021 the President of the European Commission, Ursula Von der Leyen, launched The New European Bauhaus.

In the years preceding World War II, a number of colleagues associated with the Bauhaus left Germany and contributed to building new sites of arts education. Josef Albers arrived in the US with his wife Anni Albers in 1933 to lead the Black Mountain College in North Carolina which operated from 1933 to 1957. In Chicago in 1937, The Illinois Institute of Design (after merger in 1949 known as the Illinois Institute of Technology) was founded and led by László Moholy-Nagy and called 'The New Bauhaus'. Ludwig Mies van der Rohe joined as head of architecture in 1938. The weaver Margaret Leischner emigrated to England in the 1930s and worked professionally as a textile designer. In 1948 she became Professor of textile design at the Royal College of Art, London.

While much has been published on the Bauhaus, Smith observes, 'Little to none of the current scholarship has critically analysed how the weavers shaped their craft through text, or how their textual pursuits significantly engaged with thought on craft and media more generally.' The excerpt reprinted here focuses on the weaver Otti Berger's two page essay 'Stoffe im Raum' (Fabrics in Space) published in German in 1930 and the emergence of close up photography of Bauhaus textile designs which captured the tactility of cloth. Portions of Berger's essay also appear in Judith Raum's text included in the structure section. Smith credits Berger, now less well known than her Bauhaus contemporary Anni Albers, with a 'subtle and perhaps counterintuitive response to photography' which recognized the potential of the photographic lens to convey not only optical but also tactile qualities. Rather than set touch and sight in opposition, Smith credits Berger's understanding of the 'reciprocity between optical and tactile elements within woven objects'.

Otti Berger died in 1944 in Auschwitz concentration camp in Oświęcim, Poland at the age of 46.

The Haptics of Optics: Weaving and Photography

T'ai Smith

There remains an aspect of weaving to which I have alluded in previous chapters but never properly addressed: fabric's tactility. The Bauhaus weaving workshop explored the possibilities of color and formal composition through the interlacing of threads, tacitly placing it in comparison to painterly composition and architectural function. Yet the specific palpability of threads and cloth surfaces required a new set of terms. Architecture's rhetorical strategies regarding functionality and space were only partly sufficient, so photography became the next medium whose language was harnessed. With this development, one weaving student named Otti Berger addressed the limits of the visual and the tactile within modernism and its media.[1]

From 1928, the year Hannes Meyer replaced Walter Gropius as director, until 1933, the year the Bauhaus finally closed, photographs for brochures, advertisements, and magazine articles actively marketed the weaving workshop's textile designs to a wider public of merchants and potential customers. Whereas images of the Bauhaus 1923 exhibition and one of Gropius's Weimar office from 1924, for example, displayed the workshop's carpets and wall hangings next to other furniture, as some of several elements in architectural space, the July 1931 issue of *bauhaus zeitschrift für gestaltung* revealed exquisite, carefully lit close-ups of fabrics.[2] Bauhaus textiles moved into the public image bank just as photography was beginning to flower at the school. A flurry of images quickly saturated the field of industrial design, and like all of the products generated by the workshops, weaving soon depended on the photographic medium to give it status and definition in the world. Perhaps more than any other workshop entity, weaving had the fortune of gaining a place in the spotlight, for the intimacy of a woven texture was particularly suited to the scrutiny of the lens. The slight swellings, recesses, and shadows produced by the crossing of weft and warp, the way the fabric folded or creased, or the subtlety of the tactile sensations generated by wool against cellophane seemed infinitely refined when framed by the sharp focus of a precise optical apparatus.

The beautiful full-page spreads of textiles in the special weaving issue of *bauhaus zeitschrift* fell in line with the recent advertisement photography that had been developing for at least a few years. The cover's photograph of a textile design by Margaret Leischner taken by Walter Peterhans had already been published in 1930 in the Czech journal *ReD* for a special issue on the school. Alongside an image of Anni Albers's soundproofing and light-reflective fabric documented by Zeiss Ikon (the camera lens manufacturer), Peterhans's photograph helped to present textiles as structurally, materially, and industrially sophisticated products. With detailed, close-up photography, the textures came into focus, and with framing that implied the potentially infinite dimensions of swaths of fabric, the photographs highlighted the textiles' tactile conditions.

The increased frequency of photographic presentations of weaving at this time was in part responsible for prompting Berger to theorize an aspect of cloth that had largely gone uninvestigated, until her essay "Stoffe im Raum" (Fabrics in Space) of 1930. The Bauhaus weaving workshop had been exploring the formal, structural, and functional possibilities of textiles, explicitly placing their medium in comparison with architecture, and had developed theories that harnessed the language of the Neues Bauen. But to understand further the specificity of their craft, Berger sought a different, if related, route. Through a subtle and perhaps counterintuitive response to photography, she insisted on the tactility of different materials (the smoothness of silk or the roughness of jute, for instance) as well as the fabric's contact with the kinesthetic movements of the body within architectural space (with curtains or upholstery fabric). Indeed, although Berger may not have realized just how polemical her article was (it was seemingly ignored by the larger Bauhaus circle), its theory of weaving resonated with debates that were critical to this moment. Berger's essay participated in a discussion on the sensory status of objects, drawing on a paradigm within art circles in which the optical was distinguished from—and opposed to—the tactile.[3] At the time her text appeared next to Peterhans's photograph in *ReD*, theorists and critics of photography had been embracing its status as a quintessentially modern form, what László Moholy-Nagy called the "purely optical" conditions of light through a lens.

So in order to grasp the significance of fabric's tactility, Berger turned to the medium that both brought her own object to view and simultaneously presented a counterpoint to her objectives for a theory of weaving. Drawing on her teacher Moholy-Nagy's language and proclamation of photography as an inherently optical art, Berger countered, "A fabric is not only an optical object."[4] Rather, "Most important in cloth is its tactility. The tactile in cloth is primary."[5] She sought to differentiate textiles, to give them a specifically tactile theory and identity, and so she seized, through a twist, the language that was most apparently anathema to fabric's materiality and the process of handweaving.

Still, despite Berger's passionate interest in determining what could be felt but not seen in textiles, her texts do not so much posit a strict division between visual and tactile experience as specify the latter against, but also within, the former. As I will show through an analysis of "Stoffe im Raum" and two unpublished essays, Berger often points to a reciprocity between optical and tactile elements within woven objects and as they function within space. And through an implicit consideration of a debate in photography that had been evolving since 1927, she points to a particular problem that occupied the apparently pure, optical nature of the lens. Indeed, "facture"—most explicitly revealed in the photographs of cloth texture, but also in Moholy-Nagy's interest in high-contrast photographs of wrinkles or dried fruit—was a particularly laden subject for the light-based medium's apparent immateriality. It seems Berger was aware that the tactile sense had a particularly problematic history in the discipline of art. By showing how a study of cloth requires a reflection on tactility, she also queried the limits of the visual as modernism's prized term of formal inquiry. If modernist photography claimed its identity as the conveyor of optical truth—pure light and shade—afforded by its transparent lens, then weaving reminded that the notion of photographic "objectivity" depended on a tactile, opaque surface. […]

TACTILE EDUCATION

This tension between optics and haptics in Moholy-Nagy's thought should come as no surprise. The Bauhaus, with its history of attention to craft in the workshops, was (at least initially) based on the idea that "contact with the material" was integral to artistic and technological developments.[6] But as Rainer Wick points out, more than any other teacher there, Moholy-Nagy emphasized the "haptic" sense.[7] He recognized that modernity's favor of an "eye democracy" over other senses ultimately "neglected our tactile education."[8] Thus in 1927, the Bauhaus form master developed an analysis of materiality and texture for his *Vorkurs* curriculum, which he recorded in his book *Von Material zu Architektur* (From Material to Architecture) published in 1928. Drawing on [Aloïs] Riegl's argument, Moholy-Nagy posits the tactile sense as the necessary ground of sensory experience.[9] The form master thus advocated teaching this sensory mode through the development of tactile exercises (*Tastübungen*) in part because "the sense of 'touch,' more than any other, may be divided into a number of separately sensed qualities, such as pressure, pricking, rubbing, pain, temperature, and vibration."[10] He thus established the reasoning for a group of exercises performed by students Willy Zierath and Otti Berger. Later photographed for his book, these experiments initiated an investigation of the limits of touch and vision, first by analytically piecing them out and then by setting them into conversation.

Zierath developed a particularly clever version—what he described in the object's key as a "Zweizeilige Tastleiter und optische Übersetzung" (Two-tiered Touch Scale and Optical Translation)—during the winter semester of 1927–1928. Here, rectangular samples are spread across three sets of horizontal scales, each made up of two rows, to display different tactile properties. Man-made materials are set against natural ones, and fabricated (or woven) samples are juxtaposed with raw states of wool or cotton and various metals. Below the double-tiered sampling of materials, three ink diagrams translate this touch scale into a visual model, exhibiting the properties of smooth to rough in systematically measured calculations according to the different sensory stimuli generated by each tactile sample.

Soon-to-be weaver Otti Berger's "Tasttafel" (touch panel), also created for Moholy-Nagy's course, executes the relationship between optical and tactile differently. On a long piece of metal screen that acts as both background and pedestal sits a raised layer of threads woven into triangular forms. With threads of different textures and thickness situated on a rough but pliable metal ground, Berger's "Tasttafel" attests to her early interest in the role of touch and her desire to explore the specific properties of different materials: silk, rayon, velvet, wool, organic and chemically treated cotton, and metal twisted through various threads…The colors of the threads are mostly raw or neutral, but more brilliant tones enter the composition through the placement of orange, red, yellow, green, and purple squares inside the woven triangular pockets.

Perhaps the work is not a pure touch diagram like Zierath's (it is not so "scientific" in its approach), but Berger presents a composition of colors and materials in order to explore the specific convergence of optical properties (such as color and composition) with tactile ones (such as smoothness or roughness) in a single piece. These two apparently distinct sensory modes occupy the same surface, where color literally saturates the materials. While the squared sheets of colored paper seem at first divided from the tactile qualities of the threads for the purpose of the exercise, they also

join within the structure of the panel. The optical shimmering effect of the silk is juxtaposed against the matte effect of the cotton, and as one looks at the work from different angles, one is able to see the ridges and bumps of texture from the various materials. Through her juxtaposition of material against color, or different visible textures, Berger reminds the viewer that the sense of touch is often used in concert with vision. They overlap—indeed, are fused—on the same surface.

Thus Berger's touch panel poses the questions: to what degree is it possible to "translate" or "represent" one sense into another? And to what extent can the senses be juxtaposed productively if they ultimately move in and out of each other? Her touch panel is a model of the ideas that Berger would later address in her theory of weaving, just as photographers would begin to explore the translation of material texture into the slick surface of the gelatin print.[11]

TACTILE THEORY FOR FABRIC

Although Moholy-Nagy had left his post at the Bauhaus two years before Berger published her essay "Stoffe im Raum," he had clearly played a central role in her formation as a student. No other member of the weaving workshop would address the question of tactility with the same force or consistency.[12] Though other weavers such as Gunta Stölzl or Helene Schmidt-Nonné had spoken of the functional utility of fabric and focused on weaving's objective material properties, Berger's theoretical texts emphasized the tactile as the primary quality and experience of cloth.

The young weaver from Yugoslavia entered the Bauhaus in January 1927 and completed her studies quickly, receiving her diploma in November 1930.[13] After a six-month teaching residency in Stockholm following her coursework in 1930, Berger taught weaving technique (alongside Albers) while the Werkbund designer Lilly Reich (appointed by Ludwig Mies van der Rohe, the third Bauhaus director) acted as the nominal master of an integrated interior design workshop.[14] During her teaching stint at the Bauhaus, Berger also developed and taught her own theory of materials, color, and the role of fabrics in space. In 1932, when the Bauhaus closed in Dessau, she established her own fabric design studio in Berlin, Otti Berger Atelier für Textilien. Berger had ambitions to innovate fabric structures and weaving techniques and would ultimately gain a reputation for her patented textiles for industry.[15]

The language of perceptual self-evidence that dominates "Stoffe im Raum" yields a series of shorthand notes. Berger analyzes weaving's properties and the role of fabric in space, beginning with a typical Bauhaus, manifesto-like statement: "In interior decorating, textiles command a small, but important area. In order to fulfill the demand of a living construction, we must make clear to ourselves what fabric is and further: what fabric in space is."[16] Just as Stölzl did in 1926, Berger signals her ambition to specify the identity and function of cloth as a structural and functional entity.[17] But Berger goes one step further. In addition to arguing that the "first principle" of weaving is the discovery of "the harmony . . . of materials" (thick or thin, soft or stiff), Berger stresses the importance of recognizing fabric's tactile identity within space. The order of principles, she insists, begins with the material (texture) and only afterward the structure or color of the cloth. The *Haltbarkeit* (durability, but also "hold-ability") of the object must be taken into consideration at every stage. As such, she argues, this undervalued sensory faculty is necessary in order to truly "grasp" and "recognize" a fabric:

Most important in cloth is its tactility. The tactile in cloth is primary. A cloth should be grasped (*gegriffen*). One must be able to "grasp" (*begreifen*) [its structure] with the hands. The value of a fabric should above all be recognized tactilely, through the sense of touch. The understanding (*Begreifen*) of a cloth can just as well be felt with the hands, as a color can be with the eyes, or a sound can be in the ear.[18]

In her use of repetition Berger's style is unrelenting—indeed, filled with a bursting energy regarding her observations. Short, choppy sentences are insistent and redundant. The parallel between Berger's essay and Moholy-Nagy's pedagogy is noted by Regina Lösel: "This formulation recalls the foundational teachings of Moholy-Nagy, who spoke to the large role of the sense of touch." But as Lösel also remarks, "the intensity

with which Otti Berger emphasized the sensual-tactile is specific to her own writing and theory."[19] More is at stake in Berger's writing style with the variations on the verb *greifen*. Through her verbal play with the word *begreifen*, which she sets off in quotation marks, Berger demands an attention to its different meanings: to grasp physically (with the hands, for instance), and to comprehend or to understand. She continues the play on *begreifen* by setting up an analogy with other media: *das Begreifen* can be felt (*empfunden*) with the hands just as a color can be sensed by the eyes or a sound can be heard by the ears. Although the process by which the modality of touch apprehends objects is in part coincident with vision for obtaining information about the spatial properties of objects, Berger makes clear that touch is nevertheless very specific.[20]

Berger's reference to other senses recalls the lessons learned in Kandinsky's theory courses, where the concept of synesthesia—one sense being activated by the stimulus of another—was central to his theory of color.[21] For Kandinsky, synesthesia "forms a bridge to the inner pulsation of a work of art." Kandinsky's way of explaining synesthesia was, according to historian Clark Poling,

through a generalized metaphor, that the impression provided by one sense is communicated to the organ of another sense as in the case of sympathetic vibrations in music—one instrument echoing another without itself being touched, or one part of an instrument causing the other parts to reverberate. . . . [Kandinsky] explicitly compared the nerves with the strings of the piano, so that a visual impression can cause the "cords" of other senses to vibrate.[22]

When Kandinsky refers to the tactile feelings aroused by certain colors, he finds yellow to be "hard, resistant, sharp, and prickly," whereas blue is "soft, unresistant, and velvety."

Thus on the first page of Berger's notes from a Kandinsky class, she writes: "The value of a color can be noticed not only with the eyes but also with all other senses."[23] As the first sentence of her lesson, this idea was clearly significant to Berger, who was attempting to understand her own medium and its sensory parameters. While Kandinsky's lesson went on to discuss the *Hören* (hearing), *musikalische* (musical), and *sprachliche* (lingual/vocal) qualities of colors, the faculty of touch would become the model through which Berger explores the question of sensory perception in general, thus she uses the verb "to feel" (*empfinden*), not "to see" or "to hear," when referring to both colors and sound.[24]

For Berger, different sensual properties overlap, or are of the same substance, within a woven fabric. Several years later, in response to a growing frustration she experienced trying to design textiles with the limitations of color, material, and cost set by the manufacturer, Berger would call for the "free" exploration[25] of these relationships:

> We are searching for the relationships in cloth between color and material, between color and structure, and we see that the possibilities with these means toward cloth are endless. He who knows these relationships has endless possibilities before him. He is attentive to the way the . . . material changes itself through structure, color changes itself through material and structure. Silk works differently in a raw or smooth structure. Smooth structures reflect light, but raw structures suck up the light nearby and create shadows.[26]

This understanding evidently came from her practical experience weaving materials, just as it had begun to develop in her "Tasttafel." Berger's woven experiments would determine her thoughts on the matter—revealing a consistent engagement with the visual properties of color in their combination with the tactile character of materials. So we see in Berger's experiments a concern, say, with the relationship between light-reflective synthetic fibers and matte cotton or wool. In her *Bindungslehre* (a book of her teaching methods developed while at the Bauhaus and in Stockholm between 1930 and 1931), samples juxtaposed against draft notations demonstrate how certain materials interact with different colors and structures—some drawing on the fluid character of rayon (*Kunstseide*) in pastel pink and white, others on the stiffer properties of wool in bright blues and reds.

Later she would continue to experiment with the interactions of materials: one textile from 1932 uses cellophane, a paper-like brittle material; another, a drapery fabric from 1933 (manufactured for the south-facing windows of the Landhaus Schminke in Löbau/Sachsen by architect Hans Scharoun), contrasts kapok and chenille threads.[27] The crossing of these threads in a loosely woven fabric combines the tactile feeling of scratchiness and softness but also lends the work a shimmering optical effect. In samples of her textile designs that were patented in 1934 and sold by the Schriever textile firm under the label Rosshaar Doppelgewebe, a plastic-like material known at the time as artificial horsehair (*künstliches Rosshaar*)—shiny, hard, and sharp at its edges—is double woven with softer rayon (*Kunstseide*) and cotton threads. The sets of colors alternate in each sample, with variations on the contrast between greens and red tones in one, and greens and purple tones in the other. Each plays with the two-sided, double layers of colors and materials. Seen (or photographed) from different angles and under different light conditions, the verso layer of red shows through the recto layer of green with greater or lesser intensity depending on the degree of reflection off the shining threads.

Through discussions about spatial fabrics and tactility further into the 1930s in several unpublished manuscripts and articles published in such textile journals as *Der Konfektionär* and *International Textiles*, she sets up a paradigm in which touch is a distinguished sense only to reveal how much this sensory modality is implicated in the terrain of visual experience and optical media.[28] The notion of tactility in Berger's theory is not simply posed as "fact," nor is it simply an appreciation of how tactile properties overlap with optical ones in a woven entity. Indeed, her argument for tactility becomes more complex toward the end of her 1930 essay in *ReD* when she addresses the problem of fabrics in space. And in two unpublished essays, titled "Weberei und Raumgestaltung" (Weaving and the Design of Space) and "Stoffe und neues Bauen" (Fabric and the New Architecture), both from the early thirties, Berger becomes increasingly convinced that the central concern of textiles in the modern world rests not on their visual properties but on their role within the design of haptic, spatial environments. Indeed, what begins as an argument against the optical becomes an argument for a haptic understanding of fabrics in the design of space.

In "Weberei und Raumgestaltung," Berger makes the thrust of her argument about tactility quite forceful: "A textile is not only an optical object. We come into perpetual contact with it, so it is recognized through our tactile sense. A material, therefore, also has a 'grip' ["*Griff* "]."[29] Despite her seeming matter-of-factness and straight-to-the-point style, Berger employs a single word to designate multiple ideas—*Griff*, which is set off in quotation marks and can be translated as "handle" but also means something like the texture or friction of a cloth felt to the touch and evokes the ineffable sensation of contact with an object. Moreover, by calling attention to this *Griff*, Berger acknowledges the precarious role of tactile sense perception, insofar as this contact is "perpetual" and without definite temporal boundaries. This brings to mind what Berger wrote in "Stoffe im Raum": "One must grasp the structure not only with one's brain but also feel it out with the subconscious (*Unterbewußtsein*). Then one will know about the particularity of silk, which is warmth, or of artificial silk, which is called cold."[30] In other words, through "perpetual" or mobile "contact" with textiles, as one traverses an interior space, sits down in a chair, or pulls aside a curtain, one "instinctively," even unconsciously, grasps their structures and their material properties. As Lösel notes regarding Berger's theory, her "interest in tactile experience applied not only to the physical, but also to the *psychical* sense of touch."[31]

Despite the manifesto-like quality of her writing, Berger's texts allude to something more esoteric, as indicated by her reference to Paul Klee: "Here one could say with the painter Klee: Intuition is still a good thing!—for one must listen to the fabric's secrets, track down the sounds of materials."[32] Her use of the word *erfühlen*, which means to feel or grasp instinctively (*gefühlsmässige Erfassen*), further draws out her word play on the relationship between sensing, touching, grasping, and understanding. And in the use of *erfühlen*, which she also aligns with touch, Berger differentiates instinctive feeling from the grasping (*erfassen*) of a structure with the brain, which works at a cognitive level. Berger shows that without the more

intuitive—what she refers to as "subconscious"—sense of textiles, one could not know the difference between silk (*Seide*) and viscose rayon (*Kunstseide*), which look more or less the same but through physical contact conduct different sensations of heat.[33] Thus Berger recognizes that there is more to her object than meets the eye. The visual pattern produced by the structure and colors of the woven field or the print often eclipses the perception of a fabric's texture, and the tactile contact with the surface is not always, necessarily, consciously recognized. The subject (be it the weaver or the user) may sense the cloth's *Griff*, yet within the habitual realm of contact this texture can go more or less unnoticed. "Perpetual contact" thus suggests that one approaches the object not simply through visual, conscious perception, which leads to the recognition of textiles as objects, but also through tactile (unconscious) perception, which contributes to one's overall physical experience of an environment.

Otti Berger's idea of *Unterbewußtsein erfühlen* resonates in a particular drapery fabric prototype from 1927, identified as #471 in the Bauhaus archive and attributed to the weaving workshop master Gunta Stölzl. The design draws out Berger's particular concern with *Raumgestaltung*. When hung against a window, spacing between the threads allows light to shine through, emphasizing the light-reflective quality of the rayon. As drapery, the material works with the optical effects of light, but these effects do not always appeal to vision's sense of recognition; rather, they function within the space to let light in or to protect the inhabitant from being seen from outside. Berger writes: "A curtain fabric serves different purposes and must be constructed accordingly. Either it regulates the light by day (sun-curtain) or it should hinder the view into the living space (drapery) or it is used to darken the space."[34] Alternatively, a wall covering made of cellophane works to reflect and give the impression of more light within otherwise dark rooms but also helps to warm the space during cold German winters. Anni Albers's earlier design for soundproofing fabric using cellophane with cotton chenille similarly functions to insulate the interior of the architectural space, in effect cloaking the body in a silent vacuum-like environment. The textiles appeal to the entire body's inhabitation of space. Thus even the effect of light through the fabric is registered or experienced haptically.

We can make a distinction between the terms *haptic* and *tactile* by noting that a haptic experience of space has already broken down any opposition between tactile and optical. Though "necessarily linked to the purely cutaneous perceptions generated by skin contact," writes psychologist Yvette Hatwell, the "indissociable whole labeled 'haptic' (or tactilo-kinesthetic, or active-touch) perception," is formed by "the kinesthetic perceptions resulting from [bodily] movements."[35] And these bodily movements through space are, for sighted (nonblind) experience, at once bound up in vision and touch. Blankets, curtains, pillow coverings, upholstery, wall and floor coverings (*Wand-Bespannstoff*)—all textiles occupying the interior spaces of architecture, trains, automobiles, and so on—are grasped by the subject through a combination of touch, movement, and vision.

Fabric is for Berger an integral part of the modern architectural envelope: "First it should be pointed out that these fabrics are necessarily elements and are thus to be arranged within the totality of the space."[36] Thus in "Weberei und Raumgestaltung," Berger writes several paragraphs on the function of various types of curtains:

> The Sun-curtain should diffuse sunrays, without darkening the room. Generally, it will be relatively colorless, although it may also be colored, especially if the effect of colored reflections in the space is desired. . . . The darkening-curtain should fully isolate the room from the outside world. Aside from the thickness of the material, this is achieved by the suitably chosen colors. A partitioning-curtain should at once be sound-insulating and two-sided, for it hangs between two spaces, from which both sides are seen. . . . Important for all curtains is that they hang well, that the structure of the fabrics makes this possible. . . . Also there is the fall of the folds and shadows to consider.[37]

Berger argues that colorless textiles are best for curtains, unless there is an interest in changing the color of the entire room through reflections and filtering. Thus color and light have more to do with the needs of space

than with a purely optical experience, as they might in ornamental designs. Moreover, the sculptural quality of the object (the falling and folds of the curtain) within the interior design of the space contributes to the working of shadows—ones that move with the weight of the curtain's material. Folds are at once tactile and visual: they are produced out of a specific material thickness but also yield shadows, plays of light and dark. Berger notes further that wall fabric, when used in place of wallpaper, should address multiple sensory concerns beyond the visual attributes of space: "When wall-fabrics are well developed, they must not only achieve for the space an appropriate optical effect, but also under certain circumstances insulate sound and temperature."[38]

Indeed, for Berger a fabric must always address the needs of the architectural interior—particularly as that space is not a purely formal entity but one that is experienced haptically by a subject. She would reiterate her attack on textile designs based on purely formal ideas—which she aligns with "sketches on paper"—in the essay "Stoffe und neues Bauen" from about 1933, when she was beginning to work for the interior design company Wohnbedarf AG. Developing a historical overview of textile production from hand to mechanical weaving and from wall tapestries to clothing and interior fabrics, Berger warns against pictorial weaving and printed fabrics and once again stresses the importance of the tactile:

> Sketches for pictorial weavings and printed fabrics inevitably come into being (develop) on paper. The tactile character thereby is almost completely lost [in the final product], which the sketcher, worse still, [seems to have] intended. The persons working on these cloths through the hundred-year-long constraint of paper work missed the tactile feeling almost completely. These kinds of fabrics are unfortunately still manufactured today, but they are essentially foreign to the new architecture. In order to fulfill the demands of a *living interrelation* between the new building and fabric, we must first of all make clear to ourselves their purpose in architecture.[39]

If pictorial weaving and printed fabrics are most troublesome for Berger, it is because they do not succeed in fully connecting the weaver to the process of production. So too, then, the woven object fails to have a relationship to the space in which subjects experience that textile. What we need for architecture today, Berger declares (clearly drawing on the discourse around the Neues Bauen), is a living relationship between the new building and cloth—a connection that is conceived as a necessary interrelation. Whether the design process acknowledges and meets the conditions of tactility and function in textiles determines the capability for those fabrics to have a "living interrelation" with the new building, but also with the subject that experiences that space through touch.

That Berger should have made an argument about tactility for fabrics in space and architecture is not strange, but that she should do so with such a strong invocation of photography's language of the optical perhaps is, suggesting that the immaterial aspect of the photograph (along with its subtle attention to texture) on some level *requires* a theorization of the textile medium's haptic identity for the architectural environment. Indeed, it was photography more than architecture that had Berger thinking differently about the optical and the tactile within *Raumgestaltung*, much in the way that Walter Benjamin's comments on the technical reproducibility of photographs and film led to his discussion of habit and haptic perception in architecture.[40] Consequently, Berger's writing provides a critical perspective on the studies of sense perception at this moment, particularly as they surfaced in the photograph and as they linked different media to the modern medium of photography.

THE PHOTOGRAPHIC MEDIATION OF TEXTILES: THE OPTICAL MEDIATION OF TACTILITY [...]

Where tactility was the precursor to an optical *Kunstwollen* within Riegl's teleology, the *visual* perception of texture, through photographs of textiles, became a precursor to the recognition of the tactility of fabrics. Photography acted as the lens through which texture could (literally) be seen, and through which weaving at the Bauhaus came to be recognized and sold. Fabric was mediated by the optical view presented by

the photograph, and weaving at once asserted its status as an inherently tactile art and sutured itself to magazine pages, becoming an image—a shiny, flat, black-and-white rectangle. Still missing in the photograph, of course, was any actual physical sense of the intricacy of the sensory differences activated by each piece to the touch (not to mention the color), but the textures became visible, set as they were under strong lights and against a clearly contrasting ground. In other words, the terms of tactile and optical, as exhibited in this instance of photography, served as preconditions to each other. The overlapping of visual and tactile texture in the photographs in *bauhaus* magazine points to the larger debate going on at the time about the interdependence of optical and tactile perception.

At the same time that critics debated photography's purity as an optical medium, the tactility of textiles and objects in the world was dialectically making itself felt within the photographic (and architectural) frame. By saying that a "textile is *not only* an optical object," Berger situated her argument about textiles squarely in the frame of contemporaneous debates about vision, only to reveal how tactility was necessarily entwined in that discussion. Vision cannot be distinguished from touch and even less so from texture. Berger observed that tactile contact with the surface of a textile is not always consciously recognized, but she wished to prevent the perceptual forgetting—one that Riegl's earlier discussion of "tactile memory" in the visual perception of space both acknowledged and required. So the weaver emphasized the way that certain aspects of fabric are not only felt by the hand but also sensed unconsciously. But the discussion of the tactile and the optical in photography was never uniform, and it often performed acrobatic feats, one side flipping into or before the other. So where tactility was the precursor to an optical *Kunstwollen* within Riegl's teleology, the *visual* perception of facture, through photographs of textiles, became a precursor to the recognition of the tactility of fabrics. And at the same time that Bauhaus textiles were moving into the optical public image bank, the discourse of photography had to acknowledge the centrality of the tactile to its project of visual form, especially as it helped push the medium toward commercial goals. With sensual images of textile surfaces and a good marketing strategy for their products, the weaving workshop gained a contract for the mass manufacture of their products with the Polytex-Textil company. […]

Notes

1. The tactile has been an issue for different artistic contexts throughout modernism. For a perspective on the optical and the haptic through a discussion of *Einfühlung* (empathy) in late-nineteenth-and early-twentieth-century German discourse, see Juliet Koss, "On the Limits of Empathy," *Art Bulletin,* vol. 88, no. 1 (March 2006): 139–57. See also Margaret Olin, "Validation by Touch in Kandinsky's Early Abstract Art," *Critical Inquiry*, vol. 16, no. 1 (Autumn 1989): 144–72. The question of the tactile also emerges in criticism of post-1960s installation art; Alex Potts discusses this in "Tactility: The Interrogation of Medium in Art of the 1960s," *Art History*, vol. 27, no. 2 (April 2004): 282–304. According to Potts, the emergence of "tactility" at this time is responsible for the dissolution of the medium (meaning painting and sculpture) in contemporary art. For an analysis of the issue of tactility in contemporary photography and film, see Jean Arnaud's essay on Michael Snow, "Touching to See," *October* 114 (Fall 2005): 5–16.

2. *bauhaus zeitschrift für gestaltung* 2 (July 1931). The issue includes Gunta Stölzl, "Die Entwicklung der Bauhaus-Weberei"; Amédée Ozenfant, "Mein Besuch in der Textilwerkstatt des Bauhauses"; and Johanna Schütz-Wolff, "An die Wolle."

3. It is important to note that, for example, Greenberg's use of term *optical* as the quintessential feature of modernist painting links his argument to a number of German and Austrian contributors to art history, beginning with Lessing and Kant, whom Greenberg mentions, but also to Aloïs Riegl, Robert Vischer, and Konrad Fiedler, all of whom were deeply influential in the Bauhaus context. In other words, the question of opticality—so integral to the modernist notion of medium specificity—was initially developed through the writings of Bauhaus practitioners.

4. Otti Berger, "Weberei und Raumgestaltung" (c. 1932–1934), folder 3, Otti Berger Files, Bauhaus-Archiv Berlin, 3. All translations of Berger's texts are mine.

5. Otti Berger, "Stoffe im Raum," *ReD* (Prague) 3, no. 5 (1930): 143–45, 143.

6. Josef Albers, cited in Leah Dickerman, "Bauhaus Fundaments," in *Bauhaus 1919–1933: Workshops for Modernity*, exhibition catalog (New York: Museum of Modern Art, 2009), 15–39, 32–34.

7. Rainer Wick, *Teaching at the Bauhaus* (Ostfildern, Germany: Hatje Kantz, 2000). Wick also argues, through reference to Herbert Marcuse, that Moholy's focus on the haptic was socially and politically motivated by the "loss" of this sense in the modern age.

8. In a side note to *Von Material zu Architektur*, Moholy-Nagy expressed his concern: "How neglected our tactile education is was demonstrated to me again recently in a striking way in a conversation with the director of a training school of nurses, who spoke of the difficulties she had encountered in teaching massage." Moholy-Nagy, *The New Vision*, 24.

9. For further discussion of Aloïs Riegl's work and its impact on Bauhaus thought, see T'ai Smith, *Bauhaus Weaving Theory*, pp. 32–34; 84–87.

10. Ibid., 23.

11. The grafting of optical onto tactile properties was made perhaps more poignant when photographs of various touch panels from Moholy-Nagy's course (including Berger's and Zierath's) were found in the pages of Moholy-Nagy's *Von Material zu Architecture*. See his *Von Material zu Architektur*, 22–23, 25–29.

12. More than thirty years later, Anni Albers would again address the question of tactility in fabric. See Albers, "Tactile Sensibility," *On Weaving*, 62–65; and this book's concluding chapter.

13. The first major text on Otti Berger was a German master's thesis by Regina Lösel, later published as an essay, "Die Textildesignerin Otti Berger (1898–1944): Vom Bauhaus zur Industrie," in *Textildesign: Voysey-Endell-Berger*, vol. 3 of *Textil-Körper-Mode*, ed. Gabriele Mentges and Heide Nixdorff (Berlin: Edition Ebersbach, 2002), 215–294, 31.

14. After Stölzl was forced to leave the Bauhaus due to a political scandal that pitted several students against her, Berger and Anni Albers took over many aspects of technical instruction.

15. I discuss these developments, which happened after she left the Bauhaus in 1932, in chapter 4.

16. Otti Berger, "Stoffe im Raum," *ReD* (Prague) 3, no. 5 (1930): 143.

17. See Stölzl, "Weaving at the Bauhaus."

18. Berger, "Stoffe im Raum," 145.

19. Lösel, "Die Textildesignerin Otti Berger," 237.

20. The topic of tactility was also considered by the futurist F. T. Marinetti, who published a manifesto on "tactilism" in 1921 in Italy. See Marinetti, "Manifest," in *Experiment Theater* (Zurich: Peter Schifferli Verlag AG, 1960). Quoting Moholy-Nagy, Marinetti "was a passionate advocate of a new kind of art, to be based on tactile sensations alone, and proposed tactile ribbons, carpets, beds, rooms, stage settings, etc." Moholy-Nagy, *The New Vision*, 24. Berger may have been acquainted with Marinetti's ideas, but Berger's discussion was more sustained than Marinetti's and involved a deeper reflection on the status of cloth in modern space and vis-à-vis other media, like photography.

21. See Hajo Düchting, ed., *Farbe am Bauhaus: Synthese und Synästhesie* (Berlin: Gebr. Mann; and Dessau: Stiftung Bauhaus, 1996).

22. Clark V. Poling, *Kandinsky's Teaching at the Bauhaus: Color Theory and Analytical Drawing* (New York: Rizzoli, 1986), 49.

23. Otti Berger, "Aufzeichnungen aus dem Kandinsky-Unterricht," Bauhaus-Archiv Berlin, Otti Berger files, folder 13, 6–9. The German: "Der Wert der Farbe kann nicht nur mit dem Auge festgestellt werden sondern auch mit allen anderen Sinnen."

24. Just as Aristotle had argued in *De Anima*, Berger suggests that to feel, or to touch, is primary to sense perception in general. Aristotle's point is further elaborated by Jean Luc-Nancy in *The Muses* (Palo Alto, Calif.: Stanford University Press, 1996): "The heterogeneity of the senses is not homothetic to that of the arts. . . . The classical distribution of the five senses either does not refer to five arts or raises infinite problems of the 'minor' arts (e.g., cooking, perfumery). As for touch, which is established by a very long tradition as the paradigm or even the essence of the senses in general, it does not open onto any kind of art. (When it is said that sculpture is an art of touch, one means touch at a distance—which may well be the essence of touch, but that does not do away with what, in sculpture, exceeds touch)" (11).

25. Lösel, "Die Textildesignerin Otti Berger," 234.

26. Berger, "Weberei und Raumgestaltung," 4.

27. Droste and Ludewig, Das Bauhaus Webt, 261.

28. Otti Berger, "Effect through the Material," *International Textiles* 4 (Bauhaus-Archiv Berlin, Otti Berger files, folder 27), and "Umsatzsteigerung durch Geschmacksveredelung," (Increase of Sales through the Refining of Taste) *Der Konfektionär* 47, no. 95 (November 1932), 5.

29. Berger, "Weberei und Raumgestaltung," 3.

30. Berger, "Stoffe im Raum," 145.

31. Lösel, "Die Textildesignerin Otti Berger," 237; emphasis added.

32. Berger, "Stoffe im Raum," 145.

33. *Kunstseide* translates literally as "artificial silk" and can be used to refer to either viscose silk (a material made from wood that came into widespread use in Germany during the interwar years) or rayon.

34. Berger, "Weberei und Raumgestaltung," 5.

35. *Touching for Knowing: Cognitive Psychology of Manual Perception*, ed. Yvette Hatwell, Arlette Streri, and Edouard Gentaz (Amsterdam and Philadelphia: John Benjamins B.V., 2003), 2.

36. Berger, "Weberei und Raumgestaltung," 4.

37. Ibid., 5.

38. Ibid.

39. Berger, "Stoffe und neues Bauen" (c. 1932–34), Bauhaus-Archiv Berlin, Otti Berger files, folder 3, p. 2; emphasis mine.

40. Benjamin writes, "Tactile appropriation is accomplished not so much by attention as by habit. As regards architecture, habit determines to a large extent even optical reception." Walter Benjamin, "The Work of Art in the Age of Mechanical Reproduction," in Walter Benjamin, *Illuminations*, ed. Hannah Arendt, trans. Harry Zohn (New York: Schocken, 1968), 240. For a further discussion of Benjamin and architecture with respect to this essay, see Hilde Heynen, *Architecture and Modernity* (Cambridge, Mass.: MIT Press, 2001), 107. Benjamin's essay followed Riegl's account of "modes of perception" as historical phenomena.

3

THE TACIT-TURN
Textile design in design research (2010)

Elaine Igoe

EDITOR'S INTRODUCTION

Elaine Igoe is Senior Lecturer at Chelsea College of Art, University of the Arts London and the University of Portsmouth, UK, and the author, alongside seven contributors, of the book *Textile Design Theory in the Making* (2021). Rose Sinclair's contribution to the publication appears in the community section of this book. An edited version of Igoe's 2010 article is reprinted in full here. In it she establishes several of the key topics of 'In Textasis: Matrixial Narratives of Textile Design', her PhD thesis written in the department of textiles at the Royal College of Art, London, and completed in 2014. Drawing on her BA and MA education in textile design, Igoe's research and publications articulate the importance of understanding the particulars of textile design more specifically within general design discourse. She draws on feminist qualitative research methods and autoethnography, often making use of storytelling and metaphor.

As she articulates in the text included here, 'The paucity of academic writing concerned with the idiosyncrasies of the textile design discipline marks it out as taciturn in comparison to those disciplines of design that have been instrumental in the emergence of design research.' The 'tacit-turn' in the title of this writing is a word play that recognizes Peter Dormer's use of the word 'taciturn' (commonly used to mean uncommunicative) to describe an inability to articulate knowledge as well as Michael Polanyi's writing on tacit knowledge. Igoe shares with Victoria Mitchell, the first text of this book, an instinct to build new vocabulary in an effort to convey the qualities of the textile and arrives at the word 'textiley' to describe what is hard to pin down but nonetheless familiar within the discipline.

Igoe positions textiles as 'agent[s] of tactile and visual experience'. Her writing seeks to counter what could be heard as the muteness of textile design qualities by instead offering three textile archetypes to challenge the gendered nature of textile design and articulate the unusual place of the textile as a very particular structure among other design practices: textiles is a mother, textiles is a geisha, textiles is a spinster. Throughout this writing Igoe, much like T'ai Smith's writing about Otti Berger, keeps her attention trained equally on an understanding of textile design that makes use of both sight and touch. In addressing textile design as a unique discipline within design discourse deserving of a more nuanced scholarship, Igoe reveals the disciplinary structures that guide, but can also limit, our understanding of a particular area of knowledge.

The tacit-turn: Textile design in design research

Elaine Igoe

Summary of contribution: This paper introduces some of the key topics of my PhD thesis, which seeks to conceptualise textiles to elucidate design thinking in the field. This paper aims to situate the textile design discipline into the broader remit of design research, identifying specific contexts for textile design research.

Questions about the nature of design began to emerge in the late 1950s as a result of research into creativity, decision-making and management as well as advances in computer technology and artificial intelligence for problem solving. The academic discipline of 'Design Research' developed as it became accepted that design involved a very specific and distinctive type of knowledge. Bruce Archer was a leading exponent of this view and was fundamental in the inception of the 'Design Studies journal' and academic design research in general. In the debut issue published in July 1979, Archer presents a paper entitled 'Design as Discipline' which prompts these questions from the editor, Sydney Gregory:

> "Can design be a discipline in its own right? If so, what are its distinguishing features? (What are the kinds of features that distinguish any discipline?) To what questions should the discipline address itself — in both research and teaching? What methodology does it use? What results — what applications — should it be trying to achieve?" (Archer 1979)

Over the decades, these questions have been studied from the perspective of different sectors of design, most prominently in architecture, industrial design and engineering, the results of which have formed the basis of design research knowledge and still lead the academic discourse in this area. 'Design Studies' remains one of the leading journals on design thinking and process but is heavily biased towards industrial and engineering design, as is the more recent 'The Design Journal' published since 1998. Nigel Cross has been a key research figure in the area of design thinking and his 2007 book 'Designerly Ways of Knowing' is collated as a summary of decades of his research. The book includes a chapter entitled 'Studies of Outstanding Designers' (Cross 2007:85), the three expert designers he studies approach design from an industrial or engineering perspective. Although Cross mentions that these designers are from different disciplines he does not acknowledge the similarities between those particular areas of design. Equally he does not explicitly recognise the variety of experience that may have been garnered from studying, for example, a leading ceramic designer, fashion designer or textile designer.

In relation to textile design, the context for disseminating research in the field is less developed. 'Textile; The Journal of Cloth and Culture' published since 2003 focuses on issues of materiality, and cultural and historical studies and therefore is not well placed to kindle the discourse on textiles as a design discipline. The paucity of academic writing concerned with the idiosyncrasies of the textile design discipline marks it out as taciturn in comparison to those disciplines of design that have been instrumental in the emergence of design research over the past five decades.

Peter Dormer (Dormer 1994:15) uses the word 'taciturn' as he describes the doer and maker who cannot adequately articulate their knowledge. Anni Albers (Albers 1944) states that the inability to give words to the experience of making and designing is not symptomatic of a lack of intelligence but an indication of an intelligence that expresses itself via alternative means; a type of internal intelligence that can be

---

Source: Elaine Igoe, 'The Tacit-Turn: Textile Design in Design Research', *The Duck Journal for Research in Textiles and Textile Design* (2010), pp. 1–11. Reproduced with permission.

described as awareness, intuition or tacit knowledge. Albers values the internality of knowledge and argues that its' artistic or designerly outcomes provide us with a means of verifying this knowledge. Dormer agrees and notes that this practical (tacit) knowledge is difficult to articulate but can be demonstrated and that it is possible for it to be judged. He warns of the dangers of reliance on tacit knowledge and the importance of questioning it. To question the tacit, requires the ability to begin to objectify, articulate and challenge assumptions.

As the principles of design research are so rooted within specific design disciplines from which it was developed, can we presume that they are wholly applicable to *textile* design research? I will use the questions posed by Gregory in 1979 to begin an enquiry into the notion of textile design as a sub-discipline of design with specific methodologies, tacit knowledge and modes of behaviour. In this brief paper, I hope to explore some of the inadequacies of our epistemological understanding of textile design, and identify oppor-tunities for a more integrated relationship between textile design and design research.

As Gregory ponders on how it might be possible to define a 'discipline' let us begin here too. Seminal author on tacit knowledge, Michael Polanyi (1958) provides a religious analogy that may help to explain and describe the collective mindset that drives individuals who call themselves 'designers'. He uses Christianity as an example of "...*a heuristic vision which is accepted for the sake of its unresolvable tension. It is like an obsession with a problem known to be insoluble, which yet, unswervingly, the heuristic commands; 'Look at the unknown!' Christianity sedulously fosters, and in a sense permanently satisfies, man's craving for mental dissatisfaction by offering him the comfort of a crucified God.*" (Polanyi 1958:212) In this analogy we can compare the tacitly experienced and communicated nature of religion with its collective vision of an all-encompassing and compelling unsolvable problem, to design. To profess to design also requires a shared view and an experience of a tension and a permanent dissatisfaction; one that considers that the world requires continual transformation through the creation of new objects. When judged in this way, design could

be seen as a 'broad church', structured through sub-disciplines or denominations that deliver teachings, which are largely similar but yet with some significant deviations.

A 'discipline' requires disciples; individuals who feel drawn to a particular set of teachings, tacitly learn and adopt the rules and rituals associated with the discipline allowing them to guide their thoughts and behaviours. Disciples follow and embrace the teachings, which may be explicit and written down or implicitly communicated. They will take comfort in knowing they share their fundamental beliefs, thoughts, and behaviours with others. Essentially the disciple has a tacit relationship with the discipline, which is both internal and personal and external in relation to other disciples across time and location. In a paper exploring the notion of the 'discipline' in design, Salustri and Rogers (2008:299/7) state that, "*Once we have learned to do something in a certain way, we will tend to do that thing the same way forever, or until a "better" way presents itself (and sometimes, not even then). In this way, we will tend to not try other ways to do a thing because we have learned one way of doing it.*"

So once indoctrinated in a discipline, it can remain with us almost indefinitely. This supports the notion of a quasi-religious design discipline. If we accept that the compulsion to design as well as other activities and experiences associated with designing are universal then we must also ask why most designers specialise within one area or sub-discipline of design?

In their recent paper referring to Kuhn's 1962 book '*Structure of Scientific Revolutions*', Wang and Ilhan (2009:5) "*propose a* sociological *distinctiveness to the design professions which, is really their key distinguishing signature.*" They oppose the notion that individual design professions hold specific knowledge (and note that there are social, historical and market-led reasons for this concept being maintained in academic writing) but rather that they are all centred round the '*creative act*'. They describe a '*sociological wrapping*' around the '*creative act*' and proceed in their investigation by questioning what a profession *is*. Wang and Ilhan advise that in order to define a design profession one must decipher what it does "*(with any general knowledge that assists in the creative act) in a sociological process of defining itself to the larger culture."* (Wang & Ilhan 2009:7)

The textile design discipline appears to attract a broad range of disciples. The term 'textile practitioner' can at once describe students, artists, craftspeople, hobbyists and designers of various levels of expertise, approaches and experience all with markedly different approaches to following and embracing the 'teachings' of the discipline. Certain traits in objects, behaviours or even people may be considered *'textiley'* amongst textile practitioners, a word that is difficult to define but easily understood within the discipline. Textile design encompasses teachings from the broader disciplines of design, technology, art and craft, indicating that textile design disciples have formed both a personal and collective tacit understanding of a specific blend of knowledge. What remains to be examined is whether this knowledge and its associated methodologies serve as, in Wang and Ilhan's terms, a general knowledge contributing to a more generalised creative act or design process or whether it may offer a new paradigm for design research. If sociological wrapping defines the public and professional identity of a profession or discipline, how is textiles wrapped, who has contributed to its wrapping and why so and does it need to be modified or updated?

I suggest that to begin to understand this, it is useful to consider the textile design discipline as an entity; including textile designers, designed textile objects and the textile design process. When seen in this way it is possible to identify certain traits that allow us to characterise textiles. Below, I propose particular embodiments of the character of textiles. I use the word 'Textiles' to denote an entity once again. I have selected feminine archetypes on which to explore the sociological wrapping of textiles. These roles have been selected as they draw attention to the complex and dichotomous epistemology of textiles. Textiles as an entity may at one time subscribe to all of these archetypes.

Textiles is a mother.

It is universally fundamental in its ability to enable other objects to come into existence. It is a fertile ground that invites (and requires) partners to participate in realising new creations, a site of origination. Textiles implicitly relates, adapts, communicates and gives continuously and changeably on a physical level.

Textiles is a geisha.

It must use all its performative, decorative and seductive characteristics in order to communicate its exquisiteness to patrons. Patrons are courted ritually and continuously and once a relationship has been organised, the patron receives a particular level of control over the behaviour of Textiles, who responds by expressing the potential of sensory pleasure. Textiles communicates a submissive character, which belies the reverence given to its highly accomplished and wide-ranging skills. This relationship is difficult for those from particular social cultures to understand properly, however the indigenous social perspective provides alternative readings of the situation.

Textiles is a spinster.

Textiles is considered simple, naïve and uncomplicated not forthcoming or interested in articulating what makes it special or unique. Its muteness has impeded its ability to forge relationships. Textiles can be intelligent and interesting but may be overlooked by those looking, merely, for beauty. In response Textiles sometimes opts out, preferring to remain academic, free to pursue its own interests and out of the reach of potential suitors.

These labels carry significant meaning and can be more deeply explored not least from a feminist perspective. They expose how textiles as a designed object, a way of thinking and a way of being has been gendered (Igoe 2021). The description of each archetype explains the centrality of relationality to textiles. Designed textile objects are innately highly relational, a quality of which textile designers are aware. At the same time, textile designers must regularly court manufacturers and other types of designers who are looking for textiles to help them realise their own design ideas. Most commonly, textile designs need to be bought and given an application before they can interact within society. To do this textile designers often produce a wide range of designs made to address and satisfy the market requirements as far as possible. A large proportion of perfectly acceptable textile designs will never be sold or put into production. There is of course a contingent of the most innovative textile designers who do not wish to participate in this courtship of commerce. They are encouraged by and operating within academic institutions. Some, but few, are successful in achieving both academic and commercial acclaim.

The descriptions also allude to the pleasure-giving qualities of textiles, which may be subtle and tactile or decorative and sensorial. They also point to the unspoken nature of textile design, it may be taken for granted, disregarded or unrecognised for its input in the design process and the resulting designed object. This muteness has resulted in textiles accepting a considerably less active role in the pertinent debates of design research theory as it developed.

If these labels help us to understand how textiles, as a design discipline and designed object, presents itself in the larger culture, they can also be used to uncover design theory and methodologies for textile design. Within my continued research, I seek to explore how a sociological understanding of textiles may help in articulating the form of the *'creative act'* (Wang & Ilhan 2009) for textiles.

Returning to the quotation from Gregory, he goes on to ask what kinds of questions a discipline should address itself to, and so let us apply his query to textiles. Their primary roles as designed objects are to provide shelter and modesty but also to deliver a tactile and visual experience. Of course, textiles also have functions connected with their roles, for example as filters, carrying devices or to respond to heat or light. In this paper, I want to focus on textiles' role as agent of tactile and visual experience, specifically its decorative characteristics. David Brett provides an explanation of decoration and identifies and legitimises it as transformative, alluding to its visual and tactile qualities and its role in sensory perception and social function (Brett 2005). Brett uses examples from textile design to help form his definition of 'the decorative':

" I begin to see what decoration is for. It completes. It brings buildings, objects and artefacts to completion in

and for perception, by making them easier to see, more finished, more easily focussed upon. It completes in and for social use by making them into signs and symbols for our endeavours and beliefs. It completes in and for pleasure by inviting the eye to dwell and the hand to caress. It completes in and for thought by making objects memorable. Decoration, by completing our world, completes those who live in it...." Brett (2005:264)

He continuously talks of the role of decoration in providing pleasure, but textiles can be earnestly functional and elaborately decorative at the same time, yet the multifarious qualities of textiles can often be unseen, forgotten or unspoken:

"...in many or most cases we have got so used to this ornament that we look upon it as if had grown of itself, and note it of no more than mosses on the dry sticks with which we light our fires." (Morris 1877)

Jane Graves extends Brett and Morris's inclusion of textiles as a form/mode of decoration by closely associating textiles with pattern. She gives a psychoanalytical account of pattern (Schoeser & Boydell 2002:45) in which she describes how decoration is converted through repetition into pattern. She suggests that textile *is* pattern, whether or not pattern is woven in as a design, as the natural texture resultant from weaving or knitting or as printed onto a textile surface. This approach to *'disentangling textiles'* (Schoeser & Boydell 2002) allows a deeper conceptualisation of not only the outcomes of textile design as designed objects but also the intentions, behaviours and thinking of the textile designer. Similarly to Brett and Morris, she correlates textiles (pattern *as* textiles) with pleasure and describes how, in particular the printed textile designer, is free to play with the powerful qualities of pattern and uses Freudian concepts to describe how the unconscious is drawn to pattern for it's addictive and disorientating qualities. So, textiles as designed decorative objects can be seen as sometimes imperceptible yet tacitly addictive, emotive and pleasurable but how are these 'meta-functions' of textiles understood within the discipline and how do they affect the issues to which textiles, as a design discipline, addresses itself? The nature of the ill-defined design problems that textile designers address have not yet been adequately explored or critiqued and subsequently there are no clear debates that could begin to offer answers.

Archer and Gregory (1979) also prompt an exploration of the methodology of design. Tacit knowledge is embodied in the designed outcomes of textile design and exhibited in the textile designer's cognitive and practical activities undertaken within their design process. Can a textiles orientated approach to design be correlated with a more concrete methodology within the broader remit of design research?

Design research has been understood to encompass four main areas. These were outlined in a diagram by Sanders and Stappers (2008) as critical design, participatory design, user-centred design and design and emotion. Further research into textile design from a theoretical and philosophical approach will allow for specific sites in this topography to emerge as suitable for textiles. 'Design and emotion' is represented as the smallest field within the *'topography of design research'* (Sanders 2006). It has been charted but is yet unmapped; it does not feature any distinctive research methods, tools or smaller fields of research within it. However it is this field that seems to lend itself most to the characteristics of the entity of the textiles discipline. Seeing 'design and emotion' *through* textiles could also allow for a better understanding and more overlaps with the other fields of design research. Currently, an overlap with 'user-centred design' describes the role of industrial design (including interaction design and product design) within 'design and emotion' as promoted by The Design and Emotion Society. 'Design and emotion' is led by design and by research, with the user as subject and / or partner. If it is agreed that 'design and emotion' is a field ripe for input from the textile design discipline, how might this input reshape the field or vice versa? In Sanders and Stappers (2008) diagram, 'design and emotion' is situated closer to design than research; if textiles were to adopt a more research focussed approach, what effect would this have on the nature of the textiles discipline and how it is perceived?

In recent years there has been a phenomenal growth in innovative textile design work dealing with sophisticatedly complex problems concerned with sensory perception, aesthetic and haptic pleasure and social function; for example textile designers are applying their knowledge and thinking to design for architectural, healthcare and wellbeing and automotive applications. They are working with material scientists, engineers, chemists and industrial designers. These relationships are forming because each party recognises and values a particular quality of knowledge that they wish to access in one another in order to develop and further their practice in their field. Kavanagh (2004) and Kavanagh, Matthews & Tyrer (2008) give several case studies that attest to this. The rapid growth of this type of interdisciplinary work at the cutting edge of textiles is serving to highlight its particular 'designerly ways of knowing' (Cross 2007). The activities of these textile designers will start to enlarge and stretch the 'design and emotion' methodology until more detail emerges and overlap with the other design research fields occur and will be where the specificities of textile design thinking and knowledge will be found.

Whilst it may be true that within academia, textile design is turning 'smart' and looking towards innovative interdisciplinarity, it is also true that this type of work has only a small immediate impact on the majority of textile designs that consumers wear and decorate their homes with. What links textile designers working within the commercial sector with those more concerned with innovation is that both activities require the utilisation of a tacit knowledge of textiles to make items aesthetic and/or haptic; abilities and knowledge which have not been given adequate attention, value or gravitas.

Undergraduate and postgraduate textile design students are working and playing with diverse materials as well as fabric, thread and yarn within their textile design process. It is during their education when textile designers most tangibly feel the breadth of the methodology of textile design and discover the function and meta-functions of textiles. It is only when they come into contact with industry or other fields of design do they start to tacitly understand what distinguishes the textile discipline. And it is when they see their designs in context or in use do they begin to acknowledge the relational, emotive and communicative qualities of the textiles they have designed. This knowledge continues to be implicitly communicated from designer to designer, tutor to pupil, but not explicitly articulated out towards industry or other fields of design. They tacitly synthesise this information, and therefore it remains inadequately critically evaluated in any explicit way useful for design research academia. This then creates a disjuncture between a textile designer's tacit concept of textile design and the understanding of it outside of the discipline. Many graduates of textile design degrees find that what was happily accepted and even lauded as textile design within the educational setting is inappropriate or misunderstood in industrial or commercial settings.

This disjuncture seems to be largely accepted within the textile design discipline itself, although a handful of authors have sought to address it by examining the knowledge and processes of textile design. Alison Shreeve opens up the conversation about tacit knowledge in textiles in 'Material Girls; Tacit Knowledge in Textile Crafts' (Johnson 1998) and in doing so emphasises the need for extended research in this area. James Moxey in 'The Representation of Concepts in Textile Design' (Moxey 2000) also studies textile design students. His study focuses on describing the outcomes of textile design thinking, such as moodboards and samples. These two studies focus on how the knowledge that textile designers share is communicated or displayed in an educational setting. Rachel Studd (2002) provides a detailed overview of the textile design process in a variety of industrial contexts as a way of defining a model and subsequently provides some insight into textile knowledge and thinking.

Referring back to Gregory's questions about design as a discipline and applying them to textiles shows that there is still some ground to gain before textiles is more broadly understood, and not simply practised as, a form of design. One challenge to overcome when attempting to discover the distinguishing features of the textile design sub-discipline is the requirement to make explicit the tacit knowledge closely shared amongst the textile 'disciples'. Gale and Kaur's 'The Textile Book' (2002:190) recognises that, *"In the absence of a significant interest from the chattier academic disciplines, the task of establishing such a discourse rests quite clearly with the textile community itself."*

In returning to both the title and structure of this paper it is evident that the entity of textiles, including the discipline, the designed object and the designer, is traditionally taciturn. Textiles, as a sub-discipline of design is not so much *'sociologically wrapped'* (Wang & Ilhan 2009) as 'sociologically swaddled', resulting in a lack of activity in the wider discourse of design research. This paper aims to illustrate that there are clear areas in the existing design research discourse in which textile design, could provide a unique perspective and a new voice amongst the historically *'chattier disciplines'*.

REFERENCES

Albers, A (1959) *Anni Albers: On Designing*. Connecticut: Wesleyan University Press

Archer, B (1979) 'Design as a Discipline; Whatever became of Design Methodology?' in *Design Studies* Vol 1 No 1, IPC Business Press pp.17-20

Brett, D (2005) *Rethinking Decoration*. Cambridge University Press. USA

Cross, N (2007) *Designerly Ways of Knowing*. Basel/Boston/ Berlin: Birkhauser Verlag AG

Dormer, P (1994) *The Art of the Maker*. London: Thames and Hudson Ltd

Gale, C & Kaur, J (2002) *The Textile Book*. Oxford. Berg

Graves, J (2002) 'Symbol, Pattern and the Unconscious' in Schoeser, M & Boydell, C (eds) (2002) *Disentangling Textiles: Techniques for the study of designed objects*. London: Middlesex University Press

Kavanagh, T (2004) 'Designers Managing Technology' in *Journal of Textile and Apparel, Technology and Management*, Vol 4 Iss 1. North Carolina State University. USA

Kavanagh, T, Matthews, J & Tyrer, J (2008) 'An Inter-Disciplinary Search for Innovation in Textile Design'. Proceedings of the 86th Textile Institute World Conference, 18–21, November 2008, Hong Kong, pp 409–422.

Morris, W (1877) *The Decorative Arts, their relation to modern life and progress*. [internet] Available at: https://www .marxists.org/archive/morris/works/1877/decorative.htm

Moxey, J (2000) 'The representation of concepts in textile design' in *Point: Art and Design Journal*, No.9, Spring/Summer 2000 pp 50–58

Polanyi, M (1958) *Personal Knowledge*. London; Routledge & Kegan Paul

Salustri, F & Rogers, D (2008) 'Some Thoughts on Terminology and Discipline in Design' in Undisciplined! Proceedings of the Design Research Society Conference 2008 Sheffield, UK. July 2008 pp 299/1-299/10

Sanders, E & Stappers, P (2008) *'Co-creation and the New Landscapes of Design'* [internet] Available at http://www.maketools.com/ [Accessed 11 December 2009]

Sanders, E (2006) 'Design Research in 2006' in *Design Research Quarterly* September 2006. [internet] Available at http://www.maketools.com/ [Accessed 11 December 2009]

Shreeve, A (1998) 'Material Girls – Tacit Knowledge in Textile Crafts' in Johnson, P (ed) (1998) *Ideas in the Making; Practice in Theory*. London: Crafts Council

Studd, R (2002) 'The Textile Design Process' in *The Design Journal* Vol 3, Iss 2 pp 35–49. Oxford. Berg

Wang, D & Ilhan, A (2009) 'Holding Creativity Together: A Sociological Theory of the Design Professions' in *Design Issues*, Vol 25 No 1; MIT Journals

4

FOLDS, FRAGMENTS, SURFACES
Towards a poetics of cloth (1999)

Pennina Barnett

EDITOR'S INTRODUCTION

Pennina Barnett is a writer, curator and founding co-editor of the academic journal *TEXTILE: Cloth and Culture*, first published in 2003. Her curatorial projects include 'Women and Textiles Today' held at Cornerhouse, Manchester (27 May–30 July 1988), which, together with 'Embroidery in Women's Lives 1300-1900' curated by Jennifer Harris and held concurrently at the Whitworth Art Gallery, University of Manchester, was conceived under the umbrella title 'The Subversive Stitch' exhibitions. The exhibitions drew inspiration from the late Rozsika Parker's book *The Subversive Stitch: Embroidery and the Making of the Feminine* (1984). More recently, Joseph McBrinn has also built upon Parker's writing with his book *Queering the Subversive Stitch*: *Men and the Culture of Needlework* (2021), an excerpt of which is included in the community section of this book.

Barnett's 'Folds, Fragments, Surfaces: Towards a poetics of cloth' was written for the catalogue accompanying the exhibition 'Textures of Memory: The poetics of cloth', curated by Barnett and Pamela Johnson in 1999. The exhibition was first shown at Angel Row Gallery (now closed) in Nottingham, England, followed by a UK tour, and included work by seven artists: Polly Binns, Maxine Bristow, Caroline Broadhead, Alicia Felberbaum, Marianne Ryan, Anne Wilson and Verdi Yahooda.

Barnett's writing, reprinted in full here, makes use of unconventional line spacing, inserting pauses to set apart particular passages as distinct fragments – a technique alluded to in the text's title. Cloth is proposed to be not only a poetic language – with its emotive vocabulary of fold, drape, tear and touch – but also a challenge to binary structures and their limiting categories. Drawing on the work of Gilles Deleuze and Michel Serres, she asks: 'What if the poetics of cloth were composed of "soft logics", modes of thought that twist and turn and stretch and fold?' Rather than shore up divisions or animosities, Barnett instead warns: 'To set the tactile *against* the visual is to presume the separation of the senses; to forsake soft logics for rigid boxes.'

Folds, Fragments, Surfaces: Towards a poetics of cloth

Pennina Barnett

White satin shapes and reshapes
charged like the erotic flower paintings of
                           Georgia O'Keefe,
organic forms, intimate recesses,
inner landscapes.

Soft velvet curls in upon itself
vibrating light and shade.
Pigment saturates
strokes
caresses.

A needle pierces.
Harmless
save for an empty eye, a taut posture.
Cotton, white and benign.
Silver silhouettes against black and white and
                                 black.

Small gestures pass easily by.

Yet this is a space where small gestures slide into dreams; where the familiar turns. A place of quiet intensity. Where the textures of memory are smooth and white and velvet and blue and layered with gesso and paint. Where they absorb into linen and cotton and canvas and celluloid; are of mass and material, shadow and ghost; are as fine as hair, as ephemeral as light, as sharp as pins, as random as discarded thread. Where there is the will to repair and disrepair, to reveal and conceal, to caress and embrace. And to imagine and muse, and to invent and create, and to remember and forget, and

to fold and unfold . . .

'Rigid little boxes fit inside a big one, but the reverse isn't true. It is impossible to put the big one . . . in any of the smaller ones . . . Now if there is a logic of boxes, perhaps there is a logic of sacks. A canvas or jute sack . . . is supple enough to be folded up in a sack with all the other folded sacks, even its former container. I believe that there is box-thought, the thought we call rigorous, like rigid, inflexible boxes, and sack-thought, like systems of fabric. Our philosophy lacks a good organum of fabrics.'

'. . . Let us learn to negotiate soft logics. They are only crazy if we do not understand them. Let us finally laugh about those who called rigorous what was precisely their soft discourse. And let us no longer scorn what is soft . . .'[1]

What if the poetics of cloth were composed of 'soft logics', modes of thought that twist and turn and stretch and fold? And in this movement new encounters were made, beyond the constraint of binaries? The binary offers two possibilities, 'either/or'; 'soft logics' offer multiple possibilities. They are the realm of the 'and/and', where anything can happen. Binaries exclude; 'soft logics' are 'to think without excluding'[2]— yet one is not set against the other, (that would miss the point). And if 'soft' suggests an elastic surface, a tensile quality that yields to pressure, this is not a weakness; for 'an object that *gives in* is actually stronger than one that resists, because it also permits the opportunity to be oneself in a new way'.[3]

the artist, the philosopher and the baker

An artist is watching a philosopher watching a baker. The artist is Yve Lomax; the philosopher, Michel Serres.

The philosopher: 'What does a baker do when he kneads dough? At the beginning there is an amorphous

---

Source: Pennina Barnett, 'Folds, Fragments, Surfaces: Towards a Poetics of Cloth', *Textures of Memory: The Poetics of Cloth* (Angel Row Gallery & Pitshanger Manor & Gallery, 1999), pp. 25–34. Reproduced with permission.

mass, let's say a square. The baker stretches it, spreads it out, then folds it over, then stretches it out and folds it over again. He does not stop folding the mass over on itself—an exemplary gesture . . .'[4]

The artist: 'The baker and the philosopher; and between the two a becoming. When we practice the baker's logic, theory knows no bounds; it becomes soft and flexible. Air enters into the dough; things soon will expand. To get some air in your life, practise the baker's logic'.[5]

. . . to fold and unfold and enfold . . .

. . . this is a space to curl and to clasp, to enclose and to disclose: a space of encounter . . .

'The question always entails living in the world . . . We are discovering new ways of folding, akin to new envelopments . . . what always matters is folding, unfolding, refolding'.[6]

'. . . to unfold is to increase, to grow; whereas to fold is to diminish, to reduce, "to withdraw into the recesses of a world"'.[7]

For philosopher Gilles Deleuze (1925–1995), the fold is an image of conceptual space, a mental landscape: 'the image thought gives itself of what it means to think'.[8] In classical philosophy, thought is related to truth. But for Deleuze, the task of the philosopher is to create new concepts and to alter existent meanings. This is not 'thinking' as something we automatically do, or a knowledge we already have.[9] But 'thinking' as immanent, a form of experimentation: an essentially creative and critical activity, activated when the mind is 'provoked by an encounter with the unknown or the unfamiliar . . .', or when 'something in the world forces us to think'.[10] New concepts unfold in ways we cannot anticipate, and bring into consciousness significant or important events.[11]

The Deleuzian fold is a virtual, even cinematic image—of 'points . . . referrals, spaces';[12] an infinity of folds always in motion, composing and recomposing without inside or outside, beginning or end. And in this movement disparate elements encounter and separate, continuous and discontinuous, a relation of difference with itself. It is a universe more than a world, in which

there are also spaces, not so much of rupture, but what we might call 'distribution'. Here, folds double back on themselves like ocean waves, withdraw, and almost cease to generate. Yet within the hollow of the fold, and despite its closure, a leap may still be possible: not a leap 'elsewhere (as if another world would open up) but rather leaping in place . . . and thus distorting or displacing the ground (the foundation, or its unfounding)'.[13]

. . . turning . . . inside out . . .

. . . Folds spill out from canvas into marble and architecture, and into the hurly-burly of the piazza. Inside a dark candle-lit space, the air is heavy with incense. Bernini's *St Teresa* writhes in ecstatic bliss, pleasure suffused with pain. A flaming golden arrow pierces her heart. Folds that cannot be explained by the body, multiply and become autonomous.[14] We are in the Baroque. A period of swathing draperies and billowing clothes. The Baroque, with its fantastic curves—'the fold that goes out to infinity'.[15] An art of dynamic movement, emotional display, swooning saints in spiritual and somatic rapture, all expressed through the agency of the fold, or folds. 'They convey the intensity of a spiritual force exerted on the body, either to turn it upside down or to stand or raise it up over and again, but in every event to turn it inside out and to mold its inner surfaces'.[16]

. . . The piazza empties. The Baroque fades. Yet something remains . . .

. . . for this is a space of quiet, but not one of silence, where gestures, though small, stir sense and sensation; and senses confuse and cause a vibration; where visual is tactile and tactile is visual, and what is at stake is— not representation but— the composing of folds that take place in slow motion, as intimate moments steal into view . . .

. . . From the Baroque to the white cube: the carnal to the retinal. Yve-Alain Bois writes that the modernist discourses that have come to dominate our approach to the visual deny the space that our bodies occupy. For one of the founding myths of modernism is 'that visual art, especially painting, addresses itself uniquely to the sense of sight'.[17] Even when art history does address the 'tactile', it is through a *visual representation* of tactility, which remains 'purely visual'. Drawing on Freud and Bataille, he argues that the modernist picture is conceived as a vertical section, which has implications for the way in which we experience it. For this presupposes the viewing subject as an erect being (*homo erectus*), distinct from the four-legged creature from which we evolved, a creature parallel with the ground. But this 'civilising' change of axis, he asserts, was only achieved through the sublimation of the body:

> '. . . man is proud of being erect, (and of having thus emerged from the animal state, the biological mouth-anus axis of which is horizontal), but this pride is founded on a repression. Vertical, man has no other biological sense than to stare at the sun and thus burn his eyes . . .'[18]

What he forgets, is that his feet are still in the dirt.[19]

Despite the dominance of this myth, there are, of course, many examples of painting, *within* modernism, that challenge the idea of art as an activity that alienates the viewer (and artist) from their bodies. Think of Pollock, his canvasses stretched horizontally out beneath him—they aren't addressed to *homo erectus*; or a Cézanne still life, where objects seem about to roll onto the floor in defiance of gravity.[20]

Yet myths are powerful, and perhaps it is no coincidence that cloth, with its special relationship to the body, has been largely marginalised by these dominant discourses. Always close, it has an immediacy that is part of its etymology, cloth as 'that which clings to the body'.[21] But above all, cloth addresses the most intimate of senses: touch. Limited by the reach of the body, touch marks the juxtaposition of body and world; for while it is possible to see without being seen . . .[22]

'. . . to touch is always
to be touched . . .'[23]

And one never emerges *intact* from any encounter, for to be touched involves a capacity to be moved, 'a power to be affected'. And although there are encounters which weaken our power to be affected—making us 'mean-spirited little selves'—there are others that enrich all

those involved, encounters where 'subjectivity and affectivity become inseparable, (and) enfold each other'.[24]

And if 'everything round invites a caress',[25] this is true of the baker's art of folding; it requires a caress, rather than a grip. To grip is to seek possession, possession of knowledge and thought; while to caress has the tenderness of an open gesture, open to what is not known and what is to come.[26]

. . .the texture of the intimate . . .

. . . this is an intimate space, a space of close-vision: the curl of a hair, the twist of a thread, the crease of a cloth. A place to lose oneself in the intimacy of the fold, as satin reshapes and velvet vibrates . . .

To set the tactile *against* the visual is to presume the separation of the senses; to forsake soft logics for rigid boxes. The eye, one sense-organ amongst others, does not simply look. It also feels. Its response is both visual *and* tactile. This is the affect of synaesthesia—where senses participate and merge, each enfolded in the other— where we speak of a 'white noise', a 'black mood'. The visual-tactile is a dimension of the haptic where 'there is neither horizon nor background nor perspective nor limit nor outline or form nor centre'.[27] It is what Deleuze and Guattari call a *smooth* or nomadic space,[28] like the consistency of felt. Because it is made by rolling fibres back and forth until they enmesh, felt can potentially extend in all directions, without limit, entangled in a continuous variation—a fabric, at least in principle, without top, bottom or centre. Woven cloth, on the other hand, has a fixed warp which defines its edges and limits; it has a bottom and top—a beginning and an end. This makes it a *striated or* sedentary space of long-distance vision, form and outline.[29] Yet smooth space and striated space are not set in opposition. Although striated space is more optical, the eye is not the only organ to have this capacity; the two spaces exist in mixture and passage, one giving rise to the other.[30]

folds of matter and force . . .

. . . this is a space of surface and texture, material and matter: the physical stuff from which things are made.

Of cloth that sags, and linen that wears, and acrylic that washes through warp and through weft. Of gesso that cracks like sun-bleached earth; transformed from ground in days of old, to surface and subject that starts to speak of closeness and distance, and inside and out. . . .

Cloth Folds by Tina Modotti, a platinum palladium print from the late 1920s: fabric caught in motion, creased like the cratered surface of the moon, or the flux and flow of matter. Matter, not conceived of as particles of sand, but as 'a sheet of paper divided into infinite folds'. That's how Deleuze imagines it—matter unfolding its pleats at great length, some smaller, some larger, all endlessly dividing.[31]

And now folds appear everywhere: not just in the draperies of the Baroque, but in the curling fruits and vegetables of its still life paintings; in wind and water; in sound, as it moves through the air; in the layers of sediment that make up the earth. The world becomes a body of infinite folds and surfaces, twisting and weaving through compressed time and space. But what does matter imply? Perrin speaks of 'a particular and very condensed form of energy'.[32] While for Deleuze 'matter that reveals its texture becomes raw material, just as form that reveals folds becomes force',[33] an invisible force that can be *harnessed* through art or music; and for Deleuze this, rather than the reproducing or inventing of forms, is the task of the artist. Thus he writes of Cézanne as a painter who goes beyond sensation, turning it back on itself,

> 'to render visible the force that folds the mountains, the germinative force of the apple, the thermic force of a landscape . . . '[34]

the body of folds . . .

> '. . . we are "folded" in many entangled, irregular ways, none the same . . . and . . . this "multiplicity" goes beyond what we can predict or be aware of: we are "folded" in body and soul in many ways and many times over, prior to our being as "subjects" . . . but not because we divide into distinct persons or personalities looking for a unity . . . rather that our modes of being are "complicated" and "unfold" in

such a way that we can never be sure just what manners our being will yet assume'.[35]

Folded in utero, creased in death, and between, shifting in twists and turns: are we subject to similar forces—experiencing sensations more somatic than cerebral, more felt than remembered; sensations that seem to by-pass the brain and act directly on the nervous system?[36] *Cloth Folds*, unashamedly fleshy and organic. Creased, like skin beneath a microscope. An image that permeates my surfaces, heightens my sense of corporeality. Yet what does it mean— phenomenologically—to become aware of the body?

the fragmented body . . .

My face, my back, the top my head: all elude me. I know my body only in parts. Yet my sense of totality—although an abstraction—is crucial. How else could I exist in the world? According to psychoanalytic theories developed by Freud and Lacan, for perhaps the first six months of our lives, we do not have an awareness of our bodies as fixed and bounded space encased by skin, the surface through which we mediate and encounter the world 'outside'. In Lacan's formulation, the infant—the 'subject-to-be'—is caught up in a shifting field of libidinal forces and chaotic drives which lap across it like waves,[37] as objects and part-objects merge and disappear without differentiation. Its body is experienced as disorganised and fragmented—in bits and pieces—the infant making no distinction between self and other, subject and object, inside and out.[38] An integrated sense of self, as discrete subject, gradually develops through the maternal body which gives form and meaning to the infant's internal and external worlds; and for this, the process through which subjectivity is formed, Lacan uses the metaphor of the mirror, in which the infant finds, in reflection, a unified image of itself.

'matter-materiality-maternity . . .'[39]
the body of material dissolution. . . .

If subjectivity is achieved through the sublimation of the fragmented body, the price is self-alienation: we can only know our(whole)selves, through an *external* image and this turns the subject into an object of its own gaze.[40] To become aware of the body, to 'perceive' with the body, is to trespass the boundary that maintains its closure. It is to enter our own materiality: the soft tissue of organs, the snaking folds of the intestines, the pulse of the heart: a series of body parts, each with its own impulse, one dissolving into the other, undoing the fragile unity that holds us in check. To cross the line—to encounter 'the otherness of the soma',[41] with its chaotic drives and sensations— produces uncanny affect: an otherness felt through 'the irruption of the carnal',[42] with its endless beat; a 'pulsatile effect' through which the whole body is returned to 'part objects'.[43] The mirror, the double, repetition: each are manoeuvres against dissolution, and a materiality so raw, so close, it exceeds and resists representation.[44]

To cross the line might even offer strange comfort: an imaginary fusion with the maternal body, and promise of plenitude. Yet '. . . the mother's gift of life is also the gift of death. . . the embrace of the beloved, also a dissolution of the self'.[45] What is it to become aware of the body? It is to acknowledge that material dissolution is the *presence of death in life*, not as a binary opposite— but enfolded at its very centre.[46]

'the body of sensation . . .'[47]

. . . where sky meets earth and earth meets sky, soft and diffused and without clear line. . . .

The body of sensation, what Deleuze calls 'the body without organs',[48] is the un-organ-ised body, where body and world become one, a 'body-world of non-formed elements and anonymous affective forces',[49] that corresponds to the level of pre-subjective experience. It is a body always in the process of formation and de-formation. Erwin Straus makes a useful distinction between sensation and perception. *Perception* refers to the experience of a rational, verbally mediated-world in which space and time are uniform and atomistic, with subject and object clearly demarcated; *sensation*, to the experience of a world that is prerational and alingual, where space and time are perspectival and dynamic, the difference between subject and object less clear.[50] This has parallels with aspects of the smooth and striated: sensation as smooth and unbounded, always in

movement, experienced close at hand; perception as striated, of surface and form, outline and order, meaning and sign. 'The body of sensation' is not concerned with such things. Drawing on Straus's work, Deleuze says that when we are moved by a work of art at the level of sensation, the world emerges with us, subject with object:

'. . . it is being-in-the-world, as the phenomenologists say: at the same time I *become* in sensation and something *arrives* through sensation, one through the other, one in the other. And finally it is the same body that gives and receives sensation, that is at the same time object and subject'.[51]

the space of the incomplete . . .

This is a space of fragments, a space of the incomplete. But it is not a lack or a failure. Why tie up loose ends? Penelope knew it well—weaving by day, undoing by night, 'a secret work always begun again',[52] and all the richer for this double action.

White satin shapes and reshapes: and if there are elements here of repetition in the Freudian sense[53]—where what cannot be 'remembered' returns in behaviour, the past relived in the present—it is also true that each repetition has its own inflection distinct from the first, never the same. For as with the baker kneading his dough,

'. . . each folding over changes the ensemble of the beginning into a more complex ensemble. The same square is conserved, and yet it is not the same square'.[54]

The poetics of cloth are composed of folds, fragments and surfaces of infinite complexity. The fragment bears witness to a broken whole; yet it is also a site of uncertainty from which to start over; it is where the mind extends beyond fragile boundaries, beyond frayed and indeterminate edges, expanding in the fluidity of the smooth. The surface is a liminal space, both inside and out, a space of encounter. To fold is to 'withdraw into the recesses of a world'.[55] Yet it is not a lament or a loss, for the fold is without beginning or end.

The poetics of cloth are a stretching out: an invitation to leap inside the hollow of the fold, to see what happens. And to think *inside the continuity of the fold* is to think in a continuous present. It is to believe in the presence of the moment, of the fold as the power to "begin" again . .."[56]

Pennina Barnett
June 1999

I gratefully acknowledge the support of Goldsmiths College, University of London, for granting me Leave of Absence during Spring 1999 in order to research and write this essay and to research the exhibition. I would also like to thank my colleagues Irit Rogoff and Mo Price for their suggestions and comments on this essay.

Notes

1. Michel Serres, Rome, *The Book of Foundations*, (1983) translated by Felicia McCarren, Stanford University Press, Stanford, California, 1991, p. 236. I was introduced to the work of Michel Serres through reading Yve Lomax, 'Folds in the photograph', *Third Text* 32, Kala Press, London, Autumn 1995, pp. 43–58. I am indebted to Lomax's text for the ideas it suggested to me for various sections of this essay.
2. Michel Serres, cited in Yve Lomax, 'Folds in the photograph', p. 47.
3. Max Kozloff, 'The Poetics of Softness' in *Renderings, critical essays on a century of modern art.* (1961), Studio Vista, London, 1968, p. 233. Kozloff is referring to Oyvind Fahlstrom's writing on Claes Oldenburg.
4. Michel Serres, cited in Lomax, 'Folds in the photograph', p. 51.
5. Yve Lomax, 'Folds in the photograph', p. 52.
6. Gilles Deleuze, *The Fold: Leibniz and the Baroque* (1988), trans Tom Conley, Athlone Press, London, 1993, Chapter 10, 'The New Harmony', p. 137. (See also Tom Conley's introduction 'Translator's Forward: A Plea for Leibniz', in which he explains how Deleuze developed the concept of the fold through reading the work of Leibniz (1646–1714). Deleuze considered him the 'first great philosopher and mathematician of the pleat, of curves and twisting surfaces', and the preeminent philosopher of the Baroque.)
7. Ibid., Chapter 1 'The Pleats of Matter', pp. 8–9. (Deleuze is citing Leibniz here, in a letter to Artauld of 1687.)
8. Gilles Deleuze, *What Is Philosophy?* (1991), cited in Paul Patton, 'Introduction', in Paul Patton (ed.), *Deleuze: A Critical Reader*, Blackwell, Oxford, UK and Cambridge Mass, 1996, p. 6.
9. Paul Patton, 'Introduction', ibid., p. 9.
10. Gilles Deleuze, *Difference and Repetition*, (1969) cited in Paul Patton, ibid., p. 9.
11. Paul Patton, ibid., pp. 13–14.
12. see Jean-Luc Nancy, 'The Deleuzian Fold of Thought', in Paul Patton, op. cit., p. 108.
13. ibid., p. 109.
14. Gilles Deleuze, *The Fold: Leibniz and the Baroque*, op. cit., Chapter 10, 'The New Harmony', pp. 121–123.
15. ibid., p. 121.
16. ibid., p. 122.
17. Yve-Alain Bois, 'The Use Value of "Formless"', in Yve-Alain Bois, Rosalind E. Krauss, *Formless: a user's guide*, Zone Books, New York 1997, see pp. 25–27 (catalogue of an exhibition held at the Centre Georges Pompidou, Paris, 1996).
18. ibid., p. 26.
19. ibid., p. 25.
20. ibid., pp. 27–28.
21. See Ewa Kuryluk, *Veronica and her Cloth: History, Symbolism, and Structure of a "True" Image*, Basil Blackwell, Cambridge, Mass, and Oxford, UK, 1991, p. 179. She writes that the word 'cloth' has a Germanic origin, and appears in *Kleid* (dress), *Kleidung* (clothing) and in the Dutch *kleed*. It is thought to come from the root *kli-* 'to stick' or 'to cling to', making 'cloth', 'that which clings to the body'.
22. Denis Hollier, *The Politics of Prose: Essay on Sartre*, [1986], cited in Joan Livingstone and Anne Wilson, 'The Presence of Touch', in *The Presence of Touch*, (exhibition catalogue), Department of Fiber and Material Studies, The School of the Art Institute of Chicago, Chicago 1996, p. 6.
23. Paul Rodaway, *Sensuous Geographies: Body, Sense and Place*, [1994], cited in Joan Livingstone and Anne Wilson ibid., p. 1.
24. All citations here are from 'They talk, they write, they make together, Vit Hopley and Yve Lomax on Vit Hopley and Yve Lomax', in *Make* no 75, April–May 1997, p. 15.
25. Gaston Bachelard, *The Poetics of Space*, (1958), Beacon Press, Boston, Mass, 1994, p. 236.

26. Yve Lomax, 'Folds in the photograph', op. cit., p. 32.

27. Gilles Deleuze and Felix Guattari, *A Thousand Plateaus: Capitalism and Schizophrenia* (1980), trans. Brian Massumi, University of Minnesota Press, Minneapolis, 1987. See Section 14, 'The Smooth and The Striated', p. 494.

28. Ibid., pp. 492–3. (The authors acknowledge here Alois Riegl's notion of 'close-vision-haptic space'.)

29. Ibid., pp. 475–6.

30. Ibid., p. 493.

31. Gilles Deleuze, *The Fold: Leibniz and the Baroque*, op. cit., Chapter 1, 'The Pleats of Matter', p. 6, and Chapter 9, 'The New Harmony', p. 123, respectively.

32. J. Perrin cited by Jean François Lyotard, *The Inhuman. Reflections on Time*, trans. Geoffrey Bennington and Rachel Bowlby, Polity Press, Cambridge, 1991, p. 43.

33. Gilles Deleuze, *The Fold: Leibniz and the Baroque*, op. cit., Chapter 3. 'What Is Baroque?' p. 35.

34. Gilles Deleuze, *Francis Bacon: The Logic of Sensation* (1981), cited in Ronald Bogue, 'Gilles Deleuze, The Aesthetics of Force', in Paul Patton, op. cit., p. 261.

35. John Rajchman, 'Out of the Fold', in *Architectural Design Magazine*, vol. 63, parts 3–4, March/April 1993, p. 63.

36. Francis Bacon, *The Brutality of Fact: Interviews with David Sylvester*, referred to in Daniel W. Smith, 'Deleuze's Theory of Sensation: Overcoming the Kantian Duality', in Paul Patton, op. cit., p. 32.

37. See Terry E. Eagleton, *Literary Theory* [1983], Blackwell, Oxford UK and Cambridge USA, 1993 edition, p. 154.

38. See Elizabeth Grosz, 'The Body', in Elizabeth Wright (ed.), *Feminism and Psychoanalysis, A Critical Dictionary*, Blackwell, Oxford, U.K. & Cambridge, Mass. 1992, pp. 36–7.

39. 'The unencompassable body of "matter-materiality-maternity," which indexically figures death', Elizabeth Bronfen cited in Anne Raine, 'Embodied geographies, subjectivity and materiality in the work of Ana Mendleta', in Griselda Pollock(ed.), *Generations and Geographies in the visual arts—Feminist Readings*, Routledge. London and New York, 1996, pp. 244–245.

40. See Madan Sarup, *An Introductory Guide to Post-Structuralism and Postmodernism*, Harvester Wheatsheaf, London, 1993, Chapter 1, 'Lacan and Psychoanalysis', p. 22.

41. Anne Raine, 'Embodied geographies', op. cit., p. 246.

42. Yve-Alain Bois, 'The Use Value of Formless', in Yve-Alain Bois & Rosalind E. Krauss, *Formless*, op. cit., p. 31.

43. Rosalind E. Krauss, 'Pulse: "Moteur!"' in Yve-Alain Bois & Rosalind E. Krauss, *Formless*, op. cit., p. 136.

44. Anne Raine, 'Embodied geographies', op. cit., p. 245.

45. Elizabeth Bronfen, 'Death Drive' in Elizabeth Wright (ed.), *Feminism and Psychoanalysis, A Critical Dictionary*, op. cit., p. 56.

46. Ibid., p. 53.

47. Gilles Deleuze, *Francis Bacon: The Logic of Sensation* [1981], referred to in Ronald Bogue, 'Gilles Deleuze, The Aesthetics of Force', op. cit., p. 262.

48. see Ronald Bogue, op. cit. p. 262.

49. Ibid., p. 268.

50. Erwin Straus, *The Primary World of Senses: A Vindication of Sensory Experience* [1935], in Ronald Bogue, ibid., p. 258.

51. Gilles Deleuze, *Francis Bacon: The Logic of Sensation* [1981], cited in Ronald Bogue, ibid., p. 260.

52. Michel Serres, *Rome, The Book of Foundations*, op. cit., p. 79.

53. Sigmund Freud, *Beyond the Pleasure Principle* [1920], trans. and edited by James Strachey, Hogarth Press and The Institute of Psycho-Analysis, London 1974.

54. Michel Serres, *Rome, The Book of Foundations*, op. cit., pp. 80–81.

55. Leibniz, cited by Gilles Deleuze, *The Fold: Leibniz and the Baroque*, op. cit., Chapter 1 'The Pleats of Matter', pp. 8–9.

56. Eva Mayer, 'On a matter of Folds', paper presented at Goldsmiths College, University of London, March 1999. To be published in the forthcoming edition of the journal *Parallax*.

5

MEDITATION ON TRANSLATION AND SEDUCTION (2005)

Catherine Harper

EDITOR'S INTRODUCTION

Catherine Harper's research interests include land, body, cloth and culture, with a particular commitment to 'the contested materiality of the female body in and of Ireland, its shrouded landscape of intimacy and mourning, its struggle for reproductive, sexual and cultural autonomy, and its politicised place within the Irish feminist diaspora'. Harper edited the four-volume *Textiles: Critical and Primary Sources* (2012) and is editor-in-chief of the academic journal *TEXTILE: Cloth and Culture*. Alongside her contributions to textile discourse, Harper's 2007 book *Intersex* challenges medical constructions of sex, prefiguring the more recent increase in public discourse about non-binary gender and the sexed body.

The text included in full here was first written for the exhibition catalogue edited by Lesley Millar to accompany the exhibition '2121: The Textile Vision of Reiko Sudo and NUNO', which opened at The James Hockey Gallery in Farnham, England on 21 October 2005, the year of the acclaimed Japanese textile design company NUNO's twenty-first anniversary. The exhibition then toured the HUB: National Centre for Craft and Design, Lincolnshire, England; the Museum für Kunst und Gewerbe, Hamburg, Germany; and Textile Kultur Haslach, Austria. The illustrated catalogue, printed in English and Japanese, includes an extensive interview with Reiko Sudo and Lesley Millar recorded in Tokyo in 2005; an essay by Laurel Reuter, Founding Director and Chief Curator of the North Dakota Museum of Art (and co-author with Mildred Constantine of *Whole Cloth*); as well as writing by Keiko Kawashima and Lesley Millar.

Harper shares with many of the other texts in this first section an attention to textiles as possible texts in their own right, albeit with the warning that 'translation is a tricky business'. In this catalogue writing fiction and fact are combined to create a hybrid delivered in the first person that muses on the meaning of several NUNO fabric names and the slippery boundaries of sexual interest. The text opens in the same hotel Sophia Coppola set her 2003 film *Lost in Translation* – high above the urban landscape of Tokyo, where Harper wrote the first draft of this text. She acknowledges the risk of exoticizing a culture foreign to her own, but is nonetheless forthright in recognizing the seductive qualities of many fabrics in the exhibition. What results is an evocative piece of writing that vividly brings the author's knowledge of NUNO's complex fabrics to life through touch.

Meditation on Translation and Seduction

Catherine Harper

Midnight. The Peak Lounge, Park Hyatt, Tokyo.

Fifty washi paper lanterns. An anonymous slow-tinkling piano. Smooth saki in a tiny glass.

Tokyo spreads out to left and right, in vast and awesome twinkling-throbbing glory. Somewhere out there, karaoke is in full swing, geisha listen to boasting businessmen, and grown-up schoolgirls play potent power games . . .

I stand right up to the glass and touch the city with my fingertips. It ripples and pulses under my touch.

Am I lost in translation?

I put on Reiko Sudo's *Otter Skin* (1995) and dive off into this night . . .

Otter Skin. Glinting, waterlogged, damp and loaded. Dense black, crow black, almost scaly. Affective, unsettling, brooding. Reiko Sudo's fabric holds its breath, merges into my skin and waits.

Can a textile, a piece of cloth, a woven substrate, be this potent?

Barthes writes of the 'destination' of a text as the place of its (provisional) unity, and identifies that place as lying within its reader.[1] That is, he articulates the moment of translation when the complexity of creation is in some way captured (albeit temporarily) by the reader (viewer) as a means to permit his/her subjective expression of (a) meaning. In this text, I will argue that Reiko Sudo's fabrics are such texts, for they allow this reader to peel them off and put them on for her own imaginative flight . . .

My translation may not be yours: translation is a tricky business.[2]

Lees-Maffei and Sandino quite rightly make a claim for the "machinations, seduction and jealousies of a *ménage à trois*" between Design, Craft and Art.[3] My interest in their work lies in the proposal of that territory as unstable, shifting, contingent, ultimately dangerous. It seems to me that Reiko Sudo's fabrics are potentially 'danger invested', sexually-charged, highly seductive. I believe, moreover, that she consciously mobilises the act of seduction to reveal the unspoken (unspeakable), the unauthorised (authoritatively), the uncensored (without censure) in her liaisons with cloth. . .

My seduction may not be yours: seduction is a tricky business.[4]

The pelt of the otter, and indeed that of the seal, presented to us by Reiko Sudo acts as a metaphor for a translation and re-translation between Nature and Culture which seems to resonate throughout my understandings of the dichotomies of contemporary Japan. The conceptual or material coexistence of complementary states is, for example, offered as an essentially Japanese aesthetic by Curators McCarty and McQuaid in their framing of *Structure and Surface: Contemporary Japanese Textiles* at the Museum of Modern Art, New York (1998).[5] I'm generally wary of essentialisms—there's a danger of reduction or misrepresentation—and, in cultural terms, that can lead quickly to exoticism of the worst kind. I

Source: Catherine Harper, 'Meditation on Translation and Seduction', *21:21 Textile Vision of Reiko Sudo* (2005), pp. 33–7. Reproduced with permission.

am conscious of not wishing to either reduce the cultural identification of Reiko Sudo's fabric to an exotic commodity or to code it with a 'them' and 'us' hierarchy.[6] As Greg Kwok Keung Leong notes in his articulations of 'centred' (traditional) and 'de-centred' (radical) cultural identity there is always a key "tension between the cultural identities we construct for ourselves . . . and [those] others construct for us".[7] That being said, Barthes' appeal to subjectivity in analysis is liberating in how one might then read or activate the text in the textiles.

I propose that Reiko Sudo, too, is highly conscious of the potential for exciting and even provocative narrative associations in her mobilisations of the rich textile and cultural traditions of Japan and her location of those within a highly contemporary methodology and materiality. The convergence of mechanical, technological and industrial techniques with labour-intensive handwork, plus the authoritative use of traditional and innovative materials, indicates a certain trend in Japanese textiles which arguably captures some form of essential currency,[8] and Reiko Sudo knowingly activates these essences while not allowing herself to be subsumed by them. . .

Seal and otter slip effortlessly between land and sea, solid and fluid, dry and wet. Their graceful translation from one domain or way of being to another is mesmerisingly easy. Both *Otter Skin* (1995) and *Seal Skin* (1995) appear simple: the former dark, matt, brooding, the latter a bright, shiny dense weave in celebratory red . . . But it is their potential for narrative, proposed through their titles, and then further invited through the simplicity of their surfaces that permits Barthes' textual proposition to be useful here. Both these fabrics beg to be mobilised by a viewer/reader: both resonate with a desire to be held, caressed, placed around the shoulders, swaddled over the body. My being aches to be sheathed like a seal, my body yearns for the elegant stream-lined form of the otter. I desire translation.

Interestingly, my reaction to many of Reiko Sudo's fabrics is somatic, that is my body literally speaks to this affective fabric. This is a different kind of desire for tactility to that of the hand (with its direct connection

to the head). Rather the organ that is my skin (with its direct haptic connection to the heart) responds across its area to the fabric plane . . . nerves, pores, papillae reach out to Reiko Sudo's fabrics for contact, all over contact . . .

Declan McGonagle, then Director of the Museum of Modern Art, Dublin told me of a Quaker notion of "that which speaks to one's condition",[9] and my strong sense in Reiko Sudo's most abstract work is of a visceral interiority, an animal or primal reactivity transcendent of mere material, process or technique, oblique to the conceptual, and sideways on to the triangulation of design, craft or art. It echoes in such fabrics as *Yak* (1994), *Jellyfish* (1993) or *Moth-Eaten* (1995), and activates discourses related to the notion of "fabric as envelope, as a second skin".[10] These fabrics speak to my condition as I look out over night-time Tokyo in all its animal breathing pelt-like beauty . . .

My condition may not be yours: you know the rest . . .

Undoubtedly, Reiko Sudo designs and orchestrates the making of fabrics that are sublime and extraordinary. Fabrics of enormous diversity and sophistication are her hallmark, each combining high-tech and low-tech production methods and a range of materials from the 'natural' (silk, wool, linen, banana fibre) to those that are synthetic, industrial, banal or unexpected (stainless steel, rubber, scrap fabric, laminate film, copper, oxidised metal). Reiko Sudo breaks convention in her processes as well as her materials: she characteristically interrupts the manufacture of woven fabric to manually insert feathers, she deliberately creates random rust marks on virgin cloth by scattering nails on its surface, she plies threads with incompatible shrinkages allowing applied heat to then buckle the woven results, she bonds metallic films to traditionally 'valuable' silk fabric. Reiko Sudo is a sophisticated 'avant-garde designer-craftsperson', challenging without difficulty the norms of materiality, process and technique. It's quite appropriate, for example, that Reiko Sudo played a key role in 'the space between' conference in Perth in 2004, where her habitation of the blurred territory between artisanal craft, high-end design, industrial manufacturing, and artistic creative intervention celebrated a new hybridity, a contemporary interdisciplinarity and a modern expressive synthesis in textiles.

Many of Reiko Sudo's fabrics are quite simply very beautiful, but it is those that promise a more intricate and insistent narrative that particularly interest me. Those that are the product of an abusive, even perverse, approach to the fabric substrate are especially evocative. The Nuno book *Boro Boro*, with its offer of 'Cruel and Unusual Treatment of Fabric'[11] offers a clue to a sub-text both apparent and significant to this reader . . . Sexual power games – neither essentially or exclusively Japanese, but nevertheless useful for the purposes of this text – offer abusive practices, humiliation, simulated pain, 'real tears', and vocal evidencing of 'cruel and unusual treatment'. Interestingly, the foreword to *Boro Boro* states "Mistreatment is not an end in itself (we are not textile sadists)".[12] In this collection, though, fabrics have been "roasted over burners, dissolved with acid, boiled and stewed, ripped with blades and pulled apart".[13] Other works involve baking, rubbing, moulding, weathering. . .The text itself asks "whatever did these innocent fabrics do to deserve this rough handling?", and the list of fabric treatments reads like an inquisitor's 'to do' list . . .

I'm back at the glass, looking out over mid-night Tokyo, a pelt of human culture stretching to the midnight sky. Under that pelt, countless acts of sexual cruelty, of rough trade, of sublime and seductive terror are enacted as an essential (nightly) part of human existence . . . Remember that *Otter Skin* (1995), via Barthes, permitted me to be a witness to that night-time landscape . . .

If Reiko Sudo already is an active participant in Lees-Maffei and Sandino's *ménage à trois*, then it is only a short leap of narrative faith to consider the investment of sexual, seductive, sadistic energy in certain key textile pieces. Reiko Sudo is tantalising, however, in the odd tensions she constructs between textile fabric and textile title: *Ginseng* (1995) is subtitled as "homage to the penetrating power of vegetable life",[14] and reads as a sophisticated creamy cloth, with softly decadent fringing of felted wool. It's delicious and delectable. Read the descriptor of method, however, and think again:

> The process itself literally 'damages' normal woollen weaves . . . we resorted to prolonged soaking in alternating baths of hot and cold water before pounding our wool on the 'torture rack'.[15]

It is the making explicit, as a creative act, of the method of marking the textile skin that signals some perverse delight in the hard hand labour of the work (even when ultimately it is mechanised labour that reproduces the textile). In her *Scrapyard (Nail)* (1994), rusty nails are allowed to imprint their marks onto dampened virgin rayon in a counter-intuitive act of textile offence. In *Spanish Moss* (1994) the weave structure is quite literally 'undone'. In *Cracked Quilt* (1992), chemicals etch their traces into the flesh of a rayon and wool double-fabric. And so on . . .

Always remember, my sadism may not be yours . . . sadism being a tricky business . . .

What I find unsettling, and I believe this is a deliberate and most clever strategy on the part of Reiko Sudo, is the juxtapositioning of heightened and evocative language with tender fabric and matter-of-fact explanation. It's as though she wants to remain elusive, not one thing or the other. In these creative power games, Reiko Sudo is ultimately dominant over the material, process and meanings held within her fabric, and most significantly her refusal to allow labelling keeps her dominance over us the reader/viewer.

I can speculate all I like, pull on and peel off the metaphoric layers of her designer-art-craft textiles, but I remain not her, and therefore outside the knowledge that is Reiko Sudo.

Can a textile, a piece of cloth, a woven substrate, be this potent?

Always . . .

Notes

1. R. Barthes (1977) *Image-Music-Text* London: Fontana, p. 147.
2. W. Benjamin *Task of the Translator* in H. Arendt ed. (1992) *Illuminations* London: Fontana Press, p. 75.
3. G. Lees-Maffei and L. Sandino *Dangerous Liaisons: Relationships between Design, Craft and Art* Journal of Design History Vol.17, No.3, 2004, pp. 207–219.
4. W. Benjamin *Task of the Translator* in H. Arendt ed. (1992) *Illuminations* London: Fontana Press, p. 75.
5. C. McCarty and M. McQuaid (2000) *Structure and Surface: Contemporary Japanese Textiles* San Francisco: Museum of Modern Art.
6. Diana Fuss *Essentially Speaking: Feminism, Nature and Difference* (1989) New York: Routledge.
7. G. Kwok Keung Leong *Re-Constructing Chinese* in J. Jefferies (2001) *Reinventing Textiles: Gender and Identity* Winchester: Telos Art Publishing, p. 91.
8. S.E. Braddock and M. O'Mahony (1998) *Techno textiles: revolutionary fabrics for fashion and design* London: Thames and Hudson.
9. *Interview with Declan McGonagle* in C. Harper (1991) *A Beginning* Derry: Orchard Gallery.
10. Volpe, G. and Bouillet, M. *Bodies, Clothes, Skins: A Conversation in Quebec* in J. Jefferies ed. *Reinventing Textiles: Gender and Identity* Winchester: Telos Art Publishing, pp. 29–37.
11. Nuno Nuno Books (1997) *Boro Boro* Tokyo: Nuno Corporation, p. 14.
12. Nuno Nuno Books (1997) *Boro Boro* Tokyo: Nuno Corporation, p. 15.
13. Nuno Nuno Books (1997) *Boro Boro* Tokyo: Nuno Corporation, p. 15.
14. Nuno Nuno Books (1997) *Boro Boro* Tokyo: Nuno Corporation, p. 27.
15. Nuno Nuno Books (1997) *Boro Boro* Tokyo: Nuno Corporation, p. 24.

6

THE BLANK PAGE (1957)

Isak Dinesen

EDITOR'S INTRODUCTION

The Danish author Karen Blixen (1885–1962) wrote in both Danish and English and used multiple pen names. Writing in English under the pen name Isak Dinesen, she is best known for *Out of Africa*, published in 1937. The memoir is based on her time living in British East Africa, present-day Kenya, from 1913 to 1931. When debt forced Blixen to sell her farm and return to Denmark she took up writing again. *Out of Africa* was made into a film starring Robert Redford and Meryl Streep in 1985. Her 1958 story *Babette's Feast* was also adapted into a film set in the nineteenth century about two Protestant sisters living on the western coast of Jutland, Denmark.

In Dinesen's short story 'The Blank Page', published in 1957, the textile and the act of storytelling are taken as one and the same. The story, reprinted in full here, is structured as a tale within a tale that leaves the unspoken and untold, the blank page, as a creative form of narration. Dinesen sets her story around the work of a Carmelite order of nuns in Portugal who grow flax and make the linen, including bridal sheets, used by the royal family. The preparation of the flax plant for eventual weaving into linen is humorously described from the point-of-view of cloth later in this book in the excerpt from James Fenimore Cooper's *Autobiography of a Pocket Handkerchief* (1843).

Carmelite nuns take a vow of silence, and Dinesen's decision to make her illiterate narrator – a woman who has told stories for 200 years – an expert of the oral tradition of storytelling suggests a loyalty to the adaptable and ever-shifting nature of the story. Jenni Sorkin's writing on stains included in the next section considers the stain as a mark of shame. Here the story's subject matter is an intensely private moment made public, but the blank page of the story and the unstained bridal sheet together act as loyal record keepers. Ultimately, Dinesen's textile and text provide us with multiple and beguiling conclusions.

The Blank Page

Isak Dinesen

By the ancient city gate sat an old coffee-brown, black-veiled who made her living by telling stories.

She said:

'You want a tale, sweet lady and gentleman? Indeed I have told many tales, one more than a thousand, since that time when I first let young men tell me, myself, tales of a red rose, two smooth lily buds, and four silky, supple, deadly entwining snakes. It was my mother's mother, the black-eyed dancer, the often-embraced, who in the end—wrinkled like a winter apple and crouching beneath the mercy of the veil—took upon herself to teach me the art of story-telling. Her own mother's mother had taught it to her, and both were better story-tellers than I am. But that, by now, is of no consequence, since to the people they and I have become one, and I am most highly honoured because I have told stories for two hundred years.'

Now if she is well paid and in good spirits, she will go on.

'With my grandmother,' she said, 'I went through a hard school. "Be loyal to the story," the old hag would say to me. "Be eternally and unswervingly loyal to the story." "Why must I be that, Grandmother?" I asked her. "Am I to furnish you with reasons, baggage?" she cried. "And you mean to be a story-teller! Why, you are to become a story-teller, and I shall give you my reasons! Hear then: Where the story-teller is loyal, eternally and unswervingly loyal to the story, there, in the end, silence will speak. Where the story has been betrayed, silence is but emptiness. But we, the faithful, when we have spoken our last word, will hear the voice of silence. Whether a small snotty lass understands it or not."'

'Who then,' she continues, 'tells a finer tale than any of us? Silence does. And where does one read a deeper tale than upon the most perfectly printed page of the most precious book? Upon the blank page. When a royal and gallant pen, in the moment of its highest inspiration, has written down its tale with the rarest ink of all— where, then, may one read a still deeper, sweeter, merrier and more cruel tale than that? Upon the blank page.'

The old beldame for a while says nothing, only giggles a little and munches with her toothless mouth.

'We,' she says at last, 'the old women who tell stories, we know the story of the blank page. But we are somewhat averse to telling it, for it might well, among the uninitiated, weaken our own credit. All the same, I am going to make an exception with you, my sweet and pretty lady and gentleman of the generous hearts. I shall tell it to you.'

High up in the blue mountains of Portugal there stands an old convent for sisters of the Carmelite order, which is an illustrious and austere order. In ancient times the convent was rich, the sisters were all noble ladies, and miracles took place there. But during the centuries highborn ladies grew less keen on fasting and prayer, the great dowries flowed scantily into the treasury of the convent, and today the few portionless and humble sisters live in but one wing of the vast crumbling structure, which looks as if it longed to become one with the grey rock itself. Yet they are still a blithe and active sisterhood. They take much pleasure in their holy meditations, and will busy themselves joyfully with that one particular task which did once, long, long ago, obtain for the convent a unique and strange privilege: they grow the finest flax and manufacture the most exquisite linen of Portugal.

The long field below the convent is ploughed with gentle-eyed, milk-white bullocks, and the seed is skillfully sown out by labour-hardened virginal hands with mould under the nails. At the time when the flax field flowers, the whole valley becomes air-blue, the very colour of the apron which the blessed virgin put on to go out and collect eggs within St Anne's poultry yard, the moment before the Archangel Gabriel in mighty wing-strokes lowered himself on to the threshold of the house, and while high, high up a dove, neck-feathers raised and wings vibrating, stood like a small clear silver star in the sky. During this month the villagers many miles round raise their eyes to the flax field and ask one another: 'Has the convent been lifted into heaven? Or have our good little sisters succeeded in pulling down heaven to them?'

Later in due course the flax is pulled, scutched and hackled; thereafter the delicate thread is spun, and the linen woven, and at the very end the fabric is laid out on the grass to bleach, and is watered time after time, until one may believe that snow has fallen round the convent walls. All this work is gone through with precision and piety and with such sprinklings and litanies as are the secret of the convent. For these reasons the linen, baled high on the backs of small grey donkeys and sent out through the convent gate, downwards and ever downwards to the towns, is as flower-white, smooth and dainty as was my own little foot when, fourteen years old, I had washed it in the brook to go to a dance in the village.

Diligence, dear Master and Mistress, is a good thing, and religion is a good thing, but the very first germ of a story will come from some mystical place outside the story itself. Thus does the linen of the Convento Velho draw its true virtue from the fact that the very first linseed was brought home from the Holy Land itself by a crusader.

In the Bible, people who can read may learn about the lands of Lecha and Maresha, where flax is grown. I myself cannot read, and have never seen this book of which so much is spoken. But my grandmother's grandmother as a little girl was the pet of an old Jewish rabbi, and the learning she received from him has been kept and passed on in our family. So you will read, in the book of Joshua, of how Achsah the daughter of Caleb lighted from her ass and cried unto her father: 'Give me a blessing! For thou hast now given me land;

give me also the blessing of springs of water!' And he gave her the upper springs and the nether springs. And in the fields of Lecha and Maresha lived, later on, the families of them that wrought the finest linen of all. Our Portuguese crusader, whose own ancestors had once been great linen weavers of Tomar, as he rode through these same fields was struck by the quality of the flax, and so tied a bag of seeds to the pommel of his saddle.

From this circumstance originated the first privilege of the convent, which was to procure bridal sheets for all the young princesses of the royal house.

I will inform you, dear lady and gentleman, that in the country of Portugal in very old and noble families a venerable custom has been observed. On the morning after the wedding of a daughter of the house, and before the morning gift had yet been handed over, the Chamberlain or High Steward from a balcony of the palace would hang out the sheet of the night and would solemnly proclaim: Virginem eam tenemus—'We declare her to have been a virgin.' Such a sheet was never afterwards washed or again lain on.

This time-honoured custom was nowhere more strictly upheld than within the royal house itself, and it has there subsisted till within living memory.

Now for many hundred years the convent in the mountains, in appreciation of the excellent quality of the linen delivered, has held its second high privilege: that of receiving back that central piece of the snow-white sheet which bore witness to the honour of a royal bride.

In the tall main wing of the convent, which overlooks an immense landscape of hills and valleys, there is a long gallery with a black-and-white marble floor. On the walls of the gallery, side by side, hangs a long row of heavy, gilt frames, each of them adorned with a coroneted plate of pure gold, on which is engraved the name of a princes: Donna Christina, Donna Ines, Donna Jacintha Lenora, Donna Maria. And each of these frames encloses a square cut from a royal wedding sheet.

Within the faded markings of the canvases people of some imagination and sensibility may read all the signs of the zodiac: the Scales, the Scorpion, the Lion, the Twins. Or they may there find pictures from their own

world of ideas: a rose, a heart, a sword—or even a heart pierced through with a sword.

In days of old it would occur that a long, stately, richly coloured procession wound its way through the stone-grey mountain scenery, upwards to the convent. Princesses of Portugal, who were now queens or queen dowagers of foreign countries, Archduchesses, or Electresses, with their splendid retinue, proceeded here on a pilgrimage which was by nature both sacred and secretly gay. From the flax field upwards the road rises steeply; the royal-lady would have to descend from her coach to be carried this last bit of the way in a palanquin presented to the convent for the very same purpose.

Later on, up to our own day, it has come to pass—as it comes to pass when a sheet of paper is being burnt, that after all other sparks have run along the edge and died away, one last clear little spark will appear and hurry along after them—that a very old highborn spinster undertakes the journey to Convento Velho. She has once, a long long time ago, been playmate, friend and maid-of-honour to a young princess of Portugal. As she makes her way to the convent she looks round to see the view widen to all sides. Within the building a sister conducts her to the gallery and to the plate bearing the name of the princess she has once served, and there takes leave of her, aware of her wish to be alone.

Slowly, slowly a row of recollections passes through the small, venerable, skull-like head under its mantilla of black lace, and it nods to them in amicable recognition. The loyal friend and confidante looks back upon the young bride's elevated married life with the elected royal consort. She takes stock of happy events and disappointments—coronations and jubilees, court intrigues and wars, the birth of heirs to the throne, the alliances of younger generations of princes and princesses, the rise or decline of dynasties. The old lady will remember how once, from the markings on the canvas, omens were drawn; now she will be able to compare the fulfilment to the omen, sighing a little and smiling a little. Each separate canvas with its coroneted name-plate has a story to tell, and each has been set up in loyalty to the story.

But in the midst of the long row there hangs a canvas which differs from the others. The frame of it is as fine and as heavy as any, and as proudly as any carries the golden plate with the royal crown. But on this one plate no name is inscribed, and the linen within the frame is snow-white from corner to corner, a blank page.

I beg of you, you good people who want to hear stories told: look at this page, and recognize the wisdom of my grandmother and of all old story-telling women!

For with what eternal and unswerving loyalty has not this canvas been inserted in the row! The story-tellers themselves before it draw their veils over their faces and are dumb. Because the royal papa and mama who once ordered this canvas to be framed and hung up, had they not had the tradition of loyalty in their blood, might have left it out.

It is in front of this piece of pure white linen that the old princesses of Portugal—worldly wise, dutiful, long-suffering queens, wives and mothers—and their noble old playmates, bridesmaids and maids-of-honour have most often stood still.

It is in front of the blank page that old and young nuns, with the Mother Abbess herself, sink into deepest thought.

HOW DO YOU FOOTNOTE A SMILE?
One Dialog about Two Extremes of Textile Research (excerpt) (2020)

Birgitta Nordström

EDITOR'S INTRODUCTION

The final text included in the touch section was first developed in the format of a public dialogue held in late 2018 between myself, Jessica Hemmings, and my colleague Birgitta Nordström in the weaving workshop at the Academy of Design and Crafts (HDK), University of Gothenburg, Sweden. The conversation sought to inspire colleagues to see across disciplinary boundaries to the unexpected similarities their research interests might share.

In the original article, I spoke of my interest in reading the textile through literature and focused on examples of maternal silence and loss in the writing of Yvonne Vera. Birgitta Nordström discussed her ongoing research into the woven textile as an object that can help us confront, and hold, death. The *Infant Wrapping Cloth Project* discussed in this excerpt, began in 2017 and is ongoing. Nordström explains that the woven textiles are donated to childbirth and abortion clinics in Sweden where women receive medical care for late-term abortions and miscarriages.

As part of the project's ongoing research, in 2017 and 2018 accounts were collected of midwives' use of the textile in their daily work. Our original conversation acknowledged that the research methods and research contexts under discussion arguably represent extremes along the spectrum used in textile research. Despite these differences, we share an attention to topics often treated with silence that may find useful alternative forms of communication in the textile.

The excerpt selected for inclusion here focuses on Nordström's voice and her discussion of the considerable challenges posed by her work with hand and machine woven blankets donated to clinics and hospitals in Sweden. This final piece of writing for the section offers a harrowing example of how the textile may support touch, in this case providing families with the option to hold lives which end before they begin.

How Do You Footnote a Smile?
One Dialog about Two Extremes of Textile Research

Birgitta Nordström

BN: [M]y project is about infant shrouds for small lives that die at birth or during pregnancy. It started with a question from a doctor who said to me, "I wish I had small blankets ready for these hard situations. I never know what to say when this happens to parents." We met when I was describing a blanket I had been weaving, a larger blanket to be used as a funeral pall for funeral rites. Her spontaneous wish encouraged me to really think of the textile language, and about textile actions such as holding, wrapping, and folding – to embrace these small bodies. I have been working with that initial request all the time.

[...]

BN: Weaving small blankets for hospitals is not an art practice visible to the public. But with the blankets I can argue for the importance of textile actions in relation to death. I am an artistic researcher; meaning that this research is dependent on an artistic inquiry through the weaving. First there are explorations and findings in the material process. Then how can they be tested? How can they be used? Can they contribute to memory building for the parents of a dead child? Can I learn something about trauma? Sorrow?

Over the past two years I have conducted a clinical study that placed these woven blankets in Swedish maternity wards. In the beginning it was so difficult to get a positive answer from the hospitals and the midwives about participating in the study; it took half a year to get the first positive answer. But in the last five months of the study there were departments at one hospital calling to say, "We rejected the project and we now regret this decision. We want to be part of the project. Is it too late?" The reason why they changed their minds was that they realized how the blankets were received and used in other study centers at the same hospital. It is *only* about a blanket, but that blanket is needed for these very difficult situations.

When midwives raised the question about even smaller blankets for late miscarriages and abortions the project took another step. If the parents want to be with their child the blanket is needed for viewing and leave-taking. In the other departments there may be personal blankets the parents bring, because they often know they are giving birth to a dead child. In those cases, the infant shrouds may not be needed at all. But for the very smallest, the blankets assist in the very difficult situation. Sometimes the bodies are very injured and the blankets facilitate viewing, being wrapped around the body. The midwives working in the gynaecological department said when the study started, "We have no clothing; these bodies are too small for clothing."

My response, when the question of even smaller blankets was raised, was to start handweaving again. Seven weavers joined the weaving research group at the Academy of Design and Crafts (HDK) and later in the project two more students volunteered. For the study the smallest blankets were needed urgently; it was stressful in the beginning. Handweaving is important for my artistic research into fragility, experimenting with new bindings and materials. This is a change from earlier in the project when I designed blankets that could be industrially woven, because we needed a relatively large number of blankets for the study.

Source: Excerpt from Jessica Hemmings and Birgitta Nordström, 'How Do You Footnote a Smile? One Dialog about Two Extremes of Textile Research', *TEXTILE* 18:1 (2020), pp. 100–8. Reproduced with permission.

[...]

The perspectives of medical colleagues changed once they saw the blankets being used. And I changed my language. Initially my approach was too humble and I did not have any proof that my idea was useful. At first, I also questioned the project myself. But once the midwives saw the blankets in action it helped – they were *shown* the usefulness rather than *told* the usefulness. And one important thing was also to build a team with different competences in order to create a valid study format for a clinical setting. A weaver alone would not have had enough knowledge to run the study.

For the study that was recently conducted, a questionnaire was filled in by the medical staff every time a blanket was used. The questions were about how, when, and what the blanket was used for. It may have been that several blankets were needed for one fetus or one child. Questions also related to the nurses' working conditions. My work shifted while I was writing the questionnaires and, later, working with the answers as research material, from not only developing the blankets to also learning a new language for the communication of this research.

[...]

There are moments when I have been defending the instinctive way of working, not from critical voices of others but from a more rational part of my own mind. Weaving all these blankets before even contacting the hospitals? Where does this come from? Now the midwives are teaching me; we are in a process together. I first made the blankets 90cm [35 inches] square. I had to learn that what was also needed were blankets 70cm [28 inches] square and even smaller. When we started the handweaving group for the smallest blankets, we were in a shared search to find beauty, to create variations. And that weaving was not questioned; there was a great demand for the smallest blankets.

[...]

We have learnt that the special textile action of swaddling is really about shrouding the body. Before the blankets were made available, the midwives used a towel or other hospital linen. The textile they offered was a reused thing; hospital linen goes back into the laundry and is reused. The infant shroud is not to be reused, which is a new approach. It stays with the dead body, if the parents wish.

These blankets are, in a way, anonymous. They do not carry the hospital logo or another organization's insignia. Earlier there was in one ward a church community who donated blankets. But when this research started the staffs' reaction was that the blankets in this study were useful because they were more neutral.

One midwife explained to me that, previously, if the mother or the father wanted to see the body it was shown to parents in a stainless-steel container with no linen at all. My question, to myself, is why wasn't a fetus being wrapped before?

[...]

BN: The project has affected a lot of people, but it is an anonymous undertaking. It is not an artistic search for a unique profile. Not having the origin of each blanket marked is important because I did not want this project to benefit from other people's trauma. But I think creativity is important. For this study it has been of crucial importance that the weaving of the smallest blankets came from this hand loom at the Artistic Faculty here at the University of Gothenburg. Collectively we have researched weaving and fragility. There are so many topics for a weaver to examine: the inside and the outside of the blanket; the absorbency of the blanket. But then the blanket is received by parents and the focus shifts entirely. That is enormously important. It is my hope there will be some blankets available at every hospital and they will continue to not be labelled. The blankets' mission: *to give some comfort*. Yes, but what does that mean? At the hospitals there is a sense that the blankets have the capacity to deliver a beautiful and worthy moment in a terrible situation.

FURTHER READING: TOUCH

Bristow, Maxine. 'Continuity of Touch: Textile as Silent Witness', in *The Textile Reader*, ed. Jessica Hemmings, 44–52, Oxford: Berg, 2012.

Writing is based on an expanded version of a conference paper first presented in 2007 at the 'Repeat Repeat' conference held at the University of Chester, UK. Bristow explores the hierarchical treatment of the senses and a tendency to sideline touch as a way of knowing.

Bruno, Giuliana. *Surface: Matters of Aesthetics, Materiality, and Media*, Chicago and London: University of Chicago Press, 2014.

Written by a cultural critic and theorist, this book-length study considers the place of materiality in our increasingly virtual lives. Wide-ranging examples are drawn from across art, architecture, fashion, design, film and new media.

Douglas, Mary. *Purity and Danger: An Analysis of Concepts of Pollution and Taboo*, London and New York: Routledge and Kegan Paul, 1966.

Classic text of anthropology where Douglas (1921–2007) considers the meaning of dirt and uses the now-well-quoted explanation that dirt is matter out of place. Considering contexts around the globe, she addresses ritual, religion and idea of pollution.

Hamlyn, Anne. 'Freud, Fabric, Fetish', *TEXTILE* 1, no. 1 (2003): 9–27.

In this article published in the very first issue of the academic journal *TEXTILE* Hamlyn addresses the real physical stuff at the centre of fetish: the textile. Drawing on examples from film and visual art, Hamlyn uses psychoanalytic theory to propose that a sensory connection to cloth exists beyond language.

Hauser, Jens (ed.). *Sk-Interfaces: Exploring Borders – Creating Membranes in Art, Technology and Society*, Liverpool: Fact and Liverpool University Press, 2008.

Examples of twelve artists' work that considers the possibility of a skinless society. Includes texts translated from French and German and twenty-two artistic projects.

Hill, June. 'Sense and Sensibility', in *The Textile Reader*, ed. Jessica Hemmings, 37–43, Oxford: Berg, 2012.

Hill's lecture was first presented at the conference 'Memory and Touch: An Exploration of Textural Communication' in 2008. Hill addresses the curator's response to an object's context, the power of 'gifting' as equal, if not greater, importance than the gift and the varied ways in which we understand and experience touch.

Hongisto, Ilona and Katve-Kaisa Kontturi, 'Fabulous Folds: Revolutionary Costumes in *Grey Gardens* (1975)', *Journal of Aesthetics & Culture* 12 (2020), doi:10.1080/20004214.2020.1840087.

Informed by fashion and film studies, the material agency of clothing is mapped in the American documentary film *Grey Gardens* through the concepts of the fabulous (madison moore) and the fold (Gilles Deleuze).

Mitchell, Victoria. 'Judith Scott: Capturing the Texture of Sensation', *TEXTILE* 19, no. 3 (2021): 328–39, doi:10.1080/14759756.2021.1913864.

Mitchell's article dwells on a photograph of the artist Judith Scott taken by Leon A. Borensztein in 1997. From the photograph, Mitchell discusses the meeting point of haptic and optic where once familiar boundaries, such as between interior and exterior, are breached through the photograph's affect.

Pallasmaa, Juhani. *The Eyes of the Skin: Architecture and the Senses*, Chichester: John Wiley & Sons Ltd, 2005.

First published in 1996, Pallasmaa writes from the perspective of architectural studies, tracing the dominance sight in European culture since the Greeks before proposing an approach to architecture that is multisensory.

Pajaczkowska, Claire. 'On Stuff and Nonsense: The Complexity of Cloth', *TEXTILE* 3, no. 3 (2005): 220–49, doi:10.2752/147597505778052495.

Informed by psychoanalytic theory, Pajaczkowska's article describes the textile's liminal position occupying thresholds between object and subject.

Tanizaki, Junichiro. *In Praise of Shadows*, Sedgwick: Leete's Island Books, 1977.

If touch is often set in contrast with sight, this small book instead compares different forms of ocular culture – in particular contrasting Asian cultures with Europe. First published in Japanese in 1933, Tanizaki's (1886–1965) examples include paper making and lacquerware design.

PART TWO

MEMORY

PART INTRODUCTION

The writing in this section considers the capacity of the textile to act as a record keeper of events that pass near its surface. Jenni Sorkin's writing opens the section with a discussion of benign textile stains that then confirm far less innocent violence against women's bodies. While Sorkin's essay was first published in an academic journal, her writing style challenges academic conventions and creates an engaging and emotionally seductive piece of writing that strikes a balance between the creative and the critical. Here the textile acts as an entry point into a discussion that extends far beyond the symbolic qualities of cloth.

Following Sorkin's writing on violence directed at the female body is a text translated from Spanish for this publication written by Isabel Cristina González Arango and translated by Lorna Dillon. González Arango writes of the Sonsón Memory Sewing Group who have met each month since 2009 in the Colombian city of Sonsón to sew and reflect on the violence of armed conflict in the region. Marit Paasche offers a description of repair work necessary for *We Are Living on a Star* (1958), a tapestry woven by Hannah Ryggen (1894–1970) that was damaged in 2011 by a bomb detonated by Anders Behring Breivik in Oslo's government quarter which killed eight people. Breivik killed a further sixty-nine people and injured many others on the Norwegian island of Utøya.

We then move back in time to the life of Scotsman Angus MacPhee (1916–97). As an adult MacPhee became mute, withdrawing from much of conventional life but producing countless objects knit and plaited from grasses that he would have seen produced as a child on the islands of the Outer Hebrides. Today we can only speculate that MacPhee drew comfort from childhood memories of making. In contrast, the African-American artist Faith Ringgold openly recounts expectations that her own childhood contained more trauma and distress than was in fact her experience. Turning to cloth to be able to tell her story accurately, Ringgold resists the expectations associated with her race and gender of a life of violence she explains were not her personal memories of Harlem in the 1930s.

From the intimate and individual, the memory section then shifts in scale to the institutional with writing from the perspective of the archive and museum. Decisions for the museum conservator and curator around the conservation of cloth, and the memories cloth contains, are addressed. Sue Prichard's essay considers the curator's responsibility to collect and preserve material that is 'held in trust for the nation, so that those who come after us can make sense of the past and try to understand the people, customs, and value systems related to the material held in our institutions'. Prichard considers examples of material instability weighed against the responsibilities of preservation of textiles in the collections at the Victoria and Albert Museum, London.

Sarah Scaturro's brief writing for the website of the Metropolitan Museum of Art's Costume Institute in New York City offers a complex example of what textile conversation now entails. In her discussion of Iris van Herpen's *Skeleton Dress*, Scaturro explains why one of the earliest examples of 3D printing seen on the catwalk is materially vulnerable and poses challenges for conservators' tasked with the care of artefacts made with techniques not designed with longevity in mind. In the closing text of the memory section, executive director and chief curator of the Hong Kong–based non-profit art institution CHAT (Centre for Heritage, Arts and Textile), Takahashi Mizuki, offers her account of preserving industrial textile history – not necessarily the material output of Hong Kong's once-thriving industry but instead the machinery and oral histories of the workers themselves.

8

STAIN
On Cloth, Stigma, and Shame (2000)

Jenni Sorkin

EDITOR'S INTRODUCTION

Jenni Sorkin is a critic and art historian. She completed her PhD in the history of art from Yale University in 2010 on American women potters in the 1950s and was a postdoctoral fellow at the Getty Centre in Los Angeles, California in 2011. Sorkin's first book, *Live Form: Women, Ceramics and Community* (2016), addresses gender, artistic labour and post-war ceramics. The same year she co-curated with Paul Schimmel the exhibition *Revolution in the Making: Abstract Sculpture by Women 1947–2016* in Los Angeles. Her latest book, *Art in California* (2021), is a chronicle of the state's contribution to modern and contemporary art. Sorkin is currently Professor in the History of Art & Architecture at the University of California, Santa Barbara, in the United States.

The writing included in full here was first published in 2000 with the academic journal *Third Text*. In it, Sorkin rejects the tired structures that so often communicate academic research. In place of the conventional essay format that establishes defined intentions at the outset and leads the reader from point to point, Sorkin slips from benign to harrowing material without warning. From the staining of cloth, the writing moves to the symbolic and quite literal staining of women's bodies through a writing strategy that intentionally catches the reader off guard.

Sorkin's text is an example of the creative breadth of references academic writing may draw upon. Equal gravitas is placed on all her references, which range from legal cases to song lyrics. As a result, the writing exposes the ubiquity of sexist comments, familiarity of casual language about violence and the pernicious ways guilt can be built up around violations of the, often female, body. Here, the textile's ability to remember is part of a deadly serious conversation about violence and the role of cloth as one form of record keeper of the violated body.

Stain: On Cloth, Stigma, and Shame

Jenni Sorkin

As if we could ever leave anything behind.

Pierre Joris

Cloth holds the sometimes unbearable gift of memory. And its memory is exacting: it does not forget even the benign scars of accident: red wine on a white tablecloth, water on a silk blouse, dark patches beneath arms on a humid summer day.

The ritual and expectancy of stain[1] is such that we allow for it. We designate special cloth for its usage, from birth onward: rags, bibs, diapers, wipes. Sponges. Washcloths, tablecloths, dish cloths, aprons, rubber gloves, placemats. Doormats. Sportswear: shorts, t-shirts, sports bras, leotards. Sweats: sweatbands, sweatpants, sweatshirts. Footwear: galoshes, rain boots, mud boots, snow boots, shitkickers, Gortex. Chamois, oil cloths, tarp. Q-tips, make-up applicators, cotton balls, Band-Aids, bandages, gauze. Certain underwear for certain days of the month. The convenience and abundance of paper cloth: paper towels, paper napkins, pads and tampons, toilet paper, tissue. Handkerchiefs. Stain is daily, stain is common, stain is mundane.

Stain is a negation of an area of fabric: It destroys the continuity of the cloth, supplanting the original colour and texture of a portion of the garment or textile. A true stain is permanent, forever altering the way a garment looks and therefore, is regarded.

Stains are nearly impossible to hide: The eye is drawn immediately to the damaged area. They differ in temperament, fabric to fabric. Pale, greasy, blotchy, crinkly, glossy, dark. Stains are not uniform. Like experiences, they are uneven, and irreproducible.

Stains mark the wearer: To be stained is to be dirty,[2] messy, poor, and/or careless. It infers a variety of judgements: One does not care for his or her clothing. One does not care about his or her presentation. One is unprofessional. One is obviously a slob. Many people feel embarrassment and/or scorn for the wearer of the stain. They hardly ever feel empathetic, preferring not to identify with the sloppy individual.

The wearer of the stain. What is the fabric of the wearer?

Stains are a record of what has been near, on, or is of the body.[3] Their ugliness, their offensiveness, is in their immediacy. Fresh, stains are the sores of a fabric, raw wounds that map an event. Aged, they are scars of retrospection. They function as both remainder and reminder of what has come to pass: both evidence and memory.

Nan Goldin's 1983 photograph *Brian After Coming* is an example of this kind of chronicle. Preceded by *My hand on Brian's dick* (1983), the photographic subject, Brian, lies next to marks of wetness, the spots a deeper shade of blue than the rest of the sheet. Who is the actual subject? Naked and sprawled across the bed, Brian is not alone. Who is witness to this intimacy? Who is responsible for its culmination? Here, the stain confirms Goldin's presence. She has, through the previous photograph, confirmed her participation. The sex act is not just one of self-pleasuring. Goldin inhabits the frame as much, if not more, than Brian. The stain is hers. Thus, the photographic record of this particular ejaculation acts as both validation and snapshot, laced with desire and self-witnessing.

Within the brevity of occurrence, stain taints *now* with *then*. A stain, thus, denotes the passage of time. If

Source: Jenni Sorkin, 'Stain: On Cloth, Stigma, and Shame', *Third Text* 14:53 (2000), pp. 77–80, ©*Third Text*, reprinted by permission of Informa UK Limited, trading as Taylor & Francis Group, www.tandfonline.com on behalf of *Third Text*. Reproduced with permission.

an ice cream cone drips down the front of a child's shirt, and he continues eating, the ice cream becomes a physical manifestation of a moment moments ago. Hence, stains result in an always present-past for the wearer of the damage.

Stains elicit shame: Nosebleeds, vomiting, bedwetting, incontinence. Wiping one's nose on one's sleeve. Wet dreams. Laughing so hard one begins to urinate. These are all examples of the staining one inflicts upon oneself—the self-stain. The self-stain renders the body uncontrollable: both capable and culpable of transmission, transgression and impurity, exceeding the acceptable, surpassing the boundaries of the skin. In her 1966 book *Purity and Danger*, Mary Douglas wrote, 'The mistake is to treat bodily margins in isolation from all other margins.'[4] This isolation, one of social taboo, is the source of the stigmatised stain. The action by which staining occurs is falsely tolerated, and in actuality, elicits fear and disgust. Thus the embarrassment, discomfort, and humiliation of the self-stain can be excruciating, especially when the staining occurs publicly, or becomes public. In the 1990s, no garment was more ill-famed than White House intern Monica Lewinsky's navy blue dress, marked with Bill Clinton's semen. But what of the other stain? That which is not self-originated, that which is incurred by outside action or force. Not from my own behaviour, or of my own body. That which I did not will, choose, nor want. That which is inflicted by another. That which is forced. Stain becomes, then, both an enactment and vestige of degradation, violence and coercion.

To stain another is to mark. To be marked is dark.

This darkness is constant foreboding and permanent grief. It constitutes, in its despair, a fixed sense of imperilled or impoverished destiny. Consistent and overwhelming spaces of terror specific to one's own experience interfere with living, violating the logic and assurance of reality. Memory asserts itself, rupturing and defying presence, perpetually confounding time and place, inserting, in the words of Ernst Bloch, 'this blind spot in the soul, this darkness of the lived moment'.[5]

If I am marked, I am discernible.[6] If I am discernible, I am different. If I am different, I am separate. I use discernment according to Georges Didi-Huberman's breakdown: in sifting, there is selection or deliberation. In seeing, there is visibility. In deciding, there is judgement. Huberman's signification is applicable to male assaults on women in rural Bangladesh. Over a three-year period, from 1996–1998, there were over 400 reported cases of acid attacks on women's faces and hands. Using corrosive battery acid, men have burned, blinded, and permanently disfigured women. The attacks are deliberate: most women know their attackers in the capacity of acquaintances whom have made unwanted sexual advances. The aftermath of the ordeal is one of visibility: a burned woman is considered objectionable and thus, flawed. Rural Bangladeshi women are often dependent on marriage for social and financial security. The accompanying physical marking and disfigurement ensures an unmarried status. According to Mary Douglas, differentiation is the basis for all defilement.[7] The sense of defilement or stigma that rape, incest, and all other forms of sexual violence retain in all parts of the world,[8] remains as both the individual injury and collective damage inflicted again and again upon women, before, during and after the crime. Stigma perpetuates the idea of self-stain, directing the blame at the survivor and not the perpetrator. Let it be noted that in botany, the word stigma is used to describe the part of the pistil which is the receptacle for pollen in impregnation; that is, the female region of the plant. Stigma is continually socialised as a female condition.

Sustain: the continuance and maintenance of stain. Su- is a prefix that comes from sub-: less than, not quite, lower than, secondary. A medium long considered inferior, needlework is the means by which Anne Wilson, in *Grafts #1* (1993), exaggerates and embellishes stains, holes and worn areas of table linen with human hair, re-enforcing

the repellent portions of the cloth through the careful enunciation of its flaws. The title, *Grafts*, hints at medicine, referring to living tissue transplanted to an area of the body in need of adhesion and growth. An addition or extension of life, a graft forces an injury to adapt before it can heal. Wilson's abject renderings prolong the life of the wound, magnifying and permanently altering the cloth, committing it to a state of irrevocable loss.

Stains are intrusions within a garment: Rape, incest and all other forms of sexual violence toward women are intrusive:[9] not only a disruption of normality and consistency within the life cloth, but destructive as well, discolouring all future living. If, according to Salman Rushdie, 'Repression is a seamless garment,'[10] then staining is the silent event that binds the wearer.

Stigma functions as both a form of reproach and silencing: It is the censure and condemnation of the victim rather than her perpetrator, that minimises the consequences of the violation and furthermore, relegates the rape to an inferior status than that of her attacker.

Stigma observes the dialectics of transference: In assigning culpability, the assertion of blame and subsequent burden of fault is thrust upon the survivor, essentially viewing the sadism of the perpetrator as the survivor's own masochism: that she desired the abuse, deserved the abuse, or 'asked for it'.[11]

Stigma protects the male perpetrator: In cultures socially and sexually oppressive toward women, the stigma is a natural extension of male tyranny, re-enforcing women's errant status. The preservation and maintenance of this dichotomy is a disavowal of male accountability. Evocative and ironic, Joseph Beuys' 1979 sculpture of a knife blade wrapped in gauze, titled *When you cut your finger, bandage the knife*[12] is a visual metaphor of this phenomenon of defence, cover, and sheltering. The knife, as is the penis, is the weapon of forced entry, removed from and sheltered against the damage it has incurred.

Stain is dangerous. The ownership of human residue affirms its occurrence. Cloth provides an exact topography of this marking, but the psychic implications are far graver. This essay seeks to integrate and negotiate an avowed space for the possession of sexual trauma. Stain is still disdained.

Women are almost always blamed for their perpetrator's crime. Most survivors of sexual assault and rape struggle with internal feelings of shame, humiliation, rage, and grief, which are exacerbated by the social stigma of rape: that the woman herself is at fault, or has brought shame upon herself and her family. This collective blame invalidates the trauma a survivor has been through, and creates the problem of undesirability, that is, the condemnation, avoidance and subsequent sexual and social ostracisation of the raped woman or girl.

Notes

1. Stain (n.):
   1. a discoloration produced by foreign matter having penetrated into a material
   2. a patch of colour different from that of the basic colour, as on the body of an animal
   3. a cause of reproach; stigma
   4. to bring reproach or dishonour upon; blemish
   (Webster's New College Dictionary)

2. 'No child will play with her because she is "dirty", Ngoepe 32, said of her daughter [age 6], who was raped repeatedly by Ngoepe's boyfriend and, more recently, by her own 12-year-old son.' (Chicago Tribune, 'A Plague of Rape.' [South Africa] June 1, 1999, section 1, p 1, 14.)

3. 'Torn or bloody clothing suggests a forceful struggle and supports an inference of non-consent. Clothing stained with blood or semen may identify the defendant as the perpetrator. Clothing bearing traces of semen can be introduced to show penetration or intercourse.' Legal Framework for Admissibility of Clothing at a Rape Trial, People v Pride, 833 para 2d, 643, 670–71, California, 1992, as quoted by Alinor Sterling in 'Undressing the Victim: The Intersection of Evidentiary and Semiotic Meanings of Women's Clothing in Rape Trials,' *Yale Journal of Law and Feminism*, 1995.

4. Mary Douglas, *Purity and Danger*, Routledge, London, 1993, p 121.

5. Ernst Bloch, *The Spirit of Utopia*, Translated Anothony A. Nassar, Meridian, Stanford, CA, 2000, p 198.

6. 'A *discernment*, a word whose root cernere, contains the three signifying vectors, 'sifting', 'seeing', and deciding . . .' Georges Didi-Huberman, 'The Index of the Absent Wound (A Monograph on a Stain).' *October* no 29, summer 1984.

7. Mary Douglas, *Purity and Danger*, Routledge, London, 1993, p 160.

8. The following quotes attest to this worldwide phenomenon:
'The stigma of rape is so heavy that even victims' families tell the victims to shut up.' Chicago Tribune, 'A Plague of Rape.' [South Africa] June 1, 1999, section 1, p 1, 14.

'The stigma of rape often prevents victims from identifying themselves or telling what happened. 'It's certainly taboo,' a UN official said of the rape stigma. 'Many of the women said they were afraid of how their husbands would react if they knew.'

Chicago Tribune, 'Women from Kosovo village tell of a 3-day ordeal of rape by Serb police.' April 28, 1999, section 1, p 9.

9. 'Intrusion reflect the indelible imprint of the traumatic moment.' Judith Lewis Herman, *Trauma and Recovery*, HarperCollins, New York, 1992, p 35.

10. *Shame*, Penguin, London, 1983, Ibid, p 1.

11. 'Was she asking for it? Was she asking nice? She was asking for it. Did she ask you twice?'—Hole, 'Asking for it,' *Live Through This*, Geffen Records Inc, Los Angeles, CA, 1994.

12. Elaine Scarry, *The Body in Pain*, Oxford University Press, Oxford, 1985, p 16.

9

CLAIMING THE RIGHT TO MEMORY, STITCH BY STITCH
The experience of the *Costurero Tejedoras por la Memoria de Sonsón* (the Sonsón Memory Sewing Group) (2013/2021)

Isabel Cristina González Arango

EDITOR'S INTRODUCTION

Isabel Cristina González Arango is an anthropologist who specializes in human rights and international humanitarian law. She is a researcher associated with the research group 'Cultura Violencia y Territorio' (Culture, Violence and Land), which is part of the Instituto de estudios regionales (Institute of Regional Studies) INER, Colombia. In this text González Arango discusses the Sonsón Memory Sewing Group as an important example of an initiative 'from below'. Organized at the community and individual level, women have met monthly since 2009 in the city of Sonsón, to reflect on the violence of armed conflict (experienced at its height between 1998 and 2005) while working with textiles.

The *arpilleras* stitched by women about the violence wrought during General Pinochet's dictatorship of Chile (1973–90) are now well cited in textile scholarship. But their singular example risks public misinterpretation as an isolated historical moment. González Arango's text offers another, more recent, example of violent conflict. For the Sonsón Memory Sewing Group in Colombia, sewing within community-organized women's gatherings contributes to the process of memory making.

The text included here was first published in Spanish. Excerpts of the original have been translated into English by Lorna Dillon, Research Fellow in Latin American art at the University of Cambridge. Dillon's current research considers the participatory needlework collectives (tejedoras) of Colombia, Mexico and Chile.

Claiming the Right to Memory, Stitch by Stitch:
The experience of the *Costurero Tejedoras por la Memoria de Sonsón* (the Sonsón Memory Sewing Group)

Isabel Cristina González Arango

Rituals and commemorations [sewing group meetings] are bridges between the past and the future, to the extent that they are symbolic affirmations of memory, places where individual memories come together, intersect and merge into collective memory. This is not to fixate on a past that no longer exists, but so that the past can become a catalyst for action in the present and in the future.

Maria Teresa Uribe, 2003

In Colombia, the violence – also referred to as the armed conflict or the war – is located in a complex network of empirical facts and theoretical interpretations that make it difficult to comprehend. New actors, dynamics, and disputes arise each day forcing us to rethink the contexts for the conflict moving beyond a linear historical approach. Local and regional transformations continue to emerge, blurring the nature of the conflict, not just socially and politically, but militarily, economically, culturally and environmentally (Giraldo, 2009). Indeed, the principal impact of the armed conflict and the related violence is a social phenomenon.

In the case of the city of Sonsón in the Antioquia region of Colombia, the armed conflict was most severe between the years of 1998 and 2005. The reasons for this intense period of the war are confusing and fragmented. Several milestones in the conflict help us to understand the dynamics of armed conflict in the region. These key points were a territorial dispute between the insurgent groups in the Río Verde de los Montes and Los Henao areas; the incursion of paramilitary groups supported by government forces in the urban area, and the seizure of strategic areas in the rural area, particularly in the areas of La Danta, San Miguel and Alto de Sabanas.

In this context of confrontation, the indiscriminate use of force and hostilities spread. The insurgent groups, using the 47th and 9th divisions of FARC (Revolutionary Armed Forces of Colombia), implemented a variety of war strategies, not only to contain the advance of the paramilitary groups, but also to avoid being held under siege by the government forces and losing control of territories. These violent actions severely affected the civilian population, which, in the midst of the conflict, experienced threats, selective assassinations, massacres, kidnappings, forced disappearances, minefields and a series of violations of human rights and international humanitarian law. These situations resulted in massive, forced displacements, the disintegration of families, widespread fear, terror and unspeakable pain. The victims and survivors still struggle to comprehend these things even now, as they rebuild their lives amid extreme changes in the landscapes – in the colours and dreams that they know – as well as in their day-to-day routines and the levels of autonomy that they experience.

In recent years, various social movements have emerged which draw attention to the suffering of the victims; their loss of integrity, freedom, and their experiences of citizenship when their rights were being

Source: Isabel Cristina González Arango, 'Un derecho elaborado puntada a puntada. La experiencia del Costurero Tejedoras por la Memoria de Sonsón'. Translated by Lorna Dillon, Leverhulme Early Career Fellow. Supported by the Leverhulme Trust and the Isaac Newton Trust. Published with the permission of the Revista de trabajo social del al Universidad de Antioquia, Nos 18 & 19, Julio 2013 – Junio 2014, pp. 77–100.

violated. These social movements are far removed from hegemonic discourses, which do not reflect the human face of the armed conflict, (Uribe de Hicapié, 2003). The social movements have started discourses, which include broader explanations of the contexts for the war, including people's personal and collective experiences which also helps to give meaning to lived experience.

From the 1990s onwards, and from 1997 in particular, mobilizations by civil society were driven primarily by the search for a political solution to the armed conflict by lobbying the government for the right to life and dignity, for human rights to be guaranteed and for the government to comply with international humanitarian law (Archila, 2006). The process has shown the complex relationship between civil society and the State through the implementation of strategies for the transition from war to peace. These strategies have not just come "from above", but have included views and experiences "from below". They have taken proposals that reflect unique regional experiences – proposals which have come from victims and from community organizations – as their starting point.

Numerous initiatives in eastern Antioquia provide good examples of this. In recent years these initiatives have sought to reflect on and repair the damage done by the armed conflict. They have considered its effects on the civilian population and they have sought to establish strategies for collective visibility. The initiatives have taken account of the war memories that victims of the armed conflict have, and they have also considered the different forms of peace building and empowering actions that occur when specific initiatives are carried out with a view to fostering peace and reconciliation. In this way, in 2007, a variety of victims' organizations emerged that began a process of reconstruction, using individual and collective projects to transcend the established processes for comprehensive reparations. Mika (2009) speaks of a transitional justice "from below", not as a particular type of justice, but as the inclusion of victims' perspectives on how to "do justice", to highlight proposals that challenge the State and constructively contribute to

peace through day-to-day practices that enhance the capacities of local communities. In this way, a balance is found between proposals from community figures and governmental actions. These community figures forge a pathway not as protagonists or secondary witnesses, but rather as subjects of the legal system, who demand and contribute to resistance and survival strategies, which allow them to rebuild their lives and their communities.

THE SEWING GROUP: A SPACE FOR MEMORY

In 2009, twenty adult women started to meet to sew together in a large, green house in the municipality of Sonsón. They have been meeting once a month to sew, one stitch at a time, ever since. They are mothers, grandmothers, wives, widows, and members of the Asociación de Víctimas por la paz y la Esperanza de Sonsón (Sonsón Association of Victims for Peace and Hope). They were displaced and suffered because of the armed conflict. Prior to that, most of them had worked the land, caring for animals, sowing vegetable patches, taking care of their children and husbands: entrenched rural practices that link them to the land and to a patriarchal model that determines family relations, the domestic economy and education as well as personal and social development. This paradigm continues to affect them, despite the fact that many of them are the heads of their families. Each one of these women has woven a different life for herself, but they are all united by memories of the armed conflict and the forced displacements, which, from 1998 onwards, moved hundreds of people from the countryside to the urban centre. The situation resulted in interesting processes of participation and resistance in response to the systematic violence that people were experiencing. New initiatives developed, such as the "Asamblea comunitaria Unidos por el Desarrollo y la Democracia" (The United Community Assembly for Development and Democracy); "De la casa a la plaza" (From House to Town Square) and "Jóvenes por la paz" (Young People for Peace). The situation also resulted in the formation of the group "Promodoras de Vida y Salud Mental", (Promoters of Life and Mental

Health) Provisame.[1] In May 2007, the Promodoras de Vida y Salud Mental project led to the formation of the Asociación de Víctimas por la paz y la Esperanza de Sonsón (the Sonsón Association of Victims for Peace and Hope), which provided a mechanism through which the victims of the armed conflict could claim rights, access training and gain increased visibility for victims of the conflict through ongoing local and regional peacebuilding processes.

Currently the association is comprised of about 200 people, mainly women, who hold an assembly every two months to acquire and promote skills that allow them to address the situations facing them as victims of the armed conflict. They focus on the future, exploring ongoing issues such as access to reparations via administrative processes; the restitution of lands, and participation in the local and national programmes that have been implemented as part of the attention, assistance and integral reparations designed to support victims of the internal armed conflict.

The Asociación de Víctimas por la paz y la Esperanza de Sonsón is characterised by features that would at one time have been thought of as weaknesses, but which have actually been opportunities for consolidating the group. One of these is the need for mechanisms and strategies that lead to economic sustainability and the need for opportunities for the members of the group to speak about their experiences both within the group and to the wider public in the region. This is in order to replicate the training and knowledge that different facilitators have brought in the areas of citizens' and victims' rights; psychosocial work and concepts such as memory, reparation, reconciliation, justice, forgiveness and forgetting – central themes in the struggle. These matters acquire political relevance in local and regional contexts when they are appropriated and charged with meaning, by people who have lived experiences of the dynamics of the war, and who explore the themes in light of their own experiences.

In this sense, the Association has sought to consolidate its advocacy work, proposing initiatives such as the formulation of public policy for victims in the municipality of Sonsón; participation in academic training events, and the exchange of experiences. Likewise, the group has collaborated with the Universidad de Antioquia (University of Antioquia) on a variety of linked projects financed by the Banco Universitario de Programas y Proyectos de Extensión (University Bank of Programmes and Outreach Projects) (BUPPE).[2] Through calls in 2009, 2010 and 2012, BUPPE[3] strengthened the organisation and helped facilitate reflections on memory, reparations and reconciliation. Through methodologies that facilitate both conceptual reflections and the development of new skills such as needlework, the Association recognizes the value of individual experience and builds from each participant's existing knowledge.

One important outcome of these projects was the establishment of the Tejedoras por la Memoria de Sonsón (The Sonsón Memory Sewing group), a space in which people can meet and explore memory. A variety of people have passed through the space including adults, young people and the children of the regular members, who are mostly women and who have been meeting since September 2009 to develop skills such as sewing. They have created products of great importance, not only for their artistic value, but also because of the way they highlight histories and memories. This space is conceived of as a grassroots initiative "from below" which promotes learning that

---

[1] This project involved training women from eastern Antioquia in the field of psychosocial wellbeing, so that they could provide support to groups of women affected by the armed conflict using an approach that would allow the reconstruction of the social fabric of society. The projects were facilitated by A.M.O.R, Conciudadanía and Cinep's Peace Programme.

[2] The outreach projects are projects that promote dialogue and links between the University and the wider society. Their main objective is to promote local and regional development by improving people's quality of life. Every year they release a public call for resources, which allocates human and material resources as well as funding for a set of interrelated activities that are designed to achieve specific objectives in a certain area.

[3] These projects were organised by the research group Cultura, Violencia y Territorio (Culture, Violence and Territory), which is affiliated to the Institute of Regional Studies, (INER). The researchers on the projects were Ana María Muñoz Guzmán, Verónica Espinal Restrepo, Catalina Carrizosa Isaza and Isabel Cristina González Arango.

allows the women to share their knowledge and experiences. It also validates new languages and forms of expression such as the use of stitched textiles to narrate and promote reflection on the struggles experienced by the victims/survivors of the armed conflict, and this helps to increase awareness about these experiences.

The sewing group makes objects and images that are essentially "political texts". When these items are presented to the public, they help to construct historic memory from a differential approach. The works of textile art can also be used to help communities with integration processes and integral reparations, and this, in turn, re-signifies the position of surviving victims.[4] Within the space of the sewing group, the activities that are undertaken explore the craft of sewing alongside fundamental themes related to capacity building. Different issues arising from the needs and interests of the group are explored in each session. The participants learn and practice new techniques. Since most of the women live in difficult conditions that have been exacerbated by the dynamics of the conflict, the craft techniques are presented in the workshops as methods that could potentially lead to economic opportunities. These meetings led to the emergence of the sewing group and they have ensured the space for the continuation of the project. Through the patient and dedicated practice of sewing, this project has, in its own original way provided a unique pathway for rebuilding lives.

Young people – the women's children – also participate actively in the sewing group taking on roles such as photographing the project, organising logistics and helping with housework. Sometimes they also stitch their own textiles and clothes. These young people are part of a complementary space, el Laboratorio de imágenes y Memoria (the Laboratory of Images and Memory)" which also arose from the 2009 BUPPE project. One prominent feature of that

group is the way it helped raise young people voices. The young people have spoken about the ways they identify as victims of the armed conflict, and about the ways that they have transformed the experience of being a victim: of their experiences of loss, risks and threats that continue to arise from the armed conflict, even today.

Through this project a collective memory of youth has emerged and led to specific outputs such as the documentary series "Jóvenes relatos, grandes memorias" (Youth Stories, Big Memories), and the photographic exhibition "Memorias cotidianas de Tejidos y pixels" (Everyday Memories of Fabrics and Pixels). These projects provide insight into the perspectives of those who were born in and have grown up in a context of armed confrontation. The young people have a need to understand, relate and articulate discussions and methodologies that are closer to their interests and needs to create generational insight and to support forms of collective acknowledgement about their own experiences as much as about their parents' experience.

Moreover, one of the important advances made by the Association has been an Archive of Memory.[5] This has been a key instrument in the process of increasing visibility, recognition and memorialisation. As well as being a database of cases detailing the member's individual experiences as victims of the armed conflict, it is a more personal archive of peoples' histories – of their lives and of their families' experiences past and present. The archive includes a variety of materials such as photographs and narratives that strengthen historical memorialization and inform the new strategies that are

---

[4] It is worth mentioning here that we believe that being a victim is a situation rather than a condition and so we recognise that victims as political subjects are able to have agency and to generate transformation (Blair et al. 2008).

[5] The Association's Archive of Memory emerged in 2008 through the academic practice of two technicians from the Sonsón campus of the Universidad de Antioquia, Gabriela Grisales Restrepo and Carlos Samuel Ospina. In 2010, with the objective of continuing to improve the database through the digitalization of physical documents related to the information produced by the association, a project developed entitled 'Fortalecimiento del Archivo Digital de Memoria de la Asociación de Víctimas por la Paz y la Esperanza de Sonsón' (Strenghtening of the Digital Archive of Memory of the Association of Sonsón Victims of Peace and Hope) which was funded by the BUPPE call for proposals.

being developed by the sewing group in particular, but also by other parts of the association.

Thus, the sewing group, the Laboratorio de Imágenes y Memoria and the Archive constitute a joint platform from which to the members of the Sonsón victim's association pursue causes that are important to them. The projects are supportive spaces which have become more established with time, and which help to give voice to the women and the young people. Strategically, the groups help because they make going through the process of applying for integral reparations meaningful and also because they promote integration and seek to reconstruct memory. Using the fabric metaphorically, the process can be defined as hand stitching the fabric of memory.

STITCHING ENCOUNTERS AND NEW HISTORIES

Hannah Arendt said that it is difficult to express and communicate things that happen in the personal realm; and so, she thinks that love, pain, suffering, affections and losses can only be expressed through art and literature. Whether it is in personal dialogues or in the public realm – the author assumes –, issues of intimacy can only be mentioned in terms of magnitudes and are immeasurable for the listener, since they will never be able to understand the full depth and panorama of what the other is feeling.

María Teresa Uribe, 2003: 11.

The women in the Tejedoras por la Memoria de Sonsón gather around fabric to converse, share, learn and listen. Stitch by stitch, with a rhythm of their own, images, memories and emotions emerge, goodness, why not say it, even silences emerge. Time capriciously flits from the past to the present as lives are recounted. Everyday problems are recounted in confidence and from the solidarity of the group the solution emerges: a collection is made and then an envelope with the collection is prudently given to the person that needs it. Poverty and suffering are well-known terrain, and as such, the solidarity of generosity is a strategy for overcoming it.

The sewing group is a safe space that has, little by little strengthened, making space for the women's voices. As they sew, their experiences, feelings and ideas become threads that become memory textiles and among the needles and threads, they experience sewing as a healing ritual. In this way, fears are brought out, forgetting is exorcised, and there are pauses, which allow indignation, pain and suffering to emerge in the silence, but which also protect hope and the life force that impetuously and repeatedly brings each new day helping them rebuild their everyday lives.

Each one of these women has learned to share her pain and be supportive to the others, to know that words are healing, but that, like silences, they have their time. They have been recognized as women who fight for their rights in this space, and they have been recognized as agents of change who, through their textiles, narrate truths that counter impunity and battles behind closed doors. Each seam is a vehicle of memory, transmitting experiences, feelings, and absences from the past to the present, imbuing the survivors with dignity and achieving justice for those they have lost:

> So far, we have done a lot of work together; firstly, we have been healing our souls through our sewing, and as we create dolls, we recount our memories and work on our political, social and economic project. So, we are a group of women who have managed to get ahead; if we ask any of the women here how sewing has changed their lives, all have become very empowered to speak, and so giving accounts of our disappeared no longer creates so many tears.
>
> (Member of the sewing group, November 23, 2011)

In this way, for the sewing group, exploring memory is a skill, a process, and a way of forging a relationship with time. Experience has shown that the agency of devices such as textile art, videos, photographs and exhibitions, extends beyond documenting or providing a testimony. For the women in the sewing group, fully exercising the right to memory means involving the victims as central actors in the process, not just as witnesses or as bearers of truth, but as key agents in processes, who exercise active citizenship through the process of living their lives, reconstructing their life stories, and relating to one other in solidarity. In this way they carry out politics through their day-to-day lives, claiming their places as peacebuilding agents.

For the members of the sewing group and for the young people who participate, exploring memory allows alternate ways of being; different ways of relating to others, of forming communities, of being women, sons, daughters and of claiming roles for everyone in society. The sewing group as a dynamic and creative space highlights forms of rehabilitation and ways of restoring resilience in victims. This gives strength and meaning to life among the noise of bullets and the injustices.

In each object created by the members of the sewing group a testimony is transformed into an image, takes material form, and is disseminated. This expresses the creative and conjunctural character of memory. The political dimension of memory nourishes citizen action and social reflection based on the transversality and understanding of diverse memories that narrate and interpret the past, not as a static and unique entity, but as a construction that starts from the awareness of the present experience and from a view to the future.

The embroidered cushions, the crochet fabrics, the unstitched patchwork paintings recount individual and collective experiences of the armed conflict in Sonsón. They are a materiality that validates memory, not only as a form of orality and testimony, but also since the crafts, objects and images provide another platform from which to engage in dialogue, to socialize and allow the emergence of memories "from below". In many cases, silence has been a survival mechanism in these spaces, and the word has become perceived of as a threat. The sewing group has been able to reinvent the languages and devices used to narrate lived experience, and through expression in a painting or a rag doll, generate versatile and creative methods that can elicit political transformation.

The objects created by the sewing group have become devices of memory, materialities that incorporate stories, experiences and emotions, and force us to recognize the value of the different languages the victims use to narrate the armed conflict. In the sewing group, it is the women victims who through their hands, their word and sometimes their silences, allow the exploration of feelings, interpretations and

ways of incarnating concepts such as memory, reparation and reconciliation. At the same time, they have created a space in which they can learn a skill, through which they can make artistic pieces of great value; charged with emotion and with their own language emerging in each one of the textiles, configuring scenes for processing pain, memory and the struggle for their rights and their claims.

The sewing group as a memory space constantly transits between subjective and collective histories. On occasions the textiles lead to introspection, to silence and remembrance. On other occasions they lead to speech, solidarity and the search for solutions and alternatives. In this dynamic of sewing, women have added new colours to their lives. They have reconstructed their painful histories, and they have also decorated their present, as one of them explains it when describing her experience:

> *The reason I am in the sewing group is that I have already felt very happy to be in a centre, which provides distraction and prevents you from dwelling on the bad times in life. Through these workshops, I have felt a little overwhelmed and brave. Now I hardly think of my children anymore, and that truth makes me very happy, but they know that I always carry them in my heart. I have learned a lot of skills for decorating my home, that I never thought I could manage.*
>
> (Member of the sewing group, November 14, 2011)

Thus, while the work of the sewing group, can be considered as a forum for the struggle for memory and a space for political action in the public sphere, demanding the rights of victims, it has also become a place for new histories, the creation of new relationships between friends, between women, and of ways of rediscovering yourself at a time in life, where the challenge is to be reborn from the pain, creating a new life.

The Sonsón Sewing Group, through their objects, paintings, dolls and textile art, has made visible other forms of knowledge, other stories, which are different from the official, hegemonic or institutional forms. The sewing group, as a meeting place and space for political action, helps claim the right to memory, and in that way, helps claim the rights of the victims in general, without neglecting the work of repairing their lives, of recreating the way and rebuilding the fractured everyday lives, or if you will—to continue in the metaphor of fabrics—unstitched or disrupted by war.

CONCLUSION

To work with memories, to speak about your past is to forge history. It is creating your own history and your family's history, family history with respect to what has already happened and also with regard to the future.
(Member of the sewing group, November 23, 2011)

Charged with images, memories, emotions and life experiences, the exchange needs a rhythm: a respect for silences and a time in which words can emerge. In this way, a relationship is formed between an acknowledgement of the painful grieving processes that the participants are going through and their current realities.

The implementation of methodologies based on crafts, within spaces that bring people together and continuously facilitate capacity building, generates trust, promotes the exchange of pre-existing knowledge and helps develop leadership skills. Regarding concrete and tangible outcomes, the group leans towards concepts and narratives which not only recount the conflict, but which also allow an exploration and analysis of the way the victims are reconstructing their lives. This demonstrates new ways of conceiving of the exchange between academics and people who have been victims of the armed conflict.

The sewing group creates a space for meeting, sharing creativity, being together and getting along. These are important ways of strengthening the community and accord dignity to the participants. They are also memory spaces, and spaces in which to acknowledge life stories and the way people are shaping their lives in the present. They are spaces of awareness and of self-awareness, of memories past and present, which also become spaces of social and political capacity building and spaces in which to develop citizenship, strengthening different kinds of subjectivities.

As well as learning skills in the sewing group, the process reminds the women that they are capable of doing things and it allows them to recognise what they can achieve. This increases their self-esteem enormously and helps them to feel dignity through their actions. For each member of the sewing group, feeling part of the group, and being recognised for the things they do for the group – for doing constructive and valuable things – also generates profound reflections on the wider situation.

The complexity of thinking about building peace in the midst of ongoing armed confrontation means that it is crucial to develop projects that support local initiatives and take an interest in how these new voices construct ways of practicing citizenship from their experience of the war. We believe that the reconciliation processes in the country should involve wider society in general and higher education in particular. Universities should participate in the process, disseminating the knowledge that is generated, with this including the local knowledge that is generated and knowledge about local struggles. This supports the vindication of rights that have historically been violated for these populations. The proposal for the sewing group initiative included a reflexive exercise and a concrete way of strengthening collective ties. This brought the new generation into the organisational process and implemented practices that support the struggle for political recognition. At the same time, it helped with validation for the victims / survivors, facilitating dialogues with different sectors. In this way it was possible to develop other forms of knowledge starting with explorations of individual experiences and feelings, validating new languages through which to narrate the histories of war and survival in the town of Sonsón.

The products of the sewing group are considered testimonial textiles, embroidered, and represented in images that narrate and express the historical memory of the town of Sonsón. They are means of transmitting the pain and of highlighting organisational attempts in the town and in the region. Within the sewing group, the narrative textile is a political document that recognises the victims' right to exercise citizenship, and revalidates memory as a right full of complexity, which is not exhausted in a linear reconstruction of an occurrence or in an anecdotal account of an event.

Bibliography

Archila, Mauricio. (2006). *Los movimientos sociales en Colombia y las paradojas de la democracia en Colombia.* En Controversia N°186, 10–32. Bogotá.

Blair, Elsa; Quiceno, Natalia; De los Ríos, Isabel; Muñoz, Ana María y Grisales, Marisol (2008), *De memorias y de guerras. La Sierra, Villa Liliam y el 8 de Marzo en Medellín* (Informe final de investigación). Alcaldía de Medellín, IDEA, Colciencias, Universidad de Antioquia, Instituto de Estudios Regionales —INER—, Medellín.

Giraldo, Javier. (2009). *Conflicto y Derecho Internacional Humanitario en Colombia.* Seminario Internacional sobre Colombia, Conflicto y Derecho Internacional, 1–17. Madrid.

Mika, Harry (2009), *Sobre el concepto de justicia transicional desde abajo Entrevista con el profesor Harry Mika.* En Reparar en Colombia: los dilemas en contextos de conflicto, pobreza y exclusión. Centro Internacional para la Justicia Transicional (ICTJ) y Centro de Estudios de Derecho, Justicia y Sociedad (DeJuSticia), 227–245.

Uribe, de Hicapie Maria Teresa. (2003). *Estado y sociedad frente a las víctimas de la violencia.* Estudios políticos N° 23. Medellín julio- diciembre de 2003, 9–25.

10

WE ARE LIVING ON A STAR (EXCERPT) (2019)

Marit Paasche

EDITOR'S INTRODUCTION

Marit Paasche holds a PhD in art history from the Norwegian University of Science and Technology and is the former head of research at the Norwegian Video Art Archive. She works as an independent curator and writer. Her research interests span art historiography, modernism and feminism. *Hannah Ryggen: Threads of Defiance* (2019) was awarded best art book of the year by the *New York Times* and best of book of the year by the *Times Literary Supplement*. In 2016 the Norwegian language version of the book received the Norwegian Literary Critics' Prize for non-fiction.

The artist Hannah Ryggen was born in the southern Swedish city of Malmö in 1894. She married the Norwegian painter Hans Ryggen in 1923. The couple lived on an isolated smallholding in Ørlandet, north of the city of Trondheim on the west coast of Norway. The region the couple called home would be of strategic importance during German occupation of Norway in the Second World War. Sweden remained neutral during the war and this fact, coupled with her husband's incarceration by the Nazi forces (depicted in the tapestry *Grini* from 1945), may explain, in part, why Hannah Ryggen identified as a Norwegian artist. She formalized her connection to the region towards the end of her career with the donation of a significant number of her tapestries, which she wanted to see housed in a public, rather than a private, collection, to the National Museum of Decorative Arts and Design (NKIM) in Trondheim. She died in Trondheim in 1970.

Ryggen's artistic career produced numerous tapestries of political and contemporary significance. The brief excerpt selected for inclusion here can be found at the end of Paasche's extensive book about Hannah Ryggen's life and art and briefly recounts the restoration work undertaken for the tapestry *We Are Living on a Star* (1958). The tapestry was damaged by the bomb detonated by Anders Behring Breivik outside the entrance of architect Erling Viksjø's modernist building, The Highrise (1958), in Oslo's government quarter which killed eight people. From Oslo, Breivik then drove to the island of Utøya, where he killed a further sixty-nine people and injured many others.

We Are Living on a Star

Marit Paasche

LOVE AS A POLITICAL FORCE

We Are Living on a Star was hanging in its original place in the entrance hall of the Highrise on 22 July 2011, when Anders Behring Breivik detonated an enormous bomb just outside the entrance. Immediately after the explosion Behring Breivik drove to the island of Utøya, about an hour outside Oslo. Dressed as a policeman he then attacked the participants of the Workers' Youth League's summer camp with guns, killing sixty-nine people, most of them children and youths, and injured many more.

The bomb in front of the Highrise went off at 3:25 p.m. The explosion killed eight people and injured over thirty, and was so powerful that the lobby's security gate, which weighed more than a ton, was hurled through the building and landed 20 metres (65 feet) away.[1] Yet because the tapestry is relatively soft and light, miraculously, it came through the terrorism attack with only minimal damage.

For several days after the explosion, *We Are Living on a Star* lay on the floor in a pool of dirty water, mixed with concrete rubble and shards of glass. It was then rolled up and taken to KORO (Public Art Norway) in Oslo, which in turn sent it to the Conservation Services of the Museum Centre in Hordaland, where the following assessment of its condition was recorded:

> When the tapestry arrived at Conservation Services it was damp and extremely soiled. The tapestry has a large gash in the lower right corner. The gash is not across the entire corner, i.e., the corner has not been completely severed from the rest of the tapestry, but as a result, an area is hanging loose. The loose area is especially dirty and stiff due to a brownish substance that has been absorbed deep into the textile. In the same area there are also several smaller tears of varying sizes. The tears have occurred where warp threads have frayed/been cut across. In the area around these tears, portions of the weft threads have therefore ravelled out, and long wool threads are hanging loose. In addition mould has developed in some areas due to the dampness. The uneven moisture content in the tapestry has resulted in a rippled surface. There were large quantities of broken glass, wood splinters and various building materials over the entire tapestry. Some lay loose on the surface, but much has become embedded in the tapestry.[2]

Conservator-restorers Inger Raknes Pedersen and Ida Areklett Garmann from the Conservation Services carried out a painstaking and extremely fine restoration, so that today the gash and other tears are hardly visible.

According to the final ruling in the trial of Anders Behring Breivik, the motive for the terror attack was his belief that '[a]ll the parties in Parliament (Storting), but in particular the Labour Party' were complicit in a political agenda that had transformed Norway 'into a multicultural state, one in which the Norwegian indigenous population is in the process of being exterminated'.[3] The bomb attack was aimed at social-democratic values and spokespersons for those values.[4]

A brass plaque mounted on the wall in the Highrise's lobby, next to *We Are Living on a Star*, bears this unusual inscription:

> 'We Are Living on a Star'. 1958. 400 x 300
> Property of the Norwegian State. The Government Building.
> The mysteries of the universe and love's essential place in our world.

Source: Excerpt from Marit Passche 'We Are Living on a Star', *Hannah Ryggen: Threads of Defiance* © 2019, pp. 239–43. Reprinted with permission of Thames & Hudson Ltd., London.

That this particular tapestry, which so powerfully proclaims a faith in love as a personal and political force, should be struck in the first attack on Norwegian society since the Second World War is perhaps coincidental, yet it is hard to escape being touched by the symbolic significance.

Notes

1. The bomb went off at 3:25 p.m. Immediately after the explosion Behring Breivik drove to the island of Utøya. Dressed as a policeman, he attacked the participants of the Workers Youth League's summer camp with firearms. Behring Breivik killed 69 people, most of them children and youths, and injured many more.
2. Bevaringstenestene Museumstenestene i Hordaland, Pedersen and Garmann 2012, p. 5.
3. The quotes here are from the official English translation of the judgement (TOSLO-2011-188627-24 dated 24 August 2012) in the 22 July case tried in Oslo District Court. The full text is available on the website of Lovdata (a non-profit provider of legal information services established by the Norwegian Ministry of Justice and the University of Oslo) at: https://lovdata .no/static/file/1282/toslo-2011-188627-24-eng.pdf. Last accessed: 22 November 2018.
4. This is apparent in *2083. A European Declaration of Independence, London 2011* by Andrew Berwick, a pseudonym used by Anders Behring Breivik. This compendium, or manifesto, is available on several websites. I have accessed it on the home page of *Public Intelligence*. https://publicintelligence.net/ anders-behring-breiviks-complete-manifesto-2083-a -european-declaration-of-independence/. Last accessed on 1 November 2015.

11

THE SILENT WEAVER (EXCERPT) (2011)

Roger Hutchinson

EDITOR'S INTRODUCTION

Angus MacPhee (1916–97) was born on the Scottish island of South Uist in the Outer Hebrides. As a young man he joined the last active British horse soldiers, the Lovat Scouts. Journalist Roger Hutchinson offers a detailed account of Angus MacPhee's life – as detailed as is possible to know about a man who rarely spoke during his long adult life. Hutchinson establishes the context of MacPhee's remote island birthplace, the military contribution of men from the Hebrides in the Second World War, as well as changes in medical provision for psychiatric care in Britain during MacPhee's lifetime. Hutchinson's book inspired film-maker Nick Higgins to produce a twenty-five-minute documentary titled *Hidden Gifts: The Mystery of Angus MacPhee* (2004).

During his childhood MacPhee would have witnessed the tradition of hand plaiting local marram grass and heather. The materials were made into bridles for horses, as well as baskets, ropes, thatching and even dolls, in remote crofting communities. As a child MacPhee spoke Gaelic and English. When he became uncommunicative during military service on the Faroe Islands, he was medically discharged. In 1941 he returned to Scotland as a young man and was diagnosed with catatonic schizophrenia. The diagnosis was not supported by all who spent time with MacPhee. What can be confirmed is that the reasons for his change were never known. From the grounds of the psychiatric hospital that became his home, MacPhee began to collect, plait and knit grasses, leaves and flowers.

Once completed, MacPhee showed no interest in the variety of objects he created, which were often then used as compost or burnt with other garden cuttings. The ephemeral materials he used to make his work mean the few creations that were saved are poorly suited for conservation. Today some replicas of the objects collected by the art therapist Joyce Laing have been constructed. Laing was inspired by the French artist Jean Dubuffet, who along with colleagues organized what is considered the first large public exhibition of Art Brut, known by some as 'Outsider Art', in 1949 at the Galerie Drouin, Paris. Inspired by this work, Laing collected examples of art, including MacPhee's, made by individuals in psychiatric hospital care in Scotland. MacPhee's work was first exhibited during his lifetime in 1978.

What brought about MacPhee's change and what his elected plaiting and knitting provided for him remain speculation. Hutchinson offers the explanation that MacPhee 'was afflicted with shell-shock without having been shelled'.[1] Memory of childhood making he would have seen on South Uist seems to have provided a source of comfort. The rest of the story MacPhee could not, or chose not, to tell.

Note

1. Roger Hutchinson, *The Silent Weaver: The Extraordinary Life and Work of Angus MacPhee* (Edinburgh: Birlinn, 2011), p. 25.

The Silent Weaver (excerpt)

Roger Hutchinson

Apart from making baskets and thatching outbuildings and the family home, as a young *Muranach* back in Uist Angus MacPhee would have used marram grass and heather to make rope. It was a skilled process, but straightforward once mastered. Three strands of grass were plaited into a short string. Three of the strings were then plaited into a thin rope. Three of the thin ropes were plaited to make a thicker rope. Perhaps halfway along the length of the uncompleted plait, three new strands were introduced and bound in to increase its length. The process was continued until a rope as thick and as long as its weaver wished had been created. A crofting household could never have enough rope, but hemp or sisal rope bought from a shop cost money. Well-made grass or heather cords were equally strong. They had a short useful lifespan but they were easily renewed, and were free. Crofting women knitted and sewed; the men kept their hands busy at night by mending nets and creels, and plaiting rope. In a later age plaiting rope would not be cost-effective. An hour's paid work would deliver more than enough cash to buy yards of sisal rope. But well into the twentieth century most Hebridean crofters had more hours in the day than cash. They had too little spare time and too little disposable money, but in the balance they had more of the former than the latter. However long it took them, making such essentials rather than buying them made economic sense.

[…]

After supper, rather than join his fellow patients in their armchairs and doze away the evening, he [Angus MacPhee] went outside again. There he did something unusual. 'Very untidy,' said a nurse's report. 'Takes grass and leaves into ward, these he makes into ropes, socks, etc.'

'Patient continues his weaving activities,' said others. 'Keeps himself busy outside weaving grass and leaves.'

'Continues to go about the grounds gathering long grass to make into various things.'

'Out in hospital grounds most of the day. Still makes weird and wonderful objects from grass he collects. Has to be reminded not to bring it into ward.'

[…]

Because of the mess it made in the wards, Angus MacPhee was after several years banned from weaving grass indoors at Craig Dunain. But he was allowed to knit inside with more usual fabrics. He gathered clumps of sheep's wool from the fences around the farm. He handspun this unpromising fluff into yarn – a manual process which itself would later be described and become admired as 'fibre art'. He teased out and twisted with his fingers the rough wool until it became threads of yarn. Using two pieces of wire broken from a fence, he then knitted vests and handkerchiefs and scarves and other items, most of which have long been lost and forgotten. Several of the shreds of wool were stained with bright herd markings, and those colours were carefully knitted into the garments.

'So he sat on the edge of his bed at night weaving wool,' said Joyce Laing. 'And he spun, until he got lengths of wool. He got two wires, knitting wires, and he sat with these wires. I thought he'd be knitting, but I've been told by a professional knitter that he was netting, because he'd been taught how to net for the fish. They put them down for these flat fish in Uist which are silly enough to go

Source: Excerpt from Roger Hutchinson, *The Silent Weaver: The Extraordinary Life and Work of Angus MacPhee*, pp. 47, 87, 92–3, 129. Published by Birlinn Ltd (2011). © Roger Hutchinson. Reproduced with permission of the Licensor through PLSclear.

into nets, so he knew how to make nets. He was making undergarments, vests, and mufflers, squares that looked like hankies – all from sheep's wool. He kept the sheep marking on it – it gave a punch to it, you know.'

He made obvious references to the Uist *muranach* origins of himself and his work. He made horses' harnesses and halters and reins. He made peat creels and sowing seed pouches. Some of them looked like primitive art, some of them looked like three-dimensional drafts of a still life by Van Gogh, almost all of them could under another name be shown at the Tate Modern. They were the echoes of calls from a homeland. Unable to return to *Tir a' mhurain*, he brought as much as he could of *Tir a' mhurain* to a hillside near Inverness.

[…]

Joyce Laing tried to return to Craig Dunain at least once a year after 1977.

I saw him work. He'd make six-foot long ropes before he started to make the garments, he'd have a lot of six-foot long ropes. They weren't perfectly round. He would plait. He had no tools, just fingers. So he knitted on his fingers.

His mind must have been, 'Right, I'm making a jacket.' So presumably he started from the hem upward, which you would if you were knitting. The interesting thing about the big famous jacket is it's got a basque, and a big hem in a different stitch. That means he'd worked out that the end's going to have a slightly different stitch to it, and then when it was the main body bit – you get that in a jumper or sweater – he was on to the plain sort of knitting. And then the cuffs, the huge cuffs, had the same different stitch as the basque. But the neck was a polo neck. It was just very thick. I couldn't quite see how he did it. His hands were just going like this, so quickly the whole time.

12

INTERVIEW
Faith Ringgold and Hans Ulrich Obrist (excerpt) (2019)

Faith Ringgold

EDITOR'S INTRODUCTION

The artist, activist and author Faith Ringgold was born in Harlem, New York, in 1930. Her childhood coincided with the Great Depression that began in the United States in the early 1930s with effects felt around the world. Ringgold has recalled numerous experiences of stereotyped expectations based on her identity as an African-American woman, beginning with her childhood: "I grew up in Harlem during the Great Depression. This does not mean I was poor and oppressed. We were protected from oppression and surrounded by a loving family."[1]

In 2019, the Serpentine Galleries in London showed Ringgold's first survey exhibition at a European institution. The exhibition included paintings, political posters and story quilts. By the 1970s Ringgold had moved from oil painting to work with textiles. In the 1980s she began to focus on story quilts – textiles that include text. The excerpt reprinted here is from an interview with Serpentine Galleries Artistic Director Hans Ulrich Obrist that covered questions about Ringgold's extensive artistic output which now spans more than five decades. Ringgold describes her childhood, education, artistic inspiration and eventual travel to a number of countries in Africa. She also describes her ongoing experience of expectations based on her identity as an African-American woman and the importance she places on the freedom to control her own artistic content.

In the context of the United States, art historian Julia Bryan-Wilson (whose writing appears in the politics section) acknowledges Ringgold as "one of the earliest feminists to incorporate textiles into her practice".[2] Ringgold's dialogue with Ulrich Obrist draws heavily from her own memories – a first person account of her life that differs significantly from the racial and gender stereotypes often assumed by others throughout her career.

Notes

1. Raven Holton, Curlee with Ringgold, Faith. *Faith Ringgold: A View from the Studio* Boston: Bunker Hill Publishing in association with Allentown Art Museum, 2004, p. 24.
2. Bryan-Wilson, Julia. *FRAY: Art and Textile Politics*. Chicago: The University of Chicago Press. 2017. p. 14.

Interview

Faith Ringgold and Hans Ulrich Obrist

[…]

Hans Ulrich Obrist What are your most vivid memories of growing up during the Harlem Renaissance?

Faith Ringgold It was a wonderful place to be. We had a parade at least every Sunday. The churches would participate in these because they all had choirs, children and music, and everybody went to church on Sunday. They would come down Seventh Avenue to 125th Street. Parades were very important, because they gave musicians an opportunity to perform, and it was just a joyful, beautiful experience. Growing up in Harlem was wonderful. And then it changed. Oh my God, boom! Like, overnight. And of course, it's changed again, it's changing right now. But it's such a wonderful place, because you've got the two rivers on each side and there are many bridges. The way it's laid out is just perfect. The architecture was built by the Dutch, and they made beautiful, gorgeous houses where they were painted abstract designs on the walls up the stairways. And there's always been a lot of entertainment, and many good things about Harlem. A lot of bad things, too. […]

FR My mother Willi Posey became a fashion designer. Women didn't work in those days; men worked. But my mother, and all the women, made their children's clothes. It wasn't about getting a dress that had a designer's name which every kid wore. It was about having a dress that nobody had but you, because your mother made it. That uniqueness was such a big part of my childhood.

I never thought of myself as being an artist, either, by the way. I thought of myself as making art, because women didn't work, so it wasn't about going to work or anything. But I was told I was going to college from the time I was a tiny child. […]

HUO And who were your influences when you were studying?

FR Picasso, Matisse, Rembrandt. The college didn't teach me about any black or African artists. I learned all about the European masters. I had a wonderful education in terms of technique and history and so on, but nothing about black or African art.

But I had all these African American artists living around me – I didn't have to go anywhere to study them, I just had to open my eyes and recognise who they were. […]

HUO In the 1970s you began to make soft sculpture. How did these textile elements enter your work?

FR These sculptures and the tankas were made with my mother. The idea of sewing was very important to women of her generation. I was never able to teach my daughters how to sew; they were not interested!

I loved to create forms and figures, I so wanted to sculpt, but I couldn't do it with stone or anything that made dust because it would cause an asthma attack. I started making the textile figures in the 1970s. They all have names, there's a story about each one of these as they're all people I knew. Using fabric in this way I could make a face by sewing and lining the face and putting in a stick as a support. It was so much fun.

HUO How many soft sculptures did you make?

FR I think I did about sixty-something.

HUO And what about the tankas?

FR The tankas came about because I wanted to have exhibitions all over the world. I wanted to paint big

Source: Excerpt from 'Raise Your Voice. Unite. Tell Your Story. Hans Ulrich Obrist in Conversation with Faith Ringgold', *Faith Ringgold*, ed. Melissa Blanchflower and Natalia Grabowska (Serpentine and Koenig Books, 2019), pp. 30–9. Reproduced with permission.

and stretched canvas is limited in moving it around, in picking it up. I had to wait for my husband to get home from work to move my paintings out of the house. As a woman artist, you have to [be] able to manage your work yourself. You can get an assistant, but you can't depend on your husband to help!

I went to the Rijksmuseum in Amsterdam in 1972, the guard said, 'Stop! Go downstairs – you want to see this.' And what I saw really changed my work.

HUO There was an epiphany?

FR Oh yeah, that was something. He showed me the collection of Tibetan tankas. I realised that they were great, but quilts were even better because you could make them as big as you wanted. Roll it, fold it, and pick it up myself. I just had to make a stitch between the painting, the filling and the backing, to keep it together.

People make quilts all over the world. There is nowhere you can go where the women, as it is mostly women, don't create quilts. Quilting has a long history, I believe it came to America with slavery. It was a form of art they could make easily because they needed quilts for warmth and were forced to make them for their masters. Slaves couldn't express themselves through the art that they would have made in Africa. They couldn't come to America and paint, carve sculptures or make masks, but they could make quilts.

HUO How did your stories begin to enter your quilts?

FR I decided I want to tell my story. I'd written my autobiography, *We Flew Over the Bridge*, but couldn't get it published because I was told that 'This is not your story.' Publishers were telling me, because I'm a black woman, it's not my story and their idea of 'my' story was that I was born in poverty and grew up on welfare and got raped and beat up and thrown out the window. Well, I'm sorry, that's not my story. This is my story, and I feel that freedom of speech is very important. I'm determined to have it.

I have what's called freedom of speech and that's what America has and that's what I do. The only way you're going to get it taken away from you is if you don't use it. Don't express it, you will lose it.

HUO So, you wrote your stories out instead on these quilts.

FR That's right, I will not allow anyone to keep me from voicing my story. I thought, how can I get published and get my words out there? The way to do it is to write it on my art. Nobody can stop me from doing that. It took me about fifteen years of writing and projecting my opinions on different artworks to get my memoirs published.

HUO In this you also found a way to combine words, fabric and paint and you invented the story quilt.

FR It's acrylic on canvas; it's just quilted on the back. The first one I did was with my mother: *Echoes of Harlem*, 1980.

HUO And shortly after you did the first story quilt, *Who's Afraid of Aunt Jemima*, 1983.

FR Right. It was very controversial. But I could write whatever I wanted to, because that's freedom of speech.

HUO You reimagined the story of Aunt Jemima, the fictional face of the pancake mix brand?

FR Right. It's a different story. She is an entrepreneur.

13

COLLECTING THE CONTEMPORARY
Love Will Decide What Is Kept and Science Will Decide How It Is Kept (2005)

Sue Prichard

EDITOR'S INTRODUCTION

Museums act as memory banks of the past, which is why Sue Prichard's forward-looking essay on the future of textile collecting is included here. Writing in 2003, Prichard notes the ineffectiveness of many of the traditional collection categories when applied to contemporary textile art. Prichard works through a number of acquisition examples to explain the challenge institutions, such as the Victoria and Albert Museum, London, face when taking textiles into their permanent collections. In looking to the future, she observes the importance virtual archives will have in our understanding of textiles – an observation perhaps slower in its realisation than imagined at the time of writing.

Prichard notes that in 2003/4 the V&A experienced more visitors to the museum's website than physical visits to South Kensington. Today, the ubiquity of living online makes such a comment feel unnecessary. But Prichard's 2003 writing offers a reminder that use of the Internet, at least for experiences such as museum visits, was not a given two decades ago.

The sheer scale of the V&A collections (more than 75,000 accessions, either as individual items or sets, make up the textile and fashion collection, which in turn makes up only a fraction of the museum's entire holdings) mean public access to the collections has long been a challenge. In her 'Final Thoughts' Prichard acknowledges that 'harnessing new technology will help build our collection, make them more accessible, and contribute to contemporary artistic discourse.' As the next entry in this section by Sarah Scaturro tackles, fashion and textile collections now contain objects created with digital tools, some that are materially unstable. In certain instances the digital code that produced the artefact potentially offers more longevity than the physical object.

Access to physical archives raises a further challenge, both for museums to support the volume of viewing requests received, as well as the disproportionate balance of collections housed in urban European centres. Nearly a decade after Prichard's essay, the V&A opened The Clothworkers' Centre for the Study and Conservation of Textiles and Fashion in 2013 at Blythe House in West London. Replacing the Clothworkers' Centre, the V&A East Storehouse (alongside a further outpost of the museum) based in Stratford's Queen Elizabeth Olympic Park will house the textile and fashion collection from 2024.

Sue Prichard is former Curator of Contemporary Textiles at the V&A and author of two books published by the museum: *V&A Pattern: The Fifties* (2009) and *Quilts 1700–2010: Hidden Histories, Untold Stories* (2012). She is currently Head Curator, Leeds Castle, Kent, UK.

Images:

Caroline Bartlett

Yukata Collection

Gemma Burgess

Kirsty McDougall

NUNO

Sophie Roet

Collecting the Contemporary: Love Will Decide What Is Kept and Science Will Decide How It Is Kept[1]

Sue Prichard

Eva Hesse once famously said "Life doesn't last, art doesn't last, it doesn't matter."[2] But for museum curators like myself, our role is to preserve and conserve the past, and indeed the present, for future generations. We are, for the most part, publicly funded custodians of diverse and sometimes bizarre collections of material culture, both historic and contemporary. Our remit is to ensure that these collections are held in trust for the nation, so that those who come after us can make sense of the past and try to understand the people, customs, and value systems related to the material held in our institutions. We are accountable for what we collect, and have to justify our acquisitions, both to our colleagues and to the public. This may be relatively easy when dealing with the acquisition of a unique 4,000-year-old terracotta relief of a Babylonian goddess, but more problematic when you are responsible for acquiring examples of credit cards, both come under the collecting policy of the British Museum; and virtually impossible if you are collecting moist towelettes—such a collection does indeed exist. Wearable technology, nanotechnology, smart, intelligent, and e-textiles are all buzzwords generating much interest both for academic research and commercial industries seeking opportunities for development. Given the plethora of modern design and production, what criteria do we, as curators, use when collecting the contemporary? This raises a series of further questions. When does "the contemporary" start, and how can we ensure that what was once considered relevant and significant does not rapidly become trite and meaningless? Does "contemporary" necessarily imply cutting-edge multimedia and digital processes? Is the exploration and exploitation of a traditional medium within the context of contemporary cultural discourse less significant than new technology? Does new technology drive or assist in the creative process? Should we cease physically collecting at all and concentrate on "virtual acquisitions?" How do we reconcile traditional museology, with its narrow parameters and genre hierarchy, with twenty-first century artistic practice?

HOW SHOULD MUSEUMS CLASSIFY WORK?

Classification and categorization is at the heart of what museums do; as early as 1565 the "cabinet of curiosity" was already being systematically reordered to make sense of the physical world. Objects were arranged according to their material base and these arrangements were replicated in the creation of specific museum collections and departments (Furniture and Woodwork, Textiles and Dress, Prints, Drawings and Paintings); as our knowledge of the known world expanded, collections were further divided into geographical areas (Indian, Far Eastern). However, in the twenty-first century, artistic practice and new technology is deliberately challenging the traditional categories by which we define our collections. This challenge is exacerbated by the blurring of physical and cultural boundaries that cut across traditional departmental structures and loyalties. Curators therefore need to "think out of the box" and take an active role to ensure that national collections are as representative as possible. The recognition that much contemporary artistic practice does not fit neatly into established material- and technique-based categories has resulted in the establishment of contemporary sections within some museums whose role it is to actively break down those traditional barriers that

Source: Sue Prichard, 'Collecting the Contemporary: Love Will Decide What Is Kept and Science Will Decide How It Is Kept', *TEXTILE* 3:2 (2005), pp. 150–65. Reprinted by permission of Informa UK Limited, trading as Taylor & Francis Group, www.tandfonline.com.

mitigate against an effective contemporary collecting policy. Whilst this change may have offered the potential for new ways of working on an organizational level, we still have to address the fundamental issues raised by the expanded context in which some artists choose to work.

Contemporary textile practice is acquiring its own intellectually rigorous language and methodologies. As curators we need to have an understanding of these, be capable of appropriate critical analysis, and able to communicate ideas clearly and accessibly to our public. This may sound straightforward but, for many, the term "textiles" only has resonance if it refers to traditional materials and techniques. The following example raises a number of issues regarding the categorization of contemporary textiles, as well as demonstrating the ways in which many engaged in the making of contemporary textiles explore and question its meaning and histories. In 2004, the Department of Furniture, Textiles and Fashion at the Victoria and Albert Museum (V&A) acquired a work by Caroline Bartlett called "Bodies of Knowledge Volume 5: Arbiters of Taste" (T.154-2004 [. . .]),[3] a complex arrangement of a 1934 encyclopedia, printed silk crepoline, pins and embroidery hoops. First exhibited in *Textiles in Context*, the fortieth anniversary exhibition of the 62 Group of Textile Artists,[4] "Bodies of Knowledge" explored the relationship between "text" and "textiles," making reference to the V&A as an "encyclopaedia of treasures." The artist elucidates this analogy thus: "like encyclopaedias, content and presentation reflect governing ideologies and hierarchies of taste, demonstrating the way in which society and perception change over time."[5] Bartlett is an experienced textile designer and printer who exhibits internationally, drawing inspiration from architectural elements, myths, legends, and elements of various cultures around the world. She is interested in the ways in which textile processes play a role in our concepts of organization, structure, and community. Contextual framework is of primary importance to her work, as evidenced by her public commissions, and in this she shares some of the aesthetic resonance often implicit in the work of artists such as Cornelia Parker (whose flattened brass-band installation "Breathless" can be seen in the V&A's British Galleries). Bartlett is also interested in language and the written word as systems of knowledge central to the Western view of the world that give exclusive access to those able to decode it. In 1999/2000 she participated in a touring exhibition, *The Artist's Journey*, which explored the ways in which artists refer to, and are influenced by, cultural and historical artifacts and information. The brief was to produce new work through researching the lives of Frederic, Lord Leighton, the Victorian painter and sculptor (1830–96) and Sir Richard Burton, explorer and Orientalist (1821–90), examining their travels, houses, personal experiences, collections, and their role in Victorian society. Bartlett created "On the Shelves of Memory," which referenced systems of collecting and preserving, ideas of presence and absence, and the selective process of representing an individual to the public. The work contained 492 archival labels, each bearing detailed information of individual items sold by the auctioneers, Christie's, in 1896, which were suspended in front of fragments of objects cast from fabric, and organized as though in a museum display.

So how should we categorize Bartlett's work—textiles, textile art, art installation, text? Which V&A collection should acquire her work: Furniture, Textiles and Fashion; Word and Image; Sculpture? This issue was raised recently at an open discussion to launch *Inside Out: Commissions for the City, for the Country*, an exhibition organized in 2004 by Contemporary Applied Art, in London. Sharon Elphick, who has rejected the limitations of the commercial design studio to create dynamic photographic montages of the urban landscape, was asked whether she still considered herself to be a textile designer. Her response—"I don't care what you call me, I just want someone to collect my work"—may be pragmatic, but for museum curators, working within the limitations of current museological practice, it is not so simple.

CULTURAL CONVERGENCE

The process of cross-discipline artistic practice may challenge traditional collection boundaries, but is further complicated by the process of cross-cultural fertilization or cultural intermingling. Cultural difference has now given way to cultural convergence, tearing down fixed boundaries: territorial, cultural, and creative; it is now no longer viable to define an artist by their country of origin. The following example illustrates this point. In 2004, the Department of Furniture, Textiles and Fashion was approached by the Far Eastern Department of the V&A with a donation of a bamboo-dyed silk quilted hammock (T.1–2004) and quilted cushion (T.2–2004), made from nylon. The artist, Yoshiko Jinzenji, lives in Kyoto but since 1989 has based her studio in Bali. She began quilting in the 1970s, after discovering quilts made by North America's Mennonite and Amish communities. She also takes inspiration from the Indonesian "selendang," a traditional shawl, dyed with natural tropical dyes. Jinzenji combines antique fabrics collected from around the world with innovative synthetics, such as the black metallic cloth created by Junichi Arai.

Jinzenji is a superb natural dyer and often makes quilts from fabric or fiber she colors herself, including very subtle and rich bamboo-dyed silk. In the field of natural dyes, white is a tremendously difficult technical and creative feat, and Jinzenji experimented with all the plants, roots, and trees around her studio before finally hitting upon the idea of trying bamboo. Initially she believed she had failed, as the fabric emerged from the boiled bamboo solution a dull, light brown. But it was transformed into shimmering white only when hung in the direct Bali sunlight. The dye is equally successful when applied to nylon filament, creating a flesh-colored tone. Jinzenji likens the bamboo-dyed white to the fusuma and shji sliding doors used to separate Japanese-style rooms, as well as the tradition of sumi ink drawing and calligraphy, and even the white sand of Zen gardens. When interviewed, she said that "a hammock always seems to me like the height of luxury, and particularly so when made with white quilted silk."[6] Strangely perhaps, it is not designed to hold body weight, though Jinzenji suggests it could be used in a child's room to hold a collection of stuffed animals or cushions, or at Christmas time, as a unique way of displaying gift-wrapped presents.

In choosing to use innovative synthetics at times, and at others to weave and dye her own fabric, Jinzenji has set a new aesthetic standard as a quilt-maker and maker of cloth. Her experiments with traditions and techniques reflect and challenge the concepts of globalization, ethnicity, and the blurring of cultural boundaries and influences, whilst highlighting her concern with the loss of traditional skills and individuality through increasing mass production of high-quality goods. Her choice of the Far Eastern Department through which to offer her donation was logical and based on geography; however, her use of a traditional Western technique placed her within the collecting policy of the Department of Furniture, Textiles and Fashion.

Another interesting example of cross-cultural collaboration is the British design duo Bentley and Spens' partnership with the Japanese company, Kawashima Textile Manufacturers. Originally Kawashima approached the Far Eastern Department of the V&A with the donation of their 2002 Yukata Collection (T.11–14-2004 [. . .]), but was referred to the Department of Furniture, Textiles and Fashion because the designers were British. Kim Bentley and Sally Spens design and produce one-off hand-stencilled and painted interior furnishings and screen-printed fabric. Their brightly colored, bold designs, combining traditional fabric painting and printing with increasingly exotic patterns, appealed to the Japanese love of tradition and modernism. In 2002, the designers collaborated with Kawashima to produce a range of textiles and garments for the Japanese market. In the latter half of the 1980s, the Yukata (Summer-kimono) began to make a comeback as casual summer wear amongst young Japanese women. Traditional versions were indigo and white, and, whilst today there are no restrictions on the use of color, the Yukatahas not witnessed any great variation in the basic design. The overwhelming majority employ some sort of traditional pattern such as a flower design or water pattern, with the odd ice cream cone or goldfish. The range of fabrics created by Bentley and Spens for the Japanese market has taken the traditional roots of the Yukata and embodied it with a chic and playful image, in a way that is not entirely different from Western clothing. In 2003, Bentley and Spens produced a second collection, refining their designs, simplifying pattern and motif in line with the demands of Yukata production.

Cultures only survive through self-transformation, and museum collections must reflect these transformations in order to preserve their vitality. By challenging the *status quo* of traditional demarcations, curators are able to develop new insights into their collections. Making connections between the historic and the contemporary is just as important as focusing on new developments, but we must also be wary of the ways in which we represent artists and makers in our collections— as attempts to articulate cultural identity can create as many problems as they solve. Traditionally, museums have disseminated a narrative or world view through the relationships they create between the objects they put on display. This narrative is further validated by the way in which these objects are interpreted for public consumption. In the nineteenth century, the rules of engagement with non-Western art were based on the values enshrined and safeguarded by the custodians of ethnographic collections: an object was valued because of its "purity," its ability to remain uncontaminated by the excesses of a decadent Europe. Today, globalization and innovation in communications technology has accelerated the pace of change; geographic and cultural boundaries constantly clash, combine, disintegrate, and reform. Cultural appropriation is now no longer the preserve of the West, as the example of Yoshiko Jinzenji illustrates. The concept of "the other" in contemporary society is constantly being challenged, and identities no longer presuppose continuous cultural traditions. In *Second Generation Sikhs*[7] Amrit Kaur Singh describes the cultural heritage that informs her own and her twin sister's artistic practice, citing "a number of perspectives that related not only to how we see ourselves but also to how other people have come to perceive us—as Indians, Sikhs, twins *and* artists" (Amrit's italics). Artists may indeed create works of art that are imbedded in the cultural context from which they have emerged, drawing on motifs found in indigenous cultures, reinventing them to create new works of art, but we need to continually challenge the contexts in which they will be seen and received.

Shirazeh Houshiary, nominated for the Turner Prize in 1994, was born in Iran and studied at Chelsea School of Art. She works with a range of materials and techniques, including drawing and print-making. The acquisition of a suite of etchings by the British Museum in 1995 was the result of a successful collaboration between the Department of Prints and Drawings, and what was then the Department of Oriental Antiquities. Houshiary's work is rooted in the mysticism of Islamic culture, but the choice of the Sir John Addis Islamic Gallery in which to display the suite created some tension between the museum and the artist. It was clear that Houshiary felt that her work would be better placed in the neutral environment of a prints and drawings gallery, rather than within the cultural context of a gallery devoted to the work of Islamic artists.[8] The British Museum has addressed the issue of cross-cultural and cross-discipline contemporary artistic practice by the creation of their electronic tour "Collecting the Modern World." The site is organized geographically, "reflecting the places of origin of the artists/ producers, the regions to which they owe their primary cultural allegiance, or those where they have chosen to make their careers."[9] As curators, we need to exploit new technology to help us redefine our changing world, and to create new opportunities for learning.

HOW CAN COLLECTIONS MAKE EFFECTIVE USE OF ELECTRONIC MEDIA?

A museum should and must amount to more than just an accumulation of material, it should also function as a knowledge base and provide inspiration. Online learning can help us in our quest to make cultural connections, both within our own collections and with collections regionally, nationally, and internationally. New technology can also help us to provide increased public access to objects not on display, providing a "gateway" to information and expertise concerning our collections. The Constance Howard Resource and Research Centre in Textiles (CHRRCT), at Goldsmiths, University of London, combines a rich and diverse textile collection with an archive containing slides, teaching notes, and individual interviews with artists, providing a comprehensive account of the pioneering history of textiles at the college. A new project to put records from the slide collection and material archive online will facilitate access to both the material collection and the CHRRCT itself.

In 2003/4, over four million visits were made to the V&A's website, including the On-Line Museum. This surpassed the numbers physically visiting South Kensington, proving just how successful a tool the Web is for reaching audiences. Web-based projects can also help us to collect, document, and interpret those aspects of contemporary art and design practice based on the transitory. The V&A's hugely successful "Fashion in Motion" series showcases established and emerging talent in a series of catwalk shows; by videoing the collections and interviewing the designers, we not only capture the philosophy behind the design process, but also "acquire" the event. In 1999, the Contemporary Team at the V&A was formed with the specific remit not to acquire objects, but rather to present the very best of contemporary art and design in a series of exhibitions, events, site-specific installations, and performances. Specifically targeted at a young and style conscious audience, it also brings contemporary art and design to audiences that might not otherwise experience it through reminiscence projects and "Days of Record," a series of events cataloguing applied and decorative arts in relation to the body. Past "Days of Record" have included Tattoo, April 2000; Nails, Weaves and Naturals, focusing on the hairstyles and nail art of Black British and Afro-Caribbean communities, May 2001; and the Notting Hill Carnival, August 2003. Given our limited storage resources, virtual collecting also offers real benefits in terms of ensuring that the developments in textile art and the overlap with fine art, soft sculpture, and fashion are represented in collections for the future, and are not bound by rigid collecting policies or conservation issues. Complex or large-scale installations, such as Helen Storey's "Primitive Streak" (ICA, London, 1997); "Textural Space: Contemporary Japanese Textile Art" (Whitworth Art Gallery, Manchester, 2001); or Do-Ho Suh's enormous diaphanous silk and nylon "interiors" (Serpentine Gallery, London 2002), could be successfully "acquired" and "displayed" with minimum resources.

New developments in the field of haptic technology point to even greater access to our collections, via a tactile interface that allows visitors to touch, stroke, and handle the objects they see on a computer screen. The days of the "Do Not Touch" signs are truly numbered, as individuals are able to feel and manipulate the texture of fabric and clothing, and artists are given new insights into collections. Haptic technology has already created a virtual exhibition at the British Library. "Turning the Pages" is an interactive program that allows visitors to virtually turn the pages of historic manuscripts in a realistic way, whilst keeping the original safely under glass. In April 2004, over 3,000 visitors a day viewed the selected volumes, including the Lindisfarne Gospels.[10] In February 2004, the UK Engineering and Science Research Council put out a call for proposals to establish a new research network centered around haptic technologies, interactive textiles, and haptic visuality. If successful, the network—comprising artists, engineers, computer scientists, museologists, and psychologists—would seek to examine the role of technology and touch within the area of interactive textiles from several different perspectives.

Whilst there is no doubt that new developments in technology can benefit curators and collections, are we in danger of replacing what was once defined as the fetishization of the object, with the fetishization of new technology? As the "temple-like architecture" of museums is deconstructed and remodeled, curators increasingly find themselves worshiping at the altar of the computer, driven by the need to create even more exciting ways in which to entice the public into cyberspace—the one area where funding is readily available. In "Collecting the Contemporary,"[11] Gil Saunders (2003) argues for the "primacy of the object over the digital surrogate," identifying that what makes a museum unique is its collection of objects. We need to use new technology to enhance our collection of objects, rather than replace them, and to be active in developing the methodology for using the web as a vehicle for collecting the contemporary, creating strict selection criteria that can be applied over predetermined periods of time. This will ensure that a representative set of objects can be documented for museum collections that truly reflects successful developments in the area of rapidly evolving technologies.

COLLECTING THE EPHEMERAL

In the UK, museum curators are bound by the ethical guidelines prepared by their professional body, the Museums Association, which state that we cannot ethically collect items for which the museum cannot provide long-term care and access. These guidelines provide flexible advice, but the basic principles still emphasize the long-term preservation and conservation of objects for the future. However, much contemporary art made and collected in the 1960s and 1970s, for example, when artists increasingly experimented with new materials and processes, has turned out to be very fragile. Many of the works in the Eva Hesse retrospective exhibition held at Tate Modern, London, in 2003 are now so fragile that they will never be displayed again. Whilst we may successfully argue that the Web provides the solution to such problematic conservation and collection management issues, we are still in the business of collecting material objects and face the technical and ethical challenge of how to preserve ephemeral or unstable artworks. Many contemporary artists, like Hesse, are prepared to accept the risk that the materials they deliberately choose to use will deteriorate rapidly, taking a similar view to that of Tracey Emin: "If I wanted it to last, I would make it from something else."[12] As curators we need to accept the physical limitations of each work of art, working closely not only with colleagues in our conservation departments, but with artist/makers to document and record processes.

Marielle Baylis created "Bed of Roses," a knitted wool and latex floor piece, for her final degree show in 2002 and exhibited at Decorex, the annual interior-design trade fair, held the same year. Inspired by her love of nature and her interest in domestic interiors, "Bed of Roses" was originally designed as a product for the bathroom; however, the artist was also aware of its potential as an artwork. Baylis is very fond of knitted textiles within the home and seeks to push the boundaries of how these are traditionally perceived, creating quirky and imaginative knitted toparies and hedges. "Bed of Roses" was offered to the V&A, where it was examined by the polymer scientist in the Science Conservation Department. Analysis of the materials involved revealed that the latex would degrade reasonably fast (possibly within ten years) and would become quite sticky and yellow. The conclusion of the report suggested that this degradation could cause damage to neighboring objects or cause storage problems. The solution to the problem was resolved by the Department of Furniture, Textiles and Fashion in consultation with the artist, agreeing to accept a small sample of the work, which could be easily stored and which could be used for display, study, and research purposes.

MERGING TECHNOLOGY WITH TRADITIONAL TECHNIQUES

The revival of interest in traditional techniques among young artists and designers challenges the perception that contemporary collecting is focused only on the acquisition of technologically advanced fabrics or new media. In reality, many artists use technology to assist, rather than drive, the creative process. Debbie Stack, a textile designer, who specializes in computer embroidery, believes the contemporary component provided by technology gives an additional creative edge to her work—it is the "accidents that happen during the production process that deliver the most rewarding results."[13] Gemma Burgess, who was selected as one of the young Graduate Designers of Texprint 2002, also marries traditional techniques with computer technologies, and in 2004 the V&A acquired a sample of her work for the textile collection (T.3-2004). Texprint is a nonprofit-making registered charity whose aim is to identify, select, and launch the most innovative textile design graduates of British colleges to the international textile industry. Burgess was also selected to show at New Designers 2002, her work featured in international textiles magazines, and her designs selected by both fashion and interior-design buyers. At the time of writing she is continuing her studies at the Royal College of Art in London, and is interested in exploring new relationships and arrangements for overlaying pattern, translating paperwork onto fabric, and experimenting with different processes—screen-printing, devoré, the use of digital technology, and the diverse special effects that are possible using techniques like flocking, bonding, and embossing. She is fascinated by what happens when these techniques are combined, and by the diverse tactile qualities that can be produced.

Similarly, Kirsty McDougall is interested in bringing both craft and commercial/industrial techniques to a different audience, which she has done through her participation in the knitting circle "Cast Off." Cast Off is a knitting club for girls and boys, women and men, which promotes handicrafts as a fashionable and constructive pastime. The club meets in nightclubs, bars, cafés, shops, festivals, and on public transport, and aims to incorporate an element of youth culture in traditional craft. McDougall exhibited at Texprint 2002 along with Gemma Burgess, and won the prize for weaving. But McDougall is not bound by traditional structural weaving, as is evident in her use of words such as "jumbled" and "vandalised" to describe her experimentations, and she also works in the medium of embroidery and print, exploring the boundaries between textiles and fashion. She takes her influence from areas as diverse as traditionally woven tweeds, dogtooths, and flock wallpaper found in English pubs, which she recontextualizes and redefines in a witty and subversive way. In 2004, the V&A acquired a rag-rug sample (T.4-2004), which illustrates McDougall's experimentation with technique, in which she weaves rather than hooks the fabric. It illustrates her interest in recycling, for she often uses charity-shop bargains and found objects, rich sensual fabrics with lurid market stall finds—a fusion of country casuals and the television character Pat Butcher from the UK soap opera *EastEnders*. Her interest in recycling moves beyond the objects themselves, exploring the recycling of patterns and ideas, pop art and disposable imagery. When interviewed, she explained "weaving is the physical manifestation of my ideas, fabric the messenger."[14] At the Texprint prizes held in Paris in 2002, Ronald Wesibrod of the Swiss Company Weisbrod-Zuerrer AG, who presented the awards, observed that the European textile industry could not continue to exist without maintaining a high standard of innovation and creativity, and that this was only possible if companies could constantly recruit new talent.

COLLECTING WEARABLE TECHNOLOGY AND SMART FABRICS

So what of wearable technology and smart fabrics—do they have a place in our collections? Again, a series of questions is raised. Should we be collecting cameras that can be worn as jewelry, or shawls with flexible communication screens made of glass-fiber fabric? Which collection should acquire biomedical clothing for personal healthcare—fashion, science or medicine? How innovative and cutting edge can a designer be without understanding the technical aspects of the materials at their disposal? A one-day symposium called "When is the Future" was hosted by the Crafts Council in October 2003 to discuss the complicated relationship between woven-textile designers and industry. It focused on the need for different disciplines to collaborate together to create a product that is not only scientifically innovative, but is well designed and, indeed, commercial. At the symposium Philippa Wagner, Senior Design Consultant at Philips Design, made it clear that the challenge for their product team—which includes fashion and textile designers working alongside electronic and software engineers—was to integrate electronics into fashionable clothes that people wanted to wear. In a similar vein, DuPont and Courtaulds are researching and producing innovative textiles, such as conductive fibers, which can be embroidered. The message was clear: new technology only becomes really interesting when it features a synergy between design, research, development, art, and science.

The V&A continues to collect the best of textile design with new technologies. The collection has particularly fine examples from the Nuno Corporation, a Japanese company that uses traditional fibers and techniques, as well as the most sophisticated synthetics and technology. Nuno was founded in 1984, and is Japanese for "fabric." The company is well known internationally for its ability to create exciting new fibers and weaves, drawing on traditional Japanese aesthetics and creative processes, and combining these with dynamic technological processes. Industrial by-products ordinarily discarded, such as packing material and splatter plating used by the Japanese car industry, have all inspired Nuno designers. "Jellyfish"

(T.122-1998 [. . .]) is made from an industrial vinyl polychloride fabric, developed primarily for seat covers in the motor vehicle manufacturing industry, and has a preset 50% heat-shrinkage ratio. To create "Jellyfish," Nuno has layered and partially affixed the fabric onto a polyester organdy using a special adhesive, screen-printed in a checkerboard pattern. The fabric is subjected to flash heat-treatment that causes the organdy to shrivel where adhered. Being a thermoplastic fabric, it retains the resulting crinkles even after the vinyl polychloride is peeled away. Another piece, "Pack Ice" (T.121-1998), is created from strapping tape, a common material made of flat rayon. It is very easy to tear horizontally but more difficult to tear vertically. In "Pack Ice" the rayon threads are tightly woven into large squares on a background of silk organdies. These squares are connected by unwoven rayon threads that float between the layers of the background material, suggesting spume among icebergs. Nuno is well known for its innovation, yet despite the focus on new technology, the company also continues to foster a new generation of weavers who employ traditional techniques and natural fibers, demonstrating their belief in the coexistence of contemporary and traditional technologies and techniques.

In 2001 the V&A acquired "Wandering Lines Red" (T.486-2001 [. . .]), a length of handwoven silk, nylon, and polyester monofilament that becomes phosphorescent under light. It was made by Sophie Roet, one of a small group of contemporary designers/weavers producing light-sensitive textiles. Roet says that she has "always been interested in breaking the normal rules of weave structure—creating movement within straight warp and weft thread"[15] and working with phosphorescent yarns in order to charge the textiles with glowing light. In 2000, Roet collaborated with C5 Interglas, via HITEC LOTEC, a lottery-funded organization encouraging joint working projects between industry (HITEC), and designer/craftworkers (LOTEC) to create aluminum-bonded textiles for fashion. C5 Interglas produces highly technical textiles for commercial vehicles, sports equipment, the aircraft industry, and for space flight. One of the processes they offer is bonding glass-fiber textiles to aluminum sheeting for high-quality metal building insulation facings. Roet was interested in exploring the sculptural quality produced by combining delicate, fragile textiles

and the metallic bonding process that could hold its shape without assistance "to crumble a silk organza textile (so that) it remains in its tightly crumpled state."[16] In January 2002, the V&A featured Roet's "The Aluminium Bonded Red Dress" in the front entrance display of the museum, showing what we believe to be part of the most imaginative and innovative range of technologically aware textiles produced to date in the twenty-first century.

More recently, in 2004, the V&A's *Brilliant* exhibition provided a unique opportunity to acquire a range of new lighting forms made from various materials, technologies, and visual effects. Although acquisitions were distributed throughout the museum's collections according to "traditional" material type, so that "The Ingo Maurer LED Bench and Bulb" were proposed for the glass gallery, while two specific cases of textile artists using light were proposed for the Contemporary Textile Collection, the exhibition nevertheless provided a base from which to "cherry-pick" the very best of contemporary lighting design. The Contemporary Textile Collection finally acquired "Digital Dawn" (T.155-2004), an electroluminescent and silk blind designed by Rachel Wingfield, which functions as a traditional window blind that grows in luminosity in response to its surroundings. Manufactured by Elumin8, electroluminescent technology involves applying electricity to copper dipped in zinc sulfate ink, which then emits light. This is applied using a silk-screen process to an indium/tin-oxide splattered substrate. This substrate is flexible and can be fabricated into complex shapes. Eluminescent systems have been used primarily for outdoor media-related installations (most notably the launch of the *Love Actually* DVD, where a giant red heart adorned the sides of London buses and glowed on and off as the vehicles traveled through the city). However, "Digital Dawn" moves beyond the novelty value of the technology, engaging with the problems associated with sufferers of seasonal affective disorder (SAD), by providing a constant and responsive source of light. The tension between technology and the natural world is further explored by Wingfield's choice of pattern—organic plant forms that "grow" and evolve on the blind's surface, digitally emulating the process of photosynthesis—proving that functionality and aesthetics do not have to be mutually exclusive. "Digital Dawn" was first launched at 100%

Design, where Wingfield, under the design tag "loop," was shortlisted for best newcomer 2003.

FINAL THOUGHTS

So what of the future? The V&A holds one of the most important textile collections in the world. From its foundation in the middle of the nineteenth century, the museum has always sought to include the very best of contemporary textile art and manufacture in its collections, and this policy continues to be vigorously pursued. In 2003, a new display "Recent Acquisitions 1992–2002: A Decade of Collecting Textiles" illustrated the eclectic range of contemporary objects in the collection, juxtaposing a variety of materials and textiles, and showing examples of new developments in textile design and production. The display space was deliberately chosen in close proximity to the textile study collection, to illustrate the strong tradition of textile design and production, whilst embracing and exploring the opportunities offered by new materials and technology. A commitment to making a contemporary collection that has meaning for us today will not only form a bridge between the historic collection and the present, but will also ensure the legacy of a dynamic collection for the future. Imposing limits on our contemporary collection will limit our potential to interest our audience. Realistically, the acquisition of some categories of objects, particularly those associated with new technology, are constrained by high costs and have subsequent storage and conservation issues. However, rather than limiting our collecting policies, I believe the issues involved in collecting the contemporary create new and exciting opportunities for curators to collaborate and work together. Far from replacing the hand, new technology is helping the creative process branch out in new directions, and as curators we need to learn from artists and makers. Harnessing new technology will help to build our collections, make them more accessible, and contribute to contemporary artistic discourse. Collections do not necessarily have to be all in one place, and virtual collecting offers us the ability to collect both small-scale experimental work and large-scale installations. As curators, we have yet to resolve many of the issues involved in building a contemporary collection, but I believe passionately that our role is to support both innovation and experimentation, and to continue to safeguard our collections, physical and virtual. The future, after all, is in our hands.

Notes

1. David Hockey, quoted verbally at a Crafts Council Curator's Day "Working with the Ephemeral," October 22, 2001 by Mary Brooks, Senior Lecturer, Textile Conservation, University of Southampton, UK.
2. Quoted in *Tate Modern Introduction to Eva Hesse*, November 13 2002–March 9 2003.
3. All objects acquired by the V&A are assigned a museum number. The prefix indicates the collection that originally acquires the object— "T" indicates that it has been acquired by the Textiles and Fashion section. The number is the unique, sequential number assigned independently within each collection. Numbers start at "1" at the beginning of each calendar year—154 indicates that "Bodies of Knowledge" was the 154th object to be acquired. The year indicates the year of acquisition of an object by a collection.
4. *Textiles in Context at the V&A*, September 5 2002–January 5 2003.
5. Artist's exhibition submission statement, August 2002.
6. Interviewed by the author, August 26 2003.
7. *Second Generation Sikhs*, broadcast August 1 2004, transcript www.bbc.uk/religion/ pro.
8. Francis Carey, "Elective Affinities: Collecting Contemporary Culture in the British Museum," p. 4. Paper given at Collecting Now, joint seminar between The British Museum and Kingston University, March 8 2003.
9. www.thebritishmuseum.ac.uk.
10. www.bl.uk/collections/treasures/digitisation.
11. Saunders, Gil. 2003. "Collecting the Contemporary." *Art Libraries Journal* 28(4): 5–11.
12. This statement was quoted verbally at a Crafts Council Curator's Day "Working with the Ephemeral," October 22 2001 by Mary Brooks, Senior Lecturer, Textile Conservation, University of Southampton, UK.
13. Debbie Stack interviewed in *Marmalade: The Creative Spread* 2004(2): 36.
14. Interviewed by the author, March 2003.
15. Artist's acquisition statement, 2001.
16. Artist's exhibition statement, January 2002.

(IM)MORTAL FASHION
Iris van Herpen's 'Skeleton' Dress (2020)

Sarah Scaturro

EDITOR'S INTRODUCTION

Sarah Scaturro is a conservator, curator and historian. The website text included in full here was written by Scaturro during her time as Head of the Fashion Conservation Laboratory at the Metropolitan Museum of Art's Costume Institute in New York City. Scaturro's succinct writing describes the process of 3D printing used to make Iris van Herpen's *Skeleton Dress*. The dress was part of the July 2011 *Capriole* collection presented at Paris Haute Couture week in van Herpen's debut as a guest member of the *Chambre Syndicale de la Haute Couture*. The collection included pieces from previous collections alongside five looks 'that evoke the feeling just before and during a free-fall parachute jump'.[1]

Skeleton Dress, an exoskeleton of white polyamide digitally developed with the architect Isaïe Bloch, is considered one of the earliest examples of 3D printing to walk the catwalk. The cage of 3D printed bones hangs in front and behind the model's body suggesting a glimpse of our interior. The structural references include a human skeleton, as well as 'various skeletons of different animals (snakes, birds, insects) [...] mixed into this non-existing bone structure'[2] – a precursor to the biomimicry apparent in many of the designer's later collections.

Scaturro's text offers a clear explanation not only of how *Skeleton Dress* was made, but also of the conservation challenges the object now poses. In addressing 3D printing it offers a more recent example of the challenges Sue Prichard also addresses in her writing about examples of textile art held in the V&A Collection. In the case of van Herpen's *Skeleton Dress*, the material memory of the printed nylon powder can potentially include degraded polymers from reused powder, which alongside nylon's sensitivity to light exposure, can introduce weaknesses. When 3D printing is used to create objects that are expected to have a short lifespan, this does not pose a particular problem. But when material experimentation such as van Herpen's enters archival collections, material memory and material experimentation present opposing agendas.

Notes

1. https://www.irisvanherpen.com/haute-couture/capriole. Accessed 2 November 2021.
2. Liz Stinson, 'Iris van Herpen's Extraordinary Clothes Are More like Wearable Sculptures', 19 November 2015, https://www.wired.com/2015/11/iris-van-herpens-extraordinary-clothes-are-more-like-wearable-sculptures/.

(Im)mortal Fashion: Iris van Herpen's 'Skeleton' Dress

Sarah Scaturro

In 2015 the Costume Institute acquired its first 3-D–printed dress, a startling two-piece garment called "Skeleton" that appeared in Dutch fashion designer Iris van Herpen's Fall 2011 "Capriole" collection.

Defying conventional notions of wearability, this rigid, strapless dress wraps around the body like a bony carapace, not flexing for the moving body. The novel materiality of the dress, which is made of 3-D–printed nylon, also challenges the standard conservation approaches deployed by Costume Institute conservators in the preservation of fashion.

Van Herpen created "Skeleton" without using traditional haute couture sewing techniques. Instead, she turned to a 3-D–printing process known as selective laser sintering (SLS).

The build takes place in an enclosed environment filled with nitrogen gas. Nylon powder is spread across the surface of a build platform and fused by a laser into a computer-generated shape. Once the nylon particles melt together, the build platform is lowered, another layer of powder is spread across, and the process repeats. The powder itself is maintained at a very high temperature, just below melting, to minimize warping. After the build is complete, the laser-sintered object is allowed to cool for up to 48 hours, and any excess, unsintered powder is blown off. Typical post-production processes including sanding, refining, and coating the object.

The layered manufacturing process typically gives SLS objects a ridged texture that resembles topographic lines. The fused powder also retains a porous, granular surface like that of sandstone. Van Herpen exploited the textured, naturally white, and porous characteristics of 3-D–printed nylon to evoke a bony carapace.

Unfortunately, the SLS process also damages the objects it creates. The very high temperature at which the nylon powder is kept to minimize warping shortens the material's lifespan. Furthermore, manufacturers typically use and reuse the un-sintered powder that remains to offset costs. The nylon powder used to create an object may have been held at very high temperatures during many previous build cycles, drastically damaging it.

Manufacturers are not typically concerned about damage to the nylon powder, since they use SLS to create prototypes and objects for short-term use. However, conservators in a museum are charged with ensuring that all objects that enter the collection last as long as possible—a goal difficult to achieve for an object that was only meant to live a short life.

"Skeleton" is now eight years old. When it arrived at the Costume Institute, it already showed several condition problems that are irreversible and untreatable. The dress was yellowed; its porous surface was embedded with dirt and grime; and small losses had already occurred to several fragile tips of the skeletal protrusions, indicating that the dress was becoming embrittled.

To date, there is little research on how to preserve and treat 3-D–printed objects. No one knows how long this dress—or other such objects—will

---

last, even in a controlled museum environment. Garments like "Skeleton" pose an exciting challenge for conservators, who must constantly learn new ways to approach and preserve the radical new fashions of today, as well as those of tomorrow. As van Herpen once declared:

The shortness of fashion is here.[1]

Note

1. Iris van Herpen, Mark Wilson, SueAn van der Zijpp, Jerry Stafford, and Sarah Schleuning, *Iris van Herpen: Transforming Fashion* (Atlanta: High Museum of Art, 2015).

15

HONG KONG'S TEXTILE INDUSTRIAL HERITAGE
Transformations to a place of weaving creative experiences for all (2019)

Takahashi Mizuki

EDITOR'S INTRODUCTION

Executive Director and Chief Curator of the Hong Kong–based non-profit art institution CHAT (Centre for Heritage, Arts and Textile) Takahashi Mizuki's conference lecture reprinted here is an edited version of the original. In it she addresses the task of preserving the memories of industrial textile history. The presentation was first made at the 2019 International Symposium *30th Anniversary of Yokohama Museum of Art* in Japan on the panel 'Your Museum, Your Future: For What and for Whom Do Museums Stand?'

While Sue Prichard's writing, also included in this section, addresses the complexities of the V&A's collection of textiles, predominantly as physical artefacts but increasingly also in digital versions, CHAT focuses on the legacies of textile labour and industry of Hong Kong's once thriving textile industry. In contrast to the V&A's founding in 1852 and Kensington Road location in London since 1857, CHAT opened in 2019. With the exception of the years 1941 to 1945 when Hong Kong was occupied by the Japanese, the region was a British colony from 1841 to 1997. From the mid-20th century textile manufacturing made up a significant portion of the labour force. In recent decades Hong Kong's textile manufacturing has declined dramatically and the last textile factory closed in 2014.

The work which once drew economic migration to the region and the history of local manufacturing are a significant part of the heritage conservation project CHAT. Where institutional memory keeping can be tasked with the conservation and care of artefacts for future generations, as Prichard's writing explains, CHAT operates within a different ecology. Understanding the legacies of industrial heritage includes even more ephemeral material, such as recording and preserving the importance of oral histories – the very memories – of former factory workers.

Hong Kong's Textile Industrial Heritage: transformations to a place of weaving creative experiences for all

Takahashi Mizuki

CENTRE FOR HERITAGE, ARTS AND TEXTILE (CHAT)

Takahashi Mizuki (Takahashi): Thank you for inviting me to participate in this international symposium. After moving to Hong Kong in 2016, I have been involved in establishing CHAT (the Centre for Heritage, Arts and Textile), an art center that opened in March 2019 as part of a project revitalizing a former cotton spinning mill. Our art center is different from the Philadelphia Museum of Art and Yokohama Museum of Art, whose activities center around their collections. However, my case on CHAT may be able to offer an interesting perspective for looking at contemporary art in the context of cultural heritage, because the City of Yokohama has also incorporated such perspectives in their Creative City policy. Today, I am going to talk introduce the brief historical background of CHAT and our activities.

CHAT AS PART OF THE MILLS, A PROJECT TO REVITALIZE A FORMER COTTON SPINNING MILL

Hong Kong is a familiar travel destination for Japanese people, so many of you here might have visited the city. Hong Kong consists of several islands and the Kowloon peninsula. Most of the tourist attractions, art galleries, contemporary art institutions and events, including the Peak, Art Basel Hong Kong, and the recently opened Tai Kwun Contemporary Art, are centrally located on Hong Kong Island. CHAT is located in Tsuen Wan, the last station of the MTR metro that runs north to south and connects Hong Kong Island to Kowloon.

Between the 1950s and the mid-1980s, there were many spinning mills in the Tsuen Wan district, where CHAT is located. CHAT was founded as part of a privately funded project to revitalize and utilize these former spinning mills. The name of this project is called The Mills. Besides CHAT, there are shops, cafes, and restaurants run by young Hong Kong owners, as well as the Mills Fabrica, an incubation office that supports young entrepreneurs to launch new projects inside The Mills.

The Mills was created in the renovated factories of Nan Fung Textiles. The factories were in operation until 2008. Hong Kong used to be a small fishing village, although it is known as a city of finance today. During the 1950s after the end of World War II, a lot of capitalists and workers from Mainland China came to Hong Kong to escape from the civil war and the textile, plastic, and toy manufacturing industries emerged during these years. I am often asked why the textile industry is so important for Hong Kong even today, and the answer is that it is one of the industries that built Hong Kong's economic foundation and is closely related to Hong Kong's identity. When I talk to young people today, I discover that a lot of their parents and grandparents used to work in the textile industry or garment manufacturing industry. When we look at American denim products by such brands as Levi's and Lee manufactured in the 1980s, a lot of them were actually made in Hong Kong. At its peak, one third of Hong Kong's labor force was doing jobs related to spinning, weaving, and textile manufacturing.

The renovation of the factories was done in such a way as to keep their original characteristics. Initiated by the private sector, it is an unusual project in that it

Source: Takahashi Mizuki, 'Your Museum, Your Future: For What and for Whom Do Museums Stand?' *30th Anniversary of Yokohama Museum of Art, International Symposium.* Report issued by the Yokohama Museum of Art (2019). Reproduced with permission.

conserves Hong Kong's industrial heritage. The rooftop of The Mills is a park open to the public and CHAT is located on the floor beneath it. CHAT refers to "chatting" in English, and we gave our institution this nickname with the hope that a lot of conversations and discussions would be generated here. Our logo represents two things: the relationship between warp and weft on a weaving loom as well as a hashtag used on social media such as Instagram. We adopted a symbol with this image of people coming together around a specific theme while embodying different characteristics.

Transformation from a Place for Production to a Place for Creativity

One of the galleries, the D.H. Chen Foundation Gallery, was named alter Chen Dinh-hwa, who established Nan Fung Textiles. This gallery serves to introduce Hong Kong's textile industry as a permanent exhibition. We built the gallery's spatial design concept from scratch together with Assemble, the architecture collective who received the Turner Prize several years ago, and HATO, a graphic designer based in London and Hong Kong. On one of the walls, we exhibit objects made of vintage cotton produced in Hong Kong. On another wall, the video illustrates how cotton is harvested from flower and becomes thread, as well as how many inspections are done for cotton to become thread. We hope to shed light on the workers who used to work here. For this reason, we shot many oral history videos. We have a wall that is dedicated to exhibiting documentation of the factory workers, including a pay envelope donated by a former employee.

Hong Kong's textile industry provided work not only for people in Hong Kong but also for migrants from China. There is also a section that illustrates the different kinds of training an individual worker went through to become a professional cotton spinner.

CHAT has two galleries for special exhibitions. Our opening exhibition, "Unfolding: Fabric of Our Life" is currently on view, which presents work by seventeen contemporary artists and collectives invited from the Asia-Pacific region that refer to issues related to labor and history as well as the technology behind the textile industry. CHAT Lounge is a space where people can come together to talk or relax after viewing an exhibition. We commissioned Michael Lin, a Taiwanese artist, to create work for the lounge. The work Lin created was inspired by the research into the textile market he conducted in Hong Kong. CHAT Arcade is a hallway with a unique virtual reality section. We actively incorporate the latest digital technology into our space. Since we don't have enough exhibition spaces to show what the factory was like in the past, we decided to use a virtual space. In collaboration with a Dutch VR design team, we conducted research to make an educational virtual reality video. When you put on a pair of VR goggles, you can travel back in time to the 1950s and learn how the industry landed in Hong Kong and spinning was done in the factory,

Weaving Creative Experiences for All

A factory is a place where something is manufactured, right? Since CHAT is housed in renovated former factories, we decided to give CHAT an identity as a place for creation, developed from its manufacturing past. The motto of CHAT is "Weaving Creative Experiences for All." The Tsuen Wan district used to be an industrial area and is now home to a lot of local Hong Kong families. It's very likely that people in this area haven't had many chances to visit an art museum, or aren't familiar with contemporary art. For this reason, the programs we organize always in some way or other attempt to involve the Hong Kong community and its residents in the process of collaborating with artists.

We hold a large-scale exhibition three times a year in, respectively, spring, summer, and winter. It does not necessarily have to be about textiles, but inevitably, we work with artists who understand the historical context of CHAT and its community.

The attitude of learning together is another characteristic feature of CHAT, so we host workshops to teach hand-spinning techniques almost every day at the D.H. Chen Foundation Gallery, which shares the history of Hong Kong's textile industry with visitors. In textiles, materials and texture are very important. While we use cotton every day, many people don't experience the

PART THREE

STRUCTURE

process of how it is actually produced. So here, we communicate how cotton thread is produced.

And what we value is the involvement in our activities of retired people who used to work in the textile and garment manufacturing industries. We employ and pay wages to retired workers to create work with artists. More specifically, this means they work as assistants to artists or as photography models. When contact Gonzo, a Japanese art group, did a performance at CHAT recently, we had the workers on stage with the group.

We host an international symposium related to textiles once a year, offering an opportunity for a group of people who are engaged with textiles bur have never met one another to come together. We have a different theme each year: the first was on gender, the second on textiles and community, and the third on textile and legacy. With this year's theme, "Staging Textiles," we will invite designers, artists, curators, and researchers from all over the world.

CHAT also organizes an artist residency program. Once a year, we invite an artist to Hong Kong for the duration of three months to create work. We invited Alma Quinto, a Filipino artist, lase year. She created work through a series of workshops she organized with domestic workers from the Philippines who live in Hong Kong in large numbers. There are a lot of immigrants living in Hong Kong, including myself, from many different countries. We create projects chat engage with various communities here while also thinking about a definition of what it means to be a Hong Kongers.

Additionally, in the D.H. Chen Foundation Gallery, we demonstrate the operation of the spinning machine with the help of ex-textile workers. One of the demonstrators was working as a bathroom cleaner for the Mills after retiring from a factory. One day, when one of our staff talked to her, we discovered chat she used to work in the spinning industry and knows how to run a machine. We then recruited her to work with us, and that's how she changed her job from cleaner to workshop demonstrator. She does the demonstration once a month and each time she explains the machine to our visitors with much enthusiasm. We have had many opportunities to talk to people who used to work in the textile industry, but have found chat many of them don't find any value in their work. This was the case for the cleaner. She never imagined that the work she used to do in the past could be viewed by young people with such interest and provide chem with new insights. I want CHAT to be a place like this, where we can shed light on people and things that were not valued in the past.

Our opening exhibition put the spotlight on the downsides of the textile industry, such as issues related to colonialism, labor, economy, and the environment. I have been asked whether it was okay for an art center built in a former textile factory to organize an exhibition that looks critically at the industry. I think it's important to refer to the aspects that are often overlooked or invisible. And that's precisely the point of updating the industrial heritage, and through the accumulation of these activities, we hope CHAT becomes a symbol of the civic pride in the neighbourhood. Thank you.

FURTHER READING: MEMORY

Baggott, Jean. *The Girl on the Wall: One Life's Rich Tapestry*, London: Icon Books, 2009.

Stitched and written memoir captures the author's experience of her life in the heavily industrialized West Midlands of England. Seventy-three embroidered circles establish the autobiographical chapter structure starting in 1940.

Bjørne Linnert, Lise. 'Desconocida Unknown Ukjent', https://www.lisebjorne.com/desconocida-unknown-ukjent/.

Web archive of Norwegian artist Lise Bjørne Linnert's international community art project based on mass collaboration. Name tags stitched in remembrance and protest of the women murdered in Ciudad Juaréz, Mexico, continue to be created in communities around the world in remembrance of women's lives lost around the world as the result of cultures of violence.

Evans, Caroline and Alessandra Vaccari (eds). *Time in Fashion*, London: Bloomsbury, 2020.

Anthology of writing that explores the theme of fashion and time: as seasonal rhythms of the industry, the endless recombination of motifs and fashion's capacity to dream of future alternatives. Excerpts span the eighteenth century to contemporary.

Frank, Rike and Grant Watson (eds). *Textiles Open Letter*, Berlin: Sternberg Press, 2015.

Bilingual English and German book accompanied an exhibition of the same name, with essays and interviews by Rike Frank, T'ai Smith, Grant Watson, Elissa Auther, Georg Vasold, Judith Raum, Sabeth Buchmann and Seth Siegelaub that focus on textiles in German-speaking art gallery contexts.

hooks, bell. 'Aesthetic Inheritances: History Worked by Hand', in *Yearning: Race, Gender and Cultural Politics*, 115–22, Boston: South End Press, 1990.

Long before the term 'intersectionality' became popularized, hooks called for Black women quiltmakers' work to be considered with attention to the impact of race, sex and class. hooks addresses quilting as part of enslaved labour and the considerably different requirements of creative imagination required of women living under economic and social oppression.

Hemmings, Jessica. '*That's Not Your Story*: Faith Ringgold Publishing on Cloth', *PARSE* 11 (2020): https://parsejournal.com/article/thats-not-your-story-faith-ringgold-publishing-on-cloth/.

Article begins with an account of the expectations African-American artist Faith Ringgold's race and gender placed on her writing, before discussion of the artist's storytelling quilts as a surface on which she could publish.

Lanceta, Teresa. *Adiós al Rombo / Farewell to the Rhombus*, Madrid and Bilbao: La Casa Encenida / Azkuna Zentroa, 2016.

Bilingual Spanish and English exhibition catalogue of Spanish artist's weavings influenced by Moroccan women and their textiles. Illustrated with four texts, including poetic writing by Lanceta.

Stallybrass, Peter. 'Worn Worlds: Clothes, Mourning, and the Life of Things', *The Yale Review* 81, no. 2 (April 1993): 35–50.

Originally written as a memorial lecture in memory of the author's friend Allon White, Stallybrass writes of his personal grief and the role of cloth as a mediating layer in the experience of loss. Drawing on poetry and fiction, he observes the daunting accuracy of the textile's ability to remember a departed body.

Steedman, Carolyn. 'What a Rag Rug Means', *Journal of Material Culture* 3, no. 3 (1998): 259–81.

Article that takes as a starting point an absent textile – a rag rug the author explains she incorrectly remembers reading in Elizabeth Gaskell's novel *Mary Barton* (1848). Steedman uses the rug's absence to discuss the domestic and economic realities of the novel's setting, the history of textile manufacturing and the eighteenth-century need for cotton rags by paper manufacturers.

Syjuco, Stephanie. 'What We Can Learn from Ruth Asawa', *Frieze* (online), no. 215, 30 October 2020.

Brief article opens with a photograph from the early 1940s by Dorothea Lange of Japanese American women's hand-making camouflage netting for the US war effort, before discussion of the artist Ruth Asawa (who went on to create celebrated crochet wire sculptures) and experienced detention during her childhood in several US internment camps.

Wilcox, Claire. *Patch Work: A Life Amongst Clothes*, London: Bloomsbury, 2021.

Written from the perspective of a fashion curator, micro-histories of cloth from a cardigan to a curtain provide the starting point for a series of intimate recollections about life and human mortality.

PART THREE

STRUCTURE

PART INTRODUCTION

The structures considered in this section include the physical nature of the textile and its relationship to space, as well as the linguistic comparisons between the text and textile. An excerpt of writing by the architect, art critic and Professor of architecture Gottfried Semper (1803–79) opens this section. Semper published extensively, and in the piece of writing included here he writes of his understanding of the historical importance of textiles as examples of the earliest walls in the built environment.

From Semper's historical emphasis, the writing then leaps forward to another architectural perspective focused on the future. If Semper saw the portable, flexible carpet as a wall, the architect Philip Beesley creates environments in which architecture makes use of textile structures that, with the aid of sensors, become responsive to our presence. In Beesley's early piece of writing included here, he considers several experimental projects with students that created geotextiles. Not only is the scale of textiles that Beesley constructed with his students of interest, but also the patched and pieced structure of the writing that he uses to document his work.

The brief text that follows is based on the voice of Otti Berger, a Bauhaus weaver, which the artist Judith Raum has researched extensively. Berger's writing was translated into English by Raum. In it, Berger muses on what a fabric is, first confirming, as many of the texts in the touch section write, that textiles are far more than optical. Berger moves from recognition of the importance of touch to the importance of the textile's structure and how different textile structures must be able to perform with different requirements dependent on particular spaces.

The curator Catherine de Zegher's extensive writing on the artist Cecilia Vicuña spans the realms of both physical and linguistic. De Zegher discusses the textile as a way Vicuña literally maps (precarious) spaces but also produces poetry. Here the textile is both a physical structure existing in space and a way of working with language. De Zegher likens Vicuña's early works to the game of cat's cradle – an 'inter-text' of the familiar made in thread found around the world, as well as drawing on Gilles Deleuze and Félix Guattari's ideas of smooth and striated space. A short excerpt from the writing of Deleuze and Guattari follows where the structure of woven and felted cloth is used as one of a number of examples that explore their concept of smooth and striated space to communicate thinking that extends beyond the physical reality of cloth.

The artist Sabrina Gschwandtner offers an example of how the structure of the textile can inform and inspire a range of ways of working. Knitting informs not only what she makes as an artist but how she thinks as a critic and what she orchestrates as a curator. Gschwandtner's use of knitting extends beyond the production of cloth to suggest that knitting can provide a template or model of thinking that guides a broad range of creative actions. The final entry of the section is co-authored by Kate Goldsworthy, Rebecca Earley and Kay Politowicz, who consider the structural changes necessary for circular textile design to thrive, including a call for a more nuanced appreciation of textiles and time.

16

THE FOUR ELEMENTS OF ARCHITECTURE (EXCERPT) (1851/1989)

Gottfried Semper

EDITOR'S INTRODUCTION

Gottfried Semper (1803–79) was a German architect, art critic and professor of architecture. His built work includes the Semperoper, an opera house in Dresden, Germany, that opened in 1841 and was rebuilt after a fire in 1869 to reopen in 1878. Among Semper's publications is the book *The Four Elements of Architecture* (1851) first written in German. The book attempts to establish the origins of architecture through four types: the hearth, roof, enclosure and mound, which represent the material crafts of metals and ceramics (hearth), woodwork (roof), textiles (enclosure) and earth (mound). Of interest here is the emphasis Semper placed on weaving.

Semper argued that the buildings of Ancient Greece and Rome were colourfully painted. Known as the polychromy debate, his stance brought him professional recognition. In the excerpt reprinted here Semper proposes 'hanging carpets remained the true walls, the visible boundaries of space'. He draws examples from around the world finding the influence of textile walls globally: 'even where building solid walls became necessary, the latter were only the inner, invisible structure hidden behind the true and legitimate representatives of the wall, the colorful woven carpets.' For an architect to celebrate the textile is an unusual stance. For the textile – the decorative and pliable – to be placed before the solid stuff of walls is even more rare.

The Four Elements of Architecture

Gottfried Semper

V

The Four Elements

[…]

But what primitive technique evolved from the *enclosure*? None other than the art of the *wall fitter* (*Wandbereiter*), that is, the weaver of mats and carpets. This statement may appear strange and requires an explanation.

It was mentioned previously that there are writers who devote much time to searching for the origin of art and who believe they can deduce from it all the different ways of building. The nomadic tent plays a rather important role in their arguments. Yet while with great acumen they detect in the catenary curve of the tent the norm of the Tartar-Chinese way of building (although the same shapes occur in the caps and shoes of these people), they overlook the more general and less dubious influence that the carpet in its capacity as a wall, as a vertical means of protection, had on the evolution of certain architectural forms. Thus I seem to stand without the support of a single authority when I assert that the carpet *wall* plays a most important role in the general history of art.

It is well known that even now tribes in an early stage of their development apply their budding artistic instinct to the braiding and weaving of mats and covers (even when they still go around completely naked). The wildest tribes are familiar with the hedge-fence – the crudest wickerwork and the most primitive pen or spatial enclosure made from tree branches. Only the potter's art can with some justification *perhaps* claim to be as ancient as the craft of carpet weaving.

The weaving of branches led easily to weaving bast into mats and covers and then to weaving with plant fiber and so forth. The oldest ornaments either derived from entwining or knotting materials or were easily produced on the potter's wheel with the finger on the soft clay. The use of wickerwork for setting apart one's property, the use of mats and carpets for floor coverings and protection against heat and cold and for subdividing the spaces within a dwelling in most cases preceded by far the masonry wall, and particularly in areas favored by climate. The masonry wall was an intrusion into the domain of the wall fitter by the mason's art, which had evolved from building terraces according to very different conditions of style.

Wickerwork, the original space divider, retained the full importance of its earlier meaning, actually or ideally, when later the light mat walls were transformed into clay tile, brick, or stone walls. Wickerwork was the *essence of the wall*.[1]

Hanging carpets remained the true walls, the visible boundaries of space. The often solid walls behind them were necessary for reasons that had nothing to do with the creation of space; they were needed for security, for supporting a load, for their permanence, and so on. Wherever the need for these secondary functions did not arise, the carpets remained the original means of separating space. Even where building solid walls became necessary, the latter were only the inner, invisible structure hidden behind the true and legitimate representatives of the wall, the colorful woven carpets.

The wall retained this meaning when materials other than the original were used, either for reason of

---

[1] The German word *Wand* [wall], *paries*, acknowledges its origin. The terms *Wand* and *Gewand* [dress] derive from a single root. They indicate the woven material that formed the wall.

Source: Excerpt from Gottfried Semper, *The Four Elements of Architecture and Other Writings*, pp. 103–10. © Cambridge University Press 1989. Translated by Harry Frances Mallgrave and Wolfgang Hermann. Reproduced with permission of the Licensor through PLSclear

greater durability, better preservation of the inner wall, economy, the display of greater magnificence, or for any other reason. The inventive mind of man produced many such substitutes, and all branches of the technical arts were successively enlisted.

The most widely used and perhaps the oldest substitute was offered by the mason's art, the stucco covering or bitumen plaster in other countries. The woodworkers made panels (πίναχες) with which to fit the walls, especially the lower parts. Workers handling fire supplied glazed terra cotta[2] and metal plates. As the last substitute perhaps can be counted the panels of standstone, granite, alabaster, and marble that we find in widespread use in Assyria, Persia, Egypt, and even in Greece.

For a long time the character of the copy followed that of the prototype. The artists who created the painted and sculptured decorations on wood, stucco, fired clay, metal, or stone traditionally though not consciously imitated the colorful embroideries and trellis works of the age old carpet walls.

The whole system of Oriental polychromy – closely connected and to a certain extent one with the ancient arts of paneling and dressing – and therefore also the art of painting and bas-relief arose from the looms and vats of the industrious Assyrians,[3] or from the inventions of prehistoric people who preceded them. In any case, the Assyrians should be considered the most faithful guardians of this primordial motif.

In the oldest annals of mankind Assyrian carpets were famed for their splendid colors and the skill with which fantastic pictures were woven into them. Written descriptions of mystical animals, dragons, lions, tigers, and so forth agree fully with the images we see today on the walls of Nineveh. If such a comparison were still possible, we would recognize a perfect accord not only in the objects depicted but also in the manner of treatment.

Assyrian sculpture clearly kept within limits imposed by its origin, even though the new material permitted a new means of raising the figures from the background. A struggle toward naturalism is evident, whose limits were set not by hierarchical power, but (apart from the despotic rules of a ceremonial court) by the accidental features of a technique foreign to sculpture yet still responsive to the echoes from the past. The postures of the figures are stiff but not so rigid as to have become mere characters; they only look as though they were chained. Within a composition they are already, or rather, are *still* pictorial adaptations of a celebrated historical act or a court ceremony, not like the Egyptian images, which are simply a means to record a fact and are really a painted chronicle. Even in their arrangement, for instance, in their adherence to equal head heights, the Assyrian figures are more distinguished than Egyptian images. Sharp, threadlike contours, the hard shapes of the muscles, a predilection for ornamental accessories and embroidery are indicative of their origin; there is exaggeration, but not a lifeless style. The faces do not show the slightest trace of an artistic effort to render the inner state of the soul; they are, even with their constant smiles, without any individual expression. In this respect they are less advanced than Egyptian sculpture and resemble more the early works of the Greeks.

In actual wall murals the same technique is evident. According to Layard, the wall paintings at Nimrud are surrounded and interwoven with strong black contours; the ground is blue or yellow. The freize like borders of the pictures that contain inscriptions also indicate their technical affinity with carpets. The character of the cuneiform corresponds fully with this technique. Would it be possible to invent for needlework a more convenient way of writing?

---

[2] It is highly probable that the wish to give tiles a colored glazing first led to the discovery of burnt bricks. The glazed tiles from Nineveh that I had the opportunity to examine closely in Paris are in an almost unburnt state. Their glaze must have been extraordinarily fusible. Terra cotta dressings are the forerunners to brick walls, and stone plaques the forerunners to ashlar. See further below. [In August 1849 Semper examined the Khorsabad findings in the Louvre, including some not put on public display, after having befriended the museum curator, Charles Blanc. See W. Herrmann, *Gottfried Semper*, 24 and 268n.91. - HFM]

[3] It is remarkable that most of the colors on the Assyrian alabaster panels of Khorsabad and Nimrud have disappeared, while it is evident that they must have existed to complete the remnants still surviving. In contrast to Egyptian and Greek paintings, the surviving traces are not thickly applied but appear as if stained into the surface; it is probable that the colors were composed mainly of vegetable matter.

Alongside these substitutes for the earlier carpets, the latter were still widely used as door curtains, window curtains, and so forth, as can be seen by the richly decorated rings with which they were secured. The simple inlaying of the wooden floors is a sign that they, too, were covered with carpets. Carpets were also the models for the art of mosaic, which remained for the longest time true to its origin.

The interior walls above the gypsum panels were lined with a lightly burned, glazed, or, as one might say, lacquered brick. They were glazed only on one side and covered with painted ornaments that were totally inconsistent with the shape of the stone, but that crossed over it in every direction. Other evidence shows that the stones were in a horizontal position when they were glazed. They were, therefore, first arranged horizontally, then ornamented and glazed, and finally attached to the sun-dried brick wall in proper order as a dressing (Bekleidung). This also proves that the glaze was a general covering and its idea was independent of the material to which it was applied. A late-Roman or Medieval use of colored stones for patterning a wall had not been conceived in these earliest periods of art.

If the presence of sculptured stone panels in the lower parts of the Assyrian palaces can rightly be taken as the first step to later stone construction, then the evident progress made in this direction by the well-known Persian monuments at Murghab and Istakhr is very instructive.[1] Of the original masonry walls that had been constructed in large part from crude brick, there remains only the marble corner shafts, together with the door and window frames. These frames are made of one piece, yet are hollowed out in such a way that the idea of paneling is still clearly evident. The brick wall was anchored into these cavities and connected to the marble shafts by its dressing, possibly wood panels or carpets.

With Egyptian monuments, the original meaning of the wall had already become more blurred; the hierarchical system (perhaps primordial, but in any case founded on the ruins of very old and more nature-bound cultural conditions) gave the carpet motif the fixed meaning of a stone hieroglyph. Nevertheless, the original motif is frequently rather conspicuous.

Nowhere does the stone wall appear as such, but is covered both outside and inside as if with a painted carpet. This explains the exact but nevertheless irregular joints of the stone; the wall was covered with a general coating even when dressed with granite. These ancient granite dressings, at Karnak for example, and on the interior and formerly on the exterior of the pyramids, are counterparts to the Assyrian panels.

Strangely enough, one of the few architectural members that was at the disposal of the Egyptian architect also reflected the ancient principle of paneling walls. I am thinking of the molding that rounded and edged the corners of the massive walls. It originally served to conceal the joints of the thin dressing panels, which otherwise would have easily read through the paint in an unpleasant way at the edges of the massive surfaces.[4]

The columns of Egyptian temples at times have the appearance of reed bundles, surrounded and bound together with a carpet.

Carpet imitation is again very clear and distinct on the wall paintings of the rock-tombs; among the ornaments found there the colored wickerwork and Latz predominate. The paintings recall their original character in the threadlike outlines of the parts, the wealth of color, and embroidery like details.

In China, where architecture has stood still since primitive times and where the four architectural elements most clearly have remained separate from one another, the partition wall, which is for the most part movable, retains its original meaning independent of the roof and the masonry wall. The interior of the house is divided up by such partition walls, which relate as little to the actual structure as do the outside walls, built of bricks yet hollow and dressed with braided reeds and carpets.

How these features prevailed in China, together with the ancient use of stucco and a rich general polychromy, is well known. In addition to the wealth of information on ancient conditions, they provide us with many lessons useful to our time.

---

[4] This molding is even today a very common way of concealing the joint in cabinetworks.

In India too we find similar things, and still today, as in Agrippa's time, stucco and color predominate. We even meet the same phenomenon in early American architecture.

While no trace of Phoenician and Jewish antiquity survives, the reports of famous buildings contained in the sacred and profane writings of these two racially related nations (even though vague and open to diverse interpretation) provide unambiguous and interesting illustrations of our theme. Who is not familiar with the famed Tabernacle of Moses, with the door posts clad with gold plates, the richly colored carpet-walls, and the pyramidal roof made of textiles, leather, and animal skins? This tentlike, holy shrine was imitated in stone and cedar by Solomon on Mount Moriah atop a colossal substructure, and the fact that nothing had been left undressed was celebrated in particular. Inside, the holy rooms were clad throughout with gold plates.

These reports contain the most complete history of wall fitting, and a simple reference to them would be sufficient were it not also necessary to prove that dressing walls had been a custom widely practiced among all prehistoric peoples.

With such a general diffusion of paneling, dressings, and colorful carpetlike adornments for the wall, it would be astonishing if the Greeks, who based their art on the traditions of other people, had not adhered in large part to these customs. It would be even more so, since these customs were most favorable to the cultivation of those arts in which the Greeks, as we know, had achieved what was truly sublime: the relief and painting. In favoring these two arts, they neglected what had been the pride of their Pelasgian ancestors, the terrace and stone construction, neither of which was given a prominent place in their monumental architecture.

This is evident by the custom that had long been familiar to them of paneling temple cellas and halls, as can be inferred from many passages in ancient writings and even from indications found on monuments still surviving. These were the πίναχες *tabulae* of which Pliny speaks, only those on which the great artists used to paint. They are so named because the oldest wood panels were made from spruce, although at the time of encaustic painting they certainly were not made of wood but of marble or ivory. Plates made of terracotta were also called πίναχες. Cicero speaks of them in his oration against Verres, who robbed the Temple of Minerva at Syracuse of its panels covered with the most magnificent paintings (*His autem tabulis interiores templi parietes vestiebantur*).[2]

In a similar way, all the exterior surfaces of temples that were meant to display painted sculpture were constructed for paneling. The pediment, the metopes, the frieze, the ερυματα, or balustrades between the columns, and the corresponding lower panels of the cella were thus prepared.

At the same time, or rather earlier, the principle of applying a stucco dressing to the constructive parts became generally accepted. We find it applied to all stone temples,[3] except those of marble, on which the stucco dressing was superfluous because the marble itself was a natural stucco. The probability that the use of marble went hand in hand with the adoption of a new technique in painting was noted above. The evidence that all areas were painted and that no parts of the bare stone were left undone was given in the previous chapters of this work.

I repeat once again my assertion that polychromy arose from that ancient supremacy of the wall fitter's technique over the mason's in domestic furnishings, and that only on the massive terrace walls could the mason let his own work appear independent of other work. Even the outlying rampart walls of the Assyrians, Medes, and Bactrians were, with the exception of the terrace base, richly decorated with basreliefs and paintings, as we know from the well-known descriptions of Herodotus, Diodor, Strabo, and so on. In the British Museum we find an Assyrian relief panel that clearly depicts a strong fortress with only the lowest part of the exterior wall showing squared stone. The ruins of Nimrud and Khorsabad confirm this fact, as do those of Pasargadae and Persepolis, and the temples of Egypt. Even in Greece we find the same. Thus the Parthenon, for example, stands on a terrace of beautiful Eluesinian squared stone; it was the only part uncolored.

Only at a later time, and scarcely earlier than the Roman period, did the construction of the wall (the so-called square-cut) and the nature of its material become treated as a decorative element in the main parts of the building, chiefly on the exterior walls. Before then, even the most noble materials – the granite chambers at Karnak, the alabaster panels of Nineveh, the ivory panels and paintings, even the golden joints of the temple walls no less than the columns and splendid sculpture of the Parthenon chiseled from snow-white pentelic marble – were given a coat of paint.

Yet it is possible that with simple cella-temples the walls here and there were constructed in cyclopean masonry without stucco. This phenomenon can be explained as an archaic reminiscence or allegory on the earth huts of ancestors, where the terrace might have been joined directly with the roof. One such example could be the temple at Anticyra that Kugler cites from Pausanias. Yet all of this is very uncertain, and there is no need to search for similar examples in Pausanias, who shortly afterwards mentions another building executed in irregular masonry; perhaps he meant to contrast the interior stucco of the temple with a panel or something similar he may have found in another temple. We are already acquainted with his peculiar habit of stressing the characteristics of the building's material.

Antique art completed its cycle, having run the full circle back to its origins, and became extinct with Byzantine embroideries. Its swaddling clothes became its burial shroud.[5]

* * *

[...]

Notes

1. The ruins are those of Pasargadae and Persepolis respectively.
2. Cicero, *Verrine Orations,* II.Iv,122.
3. We have followed MS78;fol.27, which reads "*allen Steintempeln*," rather than "*alten Steintempeln*," as in the published text.

---

[5] To pursue how the phoenix of art again raised itself anew in the Christian era would lead us too far astray.

17

REFLEXIVE TEXTILE (1999)

Philip Beesley

EDITOR'S INTRODUCTION

Philip Beesley is a Toronto-based architect and Professor at the School of Architecture, University of Waterloo. His research practice explores sentient architecture – a poetic realm that proposes our built environments can possess the capacity to feel. Beesley draws significant inspiration from the responsive material possibilities of textile structures. His writing on geotextiles, reprinted in full here, was first published in the *Surface Design Journal* in 1999 and earned an Award of Merit in the 1998 Surface Design Association's Critical Writing Competition.

Beesley's scale of reference for what a textile might be goes far beyond the confines of the body, or even the home, commonly associated with textile territory. In the student projects he discusses, the textile operates as a version of the landscape. The narrative he provides uses an explanatory voice 'interwoven' (quite literally) with poetic diary entries, punctuated (in the original version of the article) with visual documentation of the projects. The hand of fabric, described by the author as 'the particular interaction of nap, bias and weave that combines to give every fabric a specific quality of movement and interaction when it is handled' is extended beyond the scale of the body to apply to several distinct landscapes. The materials Beesley introduces to create these structures include cut saplings, sealed glass vessels and barbed wire shards.

Philip Beesley was the recipient of the Prix de Rome in Architecture for Canada in 1995–96. In 2010, he represented Canada at the Venice Architecture Biennale with *Hylozoic Ground*. Hylozoism refers to the ancient belief that all matter has life. Since 2013, Beesley has also regularly collaborated with the Dutch fashion designer Iris van Herpen. More than a decade after Beesley's prescient writing about sensations beyond familiar clothing, van Herpen traces her first point of inspiration with Beesley's work to *Hylozoic Ground*. Conservator Sarah Scaturro's writing about van Herpen's *Skeleton Dress* appears in the memory section.

Reflexive Textile

Philip Beesley

And the curtain of the temple was torn...[1]

This article explores hybrid textiles involving large-scale net fabrics that dress the ground, following and emphasizing topography.

The projects were produced by the author in collaboration with a number of visual artists including Warren Seelig of Philadelphia and Rockport, Maine, Seattle sculptor Katherine Gray, students of Haystack Mountain School for Crafts, DalTech School of Architecture, and the University of Waterloo Faculty of Architecture.

The discussion explores a particular approach to critique in contemporary textile art. Qualities of the work are explored using analogies to textiles in clothing and including a number of personal journal entries alluding to the projects. This pursuit leads to questions about our own bodies, and our sense of domain. The fabrics described here have immersive and *reflexive* qualities. *Reflex* is a response that suggests the textile being touched touches back. *Immersion* goes beyond the familiar sense of being clothed and surrounded by a fabric. Here the term implies animated space expanding and dissolving boundaries. In these fabrics boundaries of our selves—body and psyche—are questioned. The "hand" of fabric—the particular interaction of nap, bias and weave that combines to give every fabric a specific quality of movement and interaction when it is handled—is often referred to in descriptive reviews of textile art. We know that handling textile has a particular link to human emotion. There are poignant implications in the way textile flexes and moves with us. When we grieve, we grasp and caress and tear cloth.

This textile "hand" is a reference for the projects here in several ways. The first example shown concentrates on flexible draping that pronounces and extends the shape of the land. The next project attempts a porous, ephemeral space that opens boundaries. Other examples tend toward an intimate prosthetic relationship in which living functions are implied in the fabric. Here the hand is active, flexing and recoiling.

The projects *Haystack Veil*, *Erratics Net*, *Synthetic Earth* and *Palatine Burial*[2] attempt special qualities:

Haystack Veil is a landscape of cut saplings, thirty thousand twigs cut and bundled into a "knit" veil floating over a moss and lichen covered cliff alongside the Atlantic Ocean. *Haystack Veil* bears on the land following primordial topography, a cloak over the earth.

Erratics Net is a complex interlinked wire fabric mounted on a glacier-scoured terrain in Nova Scotia. Layers of new strata floating just above the surface of the land are developed within the foam-like filigree of this textile installation.

Synthetic Earth is a composite material involving a mass of sealed glass vessels holding digestive fluids covered by a densely layered net. The elements in this covering material are designed with springing barbed details encouraging accretive massing and clumping, a slow process of ingestion. A lurking, carnivorous quality results.

Palatine Burial is a grotto of densely massed barbed wire shards with individual links configured to grasp and puncture adjacent surfaces. Like the links used in *Synthetic Earth*, these details are ambivalent. They act as a reef supporting new growth, while at the same time their acute physical nature repels.

††††††††††

Scoured granite, solid. On the surface, giving: a thick sponge of lichen and moss crust softening every step. I moved to the bare mass below. At first hunched like before, still cradled

---

Source: Philip Beesley, 'Reflexive Textile' (1999) *Surface Design Journal*, pp. 4–10. Reproduced with permission.

on the memory of permanently floating city floors, every sidewalk hollow. But the ground here was different: not a tremor: Stone—not broken, not strained, not sailing up into vibrating light nor folded inflections trembling nor resonating with a hundred thousand voices of neighborhood. Silent.

> *My legs changed.*
> *I stood on the ground.*[3]

Haystack Veil was constructed on the glacier-formed shore cliffs flanking Haystack Mountain School of Crafts in Maine. A quarter-acre in size, the fabric is a triaxial lattice structure made from a network of repeating sapling tripods carrying long bundled twig fibers. The fibers form a continuous meshwork floating about sixteen inches above the ground. The firmly planted feet of each tripod stand toe to toe and brace each other.

This resilient anchoring makes the fabric behave like a second skin for the ground. The floating layer rolls and creases, following the earth. It spreads, wrapping over minor log falls and bridging over gullies, stretching over the dense mass of lichens and mosses at ground level while at the same time throwing into high relief the penetrations of tree trunks, ground fall branches and boulders breaking through the fabric. By filtering out the detail of the tangled forest floor, the primordial terrain of the glaciated bedrock underfoot is pronounced, telegraphing its hidden forms into the new hovering surface.

A curious sense results. On the surface, the aura of the work is of cottage industry, a hive of workers constructing an intimate cloak for the ground. At the same time an archaic presence prevails revealing deep land beneath. The result is a surface tension, a resilient meniscus.[4]

Just below my hand stirring the ocean surface, they flickered—sparks, sputtering and extinguishing, rising and sinking. A wild thicket of pulsing light close to my hand, in waves following my waving, dispersing clusters like stars. Opening into trails, carried by tiny swirling currents away from fingertips. Trails leading away from the swarm, into the dark of the water: yet out there, too, a quiet refrain of slow murmuring flashes. If my hand grew still, the phosphorescence would grow quieter, though a halo of intermittent pulses remained around

my hand—the sheer warmth of touch was enough to excite them. And, even deeper, one flash-then silence. But again, ten feet out; forty feet... Not touchable, but continually, flexing in response to my touch. Dissolving, alive.

Erratics Net is a hovering, elusive filigree extending a glacier-scoured granite terrain on a Nova Scotia shore. A scattered field of enormous rounded scoured boulders lies on the bedrock surface, the residue of the last ice age. The ground here is bare save for fragile patches of mosses and grasses clinging to hollows above the reach of the high ocean tides. The atmosphere is in constant flux, alternately bathed in thick humid washes of fog and stripped by gales rolling in from North Atlantic currents.

A special soil reinforcing mesh was developed for this shore. The mesh has two states. The first is a widespread net anchoring into the rock surface. This artificial reef encourages turf growth by means of myriad hooked clips catching windblown plant matter, holding and amassing a matted matrix serving as synthetic soil. In this state, the textile is organized in a pillowed form of alternating peaks and valleys, presenting barbs outward, catching new material, and inward for anchoring beneath. These anchors hold the net just above the bare rock, making a shallow film of still, sheltered air allowing delicate growth to emerge. The net is made with wire joints clamped by sliding flexible tubes that lock each link to its neighbor making a tough, resilient structure.

The second state responds to extended times of deep fog where the air stills and the ground is soaked in vapor. Responding to this state the net can expand into multiple layers, each outward facing peak formed within a matrix layer, in turn serving as the foot for an inward facing valley of the next layer. A foam-like cellular lattice results, a filigree extending throughout the thickened atmosphere. The natural growth encouraged by this armature is froth-like, filling space with infinitesimal mass. The material is marked by regular intervals, momentarily thickening and making a porous stratified border, then opening again. A striated penumbra emerges, an aura floating outward from the land. Like plankton phosphorescing in the ocean, *Erratics Net* offers dissociated space, an absorption into ether.

†††††††††

A skin of bull's blood. The ground was dry before she poured it. Past crimson and past rubedo, black-red. The earthen kitchen floor was the center, not like the clean porcelain inside or the planks at the front. The hearth in the back like forever, a floor with a burnished crust of red. Each fall, refreshing. Seeping into the crazed labyrinth of surface cracks, settling under to soften for a moment, then rubbing furiously and setting into gleaming skin covering the deep ground.[5]

Synthetic Earth, the collaborative installation with glass artist Katherine Gray, contains a mound of stacked wax-sealed glass vessels holding dark fluids. Each vessel bears a long collar with a holster of crimped wire joint details. These junctions form roots for fronds of intertwining twisted wire links that slide and lock together making a helical geometry of ropy strands. Each link contains outflung arms detailed with hooked barbs, acting like burrs grasping and tangling with neighboring links. A dense mass of these strands make a tangled shroud engulfing the glasswork contents of bile and blood. These contents are partly natural, from human donations, and partly synthetic, from fermented soy and salt solutions. Like feltwork, the fabric amasses complexes of individual fibers. The network rends to assemble itself by sticking to adjacent surfaces. The grasping details of the wire strands anchored to each vessel pull inward, implying that the fluids within the glasswork were ingested from without, giving a lurking, predatory presence. In spite of this outwardly aggressive posture, the interior of this material is intimate, acutely in need of its duck covering fabric. In this way the fabric is like flesh.

Swaddling: a wide band, brought down the shins, tucked under the heels then over to clamp the beginning of the shroud. Spiraling up the long thin body three full turns until the shoulders, a long serpentine edge from above to below. Bound, a coiling sheath. Turning at the shoulders, hooding up over the crown of the tiny skull, caressing the edge of exposed temples, falling behind ears and hinge of jaw. Loosening at the throat, a fibula brooch shaped like

a smooth egg holding the gathered linen. A wide smooth throat falling deep within the opening in the cloth. Eyes wider than pools receiving everything, offering to every guilt-filled gaze of the throng: for you.

A vessel shaped by clean hands, cut into the soft tufa stone beneath the gate. Barely stone: warm hued, remembering its flow from the Alban crater. Stone like bread, honey colored, shot through with shattered bits: exploded magma in iridescent bits, fused basalt shards, chalked travertines crushed and folded and worried through and through the volcanic mud. The depression cut and shaped down and out, rhythmic scorings by iron making a deep depressed circle like a world. Lined with layers of finest softest clay siftings like young skin.

Within this bed the child is laid. With him, the beaker and the bowl. The ointments are poured: frankincense, myrrh. Above is fitted the cypress threshold. My body is safe.[6]

Like *Synthetic Earth*, *Palatine Burial* is a fabric "soil," a spreading geotextile reinforcing the soil and fostering new growth. *Palatine Burial* responded to a recent excavation in Rome in which traces were found of a baby that was sacrificed and buried beneath the ancient fortifications of the city. The project involved construction of a textile cover used for reburial of the archeological site. The sacrifice was for propitiation, protecting the boundary of the city. Making sacred. A mundus, a little world offered instead of the world around. Beneath the wall at the edge of the city, a pit was dug into the volcanic mudstone tufa, fitted to the clay dolium vessel enclosing the tiny body. Sifted linings filled in the spaces closing the void between the vessel and the stone. Tiny fragments of the burial remained: a brooch; a tooth. Laid bare. What material could be adequate for covering there?

Each link of the fabric net received special details. Inside was an anatomy of transparent vessels cushioned by sprung tenons and terminated by serrated hollow needles to puncture and drain. Toward the outside, angled crampons, bent back for springing and grasping, were set up with hair-trigger antennae. Around, there was a spread of open joints with outflung guides to catch and link with neighbors.

Each of these protozoan links was thin and meager, hut by linking and clumping together they made mass and thickness. At first a bare latticework controlled by the geometry of its elements then increasingly formless and growing darker as it ingested decomposing matter. Thicker and fertile, enveloping the wire implants and making a complete turf. This cover was finally dense, redolent with growth. And within that vital new earth, a convulsion glimmered—a poise telegraphing through from the sprung armature deep within.

IMPLICATION

The physical nets constructed in these projects are a class of geotextiles, structural materials developed to reinforce and sustain natural landscapes. Engineering fabric materials used for reinforcement of large-scale civic works are a common technology involved in shaping modern landscapes. The nets use physical detailing encouraging self-assembly, invoking pursuit of artificial life. These projects can be understood as an extension of an ordinary industrial practice.

At the same time, the projects tend to question boundaries of psyche. Their large-scale field structures offer immersion, an expansion rendering our physical bodies porous and offering wide-flung dispersal of identity. This might remind us of a long mystic tradition. A recent example from modern European culture could be the mid-century writing of Georges Bataille, pursuing ecstatic *alterity: ...I stood up, and I was completely taken...Only my legs—which kept me standing upright, connected what I had become to the floor—kept a link to what I had been: the rest was an inflamed gushing forth, overpowering, even free of its own convulsion. A character of dance and of decomposing agility...situated this flame "outside of me" And as everything mingles in a dance, so there was nothing which didn't go there to become consumed. I was thrown into this hearth, nothing remained of me but this hearth...*[7] In this passage Bataille finds dark space, a spiritual encounter experienced as annihilation of identity. This work shares common interests with early strains of psychoanalysis. In a passage presented to a surrealist circle in 1937, Bataille's associate Roger Caillois studied insect behavior as an analogy for a psychopathy of dissociated identity—specifically, the assimilation of insects into space through mimicry:

To these dispossessed souls, space seems to be a devouring force. Space pursues them, encircles them, digests them in a gigantic phagocytosis[8]*... It ends by replacing them. Then the body separates itself from thought, the individual breaks the boundary of his skin and occupies the other side of his sense. He tries to look at himself from any point whatever in space...And he invents spaces "the convulsive possession"....[T]his attraction by space, as elementary and mechanical as are tropisms, and by the effect of which life seems to lose ground, blurring in its retreat the frontier between the organism and the milieu and expanding to the same degree the limits within which, according to Pythagoras, we are allowed to know, as we should, that nature is everywhere the same.*[9] The "tropisms" that Caillois speaks of are primeval turning movements of living things, turning toward the light, turning toward nourishment. But in our turn towards dissociation there is a risk that life might "lose ground." Anxiety is latent in this pursuit. At the same time that subtle dimensions of anima are revealed, loss of ordinary identity seems inevitable.

This general context suggests that the projects illustrated here are romantic, sharing the same quest as intrepid spiritualists of the late nineteenth and early twentieth century. The purpose of these works is to open boundaries allowing nascent dimensions to emerge. The artificial nature of the pursuit lends poignancy, for while anima is treated in these works as a sacred quality it is also rendered as product of geometry and material synthesis. Artificial, alive.

Then Jacob rent his cloths...[10]

Notes

1. Matthew 27:51, NRSV.
2. *Haystack Veil*, Haystack Mountain School of Crafts, Maine 1997, collaboration with Warren Seelig and students: Judith Botzan, Sophie HammondHagman, Emily Harris, Mi-kyoung Lee, Dale McDowell, Kelli Phariss, Stephanie Ross, Michele Rubin, Kristine Woods. *Erratics Net*, Peggy's Cove, Nova

Scotia, 1998, with Caroline Munk of the University of Waterloo Faculty of Architecture and DalTech Faculty of Architecture students: Kelly Chow, Chris Ferguson, Nicola Grigg, Sandra Lee, Beth Lewis, Sunil Sarwal, Vicco Yip, Thomas Wright. *Palatine Burial*, Rome, 1996, under auspices of Prix de Rome in Architecture (Canada) *Synthetic Earth*, collaboration with Katherine Gray, Glass Architecture exhibition, Canadian Clay and Crafts Gallery, Kitchener, 1996/ Design Exchange, Toronto 1997.

3. Author's journal entry, Haystack Mountain School of Crafts, August 1997.

4. The gently bulging meniscus shape signals attraction and repulsion. It can relate to surface tension in drops of liquid, or tidal gravity in oceans.

5. South African domestic ritual maintaining kitchen hearth with bull's blood, related by Caroline Munk, Toronto, 1998.

6. Author's journal entry, Palatine, Rome, 1996, documenting propitiatory sacrifice at Porticus Margataria site identified as Porta Mugonia, c. 700 BCE.

7. IV. "Ecstasy," *Inner Experience*, Georges Bataille; trans. Leslie Anne Boldt, New York, 1988 [1943].

8. Some antibiotic cells consume intruders by phagocytosis, surrounding, engulfing and digesting them.

9. "Mimicry and Legendary Psychasthenia," Roger Caillois, trans. John Shepley, in *October: the First Decade,* Cambridge, 1987 [1937].

10. Genesis 37:24, NRSV.

18

'FABRICS IN SPACE' AND 'WEAVING AND INTERIOR DESIGN'
Voice-over for the video *Discussion of Material* (excerpt) (1930/2019)

Otti Berger/Judith Raum

EDITOR'S INTRODUCTION

The German artist Judith Raum studied fine art at the Städelschule, Academy of Fine Arts, Frankfurt/Main, Cooper Union School of Arts, New York City, and philosophy, psychoanalysis and art history at the Goethe-University of Frankfurt/Main. Her artistic practice combines installation, performance and video, recently with a focus on textiles and the women who designed and wove at the Bauhaus.

The text reprinted here is the voice-over script for Raum's four-part video work which accompanies her installation *Stoffbesprechung* or *Discussion of Material* from 2019. Raum explains that in this video 'different protagonists from the [Bauhaus] weaving workshop raise their voices [Lilly Reich, Gunta Stölzl, Otti Berger], giving a sense of the conflicting work ethics each of these artists stood for, especially after the National Socialists had taken over. Otti Berger, for example, criticizes Lilly Reich bitterly for her ongoing exhibition design for the Third Reich'.[1] Parts of the video script, such as the workshop arguement are fiction written by Raum based on historical records, while other parts make use of the original, now translated, words of the weavers.

The voice in this excerpt is based on Otti Berger's writing from 'Stoffe im Raum' (Fabrics in Space) and 'Weaving and Interior Design' (Weberei und Raumgestaltung) originally published in German circa 1930 with the Czech journal *RED* which considers the potential and purpose of fabric structures. Otti Berger is also the focus of T'ai Smith's text included in the touch section about the close-up photography used to capture the texture of woven cloth designed by Bauhaus weavers.

Otti Berger died in 1944 in Auschwitz concentration camp in Oświęcim, Poland at the age of 46.

Note

1. http://judithraum.net/discussion-of-material-stoffbesprechung-2019/. Accessed 27 October 2021.

'Fabrics in Space' and 'Weaving and Interior Design' Voice-over for the video *Discussion of Material*

Otti Berger/Judith Raum

. . . .

What is fabric anyway?

A fabric is not just an optical object.

We constantly come into contact with it.

Therefore, a fabric also has a 'grasp'.

What is fabric? A mesh of threads.

What is a weave?

The way of meshing threads.

Why different weaves?

To give the necessary tautness, softness or elasticity to the fabric,

depending on its function.

Why are different materials included in the fabric? To intensify these properties even more.

We investigate the relationship in the fabric between color and material, between color and structure, and we see that the possibilities for making fabric have no limits.

The first requirement is harmony between the various materials.

Harmony between: hard and soft, thick and thin, matt and glossy.

The next requirement is balance in the structure, in other words, the floating and crossing of the various threads, in relation to durability, elasticity and hygiene.

The third requirement is harmony of color.

A final important requirement is the overall balance: between purpose and structure and quality and color.

Unlimited possibilities open up for anyone who understands these relationships within fabrics. They know that not every material is suitable for every structure, not every color goes with every material.

Material changes through structure.

Color changes through material and structure.

Smooth structures reflect light, but rough structures almost suck up the light, forming shadows.

In this context, it is possible to speak of sculpting in fabric.

Fabric becomes a form of expression.

So why do we still need flowers, vines, ornaments? The fabric itself is alive.

You have to do more than understand the structure with your brain, you have to feel it with your subconscious.

Then you will know the particular quality of silk – which is warmth – and of rayon – which is cold.

Source: Otti Berger, 'Fabrics in Space' [Stoffe im Raum] and 'Weaving and Interior Design' [Weberei und Raumgestaltung], excerpts from video voice-over *Discussion of Material* by Judith Raum. Translation Judith Raum. Reproduced with permission.

Ouvrage: Knot a Not, Notes as Knots

Catherine de Zegher

Crisscrossing the Antivero river a single white thread joins rocks and stones under and over the clear water. In this remote place, high up in the Chilean Andes, Cecilia Vicuña—an artist and a poet—is tracing the fragrance of the *ñipa* leaves and tying one verdant side of the river to the other with cord. Flexible, straight, and light, the line that she draws is a visible act. When suddenly two boys come up the river, jumping from stone to stone, they watch her carefully dropping lines inside the water. Without saying a word they slowly approach closer and closer in the trails threaded by her hands. While Vicuña is securing the yarn as into a warp—the loom of the Antivero: the river is the warp, the crossing threads are the weft—their curiosity turns into interest. Sitting on a rock they observe her gestures/signs and finally ask her what it is. When she returns them the question, the boys reply that they do not know, but that they would like very much to get the string. With a laugh Vicuña grants their request and immediately they start to untie all the rocks and plants, gradually dissolving the spatialized drawing or geometric pattern of woven lines into the current.

A DRAWN GAME

To the boys the line is a valuable length of cord used with or without a rod for catching fish. To Vicuña, the line—as a cord and as a single row of words in a poem—is a trail of communication, and the gift is the completion of the circle, in which the process of forming through disappearance is taken up again in the flow of events. Perhaps to some the line is a contour of an overtly romantic and idealistic story about "nomad space," because it blurs the borderline between the "real" and the "imaginary," between art and life—the object consumed in the act; because it circumscribes

and "protects" the mountain water as a source of life before contamination; because it alludes to joy, play and ramble; because it refers to the whole meaning in the action—even more, to the perpetual motion of "doing" and "undoing" in weaving as in language; and because it recovers in a distant past our sensory memory of a children's game at school: "cat's cradle."

Played by two or more persons, cat's cradle is a game of making geometrical string figures, looped over the fingers and stretched between the two hands. The figures change as the string is passed from one person to another. Of the games people play string figures enjoy the reputation of having been the most widespread form of amusement in the world. Over two-thousand individual patterns have been recorded worldwide since 1888, when anthropologist Franz Boas first described a pair of Eskimo string figures.[1] "The popularity of string figures derived from the novelty of being able to construct highly complex designs instantaneously in a reproducible fashion using readily available materials such as plant fibers, leather thongs, or even plaited human hair."[2] Moreover, hundreds of individual patterns can be generated from the same loop of string. Unfortunately, string figures disappeared rapidly in regions heavily influenced by European culture. Often missionaries discouraged the making of string figures because of their frequent association with pagan myths or depiction of sexual acts.[3]

As if speaking and listening to each other with the fingers alternately restricted and free, the players seek not only to take over the string, but also to recast the pattern without losing the thread. Drawing patterns of construction/dissolution, cat's cradle is a play of beginnings, an interplay between the new and the customary without which a beginning cannot take

Source: Catherine de Zegher, 'Ouvrage: Knot a Not, Notes as Knots', *The Precarious: The Art and Poetry of Cecilia Vicuña* © 1997 by Cecilia Vicuña and Kanaal Art Foundation. Published by Wesleyan University Press and reprinted with permission.

'Fabrics in Space' and 'Weaving and Interior Design' Voice-over for the video *Discussion of Material*

Otti Berger/Judith Raum

. . . .

What is fabric anyway?

A fabric is not just an optical object.

We constantly come into contact with it.

Therefore, a fabric also has a 'grasp'.

What is fabric? A mesh of threads.

What is a weave?

The way of meshing threads.

Why different weaves?

To give the necessary tautness, softness or elasticity to the fabric,

depending on its function.

Why are different materials included in the fabric? To intensify these properties even more.

We investigate the relationship in the fabric between color and material, between color and structure, and we see that the possibilities for making fabric have no limits.

The first requirement is harmony between the various materials.

Harmony between: hard and soft, thick and thin, matt and glossy.

The next requirement is balance in the structure, in other words, the floating and crossing of the various threads, in relation to durability, elasticity and hygiene.

The third requirement is harmony of color.

A final important requirement is the overall balance: between purpose and structure and quality and color.

Unlimited possibilities open up for anyone who understands these relationships within fabrics. They know that not every material is suitable for every structure, not every color goes with every material.

Material changes through structure.

Color changes through material and structure.

Smooth structures reflect light, but rough structures almost suck up the light, forming shadows.

In this context, it is possible to speak of sculpting in fabric.

Fabric becomes a form of expression.

So why do we still need flowers, vines, ornaments? The fabric itself is alive.

You have to do more than understand the structure with your brain, you have to feel it with your subconscious.

Then you will know the particular quality of silk – which is warmth – and of rayon – which is cold.

Source: Otti Berger, 'Fabrics in Space' [Stoffe im Raum] and 'Weaving and Interior Design' [Weberei und Raumgestaltung], excerpts from video voice-over *Discussion of Material* by Judith Raum. Translation Judith Raum. Reproduced with permission.

You can grasp the rawness of hemp or wool.

We don't want pictures, we want to come to the best possible, definitive, living fabric!

Now fabric in space!

This is a functional fabric and so we must ask about its function

and then about its arrangement: whether stretched out, hanging or laid flat.

The curtain material must be tested for its level of translucency or opacity.

Should it simply diffuse the sunlight,

protecting us from it or should it even darken the room?

A curtain material must fall softly, it should be yielding when we grasp it, it is pushed to one side.

The function of a wall covering is to protect the wall, insulate against heat or cold, perhaps increase the light.

First of all, it must appear to be stretched taut and must be hygienic, ideally washable.

Furniture fabric must be close-knit and impermeable, because it is subject to heavy use.

Otti Berger circa 1930 / Judith Raum 2019

19

OUVRAGE
Knot a Not, Notes as Knots (1997)

Catherine de Zegher

EDITOR'S INTRODUCTION

Catherine de Zegher is a curator and writer. In 1997 she edited *The Precarious: The Art and Poetry of Cecilia Vicuña*, which includes her essay reprinted in full here. De Zegher's extensive discussion of artist and poet Cecilia Vicuña's experimental practice likens the structure of the textile to the structure of text. Vicuña's ephemeral installations have been created since 1966 in what she describes as an effort in 'hearing an ancient silence waiting to be heard'. These fleeting explorations of space often make use of textile materials and adopt expanded, temporary textile structures.

The examples of Vicuña's early work, which de Zegher considers in this essay, are all provisional and defined to a large extent by the political instability of the artist's Chilean homeland. 'Her art is Andean, it is not *about* Andean art,' de Zegher differentiates. De Zegher maps early reference points in Vicuña's work, including the German artist Kurt Schwitters, but also earlier in the Brazilian Neoconcrete group. She refers to Deleuze and Guattari's concepts of smooth and striated space, writing that is also included as an excerpt in this section about structure.

Vicuña's work *Momio* (London, 1973) is shown on the cover of Julia Bryan-Wilson's book *FRAY: Art and Textile Politics* (2017), found in the politics section of this book. Vicuña's recent exhibitions include *Spin Spin Triangulene* at the Guggenheim (2022), *Read Thread: The Story of the Red Thread* shown at Documenta 14, Athens and Kassel (2017) and the 18th Biennale of Sydney (2012) where Catherine de Zegher was Joint Artistic Director, with Gerald McMaster. De Zegher published an anthology of her essays about women artists titled *Women's Work Is Never Done* (2014). Cecilia Vicuña is also a political activist.

Ouvrage: Knot a Not, Notes as Knots

Catherine de Zegher

Crisscrossing the Antivero river a single white thread joins rocks and stones under and over the clear water. In this remote place, high up in the Chilean Andes, Cecilia Vicuña—an artist and a poet—is tracing the fragrance of the *ñipa* leaves and tying one verdant side of the river to the other with cord. Flexible, straight, and light, the line that she draws is a visible act. When suddenly two boys come up the river, jumping from stone to stone, they watch her carefully dropping lines inside the water. Without saying a word they slowly approach closer and closer in the trails threaded by her hands. While Vicuña is securing the yarn as into a warp—the loom of the Antivero: the river is the warp, the crossing threads are the weft—their curiosity turns into interest. Sitting on a rock they observe her gestures/signs and finally ask her what it is. When she returns them the question, the boys reply that they do not know, but that they would like very much to get the string. With a laugh Vicuña grants their request and immediately they start to untie all the rocks and plants, gradually dissolving the spatialized drawing or geometric pattern of woven lines into the current.

A DRAWN GAME

To the boys the line is a valuable length of cord used with or without a rod for catching fish. To Vicuña, the line—as a cord and as a single row of words in a poem—is a trail of communication, and the gift is the completion of the circle, in which the process of forming through disappearance is taken up again in the flow of events. Perhaps to some the line is a contour of an overtly romantic and idealistic story about "nomad space," because it blurs the borderline between the "real" and the "imaginary," between art and life—the object consumed in the act; because it circumscribes and "protects" the mountain water as a source of life before contamination; because it alludes to joy, play and ramble; because it refers to the whole meaning in the action—even more, to the perpetual motion of "doing" and "undoing" in weaving as in language; and because it recovers in a distant past our sensory memory of a children's game at school: "cat's cradle."

Played by two or more persons, cat's cradle is a game of making geometrical string figures, looped over the fingers and stretched between the two hands. The figures change as the string is passed from one person to another. Of the games people play string figures enjoy the reputation of having been the most widespread form of amusement in the world. Over two-thousand individual patterns have been recorded worldwide since 1888, when anthropologist Franz Boas first described a pair of Eskimo string figures.[1] "The popularity of string figures derived from the novelty of being able to construct highly complex designs instantaneously in a reproducible fashion using readily available materials such as plant fibers, leather thongs, or even plaited human hair."[2] Moreover, hundreds of individual patterns can be generated from the same loop of string. Unfortunately, string figures disappeared rapidly in regions heavily influenced by European culture. Often missionaries discouraged the making of string figures because of their frequent association with pagan myths or depiction of sexual acts.[3]

As if speaking and listening to each other with the fingers alternately restricted and free, the players seek not only to take over the string, but also to recast the pattern without losing the thread. Drawing patterns of construction/dissolution, cat's cradle is a play of beginnings, an interplay between the new and the customary without which a beginning cannot take

Source: Catherine de Zegher, 'Ouvrage: Knot a Not, Notes as Knots', *The Precarious: The Art and Poetry of Cecilia Vicuña* © 1997 by Cecilia Vicuña and Kanaal Art Foundation. Published by Wesleyan University Press and reprinted with permission.

place: an "inter-text." Similarly, in Vicuña's work *Antivero* (1981), the two rocky banks of the river can be considered two hands, where the intertwined thread seems to function as the cradle and the communication, as the "nest" and the "text." Etymologically "nest" derives from "net,"[4] an open-meshed fabric of cord, hair, or twine used for protecting, confining or carrying. A meshwork relates to a framework of interwoven flexible sticks and twigs used to make walls, fences, and roofs in which to rear the young. To give birth and to protect the lineage, women needed to weave nests into wattle-and-daub shelters.

A POINT BETWEEN LINES

Although we can no longer recapture details of prehistoric women's lives, it seems that weaving has always been associated with caring: child care and food preparation. In *Note on the Division of Labor by Sex* Judith Brown states that whether or not the community relies upon women as the chief providers of a given type of labor depends upon "the compatibility of this pursuit with the demands of child care."[5] This is particularly the case for the crafts of spinning, weaving, and sewing: "repetitive, easy to pick up at any point, reasonably child-safe, and easily done at home."[6] Still, Brown notes "that this particular division of labor revolves around *reliance*, not around *ability*, within a community in which specialization was desirable." Being perishable, the textiles themselves at best only provide fragmentary evidence about women's lives, but materials and metaphors of weaving do inform, since they permeate both: childbearing and food. "Weaving (resulting in cloth) and parturition[7] (resulting in babies) both display women's generative capability. Tzutujil Maya use anatomical terms for loom parts (i.e., head, bottom, ribs, heart, umbilical cord), indicating that weaving is considered equivalent to giving birth. Midwives in Santiago Atitlán bind a pregnant woman's belly with the long hair ribbons that Atiteco women wind around their heads. These mimetically regulate the uterus's snake-like coils to correctly position the baby for delivery. In Chenalho, fine *huipiles*[8] are thrown into the nearby lake when women dream that the Virgin Mary needs this nourishment."[9] According

to Vicuña, caring and weaving fuse in naming: to care, to carry, to bear children, to bear a name.[10]

In South America the name *Quechua* synthesizes well this relation between text, textile, and the notion of survival in collaboration. The word designates a member of a group of Inca tribes and also the language of these tribes, still spoken among 4,000,000 Indians of Peru, Ecuador, Bolivia, and Argentina. Etymologically *Quechua* not only means the twine of two (or more) strands twisted together, but also the interlacement of two persons copulating. Significantly, in the Andes the more meanings (double, triple . . .) a word has, the higher its value in the hierarchy of words: it belongs then to the *Hatunsimi*,[11] which means "important language." Vicuña points out that language is inherited from the dead and yet again and again it is "recovered"— meaning to regain control, to repossess, to create again, or to conceal again—by the living. So words are simultaneously old and new. Their universe is "version"—in the sense of transformation—and version indicates passage, direction, action, movement.

Still, in a recent thread piece, *La bodega negra* (Barn Yarn, 1994), which was made in an old barn in the region of Vicuña's childhood near San Fernando (Chile), it is clear that the "directional" remains an important issue of her work. When the artist catches the intense sunrays inside the dilapidated barn piercing the roofholes and producing starlike points on the stone walls, earthen floor, plough share, harrow, sacks, crops, and fodder, once again dispersal and inversion take place. Dazzled when entering the barn, the viewer experiences the exterior brightness of the day turning into the interior obscurity of the night. As blind spots the constellations are cast down to earth. On her arm Vicuña is seizing a (circular) point, another one, and another, and one more: the Southern Cross. She has fastened across the space, from stones in the wall to stones on the floor, threads that, as the extension of her body, momentarily hold the suspending light. In the desire to map, this microcosmos provides protection and offers "abstracted points of identification with the human body."[12] As Henri Michaux writes in *Beginnings*: "Hands off in the distance, still farther off, as far away as possible, stiff, outspread fingers, at the self's outer limits, fingers . . . Surface without mass, a simple thread encompassing a void-being, a bodiless body."[13] Later in the evening, inversely, when the sun is setting and the angle of light is changing, the stars in the barn disappear in the twilight to reappear in the night sky. "Space is now time ceaselessly metamorphosed through action."[14]

Besides the use of roof holes by the French Revolutionary architect Etienne-Louis Boullée in his domed Cenotaph dedicated to Newton, another more recent example comes to mind in the *Sun Tunnels* of Nancy Holt. During the early seventies Nancy Holt concentrated on urban or landscape spaces as seen through holes in tunnels, pipes, and other devices that made the viewer consider both outside and inside, perceptual and physiological sensations.[15] The difference is that the tubular conduits were perforated on purpose as well as oriented in a very specific area by the artist. If land art claims to be concerned with nature as the incontestable provider of ideas and with light as the constitutive element in art and architecture, Vicuña's work introduces a different way of marking, one that addresses nature and (agri)culture in a dialogic way. *La bodega negra* is responding to a sign, it is not imposing a mark. Being a "non-site" piece, it is not about appearance, but about disappearance.

ODDS AND ENDS

Considering the linguistic relation of text, textile, and architecture, it seems appropriate to introduce the French word *ouvrage* to describe Vicuña's art practice as an open-ended work, an ongoing practice with links to writing, weaving, and constructing. Since January 1966, when Cecilia Vicuña made her first outdoor piece *Con-cón* on the beach at the junction of two waters, the Aconcagua River and the Pacific Ocean in Chile, she has examined transience and has named her work "*precario*." "Precarious is what is obtained by prayer. Uncertain, exposed to hazards, insecure. From the Latin *precarius*, from *precis*, prayer."[16] "Prayer" understood not as a request, but as a response, is a dialogue or a speech that addresses what is (physically) "there" as well as what is "not there," the place as well as the "no place," the site as well as the "non-site." Prayer is dialogue as a form of transition from what is to what could be. "Sacrifice" is an act-made-sacred and

transcendent by the awareness that this act is not only physical but retains another dimension and thus has a double meaning, is ambiguous. Vicuña quotes from a Vedic text: "the first sacrifice is 'seeing,' because the act of seeing is a response." The root of the word *respond* is "to dedicate again," to receive something and to donate it back. More or less about the same time, Lygia Clark was writing: "Art is not bourgeois mystification. What has changed is the form of communicating the proposition. It's you who now give expression to my thoughts, to draw from them whatever vital experience you want . . . This feeling of totality captured within the act should be encountered with joy, in order to learn how to live on the ground of precariousness. This feeling of the precarious must be absorbed for one to discover in the immanence of the act the meaning of existence."[17]

Born of contemplation and made of refuse, Vicuña's earth works are an answer to the land and the sun, to the lost feathers and accumulated objects. Many times she has used a stick to comb the beach into lines, circles, and spirals. Gathering flotsam and jetsam, she recognizes the inherent value of discarded materials that are lying down, and stands them up. Her desire to order things is a kind of response to their language: garbage/language, in the sense that garbage has a signifying potential and impulse that give new tension to the signifier. But whatever order she has created,[18] the wind scatters it, and long waves rolling up onto the sand—also called beachcombers—erase her work *Con-cón* at high tide. Thus, since the mid-1960s Vicuña has been producing *precarios*, which consist of small, multicolored assemblages of found materials such as fragments of driftwood, feathers, stones, lumps of shredded plastic, herbs, thin sticks, electric wire, shells, bones, and thread. Each piece is composed in such a way that every material holds another in balance. And, although not featuring any symmetry, each whole structure stands up in a fragile state of suspended equilibrium. Vicuña says of her *basuritas*: "'We are made of throwaways and we will be thrown away,' say the objects. Twice precarious they come from prayer and predict their own destruction. Precarious in history they will leave no trace. The history of art written in the North includes nothing of the South. Thus they speak in prayer, precariously."

Read in comparison with the land art of Nancy Holt or Richard Long, Cecilia Vicuña's earth works differ not only in their relationship to the environment and the body, but also in their diffusion of knowledge. In contradistinction to Vicuña's perception, these artists have staged a landscape for the viewer to colonize in order to aggrandize the self and to summon awe for the sublime Other, as a reason for obliterating it.[19] "In Richard Long's work the body is absent, though implied there is in fact a disembodied consciousness, a romantic primitivist fantasy of virgin nature projected no matter where in the world by an observing eye enjoying a sovereign isolation: residues of the colonial mind-set."[20] Again, in the case of Vicuña, the earth work is not about appearance, but about disappearance. And in Chile the *desaparecidos* (the disappeared ones) of the Junta during the seventies have a body.[21] For this reason Vicuña drew, on her first return from exile to Chile, the work *Tunquen* (1981) on the sand with colors of pigment featuring the encounter of sun and bone, life and death.[22]

BY NAME

From 1966 to 1972 Cecilia Vicuña often practiced her work in the streets of Santiago de Chile, where she created various unannounced performances and events. In 1971 she had her first solo exhibition at the National Museum of Fine Arts in Santiago with the work *Otoño* (Autumn), for which she filled the main room with autumn leaves three feet deep. In 1972 she traveled to London with a fellowship for postgraduate study at the Slade School of Fine Arts; in 1973 she had an exhibition at the Institute of Contemporary Art. When the military coup occurred in 1973 and President Allende died, Vicuña decided not to return to her country and remained in exile in Great Britain. She became a political activist and founded, together with Guy Brett, David Medalla, and John Dugger, the organization Artists for Democracy to oppose the military dictatorship in Chile. The ideas formulated by Artists for Democracy were linked to Vicuña's first revolutionary group action in 1967: the formation of the Tribu No (the No Tribe), which issued manifestos and staged public interventions. Having read the creationist manifestos of Huidobro, the futurists, and the surrealists, she believed that the only contribution of the inhabitants of the Southern Hemisphere in the second part of the twentieth century was to say "no," as proclaimed in the "No-manifesto," which circulated as a manuscript from hand to hand (Santiago de Chile, 1967). The "No-manifesto" was attended with actions such as installing the Banco de Ideas (for Allende), putting the question of "what is poetry to you?" over the telephone, circulating "circular" letters, composing a dictionary of *piropos e insultos* (sexist words and insults) and an *enclocepedia del asco* (encyclopedia of disgust). At the same time the art, poetry, and music of Violeta Parra have greatly influenced Vicuña's ideas. Violeta Parra (1917–67) was a Chilean peasant woman, whose research on the weaving, oral poetry, and music of Chile, as well as her own work, formed the foundations of the movement called La Nueva Cancion Chilena. Political and contemporary in its focus, it retained at the same time the ancient mestizo rhythms of traditional music and electrified all of South America.

Confronted with a sense of loss and isolation, Cecilia Vicuña left London in 1975 and returned to South America. She went to Bogota, where for several months she continued to make banners and sets for revolutionary theater companies such as Teatro La Candelaria. She lectured throughout Colombia about the "Chilean Struggle for Liberation," made a film at a bus stop near a *fabrica de santitos*, and made a living reading successfully her own "erotic" poetry. During this period, Vicuña stunned people with her performance of a spilled glass of milk, *Vaso de leche* (Glass of Milk, 1979). When it was estimated that every year 1,920 children in Bogota died from drinking contaminated milk produced in Colombia, and the government neither prosecuted the distributors nor took any action to stop the "milk crime," Vicuña decided to announce and perform the spilling of a glass of milk in front of a government building under a blue sky. She attached a short cord around the glass of milk, pulled it over, and thus "the poem was written on the pavement." About this performance Leon Golub once said that it was the most efficacious political work: inversely proportional to its small size and precarious content, the act had a powerful and complex impact.

In Vicuña's artistic practice, and particularly as it relates to political protest, the investigation of language and the politics of definition are always at stake, because for her "naming" is the most political act of all. *Arte precario* is the name she gives to her independent voice within the Southern Hemisphere, challenging her colonized position. Her art is Andean, it is not *about* Andean art. It belongs to this urban mestizo culture and not to the Western purist version of it appropriating "the little lama." Her work concerns *la batalla de los significados* (the battle of the signifieds). According to Vicuña, submission and poverty begin with the acceptance of definitions that others create for you. When one general designation of "indian"—at first a mistaken definition by the *conquistadores*—covered the othering of all tribes, the massacre of the native populations of the Americas was made possible. Recognition needs a name, one's own name.

NOTES AS SNOT

Small objects, much like Vicuña's *precarios*, consisting of branches and cords, as well as string figures, have appeared in many cultures as depictions of the natural environment, the material culture (tools, food, clothing sources, food gathering, and other daily activities), interpersonal relationships, legends . . .[23] Oftentimes chants and stories were recited as a string figure was displayed. Kathleen Haddon suggests that string figures merely served as a ready means of illustration for the objects or beings portrayed in the accompanying legend. The illustration was readily prepared in the absence of drawing materials, was highly reproducible, and was not dependent on the maker's artistic ability.[24] Being a sort of cultural archive, a repository for beliefs and observations deemed worthy of preserving, the objects and the stories attached to them served not only to locate people with reference to the constellation of celestial objects but also within a kinship system. Claude Lévi-Strauss states that "like phonemes, kinship terms are elements of meaning; like phonemes, they acquire meaning only if they are integrated into systems. 'Kinship systems', like 'phonemic systems', are built by the mind on the level of unconscious thought."[25]

Key elements in Vicuña's work are: *star* and *stone*, *warp* and *word*, which she defines as points of exact observation (i.e., a tall stone—for example a menhir—in a vast area indicates a fixed place from which to observe the earth and the sky; a constellation indicates a reference in the universe; etc.) constructed within models outside the self such as: constellations, weavings, and language. Moreover, although these "structured sets" or models are permanent and account for various aspects of empirical social reality, they possess an inner movement (i.e., the celestial course, the weaving grid, the alphabet), and thus call forth responses from the viewer/reader. A warp is many threads, a word is many sounds, many ideas.[26] The strangeness or otherness of the self occurs as soon as it is constructed, that is, as soon as it is symbolized; thus these structures, simultaneously constitutive and alien, are vehicles to define the self—and are thus a means of empowerment.

Any act of symbolization is both a loss and a formation of the self and its reality and should therefore remain a coming-into-language, a continuous process of defining, open to shifts in its mapping. Star, stone, warp, word: each of these points gives rise to inner movement and ambiguity and should be used only as a reference for movement within the unlimited. Motion avoids the petrifying effect implicit in the fixed gaze. Everything in Vicuña's work is about connecting, weaving, studying the relations of lines to points and references. However, once these points and references are fixed, "immovability within movement is created and along with it the Illusion of Order and Time." Cecilia Vicuña writes in May 1973:

In thinking of the form for which I am looking I can't help but find other forms for things outside my paintings, for any search must associate and connect with the search for a social way. If not, it is a castrated search, an apolitical occupation good for nothing, or good to help maintain the present structures which have been established for the benefit of the few and the destruction of the rest. But now these structures must be established taking into consideration facts other than profit or power. It will be possible to simplify these facts to these three categories: the way in and out of air, of food, of semen in the body.[27]

In this sense Vicuña proclaims "laws" as necessary, but movable and directional, written for the benefit of what goes in and out of the body: breath, snot, semen, urine, excrement, babies.

STAR, STONE, STOMACH

Vicuña's working field consists of the exploration of the symbolic function of weaving and language, stressing the fundamental place of textiles in the Andean system of knowledge. Affirming a basic congruence among the realms of writing, agriculture and weaving, the opening lines of the Popol Vuh (the Quiché Maya's ancient sacred text) have two possible translations: "This is the beginning of the Ancient Word, here in this place called Quiché. Here we shall inscribe, we shall implant the Ancient Word"; or "Here we shall design, we shall brocade the Ancient Word."[28] This multivocal translation suggests that the Maya recognize these three realms as diverse yet congruent paths of knowledge. The concept of intertextuality, linking the arts of music, weaving, oratory, architecture, and agriculture, gives insight into the permeability of the boundaries between different domains of knowledge.[29] If it seems, as Claude Lévi-Strauss writes, that the unconscious activity of the mind consists in imposing forms upon content, and if these forms are fundamentally the same for all minds—ancient and modern, primitive and civilized (as the study of the symbolic function, expressed in language, so strikingly indicates)—then a single structural scheme exists behind the chaos of rules and customs and operates in different spatial and temporal contexts.[30] Grasping in word and thread— *palabra e hilo*— the unconscious structure underlying each social institution, Cecilia Vicuña offers a principle of interpretation accurate for other institutions or systems of representation. I return to the issue of this rather totalizing thought and address the problem of it further on.

Most valued and respected products in Andean culture are textiles,[31] which construct and carry or, rather, *are* meaning and identification. Technically, a woven fabric consists of two elements with different functions: the fixed vertical threads (warp) and the mobile horizontal threads (weft or woof), which intersect the fixed threads perpendicularly and pass above them. Stake and thread, warp and woof have been analyzed in basketry and weaving as figures of "supple solids."[32] Determined by the loom (the frame of the warp), the textile can be infinite in length but not in width, where it is closed by a back and forth motion. Warp-patterned weaving, characteristic of all remaining Andean weaving today, was slow to be recognized as having value for studies of gender, social identity, economic networks, and modernization. As a strong indicator of cultural patterns—what the Maya of Mexico and Guatemala call *costumbre*—textile has communicative, but also poetic, economic, ritual, and political power. Weaving is meaning in multiple ways.

WORD AND THREAD

Compared to the privileged status given to painting, sculpture, and architecture, textile arts have been virtually ignored. Following the Bauhaus, the distinction and interrelationship of design and art were greatly elaborated in the work of Anni Albers. She overcame "two fallacious premises: that designing and making art are conflicting occupations; and that work in the fiber medium is categorically craft and not art."[33] Exploring the randomness of a discarded string in *Knot II* (1947), Albers said that, "although it is small, each thread seems charged with uninterrupted energy: the underlying units twine and intertwine with nonstop vitality, as if to say that they exist singly but also as part of something greater."[34] Working with material "is a listening for the dictation of the material and a taking in of the laws of harmony. It is for this reason that we can find certitude in the belief that we are taking part in an eternal order." Albers also came to appreciate the challenge of the discipline of weaving. Unlike painting, which allowed limitless freedom, the inherent properties of textiles (its tactile qualities, material combinations, and so forth) and the specific laws of their production (the grid) provided a framework that Albers found stimulating rather than restrictive.[35]

In the late 1920s and 1930s, Anni Albers introduced cellophane and other synthetics, as well as plastic and metallic threads that added luster and color to her weavings but were also light reflective and dust and water repellent. Taking these materials further than anyone else at that time, as Mary Jane Jacobs argues, Albers also revived long-forgotten methods, particularly those used in Peruvian textiles, which she studied and collected. The ancient Peruvians employed almost all known hand methods and their work constitutes perhaps the richest body of textile art by any culture in the world. Albers praised the Peruvians' adventurous use of threads and commented on their "surprising and ingenious ways of varying in inventiveness from piece to piece."[36] Mostly overlooked by the artworld, Andean textile arts also eloquently express transmutation of culture, women's concerns with indigenous and nonindigenous traditions, and intercultural exchanges. Cecilia Vicuña, using thread and cloth as her main medium, proposes weaving as a form of participation issuing from popular culture, but she has always perceived and understood weaving as an alternative discourse and a dynamic model of resistance (as do most indigenous Latin American women). Janet Catherine Berlo points out "that all of the cultural cross-currents and overlaps in textile art of Latin America are not, however, simply a 'making do'. They are not merely a passive, defensive response to five centuries of colonialism." In "Beyond Bricolage" she argues that "the improvisations and appropriations in women's textiles are deliberate and sometimes culturally subversive." Although world-famous as tourist items, their fabrics are signs of renewal, of new forms and topical themes, coming directly from the people. Although both women and textiles are crucial to the study of postcolonial representation, Western biases have until recently viewed women's textiles as 'sub-Primitive' art.

Using examples from two groups, the Kuna and the Maya, Janet Catherine Berlo shows that:

> ... cloth makes manifest deeply held cultural values that may otherwise be imperceptible. In fact, it may be women's very crucial job to translate these ephemeral values into material objects. In a number of Amerindian societies, men's arts are oral while women's are, literally, material: men speak, women make cloth. Hierarchical codes within our own word-obsessed culture dictate that the public, the verbal, is the area of status, autonomy, importance.

But this is not so clear within the indigenous systems. The most clear-cut dichotomy between the expressive roles of men and those of women occurs among the Kuna Indians of Panama.[37] Two types of communal gatherings, or *congresos*, are a vital part of Kuna life. At secular gatherings men gain status and prestige through public displays of their verbal fluency. Only the most eloquent men rise to positions as village chiefs who conduct sacred gatherings attended by both men and women. In this forum, chiefs display their consummate verbal skills through chanted dialogues that cover sacred history, politics, and a host of traditions. The Kuna sacred gathering encapsulates the aesthetic ideals of the Kuna universe: the chiefs, arrayed at the center of the gathering house, engage in verbal discourse. They are surrounded by rows of women, dressed in their finest garments, who work on textiles while the chiefs chant. Around the outside of the circle, sit the rest of the men.[38]

Mary W. Helms observes that "by long and arduous hours of *mola*[39] production, by the display created by *mola* wearing, and perhaps in the symbolism contained in *mola* designs, they assist the community in the furtherance of these ends by creating a form of 'silent oratory' that publicly expresses, with form and vibrant color, the same views of the 'world-as-event' and the same concepts of group cohesion and morality as are proclaimed by the spoken oratory of the men."[40] There is some evidence that a similar pattern of men's verbal and women's visual modes of expression occurs among the highland Maya. Male members of the native religious hierarchy use a style of speech in which repetition, metaphor, and patterns of parallel syntax are common. The fine nuances, repetitions, and rhythmic yet asymmetrical color and design patterns characteristic of Maya women's backstrap-loomed textiles serve in the female arena as the equivalent of Maya men's complex verbal play.[41] In her performances, Vicuña speaks while she weaves, and weaves while she sings.

MISTRESSES OF THE NEEDLE[42]

It seems that even in an excluding patriarchal culture, spaces of intervention exist where suppressed voices not only articulate their experiences and self-defined positions, but where they also express their participation in culture as active agents of transformation. The techniques of weaving allow a mobility of doing and undoing within the accumulative medium of textiles (adding brocade, embroidery, trim, and appliqué), thus increasing the meaning, power, value, and visual display. Women in Latin America transform alien objects, influences, materials, and ideas in purposeful collages, as they adapt multivocal aesthetics to indigenous culture. From this point of view textiles can be read as active texts that play out the ongoing intercultural dialogue of self-determination and cultural hegemony, as well as the dialogue of exchange between conservatism and innovation, continuity and transmutation.[43] In the material realm, Latin American women confront otherness—whether as a result of remoteness of time (colonialism) or remoteness of space (first world)—by creating a vision of indigenous culture that balances both and at the same time demonstrates its durability through the strength and vitality of their fabric. "This is a subversive act for it co-opts the hegemonic tradition that views the third world as a dumping ground for its products."[44]

Considering the work of Cecilia Vicuña, it becomes clear how actively she participates in defining culture and the social fabric of language by disrupting the grammar imposed by figures of authority and by recovering the texture of communication. Vicuña's strategies of purposeful improvisation, thoughtful linguistics, and accumulation allow her to express a multilevelled and referential body of meanings and to display this in numerous spheres of action. During the sixties, when she daily rode buses in the capital of Santiago, she decided to wear a different woven invention as a multicolored glove over her hand every day. For weeks she manufactured many types of sometimes funny gloves in all colors and forms. As an operator of signs, she wanted these handfuls of threads to function as a surprise, new— "as art"—each time she took the bus and raised her hand to reach for a hand grip. Her use of the body as a material for performance art inscribed itself in the city and its human movements. For both the artist and the "person in society" a liberating force was implicated in the awakening of each of one's gestures. Turning the familiar material (a glove) and daily gesture (reaching for the handgrip) into a question mark, she exposed the passengers' quiescent habits and tried to intensify the desire and capacity to reformulate models of signification.

Vicuña's bus performance, *El guante* (The Glove), was prompted by the necessity to restructure the language of creativity, so that the artwork could remain a means of opposing authority (be it military or multinational) and its concepts of meaning. Art here was a tool to retain independence and to nourish resistance. On the one hand, her action seems to relate to the earlier dissatisfaction of rebellious young poets, writers, and painters in South America—such as Violeta Parra, Jorge Luis Borges, Xul Solar, and the manifesto-issuing *vanguardistas*[45]—with the prevailing norm of Spanish literary language as a system of repressive and deadening constraints. For them, "a model of a perpetually reinvented language, constantly shifting to accommodate new concepts and information, was close at hand—again, in the streets of Buenos Aires, where Argentines daily enriched the staid speech of Castille with Italianisms, fragments of German and English, and their own surprising coinages."[46] On the other hand, Vicuña's glove performance seems to retrace an ancient Mapuche practice in Chile, where an old myth tells that the Mapuche women learned how to weave from observing spiders at work and from contemplating their cobwebs (both nests and traps). When a baby girl is born, mothers walk out to catch a spider and let it walk on the baby's hand: the movements of the spider will stick to her hands, and the spider will teach her.

EL MIRAR CRUZADO[47]

More recently, in 1994, two outdoor works in Chile reframe Vicuña's concern with crossing the boundaries that separate the individual and the collective, the private and the public, the local and the global, the "smooth" and the "striated," the "nomad space" and the "sedentary space."[48] For *Hilo en el cerro* (Thread in the Ridge) at Cerro Santa Lucia in the public park, the trysting place of lovers and others in the center of Santiago, she wove with a ball of red yarn spun in the house of a Mapuche woman. Was she using the thread in order to find her way out of the labyrinthine garden, or to enweb the little mountain? Does the red string indicate the solution of a problem or does it entail a question? Her *12 Hilos en un corral* (The Corral Grid) was made in the corral of a farm in the mountains near San Fernando. The corral is a trapezoidal space created by stone walls (*una pirka*) for the mestizo purpose of domesticating horses. Always falling apart, the *pirka* is periodically repaired with new stones, which are added to the ancient ones in an ongoing process. Inside the irregular corral, Vicuña's woven striation was suspended in midair at wall height. Emphasizing the

spatial "imperfection" of the corral, the weaving is an open work for the viewer to enter, by sliding one's head in to look at it. Essential in both weavings is the crossing of threads, the crossing of straightened lines at right angles, the intercrossing of opposed forces, the intertexture. Vicuña's art exists at the *crux*, where fertility sprouts and change or transformation happens through the encounter. However, while the former weaving consists of her usual unrolled woolen lines revealing an optional trajectory between trees and flowers, local linkages between parts, and multiple orientation or constant change indirection, the latter weaving represents a most regular grid structure.

In principle, a fabric has a certain number of characteristics that define it as a striated space. However, it seems that this conventional view of weaving should be suspended so as to observe some specific processes. For example, felt is a supple, solid material that has an altogether different effect; it is "an antifabric." Since it involves no separation of threads, no intertwining, but is only an entanglement of fibers obtained by fulling, it constitutes a smooth space.[49] Like paper, felt uses a matrix without entering it. But, according to Gilles Deleuze and Félix Guattari, striated space is not simply opposed to or different from smooth space. Although there is a distinction between the two, in fact they only exist in mixture and in passages from one to another. In this sense, and conversely to one's expectation about the striated nature of fabric, most of Vicuña's weavings seem to belong to smooth space, where variation and development of form are continuous and unlimited, where the lines go in all

directions, where "the stop follows from the trajectory." To quote Deleuze and Guattari: "Smooth space is directional rather than dimensional or metric. Smooth space is filled by events or haecceities, far more than by formed and perceived things. It is a space of affects, more than one of properties. It is *haptic*[50] rather than optical perception. Whereas in the striated forms organize a matter, in the smooth materials signal forces and serve as symptoms for them. It is an intensive rather than extensive space, one of distances, not of measures and properties."[51] Vicuña's sites (sand beaches, sea and river, streets, etc.) and works—be it in Chile, Bogota or New York—are "local spaces of pure connection."[52] Her linkages, signals, and orientations change according to temporary vegetation, occupations, and precipitation. The abstract line that she draws is "a line of flight without beginning or end, a line of variable direction that describes no contour and delimits no form."[53]

Yet, Vicuña's two recent outdoor weavings, *Hilo en el cerro* and *12 Hilos en un corral*, seem to enact, respectively, smooth space and striated space and, almost literally, the crossings and passages between both spaces, as though one emanated from the other, "but not without a correlation between the two, a recapitulation of one in the other, a furtherance of one through the other."[54] Her unexpected use of the woven grid in the corral piece visualizes the striation of space as a way to subordinate and measure it within anxiety in the face of all that passes, flows, or varies. As the grid since the Renaissance has been applied on a vertical plane in order to master three-dimensional space in painting, so the grid applied on a horizontal plane in Vicuña's open weaving brings to mind an archaeological method for mapping ancient sites in an "objective" and clear way. Additionally, it is important to mention that among the Quechua of Chinchero (Peru), there are profound conceptual and linguistic links between the processes of working the loom and working the earth. Here the word *pampa* refers both to the agricultural plain and to the large, single-color sections of handwoven textiles. *Khata* is a furrowed field ready for planting as well as the textile warp configuration ready for pattern formation.[55] Since Vicuña's materialization of the grid in this work seems to be projected without vantage point, it may, more importantly, figure the connection in weaving that is protecting. In this sense we can recall two examples of protective clothing: the plain weaving of Penelope's fabric that—because of its possibilities of doing and undoing—kept not only Penelope but also Odysseus alive; and the plain weaving of the poncho, which is made like a blanket with a central slit for the head. Since its structure is part of "an eternal order," as Anni Albers tells us, the open (corral) weaving 'protects' the entering viewer/reader and the land against the multinational grip of North American corporate agroindustry—which eliminates the "inferior" native corn to replace it with its own "rich" corn treated so as not to run to seed, so that the Chilean farmers become completely dependent on those corporations for production.[56]

Moreover, taking up the grid's ambivalent relation to matter and to spirit, Vicuña extends it in her work to imply the overlaying of modernity onto Andean culture, and vice versa. "Flattened, geometrized, ordered, the grid is antinatural, antimimetic, antireal . . . In the flatness that results from its coordinates, the grid is the means of crowding out the dimensions of the real and replacing them with the lateral spread of a single surface. In the overall regularity of its organization, it is the result not of imitation, but of aesthetic decree."[57] According to Rosalind Krauss, "although the grid is certainly not a story, it *is* a structure, and one, moreover, that allows a contradiction between the values of science and those of spiritualism to maintain themselves within the consciousness of modernism, or rather its unconscious, as something repressed." Because of its bivalent structure the grid portends the "centrifugal" or "centripetal" existence of the work of art. Presented as a mere fragment, arbitrarily cropped from an infinitely larger fabric,[58] the grid operates outward, compelling our acknowledgment of a world beyond the frame, this is the centrifugal reading (in relation to the operations of science, paradoxically entailing the dematerialization of the surface). The centripetal one works from the outer limits of the aesthetic object inward. "The grid is, in relation to *this* reading, a *re*-presentation of everything that separates the work of art from the world, from ambient space and from other objects. The grid is an introjection of the

boundaries of the world into the interior of the work; it is a mapping of the space inside the frame onto itself "(a reading seemingly issuing from purely symbolist origins, paradoxically opposing "science" and "materialism").[59] Krauss states that, within the whole of modern aesthetic production, "the grid has sustained itself so relentlessly while at the same time being so impervious to change." One of the most modernist aspects of the grid is "its capacity to serve as a paradigm or model for the antidevelopment, the antinarrative, the antihistorical."[60]

Apparently, in Vicuña's spatialized weaving, not only the plain surface of the grid is under consideration but also the subversion of the line. The binary discourse on the grid (nature vs. artifice, signifier vs. real, etc.) is called into question. According to Deleuze and Guattari, "the smooth and the striated are distinguished first of all by an inverse relation between the point and the line (in the case of the striated, the line is between two points, while in the smooth, the point is between two lines); and second, by the nature of the line (smooth-directional, open intervals; dimensional-striated, closed intervals). Finally, there is a third difference, concerning the surface or space. In striated space, one closes off a surface and "allocates" it according to determinate intervals, assigned breaks; in the smooth, one "distributes oneself in an open space, according to frequencies and in the course of one's crossing (logos and nomos)." Textile is a spatial construction realized by negotiating supple and fixed elements. The spatial feature of weaving occurs on several levels, through interpenetrating movements that are both external to a defined surface and at the same time create that surface. Still, there is a difference and a disjunction between the experience of space and the discourse of space, between the hand and the weaving, between the gesture and the work. As Lygia Clarks puts it: "The artisan entered into a dialogue with her/his work, while labor, increasingly automatized and mechanized, had lost every expressiveness in its relation." Thus, Vicuña's weaving opens for the artist the possibility of finding her own gestures filled with new meaning; and it wholly revises the meaning of two values—the variable and the constant, the mobile and the fixed, the supple and the solid—by bringing them simultaneously forward in the service of change. The artist's enduring transpositions are the only constant in her work. With enormous perspicacity she disorganizes and redefines the forms of meaning transmitted to her from her Andean culture and from dominant Western cultures, in order to overturn distinctions between the vernacular and the modern and to shift the international models of language. Her use of multiple fluctuating referents and of ambiguity applies to her visual art as well as to her poetry.

KNOTS IN WOOL AS NOTES

Simultaneously approaching and distancing herself from so-called international movements or institutions, such as body art, land art, and *arte povera*, Vicuña chose a flexible though firm position unassimilable to different cultural programs. Her first spatial work, *Quipu que no recuerda nada*, embraced the aesthetic of silence in an attempt to initiate a critique of the self-reflexive model and its enforced hermeticism by challenging and refusing the quietistic conditions of modernism from within.[61] By the 1950s and the early 1960s, anthologies about twentieth century European modernist thought and art[62] had been translated across the Atlantic, published in Buenos Aires, and found their way to Chile. These books were most important to Vicuña because they strengthened her independent mind and language, and, more importantly, because they demonstrated components of a geometrical abstraction, also attributed to her own Andean and pre-Columbian culture.

It is in one of these art books that she noticed a photograph of Kurt Schwitters' *Merzbau* (1923–36) in Hannover. In 1965, moved by the domestic and precarious aspects of Schwitters's work, Vicuña outlined a bare thread in her own bedroom and entitled the work, significantly: *Quipu que no recuerda nada* (The *Quipu* which

Remembers Nothing). Consisting of woolen cords with knots, the *quipu* is an Inca instrument that registers events, circumstances, and numerals. Ancient documents tell us that these registering artifacts continued to be used during the first period of the *conquista*, to be replaced later by written systems.

Nowadays, in certain very traditional communities of the Andean highlands, the use of artifacts similar to the *quipu* still persists.[63] The largest and most complex *quipu*, found within the extensive region of Tawantinsuyu, is on display in the Museo Chileno de Arte Precolombino in Santiago. According to the museum's catalogue it was excavated from an Inca cemetery in Mollepampa, in the valley of the Lluta river, near what is now the city of Arica. Seven white cords without knots, joined to the main cord by a red bow, divide six sets of ten groups of cords each. Near the end of the instrument are nine white, knotless cords and one with only one knot. The *quipu* ends in eleven sets of cords. These sets of cords, each with its knots, are formed by a main cord from which secondary ones derive, some of which produce more cords of a third category. The location of these sets and that of the cords and knots within, the way of twisting each cord, and the colors used are part of a symbolism still not completely deciphered. We know only that the positioning of the knots on the cord makes use of or refers to the decimal system. It seems that the colors encoded nonnumerological information. Recent research suggests that the *quipu* was also used as a mnemonic device for oral poetry and philosophy.

Thus, the entire *quipu* carries meaning: the length, the form, the color, the number of knots. Simultaneously the endless tying and retying of knots allows continuous marking and modification. At the most, on a literal level one could say that in contradistinction to other writing systems the *quipu* provides opportunity for infinite inscription since what is "inscribed" is never fixed. The act of doing and undoing, as in weaving, offers multitudinous possibilities or beginnings, flexibility, and mobility. In this sense Vicuña's *Quipu que no recuerda nada* synthesizes an attitude toward life, language, memory, and history in a postcolonial country, where the process of transformation generated the foundation for a new socialist collective culture. On the verge of being willing to lose any trace of representation, Cecilia Vicuña oscillates, on the one hand, between the various constructivist strategies of transparency of procedures, self-referentiality of signifying devices, and reflexive spatial organization, and on the other hand, the strategies of differentiation of subjective experience and of historical reflection. Taking into account the experience of colonialism (and even more of neocolonial dependence), with its legacies of oppression and destruction, from which her identity emerged, she holds on to the name: *Quipu*. Taking account of the desire of a new generation to be "absolutely modern," Vicuña wanted to articulate a beginning and to position herself at this beginning, but within the pre-Columbian and colonial history. She perceives "beginning" the way Edward W. Said describes it: "Beginning is making or producing difference; but difference which is the result of combining the already-familiar with the fertile novelty of human work in language."[64]

KNOT IN A HANDKERCHIEF

Perhaps at first the connection seems incongruous. However, I wish to analyze and emphasize the relationship between the work of Cecilia Vicuña and that of Kurt Schwitters in the context of Chilean colonial history. Although her earliest encounter with the German artist's work was no more than the encounter with a photograph, and although it was only much later, in the 1980s, that she learned more about his work, there is an affinity worth exploring. Both artists' oeuvres agree on several issues: nonrepresentational multimedia constructions, a "nonobjective" art, emphasis on connection and interaction—the "directional" rather than the "dimensional"; the use of refuse; the strategies of naming (*Merz* and *Precario*); and also the experimentation with other art forms, for example poetry. The elements of poetry such as letters, syllables, words, and sentences are permitted to interact and create meaning.[65] Most striking, however, is the similarity in the construction procedure of the *Merzbau*, conceived in Schwitters's house, and Vicuña's *Quipu*, which was realized in her bedroom without knowledge of the former's installation method, and would be the groundwork for all her later spatial weavings. Their thought processes seem to run parallel. As a result of the particular interest in how various materials, including the components of his own works, combine and interact, Schwitters started by tying strings in his studio from one object, picture, or work

to another to emphasize or materialize that interaction. Eventually, the strings became wires, then were replaced with wooden structures, which, in turn, were joined with plaster of Paris. The structures grew and merged, and eventually filled several rooms, resembling a huge abstract grotto.[66] (In a way this structure also reminds us of the system of suspended threads that Gaudi used in the Iglesia de la Colonia Güell (1908–14) to research construction principles and modeling methods, which would later be applied in La Sagrada Familia in Barcelona.[67] During his experiments of forms in tension, Gaudi used loose threads and weavings to visualize the constitution of walls and ceilings.)

Schwitters had called his principle of artistic creation with any material *Merz*. Since a fragment of a scrap of a bank advertisement pasted in a collage happened to show the four casual letters *MERZ*, this became the general term by which he referred to his work. His naming process is clearly based on his appreciation for the accidental, the trivial, the inconsequential. Elsewhere, he wrote that this word *Merz* came from the German *ausmerzen* (to weed out, extirpate), and that ironically it threw light on both the bright side of dadaism and the dark side of expressionism.[68] The *Merz* works are characterized by diverse materials glued and nailed on the picture surface, and by the application of color in limited sections. Schwitters used to say: "The material is as unimportant as myself. Important is only the creation. And because the material is unimportant, I take any material a picture demands. As I let different materials interact, I have an advantage compared to oil painting, as I can create interaction, not only between colour and colour, line and line, form and form, but also between material and material, e.g. wood and sackcloth."[69] A few artists among his contemporaries were also literally choosing this diversity of materials from the urban environment.[70] Later on, after World War II, many artists began to select their materials from the refuse generated by urban life and industrial "progress." Vicuña was also motivated to use discarded objects in defiance of an excluding differentiation. This impartiality (or abstractness) is maintained once the found objects are appropriated as materials. Such nonhierarchical use of materials allows reflections on balance, equality, and freedom, which are emphasized by the fragile state of equilibrium in many of her precarious objects (e.g., *Balancin*, 1981; *Pesa*, 1984; *Espiral de Jezik*, 1990).

In addition to the aesthetic considerations and the formal analogies of Schwitters's and Vicuña's work, it is of interest to compare the recurrences of both the process of naming and the use of waste materials in a specific socioeconomic environment: Schwitters in Germany before World War II and Vicuña in Chile before the dictatorship.[71] While Vicuña elucidated extensively her attention (later to become studiousness) to dadaism and its precedents in her art and poetry practices, she noticed the exaltation of memory and lament in both the pre-Columbian and German romantic poetry. Dissolving identities and shattering the communicative, representative aspect of language in favor of a dynamic conception of art, the avant-garde artists further gave rise to a theory of the subject in process, a subject equally constituted by symbolic and semiotic elements. Considering them rebels in a restraining society, Vicuña embraced the modernist vanguard aesthetic and poetry as a liberating force, contributing in one inward movement to both—on the one hand, to the newly defined social production of culture propagated by the Unidad Popular of the Marxist President Salvador Allende, and on the other hand, to the resistance against colonization and its ramifications in an emerging totalitarian regime.[72]

DESIRE OF THE HAND

If my presumed equation were based on a linear thought that implied notions of filiation and belatedness, instead of on aesthetic and socio-political recurrences and convergences in time, it would constitute yet another neocolonial attempt to create predecessors of South American art in Europe. It remains imperative to read Vicuña's work as well, which fuses the knowledge of a colonial Chilean and local Andean culture with the quest for a global avant-garde, in reference to propositions made by her contemporaries in South America. Her determination to break away from the universalist claims of geometric abstraction, without abandoning a nonfigurative, geometric vocabulary and the general social concerns of constructivism, and her

desire to take on the complexity of human reality and still remain receptive to her immediate environment, parallel the earlier attitudes of the neoconcrete group in Brazil (Lygia Clark, Hélio Oiticica, Lygia Pape, Amilcar de Castro, Franz Weissmann, Reynaldo Jardim, Theon Spanudis, the poet Ferreira Gullar, and the art critic Mario Pedrosa). These artists affirmed the values of modernity and eschewed "regionalist realism," but restated the problem of subjectivity in a specific Brazilian context. In the *Manifesto neoconcreto*[73] (1959) they attacked the positivism and mechanistic reductionism of the philosophy of Max Bill and the Hochschule für Gestaltung Ulm as ignoring the real conditions of Brazil; it was designed for an advanced capitalist/industrial society. Significantly, the neoconcrete work of Lygia Clark and Hélio Oiticica "gradually lost the technological sheen associated with constructivism and moved (in very different ways) towards the use of common and relatively valueless materials which were 'at hand' in the everyday environment of Rio."[74] Notwithstanding the isolation of these artists and the lack of communication among most countries in South America, it appears that in 1966 in Chile Vicuña was naming her works *arte precario*. That same year in Brazil Clark was describing "*precariousness* as a new idea of existence against all static crystallization within duration; and the very time of the act as a field of experience."[75] As much as Vicuña seems to rejoin the pursuit of Schwitters, Clark and Oiticica seem to reawaken visionary proposals and efforts of prewar artists (such as Duchamp, Mondriaan, and Van Tongerloo, known through the Biennals of Sao Paulo) to resist "the growing realm of the commodity." At the same time, in the 1960s and 1970s, these South American artists positioned themselves in relation to the international claims of the *arte povera*, resolutely stressing their own terminology and its intrinsic differences. In a letter to Clark (10/15/68), Oiticica states;

> For European and North American expression, this is the great difference: the so-called Italian *arte povera* is done with the most advanced means: it is the sublimation of poverty, but in an anecdotal, visual way, deliberately poor but actually quite rich: it is the

assimilation of the remains of an oppressive civilization and their transformation into consumption, the capitalization of the idea of poverty. To us, it does not seem that the economy of elements is directly connected with the idea of structure, with the nontechnique as discipline, with the freedom of creation as the super-economy, in which the rudimentary element in itself liberates open structures.[76]

According to Guy Brett, "material-linguistic objects like Oiticica's *Bolides* (*bolide* = fireball in Portuguese), his *Parangolés* (capes), *Penetrables, Nests* etc., and Clark's individual and collective 'propositions' using plastic, sacking, stones, air, string, sand, water etc., are not 'representations' but cells, nucleuses, or energy-centres. The object itself is secondary, appropriated, incomplete, existing only to initiate dialogue, and to indicate 'environmental and social wholes' (Oiticica). Literally, in many cases, they cannot exist without human support."[77] In her country Vicuña responded to the same cultural necessity and was drawn to the same tendencies of "expanding beyond the concept of the art object, beyond the gallery and the museum, into the environment, mixing media, and inviting the participation of the public."[78] Striking here are the concurrences not only in the use of "precarious" materials (netting, strings, shells), but also in the notions of space/time, of beginning, of bodily action (perception, touch, manipulation, voice, smell; the "eye-body"), of dialogue, even of another basic human creation: architecture. If for Lygia Clark a "living biological architecture" was created by people's gestures, and if Oiticica's sensory and social nucleuses, like his *Nests,* cabins, and *Penetrables*, poetically suggest new ways of constructing and inhabiting the environment—"as a metaphor of communication," then Vicuña's *Weavings* show points of interface within the semiotic/linguistic research of "nest" and "text" (discussed earlier).

LO NUNCA PROJECTADO[79]

However, in all these works it is the action of time and of "spatialization" that is most intelligible. What they mean by spatialization of the work is "the fact that it is *always* *in the present, always in the process of beginning over*, of beginning the impulse that gave birth to it over again—whose origin and evolution it contains simultaneously" (Neoconcretist Manifesto). In this sense the repetitive texture of crisscrossing straight lines, and eventually the grid, in Vicuña's woven works are formally closer to the accumulative system of joining wire cables in the kinetic *Reticulárea* (*ambientación*) (1968–76) and the *Dibujos sin papel* (Drawings without Paper) by the Venezuelan artist Gego, than to the arbitrary clusters of thread in *La Bruja* (The Broom) by Cildo Meireles (Brazil) at the Biennal of São Paulo,[80] or the earlier installation work by Marcel Duchamp at the exhibition *First Papers of Surrealism* (1942) in New York. The use of thread in these latter installation works is rather dealing with the problems of cultural institutionalization and reception to "openly denounce the validity of the retrospective exhibition and criticize the quasi-religious veneration of the acculturation."[81] At first sight Meireles's work appears as a gratuitous gesture enhancing chaotic dispersal, dust and dirt (at least the critics were heavy), but then one discovers that it is organized by this small domestic cleaning tool. Is sweeping a space not the best way to know it? Is it not about making measurements in the head with the hands?

Basting the space with large, loose stitches, Vicuña recently constructed *Hilumbres/allqa* at the Béguinage Saint-Elizabeth in Kortrijk.[82] To realize a double "weaving in space" she uses industrial black and white cotton spun in Flemish factories out of raw materials mainly imported from the so-called third world (Turkey, Egypt, Peru, etc.): "I speak to the moment in which the visible becomes invisible and vice versa," said Vicuña, "to the moment when the cognition, the definition, has not yet been formed. Moving through the room people should discover the limits and traps of their own perception, the wandering attention." *Hilumbres*, a word invented by Vicuña, is composed of two words *hilo/lumbre* (thread/ light), meaning "the thread catching light" or "the thread of light"; *allqa* is an Aymara word and a textile term that refers to a sharp contrast in the play of light and shadow. In weaving, it applies to the connection or encounter of things that can never be together: black and white. In Andean weaving this union of oppositions generates a degradation—or, as Vicuña formulates it, "a soft stairway," which argues for a model of subjectivity not rooted in binary thought: self/ other, love/hate, aggression/identification, rejection/incorporation. Similarly it should be noted that in Andean and Mayan textiles the joints between two woven panels are often the focus of articulation and elaboration. "The seam itself is not rendered unobtrusive as it is in our apparel. Instead it is emphasized by silk or rayon stitching of bold color and emphatic form. This is called the *randa*."[83] Dealing with the past and the other, the crossing of borderlines and the seams of cultural articulation are highlighted in this work.

The words of Lygia Clark about her *Trailing* (1964) express similar thoughts about a continuum, a "matrixial" space: "If I use a Möbius strip for this experiment, it's because it breaks with our spatial habits: right/left; front/back, etc. It forces us to experience a limitless time and a continuous space."[84] The exploration of another possibility of seeing that is not the phallic gaze is at stake in Vicuña's work and in this sense it rejoins the issues in the paintings of Bracha Lichtenberg Ettinger, who developed the psychoanalytical theory of "Matrix and Metamorphosis."[85] Griselda Pollock, who has systematically and profoundly analyzed the painting of Lichtenberg Ettinger, explains that modalities based on the rejection/assimilation paradigm apply to how paintings are viewed as much as to how societies treat immigrants. "What is not us, strange and unknown, be that woman for man, the other for the white European, the painting for the viewer is positioned under this phallic logic as either one of the two terms: to be assimilated and if that is not possible to be cast off as completely other."[86] Lichtenberg Ettinger argues for "a shift of the phallic" by introducing the "matrix." For

if we allow ourselves to introduce into culture another symbolic signifier to stand beside the phallus (signifier of difference and division, absence and loss and orchestrating these either/or models), could we not be on the way to allowing the invisible feminine bodily specificity to enter and realign aspects of our consciousnesses and unconsciousnesses? This will surely extend as do all these metaphors of sexual

difference to other others—issues of race, immigration, diaspora, genocide are tangled at the moment around the lack of means to signify other possible relations between different subjects—I and non-I. The matrix as symbol is about that encounter between difference which tries neither to master, nor assimilate, nor reject, nor alienate. It is a symbol of the coexistence in one space of two bodies, two subjectivities whose encounter at this moment is not an either/or.[87]

POETRY IN SPACE

Vicuña's ouvrage challenges such questions of recent art as the status of the object, the relation of the artist and the viewer/reader, bodily action, the space/time relation, the environment, inner and outer, the connection of the visual to the other senses, at once moving viewers away from their habit of compartmentalizing artistic production into separate media. At the same time it evokes a polemical attitude toward modernity, investigating a universal artistic development without negating local forms of expression. Her elaboration of popular elements shows links with bricolage and as such involves continual reconstruction from the same materials (in the sense that it is always previous ends that are called upon to play the part of means).[88] Thus Vicuña reconsiders the changes of the signified into the signifying and vice versa. Vicuña dwells in im/possibility (as did Violeta Parra and Xul Solar). She demands a laying open of the mechanisms that produce meaning: particularly, the formation of a language. Her ideal is a discourse characterized by plurality, the open interplay of elements, and the possibility of infinite recombination.[89] However, Vicuña concludes that "(visual) language speaks of its own process: to name something which can not be named."

Working with and writing about Cecilia Vicuña is a privilege and a pleasure, and I therefore thank her. For their continuous support and for critically reading this essay my warm thanks go to Benjamin Buchloh, and also to Jean Fisher and Sally Stein. Last but not least I am very thankful to my family who allowed me—but luckily not always—to disappear behind my desk.

Notes

1. Julia Averkieva and Mark A. Sherman, *Kwakiutl String Figures*, Anthropological Papers of the American Museum of Natural History, vol.71 (New York, 1992).

2. Ibid., xiii.

3. L. A. Dickey (1928), *String Figures from Hawaii*, in B. P. Bishop Museum Bulletin, no. 54 (New York: Kraus Reprint, 1985), 11.

4. Cecilia Vicuña, "Metafísica del textil," in *Revista Tramemos II* (Buenos Aires, 1989).

5. Elizabeth Wayland Barber, *Women's Work: The First 20,000 Years. Women, Cloth, and Society in Early Times* (New York and London: W. W. Norton, 1994), 29–33.

6. Ibid.

7. Cecilia Vicuña creates the new verb *palabrir*, which means "to open words," noting that *abrir* (to open) originally meant *parir* (to give birth).

8. *Huipil* is a rectangular or square shirt, sewn on the sides, with a circular opening for the head, made of cotton or wool, and usually embroidered. Worn in Mesoamerica since pre-Columbian times, it is still used in the south of Mexico and Guatemala, where indigenous women continue to weave *huipiles* both for their own use and for trade.

9. Janet Catherine Berlo, "Beyond Bricolage: Women and Aesthetic Strategies in Latin American Textiles," in *Textile Traditions of Mesoamerica and The Andes: An Anthology*, ed. Margot Blum Schevill (New York: Garland Press, 1991), 437–467.

10. Cecilia Vicuña, *Unravelling Words and the Weaving of Water* (St. Paul, Minn.: Graywolf Press, 1992).

11. Cecilia Vicuña, *La Wik'una* (Santiago, Chile: Francisco Zegers Editor, 1990).

12. Lucy Lippard, *Overlay* (New York: Pantheon Books, 1983), 106.

13. Henri Michaux, *The Beginnings*, trans. James Wanless; from *Sulfur* no. 34 (Spring 1994), 116.

14. Lygia Clark, "Nostalgia of the Body," *October* 69 (Summer 1994), 85–109.

15. Lippard, *Overlay*, 106.

16. Cecilia Vicuña, *Precario/Precarious*, trans. Anne Twitty (New York: Tanam Press, 1983).

17. Clark, "Nostalgia," 85–109.

18. Cecilia Vicuña quotes that "art" and "order" derive both from the same root, *ar* (to fit together). The word *armus* (upper arm) comes from what the arms did. In this sense the Latin *ars* (art) was "skill," and the Latin *ordo* (order) from *ordiri* (to begin to weave) was "a row of threads in a loom."

19. Jean Fischer, "1:1 Lynn Silverman," exhib. cat. (Angel Row Gallery, Camerawork, and the University of Derby, 1993).

20. Guy Brett, about Roberto Evangelista's *Immersion, in America. Bride of the Sun. 500 years Latin America and the Low Countries*, exhib. cat. (Antwerp: Royal Museum of Fine Arts, 1992), 245–246.

21. The *desaparecidos*, or the "disappeared ones," was the name given by the people of the southern cone (Chile, Uruguay, and Argentina) to men and women who were led away by the secret police from their homes or in the streets during the dictatorships of the seventies, because they were never seen again, and the military police denied having taking them in the first place. Only after years of struggle, human rights organizations were able to demonstrate that the people who had been "disappeared" by the thousands not only did exist, but had been effectively tortured to death and/or murdered by the military regimes of the three countries. Only some of the collective or individual burials have been found; sometimes their bodies were exploded by dynamite, sometimes bathed in lime and then covered by soil to render them unrecognizable.

22. Vicuña, *Precario/Precarious*.

23. Averkieva and Sherman, *Kwakiutl String Figures*, 137–150.

24. Kathleen Haddon, *Artists in String* (London: Methuen, 1930), 145; (reprinted.: New York: AMS Press, 1979).

25. Claude Lévi-Strauss, *Structural Anthropology* (New York: Basic books, 1963), 31–54.

26. Cecilia Vicuña, *Palabrir* (forthcoming; Editorial Sudamericana, Chile).

27. Cecilia Vicuña, *Sabor a mí* (Devon, England: Beau Geste Press, 1973).

28. Barbara and Dennis Tedlock, "Text and Textile: Language and Technology in the Arts of the Quiché Maya," *Journal of Anthropological Research* 41.2 (1985), 121–146.

29. Berlo, "Beyond Bricolage."

30. Lévi-Strauss, *Structural Anthropology*, 21.

31. César Paternosto speaks of "Major Art"; William Conklin of "Textile Age." See César Patermosto, *The Stone and the Thread: Andean Roots of Abstract Art* (Austin: University of Texas Press, 1996).

32. André Leroi-Gourhan, *L'homme et la matière*, Albin Michel, 244.

33. Mary Jane Jacobs, "Anni Albers: A Modern Weaver as Artist," in *The Woven and Graphic Art of Anni Albers* (Washington, D.C.: Smithsonian Institution Press, 1985), 65.

34. Ibid., 22 and plate 1.

35. Ibid., 66.

36. Ibid., 71–72.

37. Cecilia Vicuña says that this dichotomy is not a general rule in the continent. Women shamans in many indigenous societies have used words in their healing practices. Also Maria Sabina among the Mazatecs, the Machi among the Mapuche in Chile and Argentina, and the Quechua women of Ecuador have subverted this dichotomy.

38. Berlo, "Beyond Bricolage."

39. *Mola* is a rectangular piece of cotton cloth, with applique of other cotton pieces sewn in, to make designs and symbols as in patchwork. Originally worn and created by the Cuna indigenous women of Panama, today it is a flourishing form of social commentary, with *molas* carrying political messages, sports, and TV events, together with the ancient symbols, to be worn by the women themselves (as part of their shirt) and to be sold to tourists.

40. Mary W. Helms, *Cuna Molas and Cocle Art Forms*, Working Papers in the Traditional Arts, no. 7 (Philadelphia: Institute for the Study of Human Issues, 1981).

41. Berlo, "Beyond Bricolage."

42. Ruth Bunzel, *Chichicastenango: A Guatemalan Village* (Seattle: University of Washington Press, 1952), 308.

43. Berlo, "Beyond Bricolage."

44. Ibid.

45. A famous example is the "Manifesto" that Oliverio Girondo (1891–1967) wrote for the fourth issue of *Martin Fierro* (1924). "Summoning the avant-garde forces to the task of resuscitating the language, Girondo asserts that fresh life can be brought to Spanish only by finding new models outside literary Spanish: the agitated and frenetic tones of the technologized era of mass communications."

46. Naomi Lindstrom, "Live Language Against Dead: Literary Rebels of Buenos Aires," review in *Latin American Literature and Arts*, no. 31, New York (jan–april 1982).

47. *El mirar cruzado* means: looking at something from (two) different points of view, mixing the sources; in Cecilia Vicuña's unpublished manuscript *Fragmentos de Poeticas*.

48. Gilles Deleuze and Félix Guattari, *A Thousand Plateaus, Capitalism and Schizophrenia*, trans. Brian Massumi (Minneapolis and London: University of Minnesota Press, 1987), 474– 500.

49. Deleuze and Guattari, *A Thousand Plateaus*, 475.

50. Deleuze and Guattari say on p. 429 that "'Haptic' is a better word than 'tactile' since it does not establish an opposition between two sense organs but rather invites the assumption that the eye itself may fulfill this nonoptical function."

51. Ibid., 493.

52. Ibid.

53. Ibid., 499.

54. Ibid., 446–447.

55. Berlo, "Beyond Bricolage."

56. In fact this situation is part of an ongoing process of destroying native agriculture since colonial times. At first not only most of the wild wheat was devastated by the *conquistadores*— to be replaced by imported western wheat, which the Indian population had to buy— but also a great number of alpacas and llamas were killed so that these herds had to be replaced by sheep and cows sold at very high prices. See also Cecilia Vicuña, "The Invention of Poverty," in *America. Bride of the Sun*, 514–515.

57. Rosalind E. Krauss, *The Originality of the Avant-Garde and Other Modernist Myths* (Cambridge, Mass.: MIT Press, 1986), 8–22.

58. Cf. Anni Albers, who said: "It is for this reason that we can find certitude in the belief that we are taking part in an eternal order." In Jacobs, *The Woven and Graphic Art of Anni Albers*.

59. Krauss, *Originality of the Avant-Garde*.

60. Ibid.

61. Benjamin H. D. Buchloh, "Refuse and Refuge," in *Gabriel Orozco*, exhib. cat. (Kortrijk: Kanaal Art Foundation, 1993).

62. Examples are: Jean Cassou's *Panorama de las artes contemporaneas*; J. E. Cirlot's *El arte otro*; and Aldo Pellegrini, ed. And trans., *Antologia de la poesía surrealista* (Buenos Aires: Fabril Editora, 1961).

63. *A Noble Andean Art*, exhib. cat. (Santiago de Chile: Museo Chileno de Arte Precolombino), 72–73, no. 0780: *Quipu*, Camelid fibers, Inca, 1470–1532 A.D.: main cord length: 168 cms.

64. Edward W. Said, *Beginnings: Intentions and Method* (New York: Columbia University Press, 1985).

65. Kurt Schwitters said: "I let nonsense interact with sense. I prefer nonsense, but that is a purely personal matter. I feel sorry for nonsense, since, so far, it has rarely been formed artistically. Therefore I love nonsense." See Ernst Schwitters, "Kurt Schwitters—Father of *Merz—My* Father,"141.

66. *Merz = Kurt Schwitters*, Karnizawa, The Museum of Modern Art, Seibu Takanawa, Tokyo, Oct–Nov. 1983; Ernst Schwitters, "Kurt Schwitters—father of *Merz—* My Father," 142.

67. Jean François Pirson, *La structure et l'objet* (Liege: Metaphores, 1984), 29. The Iglesia de la Colonia Güell was commissioned by Eugenio Güell to Gaudi in 1898. It was constructed for a colony of textile workers and became a laboratory for experiences related to the construction of La Sagrada Familia. Gaudi collaborated with the architects, F. Berenguer and J. Canaleta, and with the engineer, E. Goetz.

68. Werner Schmalenbach, *Kurt Schwitters* (Köln, 1967), 93. *Merz* is the second syllable of *Kommerz* (commerce). The name originated from the *Merzbild*, a picture in which the word *Merz* could be read in between abstract forms. Schmalenbach quotes Schwitters as saying "When I first exhibited these pasted and nailed pictures with the Sturm in Berlin, I searched for a collective noun for this new kind of picture, because I could not define them with the older conceptions like Expressionism, Futurism or whatever. So I gave all my pictures the name 'Merz-pictures' after the most characteristic of them and thus made them like a species. Later on I expanded this name 'Merz' to include my poetry (I had written poetry since 1917), and finally all my relevant activities."

69. Schwitters, "Kurt Schwitters—Father of *Merz*—My Father," 141.

70. Yusuke Nakahara, in *Merz = Kurt Schwitters*.

71. The grandfather of Vicuña, who was the writer and civil rights activist and lawyer Carlos Vicuña Fuentes (Dean of the University of Chile and Deputate to the Chilean Parliament), had received in his home a group of refugees from the Spanish Civil War. Among the refugees were the playwriter José Ricardo Morales and the editors Arturo Soria and Carmelo Soria, who was later murdered by the secret police of Pinochet. These men and their families became part of Cecilia Vicuña's family and education. It should be remembered here that the Nazis were also instrumental in the rise of Franco and the defeat of the Spanish Republic. Carlos Vicuña Fuentes was made an "honorary jew" by the Jewish community in Santiago as a result of his antifascist activities.

72. During the nineteenth and twentieth centuries several presidents carried out an explicit policy of "Germanization" and facilitated German immigration to the South of Chile "in order," so they said, "to bring prosperity to a forsaken land and to improve the Indian race." Thus they were encouraging the "populating" of the provinces south of the Araucania (Valdivia, Osorno, Llanquihue) by taking the land from the Mapuche. During World War II a German fascist presence in the South of Chile was evident through the existence of support groups for the Nazis (National Socialist Parties) and after the war this presence was enforced by the arrival of exiled and former Nazis, from whom it is now known that they participated in the dictatorship of General Pinochet.

73. Reproduced in Ronaldo Brito, *Neoconcretisimo, Vertice e Ruptura* (Rio de Janeiro: Funarte, 1985), 12–13; reprinted in French translation in *Robho* 4, and in English translation in October 69, (Summer 1994), 91–95.

74. Guy Brett, "Lygia Clark: The Borderline Between Art and Life," *Third Text* 1 (Autumn 1987), 65–94.

75. Clark, "Nostalgia of the Body," 106.

76. "Isso é a grande diferença para a expressão européia e americana do norte: a tal povera arte italiana é feita com os meios mais avançados: é a sublimaçao da pobreza, mas de modo anedótico, visual, propositalmente pobre mas na verdade bem rica: é a assimilação dos restos de uma civilização opressiva e sua transformação em consumo, a capitalização da idéia de pobreza. Para nós, não parece que a economia de elementos está diretamente ligada à idéia de estrutura, à não-téc-nica como disciplina, à liberdade de criação como a supra-economia, onde o elemento rudimentar já libera estruturas abertas." In *Lygia Clark e Hélio* Oiticica, Sala especial do 9. Salão Nacional de Artes Plásticas (Rio de Janeiro: Funarte, 1986–87).

77. Brett, "Lygia Clark," 75.

78. Ibid.

79. *Lo nunca projectado* is the title of an album with poems by Alfredo Silva Estrada and illustrations by Gego (1964).

80. *La Brucha* consisted of 2500 km of white cotton thread unrolled in a fortuitous way through every single space all over the three floors of the Biennal Building to end up at a broom placed in a little store-room near the toilets.

81. Benjamin H. D. Buchloh, "The Museum Fictions of Marcel Broodthaers," *Museums by Artists*, ed. A.A. Bronson and Peggy Gale (Toronto: Art Metropole, 1983). "Vintage cobweb? Indeed not!" Duchamp was reported to have said.

82. Exhibition of Cecilia Vicuña in the series "Inside the Visible. Begin the Beguine in Flanders," organized by the Kanaal Art Foundation as Cultural Ambassador of Flandres, (Oct. 1–Dec. 11), 1994.

83. Berlo, "Beyond Bricolage," 453.

84. Clark, "Nostalgia of the Body."

85. Bracha Lichtenberg Ettinger, "Matrix and Metramorphosis," in *Differences: A Journal of Feminist Cultural Studies* 4.3; and 'The Becoming Threshold of Matrixial Borderlines," in *Travellers' Tales* (London: Routledge, 1994).

86. Griselda Pollock, "Oeuvres Autistes," *Versus* 3 (1994): 14–18.

87. Ibid.

88. Claude Lévi-Strauss, *The Savage Mind* (Chicago: University of Chicago Press, 1966), 21.

89. Naomi Lindstrom, "Xul Solar: Star-Spangler of Languages," *Review: Latin American Literature and Arts* 25/26, 121.

20

1440 THE SMOOTH & THE STRIATED (EXCERPT) (1987)

Gilles Deleuze and Félix Guattari

EDITOR'S INTRODUCTION

The influence of Gilles Deleuze (1925–95) and Félix Guattari (1930–92) can be found throughout the writing collected in this *Reader*. Gilles Deleuze was a French philosopher and Félix Guattari a French psychoanalyst. Among their many publications, the pair co-wrote *Capitalism and Schizophrenia: Anti-Oedipus* (1972), *Kafka: Toward a Minor Literature* (1975), *Capitalism and Schizophrenia: A Thousand Plateaus* (1980) and *What Is Philosophy?* (1991). Deleuze also wrote, among many other texts, *The Fold: Leibniz and the Baroque* (1988).

In the excerpt printed here, Deleuze and Guattari propose that smooth and striated spaces are not equal opposites. In their words, the two 'fail to coincide entirely'. A number of examples are offered – of interest here is the borrowing of various textile structures. Weaving, felt, embroidery, crochet and quilting are all used, with varying degrees of structural accuracy, by the philosophers. The knots, for example, described in reference to weaving may be applicable to carpet weaving but are an inaccurate description of plain weave, a woven structure where warp and weft [woof] are the same: 'Space of this kind seems to have a top and bottom; even when the warp yarn and woof yarn are exactly the same in nature, number and density, weaving reconstitutes a bottom by placing the knots on one side.'

Deleuze and Guattari's well-cited writing offers examples of how the textile structure has been adopted to illustrate abstract philosophical thought. Unintentionally, they also expose an occasion where descriptions of textiles can reveal misunderstandings in the specific nature of textile structures. In the first section of this book, 'Touch', Pennina Barnett draws on the idea of the Deleuzian fold, while Catherine de Zegher uses smooth and striated space in her discussion of Cecilia Vicuña's work. Deleuze and Guattari's reference to Plato's use of weaving as a paradigm for governance is also taken up by Arthur Danto in the next section about politics.

1440 The Smooth and the Striated

Gilles Deleuze and Félix Guattari

Smooth space and striated space—nomad space and sedentary space—the space in which the war machine develops and the space instituted by the State apparatus—are not of the same nature. No sooner do we note a simple opposition between the two kinds of space than we must indicate a much more complex difference by virtue of which the successive terms of the oppositions fail to coincide entirely. And no sooner have we done that than we must remind ourselves that the two spaces in fact exist only in mixture: smooth space is constantly being translated, transversed into a striated space; striated space is constantly being reversed, returned to a smooth space. In the first case, one organizes even the desert; in the second, the desert gains and grows; and the two can happen simultaneously. But the de facto mixes do not preclude a de jure, or abstract, distinction between the two spaces. That there is such a distinction is what accounts for the fact that the two spaces do not communicate with each other in the same way: it is the de jure distinction that determines the forms assumed by a given de facto mix and the direction or meaning of the mix (is a smooth space captured, enveloped by a striated space, or does a striated space dissolve into a smooth space, allow a smooth space to develop?). This raises a number of simultaneous questions: the simple oppositions between the two spaces; the complex differences; the de facto mixes, and the passages from one to another; the principles of the mixture, which are not at all symmetrical, sometimes causing a passage from the smooth to the striated, sometimes from the striated to the smooth, according to entirely different movements. We must therefore envision a certain number of models, which would be like various aspects of the two spaces and the relations between them.

THE TECHNOLOGICAL MODEL

A fabric presents in principle a certain number of characteristics that permit us to define it as a striated space. First, it is constituted by two kinds of parallel elements; in the simplest case, there are vertical and horizontal elements, and the two intertwine, intersect perpendicularly. Second, the two kinds of elements have different functions; one is fixed, the other mobile, passing above and beneath the fixed. Leroi-Gourhan has analyzed this particular figure of "supple solids" in basketry and weaving: stake and thread, warp and woof.[1] Third, a striated space of this kind is necessarily delimited, closed on at least one side: the fabric can be infinite in length but not in width, which is determined by the frame of the warp; the necessity of a back and forth motion implies a closed space (circular or cylindrical figures are themselves closed). Finally, a space of this kind seems necessarily to have a top and a bottom; even when the warp yarn and woof yarn are exactly the same in nature, number, and density, weaving reconstitutes a bottom by placing the knots on one side. Was it not these characteristics that enabled Plato to use the model of weaving as the paradigm for "royal science," in other words, the art of governing people or operating the State apparatus?

Felt is a supple solid product that proceeds altogether differently, as an anti-fabric. It implies no separation of threads, no intertwining, only an entanglement of fibers obtained by fulling (for example,

Source: Gilles Deleuze and Félix Guattari, 'Smooth & Striated Space', *A Thousand Plateaus: Capitalism and Schizophrenia*, trans. Brian Massumi (University of Minnesota Press, 1987), pp. 474–500. Copyright 1987 by the University of Minnesota Press. Originally published in *Mille Plateaux*, volume 2 of *Capitalisme et Schizophrénie* © 1980 by Les Editions de Minuit, Paris. *Bloomsbury Revelations* edition first published in 2013 by Bloomsbury Academic. Reproduced with permission.

by rolling the block of fibers back and forth). What becomes entangled are the microscales of the fibers. An aggregate of intrication of this kind is in no way *homogeneous*: it is nevertheless smooth, and contrasts point by point with the space of fabric (it is in principle infinite, open, and unlimited in every direction; it has neither top nor bottom nor center; it does not assign fixed and mobile elements but rather distributes a continuous variation). Even the technologists who express grave doubts about the nomads' powers of innovation at least give them credit for felt: a splendid insulator, an ingenious invention, the raw material for tents, clothes, and armor among the Turco-Mongols. Of course, the nomads of Africa and the Maghreb instead treat wool as a fabric. Although it might entail displacing the opposition, do we not detect two very different conceptions or even practices of weaving, the distinction between which would be something like the distinction between fabric as a whole and felt? For among sedentaries, clothes-fabric and tapestry-fabric tend to annex the body and exterior space, respectively, to the immobile house: fabric integrates the body and the outside into a closed space. On the other hand, the weaving of the nomad indexes clothing and the house itself to the space of the outside, to the open smooth space in which the body moves.

There are many interlacings, mixes between felt and fabric. Can we not displace the opposition yet again? In knitting, for example, the needles produce a striated space; one of them plays the role of the warp, the other of the woof, but by turns. Crochet, on the other hand, draws an open space in all directions, a space that is prolongable in all directions—but still has a center. A more significant distinction would be between embroidery, with its central theme or motif, and patchwork, with its piece-by-piece construction, its infinite, successive additions of fabric. Of course, embroidery's variables and constants, fixed and mobile elements, may be of extraordinary complexity. Patchwork, for its part, may display equivalents to themes, symmetries, and resonance that approximate it to embroidery. But the fact remains that its space is not at all constituted in the same way: there is no center; its basic motif ("block") is composed of a single element; the recurrence of this element frees uniquely rhythmic

values distinct from the harmonies of embroidery (in particular, in "crazy" patchwork, which fits together pieces of varying size, shape, and color, and plays on the *texture* of the fabrics). "She had been working on it for fifteen years, carrying about with her a shapeless bag of dingy, threadbare brocade containing odds and ends of colored fabric in all possible shapes. She could never bring herself to trim them to any pattern; so she shifted and fitted and mused and fitted and shifted them like pieces of a patient puzzle-picture, trying to fit them to a pattern or create a pattern out of them without using her scissors, smoothing her colored scraps with flaccid, putty-colored fingers."[2] An amorphous collection of juxtaposed pieces that can be joined together in an infinite number of ways: we see that patchwork is literally a Riemannian space, or vice versa. That is why very special work groups were formed for patchwork fabrication (the importance of the quilting bee in America, and its role from the standpoint of a women's collectivity). The smooth space of patchwork is adequate to demonstrate that "smooth" does not mean homogeneous, quite the contrary: it is an *amorphous*, nonformal space prefiguring op art.

The story of the quilt is particularly interesting in this connection. A quilt comprises two layers of fabric stitched together, often with a filler in between. Thus it is possible for there to be no top or bottom. If we follow the history of the quilt over a short migration sequence (the settlers who left Europe for the New World), we see that there is a shift from a formula dominated by embroidery (so-called "plain" quilts) to a patchwork formula ("appliqué quilts," and above all "pieced quilts"). The first settlers of the seventeenth century brought with them plain quilts, embroidered and striated spaces of extreme beauty. But toward the end of the century patchwork technique was developed more and more, at first due to the scarcity of textiles (leftover fabric, pieces salvaged from used clothes, remnants taken from the "scrap bag"), and later due to the popularity of Indian chintz. It is as though a smooth space emanated, sprang from a striated space, but not without a correlation between the two, a recapitulation of one in the other, a furtherance of one through the other. Yet the complex difference persists. Patchwork, in conformity with migration, whose degree of affinity with nomadism it shares, is not only named after trajectories, but "represents" trajectories, becomes inseparable from speed or movement in an open space.[3]

Notes

1. André Leroi-Gourhan, *L'homme et la matière* (Paris: Albin Michel, 1971), pp. 244ff. (and the opposition between fabric and felt).
2. William Faulkner, *Sartoris* (New York: Random House, 1956), p. 151.
3. On the history of the quilt and patchwork in American immigration, see Jonathan Holstein, *American Pieced Quilts* (New York: Viking, 1973) (with reproductions and bibliography). Holstein does not claim that the quilt is the principal source of American art, but he does note the extent to which the "white on white" of plain quilts and patchwork compositions inspired or gave impetus to certain tendencies in American painting: "We can see in many [quilts] such phenomena as 'op' effects, serial images, use of 'color fields,' deep understanding of negative space, mannerisms of formal abstraction and the like," (p. 13).

21

KNITTING IS . . . (2008)

Sabrina Gschwandtner

EDITOR'S INTRODUCTION

Sabrina Gschwandtner is an artist, curator and writer. She studied art/semiotics at Brown University (2000) followed by an MFA from Bard College (2008) in the United States. From 2002 to 2007 she edited and published the 'zine, *KnitKnit* now held in the permanent collections of the Museum of Modern Art, New York, the Getty Research Institute and the Harvard Fine Arts Library. Her book *KnitKnit: Profiles and Projects from Knitting's New Wave* was released in 2007. Gschwandtner's practice crosses the disciplines of textiles, video and film – often through work that observes no disciplinary boundaries between the three.

The text reprinted in full here was written for the second issue of *The Journal of Modern Craft* published in 2008. Taking knitting as her focal point, Gschwandtner considers the varied ways in which the structure of knitting has provided her with a model for her career as 'an artist, curator, writer, editor and publisher'. In this writing, knitting is an entry point into making, thinking, collaboration and conversation. As a template for interdisciplinary practice, knitting moves beyond the functional use of discrete knitted objects to instead offer a way of fostering community dialogue and commenting on the world around us.

Gschwandtner's *Wartime Knitting Circle* (2007), one of the projects illustrated in the original text, invited the public to sit together and make, but also to write, converse and reflect on American military involvement in Iraq and Afghanistan. On the walls around the interactive craft space at the Museum of Arts & Design in New York City, Gschwandtner hung machine-knit photo-blankets based on historical images of knitting during wartime. Portraying groups of men as well as women knitting gently disrupted some of the tenacious gender associations knitting continues to carry.

In the years since the article was published, knitting has continued to enjoy mainstream attention as one of the most accessible forms of textile practice. Now often cited as a useful activity in conversations about mental health, social media has played an instrumental role in sharing information not only about the technique of knitting but also about building and connecting communities. Some of the same social media platforms instrumental in building knitting communities have also been the site of posts expressing accusations of racism, a lack of representation, copyright infringement and cultural appropriation. Gschwandtner's consideration of the variety of purposes knitting may take in contemporary life remains central to an expanded understanding of what textile structures may teach us.

Knitting is . . .

Sabrina Gschwandtner

When I'm asked what I do I often reply that I'm an artist who works with film, video and textiles. To me the link between the three is instinctive and implicit—media is a textile—and my work expresses why and how I find that to be true. The model for my career as an artist, curator, writer, editor and publisher is knitting.

I started knitting in my final semester of college as an art/semiotics student at Brown University. Two of my roommates were textile students at the Rhode Island School of Design and when they came home late at night, still full of energy, they'd climb onto the yellow stools in our kitchen and chatter and spool yarn toward their needles like addicts. They showed me the basics of knitting and crochet (my mother had taught me when I was eight but I had mostly forgotten) and I was charmed. I started to knit during breaks from the dense theory I was reading for school; stitching, I was completely concentrated on the rhythm of my hands and my frenetic mind would go empty. Within a few months, although I had been rigorously devoted to experimental and avant-garde film during all four years of college, handcraft had become my guiding creative format.

I'd knit or crochet something, leave it, come back, rip it up, fix it, wear it, add some other material, hang it up, leave it, project film onto it, record that, edit it, show it, give it away and start over. Even when I'm not working with knitting as my actual medium or technique I'm still working with it as a single thread out of which emerges a surface, a fabric, a narrative, an outfit, a pattern, a text, a recording, and even, despite my seemingly erratic way of working, a form that encompasses all of these things.

KNITTING IS SCULPTURE

Stitching was how I first conceived of working with film as a sculptural material. For an early project, I sewed onto 35 mm slides that had come back from the lab blurry and unusable as the documentation I'd intended. I found that when the sewn slides were projected, the pattern of the thread and the holes left by the sewing needle became the foreground imagery, instead of the photographic image on the slide. The fan of the slide projector blew the loose threads in all directions, which also caused an unusual kind of animation. The slide projector's automatic focus mechanism struggled to focus on the three-dimensional thread hanging in front of and behind the slides and it sometimes gave up, leaving the viewer to inspect a blurry field in between thread and image. I selected a group of eighty slides, put them into the carousel and let them project for ten seconds each in a continual loop. This was the piece; all the ways in which the slide projector abstracted and activated a non-narrative about space. In conceiving of an approach to filmmaking that was in part defined by the craft ethos of mending and recycling but still devoted to the history of avant-garde cinema, I was able to expand on the potential for the projected image, but place it within the context of handcraft.

KNITTING IS PARTICIPATION

The more I worked with handcraft materials, the more I came to think about the social spaces they implied. I swung from making quiet, sculptural spaces to creating sites of conversation. I realized that knitting had potential to reach out to a different audience and that collective crafting and dialogue could be part of the art experience: it could catalyze a different kind of exchange, outside of traditional art audience boundaries. This reflected a new interest in the public sphere and in creating artwork with social and political components.

Source: Sabrina Gschwandtner, 'Knitting is . . .', *The Journal of Modern Craft* 1:2 (July 2008), pp. 271–8. Reprinted by permission of Informa UK Limited, trading as Taylor & Francis Group, www.tandfonline.com.

I started thinking about handcraft as a site of resistance—to an oppressively commodity-based art market and to an omnipresent, excessive, and high-speed communicative landscape—but also as a site of empowerment and activism. Knitting has, after all, become popular during every major American war.[1] During wartime, knitters have used their craft for civic participation, protest, therapeutic distraction, and even direct attack.[2]

For my piece *Wartime Knitting Circle*, an interactive installation created for the Museum of Arts & Design's 2007 exhibition "Radical Lace and Subversive Knitting," I wanted to exploit these different uses of wartime knitting in order to incite political conversation between different kinds of people. Knitters represent a diverse audience group in terms of age, race, politics and economics (for every knitter using qiviut, spun copper, or other high-priced yarns there is a knitter making clothes out of economic necessity).

The installation consisted of nine machine-knitted photo blankets—which in 2005 became a popular way for families to honor their relatives who had been deployed to Iraq and Afghanistan—depicting images culled from newspapers, historical societies and library archives that all showed different ways knitting has been and is being used during war. The installation provided a space and materials for knitters to work on wartime knitting projects; it was also a place for them to consider the role their handcraft could play in the Iraq war. Knitters were allowed to bring in their own projects, or they could choose to work on one of four wartime knitting patterns that were provided. The patterns included Lisa Anne Auerbach's Body Count

Mittens,[3] which memorialize the number of US soldiers killed at the time the mittens are made; a simple square to be used for blankets, which were either mailed to Afghans for Afghans[4] or to US soldiers recovering in military hospitals; balaclavas to be sent either to troops in Iraq and Afghanistan or to Stitch for Senate, microRevolt.org's war protest project;[5] and *USS Cole* Slippers, sent to troops on ships. Many of these items were knit by several different people; one knitter would cast on, add a few stitches or rows, then put the project down and later another knitter would advance the piece.

I witnessed several heated arguments at the knitting table and I participated in one of them.

A visitor comment book included in the installation recorded some of what happened when I wasn't there:

Political associations made for a more interesting group knitting experience. *Devon Thein*

Added a bit to the helmetliner—Kay worked a square, of course. *Ann Shayne*

Knitting in public is a radical act. *Bonnie Gray*

My earliest memories are the clack of knitting needles (on the therapeutic theme)—my grandmother knitted continuously as we sat in the air-raid shelters in Scotland 1942–45. *S. Holton*

KNITTING IS COMMUNITY

When I started KnitKnit in 2002 it was a very personal format for my thinking through the connections between handcraft and fine art. I had been making one-of-a-kind knit and crochet clothes by hand and selling them to boutiques in Manhattan for about two years when I decided that I wanted to return to art making. I interviewed two friends who had come to handcraft, like me, after studying fine art in college and I put that text into a very rough, photocopied and stapled booklet with spray-painted stencils. *KnitKnit* became a biannual 'zine that took different formats each time and included contributions by all kinds of artists, designers, writers and makers: producing KnitKnit, distributing it, and organizing KnitKnit launch events and art exhibitions were ways to create a far-flung community of people interested in displacing the boundaries between art and craft.

When I initiated a KnitKnit book in 2006, I purposely situated it as a craft *and* an art endeavor, working with a craft book editor at Abrams, a publishing house that also makes and distributes art books. With the publisher committed to sending the book to major chains, art bookstores and yarn shops, I chose to profile a mix of knitters making clothing, sculpture, graffiti, therapy, protest and performance, juxtaposing political and conceptual gestures with functional and technical achievements.

KNITTING IS WRITING

This is why so many knitters blog; they're dauntingly aware that making a sweater is, in a way, writing history. As Jim Drain told me when I was interviewing him for my book, ". . . knitting is a living tradition—it's physical knowledge of a culture. Knowledge of language dies so quickly. It's awesome to find a sweater and look at the language of it—to see how it's made, what yarn was used, and how problems were solved. A sweater is a form of consciousness."[6]

My 2007 video, *A History of String*, includes a chapter on quipus, which are recording devices from the Inca Empire. Quipus are beautiful bundles of twisted and knotted colored threads that were continuously tied and retied and presumably read by touch and sight. Each part of the quipu—length, color of string, number of knots, and type of knots—is thought to contain meaning. Because the Spanish destroyed as many quipus as they could find during their colonial conquest, only about 600 pre-Columbian examples survive, preserved in private and museum collections. Although quipus are generally believed to contain numerical information, some anthropologists are working to translate them into language, reading them as three-dimensional binary code (similar to the way computers translate eight-bit ASCII into letters and words).[7]

One has to wonder how future generations might read our sweaters if written and photographic records of them are lost.

KNITTING IS GIFT

I co-curated (with Sundown Salon founder Fritz Haeg and producer Sara Grady) a salon called the KnitKnit Sundown Salon in 2004. The daylong event included a meeting of the Church of Craft, an exhibition of art and craftworks, a film/video screening, a performance and several impromptu fashion shows, among other happenings. It wasn't just the quality of the work inside the geodesic dome where the event was held, nor the abundant activities there that made the salon so memorable; it was the complete reciprocity with which the work was given and received. For eight

hours on a cold February day in Los Angeles, the KnitKnit Sundown Salon existed as a utopian, three-tiered marvel of handmade wonders and a communal undertaking that gave me hope for the rise of a new social order.[8]

KNITTING IS PLEASURE

As my mentor Leslie Thornton wrote to me by email:

> I know I've told you this, many women my age must tell you the same thing, but making things, sewing, designing all of my own clothes, knitting, even making beads, but that was much later, when the train to Providence was driving me crazy, so anyway, I was saying, in this very long sentence, possibly the longest I've ever written in my life, I made things nearly constantly when I wasn't in school, studying, going to rock concerts or sleeping, playing kickball, or riding my bike or picking flowers in our huge beautiful yard or catching frogs, from the age of three on.

KNITTING IS HOME

Through my friend Alysa Nahmias, who had at the time just started her architecture degree at Princeton, I learned of Gottfried Semper, the nineteenth-century architect and theorist who asserted that woven and knitted materials effectively separated inner and outer life to create what we know as "home." After a trip to a library, where I read more of his writings, I ended up reprinting one of his texts in *KnitKnit's* third issue. Brian Sholis, an art critic, wrote an introduction to the issue that included the following lines: "Semper not only rehabilitates arts and crafts, integrating them more fully with our understanding of architecture and other fine arts; he also smudges the line between 'advanced' and 'barbaric' contributions to culture, reincorporating the contributions of minority citizens to the achievements of ancient Greece, Egypt, and beyond."[9]

At a "Stitch In" at the Jersey City Art Museum in October 2007 I gave a short talk about war and handcraft. It concluded with a recollection of someone telling me that she thought women did housekeeping/

homemaking activities with a kind of irony these days. I asked how the audience felt about that. It really got people going—everyone has an opinion about their home. One by one people spoke up and their responses ranged from detailed explanations of 1970s fiber art to Martha Stewart's design influence on the marketplace to the agony of making a decision about whether to hire a housekeeper to ideas about post 9/11 nesting.

Swedish critic Love Jönsson put this forward during a recent lecture: avant-garde art proposes an access to the everyday that craft, through its traditional link to utility and material culture, already has. Young artists working with handcraft do not need an art world seal of approval, he said, and in reevaluating the craft tradition they have emphasized that:

- making things by hand is joyful; and
- "the functional object is the most interesting one."[10]

Whether knitting is high architecture, hip Home Ec, functional art, or a reaction to terrorism, it is helping us think through our notions of domesticity.

KNITTING IS MEDIA

It's true that people pick up crochet hooks as an escape from the computer. In the face of everything fast and glinting, they want something real—a reinjection of the artisanal or some sense of the integrity of labor. But handcraft will usually send them to the web, which is a contemporary Whole Earth Catalog if you know where to look. When crafters go online searching for instruction they usually end up commenting on other crafters' blogs or posting to myriad threads on craft community boards. In contrast to the lifestyle associated with the professional craftsperson of the late twentieth century (which is still the academic craft model), DIY crafters fluidly use technology to market and sell their work and participate in their communities. As artist and knitwear designer Liz Collins has remarked, "putting together a MySpace page is not that different from collaging or quilting. You're using different materials, to different ends, but along the way you're starting with matter and transforming it into something else, using your hands and your brain."[11]

Knitting is a site, and it can and should be used as a form of broadcasting, just like the Internet, television, or any other public media.

Notes

1. Allison Smith, *The Muster* (New York: Public Art Fund, 2007).
2. Anne MacDonald, *No Idle Hands: the Social History of American Knitting* (New York: Ballantine Books, 1990).
3. See www.stealthissweater.com/patterns/mittenpattern.pdf.
4. See www.afghansforafghans.org.
5. See www.stitchforsenate.us.
6. Sabrina Gschwandtner, *KnitKnit: Profiles and Projects from Knitting's New Wave* (New York: Stewart, Tabori and Chang, 2007), p. 52.
7. Sabrina Gschwandtner, "A Brief History of String," *Cabinet* 23 (Winter 2006): 38–41.
8. Fritz Haeg (ed.), *Sundown Salon 2001–06 In Words and Pictures* (New York: Evil Twin Productions, 2008).
9. Brian Sholis, "Writings of Nineteenth Century Architect Gottfried Semper," in Sabrina Gschwandtner (ed.) *KnitKnit* 3 (January 2004): 1.
10. Urban FIELD symposium, University College for the Creative Arts, Farnham, England. November 14, 2007.
11. Julia Bryan-Wilson (ed.), "The Politics of Craft," *Modern Painters* (February/March 2008): 78–83.

22

CIRCULAR SPEEDS
A Review of Fast & Slow Sustainable Design Approaches for Fashion & Textile Applications (2019)

Kate Goldsworthy, Rebecca Earley and Kay Politowicz

EDITOR'S INTRODUCTION

Co-authors Kate Goldsworthy, Rebecca Earley and Kay Politowicz were each associated with the research group Textiles Environment Design (TED) at the University of the Arts London before Earley and Goldsworthy co-founded the Centre for Circular Design, also based at UAL, in 2017. The article reprinted here presents a summary of some of the key themes all three researchers have tackled over the past decade. While sustainability research may seem more appropriately placed under the heading of production in this book, this article is included within the structure section because of the expanded shift in emphasis their writing explores. In place of oversimplified debates that focus solely on production, this article takes a broader view of textiles and fashion that instead summarizes some of the structures that may eventually epitomize future consumption and production alternatives.

In this writing the co-authors question, 'how a polarization of thinking in relation to "speeds" has occurred'? (abstract). Drawing material from the first phase of the Mistra Future Fashion research project, the article contextualizes how and when an emphasis on 'slow design' emerged before moving to suggest that it is in fact a combination of both 'slow' and 'fast' approaches that may provide the most feasible contribution to designing for a circular economy. Alongside alternative approaches to production is an acknowledgement of the businesses that support not only repair of their products but also short-term loans and rehoming. This article shares with Ursula K. Le Guin's writing about community an attention the importance of open dialogue that is necessary to accurately understand the limitations of textile manufacturing.

The original article contains charts and images that have not been reproduced in this version of the text.

Circular Speeds: A Review of Fast & Slow Sustainable Design Approaches for Fashion & Textile Applications

Kate Goldsworthy, Rebecca Earley and Kay Politowicz

INTRODUCTION

This article aims to further the understanding of designing for textile product speeds in a circular fashion context, by examining theoretical, industry and practice-based research contexts (Earley et al. 2016).

Design and production has changed to meet the need for speed, growing populations and the cultivated fast fashion appetite. Conversely, the idea of designing durable and long-lasting fashion textiles has been a part of the fashion industry from the outset – long before product obsolescence had been dreamt up in the 1950's, yet the idea of slow fashion has been promoted in recent years as a new counter approach to *fast fashion*. In this paper the authors propose another way of viewing the speed of fashion products by building on the work of Fletcher & Tham around *rhythms* (Lifetimes, 2004), and also drawing insights from the authors' practice-based work during MFF Phase 1 (2011–2015).

The concepts of fast and slow fashion have gained increased attention during recent years. This may in part be due to a renewed and intensified media coverage of the unwanted implications of the fast fashion industry, which can be seen on a local, regional and worldwide scale (including water, air and soil pollution, climate impact, shortage of arable land, harmful and unsafe working conditions, poor workers rights', fatal factory accidents, etc.). In addition, the slow movement, which has been promoted by NGOs and other groups and individuals, is growing stronger. Slow living, spanning from food to fashion to other daily practices, is now an established phenomenon of the Western world – offered as an antidote to the fast-paced living that dominates our societies.

Furthermore, the notion of a circular economy, as promoted by the Ellen MacArthur Foundation, and its associated principles has gained rapid ground and widening political support over the last years. Circular approaches are now being explored by many fashion companies, and new technological advances bring us ever closer to a truly circular materials system.

CIRCULAR DESIGN

Circular design first became relevant to textile designers through McDonnough and Braungart's *The Hannover Principles* (1992) followed by the more widely cited *Cradle to Cradle* (2002), where the sixth principle "eliminate the concept of waste" pointed towards a far more holistic notion of materials recovery as compared to the then common "reduce, reuse, recycle" mantra. They called for the optimisation of the "full lifecycle of products and processes to emulate natural systems, in which there is no waste", and suggested that current methods perpetuated a cradle-to-grave strategy, which was ultimately a linear one. Circular design aims to redefine sustainability models as a more cohesive and connected approach. It is not simply about recycling materials, or even about closed-loops of material recovery. Circular design is at its very core a concept of systems thinking with cycles of every size and speed considered.

Fast, Slow and Everything in Between

The research on fashion and speed is well underway, starting with the research of Fletcher and Tham through their definition of "clothing Rhythms" (2003) and the Lifetimes project (2004) which explored rhythms

---

Source: Kate Goldsworthy, Rebecca Earley and Kay Politowicz, 'Circular Speeds: A Review of Fast & Slow Sustainable Design Approaches for Fashion & Textile Applications', *Journal of Textile Design Research and Practice* 6:1 (2018), pp. 42–65. © Kate Goldsworthy, Centre for Circular Design, University of the Arts London https://www.circulardesign.org.uk/. Reproduced with permission.

through wardrobe studies and classification of existing clothing archetypes. More recently these concepts have been explored through practice-based research with the work of Earley, Goldsworthy, Politowicz and researchers at University of the Arts London (Textile Toolbox, 2014), as part of MFF, Phase 2. This study aims to further add to the slow-fast fashion framework, by setting the scene in theoretical, industry and practice-based research contexts.

Carl Honoré's "In Praise of Slow" (2004) proposed that we seek balance – the right speed – and that we question the notion that faster is always better. This sits at ease with the sustainability discourse which calls for slower consumption and more durable products. But equally there are examples of all speeds in the natural world which point towards positive appropriation of both fast and slow systems. We see the same positive and expansive examples of the full spectrum from fast to slow in other industries, for example food and architecture. Street food offering fast yet authentic and healthy alternatives to the processes and mass-produced fast-food on offer in another part of the market, and even "fast architecture" providing appropriately temporary building structures for disaster zones or short-life exhibition concepts. Perhaps slowing down is not the only solution to the environmental challenges we face.

In the natural world, "small and fast" lifecycles exist in combination with "large and slow", to arrive at a suitable ecosystem for survival. The combination of different natural speeds related to durability enables the entire system to continue. Brand (1985) proposes that we should "adopt this approach in the imaginative design of systems". Fletcher suggests in "The Speed Factor" (2011) that, "applying ideas of speed and rhythms of use to fashion and textiles helps us develop a new vision for the sector that has the potential to reduce some of the negative impacts of consumerist 'fast' fashion. If we look at how speed is dealt with in nature, we see combinations of fast and slow. Ecosystems achieve balance and long-term resilience of the larger system by adjusting to change at different paces."

Rather than pursue a polarised approach to viewing "speed of use" (which often limits attention to a small part of the whole lifecycle), the authors here argue that a more nuanced method of analysing speed is needed which acknowledges the entire lifecycle of a product. We should in fact be considering the right speed for each garment within specific lifecycle stages.

[…]

The Role of Design in a Creative and Collaborative Methodology

Integral to the development of good design practice are the current ideas from relevant disciplines: anthropology, business studies, materials science, behavioural economics, design studies, histories of dress and theories of sustainability. This multi-disciplinary integration is at the very heart of the project. Systemic solutions, such as is its remit, cannot be nurtured and developed in academic silos and so research is being developed in four discipline-crossing themes in order to promote a truly collaborative process.

Design research serves as a vital means of connection between these scientific practices. In 1986, Appadurai described the social role of artists as critical as "they are thinking about new ways to arrange things". He commends their ability to imagine new possibilities and form alliances with other disciplines, which can have practical applications. To benefit social progress, the imagination of artists and designers needs to be connected to innovation in science and technology. In an interview, Tonkinwise (2015) pointed out that the job of design is not confined to "the creation of artifacts, whether communications, products, or environments. But the practice of design is actually about persuading a wide range of actors – fellow designers, suppliers, investors, logistics managers, users in households, workplaces or public spaces, etc. – to work together on materializing a future in which such an artifact exists."

Design can play a pivotal role in improving performance at every stage of the socio-material lifecycle. By working in communities of practice, designers can identify both the physical and psychological barriers to more sustainable solutions, translating them into creative proposals for transformation.

Design can work at both micro and macro scale (both materials/ products and systems innovation) to avoid the often unintended con- sequences which can come from looking only at parts of the lifecycle and value chain. Designers need to work with circularity principles within a sustainability framework and to fully understand the technical and biological cycles within the circular economy. Yet innovation in the field has shown us that for textile designers, circular design also needs to consider how these cycles can interconnect; and how understanding the speed of these cycles is also important in making appropriate design choices. The inter-disciplinary practice-based textile design being carried out in this project aims to generate new insights for this emerging design field.

The overwhelming complexity and lack of trans- parency of environmental problems can be discoura- ging. But designers have an ability to apply systems thinking, in a creative method that Ackoff (2006) terms "problem dissolving", which shifts the problem into a new context. Designers can then construct new approaches based on reflection, logic and the generation of creative, speculative ideas. To do this, the poetic and lateral-thinking outcomes of the design process are best achieved in collaborative communities of practice. In order to be influential to innovation on a large scale, design outcomes need to be pre-emptive rather than reactive and locate physical products as part of material and immaterial systems.

We are seeking to relate these material (in the broadest sense) choices appropriately to a specific lifecycle context. All garment journeys are not the same and all users are not uniform in their behaviour and wardrobe curation. Each fashion consumer will have a complex and varied collection of garments in their care and this variety and complexity is essential in any consideration of a solution.

Circular Design Through the Prototype

Designers are intrinsically connected to materials in proposing their transformation into objects, which have both meaning and practical application. However, a C21st understanding of the expenditure of energy, water and valuable material commodities to make artefacts, is also leading us to seek "immaterial" extensions of objects in use, as propositions to lighten the material load. A way forward for the fashion designer is to study the preferences and behaviour of a particular social group. Understanding their aspirations and the triggers to purchases can enable designers to propose desirable models for an improved fashion system.

To achieve sustainability and circularity through design, an understanding of impacts through all stages of the life-cycle must be understood in order to tackle the reduction of damage resulting from existing practices. A product can be redesigned to improve its overall performance, by understanding its context in this lifecycle system. "Re-directive practice" results in what Fry describes as design "re-coding": "the exposure of the unsustainable and the declaration of means of sustainment" (2009). When this is embodied in a prototype, the reflective "conversation" takes place in a series of project revisions. As a result of surprise realisations or "backtalk" from the prototype, the designer can test, redesign and collaborate with other disciplines and ultimately, with the consumer, who can become part of the prototype community (Winograd 1996). In this way we are using the prototype alongside multi-disciplinary collaboration in order to question and find insight on these circular models. First to expose the unsustainable elements in order to then design them out of the system.

But how can designers know that they are not simply sustaining the unsustainable, in working towards reduced impacts? They cannot. Popper (1984) summ- arized the dilemma: "It is important that we realise just how little we know about these unforeseeable conseq- uences of our actions. The best means available to us is still trial and error: trials that are often dangerous and even more dangerous errors. What remains is the problem of selecting among our tentative solutions, "our guesses" according to a method that is open to us." Designers can only integrate the components they believe are necessary for sustainability, while making key trade-offs in search of better design solutions. The "re-direction" of generic design observed in all individual and social activity, is best complemented and reinforced by a systems approach in "transition design" (Irwin, Tonkinwise and Kossoff 2015).

However, we are mitigating this uncertainty through developing relationships between the hard and soft elements of the research. By working closely with both science and industry partners on the project we aim to reveal deeper insight and map metrics into the design process (Goldsworthy et al., 2017). Further work with stakeholder groups and a programme of designers-in residence (both with science and industry partners) will expand and evolve the understanding of issues.

[…]

SLOW: BRANDS DESIGNING FOR PRODUCT LONGEVITY

Context of Slow

The original model of "slow" in fashion is a long-standing one, being a solution throughout history of applying craft-skills to make products of physical and (arguably) aesthetic longevity. In fashion terms "haute couture" has always adopted this approach. Affluent clients can select garments from beautifully made collections, with opportunities for "bespoke", customised detailing.

In the market today "slow fashion" has become synonymous with "sustainability" and to represent "high quality, durability and low impact production". Ironically this often relates only to the slowing of use and production phases and often fails to acknowledge the slow nature of synthetic materials in the raw material part of the lifecycle. Oil based synthetic fibres are based on fossil material built up over millions/billions of years, synthesised into fibres such as polyester, which in itself takes 200 years to degrade in nature.

There are many contemporary industry responses to "slow" which are having impact. In this section we look at ways to extend "product longevity" by design through the following framework.

Extending Single-User Lifetimes

This approach is achieved through functionally durable materials, timeless style & care/repair services.

This approach seeks to keep products in use as long as possible during their first life. There are many examples of companies, both traditional and contemporary focusing on material quality and durability as their manifesto, with some even guaranteeing extended durability. Many of the brands seek to use design to achieve a "classic" product– one that does not adhere to changes through trends. A few of the brands in this section invest resources in offering the user extended care and repair options or advice to the user for home care in order to maximise the life of each garment. Often companies provide all these services and approaches in tandem.

Companies who provide a focus on durable materials, timeless style or care & repair services aiming to prolong the life of a garment include; leading sustainable fashion brand Filippa K (Sweden) who develop their "Front Runners" collections to be covered by a "10 years of care" warranty system. Care of garments is emphasised with a simple guide available online giving the consumer information on how to wash mend and care for their garments; Tom Cridland (UK), created the "30-year collection" of T-shirts, sweatshirts and jackets that have a 30-year guarantee. Designed to last, any item within the range can be returned to be mended for three decades, and have been shrink-tested over 100 wash and dry cycles; outdoor company Houdini (Sweden), offer a repair programme in store to avoid replacing products that can still be used, and also promote customer involvement with garment care extending life with a set of comprehensive guidelines available online.

Other companies offering a repair service as standard include; Eileen Fisher (USA) who offer a free repair service covering moth holes, missing buttons and broken zips; Nudie Jeans (Sweden) place their repair stations visibly in store and repairs are conducted on the spot or if no longer wanted are washed, repaired and resold as second hand; Hiut Denim (UK) provide free repairs for life on all their jeans, which come with a unique number that the consumer can use to sign up the Hiut HistoryTag website. This allows customers to update the story of their jeans, where they have been, and the memories that go with them. If the jeans end up in a second hand store the story can go with them.

Enabling Multiple-User Lifetimes

The focus here is on brand leasing and clothing libraries, peer-to-peer sharing platforms and resale, charity and branded resale.

These business models provide services to give existing products new life opportunities through multiple users without material changes. All of the featured examples offer services which give products a new user life through leasing, sharing, charity options and branded resale.

Multiple-user lifetimes can be enabled in many different ways but many fashion brands are beginning to offer leasing services as part of their portfolio; Filippa K (Sweden) Lease collections are available to be leased, at a cost of 20% of the full price (this includes the cost of cleaning) for a loan of 4 days. Taking this even further the brand has developed the "Filippa K Collect" a return program which invites customers to bring unwanted garments to be resold in dedicated stores and are rewarded with a 15% voucher off the next purchase; Uniforms of the Dedicated (Sweden) runs a service called "Time Share" which is a way to rent selected suit jackets and outerwear. The scheme is offered at 15%-20% discount on the full price depending on loan period; MUD Jeans (Netherlands) was one of the earliest examples of lease wear with their "Lease A Jeans", which functions through a monthly subscription for 12 months. At the end of the year, the jeans can be kept at no further cost or exchanged for a new pair with a continued monthly fee.

Other brands are basing their whole business on a "clothing library" model; Klädoteket (Sweden) is a fashion library made up of second hand, vintage and designer collaboration pieces. Garments are categorised, and each category is worth a certain number of points to allow for a range of price-points to be included in the service; Vigga (Denmark) is an online rental service that gives parents subscription for organic children's clothing and maternity wear. Items can be returned and exchanged for the next appropriate size when needed; Rentez Vous (UK) is also an online rental service that has two strands with its business model. The first is a collaboration with designers allowing its customers to rent garments that they otherwise might not be able to afford. The second approach allows the consumer to profit from the rental of their own clothing which they can list online; Curatorz (Sweden) is a high-end fashion rental business that allows its customers to lease quality fashion items for 3 or 7 days at a time and returned to be laundered.

Peer-to peer sharing and resale platforms are also growing in popularity; Sellpy (Sweden) works as a resale tool for unwanted items with more of a focus on customer convenience than other more well- known peer to peer resale sites. A Sellpy bag is ordered and filled with unwanted items and collected from your door. Items are sorted, photographed and sold via the Sellpy website on behalf of the customer and a percentage charged on the sale. Anything not sold is either donated to charity or recycled; Shareware (Sweden), is an initiative which works with the use of social media platform Instagram. Using the hashtag #sharewear users can comment on a garment they would like to share. Once the owner has been contacted, a meeting is arranged for the garment to be handed over. Consumers are encouraged by a set of "rules" to only keep the item for one week, and then to pass the item forward in the same way they received it; Swishing (UK) was originally established by Futerra, who describe Swishing as "to rustle clothes from friends". Swishing parties, as they are known, are formally or informally organised on the premise that each person in attendance brings at least one item of unwanted clothing to contribute.

Charity and branded resale businesses include; Eileen Fisher (USA) who have a service called "Fisher Found", a national take-back programme launched in 2009 to take back any Eileen Fisher items to any store where they are resold with all profits of the second-hand resales going to charity; Myrorna (Sweden) is the largest retail chain of second-hand goods with the largest collection of goods in Sweden. All items are donated from the public or businesses and are sold within stores around Sweden or overseas; Oxfam (UK) is a charity based on public donations of unwanted clothes and sells them on in a large network of UK stores as well as an online store (Oxfam vintage); Remake (Sweden) is a design brand offshoot from Stockholm's Stadmission second hand stores. Although it has been around for fifteen years it is only in 2016 that the designs have been sold in a dedicated remake store.

All of these initiatives could encourage product longevity through multiple-user lifetimes.

Product Reconstruction & Recycling

This approach involves reinventing existing products through design intervention.

The approaches discussed so far achieve longevity with little or no "recycling intervention". These next examples create new product life-times through designer-upcycling, product reconstruction, remanufacture and mechanical recycling. Examples represent the first stage of material reinvention in order to re-elevate the value of existing products and make them suitable for further lives. This group of brands use remanufacturing approaches – achieving longevity through reinventing existing products with design intervention; Christopher Raeburn (UK) is a luxury fashion designer who has made his name as through various innovative collections and collaborations re-appropriating military material to create contemporary clothing and accessories; Rood by Rens (Netherlands) is a clothing collection that is "connected by the colour red" giving unwanted clothing a new lease of life through dying it with the same red dye to create a varying shaded collection. The red shade of each garment is dependent on the original colour, and raw materials of the garment; Lindex Re:Design (Sweden) collaborated with Re:textile at The Swedish School of Textiles in Borås to work on a pilot project, launched March 2017 upcycling denim garments collected from their previous collections; C/O Cheap Monday (Sweden) is an "upcycling project made entirely from recycled textiles" that was launched in 2016. The 500-piece unisex capsule collection is formed by disassembling and reforming unwanted clothing, many of which were collected through the bins in store, and upcycled at the Cheap Monday Stockholm HQ studio.

But material reconstruction can also happen at a more material level through mechanical recycling methods. Many craft-focussed designers are finding innovative ways to reuse waste textile materials and fibres, from crafted reconstruction of post-consumer fibres back into yarn or nonwoven textiles or into composite materials for other industry uses. Anneka Textiles (UK) is a startup business using post-consumer fashion waste to create new materials. Collecting unwanted knitted garments comprised of a mix of fibres and blends, they are colour sorted into shades ready to be mechanically pulled back to fibre, before finally spinning or felting into new materials; Sophie Rowley (UK) collects waste materials, such as denim offcuts and using a bio-resin, creates sculptural pieces that can be carved into products. In this process the layers and patterns appear, which resemble marble; Precious Waste (Netherlands) by designer Michelle Baggerman was a project that created a new material by spinning used plastic bags and weaving a cloth, that can be used to make new bags with an extended life span. This process is all done by hand without chemicals, heat or electricity and is still able to be recycled at the end of life.

Larger commercial entities are also improving on mechanical fibre recycling of predominantly pre-consumer (industrial) waste materials which provide a scalable and reliable source of raw materials; Recover (Spain) takes post-industrial cotton waste, and shreds the fibre to upcycle it into yarn. By colour sorting the waste materials, they have developed a "colourblend" blends selected colour fibre waste with a carrier fibre to strengthen the yarns, such as recycled plastic bottles; Pure Waste (Finland) is a fashion company using industrial cutting waste from garment manufacturing. The waste is sorted by colour, and spun into yarn without using dyes or fresh cotton and saving the environmental impacts created in virgin cotton production; Bright Loops (Netherlands) mechanically recycles post-consumer woollen jumpers, sorting them by colour, and blending with post-industrial waste or new durable fibres to create a new strong yarn.

FAST: BRANDS WORKING TOWARDS MATERIAL RECOVERY

Context of Fast

The increasing dominance of "fast fashion" in the current commercial context, results in a fast-moving market full of products designed to be cheap and economically efficient in production. This in turn results in the use of low-cost materials and labour, short lead times and high volume production systems. The consumer often places little value on these seemingly expendable items, buying in bulk and discarding quickly. A key insight from the 2017 Ellen MacArthur Foundation report showed a trend towards the increased volume of clothing sales and the corresponding decline in clothing utilisation (or longevity). Namely, more items worn fewer times before disposal.

This is the total antithesis of the aim of the sustainable design movement in fashion and it seems that a link between fast fashion and sustainable development would be impossible. But something exciting is happening in the materials recovery space. We are beginning to see the emergence of some truly spectacular leaps in technology towards full "fibre to fibre" recycling. There are many technologies in development which can handle a supply of mixed fibre waste which is the reality of most post-consumer waste streams. This may allow us to think of longevity in a very different way, from a materials perspective: longevity could be enabled through the recovery and reuse of materials at resource level (material longevity), and not only through product longevity.

These technologies are emerging and not yet at commercial full-scale but as progress gathers momentum we can begin to imagine the potential. Some garments may come to the end of their useful life sooner others, but if reduced impacts in the production or recovery stages (as compared to virgin production) can show an overall reduction in "cost per wear", then this may be equally beneficial in the long-term.

In this section we review the approaches & technologies which may point us towards a reconsidering or reshaping of the mass-fashion market and even a positive assessment of those garments which are unable to utilise a "slow approach". The reality is that not all garment archetypes can aspire to this.

Advances in Material Recovery

The focus here is on technologies which can recover virgin quality materials from existing textile waste streams; chemical recycling of PET, cellulose, mixed waste, and sorting technologies.

The "Well Dressed" report (Allwood et al. 2006) stated that there had been "no innovation in the recycling of textile fibres for over 200 years". Whilst this was the case in 2006, it certainly can't be claimed today. There has been unprecedented innovation and progress in technologies which can recover virgin quality materials from existing textile waste streams in the last ten years and many promising processes are now moving from the lab to pilot stage. In this section we review the current leaders in this "space race" and set the scene for a very different landscape of raw materials, making vast amounts of currently unusable materials available. Here we look at two key areas of growth, fibre-to-fibre recycling and food waste as a raw material for many of the new fibres coming to market. We are not reviewing the entire landscape of existing processes (mechanical recycling and composting which will be covered later in the project) but rather we point to the potential for virgin-quality recovered fibres as a way to improve the sustainable credentials of a material and even clean up other industries waste streams.

The chemical recycling of PET (polyester) has continued to be developed since Teijin, based in Japan, were the first to bring fibre-to-fibre technology to market with ECO CIRCLE™ in 2006. The process resulted in virgin equivalent polyester and was reported to have reduced CO_2 emissions by 77% and energy use by 84% when compared with conventional polyester. However it also commanded a 20–30% higher price (EMF, 2017: 99). Recycling innovators such as JEPLAN and Ioniqa are continuing to push this technology closer to market and research consortia including scientists in the Trash-2-Cash, Mistra Future Fashion (www.mistrafuturefashion.com) and Resyntex projects are also driving progress in the lab.

Cellulose-based textile waste can also be chemically recycled into a high quality regenerated fibre source. Evrnu (US) developed a pair of jeans made from regenerated cotton from five old t-shirts; The Infinited Fibre Company (Finland) has developed a process that processes cotton rich textile waste into new fibre without degrading the quality; Re:newcell (Sweden) takes high cellulosic content post-consumer waste to create a lyocell or viscose fibre, that is high quality in terms of tensile strength and abrasion; Ioncell-F technology (Finland) can convert waste cotton into new textiles using a 'non-toxic and environmentally friendly' Lyocell-type spinning process.

Blended materials, which are challenging to recycle, are also being explored with success. For example, recycling start-up Worn Again (with H&M and Kering) has developed a process that can separate and recapture polyester and cotton from pure and blended materials into virgin- equivalent polyester and a cellulose pulp that can be used to produce lyocell or viscose. The Hong Kong Research Institute for Textiles and Apparel in partnership with the H&M Foundation also recently developed a new process to separate cotton-polyester blends, as have researchers within the MFF project with the ReBlend initiative from RiSE (Sweden).

Waste streams from other industries, in particular agriculture and food waste, are also being utilised to create new materials, with both natural and man-made processing. This not only creates new and interesting materials which are often bio-compatible but also provides a solution for eroding waste streams for other industries. Orange Fiber (Italy) uses the tonnes of waste citrus fruit peels produced by the pressing and processing of oranges to create regenerated cellulose fibre (viscose); Fruitleather (Netherlands) is developing a new alternative leather made from fruit waste by collecting local wasted fruit and processing through mashing, cooking and drying; Ananas Anam – Pinatex (UK) has developed a leather alternative non-woven material from pineapple leaves. This innovative and high-performance textile is the by-product of pineapple harvest, and requires no additional land, water or fertilisers. Effectively, the raw materials for this group of fibres are bringing positive impacts to the industry they originate from.

Designing FOR Recovery

Here we explore in-built design features which enable more efficient recovery to support material recovery; design for disassembly, mono-materials, biocompatibility.

These imminent technology breakthroughs provide an interesting challenge for design in the future. The increased take-up of circular design thinking is already changing the way industry responds to sustainability challenges and approaches. Many companies are embedding these principles into their product development at the outset, creating garments which are specifically designed for an end-of-life recovery route; either biodegradation or closed loop chemical recovery.

Designing products for composting or biodegrading safely requires the use of wholly biocompatible materials and finishes. Adidas/Biosteel (Germany) collaborated with AMSilk to develop a pair of trainers with an upper made from Biosteel, a material that can be dissolved at home using an enzyme and water; C&A (Switzerland) and DyStar (Singapore) collaborated to create compostable t-shirts made of 100% organic cotton with no exposure to harmful chemicals and using renewable energy; Lauffenmuehle (Germany) produce Reworx, a "regenerative fabric" launched in 2017 which can be safely returned to earth as a biological nutrient including textile fibres and chemicals; Freitag (Switzerland), usually known for their upcycled "truck tarp" bags, have launched a fabric for use in workwear called "F-abric, Broken Twill". The material is 100% naturally biodegradable – including threads and selvage, with metal buttons designed to unscrew for re-use.

Designing recoverable polyester products for closed loop recycling requires, at present, the need for monomaterial (or close to monomaterial) fibre content. reWEARness (Netherlands) has developed a circular service model for its work wear, with garments made of 100% recyclable materials that can be broken down and remade into new woven material ready to be used again; Wear2 (UK) have created a thread which can be "dissolved" using microwave technology thus allowing garments to be disassembled at the end of life; Natulon (USA) has developed zips made completely from post-consumer polyester including the zip pull, teeth and tape, so that the whole zip can be perpetually recycled through a chemical recycling system.

Reducing Production Impacts

There is great potential in innovative production systems which reduce overall impacts of garments; streamlined and vertical manufacturing, redistributed production, automation, mass customisation.

Early analysis of life-cycle thinking resulted in a visualisation tool named the "Speed Cycle" (Goldsworthy, 2017), which showed that the same impact savings might theoretically be possible through reducing production impacts as for increasing garment usage. i.e. halving production impacts could have the same result as doubling the use phase. This can mean reducing impacts in an existing production system through energy efficiency, reduction in materials use and increased use of recycled materials. But it can also relate to more radical thinking. Research from Roos et al. (2015) showed that there are considerable environmental cost savings to be gained through the adoption of non-woven materials for fashion applications due to the reduction of processing steps required in the fabric production phase. There are also several examples of companies focused on this streamlining of production which show promise, including localised and on-demand production (re-distributed production), mass-customisation, vertical and merged manufacturing processes and augmented reality applications.

In particular the explosion of RdM (Re-distributed Manufacture) could be at the forefront of the next "industrial revolution". According to a recent UK research project Future Makespaces (Stewart & Tooze, 2015), RdM can be understood to be: technology, systems and strategies that change the economics and organisation of manufacturing, particularly with regard to location and scale. There is a drive towards smaller-scale local manufacturing caused by changes in transport and labour costs, the availability of materials and energy, the need for sustainability, the availability and cost of small-scale equipment, and access to information. "The potential for smaller-scale manufacture has been made possible by a combination of new technologies, small-scale flexible manufacturing equipment, and new manufacturing processes. In turn, these changes are driving the development of new business models and supply chains, changing dynamics of work and communities, and have immediate implications for industrial and social policy".

Local, automated & customised production could be set to have a huge impact on the "long tail" (Anderson, 2006) of small fashion businesses and as

such, the industry as a whole. Unmade (UK) has developed software linked to electronic knitting machines allowing quick and interactive knitwear products to be produced according to individual requirements. Using this method, the company has no need to mass produce products, and works on a made to order, local basis; Post Couture (Netherlands) offers an alternative to modern day production by embracing the "maker movement". Each design is developed to be laser cut and assembled by the consumer, either sent pre-cut to or downloaded as a digital file to be customised, inputting your measurements and laser cutting from your own material at a local machine; Open Knit Project (UK) is a kickstarter that aims to create a low cost automated digital knitting machine available to anyone, with software that allows you to adapt pre-prepared adaptable patterns or the ability to upload your own. Users can create garment pieces that are personalised and available "at the click of a button" while small companies could reduce industry lead times with quick prototyping of small collections of garments according to demand.

These emerging production models are becoming more accessible and have huge potential in lowering the impacts associated with mass production which often happens at a great distance from the eventual consumer.

CONCLUSIONS AND CIRCULAR DESIGN PROPOSALS

Through reviewing current industry activity through the lens of lifecycle speeds, we can more clearly see the opportunities for design to innovate more effectively in the circular fashion economy. Slowing down the system at product level involves extending garment lifetimes but also enabling multiple lifetimes (not necessarily long) with different users and even a level of reinvention. Where product longevity is impossible then there are options to focus on "material longevity" through the use of closed-loop fibres and progressively improving these recovery systems through design for recycling. We can also consider the reduction of production and use impacts to be as effective as the increasing of time in use where a short-lifetime is the only option.

Fundamentally we need to consider appropriate design decisions based on a realistic and defined context.

All too often approaches to sustainability and circularity are at odds, with competing strategies seemingly incompatible. Yet the potential for circular design is that it "connects" through holistic relationships, participation and collaboration. The model we should aspire to is based on a synergistic network of cycles and open loops which feed each other at multiple scales and speeds. These are complex and sophisticated transformations of materials and living matter. Within this network we will undoubtedly see both old and new technologies and processes contribute to the whole, with hi- and low-technology working together. The very same system could include slow garments, upcycled from pre-loved ones or fibres chemically recycled back to virgin quality in a closed loop system where nothing is lost.

We conclude this paper with a reflection on these approaches from a design-driven perspective. How might these approaches be turned into useful design briefs for future development?

[…]

Slow and Slower

Extending Single-User Lifetimes: design to keep products in use as long as possible for their first life. This can be achieved through the careful selection and development of functionally durable materials, which retain their quality throughout an extended life and wear appropriately for the intended time frame for use. If these materials can be paired with design intended to last beyond the short fashion cycle and so that they have maximum uses during their time in service there could be additional benefits. And services which enable careful laundry and repair either through a brand or at home could additionally extend the life of the garment.

Enabling Multiple-User Lifetimes: services which give existing products a new life opportunity. As well as the above material characteristics this approach requires connection to new models for distributing and recollecting our garments. Both industry and the consumer have a part to play here in the use of leasing and peer-to-peer sharing services, and the passing on of unwanted, but serviceable items through charity and branded resale.

Scaling Garment Upcycling: reinventing existing products with design intervention. This is where designers can create augmented value in products through their recreation and physical transformation or upcycling. Whilst often these responses are based in small or niche fashion brands there might be scope to develop upcycling practices at a larger scale through the examination of remanufacturing processes in other industries. Advances in technology and a pre-designed second life built into new garment design could be used to accelerate this shift.

Fast and Forward

Advancing Material Recovery: technologies which can recover virgin quality materials from existing textile waste streams. The rapid progress of recycling technology is providing real hope for the future of material recovery. Designers have a role to play here in spreading understanding of this constantly changing field. These step changes are not only in the area of fibre-to-fibre recycling technologies which promise "virgin quality" materials from discarded textile materials; cellulose, polyester and nylon recovery is now possible at pilot scale if not always commercially available. The recovery of mixed fibre waste is getting ever nearer, and even waste streams from other systems, such as food waste, are being utilised to a much higher value than ever before. Designers are becoming ever more involved in these technological and scientific developments, bringing new insight and innovation to many developments.

Designing FOR Recovery: in-built design features which enable more efficient recovery to support material recovery. Designers now need to understand and assess which of these end of life opportunities is most relevant to their design process and be able to respond accordingly to the requirements of the system. Ease of recyclability can be built into design practices in a multitude of ways; through design for disassembly, use of monomaterials, which relate either to the biological or technical system, and use of biocompatible or technical finishes and production processes which also fit the end of life intention. This is a difficult brief to follow as the speed of change is potentially high but there is also an increasing understanding of the features of "design for recycling" through collaborative projects such as MFF which brings together stakeholders from all areas of the value chain to create a progressive and common understanding.

Reducing Production Impacts: innovative production systems which reduce overall impacts of garments. This concept of "lighter" production systems which impact more gently on our environmental and economic systems is a huge are of potential improvement. We must enable more streamlined and vertical manufacturing opportunities, redistributed production, automation and mass customisation. Local and decentralised production can be connected to highly technological solutions.

The production of novel materials based on nonwoven technologies is crucial here and has clear environmental benefits as compared to traditional processes.

Synergies, Trade-offs and Next Steps

Whilst there are often trade-offs to be made between designing for durability and recyclability which make it difficult to choose one over the other, there are also opportunities for synergy and double-wins.

A "slow" approach may include multiple "fast" lives which build over time to reveal a super slow product. Whereas a "fast" approach might entail an ultra-short-life compostable or easily recyclable product which is designed with only a few or even a single use in mind at the outset, but by recovering it over and over again actually keep the materials in use over the longest time.

In the exploration of these extreme poles of fast and slow we begin to see a middle ground, where light production methods might be used to produce "slow garments" or distributed manufacture hubs utilised as hubs for recovery and repair; or "fast garments" being produced in such a way as to enable extended use within a limited timeframe in order to further increase the benefits to the environment.

Wardrobes contain a spectrum of archetypes and speed stories. Certain clothes in our wardrobe can be the "quality" agents we need to carry the bonds to permanence and connect to memories. They improve in value with age and are cherished. Others can be designed to be durable and connect with a system for revision, repair and renewal, where the whole or in part they could be replaced and redesigned. Others can function in a way that engages us in collective interaction, provides services and operates through temporary ownership to allow us "guardianship" for a specific period. Still more can be the outcome of mass production for a positive form of "planned obsolescence", where the material is recovered for re-manufacture, after a short time in use, because the purpose of the artefact has been served and the polluting effects of laundry outweigh the effects of production. The meaning of an object is timeless, whereas an individual garment might last only weeks before "recovery". A mixed economy for fashion and textile design can then be developed that relies on a range of engagements with users.

[…]

ACKNOWLEDGEMENTS

The research was conducted by the Centre for Circular Design (CCD, formerly TED) team of University of the Arts London (UAL) – textile design researchers who are part of the Swedish funded multi-disciplinary Mistra Future Fashion (MFF) consortium. A number of key people have further contributed to this report through supporting the CCD team in the research tasks. These include: Cathryn Hall and Helen Paine, CCD Research Assistants at UAL and Anna Brismar, Green Strategy who all contributed to the compilation of industry case study research.

References

Ackoff, R. 2006. *Idealised Design*. Upper Saddle River, NJ: Prentice Hall.

Allwood, J.M., Laursen, S.E., Malvido de Rodriguez, C. and Bocken, N.M.P. 2006. *Well Dressed?* Cambridge: University of Cambridge Institute of Manufacturing.

Anderson, C. 2006. *The Long Tail*. New York: Hyperion.

Appadurai, A. 1986. *The Social Life of Things*. Cambridge: Cambridge University Press.

Brand, S. 1985. *The Clock of the Long Now: Time and Responsibility*. New York: Basic Books.

Earley, R., et al. 2016. *The Textile Toolbox: New Design Thinking, Materials and Processes for Sustainable Fashion Textiles*. Project Report for Mistra Future Fashion, Sweden.

Earley, R. and Goldsworthy, K. (2014). *The Textile Toolbox Exhibition*. Available online at: http://www.textiletoolbox.com/ (accessed December 20, 2017).

Ellen MacArthur Foundation. 2017. *A New Textiles Economy: Redesigning Fashion's Future*. Available online at: http://www.ellenmacar- thurfoundation.org/publications (accessed February 20, 2017).

Fletcher, K. and Tham, M. 2003. "Clothing Rhythms." in E. van Hinte (ed.) *Eternally Yours: Time in Design*, pp 254–274. Rotterdam: 010 Publishers.

Fletcher, K. and Tham, M. 2004. Lifetimes Project. Available online at: http://katefletcher.com/projects/lifetimes/ (accessed January 8, 2018).

Fletcher, K. 2011. "Fashion & Sustainability: the speed factor," *HEIA Journal*, 18(2): 26–34.

Fry, T. 2009. *Design Futuring: Sustainability, Ethics and New Practice*. Oxford: Berg.

Goldsworthy, K., Roos, S., Peters, G. and Sandin, G. (2017). *Towards a Quantified Design Process: bridging design and life cycle assessment*. CT Conference Proceedings. Available online at: http:// circulartransit ions.org/media/downloads/Circular-Transitions-Pro-ceedings.pdf.

Goldsworthy, K. 2017. "The Speedcycle: a design-led framework for fast and slow circular fashion lifecycles." *12th EAD Conference, Design Journal* 20(sup1): S1960–S1970.

Honore, C. 2004. *In Praise of Slow: How a Worldwide Movement is Challenging the Cult of Speed*. London: Orion.

Irwin, T., Kossoff, G. and Tonkinwise, C. 2015. Transition Design Provocation. *Design Philosophy Papers*, 13(1): 3–11. doi: https://doi.org/10.1080/14487136.2015.1085688.

McDonnough, W. and Braungart, M. 1992. *The Hannover Principles*.

Hannover: Prepared for EXPO 2000 The World's Fair.

McDonnough, W. and Braungart, M. 2002. *Cradle to Cradle; Remaking the Way We Make Things*. New York: Northpoint Press.

Mistra Future Fashion Programme. Available online at: http://www.mistrafuturefashion.com (accessed December 21, 2017).

Popper, K. 1984. *In Search of a Better World: Lectures & Essays*. London: Routledge.

Roos, S., Sandin, G., Zamani, B. and Peters, G. M. 2015. *Environmental assessment of Swedish fashion consumption*. Available online at: http:// mistrafuturefashion.com/wp-content/uploads/2015/06/Environmental-assessment-of-Swedish-fashion-consumption-LCA.pdf (accessed December 20, 2017).

Stewart, H. and Tooze, J. 2015. "Future Makespaces and Redistributed Manufacturing," *Making Futures Journal*, 4: 1–9. Available online at: http://makingfutures.plymouthart.ac.uk/media/75718/hs_jt.pdf (accessed February 20, 2018).

Tonkinwise, C. 2015. *Responses for "21st Century. Design After Design"*, XXI Triennale di Milano. Available online at: https://cmu. academia.edu/camerontonkinwise.

Winograd, T. (ed.) 1996. *Bringing Design to Softwear*. Reflective Conversation with Materials. Donald Schon & John Bennett. Addison-Wesley. Palo Alto, CA: Stanford University Press.

FURTHER READING: STRUCTURE

Albers, Anni. 'The Pliable Plane: Textiles in Architecture', in *Selected Writings on Design*, ed. Brenda Danilowitz, 44–51, Middletown: Wesleyan University Press, 2000.

The celebrated weaver Anni Albers (1899–1994) is equally celebrated as a writer of early textile theory. Fifteen essays address the challenges of modern design and the role of the modern designer, with 'The Pliable Plane' focusing on the built environment.

Barthes, Roland. *The Pleasure of the Text*, trans. Richard Miller, New York: Hill and Wang - Farrar, Straus and Giroux, 1975, 64.

French literary theorist Roland Barthes's (1915–80) well-cited interest in, among other lines of thinking, the materiality of language appears here in his writing of text as tissue with meaning the result of endless interweaving.

Calvino, Italo. *Invisible Cities*, London: A Harvest Book/Harcourt, Inc. 1972.

Cuban-born Italian writer Italo Calvino (1923–85) uses the explorer Marco Polo as a central narrative voice in the novel that travels through a number of imagined sites that include the nomadic city of Ersilia whose inhabitants leave only a network of threads behind.

Connor, Steven. 'Witchknots, Knitwits and Knots Intrinsicate', http://www.stevenconnor.com/knots/knots.pdf.

Connor's exhibition essay reveals the numerous connotations the knot has commanded in the English language over the centuries – from innuendo to metaphor: literature, myth, folklore, lyrics are all cited to build up our understanding of what the simple structure of the knot has been used to represent.

Deleuze, Gilles. *The Fold: Leibniz and the Baroque*, Minneapolis: University of Minnesota Press, 1993, 3–13.

Gilles Deleuze (1925–95) was a French philosopher. In *The Fold* he considers the folds of space, movement and time that surround us. The writing influenced architectural thinking and has become a familiar reference in textile writing. Deleuze is also celebrated for his writing with psychoanalyst Félix Guattari.

Guss, David M. *To Weave and Sing: Art, Symbol, and Narrative in the South American Rain Forest*, London: University of California Press, 1990.

Ethnographic study of ritual and material role of basketry for the Yekuana's of Venezuela. Guss warns that to understand the symbols of Yekuana basketry, contextualization as collective, rather than individual, artefacts is necessary.

Krüger, Sylvie. *Textile Architecture/Textile Architektur*, Berlin: Jovis Verlag, 2009.

Predominantly visual study comprising a broad range of examples of textiles used in the built environment. Bilingual English and German text.

Millar, Lesley. *Textural Space*, The Surrey Institute of Art and Design University College, Surrey: James Hockey Gallery, 2001.

Bilingual Japanese and English exhibition catalogue for *Textural Space*, curated by Lesley Millar. The exhibition introduced thirteen Japanese textile artists to UK audiences many working in the format of large-scale installations.

Padovani, Clio and Paul Whittaker, 'Twists, Knots and Holes: Collecting, the Gaze & Knitting the Impossible', in *In the Loop: Knitting Now*, ed. Jessica Hemmings, 10–17, London: Black Dog, 2010.

The structure of knitting – the basic loop and more importantly the void at the centre of that loop – is proposed as a system for seeing the world. The pair test the psychoanalytic 'gaze' and the notion of 'collecting' as systems for the analysis of knitting in the photographs of Margi Geerlinks and the installations of Louise Bourgeois.

Quinn, Bradley. 'Textiles and Architecture', in *The Handbook of Textile Culture*, ed. Janis Jefferies, Diana Wood Conroy and Hazel Clark, 51–64, London: Bloomsbury Visual Arts, 2016.

Quinn has published extensively on architecture and fashion. This chapter reviews some of the textile innovations to appear in architectural work in recent decades.

Turney, Joanne. *The Culture of Knitting*, London: Bloomsbury, 2009.

Turney takes a broad and accessible approach to her research. Examples from amateur to high fashion cut across typical disciplinary hierarchies and instead place one specific textile structure – knitting – at the centre of her research.

von Busch, Otto. *Notebook on Textile Punctum: Embroidery of Memory*, selfpassage.org, 2005, http://selfpassage.info /textilePunctum/textPunctum.pdf.

Organized as twenty-eight vignettes, part-autobiographic and part-academic writing that muses on the Roland Barthes' levels of reading in *Camera Lucida*: the general 'studium' and 'punctum', or personal jolt or prick applied to the context of fashion and the act of embroidery.

PART FOUR

POLITICS

PART INTRODUCTION

In the politics section contributors address how the textile relates to power and social relations. The section opens with an excerpt from James Fenimore Cooper's humorous *Autobiography of a Pocket Handkerchief*, which offers a thinly disguised attack on the social values of America during Fenimore Cooper's time and a critique of the harsh division of wealth and opportunity existing in France. The story is communicated via the main character – one uncommonly articulate handkerchief. Fenimore Cooper brushes metaphors aside and turns the textile into the storyteller, using its nonhuman identity as a shield for his criticisms of class and economics.

Arthur Danto follows with a reminder that the ancient Greeks used the woven structure to explain the responsibilities of citizenship and government. Interestingly, this metaphor is not applied in a restrictive sense. Instead, Danto reminds us of how Plato used the structure of weaving to suggest the adaptable nature of decision-making in the absence of laws.

Sarat Maharaj's writing on the textile in relation to Britain's waning identity as a colonial power opens a group of postcolonial texts. Susan Bean considers the remarkable influence of textiles in the life of Mahatma Gandhi (1869–1948) and his non-violent resistance movement, which contributed to Indian independence. Pamela Johnson then uses the genre of poetry to take up ideas of cultural identity and the movement of cultural traditions and language. Her poem offers a reminder of the many ways Britain's contemporary multicultural identity operates in daily life.

Focus then moves to the Russian city of Ivanovo, coined in the nineteenth century the 'Russian Manchester' or 'Red Manchester' because of its textile manufacturing. Translated from Russian by Sophie Abasheva for publication here, Galina Kareva introduces some of the Ivanovo's Agitprop printed textiles held in the Ivanovo Calico Museum collection of the Ivanovo State Museum of History and Local Lore. Soviet desire to immerse citizens in the values of Socialism included new household items such as the printed textiles Kareva discusses.

The final three texts in the politics section share a feminist outlook. Elissa Auther writes about fiber art made in America with attention to the power structures that have contributed to its misunderstood and devalued status. Auther refers to the 'extra-aesthetic forces affecting the formation of the fiber movement' and reveals the numerous individuals who, intentionally and unintentionally, contributed to the identity of American fiber art. An excerpt from Julia Bryan-Wilson's book *FRAY: Art and Textile Politics* (2017) addresses the research strategy she uses throughout the book. Setting professional and amateur side by side, Bryan-Wilson foregrounds the place of textile making in claiming the personal as political and establishes the role textiles have contributed to the gay liberation movement.

The final writing in this section steps back over a century to Charlotte Perkins Gilman's short story 'The Yellow Wallpaper'. Gilman uses pattern as the basis for a narrative about the expectations and demands placed on women's identity. The story is communicated to us via an unreliable narrator and we are left wondering if Gilman's yellow wallpaper is a physical prison or a mental one. Perhaps it is both. Time has moved on, but some may fairly wonder if the doubts Gilman raises have in fact progressed significantly in the 130 years since the story was first published.

23

AUTOBIOGRAPHY OF A POCKET HANDKERCHIEF (EXCERPT) (1843)

James Fenimore Cooper

EDITOR'S INTRODUCTION

The American author James Fenimore Cooper was born in 1789 and died in 1851, publishing numerous novels during his lifetime. He is perhaps most famous for the 1992 film adaptation of his novel, *The Last of the Mohicans*, set in 1757 and starring Daniel Day-Lewis. An excerpt from his *Autobiography of a Pocket Handkerchief* is printed here. The story was first published in a magazine in 1843, with subsequent, slightly different, versions released.

The idea of an object acting as a narrator is now a familiar literary strategy, but when Fenimore Cooper wrote the story the premise of an embroidered handkerchief acting as lead narrator was less familiar. The earliest examples of object narration are credited to writers a century earlier. The strategy provides us with a real, if humorous, example of the textile literally remembering and recounting the course of its life. The technique provided Fenimore Cooper with a thinly veiled cover for his criticism.

The entrenched politics of Paris and the vacuous values of New York City's nouveau riche are experienced by the textile, who recounts the modest payment earnt by the French woman who spends two months first stitching the finest embroidery, contrasted with the extreme price the woman's handkerchief eventually commands when sold in New York after passing through several middlemen, before briefly returning by chance to the same woman who stitched the linen, now working as a governess in New York. Even the linen itself carries a critique of aristocratic lineage, hailing from common flax grown beside the Connecticut River, rather than European linen.

'The handkerchief is thus an "American by origin, European by emigration, and restored to its parental soil by the mutations and calculations of industry and trade," an "aristocratic" artifact of humble birth, eminently qualified to address an American audience.'[1]

Note

1. Hannah Carlson, 'Vulgar Things: James Fenimore Cooper's "Clairvoyant" Pocket Handkerchief' http://commonplace .online/article/vulgar-things/. Accessed 4 November 2021.

Autobiography of a Pocket Handkerchief

James Fenimore Cooper

It is scarcely necessary to dwell on the scenes that occurred between the time I first sprang from the earth and that in which I was 'pulled.' The latter was a melancholy day for me, however, arriving prematurely as regarded my vegetable state, since it was early determined that I was to be spun into threads of unusual fineness. I will only say, here, that my youth was a period of innocent pleasures, during which my chief delight was to exhibit my simple but beautiful flowers, in honor of the hand that gave them birth.

At the proper season, the whole field was laid low, when a scene of hurry and confusion succeeded, to which I find it exceedingly painful to turn in memory. The 'rotting' was the most humiliating part of the process that followed, though, in our case, this was done in clear running water, and the 'crackling' the most uncomfortable.[1] Happily, we were spared the anguish that ordinarily accompanies breaking on the wheel, though we could not be said to have entirely escaped from all its parade. Innocence was our shield, and while we endured some of the disgrace that attaches to mere forms, we had that consolation of which no cruelty or device can deprive the unoffending. Our sorrows were not heightened by the consciousness of undeserving.

There is a period, which occurred between the time of being 'hatchelled'[2] and that of being 'woven,' that it exceeds my powers to delineate. All around me seemed to be in a state of inextricable confusion, out of which order finally appeared in the shape of a piece of cambric, of a quality that brought the workmen far and near to visit it. We were a single family of only twelve, in this rare fabric, among which I remember that I occupied the seventh place in the order of arrangement, and of course in the order of seniority also. When properly folded, and bestowed in a comfortable covering, our time passed pleasantly enough, being removed from all disagreeable sights and smells, and lodged in a place of great security, and indeed of honor, men seldom failing to bestow this attention on their valuables.

It is out of my power to say precisely how long we remained in this passive state in the hands of the manufacturer. It was some weeks, however, if not months; during which our chief communications were on the chances of our future fortunes. Some of our number were ambitious, and would hear to nothing but the probability, nay, the certainty, of our being purchased, as soon as our arrival in Paris should be made known, by the king, in person, and presented to the dauphine, then the first lady in France. The virtues of the Duchesse d'Angoulême[3] were properly appreciated by some of us, while I discovered that others entertained for her any feelings but those of veneration and respect. This diversity of opinion, on a subject of which one would think none of us very well qualified to be judges, was owing to a circumstance of such everyday occurrence as almost to supersede the

---

[1] 'Rotting' (or 'retting') is the process of soaking flax in water, to soften it in preparation for weaving. Its fibers are then separated out by beating, which is probably what Cooper means by 'crackling'.
[2] Combed, the final stage of preparing the flax for weaving.

[3] Marie Thérèse d'Angoulême (1778-1851), the only daughter of Louis XVI.

Source: Excerpt from James Fenimore Cooper, *Autobiography of a Pocket Handkerchief* (1843).

necessity of telling it, though the narrative would be rendered more complete by an explanation.

It happened, while we lay in the bleaching grounds,[4] that one half of the piece extended into a part of the field that came under the management of a *legitimist*, while the other invaded the dominions of a *liberal*.[5] Neither of these persons had any concern with us, we being under the special superintendence of the head workman, but it was impossible, altogether impossible, to escape the consequences of our locales. While the *legitimist* read nothing but the *Moniteur*, the *liberal* read nothing but *Le Temps*, a journal then recently established, in the supposed interests of human freedom. Each of these individuals got a paper at a certain hour, which he read with as much manner as he could command, and with singular perseverance as related to the difficulties to be overcome, to a clientele of bleachers, who reasoned as he reasoned, swore by his oaths, and finally arrived at all his conclusions. The liberals had the best of it as to numbers, and possibly as to wit, the *Moniteur* possessing all the dullness of official dignity under all the dynasties and ministries that have governed France since its establishment. My business, however, is with the effect produced on the pocket handkerchiefs, and not with that produced on the laborers. The two extremes were regular *côtés gauches* and *côtés droits*.[6] In other words, all at the right end of the piece became devoted Bourbonists, devoutly believing that princes, who were daily mentioned with so much reverence and respect, could be nothing else but perfect; while the opposite extreme were disposed to think that nothing good could come of Nazareth.[7] In this way, four of our number became decided politicians, not only entertaining a sovereign contempt for the sides they respectively opposed, but beginning to feel sensations approaching to hatred for each other.

The reader will readily understand that these feelings lessened toward the center of the piece, acquiring most intensity at the extremes. I may be said, myself, to have belonged to the *centre gauche*,[8] that being my accidental position in the fabric, when it was a natural consequence to obtain sentiments of this shade. It will be seen, in the end, how prominent were these early impressions, and how far it is worth while for mere pocket handkerchiefs to throw away their time, and permit their feelings to become excited concerning interests that they are certainly not destined to control, and about which, under the most favorable circumstances, they seldom obtain other than very questionable information. […]

4

From this time, the charming Adrienne frequently visited the bleaching grounds, always accompanied by her grandmother. The presence of Georges was an excuse, but to watch the improvement in our appearance was the reason. Never before had Adrienne seen a fabric as beautiful as our own, and, as I afterwards discovered, she was laying by a few francs with the intention of purchasing the piece, and of working and ornamenting the handkerchiefs, in order to present them to her benefactress, the dauphine. Madame de la Rocheaimard was pleased with this project; it was becoming in a de la Rocheaimard, and they soon began to speak of it openly in their visits. Fifteen or twenty napoleons[9] might do it, and the remains of the recovered trousseau would still produce that sum. It is probable this intention would have been carried out, but for a severe illness that attacked the dear girl, during which her life was even despaired of. I had the happiness of hearing of her gradual recovery, however, before we commenced our journey, though no more was said of the purchase. Perhaps it was as well as it was; for, by this time, such a feeling existed in our extreme *côté gauche*, that it may be questioned if the handkerchiefs of that end of the

[4] Open spaces where new linen is stretched out on the ground to whiten in the sun.
[5] *Legitimist*: a royalist who supported the claims of the representative of the senior line of the house of Bourbon to be the legitimate king of France. Leftist *liberals* argued for reform.
[6] 'Left side' liberals and 'right side' *legitimists* (French).
[7] "'Nazareth! Can anything good come from there?'" (John 1:46)

[8] Center left (French).
[9] Gold coin minted in the reign of Napoleon I, equal to twenty francs.

piece would have behaved themselves in the wardrobe of the dauphine with the discretion and prudence that are expected from everything around the person of a princess of her exalted rank and excellent character. It is true, none of us understood the questions at issue, but that only made the matter worse; the violence of all dissensions being very generally in proportion to the ignorance and consequent confidence of the disputants.

I could not but remember Adrienne, as the *commissionaire* laid us down before the eyes of the wife of the head of the firm, in the rue de-. We were carefully examined, and pronounced '*parfaits*;'[10] still it was not in the sweet tones, and with the sweeter smiles of the polished and gentle girl we had left in Picardie. There was a sentiment in *her* admiration that touched all our hearts, even to the most exaggerated republican among us, for she seemed to go deeper in her examination of merits than the mere texture and price. She saw her offering in our beauty, the benevolence of the dauphine in our softness, her own gratitude in our exquisite fineness, and princely munificence in our delicacy. In a word, she could enter into the sentiment of a pocket handkerchief. Alas! how different was the estimation in which we were held by Desirée and her employers. With them, it was purely a question of francs, and we had not been in the *magasin* five minutes, when there was a lively dispute whether we were to be put at a certain number of napoleons, or one napoleon more. A good deal was said about Mme la Duchesse, and I found that it was expected that a certain lady of that rank, one who had enjoyed the extraordinary luck of retaining her fortune, being of an old and historical family, and who was at the head of fashion in the *faubourg*,[11] would become the purchaser. At all events, it was determined no one should see us until this lady returned to town, she being at the moment at Rosny, with Madame,[12] whence she was expected to accompany that princess to Dieppe, to come back to her hotel, in the rue de Bourbon, about the last of October. Here, then, were we doomed to three months of total seclusion in the heart of the gayest capital of Europe. It was useless to repine, and we determined among ourselves to exercise patience in the best manner we could.

[...]

We had been near a month in the drawer, when I recognized a female voice near us, that I had often heard of late, speaking in a confident and decided tone, and making allusions that showed she belonged to the court. I presume her position there was not of the most exalted kind, yet it was sufficiently so to qualify her, in her own estimation, to talk politics. '*Les ordonnances*'[13] were in her mouth constantly, and it was easy to perceive that she attached the greatest importance to these ordinances, whatever they were, and fancied a political millennium was near. The shop was frequented less than usual that day; the next it was worse still, in the way of business, and the clerks began to talk loud, also, about *les ordonnances*. The following morning neither windows nor doors were opened, and we passed a gloomy time of uncertainty and conjecture. There were ominous sounds in the streets. Some of us thought we heard the roar of distant artillery. At length the master and mistress appeared by themselves in the shop; money and papers were secured, and the female was just retiring to an inner room, when she suddenly came back to the counter, opened our drawer, seized us with no very reverent hands, and, the next thing we knew, the whole twelve of us were thrust into a trunk upstairs, and buried in Egyptian darkness. From that moment all traces of what was occurring in the streets of Paris were lost to us. After all, it is not so very disagreeable to be only a pocket handkerchief in a revolution.

Our imprisonment lasted until the following December. As our feelings had become excited on the questions of the day, as well as those of other irrational beings around us, we might have passed a most uncomfortable time in the trunk, but for one circumstance. So great had been the hurry of our

[10] Prefect (French).
[11] Neighborhood (French).
[12] The Duchesse d'Angoulême (see note 9).
[13] Four decrees establishing absolute rule, issued by King Charles X on 25th July 1830, which touched off the July Revolution.

mistress in thus shutting us up, that we had been crammed in in a way to leave it impossible to say which was the *côté droit*, and which the *côté gauche*. Thus completely deranged as parties, we took to discussing philosophical matters in general, an occupation well adapted to a situation that required so great an exercise of discretion.

One day, when we least expected so great a change, our mistress came in person, searched several chests, trunks and drawers, and finally discovered us where she had laid us, with her own hands, near four months before. It seems that, in her hurry and fright, she had actually forgotten in what nook we had been concealed. We were smoothed with care, our political order reestablished, and then we were taken below and restored to the dignity of the select circle in the drawer already mentioned. This was like removing to a fashionable square, or living in a *beau quartier*[14] of a capital. It was even better than removing from East Broadway into bona fide, real, unequaled, league-long, eighty feet wide, Broadway!

We now had an opportunity of learning some of the great events that had recently occurred in France, and which still troubled Europe. The Bourbons were again dethroned, as it was termed, and another Bourbon seated in their place. It would seem *il y a Bourbon et Bourbon*.[15] The result has since shown that 'what is bred in the bone will break out in the flesh.' Commerce was at a standstill; our master passed half his time under arms, as a national guard, in order to keep the revolutionists from revolutionizing the revolution. The great families had laid aside their liveries; some of them their coaches; most of them their arms. Pocket handkerchiefs of *our* caliber would be thought decidedly aristocratic; and aristocracy in Paris, just at that moment, was almost in as bad odor as it is in America, where it ranks as an eighth deadly sin, though no one seems to know precisely what it means. In the latter country, an honest development of democracy is certain to be stigmatized as tainted with this crime. No governor would dare to pardon it.

The groans over the state of trade were loud and deep among those who lived by its innocent arts. Still, the holidays were near, and hope revived. If revolutionized Paris would not buy as the *jour de l'an*[16] approached, Paris must have a new dynasty. The police foresaw this, and it ceased to agitate, in order to bring the republicans into discredit; men must eat, and trade was permitted to revive a little. Alas! how little do they who vote, know *why* they vote, or they who dye their hands in the blood of their kind, why the deed has been done!

The duchesse had not returned to Paris, neither had she emigrated. Like most of the high nobility, who rightly enough believed that primogeniture and birth were of the last importance to *them*, she preferred to show her distaste for the present order of things, by which the youngest prince of a numerous family had been put upon the throne of the oldest, by remaining at her château. All expectations of selling us to *her* were abandoned, and we were thrown fairly into the market, on the great principle of liberty and equality. This was as became a republican reign.

[…]

5

The holidays were over, without there being any material revival of trade, when my deliverance unexpectedly occurred. It was in February, and I do believe our mistress had abandoned the expectation of disposing of us that season, when I heard a gentle voice speaking near the counter, one day, in tones that struck me as familiar. It was a female, of course, and her inquiries were about a piece of cambric handkerchiefs, which she said had been sent to this shop from a manufactory in Picardie. There was nothing of the customary alertness in the manner of our mistress, and, to my surprise, she even showed the customer one or two pieces of much inferior quality, before we were produced. The moment I got into the light,

[14] Good area (French).
[15] There are Bourbons and there are Bourbons (French).
[16] New Year's Day (French).

however, I recognized the beautifully turned form and sweet face of Adrienne de la Rocheaimard. The poor girl was paler and thinner than when I had last seen her, doubtless, I thought, the effects of her late illness; but I could not conceal from myself the unpleasant fact that she was much less expensively clad. I say less expensively clad, though the expression is scarcely just, for I had never seen her in attire that could properly be called expensive at all; and, yet, the term mean would be equally inapplicable to her present appearance. It might be better to say that, relieved by a faultless, even a fastidious neatness and grace, there was an air of severe, perhaps of pinched economy in her present attire. This it was that had prevented our mistress from showing her fabrics as fine as we, on the first demand. Still I thought there was a slight flush on the cheek of the poor girl, and a faint smile on her features, as she instantly recognized us for old acquaintances. For one, I own I was delighted at finding her soft fingers again brushing over my own exquisite surface, feeling as if one had been expressly designed for the other. Then Adrienne hesitated; she appeared desirous of speaking, and yet abashed. Her color went and came, until a deep rosy blush settled on each cheek, and her tongue found utterance.

'Would it suit you, madame,' she asked, as if dreading a repulse, 'to part with one of these?'

'Your pardon, mademoiselle; handkerchiefs of this quality are seldom sold singly.'

'I feared as much - and yet I have occasion for only *one*. It is to be worked - if it-'

The words came slowly, and they were spoken with difficulty. At that last uttered, the sound of the sweet girl's voice died entirely away. I fear it was the dullness of trade, rather than any considerations of benevolence, that induced our mistress to depart from her rule.

'The price of each handkerchief is five and twenty francs, mademoiselle –' she had offered the day before to sell us to the wife of one of the richest *agents de change*[17] in Paris, at a napoleon a piece - 'the price is five and twenty francs, if you take the dozen, but as you

appear to wish only *one*, rather than not oblige you, it may be had for eight and twenty.'

There was a strange mixture of sorrow and delight in the countenance of Adrienne; but she did not hesitate, and, attracted by the odor of the eau de cologne, she instantly pointed me out as the handkerchief she selected. Our mistress passed her scissors between me and my neighbor of the *côté gauche*, and then she seemed instantly to regret her own precipitation. Before making the final separation from the piece, she delivered herself of her doubts.

'It is worth another franc, mademoiselle,' she said, 'to cut a handkerchief from the center of the piece.'

The pain of Adrienne was now too manifest for concealment. That she ardently desired the handkerchief was beyond dispute, and yet there existed some evident obstacle to her wishes.

'I fear I have not so much money with me, madame,' she said, pale as death, for all sense of shame was lost in intense apprehension. Still her trembling hands did their duty, and her purse was produced. A gold napoleon promised well, but it had no fellow. Seven more francs appeared in single pieces. Then two ten-sous[18] were produced; after which nothing remained but copper. The purse was emptied, and the reticule rummaged, the whole amounting to just twenty-eight francs seven sous.

'I have no more, madame,' said Adrienne, in a faint voice.

The woman, who had been trained in the school of suspicion, looked intently at the other, for an instant, and then she swept the money into her drawer, content with having extorted from this poor girl more than she would have dared to ask of the wife of the *agent de change*. Adrienne took me up and glided from the shop, as if she feared her dear bought prize would yet be torn from her. I confess my own delight was so great that I did not fully appreciate, at the time, all the hardship of the case. It was enough to be liberated, to get into the fresh air, to be about to fulfill my proper destiny. I was tired of that sort of vegetation in which I neither grew, nor was watered by tears; nor could I see those stars on which I so much doted, and from which I had learned a wisdom so profound. The politics, too, were rendering our family unpleasant; the *côté droit* was becoming supercilious - it had always been illogical; while the *côté gauche* was just beginning to discover that it had made a revolution for other people. Then it was happiness itself to be with Adrienne, and when I felt the dear girl pressing me to her heart, by an act of volition of which pocket handkerchiefs are little suspected, I threw up a fold of my gossamer-like texture, as if the air wafted me, and brushed the first tear of happiness from her eye that she had shed in months.

[...]

When Adrienne laid me on the frame where I was to be ornamented by her own pretty hands, she regarded me with a look of delight, nay, even of affection, that I shall never forget. As yet she felt none of the malign consequences of the self-denial she was about to exert. If not blooming, her cheeks still retained some of their native color, and her eye, thoughtful and even sad, was not yet anxious and sunken. She was she felt the importance of keeping her in ignorance of her own value. By paying the franc it might give her assistant premature notions of her own importance; but, by bringing her down to fifteen sous, humility could be inculcated, and the chance of keeping her doubled. This, which would have defeated a bargain with any common *couturière*,[19] succeeded perfectly with Adrienne. She received her fifteen sous with humble thankfulness, in constant apprehension of losing even that miserable pittance. Nor would her employer consent to let her work by the piece, at which the dear child might have earned at least thirty sous for she discovered that she had.to deal with a person of conscience, and that in no mode could as much be possibly extracted from the assistant as by confiding to her own honor. At nine each day she was to breakfast at a quarter past nine, precisely, to commence work for her employer; at one, she had a remission of half an hour; and at six, she became her own mistress.

'I put confidence in you, mademoiselle,' said the *marchande de mode*, 'and leave you to yourself entirely. You will bring home the work as it is finished, and your money will be always ready. Should your grandmother occupy more of your time than common, on any occasion, you can make it up of yourself, by working a little earlier, or a little later; or once in a while, you can throw in a day, to make up for lost time. You would not do as well at piecework, and I wish to deal generously by you. When certain things are wanted in a hurry, you will not mind working a hour or two beyond time, and I will always find lights with the greatest pleasure. Permit me to advise you to take the intermissions as much as possible for your attentions to your grandmother, who must be attended to properly. *Si* - the care of our parents is one of our most solemn duties! *Adieu, mademoiselle; au revoir!*'

[...]

'Who is your boss, pocket handkerchief?' demanded the shirt, a perfect stranger to me, by the way, for I had never seen him before the accidents of the washtub brought us in collision; 'who is your boss, pocket handkerchief, I say? -you are so very fine, I should like to know something of your history.'

From all I had heard and read, I was satisfied my neighbor was a Yankee shirt, both from his curiosity and from his abrupt manner of asking questions; still I was at a loss to know the meaning of the word *boss*, my clairvoyance being totally at fault. It belongs to no language known to the *savans*[20] or academicians.

'I am not certain, sir,' I answered, 'that I understand your meaning. What is a boss?'

'Oh! that's only a republican word for "master." Now, Judge Latitat is *my* boss, and a very good one he is, with the exception of his sitting so late at night at his infernal circuits, by the light of miserable tallow candles. But all

---

[19] Seamstress (French).

[20] Learned people.

the judges are alike for that, keeping a poor shirt up sometimes until midnight, listening to cursed dull lawyers, and prosy, caviling witnesses.'

'I beg you to recollect, sir, that I am a female pocket handkerchief, and persons of your sex are bound to use temperate and proper language in the presence of ladies.'

'Yes, I see you are feminine, by your ornaments - still, you might tell a fellow who is your boss?'

'I belong, at present, to Colonel Silky, if that is what you mean; but I presume some fair lady will soon do me the honor of transferring me to her own wardrobe. No doubt my future employer - is not that the word? - will be one of the most beautiful and distinguished ladies of New York.'

'No question of that, as money makes both beauty and distinction in this part of the world, and it's not a dollar that will buy you. *Colonel* Silky? I don't remember the name - which of *our* editors is he?'

'I don't think he is an editor at all. At least, I never heard he was employed about any publication, and, to own the truth, he does not appear to me to be particularly qualified for such a duty, either by native capacity, or, its substitute, education.'

'Oh! that makes no great difference - half the corps is exactly in the same predicament. I'fegs![21] if we waited for colonels, or editors either, in this country, until we got such as were qualified, we should get no news, and be altogether without politics, and the militia would soon be in an awful state.'

'This is very extraordinary! So you do not wait, but take them as they come. And what state is your militia actually in?'

'Awful! It is what my boss, the judge, sometimes calls a "statu quo."'

'And the newspapers - and the news - and the politics?'

'Why, they are not in "statu quo"- but in a "*semper eadem*"[22] – I beg pardon, do you understand Latin?'

'No, sir - ladies do not often study the dead languages.'

'If they did they would soon bring 'em to life! "*Semper eadem*" is Latin for "worse and worse." The militia is drilling into a "statu quo," and the press is enlightening mankind with a "*semper eadem*."'

After properly thanking my neighbor for these useful explanations, we naturally fell into discourse about matters and things in general, the weather in America being uniformly too fine to admit of discussion.

'Pray, sir,' said I, trembling lest my *boss* might be a colonel of the editorial corps, after all – 'pray, sir,' said I, 'is it expected in this country that the wardrobe should entertain the political sentiments of its boss?'

'I rather think not, unless it might be in high party times; or, in the case of editors, and such extreme patriots. I have several relatives that belong to the corps, and they all tell me that while their bosses very frequently change their coats, they are by no means so particular about changing their shirts. But you are of foreign birth, ma'am, I should think by your dress and appearance?'

'Yes, sir, I came quite recently from France; though, my employer being American, I suppose I am entitled to the rights of citizenship. Are you European, also?'

'No, ma'am; I am native and to the "manor born," as the modern Shakespeare has it.[23] Is Louis Philippe likely to maintain the throne, in France?'

'That is not so certain, sir, by what I learn, as that the throne is likely to maintain Louis Philippe. To own the truth to you, I am a Carlist,[24] as all genteel articles are, and I enter but little into the subject of Louis Philippe's reign.'

This remark made me melancholy, by reviving the recollection of Adrienne, and the conversation ceased. An hour or two later, I was removed from the line, properly ironed, and returned to my boss. The same day I was placed in a shop in Broadway, belonging to a firm of which I now understood the colonel was a sleeping partner. A suitable entry was made against me, in a private memorandum book, which, as I once had an opportunity of seeing it, I will give here.

Super-extraordinary Pocket handkerchief, French cambric, trimmed and worked, in account with Bobbinet & Gull

---

[21] An archaic exclamation derived from 'In faith'.
[22] Always the same (Latin). The shirt is presumably being ironic.
[23] 'To the manner born,' from *Hamlet*, 1.4.14ff, frequently misquoted as 'to the manor born'.
[24] Supporter of King Charles X.

DR.

To money paid first cost, francs 100, at 5.25 - $19.04

To interest on same for- 00.00

To portion of passage money- 00.04

To porterage - 00.00 1/4

To washing and making up - 00.25

(*Mem.* - See if a deduction cannot be made from this charge.)

CR.

By cash, for allowing Miss Thimble to copy pattern - not to be worked until our article is sold - $1.00

By cash for sale, &c. -

Thus the account stood the day I was first offered to the admiration of the fair of New York Mr. Bobbinet, however, was in no hurry to exhibit me, having several articles of less beauty, that he was anxious to get off first. For my part, I was as desirous of being produced, as ever a young lady was to come out; and then my companions in the drawer were not of the most agreeable character. We were all pocket handkerchiefs, together, and all of French birth. Of the whole party, I was the only one that had been worked by a real lady, and consequently my education was manifestly superior to those of my companions. *They* could scarcely be called comme il faut, at all; though, to own the truth, I am afraid there is *tant soit peu de*[25] vulgarity about all *worked* pocket handkerchiefs. I remember that, one day, when Mme de la Rocheaimard and Adrienne were discussing the expediency of buying our whole piece, with a view of offering us to their benefactress, the former, who had a fine tact in matters of this sort, expressed a doubt whether the dauphine would be pleased with such an offering.

[…]

11

And here I will digress a moment to make a single remark on a subject of which popular feeling, in America, under the influence of popular habits, is apt to take an ex parte view. Accomplishments are derided as useless, in comparison with what is considered household virtues.

The accomplishment of a cook is to make good dishes, of a seamstress to sew well, and of a lady to possess refined tastes, a cultivated mind, and agreeable and intellectual habits. The real *virtues* of all are the same, though subject to laws peculiar to their station; but it is a very different thing when we come to the mere accomplishments. To deride all the refined attainments of human skill denotes ignorance of the means of human happiness, nor is it any evidence of acquaintance with the intricate machinery of social greatness and a lofty civilization. These gradations in attainments are inseparable from civilized society, and if the skill of the ingenious and laborious is indispensable to a solid foundation, without the tastes and habits of the refined and cultivated, it never can be graceful or pleasing.

Eudosia had some indistinct glimmerings of this fact, though it was not often that she came to sound and discriminating decisions even in matters less complicated. In the present instance she saw this truth only by halves, and that, too, in its most commonplace aspect, as will appear by the remark she made on the occasion.

'Then, Clara, as to the *price* I have paid for this handkerchief,' she said, 'you ought to remember what the laws of political economy lay down on such subjects. I suppose your Pa makes you study political economy, my dear?'

'Indeed he does not. I hardly know what it means.'

'Well, that is singular; for Pa says, in this age of the world, it is the only way to be rich. Now, it is by means of a trade in lots, and political economy, generally, that he has succeeded so wonderfully; for, to own the truth to you, Clara, Pa hasn't always been rich.'

'No?' answered Clara, with a half-suppressed smile, she knowing the fact already perfectly well.

'Oh, no - far from it - but we don't speak of this publicly, it being a sort of disgrace in New York, you know, not to be thought worth at least half a million. I dare say your Pa is worth as much as that?'

'I have not the least idea he is worth a fourth of it, though I do not pretend to know. To me half a million of dollars seems a great deal of money, and I know my father considers himself poor - poor, at least, for one of his station. But what were you about to say of political economy? I am curious to hear how *that* can have any thing to do with your handkerchief.'

---

[25] Ever so little of (French).

'Why, my dear, in this manner. You know a distribution of labor is the source of all civilization - that trade is an exchange of equivalents - that custom houses fetter these equivalents - that nothing that is fettered is free - '

'My dear Eudosia, what is your tongue running on?'

'You will not deny, Clara, that any thing that is fettered is not free? And that freedom is the greatest blessing of this happy country; and that trade ought to be as free as any thing else?'

All this was gibberish to Clara Caverly, who understood the phrases, notwithstanding, quite as well as the friend who was using them. Political economy is especially a science of terms; and free trade, as a branch of it is called, is just the portion of it which is indebted to them the most. But Clara had not patience to hear any more of the unintelligible jargon which has got possession of the world today, much as Mr. Pitt's celebrated sinking fund scheme for paying off the national debt of Great Britain did,[26] half a century since, and under very much the same influences; and she desired her friend to come at once to the point, as connected with the pocket handkerchief.

'Well, then,' resumed Eudosia, 'it is connected in this way. The luxuries of the rich give employment to the poor, and cause money to circulate. Now this handkerchief of mine, no doubt, has given employment to some poor French girl for four or five months, and, of course, food and raiment. She has earned, no doubt, fifty of the hundred dollars I have paid. Then the custom house – ah, Clara, if it were not for that vile custom house, I might have had the handkerchief for at least five-and-twenty dollars lower-!'

'In which case you would have prized it five-and-twenty times less,' answered Clara, smiling archly.

'*That* is true; yes, free trade, after all, does *not* apply to pocket handkerchiefs.'

'And yet,' interrupted Clara, laughing, 'if one can believe what one reads, it applies to hackney coaches, ferry boats, doctors, lawyers, and even the clergy. My father says it is – '

'What? I am curious to know, Clara, what as plain speaking a man as Mr. Caverly calls it.'

'He is plain speaking enough to call it a – *humbug*,' said the daughter, endeavoring to mouth the word in a theatrical manner. 'But, as Othello says, the handkerchief.'[27]

'Oh! Fifty dollars go to the poor girl who does the work, twenty-five more to the odious custom house, some fifteen to rent, fuel, lights, and ten, perhaps, to Mr. Bobbinet, as profits. Now all this is very good, and very useful to society, as you must own.'

Alas, poor Adrienne! Thou didst not receive for me as many francs as this fair calculation gave thee dollars; and richer wouldst thou have been, and, oh, how much happier, hadst thou kept the money paid for me, sold the lace even at a loss, and spared thyself so many, many hours of painful and anxious toil! But it is thus with human calculations: the propositions seem plausible, and the reasoning fair, while stem truth lies behind all to level the pride of understanding, and prove the fallacy of the wisdom of men. The reader may wish to see how closely Eudosia's account of profit and loss came to the fact, and I shall, consequently, make up the statement from the private books of the firm that had the honor of once owning me, viz.:

Super-extraordinary Pocket handkerchief, &c., in account with
Bobbinet & Co.

    DR

To money paid, first cost, francs 100, at 5.25 - $19.04
To interest on same for ninety days, at 7 percent - 00.33
To portion of passage money - 00.04
To porterage - 00.00 1/4
To washing and making up - 00.25

$19.661/4

    CR

By cash paid by Miss Thimble - $1.00
By cash paid for article - 100.00
By washerwoman's deduction - 00.05

101.05

By profit - $81.39?

---

[26] In 1786 William Pitt the Younger (1759-1806) introduced a sinking fund to underpin national finances.

[27] 'Fetch me the handkerchief,' from Shakespeare's *Othello*, 1.4.98.

24

WEAVING AS METAPHOR AND MODEL FOR POLITICAL THOUGHT (2006)

Arthur C. Danto

EDITOR'S INTRODUCTION

American art critic Arthur Danto (1924–2013) published numerous books on philosophy and art. His essay 'Weaving as a Model and Metaphor for Political Thought' was included in the monograph of American artist Sheila Hicks's miniature weavings published in 2006. Hicks has made a lifelong commitment to working with textiles. Her introduction to fiber is first credited as occurring in South America, where she travelled to Chile in 1957–8 on a Fulbright scholarship. Today her extensive exhibition record includes the Venice Biennial (2017), the Whitney Biennial (2014) and the São Paulo Biennial (2012).

In the writing reprinted in full here, Danto begins with the observation that we often look beyond our local cultures to learn about the meaning of textiles. He writes, 'Our culture rests on Greek foundations, and weaving is as much a part of our conceptual scheme today as it was in the time of Homer.' The 'our culture' Danto refers to is presuming European roots – an assumption now regularly questioned by decolonial work. What Danto saw in the textile metaphors frequently found in Greek literature is that the 'woven object is at once a symbol of protection and of betrayal'.

While attention to the metaphors of textiles has arguably fallen out of academic style in recent years, Danto's writing nonetheless establishes one important historical reference point for textile scholarship. His essay goes on to consider the use of weaving by the ancient Greeks as a model and metaphor for public life and observes that textile metaphors were held in 'high regard' by Plato and 'serve him as the root metaphor in his mature reflections on the art of ruling'. Danto focuses on Plato's *Republic* where the metaphor of weaving stood for the 'the ability to make decisions in the absence of rules or laws', a quality Danto acknowledges that the philosopher Immanuel Kant defined as 'genius'. In the structure section of this book, Gilles Deleuze and Félix Guattari briefly refer to Plato's use of weaving when writing of smooth and striated space.

Weaving as Metaphor and Model for Political Thought

Arthur C. Danto

Contemporary writers on the meaning of textiles and of weaving often draw their illustrations from cultures very distant from ours. This is valuable in that it shows what meanings are humanly possible, even if they are not especially our meanings. I instead shall briefly examine the way weaving figures, as model and metaphor, for the Greeks. Our culture rests on Greek foundations, and weaving is as much a part of our conceptual scheme today as it was in the time of Homer.

The complex Western attitude toward the fine arts—that they are simultaneously dangerous and frivolous—was famously articulated in the core writings of Plato two and a half millennia ago.[1] The most familiar of Plato's disenfranchising texts on the subject is, of course, *The Republic*, where he develops a metaphysics of reality and at the same time a visionary political order, in both of which the arts are marginalized: they are marginal in the universe as a whole, having only the substance of illusions, and they are more than marginal in Plato's ideal state, because the artists are to be driven into exile as inimical to the political well-being of its citizenry. But the deep mistrust stains the entire fabric of Platonic speculation—to compound a metaphor from the crafts of dyeing and especially of weaving, for which Plato had a particularly high regard and which serves him as the root metaphor in his mature reflections on the art of ruling. Since Plato stands at the origin of Western reflection on the status of the arts, it is perhaps excusable to attempt to weave into an essay on fabric and fine art a discussion of the metaphorical uses Plato makes of weaving, and to explore some of the ways fabric and its forms figure in Greek literature.

In one of the less frequently consulted dialogues, known as *Statesman*, an anonymous spokesman, identified only as the Stranger, undertakes to instruct a young thinker (identified as the Younger Socrates) in a form of philosophical method, which, if rigorously enough pursued, will yield up a definition of whatever we seek to understand. The task at hand is to define the statesman or ruler, and as the dialogue evolves, it turns out that ruling is itself a kind of art, in the sense that the ruler must make decisions often in the absence of laws. There cannot, after all, be laws for everything, and the ruler must be able to act wisely in their abeyance. What kind of art is the art of statesmanship? In the course of an exhaustive review of possibilities, Plato, predictably enough, disparages the fine arts, which the Stranger identifies as "every art which produces artistic representations whether in the visual arts or for the ear in poetry and music."[2] These "are wrought simply to give pleasure," the spokesman states without opposition. "None of them has a serious purpose; all are performed for sheer amusement." This is the "arts are frivolous" part of the Platonic indictment, which he had taken up in those dismissive passages of *The Republic* and of *Ion*, where he is bent on denying that artists have knowledge and on asserting that works of art are at best forms of illusion. Still, the investigation is governed by the thought that ruling itself is some kind of art, whatever the form of government, and the question remains: if not one of the fine arts, what sort of art can it be? Interestingly enough, in view of the invidious contrast sometimes drawn between craft and the so-called fine arts today, Plato's spokesman locates his paradigm in the art of weaving:

> What example is there on a really small scale which
> we can take and set beside kingship, and which,
> because it comprises an activity common to it and to
> kingship, can be of real help to us in finding what we

Source: Arthur C. Danto, 'Weaving as Metaphor and Model for Political Thought', *Sheila Hicks: Weaving as Metaphor*, ed. Nina Stritzler-Levine (Bard Graduate Center for Studies in the Decorative Arts, Design, and Culture/Yale University Press, New Haven, CT, 2006) pp. 22–36, 384. Reproduced with permission.

are looking for? By heaven, Socrates, I believe I know one. Do you agree that, if there is no other example ready to hand, it would be quite in order for us to select the art of weaving for the purpose?[3]

After considerable further analysis, in which the Stranger and his interlocutor identify the various "arts" necessary to the state—legislation, judging, and the like—they go on to the view that "there is an art which controls all these arts. It is concerned with the laws and with all that belongs to the art of the life of the community. It weaves all into it sunified fabric with perfect skill."[4] And to make certain that more than a useful metaphor is involved in this claim, the Stranger immediately says:

> We must describe the kingly weaving process. What is it like? How is it done? What is the fabric that results from its labors?

It is not necessary perhaps to press further into the details of the discussion here, but it is interesting to note a certain analogy between this way of thinking about "the kingly art of weaving" and what one might call the art of justice, as discussed by Plato in *The Republic*. There the aim was to find what kind of virtue justice was, in a list consisting of bravery, temperance, and wisdom; and the conclusion was that justice itself is not another item on the list, but a way of harmonizing the other virtues in the interest of producing a unity. And it must be clear that had the image of weaving occurred to him in this earlier discussion, Plato would certainly have used the art of weaving as the illuminating analogy he finds it to be in *Statesman*. Injustice, after all, is disunity or disharmony in *The Republic*, and this means a failure in the weave of the state or, since "the state is man writ large," in the fabric of the human soul. In any case, the dialogue ends with a rather exalted speech on the Stranger's part:

> Now we have reached the appointed end of the weaving of the web of the state. It is fashioned by the statesman's weaving: the strands run true, and these strands are the gentle and the brave. Here these strands are woven into a unified character. For this unity is won where the kingly art draws the life or both types into a true fellowship by mutual concord

and by ties of friendship. It is the finest and best of all fabrics.[5]

It is at times thought remarkable that Plato should have drawn so exalted a metaphorical use of what some today might dismiss as a mere craft, and one, moreover, that was associated with women in ancient Greece. Weaving is almost always an attribute of female characters in Greek literature, much as armor or weaponry is the attribute of males. When we first encounter the radiant Helen in *The Iliad*, she is "weaving a growing web, a dark red folding robe, / working into the weft the endless bloody struggles / stallion-breaking Trojans and Argives armed in bronze / had suffered all for her at the god of battle's hands."[6] Helen's red web symbolically reproduces the web of violence her beauty has unleashed upon the world, and in general, like arms, weaving is not a simple emblem of domestic order and harmony: it can even be a weapon in its own right, through which women are able to achieve their ends. Weaving—and unweaving—famously emblematizes the means through which faithful Penelope, the crafty and exemplary wife, keeps her suitors at bay while her husband makes his zigzag way home. But the tapestries Clytemnestra and her maids wove for the homecoming of Agamemnon were a trap: Agamemnon, urged by his treacherous wife to walk on purple cloths, is entangled and tethered, and, rendered helpless by what was presented in a ceremony of welcome, he is slain. Andromache weaves a warm cloak for her noble husband, Hektor, but Medea weaves a poisoned garment through which she kills the princess her unfaithful husband has fallen in love with. The woven object is at once a symbol of protection and of betrayal. But Plato is anxious to play down female superiority in such domestic accomplishments as weaving in order to argue that there is no "feminine mystique" that would bar women from the role of administration in the state: "Must we make a long story of it by alleging weaving and the watching of pancakes and the boiling pot, whereon the sex plumes itself?"[7] So a state can be just as well ordered if men were to do the weaving and women the ruling as the other way round—the only serious damage is done when someone capable of ruling is wasted in other tasks, whatever their gender.

However reactionary we find Plato on the subject of the fine arts, he was singularly enlightened in his readiness to admit women to the highest functional rank of the ideal society.

Weaving remains a powerful metaphor for certain integrative activities—we weave stories, for example, and poets, speaking in a metaphysical voice, have spoken of the way Will "has woven with an absent heed / since life first was; and ever so will weave."[8] But the industrialization of the weaving process has set between most of us and the reality of weaving a cognitive barrier opaque enough that it must come as a surprise that Plato should have found common to the arts of weaving and of statesmanship a quality of mind that is very central to the practice of an art, namely a certain kind of creative judgment—the ability to make decisions in the absence of rules or of laws—that Kant, in his great work on aesthetic judgment, should have identified as genius. The concept of genius has created great mischief for the distinction between art and craft in post-Romantic times, and it is worth highlighting Kant's way of thinking about it, inasmuch as it corresponds exactly to the way Plato thought of ruling and, by analogy, of weaving.

Kant defines genius as follows: "(1) Genius is a *talent* for producing that for which no definite rule can be given; it is not a mere aptitude for what can be learned by rule. Hence *originality* must be its first property. (2) But since it can also produce original nonsense, its products must be models, i.e., *exemplary*, and . . . must serve as a standard or rule for others."[9] Plato thinks of weaving as exercising a certain kind of judgment, which cannot be formulated nor, in consequence, applied mechanically. It is a judgment that guards against exceeding the due measure or falling short of it. It is precisely by "this effort they make to maintain the due measure that they achieve effectiveness and beauty in all that they produce."[10] Some pages further on, Plato speaks of "the kingly weaving process" in which different and even opposed human materials are combined and interwoven.[11]

This perhaps helps to explain why weaving should have struck Plato as so natural a metaphor for statecraft, and why the fine arts, as he understood them, are of no use in thinking about politics at all. It is because Plato held to the theory that the fine arts are mimetic, or imitative, and hence involve nothing he would recognize as originality, since they involve merely copying an external reality. The artists are as passive in this respect as the camera would be. (Aristotle knew the principle of the *camera obscura*, but Plato uses the mirror as his paradigm of the sheer passivity he ascribes to such arts as painting and sculpture.) Imitation, of course, played a central role in the educational programs of his ideal state, but the problem for him would be one of finding the right models to imitate rather than the problem of imitating itself, which he must have regarded as relatively natural. The beauty of the weaving metaphor is that each move made by the weaver has the whole fabric in view, and although we know that this would be something of concern to painters, concerned as they were to make, as nineteenth-century terminology has it, *tableaux* rather than *morceaux*—works rather than fragments—none of this seems to have struck Plato in his discussions of mimesis, though it is the primary consideration in regard to constructing the state. The aim of state making is justice, which means, in effect, weaving together the various social virtues without allowing one more than the other to dominate. And it is that which makes weaving so apt a metaphor for statesmanship. The task is "to make the city as a whole as happy as possible . . . not modeling our ideal of happiness with reference to any one class."[12]

I want to stress that Plato's appropriation of the weaving metaphor is enough more than casual that we can see how natural it would be in the discourse of a business executive today. Plato saw two basic and often opposed kinds of human materials needed to fabricate an enduring society: "Those to whom courage predominates will be treated by the statesman as having the firm war-like character as one might call it. The other will be used by him for what we may likewise call the woof-like strands of the web. He then sets about his task of combining and weaving together these two groups exhibiting their mutually opposed characters."[13]

Plato thought of human beings as having very different natural endowments. As he put it in his last great treatment of these matters, *The Laws*:

Now just as in the case of a web or other piece of woven work, woof and warp cannot be fashioned of the same threads, but the material of the warp must be of a superior quality—it must be tough, you know, and have a certain tenacity of character, whereas the woof may be softer and display a proper pliancy. Well, the distinction shows that there must be some similar distinction made between citizens. For you must know that there are two things which go to the making of a constitution. The conferring of office on individuals is one; the other is the providing of a code of laws.[14]

Plato had a very vivid sense that various irreducibly different kinds of skill are required if there is to be what we today would call a "sustainable" political order. We need philosophers, guardians, and producers, all of them necessary and none of them dominant. And weaving naturally suggests itself as a metaphor to him because of the way in which these disparate but necessary elements can he held together in a whole that offers shelter, protection, and fulfilment.

Notes

1. This piece was originally written as part of an essay on philosophy and the concept of fabric that was commissioned by the Fabric Workshop in Philadelphia. Its title was "The Tapestry and the Loincloth." A very large section of the essay was published in the celebratory volume that marked the twenty-fifth anniversary of the Fabric Workshop. I hope and expect that one day the entire essay will appear as an integral whole. Meanwhile, it gives me pleasure to have the section on weaving appear in a volume dedicated to the work of the artist Sheila Hicks.

2. Plato, *The Statesman* (288c), translated by J.B. Skemp, in *Plato: The Collected Dialogues, including the Letters*, edited by Edith Hamilton and Huntington Cairns (Princeton: Princeton University Press, 1989).

3. *Statesman* 279a–b.

4. *Statesman* 305e.

5. *Statesman* 311e.

6. Homer, *Iliad*, translated by Richmond Lattimore (Chicago: University of Chicago Press, 1951): III.125–28.

7. Plato, *The Republic* (V.455c), translated by Paul Shorey, in Hamilton and Cairns, eds., *Plato: The Collected Dialogues* (1989).

8. Thomas Hardy, *The Dynasts, a drama of the Napoleonic wars, in three parts, nineteen acts, & one hundred and thirty scenes, the time covered by the action being about ten years,* part I, *Fore-Scene* (London: Macmillan, 1925).

9. Immanuel Kant, "Beautiful Art is the Art of Genius," *Critique of Judgment*, translated by J.H. Bernard (New York: Hafner, 1951): 150–51.

10. *Statesman* 284a.

11. *Statesman* 309b.

12. *Republic* V.466a.

13. *Statesman* 309 b.

14. Plato, *The Laws* V.734e–735, translated by A.E. Taylor, in Hamilton and Cairns, eds., *Plato: The Collected Dialogues.*

25

ARACHNE'S GENRE
Towards Intercultural Studies in Textiles (1991)

Sarat Maharaj

EDITOR'S INTRODUCTION

Sarat Maharaj is Professor of Visual Art & Knowledge Systems, Lund University and the Malmö Art Academies, Sweden. His often-cited essay, reprinted in full here, was first published in 1991 in the *Journal of Design History*. Maharaj begins by revisiting the Greek myths of Athena and Arachne and discovering two models of textile production and knowledge: the ordered, polite, conformist (Athena) versus the challenging, questioning and inescapably messy (Arachne). Maharaj observes differing ways of seeing (via the textile) the world that reveal the problematic Europe versus 'other'; rational versus exotic; West versus East thinking confronted by postcolonial thinking. As Maharaj writes, 'The Athena/Arachne poles, in various guises, have tended to underpin modern versions of the Eurocentric gaze in art and design history and theory.'

The essay then moves its attention to the British trade journal *Textilia*, published between 1918 and 1920 and directed at colonial textile buyers to improve morale post–First World War. Here, Maharaj finds another power struggle organized in terms of gender (the trader versus consumer of textiles) and also between the past and the near future that will bring with it the decline of the British colonial power and textile trade. The third section turns to Gandhi's writings, which Maharaj suggests stand for the modern version of the Indian epic the *Mahabharata*, a '"de-feminising" of the textile terrain' is observed as a move to situate textile production as a 'sexually indifferent practice'.

Maharaj writes that Gandhi's 'focus is on the unequal relations of the imperial system [. . . a]t one end, prosperity in 'Lancashire' developed with protective laws: at the other, pauperism with the indigenous textiles industry run down and reduced to consumer, client status'. Both Gandhi and Lancashire reappear as topics in the following entries by Susan Bean and Pamela Johnson. The essay concludes with the 'ethnic look' that took to the catwalk in the late 1980s and finds the textile to be a discipline that takes joy in re-making and escaping the categories set for it.

The original publication of the essay included a number of images: Rubens's *The Fable of Arachne* (c. 1636); Velasquez's *Las Hilanderas* (c. 1657–9); Peter Brook's *Mahabharata* at the Tramway, Glasgow (1988); Pintoricchio's *Scenes from the Odyssey* (1509); William Roberts's *Study for the Return of Ulysses* (1913); four images from the publication *Textilia*; Judy Chicago with Judy Kendall, Judith Meyers, Jacquelyn Moore and group in Greeley, Colorado *Birth Project: Mother and India* (1985); catwalk and advertising images of the 'ethnic look' and, finally, Magdalena Abakanowicz's *Abakan – Situation Variable* (1970).

Arachne's Genre: Towards Inter-Cultural Studies in Textiles

Sarat Maharaj

ARACHNE VERSUS ATHENA

'Do' and 'Do not' says the law of genre. (Derrida)

Arachne or Athena? Who ends up the more wronged, the more shabbily-treated in the fateful contest to decide who is the better textile-maker of the two, 'the champion'? The question is not easily shaken off—something of it unsettles even the most clipped, zero-degree renderings of the Arachne story. The more we feel for Arachne the more we seem to stop short of taking her side altogether: at the same time, we become less and less sure about Athena's wisdom.

It is this ebbing double movement which Ruskin strives to counteract in telling the Arachne story, part of his Address on prize-giving day, 13 December 1870, to the Woolwich section of the Art and Science Department.[1] He does not simply run through the story start to finish. He cuts into his own narration just before the climax to make a special plea for Athena and to caution his audience: they should not be taken in by the fact that everything appears to end quite disgracefully, demeaningly for the goddess. To set things in her favour he paces his audience through a reading of the fable.

Why the desperate need to shore up Athena's reputation? What clues does it give about how we have come to think of textiles and textiles-making and the world of idea and imagination associated with it? To explore this we might perhaps recall the bare bones of the myth.

Arachne, a Lydian woman renowned for her needlework, sewing, and stitchery, challenges Athena, goddess of the crafts, to a contest of textile skills. Athena, disguised as an old woman, tries to dissuade her. But Arachne persists with her challenge. The test begins, Arachne's hands fly across the taut loom-netting with the shuttle as swiftly, as ably as Athena's. Athena inspects the completed piece, finds it faultless, as lovely as her own. The dénouement is best left in Ruskin's words: 'She loses her temper; tears her rival's tapestry to pieces, strikes her four times across the forehead with her boxwood shuttle. Arachne, mad with anger, hangs herself; Athena changes her into a venomous spider.'

Ruskin's staging of the myth projects a norm for textiles-making and womanhood, for 'proper' textile work, and 'proper' sexual identity. 'Athena' serves as the device through which this feminine/ textiles norm is constructed and dramatized. He justifies her wrath by presenting her as a corrective, sobering force exercised in the name of the law, the norm. How she enforces it—the matter of her aggressive jealousy, her violent fury, the all-too-final punishment meted out to Arachne, is side-stepped.

Athena, figure of the notion of 'proper' genre and gender? Arachne, at the opposite pole, sign of everything improper, deviant? The opposition is summed up in their embroidery. Through the 'trim-leaved olive of peace' motif the former signalled a sense of poise, control, restraint. The latter's imagery of ivy leaves, as Ruskin puts it, 'in their wanton running about everywhere' spoke of wild abandon, of Bacchus—disruptive forces of a topsy-turvy world of tabooed desires, unchecked longings, feelings quite outside 'the law'.

Athena had embroidered the council of the gods—a serious, weighty theme. It celebrated order, reasoned exchange, measured discourse. The composition touched on the sense of civic manners, virtues, morals,

Source: Sarat Maharaj, 'Arachne's Genre: Towards Inter-Cultural Studies in Textiles', *Journal of Design History* 4:2 (1991), pp. 75–96. Reproduced with permission.

on the civilizing force, the laws of men. What Arachne had pictured might be called 'the unmentionable'. Ruskin describes it as 'base and abominable'. It demystified the lives of the gods—exposing their trickery, the devious means to which they stooped to get their way. Arachne had driven home the point by depicting the 'Rape of Europa' and twenty other episodes involving the gods' abduction and violation of women.[2]

For Ruskin, Athena's idiom and imagery are at one with the established order of sensibility—bringing together ideas of 'needlework within the bounds of good taste' with those of 'the decent, respectable woman'. How he constructs the 'textiles/feminine' is underscored by the fact that the goddess had sprung fully-created from Zeus's head—something of a male-centred projection of the feminine? At odds with this order, Arachne's work seems unbecoming, lewd, in poor taste. It smacked of the shameful and licentious. Athena was 'legitimately' provoked into curbing, as Ruskin puts it, 'her fault of a poisonous and degrading kind, sensual, insolent, foul'.

His address seems fine-tuned for the women in his audience, at times as if for their ears alone. A confessional mood is evoked. Do young girls still sew samplers he asks in an aside? Let's hope they have not let such sound, Athena-work lapse. It would amount to courting Arachne's fate. The intense terms in which he describes her transformation into the 'meanest and most loathsomely venomous of creatures' impresses, repels, instructs. With allusions to Penelope, faithful at her loom, and to 'the Queen of our own William the conqueror, maker of Bayeux tapestry', his model of 'proper needlework/womanhood' is rounded off and heightened—against any temptation to stray onto the reckless path Arachne had taken.

What Ruskin subsumes under the term 'textiles' seems surprisingly all-embracing 'good stout clothes to knit and weave but also to make pictures on them'. It seems to take in the spectrum of textiles genres, cutting across all its modes and effects—everything from production of cloth, through commodities and goods, to textiles as art practice, as something which may be read as fine art statement or object. Should we take this, in the spirit of Barthes' 'endless garment',[3] as a seamless, unending textile text worthy of attention at any of its countless points?

Ruskin, however, privileges and validates simply one site of this vast textile text—Athena's genre. He sees its force as essentially institutionalizing—at the four corners of her tapestry she had embroidered 'admonitory panels' depicting the dreadful fate of those who dare question the established order. He favours its capacity to replay received imagery and iconography, to cite and recite an approved, accepted system of attitudes and values—a logic encapsulated by the notion of 'sewing sampler'.

He excludes Arachne's space, subordinates it—sensing in it a swirling stream-of-consciousness energy, the destabilizing force of tinkering at will with elements of received representations, for playing them off and turning them against themselves. What he is denouncing is its potential for prising open a gap through which other versions and voices, other inflections and differences may appear. It is on the drive towards such an exploring, experimenting sensibility—on a questioning, independent creativity—that he comes down heavily towards the end of his address.

The genre of Athena as repetition; that of Arachne as resistance? The former as sheer production, as prescribed representation, as saying the same thing again, as 'naked repetition'; the latter as expressive, self-reflexive practice, saying it again with a difference no matter how apparently small, as 'clothed repetition'?[4]

These may serve as signposts in mapping textiles today. We may see Arachne's space as a metaphor for avant-garde textiles practice—in which handed-down notions of art practice/genre/ gender come to be cited and overturned, displaced and played out. A space on the other side of Athena's male-order decencies—one shot through with a sense of the obscene, orgasmic?

ARACHNE—EXOTIC EMBROIDERESS?

To the blonde goddess's eyes, Arachne's tapestry border of ivy leaves was 'faultless': she tore it to shreds. To Ruskin's eyes it is 'exquisite': he condemns it as signifying everything 'wanton, foul, abominable'. It suggests something not unlike that split in the gaze which constructs the exotic object—between irresistible attraction to the thing and a sense of revulsion for what it is taken to mean—the split of the Eurocentric gaze.

Arachne is a Lydian needlewoman, 'a poor little Lydian girl' for Ruskin. Lydia, in Asia Minor, stands as part 'the Greek world'. But it is also too much at its edge, at that dangerous point where 'the Attic' must meet and tussle with whatever it constructs as other than itself, as different. The word 'Lydian' connotes a sense of the voluptuous as against 'Attic' restraint, self-control. As a musical mode, against the latter's manly, robust clarity, its strains are orientalizing, effeminate. It serves as a metaphor for the exotic, the Oriental Other— impossibly necessary and unacceptable in one go.

The Athena/Arachne poles, in various guises, have tended to underpin modern versions of the Eurocentric gaze in art and design history and theory. 'When the Attic migrates eastwards', Winckelmann, founder of the discipline's modern career, observes, it risks 'lapsing into Asiatic luxury, becoming voluptuous, wanton'.[5] The artistic norm, the idea of the beautiful in 'the Greek' he counterposes to the wayward extra-ordinariness of 'the Eastern other'—grotesque, non-manly, excessive.[6] For Hegel, too, 'the bizarre extraordinary' signals the exotic other; he situates it in Indian art, which he constructs with formidable consistency as the split sign—at once shamelessly sensual and sublime.[7]

Ruskin's split view of the Lydian as the exquisite or foul is not separate from this tradition of looking. It is tied to his own distinction between the Greek ideal, 'Daedalus work', and what he sees as Indian art's excess and moral inferiority.[8] Indian textiles, design and craftwork count as exquisite in his scheme only because he hives it off from the distasteful content he finds in Indian art.

The pattern persists even where we would have expected change. Fry attempts in the 1930s, under the impact of modernism and primitivism, to dethrone the Attic norm. He ends up constructing Indian art in terms of exotic excess, as a sign riven by lush lifelikeness and pornographic content—summed up in what he sees as its 'provocative dehancement of the female figure'.[9]

For inter-cultural studies the concern is not only with how the Eurocentric gaze constructs itself historically. It is with the fact that it is the inescapable factor in analysis.[10] Athena's piercing eyes dart across the Lydian's embroidery—scanning, scrutinizing—till she lashes out. How do we go beyond the relations of power and domination of the Eurocentric gaze which constructs the 'otherness' of non-European cultures— beyond the violation following on Athena's gaze?

But could she have made sense of Arachne's embroidery as a Lydian might have? The possibility of an epistemic barrier needs to be admitted. To speak of cultural orders whose ways of patterning and picturing experience are 'radically at odds with ours' is to face up to incommensurable elements of systems which cannot be decoded one to another. There is no 'common idiom' in which to do so, hence their 'radical difference'.[11] Foucault highlights this by reference to the 'bafflingly fantastic way' in which animals are classified in Borges' Chinese encyclopaedia:

> (a) belonging to the Emperor, (b) embalmed, (c) tamed, (d) sucking pigs, (e) sirens, (f) fabulous, (g) stray dogs, (h) included in the present classification (i) frenzied, (j) innumerable, (k) drawn with a very fine camelhair brush, (l) et cetera, (m) having just broken the water pitcher, (n) that from a long way off look like flies.[12]

Its impact on 'our own' logic of representation is to show it up as only one of many ways of arranging things. It makes us rethink the view of inter-cultural studies as simply stepping out of 'our' ways of knowing and feeling into those of another culture. It is more likely we are thrown into tussling with 'radical difference', with an epistemic barrier we might never quite pass. The more we strive to get under the skin of another system the more we find ourselves glancing over our shoulders to see how 'our system' is reshuffled. By the inter-cultural stance we would need to understand something like this anxious, two way, self-searching process—scene of never-ending exchange?

The view seems not unrelated to post-war economic and cultural developments.[13] It is not easy to see how we could continue to speak of cultures as discrete entities, separate worlds of life and living closed in on themselves. As Clifford notes, the forces of post-war communications and internationalization, of global economics, cultural centralization, of 'entry into modernity', have produced what may be spoken of as a world-system. The exotic, once tantalizing far-away, is now increasingly part of our local, everyday; at the same time, we stumble over the familiar in the most unexpected, 'exotic' of places.

It suggests a breaking down of differences between cultures, a levelling out of those distinctions, oppositions, contrasts, on which received ideas about culture were based. At least, of notions of clear-cut, essential forms of difference centred on stabilities and continuities such as tradition, roots, clothing and custom, language. The breakdown of the 'old orders of difference' might be understood as a process of loss, of homogenization. Or as an opening for creating new, critical statements of difference and identity. Neither seems to tell the whole story. Each undermines the other and slips out of the privileged grasp of a totalizing account.

In this setting we might think of culture less in terms of a final, enclosing identity, more as an unceasing activity of unmaking and remaking. It stages itself as a stalling, a perpetual putting off the point of arrival. We might see it as play of inflections of difference, images of self rubbed out even as they are written up. By the idea of post-imperial identity we thus grasp something not unlike 'a fable of our Caribbean selves'—metaphor for a sense of self as a process of uprooting, grafting, copying.[14] It makes itself up as it goes along out of the dizzying mix of elements of the late modern world.

But it remains arguable whether this breath taking spectacle of diversities amounts to a realm of expressive liberties or to one of repressive tolerance. It is not unlikely that what we gain on a micro-level in terms of expressing difference through dress, fashion, clothing, style, we lose on a macro-level to a tighter, intensified standardization and corporate uniformity.

It suggests an interplay of liberating and imprisoning forces—or even perhaps their stalemate. What sense should we thus give the claim that the Eurocentric gaze has been met and scattered?[15] Does it persist through this scene in the guise of fashion-textiles up-to-dateness, the 'Ethnic Look', or is the latter a travestying of Athena's gaze, turning it against itself?

TEXTILES' PRIMAL SCENES

The Arachne Story or The Tapestry Weavers—is Velasquez's Las Hilanderas on a mythological or historical theme? For all the hard evidence now in the former's favour the verdict remains open because so much in the picture does not fit the case made out by either side. Ortega suggests that Velasquez turns myth 'inside out': he does not let it run away with representation into makebelieve, he draws it into the real world, he historicizes myth. 'He finds the root of every myth in its logarithm of reality.'[16]

The view echoes the long-standing counterposing of the mythic to the historical—the former as representation on an imaginary, timeless plane; the latter as in specific time and place. The one an order wrought out of idea and concept, the other out of sticking to the empirical facts. Myth as running on the spot, replay—as 'naked repetition'—how textiles tend to be written about. History as cutting through myth in steady advance towards progressive enlightenment, a chronicle of bursts of originality and creative leaps—the way fine art practice is written.

It loses its force as we grasp the complex ways in which myth intertwines with enlightenment, metaphor with unembellished historical fact.[17] Historical writing may thus be seen as a 'white, colourless light' spun *out of* the colour spectrum that is epic and myth, rather than as something entirely separate from it.[18] The force of metaphor in historical writing, in what stages itself as a meticulous representation of 'things as they actually happened' seems inescapable. We rarely, though, see anything of the machinery, the figures and tropes, with which it pulls off the effect.

Such metaphors are not unlike wornout images on coins, defigured through use and rendered 'invisible'. Drained of their lifeblood, a 'white mythology' they figure forth representation which has the look of a flat, factual, 'historical' account of things, of 'literalmeaning'.[19] We would have to think of textiles in the spirit of this interleaving, beyond the 'reassuring opposition of metaphor and proper meaning', myth and history. It would be to alert ourselves to metaphor's and myth's force in language—how it shapes the social, political, institutional discourses in which textiles are imagined and made.

The myth of the primal scene serves as a device for imagining that 'origin' through which the textiles world comes to be decisively carved out. At the same time the idea of an 'originary moment' is cancelled, for we reach back to more than one scene, more than a single 'origin'—to the high modernist avant-garde, to ancient Greece and India, to the *Odyssey* and the *Mahabharata*— to Penelope in the former and Draupadi in the latter— epics in which textiles function as preeminent signifiers.

For much of the epic we have a portrait of Penelope, drawn by a male-order placing of the feminine, as patient, prudent, adamant. We witness her highly praised loyalty to Odysseus who has not returned from the Trojan war. She waits faithfully at her loom as the years pass, managing to keep at bay the suitors who lodge themselves in her home and who refuse to leave till she has chosen to marry one of them.

It is at odds with how she is portrayed in the final book, the Hades section of the epic. There the suitors, recounting the events leading to their slaughter by Odysseus on his return, see her as deceiving, double-dealing. They complain of the calculated way in which she misled them into waiting. She had promised to make up her mind about whom to marry when she had finished weaving her husband's shroud. But she had only pretended to be doing this. All day she would weave at the loom. By night she would sneak out to undo her day's work.[20] She had devised a delay tactic, a way of stalling for time.

The ruse stamps something of the motif of the guileful, weaving woman, the notion of feminine craftiness across the textiles scene. Penelope herself seems to come through largely unscathed in literary, artistic representations. As we have seen, Ruskin invokes her image as the 'good needlewoman' and endorses it. But the point is not that we rarely, if ever, see Penelope herself cast as the cunning 'bad needlewoman'. It is that 'good or bad needlewoman', they amount to two sides of the same male-order coin of feminine images.

In the *Mahabharata*, Yudistra stakes himself, his brothers, even Draupadi, their collective wife, in a game of dice he loses to his greedy cousins. She is dragged by her hair, out of the seclusion due to her at the time of menstruation, into the assembly hall, as the Sabha

Parva section of the epic notes, 'trembling like a plantain in the storm'.[21] The victors try to disrobe her in public. The final humiliation they wish on her, however, does not quite come off.

For every yard of her sari her tormentor manages to pull off another seems to add itself on. He ends up in a tangle of cloth. Draupadi asks, 'has the house of the Kurus sunk so low that women are not respected?' Draupadi's violation mirrors the even more ancient figure of feminine hurt, Amba, whose name means 'the womb' and who haunts the epic's events. Both voices counterpoint through the epic a complaint which is never silenced against male-order and its power.

Penelope's suitors, Draupadi's husbands; Penelope's unending shroud, Draupadi's endless sari; a weaving and a denuding which never reaches finality, a stalling tactic, a perpetual deferring which encapsulates something of their 'recalcitrance', the sense of feminine resistance. The motifs come to be echoed and inflected in the avant-garde, in the Bachelors' attempt at disrobing the Bride which is part of the turbulent narrative of desire in Duchamp's *Large Glass* or *The Bride Stripped Bare by her Bachelors, Even* (1915–23; Philadelphia Museum of Art).

In the *Large Glass* drama the Bride's 'intense desire for orgasm' leads her to take charge of her own undressing. That is, even when the Bachelor machine—'9 malic moulds, a cemetery of uniforms and liveries', as Duchamp describes his cross-section of the hierarchy of male stereo-types—assumes the initiative in her stripping, in which she aids and abets. But she backs off and rejects his brusque offer. Frustrated, the bachelor turns to autoeroticism, 'grinds his own chocolate', culminating in its own spectacular splash.[22]

Against this Duchamp sketches the Bride's struggle to go it alone, to work out and achieve climax under her own steam. Her desire springs from a voluntary stripping imagined by herself. Duchamp pictures her effort in terms of a motor car climbing a slope in low gear. 'The car wants more and more to reach the top while slowly accelerating. As if exhausted by hope, the motor of the car turns faster and faster until it roars triumphantly.'[23] It dramatizes something of a sense of independent feminine desire, activity and achievement.

It is not without significance that *The Large Glass* is subtitled 'A Delay in Glass'. We might understand it as a holding back in a double sense—in terms of the work's theme and its genre. The encounter between the Bride and the Bachelors is fraught, incomplete. It puts off the idea of some final coming together, a moment of total erotic fulfilment—metaphor for the notion of the inundating, full presence of meaning? The search for such a moment is left open-ended.

But *The Large Glass* as 'delay' also refers to holding back from identifying with any particular genre. Duchamp conceived the piece as a resisting of the 'painterly visual', of its mindless excess, in favour of the conceptual. His notes on how to render the orgasmic cloud—Milky Way imagery in the topmost part of the work—recoils from a full, grandiose fine art treatment of pigment. A lush, expansive painterliness, smeary impasto flourish and facture is cited but held at bay by more reserved, laconic, 'taste-neutralizing' forms of marking and imprinting based on varnish, dust-breeding techniques, on lead-wire thread and threading.[24]

The work stops short of the genres of fine art statement, holding them up for long as possible. The painterly institution of the canvas as window on the world, its perspective conventions are played *ad absurdum*. Our sight passes from the glass surface, through and beyond it into the extra-pictorial. The piece is not a 'painting on the wall'; if it is a freestanding object it is not quite so in a 'sculptural sense'. It has a craft dimension to it, a sense of meticulously-calculated design set off against ready-made, manufactured elements. The myths of a painterly genre, the sense of free expressivity and its flourish are detoured and side-tracked.

A genre which cuts across genres—which seems both less than painting, the readymade, sculpture, the craft-design object, visual and conceptual statement, and yet more than them. A genre which keeps itself at play between them, eluding them, not unlike the Bride's 'going it alone'. With this configuration of genre and the sexual identity do we begin to approach Arachne's space?

The historical moment of Duchamp's *Large Glass*—from 1915 to 1923—saw the opening of two discourses

grappling with 'the cloth famine' from opposite ends of the world system of textiles: in England, a discourse centred on the new journal *Textilia* (1918–20)—trade and corporate interests searched for the way forward after the Great War, to recover imperial normality 'without delay'.[25] In India, Gandhi's views and debates on textiles addressed to Indians struggling to shake off British rule 'without delay', centred on the paper *Young India*, collected and reprinted in the thick of the independence movement as *Wheel of Fortune* (1918–22).[26]

TEXTILIA: 1919–20

Never was a time more inauspicious than the present, it would seem, for the publication of a new journal—when all the great nations are engaged in the greatest war ever waged, when industry and commerce are plunged in difficulties hitherto never dreamed of and new anxieties appear on the darkened horizon almost every moment.[27]

Textilia was launched with these words in July 1918—a monthly journal but published quarterly because of wartime economies. It embraced some fairly long-standing journals and bulletins acting as the mouthpiece of the spectrum of established textiles trades.[28] They grouped under the *Textilia* umbrella to speak with one voice, a common front in the face of an important element of the wartime crisis—buyers at home and abroad felt that the trade was taking unfair advantage of war shortages to push up prices; there were allegations and suspicions of outright profiteering.[29]

It was a prime factor in *Textilia's* original reasons for appearing at what seemed an inauspicious time. It saw its purpose as 'created by the exigencies of the present and writ large on its pages': 'to tell in the language of truth the real position of the Textilian and allied industries of Great Britain and Ireland at the present time, their struggles to maintain output in the face of the gravest difficulties which have ever beset the trade, and their loyal services to their country in its hour of peril'. It set out to reveal the facts behind 'abnormal prices, the vital details of which are perhaps not fully grasped or understood'.[30]

'Vital details'—a sustained commentary on them. That is how we might look on *Textilia*, a 'fair-minded' defence of the trade's views on the rising textiles prices, an issue which dogged it to its final number in 1920. With an eye on the big South American market, it resorted to quoting a Brazilian minister on the trade's bona fides: he vouched for the fact that Britain's name was synonymous with 'reliability, sound workmanship and good faith, punctuality and straightforwardness'.[31] The testimonial unwittingly spotlights the very problems which made for the textiles crisis!

The journal sought to dispel worries about inordinate rises in prices, the future of the trade given the cloth famine and bleak world-wide shortages. It aimed at boosting morale—at encouraging colonial buyers who were fighting shy of placing firm orders in the hope that prices might come down. Against crashes, breakdowns, distortions in the wake of the government's diverting of massive textiles resources for the war effort, it sought to inspire confidence in the trade, in a return to something like pre-war normalities.[32]

To restore trust, to reaffirm old alliances and contacts—*Textilia* embarked on a robust publicity drive on the trade's will to weather the crisis. Its advertising campaign promised 'business as usual' after the war. For 'textilian entrepreneurs and tradespeople' it was not unlike a pep talk, a barometer of market fluctuations. For the British public, colonial buyers, new consumers— it saw itself as an exercise in persuasion and propaganda to stave off growing competition.

'Vital details'—the issue of rising yarn and cloth prices—which *Textilia* tried to account for so tirelessly so 'that nothing might besmirch that fair character attaching to British production' thus comes to signal two conflicting desires. The wish to go back to 'familiar prices', stabilities and normalities of the pre-war imperial textile system at odds with the awareness that there was no going back, that 'abnormal prices' had come to stay. The desire to restore the old order plays off against the desire to move forward, the pull of the traditional against that of modernity and change.

Textilia's discourse structures itself in this double movement. On one plane a narrative of past enterprise, achievement and success which runs as a series of tales on specific sectors of the trade: each becomes a mythic, heroic saga of determination, skill, triumph.[33] Against this, on another narrative plane, run reports on the actual, contemporary condition of the trade—glimpses of hardship, loss, adaptation, grappling with modernity.

In this sense, it structures itself as 'representation of representation'. The textiles narrative it constructs is through other narratives on the subject. We have a heightened sense of the mode with the 'Great Trade Novelists' series.[34] The textiles world is depicted through citing other depictions. Literary/historical, fictive/documentary, statistical/imaginary—the lines between them blur in the journal's representation of the trade.

The visual representation of textiles it constructs is in not dissimilar mode, through representations of art works related to textiles-making. Pieces by the great masters build up into the sense of an unbroken, grand tradition.[35] What is evoked is a textiles culture at one with fine art masterpieces and the world of high culture—sign of traditional order, wholeness, stability of value.

That the journal should have been subtitled 'Argosy of Informative Textilian Commerce and Industry' takes on some significance in this context. It seems to connote little more than a formal, literary convention as we might understand in a 'treasury' of stories and reports. But against the background of crisis, the desire for 'the homecoming' to stable values and prices, the framing power of the Odysseus myth is not far away—ideas of survival against all odds, sacrifice and ordeal, of adventure and exploration, even conquest and colonization. Audley Gunston's cover design pictures a safely berthed, textile-laden argosy to dramatize the point—an inspiring image for the trade striving to make it through the stormy times.

As if to stress the homecoming theme, the April 1919 issue featured, at a dark hour of the crisis, Bernardino Pintoricchio's *Scenes from the Odyssey*. It entitled it *The Return of Penelope* to *Ulysses* which, though not inaccurate, tends to inflect our reading in a more positive, affirmative register. We see Penelope at her loom and Ulysses (though it is more likely Telemachus) as striking figures in their prime—not, as the epic text might have led us to imagine, somewhat aged and ravaged by testing years of separation and exile.

Through the window we catch a glimpse of the 'argosy' safely in harbour (though it is more likely a snapshot of the tormenting Sirens episode). In the journal's context, the picture comes to be projected as an idealized sign of reunion—at any rate, a shorthand image of homecoming as a sense of total completeness and reprise which mirrors the journal's narrative of the trade weathering the crisis back to the productive fullness of its imperial heyday.

As Renaissance art work, the Pintoricchio itself stands as a sign of 'the standard of value' as opposed to its breakdown in the contemporary avant-garde. *Textilia's* projection of this version of the myth may be contrasted to two other avantgarde uses of it around the time. In Joyce's *Ulysses* (1915–23), the heroic myth is at every turn punctured by the mundane, the contemporary every day. Bloom's return is to a 'cold, cuckolded bed': Molly is modelled on the tradition of the 'disloyal' Penelope who was said to have chosen to sleep with her suitors rather than to have saved herself for her husband. Joyce holds back on the notion of a grand reunion—everything is left open-ended, in flux.

His language would not permit otherwise. Meanings slide across other meanings, a perpetual staving off safe arrival at some enclosing finality of meaning. It is not unlike the Vorticist language of William Roberts' *Return of Ulysses* (1913); angular, jagged forms keep at bay the sense of organic totality. They discourage and interrupt buildup of sentiment and feeling associated with the reunion theme. Swerving, dissonant juxtaposings of planes and perspectives, a terse, speeded-up idiom break up the received regularities of our ways seeing and picturing things.

Textilia's inaugural number signalled the idea of 'the homecoming' both as a return to the pre-war imperial order of textiles and as a reclaiming of the 'essence of British identity'. The trade's resilience, its capacity to fight and win back its preeminence is tied to grit and determination, 'the characteristic of the British race'. Its capacity to prove its strength and resolution against all odds, in the darkest hour of crisis, is presented as 'an axiom' of the national identity. The tenacity which brought its military captains such success is linked with the spirit of its industrial and commercial adventurers who managed by 'their indomitability in penetrating to the uttermost parts of the earth'.[36]

The journal noted a year later that the portrait it had penned had not been unjustified. It sprang from 'the sure record of our national history, where there is no instance to be found of our defeat, when to the world it seemed inevitable'.[37] But, from the October 1918 issue onwards, there was growing awareness that it had become less easy to speak of Britishness in terms of the received grand myth: other voices, of textiles workers and the public of consumers, now cut across it. If the lead article, 'Renascens Britanniae', continued to couch Britishness in rather grandiose figures of the fifteenth-century revival, the imagery was also deployed to dramatize the possibility of regress, of lapse 'into decadence and decline'.

The concern was that despite the forging of a new sense of Britishness—'pulsating with new aims, new hopes, new visions of the future'—injustices, vices, evils of the industrial past[38] would linger on. The inflection it was adding sought to appeal to both ruling and subordinate elements of society. The search was for an identity built on a spirit of cooperation and togetherness. In a rather laboured tapestry metaphor the lead article, 'Dawn', was to speak of the 'Great Design that now had to be woven', of 'New units in a harmonious whole', of unity through interdependence.[39]

The corporatist overtones of this vision of Britishness, centred on an organic unity of 'head/ hand, brain/brawn, capital/labour',[40] were not uncoloured by the period's new order political ideologies. It reflected its classic oppositions: keenness to thrust into the industrializing future set off against the wish to reaffirm what was seen as the human, personal quality in pre-industrial work relationships. As its scan of Britain's historical development reveals, *Textilia* favoured an idealized model of close, individual contacts, family-community bonds of workers associated with the era of artisanal labour.[41]

If the age of machinery had created great manufacturing concerns, workmen's combinations, and federations, it had also unleashed bureaucratizing forces—'a maze in which the individual is lost', a wounding division between 'soulless corporations called employers and soulless combinations called employees'. The journal held out little hope for schemes of betterment for workers until the 'old relationship could be restored without being attended by the old evils'; a restorative and transformative desire in one go—not the first time we see this pattern in its discourse.

The 'Britishness' *Textilia* pondered was understood as forged within the network of Britain's relationships with the colonies—national identity as something defined through 'other worlds' and against them. 'Lancashire', textilian symbol for Britain, was seen as both tied to and set off against India, sign of the colonial world. The latter's purchasing behaviour came in for anxious scrutiny—sustained speculation about whether Indian dealers would follow up price inquiries with commitments to buy. If Lancashire was to be baled out of the slump this was crucial. What is unwittingly conveyed is that India—portrayed as Lancashire's special dependent, steady and subordinate client—is really its prop and lifeblood, its *raison d'être*!

The anxiety was over the colonial other's 'bewildering' behaviour which did not appear as legible as in the past. If it provoked a feeling of the loss of grip over 'the other' it also had something of an unnerving impact on the sense of self. There was fear that the 'fat days of Lancashire were over'.[42] It was expressed in tetchy, exasperated remarks about the colonial market: 'Frankly India so far has been disappointing.'[43] It was suggested that she might have 'burnt her fingers'[44] in holding back with firm orders: 'Calcutta was a particularly bad sinner in this respect. Bombay was not very much behind, with Karachi a good third'.[45] There was worry that this meant 'competition, menace, a threat' from the 'greatest of outlets for Lancashire' which would 'put in jeopardy its supremacy'.

In this respect, *Textilia* saw matters almost exclusively in terms of a return to the prewar, imperial pattern of trade. It was keenly aware that 'upcountry India had been swept clean of cloth and starved of yarn'.[46] Why the delay in placing orders? It marked the limits of its response. Many factors were involved in the tardiness of Indian buyers—whether colonial British or native—which are not at issue here. The striking thing is that throughout the journal there is no hint of the swelling resistance in India to dependency on Britain—a movement which, ironically, was making Lancashire cloth and yarn the very issue of struggle.

Notions of Britishness touched on in *Textilia* were mainly in the 'masculine mode'. Audley Gunston's cover design dramatizes this. An argosy laden with materials and garments stands safely at anchor. From it a man carries forward fabrics and offers them, ritual fashion, to 'woman'—pictured as an ideal, classical nude with attendants. The two activities involved seem to be centred in the masculine, or at any rate initiated from its standpoint: the seafarer's business of gathering and bringing back exotic cloth and the issue of constructing the 'feminine' by dressing it up, fashioning it, condense into one.

The image seems to capture the journal's overriding concern with the sphere of trade and trading: textiles and the feminine become signs of a male-centred exchange and turnover of commodities. By depicting the business of obtaining textiles and its usage as very much in the hands of men the image suggests a linking of sexual place, position and power. The division it implies seems to be between 'masculine' obtaining of materials through trade, putting them to 'manly' use as necessities, at the service of 'woman': this is set off against the 'feminine' receiving of textiles, displaying them as part of the spectacle object.

It is a scene of relationships carried through in no small measure in other pictures on the theme of 'textile goods and exchange' reproduced in the journal. The Gunston cover design shares much the same ground of ideas and attitudes as Lord Leighton's *Phoenicians Bartering with the Ancient Britons*.[47] The field encompasses the dramatic Derry and Toms' advertising image on the subject. The journal notes: 'The scene represents the Port of London, where are gathered together merchants from four quarters of the globe, laden with the choicest fabrics, the most costly furs and exquisite textiles that their countries produce for the adorning of women and beautifying of the home.'[48] Across the spectrum of representation—fine art to advertising images—the turnover of textiles commodities seem to be depicted in and through the image of woman, the consumer-spectacle.

With the journal's emphasis on the sphere of textiles exchange and consumption the Viyella advertisement it almost regularly featured as its back cover may seem unusual in showing women in the act of textile production. But it is also phrased to evoke a sense of the glamorous, exotic spectacle object—women exhibiting cloth and themselves 'as if only to themselves'. Beyond this double-edged image, *Textilia* reveals little about the sexual division of labour and its coding in the sphere of production.

In *Textilia's* pronouncements on taste and its orders—through which it signalled notions of difference of culture, class, nation and ethnic provenance—we see a condensed version of those oppositions which characterize its wider reflections on Britishness. 'Each nation's taste is different, each demands a different line of design—Africa, on the Gold Coast requires more brilliance than the sea-girt islands of Japan.' The view, however, was not so much part of an open pluralism of taste as a fixed stereotyping of difference based on market demands.[49]

It marked out something like a universal ground of fine taste—'educated taste'. This centred on a rather rough and ready distinction between garish, brilliant colour as sign of 'less educated, provincial, crude taste', and 'softer, muted colour as that of fine taste'. It is not unlikely the view reflected, in broad terms, dominant norms of colour and taste of Britain of the day. It was evoked in the face of workers 'tasteless', high spending on costly silks. If the aim was to give guidance on good taste it was no less to regulate buying, to steer it out of the 'elysium of luxury goods' towards more sober, mainstream textiles on the market.[50]

In these respects, *Textilia* seemed to conform to the old orders of taste. But it was not completely sealed off from the new, as may be noted in its reaction to the Mayor of Brighton's criticism of the English as 'the most inartistic nation on the face of the earth'. 'In our homes, our furniture, decorations, pictures and ornaments are all hideously ugly. All middle class and working-class homes throughout the country want refurbishing.'[51] The journal seemed to demur before the sweeping, almost Vorticist ring of his views. But it called for a positive response to the simpler, cleaner line of the modernist style coming into vogue—away from the 'old stodgy standard of Victorian taste'.

The switches of focus from traditional to modernist orders of taste are part of the overall double movement of the journal's discourse. It also depended on the particular area of textiles on which it was commenting. At one end, a conservatism of taste: matter of fact acceptance that little could be changed with straw hats, 'the boater design',[52] or the desire to catch up with Parisian *haute couture*, sign of established fine taste. At the other, an incipient modernist taste: rejection of muted colours associated with the old world in favour of colour suggestive of the 'brass band with more stridency than tune', a taste for the vibrant, easygoing, dissonant, for experiment, futurism and modernity.[53]

One item captured the sense of these switches: government promises to put aside cloth for something like mass-produced, reasonably priced suits. From the outset the project appeared to get bogged down by delays, diversions of promised material, high prices. *Textilia's* last issue comments on the innovative scheme's failure; the trade and its customers are urged to report unfair prices to the Committee on Profiteering.[54]

The idea of constructing a textiles world based on 'standardization and concentration'—mass-produced goods and special items, ready-made and one-off, made-to-measure clothes—appeared to have to come to grief. The standardized suit, recalling Penelope's incomplete shroud, turns up as a pre-eminent signifier of the unfinished product of modernity—'new order Britishness'.

GANDHI'S WHEEL OF FORTUNE: 1918–22

Who has denuded India? The question reverberates through the Gandhi texts centred, not unlike *Textilia*, on the desire to remake the world of textile-making. The latter serves as both practical instrument and metaphor for 'Swaraj'—the remaking of India, of something like an Indian identity quite independent of British rule and outside the network of colonial subordination.[55]

The stripping of Draupadi replays itself in the actions of the modern denuders of India who strip her of wealth and assets. Gandhi identifies them as representatives of the colonizing power, Messrs Bosworth Smith & Co. and the O'Briens and native agents, the Shree Rams and the Maliks. He links them with the insolent power of men who 'lift women's veils with their walking sticks', to peer at them as if they were commodities—disrespect and violation no less than that suffered by Draupadi.[56]

The tone seems unusually sharp—he is responding to the British shooting of unarmed Indians at Amritsar in April 1919. The backdrop is the jittery reaction of the colonial authorities to the Russian Revolution's impact on agitation for home rule. The moment is the aftermath of the Great War. The 'Mahabharata', a figurative expression in many Indian languages, had come to mean literally the 'Great Conflict'.[57] In this sense, we might say, the Gandhi texts speak to 'the time of the modern Mahabharata'.

His focus is on the unequal relations of the imperial system. It has brought poverty, 'a famine of cloth in India'.[58] At one end, prosperity in 'Lancashire' developed with protective laws: at the other, pauperism with the indigenous textiles industry run down and reduced to consumer, client status. Indians had themselves come to believe that cloth could not be manufactured in India, that they were at the mercy of imports. They had been 'amputated in a figurative sense'—crippled, rendered into state of dependency.[59] Gandhi's allusion is to the trauma of East India Company rule, of control over textile production sometimes enforced by mutilating workers, by chopping off their fingers.

How do the colonized break the bonds of dependency? Gandhi saw only part of the answer in 'Swadeshi'—the boycott of British cloth. To give up foreign clothes is 'to decline to wear the badge of slavery'.[60] But could this be anything more than an aggressive desire to punish 'the English'—a sign of weakness?[61]

For Gandhi the post-colonial self could not be forged in a clear-cut instant by simply negating the colonizing other: independence, self-determination were not so much ready-made states of being and mind as a self-creating process on the part of the colonized—a struggle to awaken new capabilities and qualities in themselves no less than in the colonizer. A mutually transforming, binding project, a 'sacrificial quest'— they redefine themselves and the colonizer without feeling the latter could be simply bypassed.

Gandhi grounds the search in homespun—the 'rudimentary' mode of textile-making, but something not out of people's reach, even the poor. They, above all,

would need to experience through spinning and weaving a sense of what it might mean to do things for themselves, to stand on their own feet. Gandhi put great store on it as a practical-symbolic mode for shaking off the sense of dependency, for grasping the idea that deliverance from colonial subjugation lay in their own hands. He is thus wary of mill-loom, machine-made cloth not because of a backward-looking glorifying of artisanal modes. It is because he assesses it, in the circumstances, as the less effective instrument for undoing the structures of colonial power.

He codes the homespun/mill-made divide thus: the former, has a potential for activating the mass of people into making of cloth—drawing them into the arena of reforging themselves and their energies, of rethinking identities and subjectivities. Mill-made cloth, on the other hand, no matter how 'native' in origin, remained a product churned out over their heads: it tended to leave relationships of subordination and dependency largely intact.

Gandhi is also aware that to opt totally for mill-cloth would be to hand over to the colonizers the lever of a 'machinery blockade' of native mills. It would mean stepping out of the old order of dependency on foreign cloth only to step into the new one of dependency on imported technology and machinery.

Homespun/mill-made—signs of counterposed economic systems and politics? 'Capitalists do not need popular encouragement', Gandhi notes drily, in associating mill-cloth with a rising class of native industrialists, entrepreneurs, and merchants.[62] Their aspirations, however movingly expressed 'in the name of the nation and independence', amount to stepping into the colonizing power's shoes.

Homespun, at the other pole, he links to the making of a people, their coming to awareness in personal ways of fresh connections and contacts which cut across caste and class in new cooperative communities.[63] In this sense it serves as a critical gloss on the prevailing system of textiles production. Where mill-made cloth signals a consolidating of corporate forces, hand-spun, based 'anarchically' in individual desire and demand, comes to signify resistance.

But is it 'manly' activity?[64] The question is put by Swadeshis not at ease with the spinning and weaving regime Gandhi recommends for men and women alike. It seemed radically at odds with accepted ways of being men and women, with received ideas about 'virile labour' and 'women's activity', productive work time and leisure time.

Gandhi suggests a kind of 'de-feminizing' of the textiles-making terrain, displacing its traditional axis of sexual position and power. He seeks to shift it into a space where it might be seen more as a sexually indifferent practice, where it might become 'as graceful for either sex as music'[65]— something like an unmotivated sign system, an abstractive notation all the more flexible for that for constructing sexual identities in fresh ways.

A sexually indifferent 'gracefulness', the sense of stepping out of the state of dependency towards co-operative living—Gandhi pictures the post-colonial self as a site of transformation where the orders of taste come to be turned inside out. People would have to consider revising their sense of fashion and feeling for cloth textures. It would involve training themselves to revalue the lowly, subordinate product of homespun, to see 'art and beauty in its spotless whiteness', to appreciate its soft unevenness.[66] It would mean cultivating a different textiles sensibility altogether—an aesthetic more responsive to elements of the raw, native, vernacular.

'Will the nation revise its taste for Japanese silks, Manchester calico or French lace and find all its decoration out of hand-spun, hand-woven cloth, that is, Khaddar?'[67] Gandhi is responding to reports sent in by women's groups on debates and discussion over tastes, fabric textures, a new textiles sensorium.

The activist Sarladevi writes from a Swadeshi meeting at Sialkot attended by 1,000 women: they are sorry she has given up costly fine silks for a heavy, coarse, homespun white sari. She answers that it is easier to bear than the weight of helpless dependence on foreign manufactures however apparently fine and light.[68] Her sari impresses more than her speech: as with Draupadi, it stands out as the signifier pre-eminent.

ARACHNE—'GENRE DÉBORDÉ'?

Athena or Arachne? In one of his *Irish Tracts*, Swift sides with the latter in the name of 'colonized Ireland'. In another, no matter its doubtful and suppositious status in the Swift canon, he sides with the former in the name of 'colonizing England'. Each stance comes to over run its own borders into the other. An 'undecided' space opens up.

Swift recounts the Arachne story in *A Proposal for the Universal Use of Irish Manufacture in Cloaths and Furniture of Houses etc. Utterly Rejecting and Renouncing Every Thing Wearable that comes from England* (1720).[69] 'From a Boy, I always pitied poor Arachne', he confesses. 'I could never heartily love the Goddess, on account of so cruel and unjust a sentence'. He likens it to the even more painful sentence of English exploitation of Ireland: 'for the greater Part of our Bowels and Vitals is extracted, without allowing us the Liberty of spinning and weaving them.'

Swift speculates on a boycott of materials and yarns not grown in Ireland or made there. Would that all 'silks, velvets, calicoes and the whole lexicon of female fopperies' were excluded in favour of Irish stuffs. He suggests a 'firm resolution by Male and Female, never to appear with one single shred that comes from England'. Would Ireland then stand on her own feet, this land where 'the faces of the Natives, their manner and dwellings' spoke of 'universal oppression'?

His counter-tract *A Defence of English Commodities Being an Answer to the Proposal for the Universal Use of Irish manufactures . . . etc.* (1720),[70] portrays Arachne as ungrateful, guilty of presumption and pride. Her sentence is seen as fair, as a warning against the ill-consequences of her putting her trust in herself, of contending with superiors. The stress is on the old woman's advice to Arachne: to accept her subordinate position, to obey so that the blessings given to her might not be revoked. Swift's arguments on her behalf are seen as misleading—a topsy-turvy interpretation in which he makes 'Madness pass for Wisdom and Wisdom for folly'.

It calls into question his account of the downtrodden, 'native Irish'. 'They have been chastised by England with great severity; if they shared Arachne's fate it was for the same crime— Madness, Pride, Presumption.' But it claims the punishment had its creative, transforming side, eliciting from them skills and sensibilities for a new world. 'They have been metamorphosed not into spiders but Men—transformed from savages into reasonable creatures, delivered from a state of nature and barbarism, and endowed with Civility and Humanity'.

If we have a striking picture of the violent, wounding induction of the colonized to modernity it is a double-edged one. Fiercely corroding as this force is, it is paradoxically creative: it brings into being conditions in which the colonized come to reforge themselves as identities in a modern world.

The Swift tracts tend to leave us less sure about imagining power as a dominating force radiating outwards from a focal, colonizing source. We are alerted to the possibility of its being something like a two way, destructive/creative process—even when 'the one' seems to be calling all the shots. The idea of stepping out of the 'state of dependency' would not be easily grasped without taking this field of interconnectedness into account.

Swift's eye for elements of this intertwined relationship of demand/response is keen: 'biass among our people', he notes, 'is in favour of things, persons and wares of all kinds that come from England.' They admire English things and are attached to them, desire for foreign textiles not easily shed off—an issue not unfamiliar to Gandhi in the Indian setting. To interpret such desire simply in terms of abject dependency and collusion, as artificial and false needs, seems limiting, brittle, not least belittling. It is better to see here a field of needs and wants in interplay: they mutually define, mould and elaborate one another, often taking on a momentum of their own.

The discourses of both *Textilia* and Gandhi are not unaware of this and have to reckon with it. Their constructions of 'Britishness' or 'Swaraj' come face to face with a world-system of interlinking needs and wants, symbolized by the Lancashire/India connection, and, wittingly or not, are conceived in its terms.

In the post-war setting of avant-garde textile practice, by 'Arachne's space' would be signalled something less than the absolutely separate and totally autonomous and something more than it. At any rate, not simply a self-enclosed space with clear-cut, fixed boundaries demarcated in straight opposition to that of Athena's. We would have to imagine it as approaching a condition not unlike that 'state of débordement' with which Derrida rethinks genre:[71] a marking out of borders with their spoiling, a spilling out and beyond them, a taking into itself 'its outside and other'—Athena's space.

Judy Chicago's *Mother India* is a principal landmark in this textiles field. It situates itself squarely in Arachne's space—terrain on the 'other side of male-order' from where it launches its powerful critique of the actual subordination of women, the devaluing of the female body and childbirth in institutions of Indian life and living. But in drawing Athena's gaze into itself can we say it manages to turn it inside out and displace it—to make it speak about, even against, itself? Or does it simply replicate its way of seeing? A Eurocentric gaze at the heart of a feminist critique and at odds with it—deadlock of insight and blindness?

The Chicago piece stages itself through Katherine Mayo's *Mother India* (1927)[72]—a controversial report, at a high point of the Swaraj movement, on the condition of women in India, on Gandhian action for change. The Mayo work does battle with the Mother India of tradition and 'obscurantism'. The myth had been remobilized in the 'Bande Mataram'—Hail Mother India!—movement against colonial rule. She sought to combat the forms it took in native practices attending women's health care and childbirth, to cut through the latter's 'superstitious world' in the name of progress, humane medical knowledge.

The female 'child-fabric'—how it is rent and ripped by the force of the Indian male-order—is the focus of Mayo's moving account of Indian women.[73] Her story is devised through figures and imagery which share not a little with Orientalist narratives of the colonized other. She documents shocking, unspeakable conditions. But the more harrowing the data the more everything tips over into an Orientalist fable of exotic brutalities and horrors.

Through vivid anecdotes and vignettes, a spellbinding tale of bizarre habits, practices, and morals emerges which is no less 'factual' for that. In querying Mayo's sources, Wyndham Lewis was to draw attention to this phenomenon. It makes his critique of *Mother India* significant for our review of Athena's gaze if in other ways it simply expresses the imperial male's embarrassed defence of the 'great Indian people' against the 'suffragette outsider'.[74]

If Mayo's insights were crucial they were also not easy to dissociate from a sense of the Western, medical gaze as invasive, punitive. We see something of a collision between a traditional symbolic ordering of divisions between pure/polluted and a modern, 'literal', clean/dirty hygienic code. As systems of representation they seem utterly closed off to each other, incommensurate: we reach something like an epistemic barrier.

Chicago's own focus on the 'hygienic body' tends to replicate this framework. As such it seems at one with the period's forceful assertion of this stance, with Naipaul's troubling double-edged, sanitizing scan of the Indian body.[75] She notes that the hospital system for childbirth might be a questionable blessing for modern Indian women.[76] For a moment it seems she is leading up to opening a gap for a critical review of the gaze; the moment seems to slip by.

Chicago voices far more explicitly and strikingly the politics of 'stepping out of dependency' than Mayo. But her desire to take 'an enlightened, compassionate' view of the 'Indian other's world' suggests less of that self-reflexive element with which the latter accounted for her forth-right, plain-speaking and brisk 'truth-telling'. Mayo was putting together 'living facts of India today'—however problematical such an enterprise might be. Its equivalent, a sense of the 'living facts' of the post-colonial contemporary condition of women in India, appears to be the missing—at least unnegotiated—dimension of the Chicago world.

Hence the work's repetition of an array of received, 'sensationalized' scenes: arranged and child marriages, infanticide, sati, purdah and the like. Mayo speaks of midwives inserting balls of hollyhocks roots into the uteruses of women in labour.[77] The Chicago piece pictures them in the 'Birth Scene' probing the woman's body with a whole hollyhock stem—a raising of the horror stakes, a heightening turn not out of keeping with the Orientalist mode. The decorative elements add not a little to this sense of stereotyping.

A sense of the static, unchanging 'other' comes to be reaffirmed. The tendency is for the grand received text of the Eastern world of 'self-inflicted sorrows' to reinstall itself. Perhaps even quite against its intentions, the piece veers towards depicting the other

unremittingly as victim. It is as though everything is seen through Athena's gaze—as a world waiting to be uplifted and in which the 'other' cannot speak and must be spoken for.

Against this force, to make room for this voice, Chicago tries to allude to 'stepping out of dependency' by means of strips of mirror-worked Gandhian homespun. The device is perhaps too muted to mark itself off as critical, counterpointing inflection against the rest of the representation. In staging a tableau on the suffering of Indian women the Chicago piece gets inexorably caught up in an eyeball to eyeball encounter with the 'Athena vision': the showdown tends to leave it somewhat transfixed by it, even captive to it.

Mayo had confronted the grand mythologies of feminine power, 'Mother India' goddesses, with the desperate condition of women in India of the day. The Chicago piece, ironically, tends to take up her diagnosis and to institute it as a negative, fixed mythology. We sense little of the condition of women in the India of Chicago's day.[78]

It is as if a half-century of the story of Indian women—signposted by the popular post-independence film *Mother India*, which had such an impact across the decolonizing world, picturing a woman's and a people's struggle 'to step out of dependency'—should go missing. Its upshot is to vacate the field for the unintercepted sway of Athena's gaze, blunting the vigorous sense of exposé which inspired the piece.

'Ethnic, ethnic everywhere', observes Katherine Hamnett, commenting on the late 1980s fashion textiles craze for the 'Ethnic Look'.[79] Its lexicon is derived from elements of 'tribal raffia work and dress', references to colonial clothing, 'ethnic design, motifs and decoration', pop synthetic sari fabrics, 'folk-kitsch' materials, 'native embroidery, bead and sequin work and stitchery'. These collage into some topsy-turvy statement about 'self as the other'—at least, some blurring of the received demarcating lines between them. But does the Eurocentric gaze gain a further lease of life in this masquerade, in the guise of the 'Ethnic Look'?

Does the latter simply mime and endorse the former, as a straightforward mirroring and celebrating of Eurocentric textile-fashion-costume constructions of otherness? The heightened manner in which it stages its borrowed and lifted elements suggests otherwise. In parading them in a larger than life register it tends to open up a self-reflexive gap between 'source and cited version', 'original and copied item'.

Hence the air that everything has been 'expressed to the second power'—whether they are quite placed in quotation marks or not. In uneven ways the elements come to be rendered in an ironic mood. Each item—fabric, texture, threading, stitching, pleating, motif, design, imagery—is mimicked in a version which sets it all askew enough for new inflections and tones to be marked. Is it in the 'Ethnic Look' that Athena's gaze is met, splintered, deflected—its codes brusquely scrambled?

Arachne's genre, where everything surges beyond its borders and overruns it in an endless referring to something other than itself may be contrasted to the self-referring character of the modernist conception of genre. At least, to the version which came to post-war pre-eminence with Greenberg.[80] For him the modernist genre, *par excellence*, involved a reductive, involuting process—a paring down by each art of its medium to its essential qualities.

The stress is on each art alluding back to the logic of its own idiom and shadowing it, divesting itself of every element of the 'extra-pictorial'. It amounts to a sense of the strict autonomy of each art practice—an underlining of firm boundaries and borders between them. Everything in this view of genre is driven by a self-enclosing force: to use Greenberg's words 'the arts, then, have been hunted back to their mediums, and there they have been isolated, concentrated and defined'.

Amongst the many reasons for this purist conception of genre, we need mention only one: 'the threat' to fine art's autonomy posed by both 'art in the service of politics' and the spectacular growth of mass culture forms. Strictly defined, genre was part of a holding operation against this dynamic of dissolution. It aimed at staunching the outward flow of representation, out of its received generic confines, at curbing tendencies towards the flattening out of differences between artistic practices.

Greenberg recalled not only Lessing's Enlightenment project of defining the classic, clear-cut spheres of each

of the arts against what was seen as the medieval confusion of the arts, their undifferentiated mix.[81] He echoed Babbitt's rearguard project which had appeared with high modernism. Babbitt was against the 'effeminate' mixing and blending of the arts into one another in a 'mélange des genres'. Against their 'restless striving away from their own centres toward that doubtful periphery where they pass over into something else' he sought to assert a more strict, 'manly' division of the arts, 'genre tranché'.[82]

The 'uneven undecidedness' of Arachne's genre might be seen as placed both between the world of 'genre tranché' and that of a 'mélange des genres'—and beyond them. Between the former's manly power, its strict demarcations and steely divisions and the latter's 'effeminate' force, its yielding, submissive lines—and beyond them in something like a sexually indifferent terrain? Avant-garde textiles practice thus begins to map out an inside/outside space. An 'edginess'—it cites established genres and their edges even as it cuts across and beyond them.

We would perhaps have to remind ourselves that it is not, therefore, so much a matter of elevating it from its 'subordinate' place in the hierarchy of art practices, of legitimating and adding it to the official list of genres. This would be to see things simply in terms of extending the list—as if the idea were to equal or top the breathtaking range of art genres recognized in the *Kama Sutra* and *Sukraniti*.[83]

It is rather that it throws out of joint the list itself, its ordering of the arts. As a genre of 'boundaried boundarilessness' it marks that protracted exit out of the modernist landscape of genres into the post-modern scene of art practices. This uneven passage might be signposted by Magdalena Abakanowicz's invention of the 'Abakan genre' which spans the years 1964–75. Hanging forms, genre between wall and floor, a 'débordement' in which all genres are played and deferred the series is perhaps best summed up by the piece *Abakan—Situation Variable*.[84]

The two orders of genre sketched by Derrida are centred on the issue of borders.[85] They might be related to the 'edgy matter' Ruskin made of the borders embroidered by the Goddess and the Lydian needlewoman. A law of genre based on purity—clear demarcations of a practice's

edges and boundaries. We might liken this to Athena's trim-leaved olive of peace border: measured interval, decisive, crisp outlining. It suggests a manly territorializing force constantly staking its ground, hemming in things, patrolling its frontiers to find out what belongs inside and what outside. A regulating, self-enclosing drive keen to ensure, to use Chicago's words, that 'borders should not be wonky'.[86] Against this, is Derrida's counter-law of genre based on contamination and impurity in which everything belongs by not belonging, scene of the undecided, unsteady. We might liken this to Arachne's border of ivy leaves, with its 'wanton running about everywhere', hither and thither—a dispersing, incontinent force, 'genre débordé', to use Derrida's words, a 'fabric of traces'.[87]

NOTES

My special thanks to Tag Gronberg for help with this research. One version took the form of an address to the Arts Council of Great Britain in September 1989, another a paper to the 'Textiles Today Symposium' held at Bradford University in April 1990. Thanks also to Ian Paggett, Central Saint Martins, the London Institute, for photos of students' work.

Notes

1. J. Ruskin, *Complete Works*, GeorgeAllen,1905, vol. XX, pp. 371–80.
2. Ovid, *Metamorphoses*, Harvard University Press, 1977, vol. 1, lines 1–145, pp. 289–99.
3. R. Barthes, *The Fashion System*, Hill & Wang, 1984, p.42.
4. G. Deleuze, *Différence et repetition*, Presses Universitaires de France, 1968, pp. 36–7.
5. J.J. Winckelmann, *Reflections on Painting and Sculpture of the Greeks* (1756), Scolar Press, 1968, pp. 160–1.
6. J. J. Winckelmann, *History of Ancient Art* (1764), Low, Marston, 1881, vol. 1, p. 162 (17) & (18).
7. G. W. F. Hegel, *Aesthetic* (1835), Clarendon Press, 1975, pp. 322–47.
8. Ruskin, op. cit., p. 347.
9. R. Fry, *Last Lectures* (1933–4), Cambridge University Press, 1939, pp. 150–69.
10. E. Said, Orientalism, Penguin, 1987, pp. 1–28.
11. J.L. Lyotard, *The Postmodern Condition*, Manchester University Press 1984, pp. 15–27.
12. M. Foucault, *The Order of Things*, Tavistock Publications, 1970, p. xv.
13. F. Jameson & S. Hall, *Marxism Today*, September 1990, pp. 28–31.
14. J. Clifford, *The Predicament of Culture*, Harvard University Press, 1988, p. 182.
15. Ibid., p. 256.
16. Ortega y Gasset, *Velasquez, Goya and the Dehumanization of Art*, Studio Vista, 1972, pp. 101–2.
17. T. W. Adorno, *Dialectic of Enlightenment*, Verso, 1979, pp. 43–80.
18. W. Benjamin, *Illuminations*, Fontana, 1970, p. 95.
19. J. Derrida, *Margins of Philosophy*, Harvester Press, 1982, pp. 209–29.
20. *Odyssey*, Clarendon Press, 1932, Book XXIV, lines 114–50, pp. 496–7.
21. *Mahabharata*, Indian Press, 1915, Sabha Parva.
22. M. Duchamp, *The Green Box*, 1915. M. Sanouillet & E. Peterson, *The Essential Writings of Marcel Duchamp/ Marchand du Sel*, Thames & Hudson, 1973, pp. 62–8.
23. Ibid., p. 43.
24. Ibid., p. 36.
25. *Textilia* (An Informative Journal of Textilian Industry and Commerce), London, 1918–20.
26. M. K. Gandhi, *The Wheel of Fortune*, Ganesh, 1922.
27. *Textilia*, no. 1, vol. 1, July 1918, p. 2.
28. *Textilia* (Woollens, Cottons, Silks etc.): *Linen* (Organ of the Linen Trade); *British Lace* (Journal of British Lace, Embroidery & Curtain Trade); *Hosiery and Underwear; British Clothier; British Glovemaker; British Hatter.* With the April 1919 issue Textilia took under its wing *The British Spinner* and *the Carpet Maker*.
29. No. 4, vol. 1, April 1919, p. 232.
30. No. 1, vol. 1, July 1918, p. 2.
31. No. 1, vol. 1, July 1918, p. 2.
32. No. 1, vol. 1, July 1918, pp. 2–5.
33. 'Story of the Sailor Suit', no. 1, vol. 1, July 1918, pp. 33–92; 'Story of Hosiery', no. 1, vol. 1, July 1918, p. 93; 'History of Hats', no. 1, vol. 1, July 1918, p. 98; 'History of Lace', no. 3, vol. 1, Jan. 1919, p. 127; no. 4, vol. 1, April 1919, p. 257; 'History of Gloves', no. 3, vol. 1, Jan. 1919, p. 146.
34. The first featured Mrs Henry Wood, 'Novelist of the Glove Trade', with reference to her novel *Mrs Halliburton's*

Troubles, no. 1, vol. 1, Jan. 1919, pp. 143–6; the second Mrs Gaskell, 'Novelist of the Cotton Trade', in a discussion of *Mary Barton*, no. 4, vol. 1, April 1919, p. 185.

35. Vermeer's *The Lace Maker*, no. 2, vol. 1, Oct. 1918, p. 76; Rembrandt's *The Syndics*, no. 1, vol. 1, July 1918, p. 7; Hals' *Man with Glove*, no. 1, vol. 1, Oct. 1918, p. 86; Velasquez's *Las Hilanderas* and *Lady with Fan and Gloves*, no.1, vol. 4, April 1919, p. 209; no. 2, vol. 1, Oct. 1918, p. 85; Van Dyck's *The Embroidery Age*, no. 3, vol. 1, Jan. 1919, p. 135; Titian's *Man with Glove*, no. 3, vol. 1, Jan. 1919, p. 144; Lord Leighton's *Phoenicians Bartering with the Ancient Britons*, no. 4, vol. 1, April 1919, p. 214; Moore's *Blossoms*, no. 2, vol. 2, Oct. 1919, p. 155. Only the Irish linen industry engravings and Spenser-Pryse's *The Workers' Way*, no. 3, vol. 2, Feb. 1920, p. 207, go against the grain of the myth thus woven.
36. No. 1, vol. 1, July 1918, p. 2.
37. No. 4, vol. 1, April 1919, p. 50.
38. No. 4, vol. 1, April 1919, p. 51.
39. No. 3, vol. 1, Jan. 1919, p. 127.
40. No. 4, vol. 1, April 1919, p. 3.
41. No. 1, vol. 2, July 1919, p. 3.
42. No. 4, vol. 1, April 1919, p. 233.
43. No. 1, vol. 2, July 1919, p. 12.
44. No. 3, vol. 2, Feb. 1920, p. 241.
45. No. 2, vol. 2, Oct. 1919, p. 135.
46. No. 3, vol. 1, Jan. 1919, p. 162.
47. No. 4, vol. 1, April 1919, p. 214.
48. No. 1, vol. 2, July 1919, p. 90.
49. No. 2, vol. 2, Oct. 1919, p. 137.
50. No. 1, vol. 1, July 1918, p. 55.
51. No. 1, vol. 2, July 1919, p. 34.
52. No. 4, vol. 1, April 1919, p. 289.
53. No. 3, vol. 2, Feb. 1920.
54. No. 1, vol. 1, July 1918, p. 17; no. 2, vol. 2, Oct. 1919, pp. 222–3; no. 3, vol. 3, Feb. 1920, p. 313.
55. M.K. Gandhi, *Wheel of Fortune*, 1922, pp. 8–14.
56. *Young India*, 7 July 1920, p.29.
57. The Spenglerian grand cycles of conflict and decline in which D. Tagore places Western civilization and the Great War in his introduction to the Gandhi texts adds to the sense of a modern Mahabharata (pp. i–xii). See also A. Besant, *The Great War*, Theosophical Publishers, 1899. Gandhi explicitly tied the wheel (chakra) to the symbolism of the Gita

section of the Mahabharata (*Young India*, 20 Oct. 1921), pp. 93–6.
58. Gandhi, op. cit., p. 11.
59. Ibid., pp. 24–5.
60. Ibid., p. 45 (*Young India*, 6 July 1921).
61. Ibid., pp. 2–5.
62. Ibid., p. 20 (*Young India*, 18 August 1920).
63. Ibid., p. 54 (*Young India*, 6 July 1921).
64. Ibid., p. 78 (*Young India*, 10 Nov. 1921).
65. Ibid., p. 12.
66. Ibid., p. 8.
67. Ibid., p. 6.
68. Ibid., p. 27 (*Young India*, 7 July 1920).
69. J. Swift, *Irish Tracts* (1720–3), Basil Blackwell, 1948, vol. IX, pp. 15–22.
70. Ibid., pp. 269–77.
71. J. Derrida, 'Living On Borderlines', *Deconstruction and Criticism*, RKP, 1979, pp. 75–176 and 'The Law of Genre', *Glyph*, 7, 1980, pp. 202–32.
72. K. Mayo, *Mother India*, Jonathan Cape, 1935, pp. 76–98.
73. Ibid., p. 51.
74. W. Lewis, *Paleface*, Chatto & Windus, 1929, pp. 289–300.
75. V.S. Naipaul, *India—A Wounded Civilisation*, Deutsch, 1977.
76. J. Chicago, *Birth Project*, Doubleday, 1985, p. 180.
77. K. Mayo, *Mother India*, 1935, pp. 80–3.
78. Even though she mentions three works on post-war India (1985, p. 231).
79. L. White, 'The Empire Strikes Back', *Vogue*, no. 6, whole no. 2305, vol. 153, June 1989, p. 168. Also see *L'Image*, no. 2, Summer1989, pp. 42–3.
80. C. Greenberg, *Towards a Newer Laocoon, the Collected Essays and Criticism*, vol. 1, 1939– 44, University of Chicago Press, 1988, p. 88.
81. G. Lessing, *Laocoon* (1766), Bobbs-Merrill Publishing, 1977.
82. I. Babbitt, *The New Laocoon*, Riverside Press, 1910, pp. viii, 159.
83. Vatsyayana, *Kama Sutra*, Taraporevala, 1961, pp. 75–80; Sukracharya, *Sukraniti*, Manoharlal Publishers, 1975, pp. 156–60.
84. *Magdalena Abakanowicz*, Museum of Contemporary Art, Chicago, 1983, pp.46–50.
85. Derrida, op. cit., pp. 201–10.
86. Chicago, op. cit., p. 133.
87. Derrida, op. cit., 1979, p. 82.

26

GANDHI AND *KHADI*, THE FABRIC OF INDIAN INDEPENDENCE (1989)

Susan S. Bean

EDITOR'S INTRODUCTION

One of the most notable examples of the textile's power, in terms of sheer scale, can be found in Mahatma Gandhi (1869–1948) and his use of the textile as a tool in the ultimately successful Indian independence movement. The essay reprinted in full here, by anthropologist, art historian and curator Susan Bean, first appeared in the often-cited collection of essays titled *Cloth and Human Experience*, edited by Annette B. Weiner and Jane Schneider. When published in 1989, Susan Bean was Curator of South Asian and Korean Art at the Peabody Essex Museum in the United States. Since her retirement in 2012, she has chaired the Art & Archeology Centre of the American Institute of Indian Studies and is an associate of the Peabody Museum at Harvard University.

Bean outlines Gandhi's use of the textile, noting that 'From 1908 on, these two elements – the economics of cloth and the semiotics of cloth – united in Gandhi's thought'. The essay charts Gandhi's own experience of dress as a tool for expressing identity and status and the evolution of these ideas into his use of the textile as a method for non-violent resistance. Creating and wearing *khadi* became a powerful instrument as Bean explains of India, 'English cloth had become the most potent symbol of English political domination and economic exploitation.'

Gandhi's use of textiles remains a significant example of the ability of cloth to not only comment on but also bring about change. Despite his aura of infallibility, more recent scholarship has brought attention to Gandhi's racist treatment of African cultures in his early writing and, late in his life, his decision to test his willpower and commitment to celibacy by sharing his bed with young women. In Bean's writing we are reminded that Gandhi's choice of dress to communicate his political values was of crucial importance to a nation with multiple languages and high illiteracy rates, which made visual (rather than written or spoken) communication all the more vital.

Gandhi and *Khadi*, The Fabric of Indian Independence

Susan S. Bean

Cloth was central to the Indian struggle for national self-government—cloth as an economic product and cloth as a medium of communication. Cloth was officially incorporated into the nationalist program in 1921 when the Indian National Congress resolved to campaign for the boycott of foreign cloth, to require its officers and workers to spin cotton yarn and wear hand-spun, hand-woven cloth (*khadi*), and to adopt a flag with the spinning wheel in the center. Mahatma Gandhi was the force behind the adoption of these resolutions, but they were successful because Gandhi had achieved an understanding of the role of cloth in Indian life, the culmination of decades of experimentation with cloth as a medium of communication and means of livelihood.

Gandhi's changing sociopolitical identity can be traced through his costume changes as well as through his speeches, writings, and activities. As he came to appreciate the semiotic properties of cloth, he learned to use it to communicate his most important messages to followers and opponents and to manipulate social events. Once he had appreciated the economic importance of cloth in India, he made it the centerpiece of his program for independence and self-government. [...]

LESSONS IN THE SOCIAL MEANING OF COSTUME

When Mohandas K. Gandhi disembarked at Southampton in 1888, he was wearing white flannels given to him by a friend and saved especially for the occasion, because he "thought that white clothes would suit [him] better when [he] stepped ashore" (Gandhi 1957: 43). On his arrival at Southampton he realized that white flannels were not worn in late September. Later he replaced his Bombay-style clothing, which he thought "unsuitable for English society"(Gandhi 1957: 50), with an evening suit from Bond Street, patent leather shoes with spats, and a high silk hat, "clothes regarded as the very acme of fashion" (Fischer 1982: 37). Gandhi was sensitive to the connection between costume and social status, and perceived that changes in social position required changes in costume. His sensitivity became self-consciousness because Gandhi, the student from India, was so ignorant of how Gandhi, the London barrister, should appear.

In 1891 when Gandhi returned home to Rajkot, a barrister, he promoted the westernization of his household, begun for him by his brother, by adding items of European dress (Gandhi 1957: 92). Gandhi believed his success was dependent on westernization. Later, in the harsher, more repressive, and openly racist South Africa where he went to work as a barrister in 1893, he confronted his indelible Indianness.

On this third day in South Africa, he visited the Durban court. It was explained to him that Hindus had to remove their turbans in court, though Muslim Indians were permitted to keep their turbans on. Turbans were not like hats: In this context, removal was not deferential, it was demeaning. Gandhi thought he could solve the problem by wearing an English hat, but his employer warned him that he would be undermining efforts for recognition of the Indian meaning of the turban and for permission to keep it on in court. His employer added, in appreciation of Indian dress: "An Indian turban sits well on your head." Besides, he said, "If you wear an English hat you will pass for a waiter"

Source: Susan S. Bean, 'Gandhi and *Khadi*, The Fabric of Indian Independence', *Cloth and Human Experience*, ed. Annette B. Weiner and Jane Schneider (Smithsonian Institution, Washington, DC, 1991), pp. 355–76. Reprinted with permission of Smithsonian Books. Copyright 1991.

(Gandhi 1957: 108). (Most waiters in South Africa were Indian converts to Christianity who wore English dress.)

Gandhi kept his turban and began to appreciate the limits of his Englishness—limits imposed by the colonial regime and by his pride as an Indian and a Hindu. But still he thought he could make his Indianness compatible with Englishness. He wore a fashionable frock coat, pressed trousers, and shining shoes with his turban (Fischer 1982: 57). After he was thrown off the train to Pretoria for traveling first class, he reapplied for a first-class ticket, presenting himself to the station master "in faultless English dress" (Gandhi 1957: 116). He succeeded. The station master said, "I can see you are a gentleman" (Gandhi 1957: 117).

Gandhi later also succeeded in persuading the railway authorities to issue first- and second-class tickets to Indians "who were properly dressed" (Gandhi 1957: 128). He sought to demonstrate that Indians could be as civilized as Englishmen and therefore were entitled to the same rights and privileges as citizens of the British Empire. This belief seemed to be supported by the Empress Victoria herself, who stated that there was a distinction between "aliens and subjects of Her Majesty [and] between the most ignorant and the most enlightened of the natives of India. Among the latter class there are to be found gentlemen whose position and attainments fully qualify them for all the duties and privileges of citizenship" (Queen Victoria, quoted in Erikson 1969: 172–3).

When Gandhi brought his family to South Africa in 1896 he believed "that in order to look civilized, our dress and manners had as far as possible to approximate the European standard. Because, I thought, only thus could we have some influence, and without influence it would not be possible to serve the community. I therefore determined the style of dress for my wife and children. How could I like them to be known as Kathiawad Banias? The Parsis used then to be regarded as the most civilized people amongst Indians, and so, when the complete European style seemed to be unsuited, we adopted the Parsi style. Accordingly my wife wore the Parsi sari, and the boys the Parsi coat and trousers. Of course no one could be without shoes and stockings. It was long before my wife and children could get used to them. The shoes cramped their feet

and the stockings stank with perspiration" (Gandhi 1957: 186).

Soon the prospect began to fade that one could be an Indian and a full citizen of the British empire by wearing Indian headgear with an English suit. For one thing, it had become clear that the color of one's skin was as much a part of one's costume as a frock coat, and this fundamental Indianness Gandhi would not have changed even if he could. He began to admire Indian dress. In 1901, back in India for a visit, he met some rulers of Indian states at the India Club in Calcutta. Gandhi recalls, "In the Club I always found them wearing fine Bengalee *dhotis* [Hindu garments of seamless cloth, wrapped and folded around the lower body] and shirts and scarves. On the darbar day [Viceroy's audience] they put on trousers befitting *khansamas* [waiters] and shining boots. I was pained and inquired of one of them the reason for the change. "We alone know our unfortunate condition [began the reply]. We alone know the insults we have to put up with, in order that we may possess our wealth and titles. 'But what about these *khansama* turbans and these shining boots?' I asked. 'Do you see any difference between *khansamas* and us?' he replied, and added, 'They are our *khansamas*, we are Lord Curzon's *khansamas*. If I were to absent myself from the levee, I should have to suffer the consequences. If I were to attend it in my usual dress, it would be an offence'" (Gandhi 1957: 230). As in the Durban court, the sartorial dictates of the Empire were demeaning for its Indian citizens. During the same visit he remarked on his mentor, Gokhale: "In the Congress I had seen him in a coat and trousers, but I was glad to find him wearing a Bengal *dhoti* and shirt [at home]. I liked his simple mode of dress though I myself then wore a Parsi coat and trousers" (Gandhi 1957: 234). Gandhi began to experiment with his own costume. Soon he embarked on a tour of India to learn about its people; he traveled third class. For clothing he took a long woolen coat, a *dhoti*, and a shirt. But on his return to Bombay in 1902 he resumed the life of the well-dressed, well-housed barrister riding first class on the trains.

Gandhi's responses to the costumes of others and his experiments with his own attire indicate a growing awareness of the meaning of clothes—their importance as indicators of status, group identity, social stratification, and political beliefs. He had begun to doubt the possibility of being both a dignified Indian and an English gentleman. The sartorial requirements of the Empire forced Indians to humiliate themselves, and revealed the true relationship—of master and slave—between the English and the Indians. Gandhi's experiments with simple, inexpensive Indian garments expressed his growing disdain for possessions and his growing identification with the poor.

By 1908 he had come to believe that Indians could not be Englishmen and that India should be ruled for the benefit of India by Indians. He set forth these views in *Hind Swaraj* (*Indian Home Rule*) (1908), where he also said: "If people of a certain country, who have hitherto not been in the habit of wearing much clothing, boots, etc., adopt European clothing, they are supposed to have become civilized out of savagery" (Gandhi 1922: 32). He himself had believed this when in 1893 he appealed to the railroad authorities to allow Indians in European dress to ride first class, and in 1896 when he brought his family to South Africa and insisted on the further westernization of their dress. By 1908, he no longer believed that European garments were an index of civilization and Indian ones of its lack.

In *Hind Swaraj*, Gandhi first articulated the importance for India of the economics of cloth. For fifty years, an economic nationalism (whose roots were in fact much older) had been evolving in India. British rule had not benefited India, as the British maintained. On the contrary, British rule had destroyed the economy of India by taking its wealth back to England, by overtaxing its farmers, and by destroying Indian industries that might compete with English ones, thus causing poverty, famine, and disease. Cloth manufacture had been the premier industry of India and its decline was a chief cause of Indian poverty. These views were set out in detail in R.C. Dutt's two-volume *Economic History of India* (Dutt 1901 & 1903). Gandhi commented in *Hind Swaraj*: "When I read Mr. Dutt's *Economic History of India* I wept; and, as I think of it, again my heart sickens. It is difficult to measure the harm that Manchester [the seat of the English mechanized textile industry] has done to us. It is due to Manchester that Indian handicraft has all but disappeared" (Gandhi 1922: 105).

From 1908 on, these two elements—the economics of cloth and the semiotics of cloth—united in Gandhi's thought. By 1921, *khadi* (homespun cloth) had become central to his politics. The intervening years were full of experiments with costume and with the production of handmade cloth.

CLOTH IN ECONOMIC NATIONALISM

Gandhi's campaign for *khadi* was a product of economic nationalism. Gandhi's views on cloth and clothing were unique, but the elements of which they were composed were not. According to the economic nationalists, India's decline was due largely to British destruction of Indian manufactures beginning in the late eighteenth century. Cotton textiles had been India's premier industry. Weavers and dyers so excelled in producing both coarse, inexpensive textiles and fine, exquisitely dyed, luxury textiles that Indian cloth was prized in Rome, China, Egypt, and Southeast Asia.

As early as 200 b.c. the Romans used a Sanskrit word for cotton (Latin, *carbasina*, from Sanskrit *karpasa*). In Nero's reign, delicately translucent Indian muslins were fashionable in Rome under such names as *nebula* and *venti* textiles (woven winds) the latter exactly translating the technical name of a special type of muslin woven in Bengal up to the modern period. The quality of Indian dyeing, too, was proverbial in the Roman world, as we know from a reference in St. Jerome's fourth century Latin translation of the Bible, Job being made to say that wisdom is even more enduring than the "dyed colors of India" (Irwin 1962).

In the fifth century a.d. an Indonesian diplomatic mission carried textiles from India and Gandhara to China. In the eleventh century, "500 Jewish families on their way to settle in the Northern Sung capital of China, bought cotton goods in India to take as gifts" (Gittinger 1982:13). Fifteenth-century fragments of Indian cloth found at Fostat, near Cairo, show that the trade was not exclusively in fine textiles. The fragments are "often lacking in care or precision [in dye craftsmanship] and only occasionally showing exceptional skill. Inescapable is the sense that these were made for a modest clientele and do not represent elements of a 'luxury' trade" (Gittinger 1982: 33).

Until the sixteenth century, Indian and Arab merchants dominated the trade in Indian cottons. From the late sixteenth century, Europeans gained increasing control of the world trade in Indian cottons (Chaudhuri 1978). At first European traders were interested in Indian cottons as trade goods which could be exchanged in South-east Asia for spices. By the middle of the seventeenth century, the traders had discovered that if they supervised the design of the textiles made in India, these could be sold at a reasonable profit in London. At the end of the seventeenth century, the demand for Indian painted cottons had become so great that France banned chintz imports to protect its own silk industry (Irwin and Brett 1970: 3, 4). England followed suit a few years later. So popular were these fabrics that the prohibitions were ignored. In 1720 "a second prohibition was introduced . . . to forbid 'the Use and Wearing in Apparel' of imported chintz, and also its 'use or wear in or about any Bed, Chair, Cushion, or other Household furniture'" (Irwin and Brett 1970: 5).

The great popularity of Indian cottons was due both to the cheapness and to the superiority of Indian products. Indian hand-spun yarns were superior to those produced in England and were imported for the weaving of fine cloth. Indian dyers were expert in the technology of mordant dyeing, which produced washable cottons in vibrant colors (Chaudhuri 1978: 237ff). While the competition from Indian cloth could be fought with duties and prohibitions, the technological superiority remained unchallenged until the industrial revolution.

From the late eighteenth century, with the development and growth of machine spinning and weaving and the adoption and modification of Indian cotton-dyeing technology (Gittinger 1982: 19), England began to produce quantities of inexpensive cotton textiles. English political control of India permitted adjustments in tariffs (and import prohibitions) to assure the advantage of Lancashire cottons in trade. English cotton-spinning mills secured supplies of raw cotton from India, and British traders succeeded in competing in India with the local hand-loom industry,

thus opening a vast new market for the products of the Lancashire mills. The hand-spinning of cotton yarns had virtually died out in India by 1825. Only the highest counts of cotton yarns could not be reproduced by machinery. Even Indian hand-loom weavers used the cotton yarns produced in Lancashire. During the nineteenth century, exports fell drastically and the world's greatest exporter of cottons became a major importer of cotton yarns and piece goods. "In the first four years of the nineteenth century, in spite of all prohibitions and restrictive duties, six to fifteen thousand bales [of cotton piece-goods] were annually shipped from Calcutta to the United Kingdom After 1820 the manufacture of cotton piece-goods declined steadily, never to rise again" (Dutt 1906: 296). Between 1849 and 1889, the value of British cotton cloth exports to India increased from just over 2 million pounds a year to just less than 27 million pounds a year (Chandra 1968: 55). At the end of the nineteenth century, the development in Europe of inexpensive, easier-to-apply chemical dyes dealt the final blow to Indian technological superiority in textile production.

The interpretation of these changes has long been a subject of heated debate among historians and economists. Did British cloth destroy the demand for Indian hand-looms or supplement it? Did indigenous production really decline or was it simply consumed in the domestic market? Did British policy destroy Indian manufactures or was the demise of Indian industry the inevitable result of the competition between artisans and machines? Did India fail to industrialize because British policy prevented it or because Indian society was infertile soil for industrialization?

During the late nineteenth century, an interpretation of England's economic relations with India evolved that became the economic basis of Indian nationalism. In this economic nationalism, the history of cotton production and trade was central. Especially significant was the transformation of India from the world's most advanced producer of cotton textiles to an exporter of raw cotton and an importer of cloth.

Dadabhai Naoroji was the recognized leader of this movement and codified the theory of economic nationalism. In his view, "the continuous impoverishment and exhaustion of the country" (Naoroji 1887) was unquestionably the result of British rule. Wealth was taken from India to pay the Englishmen in London who ruled India and to pay large salaries and pensions to English civil servants, who spent much of this wealth in England. Grinding poverty and severe famines resulted from the enormous tax burden on the cultivators. British protection of English industries, through trade advantages in the structure of tariffs, destroyed indigenous artisanry and prevented the development of machine industry.

Naoroji and other early nationalists (e.g., Ranade, Tilak, Gokhale) believed that the low tariffs on British yarns and cloth coming into India and the high tariffs on Indian textiles taken out of India caused the decline of the textile industry, forced more people onto the land, and created an unbalanced economy that exacerbated the poverty of India. Furthermore, they believed that the tariff structure on cotton goods revealed the true nature of British rule:

> Be that as it may, as regards this question of the cotton duties, the mask has now fallen off the foreign English administration of India. The highest officials in the country, nay the entire official body and the leading newspapers in England, have had to make the humiliating confession—The boast in which we have been so long indulging, the boast that we govern India in the interest and for the welfare of the Indians, is perfectly unfounded; India is held and governed in the interests of the English merchants (*The Bangabasi*, 17 March 1894, quoted in Chandra 1966: 235).

The national leadership united on this issue, and on the importance of protection for India's artisans and nascent industries. Moreover, for the first time they united in action, around the issue of cotton tariffs. In 1896 they urged the boycott of foreign goods (Chandra 1966:250). The tactic of appealing to the English government of India to practice what it preached—just government—had begun to give way to active opposition. The seeds of opposition, the idea of *swadeshi* (the promotion of indigenous products), had already been planted:

> In 1872 Justice Ranade delivered a series of public lectures at Poona on economic topics, in which he popularized "the idea of *swadeshi*, of preferring the goods produced in one's own country even though they may prove to be dearer or less satisfactory than finer foreign products." These celebrated lectures so inspired the listeners that several of them including Ganesh Vasudeo Joshi . . . and Vasudeo Phadke . . . enthusiastically "vowed to wear and use only swadeshi articles." Joshi used to spin yarn daily for his own *dhoti*, shirt and turban; he started shops at several places to popularise and propagate *swadeshi* goods, and, at the Delhi Durbar of 1877 and in the midst of pageantry and flamboyancy, he represented the Sarvajanik Sabha dressed in pure self-spun khadi (Chandra 1966: 122–3).

Indians could fight the destructive power of the English government by using Indian products in preference to foreign ones. The ideology and practice of *swadeshi* grew among nationalists and then, when the English government of India imposed excise duties on Indian cloth, *swadeshi* promoters turned to their most powerful weapon, boycott. In 1896, many people in Dacca resolved to boycott Manchester cloth and to patronize Indian mills (Chandra 1966: 126). The center of activity was the Bombay Presidency, home of the nascent textile industry (the first mill opened only in the 1850s). Indians showed their opposition to English clothing by refusing to buy it or wear it, and by burning it. "According to the *Nyaya Sindu* of 2 March 1896 huge bundles of English clothing were thrown into the Holi fire that year" (Chandra 1966: 130, n.167). A *Times* correspondent reported that "It was impossible for a respectable citizen to go with a new English piece of cloth without being asked a hundred perplexing questions" (Chandra 1966: 130). Even though agitation subsided in subsequent years, *swadeshi*, the promotion of indigenous products, with cloth as its main platform, became a permanent feature of the nationalist movement.

English cloth had become the most potent symbol of English political domination and economic exploitation. As cloth is used mainly in clothing, the results of English exploitation—the demise of indigenous industry—were constantly there for all to see, on the backs of Indians who wore Manchester cloth made into British-style garments, and on Indians who used Manchester cloth for turbans, *kurtas* (shirts), *saris*, and other Indian garments. *Swadeshi*, an attempt to revive and promote Indian industry, required that each person be counted as a patriot-nationalist or a supporter of English domination and exploitation. An individual's political views, encoded in his or her costume, were exposed to public view.

Indeed, part of the reason for the decline of the *swadeshi* movement was the difficulty in procuring, and resistance to wearing, *swadeshi* costume. In the late nineteenth century, the Indian mills and handloom weavers together did not have the capability to clothe the nation. More significantly, most nationalist leaders, including Gokhale and Naoroji (but not the more militant Tilak), continued to wear English costumes with Indian headgear in public. They still believed that the way to gain a just administration of India was to show the English rulers the errors of their ways, so that English fair play and justice would prevail, Indians would be given a greater voice in the government of their land, and artisanry and industry would be revived. Like Gandhi when he appealed to the railway authorities in South Africa in 1893, they seemed to believe that they had to show their English rulers that they were like the English, that they were English gentlemen, and were entitled to all that the English government would give to its own people.

Thus a fascinating paradox was generated from the semiotic and economic characteristics of cloth. These early nationalists wanted to revive and modernize Indian manufactures, especially the textile industry. But their political beliefs stood in the way of utilizing its products. Cloth is made to be worn and to express the social identity of its wearer. They expressed their belief in English values and their right to English justice by comporting themselves as English gentlemen in English dress (albeit with a special hat or turban to signify a slight cultural distinctiveness). Because they were still committed to this Englishness of dress, they were incapable of carrying out their own program of *swadeshi*.

Gandhi, following the lead of Tilak, Joshi and others, came to the more radical position that to promote Indian industry, foreign notions of civilization and gentlemanliness would have to be discarded. Economic Indianization was intrinsically connected to sociocultural Indianization. One could not promote the Indian textile industry without wearing its products and one could not wear its products and remain a proper Englishman. And if one gave up frock coats and morning suits, one would no longer be an English gentleman entitled to treatment as such. A new strategy would be required to achieve the nationalists' goals for India, a strategy based more on confrontation and opposition than on persuasion and cooperation.

THE MAHATMA AS SEMIOTICIAN

Gandhi began his conscious experimentation with costume on his trip to India in 1901. He had begun to question the political efficacy of gentlemanly dress. The experiments intensified during the *satyagraha* (truth force) campaign of militant non-violence in South Africa, from the 1906 opposition to the Black Act until his departure in 1914. In 1909, when Gandhi settled at Tolstoy Farm, he is said to have put on "laborer's dress"— workman's trousers and shirt in the European style, which were adapted from prison uniform (Nanda 1958: 109). There is a photograph of him during the *satyagraha* campaign wearing *lungi* (South Indian wrapped lower garment), *kurta* and coat. His head and feet are bare; he carries a staff and a bag slung across his shoulders. This costume was similar to the one he wore on his third-class pilgrimage through India in 1901. The transformation was so radical and unfamiliar that the Reverend Andrews, who arrived to join the movement in 1913, did not recognize the "man in a *lungi* and *kurta* with close cropped head and a staff in hand," reported Prabhudas Gandhi who added "probably he took him for a *sadhu* (ascetic holy man)" (Gandhi, P. 1957: 176).

That same year, after being released from jail, he attended a meeting in Durban in a *dhoti* (perhaps a *lungi*). His feet were bare and he had shaved his moustache. He was in mourning for the dead coal strikers (Ashe 1968: 124). However, when he sailed for England in 1914 he was dressed as an Englishman (Fischer 1982: 151), and when he landed in India the following year he was dressed as a Kathiawari (Gujarat) peasant, in *dhoti, angarkha* (robe), upper cloth, and turban, the most thoroughly Indian of his costumes.

His *satyagrahi* garb was his own design, and expressed simplicity, asceticism, and identity with the masses. His Kathiawari dress was more formal. It identified his region of origin and presented him as a totally Indian gentleman. In his autobiography he comments on this costume "with my Kathiawadi cloak, turban and *dhoti*, I looked somewhat more civilized than I do today" (1982: 374). The costume was an attempt to provide an Indian resolution for the contradiction between being civilized and being Indian.

His colleagues were not sure what to make of him. He "was an eccentric figure, with his huge white turban and white clothing, among the western attired delegates" (Gold 1983: 63). By appearing in this eccentric fashion he forced his colleagues to notice and accommodate his view of a truly Indian nationalism. He deliberately used costume not only to express his sociopolitical identity, but to manipulate social occasions to elicit acceptance of, if not agreement with, his position.

Despite the thoroughgoing Indianness of his Kathiawari costume (actually because of it) it was inadequate for Gandhi's purposes because it indicated region, class, and religion. Gandhi's program called for the unity of all Indians throughout the subcontinent, rich and poor, Hindu, Sikh, and Muslim. He needed a costume that transcended these distinctions. His experiments continued. He arrived in Madras in 1915 traveling third class and wearing a loose shirt and pair of trousers (Erikson 1969: 279). He was photographed in Karachi in 1916 wearing a dark-colored hat similar in shape to what has become known as a "Gandhi cap" (Gold 1983: 59). Again during the Kheda *satyagraha* in 1918 he was photographed in his Kathiawari turban. At the 1919 Amritsar Congress he first wore the white homespun "Gandhi cap." Some believe it was derived from South African prison garb (Ashe 1968:199). The cap also resembles some worn by Muslims and it may be important that Gandhi began to wear it during the campaign to support the Caliph of Turkey, a campaign important to Gandhi for its promotion of Hindu-Muslim unity. The cap, which Gandhi discarded two years later, was to become part of the uniform of Indian nationalists.

Gandhi's final costume change took place in 1921 when he began his national program for the revival of handmade cloth. *Khadi* (homespun) was scarce and expensive, so he urged his followers to wear as little cloth as possible:

> I know that many will find it difficult to replace their foreign cloth all at once ... Let them be satisfied with a mere loin cloth ... India has never insisted on full covering of the body for the males as a test of culture. ... In order, therefore, to set the example, I propose to discard at least up to the 31st of October my *topi* (cap) and vest, and to content myself with only a loin cloth, and a *chaddar* (shawl) whenever found necessary for the protection of the body. I adopt the change, because I have always hesitated to advise anything I may not myself be prepared to follow I consider the renunciation to be also necessary for me as a sign of mourning, and a bare head and bare body is such a sign in my part of the country I do not expect coworkers to renounce the use of the vest and the *topi* unless they find it necessary (29 September 1921, quoted in Jaju 1951: 98).

Later recalling the same event, Gandhi added he "divest[ed] [him] self of every inch of clothing [he] decently could and thus to a still greater extent [brought himself] in line with the ill-clad masses in so far as the loin cloth also spells simplicity let it represent Indian civilization" (quoted in Jaju 1951: 99). Gandhi had completely rejected the English gentleman and replaced him with the Indian ascetic, the renouncer, the holy man. When he visited the Viceroy in 1921 (and still later, when he attended the Round Table Conference in London in 1931 and visited King George and Queen Mary at Buckingham Palace) wearing his *mahatma* garb, nothing could match the communicative power of a photograph of Gandhi in loincloth and *chadar* sitting among the formally attired Englishmen. He communicated his disdain for civilization as it is understood in the West, his disdain for material possessions, his pride in Indian civilization, as well as his power—an ordinary man would not have been granted entry. By dealing openly with a man in *mahatma* garb, the British accepted his political position and revealed their loss of power.

The communicative power of Gandhi's costume was, however, uniquely Indian. Paradoxically, as his popularity grew, the messages he brought to the Indian public in his speeches and writings had increasingly limited range. Gatherings were huge, running to a hundred thousand or more. Only in the cities were public address systems available to him. Most people who went to see him could not hear him. Even if they could hear him the Gujarati or Hindustani or English in which he spoke could not be understood by many, sometimes most, of his audience. In a nation about three-quarters illiterate, his writings were available to still fewer.

Gandhi needed another medium through which to communicate with the people of India. He used his appearance to communicate his most important messages in a form comprehensible to all Indians. Engaged in the simple labor of spinning, dressed as one of the poor in loincloth and *chadar,* this important and powerful man communicated the dignity of poverty, the dignity of labor, the equality of all Indians, and the greatness of Indian civilization, as well as his own saintliness. The communicative power of costume transcended the limitations of language in multilingual and illiterate India. The image transcended cultural boundaries as well. His impact on the West was enhanced by his resemblance, in his simplicity of dress and his saintly manner, to Christ on the Cross.

In India, visual communication has a unique force. The sight of the eminent or holy blesses and purifies the viewer; the experience is called *darshan*. People came, literally, to *see* Gandhi. Through *darshan*, the power of Gandhi's appearance surpassed his message in words. "For the next quarter of a century, it was not only for his message that people came to him, but for the merit of seeing him. The sacred sight of the *Mahatma*, his *darshan*, was almost equivalent to a pilgrimage to holy Banaras" (Nanda 1958: 213).

During this same period, Gandhi was experimenting with the economics of cloth production. Gandhi recalled: "It was in London in 1908 that I discovered the wheel. I saw in a flash that without the spinning wheel there was no *Swaraj* [self-government]. But I did not then know the distinction between the loom and the wheel, and in *Hind Swaraj* used the word loom to mean the wheel" (quoted in Jaju 1951: 1). "I do not remember to have seen a handloom or a spinning wheel when in

1908 I described it in *Hind Swaraj* as the panacea for the growing pauperism of India. In that book I took it as understood that anything that helped India to get rid of the grinding poverty of her masses would in the same process also establish *Swaraj*. Even in 1915 when I returned to India from South Africa, I had not actually seen a spinning wheel" (Gandhi 1957: 489). By the time Gandhi returned to India in 1915, cloth production had become central to his program.

Like most leaders of the nationalist movement, Gandhi thought the reindustrialization of India to be of paramount importance, but unlike most of them he was opposed to mechanized industry, which he viewed as a sin perpetrated on the world by the West. He wanted to revive artisanry. From the establishment of Phoenix farm in 1904, Gandhi had committed himself to the simple life of labor. Machines were labor-saving devices that put thousands of laborers out of work, unthinkable in India where the masses were under employed. Factory production facilitated the concentration of wealth in the hands of a few big capitalists, and transformed workers into "utter slaves."

Gandhi selected Ahmedabad, the Manchester of India, as the site for his settlement because this "great textile center was best suited for experiments in hand-spinning and weaving which appeared to him the only practicable supplementary occupations for the underworked and underfed masses in the villages of India" (Nanda 1958: 134), and ". . . as Ahmedabad was [also] an ancient centre of hand-loom weaving, it was likely to be the most favourable field for the revival of the cottage industry of hand-spinning" (Gandhi 1957: 395). Erikson, who has written so brilliantly on the early years in Ahmedabad, observes that "Gandhi blamed the disruption of native crafts [not only for the poverty of India, but also] for the deterioration of Indian identity. He was soon to elevate the spinning wheel to significance as an economic necessity, a religious ritual and a national symbol . . . Gandhi wanted to settle down where both tradition and available materials would permit him and his followers to build a community around the cultivation of spinning and weaving" (Erikson 1969: 260).

By the time he settled at Ahmedabad his goal for India was the achievement, through *satyagraha*, of the reduction of poverty, disease, and immorality, and the restoration of dignity. Spinning offered solutions to all these problems. The English had destroyed the greatest cotton producer in the world in order to protect their own industries from competition, to create a source of raw materials not available in the British Isles, and to make a ready market for their finished products. Gandhi sought to restore India's lost supremacy, to revive this "second lung" of India (the first was agriculture). His reasoning was simple: If Indians returned to the production of their own cloth there would be work for millions of unemployed, Indian wealth would not be taken to England and Japan, and Indians would again be their own masters (See Jaju 1915:8). "*Swadeshi* is the soul of *Swaraj, Khadi* is the essence of *Swadeshi*" (Gandhi quoted in Jaju 1951: 12).

Until its demise in the 1820s, spinning had been a supplementary occupation of women all over the country. Weaving, by contrast, had always been a caste occupation. Though at first Gandhi concentrated on reviving spinning among women, he soon broadened his program. Spinning would become the leisure pursuit of all. The wealthy would spin as service; the poor to supplement their incomes. Through spinning, India would be able to clothe itself, and thereby free itself from foreign exploitation and domination. Through spinning, all Indians, rich and poor, educated and illiterate, would be laborers, equal and united through their labor (see Bean 1988):

> Originally there was one specific objective: to give work and clothing to the half-starved women of India. To this was related from the beginning the larger objective of khadi—the cloth itself as a means of economic self-sufficiency (*swadeshi*) which in turn must inevitably produce self-government (*swaraj*). This progression, *Khadi = swadeshi = swaraj*, was Gandhi's incessant preachment for the rest of his life. His genius had found a tremendous symbol which was at the same time a practical weapon . . . for the liberation of India. . . . The symbol he had found, the wheel itself, assumed enormous importance with the passage of time: it related itself to the whole of life, to God, to the pilgrimage of the spirit. (Sheean 1949: 154, 157, 158, see also Bayly 1986).

Gandhi had returned from South Africa determined to wear handmade cloth. He brought a weaver to the ashram, but there was no hand-spun yarn available for the loom, so Gandhi began looking for a spinner. It was not until 1917 that his associate Gangabehn located spinners who would produce yarn to be woven at the ashram—if slivers, carded cotton for spinning, could be supplied to them. Until then, Gandhi had relied on machine-spun yarn from Ahmedabad mills for his looms, but he still had to get the slivers for hand-spinning from the mills. Gandhi's *khadi* had to be entirely handmade, so he asked Gangabehn to find carders who could provide the slivers. Gandhi "begged for [the raw] cotton in Bombay" (Gandhi 1957: 492). Finally the entire process of making cloth could be done by hand.

At this time, Gandhi's *dhoti* was still of Indian mill cloth. The *khadi* manufactured at the ashram was only 30 inches wide. Gandhi "gave notice to Gangabehn that, unless she provided a *khadi dhoti* of 45 inches width within a month, [he] would do with coarse, short *khadi dhoti*. . . . well within the month she sent [him] a pair of *khadi dhotis* of 45 inches width, and thus relieved [him] from what would then have been a difficult situation." (Gandhi 1957: 493). Perhaps Gandhi was looking for an opportunity to change to a loincloth, a change he accomplished two years later. From 1919 on, he was clothed entirely in *khadi*, and instead of the turban, he began wearing the white *khadi* "Gandhi cap." *Khadi* was much too coarse for wrapping as a Gujarati turban.

In 1920 as part of the Non-cooperation Movement, the leaders of the Indian National Congress endorsed hand spinning and weaving, to supply cloth to replace boycotted foreign cloth and to engage the masses in the nationalist cause. In this they followed Gandhi, but they were by no means in full agreement with him. "Tagore argued that trying to liberate three hundred million people by making them all spinners was like urging them to drown the English by all spitting together: it was 'too simple for human beings.' Complaints came in against *khadi* as a material in the conditions of modern living. It wouldn't stand up to the wear and tear of a factory. It was too heavy. It was hard to launder and therefore unsuitable for children.

Gandhi's answer was that with more skill there would be better *khadi*" (Ashe 1968: 249).

Most nationalists disagreed with Gandhi's opposition to mechanized industry. Many, including Jawaharlal Nehru, believed industrialization crucial for India's economic wellbeing. Few felt Gandhi's love for the purity and simplicity of coarse white *khadi*. Jawaharlal Nehru's sister Vijayalakshmi Pandit thought *khadi* rough and drab. She felt deprived to have to wear a wedding sari of *khadi*, though it had been spun and woven by Kasturbai Gandhi and dyed the traditional Kashmiri pink. Their father Motilal Nehru, at the meeting of the Congress Working Committee in Delhi during November 1921, burst out laughing when he heard Gandhi say that a person must know hand-spinning in order to participate in civil disobedience (Nanda 1958: 235). In a letter to his son, the elder Nehru spoke of the *khadi* movement as one of Gandhi's hobbies.

Despite their disagreement, the Nehrus and other nationalist leaders supported hand-spinning and *khadi* because they recognized its symbolic and economic importance in the programs of *swadeshi*, boycott, and noncooperation. Mrs. Pandit noted the effects of wearing *khadi* "Gandhi caps," *kurtas*, and *dhotis*: She could no longer detect the social class of the visitors to her family's home. The uniform was a leveler, all Congressmen were the same (Pandit 1979: 82). Accommodations were made for intranational variation: *dhotis* for Hindus, *pyjamas* (trousers) for Muslims, turbans distinctive for Sikhs or southern Brahmins. *Khadi*, the fabric of nationalism, transcended and encompassed these distinctions. Gandhi had taught his followers that costume can transform social and political identities. When Gandhi, clothed in loincloth and *chadar*, was received by the Viceroy Lord Reading in 1921, his followers (and his opponents) also saw that costume can be used to dominate and structure a social event. The most important result of those meetings was that Gandhi, wearing his opposition to English values and representing the people of India, was accepted to negotiate as an equal with the representatives of the British Empire in India. Gandhi forced the Empire to compromise its standards and thus demonstrated the power of the freedom movement he led.

By 1921, all Congressmen were dressed in *khadi*. The Governor of Bombay Presidency, C.R. Das, made *khadi* the uniform of civic employees. From July 1922, no member of Congress was allowed to wear imported cloth, and dues were to be paid in hand-spun yarn instead of cash. Hand-spinning and *khadi* had become a fixture in the freedom movement. Economic revitalization and self-government would be accomplished through mass organization, carried on by khadi-clad Congress workers promoting indigenous industries and mass action by teaching spinning to everyone, spreading the boycott of foreign products to the most remote villages, and preparing the way for mass civil disobedience.

Khadi had become, in Nehru's words, "the livery of freedom."

References Cited

Ashe, Geoffrey (1968) *Gandhi*. New York: Stein and Day.

Bayly, C.A. (1986) 'The Origins of Swadeshi (Home Industry): Cloth and Indian Society, 1700–1930' In *The Social Life of Things*. Arjun Appadurai, ed. Cambridge: Cambridge University Press.

Bean, Susan S. (1988) 'Spinning Independence' In *Making Things in South Asia: Proceedings of the South Asian Regional Studies Seminar*. Michael Meiter, ed. Philadelphia: University of Pennsylvania.

Chandra, Bipin (1965) 'Indian Nationalists and the Drain, 1880–1905'. *Indian Economic and Social History Review* 2(2):103–44.

(1966) *The Rise and Growth of Economic Nationalism in India*. New Delhi.

(1968) 'Reinterpretations of Nineteenth Century Indian Economic History'. *Indian Economic and Social History Review* 5:35–75.

Chatterji, Basudev (1980) 'The Abolition of the Cotton Excise, 1925: A Study in Imperial Priorities'. *Indian Economic and Social History Review* 17(4):355–80.

(1981) 'Business and Politics in the 1930s: Lancashire and the Making of the Indo-British Trade Agreement'. *Modern Asian Studies* 15:527–74.

Chaudhuri, K.N. (1968) 'India's International Economy in the 19th Century'. *Modern Asian Studies* 2:31–50.

(1978) *The Trading World of Asia and the English East India Company 1660–1760*. Cambridge: Cambridge University Press.

Cohn, Bernard (1988) 'Cloth, Clothes, and Colonialism: India in the Nineteenth Century'. In *Cloth and Human Experience*. Annette B. Weiner and Jane Schneider, eds. Washington, DC: Smithsonian Institution.

Dewey, Clive (1978) 'The Eclipse of the Lancashire Lobby and the Concession of Fiscal Autonomy to India'. In C. Dewey and A.G. Hopkins, eds. *The Imperial Impact*. London: Althone Press.

Dutt, Romesh Chunder (1968) Romesh Chunder Dutt. Delhi: Government of India, Ministry of Information and Broadcasting.

(1901, 1903) *The Economic History of India*, 2 vols. London.

(1906) *India Under Early British Rule*. London: Kegan Paul

Erikson, Erik (1969) *Gandi's Truth*. New York: W.W. Norton.

Fischer, Louis (1982 [1951]) *The Life of Mahatma Gandhi*. London: Granada.

Gadgil, D.R. (1942) *The Industrial Evolution of India in Recent Times*. Calcutta.

Gandhi. M.K. (1922 [1908]) *Indian Home Rule*. Madras: Ganesh & Co.

(1941) *Economics of Khadi*. Ahmedabad: Navajivan Press.

(1957 [1927–29]) *An Autobiography: the Story of My Experiments with Truth*. Boston: Beacon Press.

Gandhi, Prabudas (1957) *My Childhood with Gandhiji*. Ahmedabad: Navajivan Press.

Ganguli, B.N. (1965) 'Dadabhai Naoroji and the Mechanism of External Drain'. *Indian Economic and Social History Review* 2(2):85–102.

Gittinger, Mattiebelle (1982) *Master Dyers to the World*. Washington, D.C.: Textile Museum.

Gold, Gerald (1983) *Gandhi: A Pictorial Biography*. New York: New Market Press.

Irwin, John (1962) *Indian Textiles in Historical Perspective*. Marg XV(4).

Irwin, John and K. Brett (1970) *The Origins of Chintz*. London: Victoria and Albert Museum.

Jaju, Shrikrishnadas (1951) *The Ideology of Charka*. Tirupur.

Masani, Rustom Pestonji (1939) *Dadabhai Naoroji: The Grand Old Man of India*. London: Allen & Unwin.

Mehta, Ved (1977) *Mahatma Gandhi and His Apostles*. New York: Penguin Books.

Nanda, B.R. (1958) *Mahatma Gandhi*. Boston: Beacon Press.

Naoroji, Dadabhai (1887) *Essays, Speeches and Writings*. C.L. Parekh, ed. Bombay.

Pandit, Vijayalakshmi (1979) *The Scope of Happiness*. New York: Crown.

Pradhan, G.P. and A.K. Bhagwat (1958) *Lokamanya Tilak*. Bombay.

Sarkar, Sumit (1973) *The Swadeshi Movement in Bengal, 1903–1908*. Calcutta.

Sharma, Jagadish (1955, 1968) *Mahatma Gandhi: A Descriptive Bibliography*.

Sheean, Vincent (1949) *Lead Kindly Light*. New York: Random House.

Sitaramayya, Pattabhi (1969) *History of the Indian National Congress*, vol. 1 (1885–1935). Delhi: S. Chand.

Wolpert, Stanley (1962) *Tilak and Gokhale*. Berkeley: University of California Press.

27

100% COTTON (2011)

Pamela Johnson

EDITOR'S INTRODUCTION

In '100% Cotton', the novelist and poet Pamela Johnson explores Britain's postcolonial identity. Shifting between the perspectives of a father and daughter, the poem appropriates textile terms and garment shapes to show how culturally specific details are adopted, often with little recognition of the past. Following antagonism between neighbours, the poem opens out to glimpse the wider community.

The town of Oldham to which Johnson refers – formerly in the county of Lancashire – now falls within Greater Manchester, England. In the nineteenth century Oldham experienced rapid growth in textile manufacturing to become one of the first industrialized towns. The area was badly impacted by the Lancashire Cotton Famine (1861–5) caused by overproduction of textiles and disruption of cotton shipping from the United States during the American Civil War. Nonetheless, in the 1860s and 1870s Oldham was considered one of the most productive cotton spinning towns in the world, a claim it held into the 1960s. The last cotton spinning mill closed in Oldham in 1998.

In the memory section of this book, Takahashi Mizuki discusses the decline of Hong Kong's textile manufacturing industry where the last factory closed in 2014. An excerpt of the film script from *The Man in the White Suit* (1951) is included in the production section of this book set in an unnamed textile manufacturing town in the north of England. In Johnson's writing, the textiles she evokes throughout the poem carry cultural identities and unavoidable – if unspoken – politics.

100% Cotton

Pamela Johnson

I'll defend my own land, Frank shouts across
the privet at the man, in shalwar
and t-shirt, who's moved in next door.

It's only a hedge. Isn't 'land' a bit grand
for your handkie-sized plot? Blood on the boil,
I fought for this country, Frank cries as he falls.

His gashed head lies wrapped in soft lint,
morphine eases the rage from his brow.
Not knowing how to care for a bully,

she brings new pyjamas, finest white cotton,
blue piping, remembering that day when
her mum bought him two-for-the-price-of-one,

polyester, 'seconds' from the market, a fiver,
and his temper sent static crackling
between them that went on for a week.

Did he think he was bettering himself
drawing in the cord, tied tight,
an Englishman, one-hundred-percent cotton?

A buddleia grows where smoke
once belched as thousands swarmed
to the sound of the hooter, three shifts a day,

and alongside the crumbling chimney
a minaret rises and men, loose-trousered,
fill the close-packed streets

drawn by the call of the muezzin, hugging
woollen coats against an Oldham winter
while she, at his bedside, waits to offer nightwear

adopted, adapted from an ancient design
of tailors in the markets of Kharachi,
not sure if he knows *payejama* is an Urdu word.

28

IVANOVO'S AGITPROP TEXTILES
Design and Inscriptions (2011/2021)

Galina Kareva

EDITOR'S INTRODUCTION

Galina Kareva is the Head of the department Ivanovo Calico Museum of the Ivanovo State Museum of History and Local Lore, named after D. G. Burylin. The museum is located in the Russian city of Ivanovo 254 kilometres (158 miles) north-east of Moscow. In the nineteenth century Ivanovo was known as the 'Russian Manchester' or 'Red Manchester' because of its textile manufacturing. The museum was founded in 1912 and includes an extensive collection of Ivanovo cotton printed textiles.

The term 'agitprop' found in this writing is an abbreviation of the Russian terms 'agitation' and 'propaganda' (agitatsiya and propaganda) used by the department of Agitation and Propaganda Section of the Central Committee Secretariat of the Communist Party established in the early 1920s in the Soviet Union. Official information, including education and mass communication, was overseen by the department. When used in English, the term 'agitprop' has come to connote strategies that use the arts for political indoctrination.

Agitprop textiles exemplify the Soviet desire to immerse citizens in the values of socialism, which included the introduction of new household objects. In the writing reprinted in full here, Kareva not only vividly describes particular examples of the collection's roller printed cotton textiles but also notes specific design strategies such as the nearly hidden acronyms embedded in some of the designs.

This article was first published in Russian and has been translated in full here by Sophie Abasheva.

Ivanovo's Agitprop Textiles: Design and Inscriptions

Galina Kareva

The 1920s and 1930s became a new milestone in the history of Ivanovo-Voznesensk, dubbed 'the Red Manchester' and 'the Third Proletarian Capital'. The Soviet architects' stylistic experiments, the large-scale housing, social and industrial construction projects and the production of Ivanovo fabrics were all carried out in a single ideologized sphere. Through a utilitarian consumer product, both at the conscious and subconscious level, a powerful propaganda machine was launched for decades at a much larger and more thorough scale, multiplied by the potential of nationalized industry.

In a vivid, imaginative form, the Ivanovo agitprop designs reflect the era of great transformations expressed in electrification, industrialization, collectivization and changes in the army and sports. Notwithstanding a whole range of new subjects, the designs remained tradition-bound. Their content, in most cases, strictly conformed to the traditional methods of repeat composition. A low-key colour scheme, the small scale of the design and its graphic quality somewhat reduced the power of the revolutionary impact. Inscriptions and slogans were extremely rare at that time on agitprop garments, and their use is of great interest to researchers and designers.

A series of headscarves produced by the Teykovo Textile Factory in 1922 to commemorate the 5th anniversary of the October Revolution could be considered the earliest experiment in the production of agitprop textiles. Two types of scarves from this series have been preserved bearing the mottos 'Vsya vlast' Sovetam!' (All power to the Soviets!) and 'Proletarii vsekh stran, soyedinyaytes'!' (Proletarians of all countries, unite!) based on the drawings of the artist Leonid Chernov-Plessky. The first of them contains a complex multi-layered ornamental composition with a central piece — *The Dispersal of the Constituent Assembly by the Bolsheviks*, while portraits of political leaders — Vladimir Lenin, Yakov Sverdlov, Mikhail Kalinin — occupy modest angular motifs and are blended in the outline of a common border pattern narrating revolutionary events. The design of the kerchief contains a large number of inscriptions explaining the plots: *The Capture of Perekop*, *The Annexation of the Far Eastern Republic*, etc. This is the only headscarf with portraits created for actual wearing, hence the rotation of the composition around the central axis. Another kerchief of the same factory is perceived as a poster, with its utilitarian nature disappearing. A portrait of V.I. Lenin from this headscarf later was printed on the mourning armbands of the delegates from Ivanovo-Voznesensk Governorate[1] at Lenin's funeral. The scarves were presented at the First Exhibition of the Trust Industry in Moscow in the same year. Production of souvenir headscarves commemorating remarkable occasions used to be an old tradition in pre-revolutionary Russia. The Russian Civil War exerted a heavy toll on the Ivanovo-Voznesensk textile industry. Raw materials — cotton and yarn — were lacking, but the shortage of fuel was especially acute at the enterprises. Many factories in the province were shut down as all attempts to breathe new life into the industry failed. Factories produced plain dyed or grey fabrics. Clearly, the production of themed headscarves with revolutionary leaders' portraits was planned by the Ivanovo-Voznesensk Textile Trust as a special symbolic gesture to mark the revival of the textile industry.

The most unusual fabrics with slogans are calicos *Proletarians of All Countries, Unite* designed by Sergei

Source: Galina Kareva, 'Ivanovo's Agitprop Textiles: Design and Inscriptions'. Translated from Russian by Sofia Abasheva. Reproduced with permission.

Loginov. The artist has developed several designs for calico which could have been called traditional since they were decorated with floral ornaments, but upon closer examination, the slogan 'Proletarians of all countries, unite!' is visible in the finest rendering. The patterns of these fabrics are regarded as masterpieces of engraving art. They were developed in 1926, when, despite a massive propaganda campaign, agitprop fabrics were produced in small quantities. The designs, called *perekat* (top printing) in Ivanovo, are examples of the technology in the conditions of an extreme raw material crisis. The acute shortage of dyes in the 1920s and the great need for fabrics obliged artists to be as economical as possible when choosing artistic means. The transfer of the textile motif into stylized graphics produces an interesting ornamental solution; the image appears to vibrate due to the thickness and frequency of hatchwork. Thanks to this technique, the pattern on the fabric acquires a dynamic play of silhouette and linear images, and the repetition of identical elements is not perceived as monotonous and dye is used sparingly. Single-roller fabrics with a new image interpretation technique were especially popular in the 1920s. Within one and the same colour — red, dark blue or black — against a background, the artists were able to achieve amazing decorative expressiveness. The calico *Proletarians of All Countries, Unite* is the only example of the use of inscriptions in *perekat* prints, although many Ivanovo artists worked in the same manner: Sergei Burylin, Raisa Matveyeva, Darya Preobrazhenskaya, Pavel Nechvalenko.

The creation of agitprop textile prints in Ivanovo-Voznesensk is a complex and contradictory phenomenon, many of the ornaments are perceived not just as attempts to find a compromise between the traditional form and the new content, but also as attempts to preserve the tradition of Ivanovo design. Among the Ivanovo textile artists of the Soviet period Pyotr Leonov is a legendary figure who took the lead in regional drawing workshops during the difficult years of the formation of the Soviet industry. In 1939, he was the first among textile artists to be awarded the USSR State Prize, and by decree of the Presidium of the Supreme Soviet of the USSR on April 7, 1939, he was awarded the Order of Lenin. Pyotr Leonov was not only a good administrator, but also a talented artist. Having become the head of the central artistic workshop, which, according to the art critic of the 1930s Frida Roginskaya, was supposed to be a kind of ideological centre for the creation of new drawings and colour ways (Roginskaya 1930: 78–81), when working on thematic drawings Leonov sought to ensure that they meet the specifics of the textile ornament. It is not unlikely that thanks to Pyotr Grigoryevich Ivanovo agitprop fabrics escaped poster-like quality, there are no brute-force solutions in the presentation of new subjects, and inscriptions and slogans are veiled in traditional ornaments.

An example of the use of acronyms in a traditional textile pattern can be considered in the calico *VKP(b)* (All-Union Communist Party (bolsheviks)), produced at the factory of the trust Ivtextil. A single-roller small pattern, in which the background colour is very active, at a first glance is perceived as floral and not corresponding to its dominant name. The dashed fractional rendering of the drawing creates a virtuoso dynamic composition, but makes the letters of the acronym almost illegible.

Examples of the use of inscriptions could also be found in the plot designs for decorative fabrics of 1927–1928. The theme symbolizing the daily routine of the Soviet village and agricultural sector transformations is seen in drawings of a realistic, sometimes even naturalistic character. Decorative fabrics that are noteworthy in their construction, colour solution and stylization by Vladimir Maslov *Sel'skoye potrebitel'skoye obshchestvo* (Rural Consumer Society) and Sergei Burylin *Novaya derevnya* (New Village) are missing from the Ivanovo museum collection. In their panoramic works, the linkage of the city and the village, the mechanization of agriculture and the new way of life found a good pictorial solution, large-scale and beautiful in colour. Evaluating the agitprop fabrics of this direction, the well-known theorist of propaganda textiles Frida Roginskaya noted that the drawings were made 'almost in the manner in which Sytin rendered his lubok prints — cloyingly, excessively naturalistic, with a taste of rusticism...' (Ibid., 35–36). Bright colour schemes, large-scale repeat compositions and contrasting local combinations make the composition easily perceived at a distance.

All these compositional and plot fabrics are distinguished by the complexity of the process, which requires bright colours, a large number of rollers for the printing machine, and complex engraving of the drawing.

The largest group of fabrics with inscriptions are drawings using various acronyms: *KIM* (Communist Youth International), *MOPR* (International Workers Aid Society), *SSSR* (Union of Socialist Soviet Republics), *RSFSR* (Russian Soviet Federative Socialist Republic), or the numbers 4 and 5, conveying the popular slogan '*Pyatiletku v chetyre goda*' (Five-year plan in four years).

The actual abolition of the NEP provided the avantgardists with ample opportunities to turn the fabric into a kind of calico tribune. The main driver in this trend was not the government or party ideologists, but the artists themselves, who formed influential organizations. The role of the Art Council of the All-Union Textile Syndicate increased significantly, it assumed leadership and administrative functions in the evaluation of textile patterns. Young artists were the core of the Art Council formed under the Syndicate. In 1926, a branch of the *AKhR* (Association of the Artists of Revolution) appeared in Ivanovo-Voznesensk, in 1930 its textile section was organized. Thus, the artists had the opportunity of ideological control over most of the drawings that went into production. New designs produced in workshops had to be approved by the Art Council, which established strict Marxist social and class requirements. The Council saw its task in eliminating all those drawings that were traditional and ideologically neutral. A massive attack was launched on factory archives and studios, subjecting thousands of old sketches to an ideological compliance test. In the period from late 1929 to early 1931, 24,000 textile drawings were destroyed, most of them based on floral compositions, and thousands of rollers with traditional patterns were all at once ground off. Only about one third of submitted designs were found to comply with the ideological requirements of the Council (Douglas 1992: 642).

The presence of certain specified design directions is indisputable and clearly visible from the materials of the Central Art Workshop of the Ivanovo-Voznesensky Trust. The *KIM* designs submitted by Sergei Burylin

and Darya Preobrazhenskaya differ in their stylistic features. Sergei Burylin, a representative of the pre-revolutionary school of textile design who mastered the craft in the workshop of Kuvayevskaya Textile Factory, uses revolutionary symbols as a mere decorative textile ornament. The design uses a traditional, very conservative pattern construction scheme and a colour scheme close to pillowcase chintz. The artist masterfully enhances the red colour with colour splashes, using the second colour for the background and contour rendering of the drawing. The acronym is inscribed with lines of different sizes, muted with the introduction of an additional ornament into the drawing. Fabrics printed with this pattern were sold not only in domestic markets, but also exported to China.

In Ivanovo-Voznesensk, a shift to new subjects was associated with the creative work of young enthusiastic artists, graduates of VKHUTEIn — Liya Raitser, Darya Preobrazhenskaya, Liubov Silich, Mikhail Khvostenko, Olga Fedoseyeva, and others.

Daria Preobrazhenskaya's design could be considered an example of a bright revolutionary breakthrough in thematic pattern. The work of the young artist is quite peculiar. The avant-garde vibe, contrasting colour and restless rhythm caused by the use of the inscriptions *KIM* and *MYuD* (International Youth Day), distinguish this pattern among other ornaments. The accentuated variegation of colour and the relief structure of the fabric enhance the intricacy of the pattern.

Another popular inscription in 1929–1930 fabric design was the slogan 'Five-year plan in four years'. Within the framework of this trend in textile ornament, Darya Preobrazhenskaya's work *Five-year Plan in Four Years*, sometimes referred to by researchers under another name — *Electrification*, should be highlighted. The diagonal arrangement of the ornament, relative geometrization of the drawing and the use of two clearly alternating contrasting colours convey the rhythm, increase the intensity of transformations and contribute to a bright dynamic composition. The use of bold electric lights and the numbers 5 and 4 encoding the slogan as equivalent semantic units seems to be a well-conceived move. Next to this design, an ornamental composition by the older generation artist

Ivan Mityayev is perceived to be rythmically much more sedate. This is one of the most popular designs for Ivanovo agitprop textiles which was printed on fabric by two major factories: the Bolshaya Kokhomskaya Textile Factory and the Novaya Ivanovo-Voznesenskaya Textile Factory. The layout of the pattern and its sophistication in many ways make it akin to the *mille-fleurs*. The emphasis placed by the artist on the number 4 and the factory pipes with red colour is muffled by fine elaboration and thin lines. The design does not appear heavy, so it was printed not only on dense textured, but also on thin fabrics, including the most refined — armure and foulard.

In comparison with these works, the designs by Sergei Burylin and Olga Bogoslovskaya are perceived as very ascetic. The use of a suppressed colour scheme, the denseness of the pattern and the absence of decorative ornamental motifs in many ways make these two designs similar.

The history of Ivanovo agitprop textiles came to an end with the exhibition of 1934 *Brak v proizvodstve* (Manufacturing Defect) where among other defective fabrics those of propaganda were also exhibited. The brilliant Soviet figurative ornament, having fulfilled its mission, became a museum treasure. Agitprop textiles were produced until the end of the 1930s.

Ivanovo State Museum of History and Local Lore named after D.G. Burylin and its department 'Ivanovo Calico Museum' keep one of the most complete and multifaceted collections of agitprop textiles, designs and sketches in Russia (about 1,000 storage units, of which 790 are samples of fabrics). A comprehensive picture of Ivanovo textiles is presented in the book *100% Ivanovo* as part of the programme *Pervaya Publikatsiya* by Vladimir Potanin Foundation.[2]

Notes

1. For more information, see: Kuskovskaya 1990: 57.
2. See the review in *Fashion Theory* (*Russia*). No. 21 (3/2011), pp. 273–277. (Ed.)

References

Douglas, C. (1992), 'Russian Fabric Design, 1928–32', in: *The Great Utopia: The Russian and Soviet Avant-Garde, 1915–1932*, 634–48, New York: Solomon R. Guggenheim Museum.
Kuskovskaya, Z. (1990), 'Portrety Lenina na tkani (Portraits of Lenin on Fabric)', *Krayevedcheskiye zapiski*, Ivanovo: RIO Uprpoligrafizdata Ivanovskogo oblispolkoma.
Roginskaya, F. (1930), *Sovetskiy tekstil'*, [Soviet Textiles] Moscow: AKhR.

FIBER ART AND THE HIERARCHY OF ART AND CRAFT, 1960–80 (2008)

Elissa Auther

EDITOR'S INTRODUCTION

Elissa Auther lays out many of the ideas that are explored in her book-length project, *String, Felt, Thread and the Hierarchy of Art and Craft in American Art* (2009), in this essay reprinted in full and first published in the inaugural issue of the *Journal of Modern Craft*. The original writing included images that have not been reproduced here. Auther considers the use of textile materials and techniques in American art of the 1960s and 1970s, and the efforts of Mildred Constantine and Jack Lenor Larsen to 'elevate' this work from what was understood at the time as the devalued category of craft to the rightful domain of art.

Auther's research pays attention to the factors, seemingly peripheral, to the actual objects under discussion. In adopting this broader view, the curators, galleries, collectors and social networks that have had a significant impact on the reception and definition of work as sculpture (made from fiber) or fiber art (struggling for validation) are brought to light. Auther shows that the value systems that are used to legitimize much of our visual art often involve considerations and loyalties that go well beyond the physical object in question.

In this essay, Auther pinpoints Lenore Tawney's 1961 solo exhibition at the Staten Island Museum as the moment 'fiber art as it would be recognized in the following two decades made its public debut in a fine-art context'. She goes on to credit Mildred Constantine and Jack Lenor Larsen's exhibition *Wall Hangings*, which toured the United States in the late 1960s, as 'the first major American exhibition of the new genre of fiber art'. While Constantine and Larsen's efforts to raise the profile of fiber art struggled for public recognition at the time, their efforts influenced the next generation of curatorial work with individuals such as Mary Jane Jacob's work continuing to question implicit material and gender hierarchies. In the past decade, textiles have generally received a warmer reception since the period of the 1960s and 1970s Auther discusses. Fiber art as a descriptive category remains little used as a term outside North America.

At the time of writing this essay, Auther was Associate Professor of Modern and Contemporary Art at the University of Colorado at Colorado Springs. She is currently Deputy Director of Curatorial Affairs and William and Mildred Lasdon Chief Curator at the Museum of Arts and Design (MAD) in New York City. From 2007 to 2017, she co-directed the public program *Feminism & Co.: Art, Sex, Politics*.

Fiber Art and the Hierarchy of Art and Craft, 1960–80

Elissa Auther

Alan Saret's *Untitled* (1968), a work of rope and wire and Alice Adams's *Construction* (1966), of rope and steel cable, share significant formal similarities. Both works are floor based, of similar size and shape, and both utilize materials associated with "craft," hand labor or industry. Indeed, one could conclude that the same artist made both works. But this is not the case, and the two artists were associated with very different artistic circles in the 1960s: Saret was an anti-form sculptor, whereas Adams was associated with what came to be known as the fiber art movement. Moreover, the works were exhibited and received very differently.

Comparing the varied reception of these two similar objects reveals not only fiber's arrival as a new medium of "high art" but also how this elevation of fiber issued from multiple sites or positions, each with a distinct location within the complex network of power relations governed by the application of the term "craft" in the United States in the 1960s and 1970s.

In 1972, Mildred Constantine—a former curator of architecture and design at the Museum of Modern Art (MoMA), New York—reproduced Adams's *Construction* in *Beyond Craft*, the first in-depth study of the emerging fiber art movement.[1] This important text, co-authored with textile designer Jack Lenor Larsen, chronicled the movement's evolution, defined its aesthetic priorities and defended work made of fiber as "fine art." In 1963, Adams's unorthodox woven works had been included in New York's Museum of Contemporary Crafts' exhibition *Woven Forms*, a show that Constantine and Larsen's study singled out as groundbreaking.[2]

Significantly, critic Lucy Lippard also exhibited Adams's *Construction* in her eclectic, "post-minimalist" show *Eccentric Abstraction*, at the Fischbach Gallery in New York in 1966. Unlike *Beyond Craft*, *Eccentric*

Abstraction situated Adams's *Construction* among avant-garde work by such emerging artists as Eva Hesse, Bruce Nauman and Keith Sonnier. The show's works utilized a variety of non-traditional, flexible media, including wire mesh, vinyl, cloth and rope.

Saret exhibited *Untitled* in 1970 in New York's Sidney Janis Gallery's January group show *String and Rope*, alongside works by Christo, Fred Sandback, Bruce Nauman and Robert Morris. *Arts Magazine*, one of the era's major fine-art periodicals, reproduced Saret's piece and a critic writing for the *Christian Science Monitor* noted the use of fiber as an autonomous abstract element. The "artists included," he wrote, "use string or rope (or thread), not as line, but as falling, tangling, stretching, or coiling matter" (Andreae 1970: 58).[3]

Studies like *Beyond Craft* (1972), exhibitions such as *Woven Forms* (1963), *Eccentric Abstraction* (1966) and *String and Rope* (1969), and works in fiber like Saret's and Adams's are representative of a number of projects in the 1960s and 1970s that signaled fiber's potential as a fine-art medium and illustrate different relations to the art world's center of power. In each case, fiber, that is, craft—typically dismissed or even invisible as a force shaping the art world in this period—was in actuality central to its constitution. *Beyond Craft* and *Woven Forms* attempted to elevate fiber from the realm of "craft" to that of "art" and were undertaken by individuals and institutions dedicated to legitimating new work in materials traditional to craft. The goal of legitimating so-called fiber art as "Art" sets these projects apart from exhibitions such as *Eccentric Abstraction* and *String and Rope*, which attempted to capture sculpture's latest vanguard. Here craft functioned as a conceptual limit, essential to the elevation of art—in the words of Glenn

Source: Elissa Auther, 'Fiber Art and the Hierarchy of Art and Craft, 1960–80', *The Journal of Modern Craft* 1:1 (2008), pp. 13–33. Reprinted by permission of Informa UK Limited, trading as Taylor & Francis Group, www.tandfonline.com.

Adamson, as "a border that can never be reached, but is nonetheless intrinsic to any sense of position" (Adamson 2007: 2). *Eccentric Abstraction* and *String and Rope* were both produced by members of the art world whose authority in itself legitimated the work in question, a privilege not fully extended to Constantine and Larsen. Rather than focusing on whether Saret's *Untitled* was a work of art, these exhibitions theorized the artistic use of fiber and fiber-like materials in relation to previous examples of non-traditional media in sculpture and to other conditions, such as craft, that oppose the definition of art.

Despite these differences in the projects' orientations and goals, they all probed fiber's symbolic power, paradoxically generated by its subordination in the history of art through deep-rooted associations with utility or craft, a phenomenon Saret's and Adams's works also illuminate. In challenging the subordination of fiber as a medium of craft or of primarily utilitarian value, Adams's and Saret's works additionally illustrate the role fiber played in testing the art world's aesthetic boundaries in the 1960s and 1970s. Yet, with the exception of Adams's *Construction*, which circulated widely, the status of "high art" remained elusive for the objects that Constantine and Larsen featured in *Beyond Craft*. In fact, fiber art in this period was typically viewed as neither art nor craft, but as between the two categories, thwarting the works' potential to undermine the hierarchy of media responsible for fiber's low aesthetic status.

This article examines the efforts of Mildred Constantine—the movement's principal architect and supporter—and her collaborator Jack Lenor Larsen to eliminate this ambiguity, securing fiber's identity as a medium of high art. Their strategy was defined by the goal of assimilating fiber-based work to the fine arts and did not address the fact that the boundary separating art from craft is constructed rather than natural. Although this strategy led to an unfortunate collusion with the very hierarchy of media they sought to transform and in hindsight might seem obviously flawed, my analysis suggests that the options available to them as defenders of fiber art were tremendously constrained by the period's artistic discourse defining the work of art, particularly its autonomy from social contexts and practices outside the art world with which fiber was

intimately connected. The reasons surrounding the art world's resistance to fiber art were complex and varied, involving the cultural connotations of fiber, popular trends in fiber crafts and gender bias deriving from fiber's association with women and the domestic realm; with such factors working against their project, perhaps no curatorial strategy Constantine and Larsen could have adopted at the time would have fared better.

THE AESTHETIC STATUS OF FIBER IN THE 1960S AND 1970S

In 1961, with Lenore Tawney's solo exhibition at the Staten Island Museum, fiber art as it would be recognized in the following two decades made its public debut in a fine-art context. The show consisted of forty works produced between 1955 and 1961 in a technique now referred to as open-warp weave: a structure in which large parts of the warp are left unwoven. The reception of this and subsequent work demonstrates that from the start fiber artists experienced considerable resistance from the realms of both craft and fine art for the way their work violated conventions of both practices. Tawney recalled that her early "open-warp weaves caused quite a controversy [amongst weavers]. No one had done this kind of weaving ... It's against the rules and those people who go by the rules were against it" (Tawney 1978: n.p.).

However, posing a challenge to the definition of weaving in the 1960s did not automatically confer the status of "art" on Tawney's work; in the "high" art world too, her work's identity was unstable. For instance, the small catalog for Tawney's 1961 exhibition reveals that on the one hand the show was sponsored by the "Section of Handcrafts" but elsewhere attempts to position Tawney as a "fine artist." In particular, the appreciation written by Tawney's close friend, painter Agnes Martin, defends her artistic identity, praising the work's "originality" and its relation to larger art-world trends toward exploring new media.

Before Tawney's Staten Island Museum show was even mounted, the artist had started using her open-warp method to combine different weave structures in a single work by dividing and redividing the warp as the weave was in progress. The resulting works, which she called "woven forms", were monumental in scale, departed from the rectilinear shape of loom-woven fabrics and were not even remotely utilitarian. Given their size, which ranged from 11 to 27 feet (3.3 to 8.1 m) in height, their abstraction (like some of her earlier open-warp weaves, the "woven forms" have no pictorial content) and Tawney's method of hanging them from the ceiling, her work sharply departed from the conventions of the "decorative wall hanging," the category in which weaves without everyday utility were normally classified in the 1960s.

Yet this work too fell between accepted divisions between art and craft. For instance, Tawney's 1962 solo exhibition at the Art Institute of Chicago was installed in the Textiles Department and *Woven Forms*, the 1963 group show at the Museum of Contemporary Crafts that included her work, also institutionally situated her weaving as craft. Even so, a reviewer for the *New York Times* remarked that Tawney "is more than just a weaver—she is also an artist. Unfortunately, craft work has for many years implied to the general public work done by amateurs ... with little merit ... Miss Tawney's craft is in marked contrast to this mistaken concept and her woven forms are considered by experts to be works of fine art" (O'Brien 1963).

This reviewer's willingness to embrace Tawney's work as "fine art" against prevailing sentiment that connected craft media to the amateur or hobbyist, however, was more the exception than the rule. Subsequent reviews continued to question her work's artistic status. As late as 1990, on the occasion of Tawney's retrospective at the American Craft Museum, Roberta Smith drew a negative conclusion in her review for the *New York Times*, leaving the impression that the intervening years had done little to resolve questions about the works' status and identity within the art world: "Mrs. Tawney's work exists in a limbo that is endemic to much contemporary craft: it has departed from craft and function without quite arriving at art ... Handsome and impressive as her best efforts often are ... [m]ost of them sustain comparison neither to such achievements in weaving as Navajo blankets, nor to contemporary painting and sculpture" (Smith 1990).

Smith's evaluation presents another facet of the picture that often consigned Tawney's work to an art world "limbo," the artist's refusal of the utilitarian

associations of craft. Instead of exploring this aspect of her work, however, Smith uses Tawney's departure from utility or function to reassert the differences between craft (Navajo weaving) and art (painting and sculpture) that the woven forms actually complicated.

These equivocations over the value of Tawney's woven work indicate the institutional obstacles artists, critics and curators of fiber art faced in trying to legitimate their work or the genre of fiber art. Examining Constantine and Larsen's efforts to consecrate fiber art provides an opportunity to look more systematically at the questions of artistic legitimacy that Tawney's work provoked.

WALL HANGINGS

The first major American exhibition of the new genre of fiber art was MoMA's *Wall Hangings*, co-curated by Constantine and, at her invitation, Larsen. With this exhibition, the two established themselves as the fiber movement's leading experts and also set the canon of vanguard fiber art (or "Art Fabric," as they called it). *Wall Hangings* presented to the American museum-going public the first international survey of primarily large-scale, abstract woven and off-loom work in fiber. Planned by Constantine since 1966, the exhibition toured eleven cities in 1968, returning in early 1969 to MoMA, where it was installed, at Constantine's insistence, in the museum's first-floor special exhibition galleries, rather than in the Department of Architecture and Design. To the American fiber world's leading triumvirate of Lenore Tawney, Sheila Hicks and Claire Zeisler, Constantine and Larsen added Kay Sekimachi, Walter Nottingham and Ed Rossbach, among others. Some of the exhibition's most advanced work came from abroad, including that of the Swiss Françoise Grossen, Yugoslavian (Croatian) Jagoda Buic, and Poles Magdalena Abakanowicz and Wojcieh Sadley, whose woven forms radically departed from the conventions of tapestry as practiced in Europe at the time.

Regrettably, given the exhibition's importance in the history of the American fiber movement, the only national art-world press *Wall Hangings* received was a review that *Craft Horizons* commissioned from sculptor Louise Bourgeois.[4] Bourgeois's response to the show contrasts strikingly with the curatorial statement written by Constantine and Larsen for the exhibition catalog. Whereas they asserted: "During the last ten years, developments in weaving have caused us to revise our concepts of this craft and to view the work within the context of twentieth-century art" (1969: n.p.), Bourgeois concluded:

> The pieces in the show rarely liberate themselves from decoration ... A painting or a sculpture makes great demand on the onlooker at the same time that it is independent of him. These weaves, delightful as they are, seem more engaging and less demanding. If they must be classified, they would fall somewhere between fine and applied art. (Bourgeois 1969: 33f)

These opposing evaluations speak to the period's symbolic boundaries between art and non-art and such boundaries' centrality to maintaining a hierarchy of media separating fine art from craft. They also point to a set of real and conceptual obstacles heavily borne by fiber artists and their supporters, who sought to transcend the aesthetic boundaries structuring the art world in the 1960s and 1970s. It is clear that although Bourgeois disagreed with Constantine and Larsen about the works' value, the question of their identity preoccupied them all. This preoccupation continued to burden Constantine and Larsen and subsequent scholars of fiber art, who took up issues of category over the nature of the work itself. Bourgeois also exhibits concern about categories of art, which she strategically upheld in this review by using fiber art to explain what painting and sculpture were not.

Bourgeois's evaluation of the works in *Wall Hangings* as "decoration" traded upon the distinction between art and craft, reasserting the aesthetic boundaries fiber artists and their supporters sought to overcome.[5] In her words, the objects were "delightful" and "engaging." In the writing of modernist critics such as Clement Greenberg, to be either was to succumb to the decorative by making "immediately pleasing" what true artists achieved through rigorous intellectual struggle and risk-taking (Greenberg 1945; 1986: 41). Bourgeois reasserts the high-art status of painting and sculpture by claiming that these genres place a "demand" upon the viewer absent in fiber art. The opposition she reinforces—that between the merely attractive object

and that which requires sustained attention—is central to the hierarchy of art and craft, which associates art with the cognitive realm, craft with mere surface effect.

In an interview, Constantine related her reaction to Bourgeois's review of *Wall Hangings*: "I was furious," she reported. "It represented exactly the attitude we were trying to work against" (conversation with the author 1999). Despite their awareness of the negative art-world attitudes concerning media traditionally associated with craft, Constantine and her co-curator attempted to assert fiber's art status by introducing the new genre into the fine art world on the terms set by that world. This strategy required that they adhere to the dominant philosophy of art voiced by Bourgeois and that they collude in maintaining the hierarchy of media responsible for fiber's general exclusion from "high art."

Two factors in particular made this strategy meaningful to Constantine and Larsen, factors that were themselves effects of the hierarchy of art and craft and indicate its self-perpetuating nature. The most important such factor was that contesting the hierarchy of art and craft rather than assimilating select objects (those without utility, for instance) into the category of "high art" would have been to destabilize the very artistic status they claimed for fiber artists. The identity of fiber artists, because they worked in a medium traditional to craft, required authorization different from that bestowed upon artists working securely within the "high art" world. The necessity of establishing one's art *as art* was a handicap that belonged only to the artist working in craft media. An excellent example of the nearly automatic security afforded the artist with a position within the "high art" world is demonstrated by the critic Hilton Kramer's review of Lucy Lippard's 1966 exhibition *Eccentric Abstraction* for the *New York Times*. About the show, which featured work that radically flouted sculptural conventions of the time, Kramer wrote: "[although the] work is neither painting nor exactly sculpture ... art—of some sort—it is" (1966). The lack of legitimacy afforded an exhibition such as *Wall Hangings* illustrates that this basic security was not extended to fiber artists in the 1960s and 1970s.

A second factor informing Constantine and Larsen's approach was the fact that overtly challenging the hierarchy of art and craft might also undermine their authority as curators, with negative consequences for fiber art's legitimation. Constantine, like others of her generation at MoMA (she joined the staff in 1948), was committed to the museum's mission of identifying and collecting modern works of the highest achievement in art and design, a goal that included examples of applied art or craft to the extent such objects conformed to modernist norms of innovation and abstraction. Anni Albers's solo exhibition in 1949, MoMA's first exhibition of weaving, exemplifies this approach to craft and design. Albers's association with the Bauhaus, her commitment to experimentation and her adaptation of non-objective form to weaving all reflected the museum's vision of the modern in art.

In the 1960s, exemplary objects of craft and design were still subject to this form of evaluation, which helped to shape Constantine's curatorial vision for *Wall Hangings*. An anecdote of Constantine's about her experience as a curator while MoMA was directed by René d'Harnoncourt is revealing in this regard. Sometime in the mid-1960s a hand-thrown vessel by the celebrated Japanese potter Kitaoji Rosanjin was under consideration for acquisition. In Constantine's account, d'Harnoncourt put this rhetorical question to his curators at the acquisitions meeting: "Do you know when a pot is no longer a pot but a work of art?" (in conversation with the author).[6] To Constantine, such a question affirmed that the distinction to be found between art and craft resided *in* the object rather than being culturally projected onto it. Such an assumption underscores Constantine and Larsen's confidence regarding the art status they asserted for the objects exhibited in *Wall Hangings*.

The story also foregrounds the authority that rested in the curator (in the capacity of his or her "eye") to discern quality in objects of cultural significance—that is, to distinguish between good and bad, "high" and "low," "fine art" and mere "craft."[7] A theory of boundary maintenance in the arts that pointed to the role of extra-aesthetic factors such as gender, different contexts of production, or cultural presumptions about craft in the production of distinctions of value had the potential to undermine this curatorial and ultimately institutional form of power in the 1960s. To the extent that the authorization of an object as art is only as good (that is,

as convincing) as the authority of the authorizer, undercutting the myth of the "good eye," could result in the forfeiture of institutional validation required by a new genre or movement.

A straightforward way of approaching the conception of value that Constantine and Larsen used—a conception of value as intrinsic to an object—is to consider it alongside the recontextualization of non-Western objects from ethnographic specimens to works of art, a taxonomic shift to which Constantine and Larsen's conception is related. Recent anthropological and art historical considerations of shifts in classifying objects previously recognized for their ethnographic value demonstrate that museum strategies of acquisition and display that elide issues of context, technique and utility in favor of disinterested contemplation of an object according to a modernist theory of art are premised upon art's autonomy from the social realm.[8] As Mary Anne Staniszewski has shown in her study of the history of exhibitions at MoMA, the type of installation now considered standard in fine-art museums—in which works are spotlit, arranged at eye level on a neutral-colored wall and widely spaced— emerged in the US in the 1930s.[9] This type of installation, which "facilitated appreciation of the singular artwork," was also applied to the exhibition of ethnic "artifacts" in museums in the 1930s and 1940s, reflecting a growing aesthetic appreciation of non-Western objects. In general, the aestheticized display of ethnographic objects suppressed issues of utility and highlighted form, creating an atemporal, formalist viewing experience unencumbered by the social formations that gave rise to the work. As scholars of exhibition history have pointed out, this reconceptualization confirms the aesthetic categories and assumptions of the West's "high art," leaving intact the hierarchy of the arts and stripping those aspects of non-Western objects in conflict with that hierarchy's values.

Constantine, who assisted d'Harnoncourt in a major exhibition that employed this strategy—1954's *Ancient Art of the Andes*—was familiar with such a curatorial strategy and it undoubtedly influenced the conception of *Wall Hangings* and subsequent fiber-art projects. As installation photographs of the show suggest, Constantine and Larsen hung the work according to a method of displaying painting and sculpture calculated to enhance the objects' visual impact and autonomy. Although such installation was by then typical at MoMA for painting and sculpture, its adoption in *Wall Hangings* can be seen as strategic given fiber's lack of autonomy—that is, its extensive use in cultural and practical contexts outside the art world. The exhibition displayed works in relative isolation within the austere, white-walled special exhibition galleries. This strategy was carried over to the catalog, which lacked detailed information about technique and enhanced the works' formal qualities by using photographs in which each object was suspended in space against a dark ground, a classic mid-century method of photographing ethnic objects that privileged form over implied utility.[10]

Constantine and Larsen's approach to the consecration of fiber art has a logic rooted in a belief in formalism as a democratic, legitimating discourse capable of transforming any work into an object of pure, aesthetic contemplation. As the negative reception of *Wall Hangings* suggests, however, applying a formalist exhibition strategy did not resolve the hierarchy of art and craft Constantine and Larsen sought to transcend.

An important factor at play here is the way fiber's "low" aesthetic status derived in part from its extensive use in cultural and practical contexts outside the art world. Briefly examining these contexts illuminates the larger challenge that Constantine and Larsen faced in attempting to elevate fiber as a medium of "high art."

UTILITY AND AMATEURISM

Outside the "high" art world, fiber gained a new visibility in the United States in the 1960s and 1970s with revivals of the traditional crafts of hand weaving, quilting, embroidery, dyeing, knotting and basketry. The social and artistic contexts and practices surrounding these revivals included the back-to-the-land and hippie movements, the renewed interest in folk art around the American Bicentennial, trends in the personalization of clothing like the adoption of African dress by African Americans, the feminist recuperation of women's history, the revival of traditional arts of minority communities in the South and Southwest, and the popular craze of macramé. Increased funding from the National Endowment for the Arts to support regional arts and a burgeoning commercial

market for craft and folk art bolstered interest in such work.[11] These contexts and practices demonstrate both the richness of what ought to be defined as a major craft revival in the United States in the 1960s and 1970s and the difficulty, for fiber artists, of distinguishing their work from this nebulous conglomeration.

The frequent connection made between fiber art and macramé—an association encouraged by fiber artists' extensive use of off-loom techniques such as knotting, looping, linking and plaiting—shows why fiber artists strove to distinguish their work from popular craft. The term macramé, which denotes a form of lateral knotting probably Arabic in origin, referred in the late 1960s and 1970s to a genre of useful objects (jewelry, belts, handbags, lampshades, plant holders and hammocks, for instance) produced using "decorative" knotting techniques. Macramé's enormous popularity is attested to by the fact that fiber artist and macramé specialist Mary Walker Phillip's best-selling book *Step-by-Step Macramé* (1970) had sold more than a million copies by 1976. In 1971, macramé's mass cultural appeal even led the Museum of American Folk Art in New York to organize a major exhibition on the subject as part of its NEA-funded series, *Rediscovery of Grass Roots America*.[12] Unusually, this exhibition placed contemporary macramé within the larger history of knotted-fabric construction, bringing together, among other examples, seventeenth- and eighteenth-century European lace, knotted fabrics and jewelry of North American Indians, the decorative knotted work of sailors from the nineteenth and twentieth centuries, and the large-scale knotted work of fiber artist Françoise Grossen, which emphasized the fiber art-macramé connection.

The macramé hobby craze was problematic for the fiber movement because it reinforced assumptions about fiber as a woman's medium or of "low" art status. In her 1979 interview for *Arts Magazine*, Claire Zeisler took advantage of a question about technique to distinguish her knotting (often in macramé) from the "decorative" knots used by "macramé artists," suggesting the sensitivity of the topic for artists working in fiber.

J. PATRICE MARANDEL: In your own mind, do techniques such as knotting or cutting... set you apart from other fiber artists?

CLAIRE ZEISLER: When I first started knotting, it was not a trend ... You certainly have heard the word *macramé*. Some people referred to my work as Claire Zeisler's macramé. That's when I hit the ceiling ... I do mind the word macramé because macramé today means a decorative knot and I use my knotting technique as structure ... The knot becomes the base for the piece, like the canvas is the base for a painting. (*Arts Magazine* 1979: 151f)

Zeisler's insistence on distinguishing between her work and popular craft underscores the degree to which macramé had become a cultural phenomenon that impinged upon the fiber movement's bid for status as art. It is likely that Zeisler's discussion of technique in the pages of *Arts Magazine*—then a leading periodical of contemporary art that rarely dedicated copy to work in traditional craft media—was a deliberate attempt to persuade readers that work in fiber shared important features with art rather than the popular hobby of macramé. Her reference to knotting as integral to the "structure" of her pieces emphasizes her art's formalist nature, as does her explicit parallel between her work and painting. The latter comparison places her work firmly in the category of "high art" by invoking its pre-eminent medium to highlight not craft-oriented technique but art-oriented practice. Zeisler's rhetorical strategy was similar to that adopted by numerous fiber artists and their supporters who were working to change the place of fiber in the art world's traditional hierarchy, dismissing its connections to activities classified as "non-art."

This effort was actually initiated some years earlier by Anni Albers, who in 1940 entered into a debate over the function and value of hand weaving with Mary Atwater, America's leading spokesperson for the non-professional weaver, in the pages of *The Weaver*, a nationally distributed quarterly for the American hand-weaving community. Atwater and Albers's conflict over the meaning and role of textiles not only helps to demonstrate how deep the association of amateurism with fiber runs, but also points to another serious hurdle fiber artists (working on or off the loom) faced in defining their work as art in the 1960s and 1970s—fiber's gendered associations.

Atwater, perhaps best known as the founder of the Shuttle Craft Guild and its correspondence course in

weaving in 1920, advocated a view of weaving as a leisure-time or therapeutic activity. She also researched nineteenth-century weaving traditions, publishing her findings alone or in publications for hand weavers. Her research was instrumental to the survival of these historical and regional practices, but her practical how-to approach ran counter to the idea of weaving as an art form. As Ed Rossbach put it, "She told Americans what to weave, how to weave, [and] what to do with their weavings" (Rossbach 1983: 22).[13]

Unlike Atwater, Albers regarded herself as an artist and was particularly outspoken regarding hand weaving's potential to move beyond a leisure pursuit with utilitarian imperatives. She encapsulated her views in a statement from 1959 that implored, "let threads be articulate ... and find a form for themselves to no other end than their own orchestration, not to be sat on, walked on, only to be looked at" (Albers 1959: 5).

Albers's article for *The Weaver* commented upon the state of contemporary hand weaving in the United States and illustrated textiles produced by her students at Black Mountain College in North Carolina.[14] The publication coincided with the height of the Appalachian craft revival, in which weaving played a major role, providing the immediate context for her sharp critique of "recipes" and "traditional formulas, which once proved successful" (Albers 1940: 3). Albers argued that "such work is often no more than a romantic attempt to recall a *temps perdu*" and that it reflected the state of "isolation" and "degeneration" of US hand weaving in the period (Albers 1940: 3). Albers called for a return to "fundamentals" and free experimentation on and off the loom to foster innovation and she suggested that the resulting development of new forms in fiber could be art.

Atwater, who had no interest in the imperatives of industry, modern design, or art, responded to Albers with the predictably titled piece "It's Pretty—But is it Art?" which she published in her advice column for *The Weaver*.[15] Not surprisingly, Atwater took offense at Albers's criticisms of faithfulness to tradition and reproduction of historical patterns (or "recipes," as Atwater called them). Atwater found the idea that a textile might lack utility or be considered art preposterous and she asserted that fiber and weaving were essentially useful and of value primarily as an "escape from the distresses or the hum-drum detail of our daily lives" (Atwater 1941: 13). Atwater responded to Albers's emphasis upon experimentation, imagination and the creation of new forms (key elements of modernism in the arts) with similar disdain, defending the right of her readers (mostly women isolated at home with little access to artistic training) to draw aesthetic pleasure from weaving regardless of their level of expertise or whether they relied upon a pattern. Atwater's acceptance, even promotion, of her audience's amateurism raises the issue of fiber's connections to femininity and domesticity, associations that plagued fiber artists in the 1960s and 1970s.

FEMININITY AND DOMESTICITY

As Rozsika Parker and Griselda Pollock asserted over twenty-five years ago in their groundbreaking study *Old Mistresses: Women, Art and Ideology*, "the sex of the artist matters. It conditions the way art is seen and discussed" (Parker and Pollock 1981: 50). This is nowhere more evident in the late twentieth century than in the history of the fiber movement, whose status and reception was affected by weaving's near-universal association with women and the domestic realm.

At its worst, the effort to challenge the gendering of fiber as "women's work" actually reinforced its association with femininity and its low place in the art-world hierarchy. In the late 1960s, when off-loom techniques rose to prominence, the work of fiber artists adopting these techniques was interpreted as free from the craft tradition's conventional values by virtue of their rejection of the loom. Critics such as Rose Slivka posited an antithesis between loom and off-loom construction techniques, praising the latter's superior artistic quality. In the provocatively titled piece "Hard String," her review of the 1972 group exhibition *Sculpture in Fiber for Craft Horizons*, Slivka characterized the loom as an impotent instrument, a gendering of technology that had the unintended effect (as did the title of the show) of associating off-loom fiber art with the perceived masculine virility of modern art.[16]

Not surprisingly, given this context, the housewife is a key figure in critical considerations of fiber art, where she signifies amateurism and lack of creativity. In criticism about fiber art, this set of associations often

had to be overcome before the writer could consider a work of fiber art worthy of discursive attention.

Fiber's problematic association with the domestic accounts for the distinctly confessional tone or hedging found in fiber-art criticism that invokes the figure of the housewife. Katherine Kuh's article about the work of Lenore Tawney and Claire Zeisler for *Saturday Review* in 1968, "Sculpture: Woven and Knotted," is typical. Despite her eventual enthusiasm, Kuh opens the article by admitting her own negative assumptions about weaving, shared, presumably, by her readers: "Until recently, I always considered weaving a ladylike pursuit for frustrated housewives, but I am drastically changing my mind. The best weavers are, to be sure, still women, but some of them are also first-rate artists" (Kuh 1968: 36). The use of the qualification "also," as in "also first-rate artists," echoes George O'Brien's language in his review of Tawney's work in the 1963 exhibition *Woven Forms* cited earlier. In that piece, Tawney is "more than a weaver—she is also an artist," a qualification that O'Brien used later in the review to question craft's amateur associations. In Kuh's assessment, the amateur associations of craft are now inflected by gender, yet another barrier to participation in the art world in this period faced by fiber artists—a problem shared by female artists generally, in fact. Critic Gregory Battcock's review of Claire Zeisler's show at the Richard Feigen gallery in 1969 provides another example of how the image of the housewife was used to great effect in backhanded compliments during the 1960s:

> Mops, floppiness and house-wifey dumpiness might distract the viewer, but only momentarily. The colors are certainly more arresting than the Sheriff in Darien Conn. and the general tone is more elegant than The Hilton Inn. Zeisler's sculptures emphasize texture at the expense of form and since texture is emphasized in just the right way, it's O.K. (Battcock 1969: 65)

For Kuh the housewife is capable but frustrated, while for Battcock she is dumpy—differences that might have to do with the differing gender of the two critics or the audience for whom they were writing. In any case, Battcock's idea of the housewife and the comparison of Zeisler's work to mops remove fiber from even the sphere of craft, downgrading it to drudgery. Ultimately,

Kuh's and Battcock's language permits notice of Zeisler's work only to the extent that their own critical authority regarding the evaluation of art is assured.

This brief examination of fiber's extra-aesthetic associations sheds additional light on Constantine and Larsen's approach to elevating fiber in a manner that completely elided its history as a craft and its presence in numerous contemporary non-art contexts. Alternate approaches proved no more successful and further demonstrate the severity of the constraints they faced in championing a material historically categorized and marginalized as craft.

For instance, hybrid categories that could bridge the divide between "art" and "craft," presumably better accommodating fiber art, also faced serious resistance in the art world. Two such categories were "soft art" and "soft sculpture." Both functioned as organizing rubrics for several shows in the late 1960s and 1970s such as the New Jersey State Museum's *Soft Art* (1969), curated by Ralph Pomeroy; Lucy Lippard's traveling exhibition for the American Federation of the Arts, *Soft and Apparently Soft Sculpture* (1968–9); and the New York Cultural Center's traveling exhibition, *Softness as Art* (1973). *Soft Art* included work by Tawney as well as Richard Tuttle, Robert Morris, Eva Hesse and Claes Oldenburg. *Softness as Art* included one work by Françoise Grossen, amongst that of Jackie Ferrara, Harmony Hammond, Richard Serra, Robert Morris and Hannah Wilke. Fiber artists recognized the potential of the categories "soft art" or "soft sculpture" to bridge the divide separating art from craft. In a 1970 article for *Craft Horizons*, "When Will Weaving Be an Art Form?" Virginia Hoffman observed that "soft sculpture"

> could logically include any three-dimensional form made by flexible joinings, fibrous materials, modules with no fixed beginning or end, soft materials made hard and vice versa ... One thinks of ... works by Eva Hesse, Alan Saret, Robert Morris, [and] Alice Adams. (Hoffman 1970: 18)[17]

However, art critics were not as enthusiastic about the soft art phenomenon. Some went to great lengths to reassert boundaries between genres and materials that the rubric blurred. In his *Artforum* review of the New York Cultural Center's exhibition, *Soft as Art*, James Collins asserted, "one of the things artists shouldn't do today is to make art with anything soft" (Collins 1973: 89). Most problematic for him was the category itself, which "denies criticism the luxury of a single critical framework" (Collins 1973: 89). His response to this dilemma was to divide the work in the show into four categories: "process," "revamped painting," "craft/fetish," and "novelty art." In his review these categories redrew boundaries distinguishing "art" from "craft" through a separation of works in fiber into either the "process" category or the "craft/fetish" category. In the "process" category, Collins singled out a felt work by Robert Morris (along with a work by Richard Serra) as worthy of attention for its "theoretical underpinnings" (Collins 1973: 89). The rest of the work in the exhibition was "neither experientially nor theoretically interesting" (Collins 1973: 90). In the "craft/fetish" category, Collins placed the work of Françoise Grossen, Jackie Ferrara and Brenda Miller, all of whom exhibited work in fiber.

Anticipating readers' objections to his application of the term craft to the work of three female artists working in rope and other forms of fiber, Collins asserted that "labeling a work as craft orientated isn't an attack on women" (Collins 1973: 90). He continued:

> [it] is only to say they give the impression of manual over mental dexterity and people who are manually dextrous aren't necessarily interesting artists ... Both Jackie Ferrara with her *Four Balls II* made of cotton bailing, rope and chains and Brenda Miller's *Abscissa*, consisting of a numbering system dictating the structure of a twine wall piece just by the use and association of their materials suggest a "grass skirt" reference—a gender neutral one. (Collins 1973: 90)

That the term "grass skirt" in this context is not gender neutral hardly requires elucidation. By rejecting the hybrid category "soft art" and reinforcing fiber's association to femininity and primitiveness, Collins neatly maintains the boundary between art and craft. Given the degree to which fiber's associations to craft overwhelm Collins's response to Ferrara and Miller's work, one can imagine how easily the hybrid character of work by fiber artists such as Grossen, Sheila Hicks, or Ed Rossbach could be dismissed as illegitimate.

Thanks to such challenging associations, Constantine and Larsen's goal of elevating fiber art, in *Wall Hangings* and subsequent projects, was difficult if not impossible to accomplish in the 1960s and 1970s. In addition, their acceptance of the division between "high" and "low" art—and, one might argue, their refusal to engage with the very non-art connotations of fiber that were so problematic for their goals—left art-world prejudices intact. Despite Constantine and Larsen's efforts, the work of Alan Saret—a male artist who had worked previously in other media and was part of the "high" art world—was critically received as art, while Alice Adams's remarkably similar work— emerging from her previous practice as a weaver—was viewed with skepticism.

Despite these setbacks, however, evidence suggests that Constantine and Larsen's work did make an impact, albeit one that did not come to fruition until fairly recently. In 1993 the well-known independent curator Mary Jane Jacob wrote about the influence of Constantine upon her own innovative, unorthodox, curatorial mission, which has been instrumental in promoting an open use of non-traditional materials without regard to the art world's hierarchical distinctions:

Unbeknownst to me, I began following [Constantine's] work as a young visitor to The Museum of Modern Art on frequent occasions from 1965 to 1969. Reading and just looking at the images in *Beyond Craft* sent my own curatorial work in another direction. Most of all, her avant- garde philosophy of inclusionism remains compelling and her career—battling to bring into the mainstream art and artists from the outside—is a model of independent vision and courage. (Jacob 1993: 9)

Dramatic change in the use and reception of fiber in the art world *has* occurred since the 1970s, thanks in part to curators such as Jacob, as well as artists of the first-wave feminist art movement, who set as one of their goals the analysis of the hierarchy of art and craft and women's low position within it through the incorporation of fiber into their work. For feminists, fiber craft played a role in the construction of an alternate history of art making. A shared marginality between the female traditional artist and the contemporary feminist artist helped the latter

negotiate the paradoxical goal of seeking recognition in the mainstream art world, while at the same time attempting to critique it. In this context, the once negative associations of fiber or craft with femininity and the home were recast as distinctive and culturally valuable features of an artistic heritage specific to women.

While I'm not convinced that the use of fiber by artists today demonstrates the complete effacement of the hierarchy of art and craft, the medium's ubiquitous use in contemporary art no doubt represents an important stage in a decades-long process of art-world assimilation of the medium. The evolution of Louise Bourgeois's attitude toward fiber—from one of dismissal in the 1960s to full embrace with her latest soft sculptures made from her personal collection of linens and fabric remnants—is only one example of the medium's new currency. The limitations of their strategy aside, the work of Constantine and Larsen in the 1960s and 1970s to legitimate fiber as a medium of art represents a historically important moment in this process.

Notes

1. Constantine, Mildred and Larsen, Jack Lenor. 1972. *Beyond Craft: The Art Fabric.* New York: Van Nostrand. For an assessment of Constantine's career see Sorkin, Jenni. 2003. Way Beyond Craft: Thinking Through the Work of Mildred Constantine. *Textile* 1(1): 30–47.
2. *Woven Forms.* 1963. New York: Museum of Contemporary Craft.
3. See also Atirnomus, "String and Rope at Janis." *Arts Magazine.* February 1970: 58.
4. Bourgeois, Louis. 1969. "The Fabric of Construction." *Craft Horizons* 29 (March): 31–35.
5. On the subject, see my 2004 essay "The Decorative, Abstraction and the Hierarchy of Art and Craft in the Art Criticism of Clement Greenberg," in *Oxford Art Journal* 27(3): 339–64.
6. Constantine also recounts this experience in *The Art Fabric: Mainstream* (New York: Van Nostrand Reinhold, 1981, p. 8).
7. Thanks to Judith Bettelheim, Constantine's daughter, for helping me clarify this point.

8. On the subject, see Marcus, George E. and Myers, Fred R. (eds). 1995. *Traffic in Culture: Refiguring Art and Anthropology*. Berkeley: University of California Press.

9. Staniszewski, Mary Anne. 1998. *The Power of Display: A History of Exhibition Installations at the Museum of Modern Art*. Cambridge, MA: MIT Press, chapter two, passim.

10. See Price, Sally. 1989. *Primitive Art in Civilized Places*. Chicago: University of Chicago Press; and Staniszewski (1998).

11. See National Endowment for the Arts. 1977. *To Survey American Crafts: A Planning Study*; and McLean, John. (ed.). 1981. *National Crafts Planning Project*. National Endowment for the Arts.

12. See *Macramé*. 1971. New York: Museum of American Folk Art. See also Mary Walker Phillips's review of the exhibition for *Craft Horizons* (December 1971): 62.

13. Rossbach also reported that "[Atwater's] writings were consulted (often a bit sheepishly) by many who deplored her approach to textiles, who did not believe that weavers should be provided with 'recipes,' as she called them, for works that ought to have been creative and individual. I remember the small regard I once felt for Atwater and her coverlet weaves, even though my first weaving experience consisted of following a pattern carefully selected from her book" (1983: 22).

14. Albers, Anni. 1940. Hand Weaving Today: Textile Work at Black Mountain College. *The Weaver* 6(1): 3–7.

15. Atwater, Mary. 1941. It's Pretty, But is it Art? *The Weaver* 6(3): 13–14 and 26.

16. Slivka, Rose. 1972. Hard String. *Craft Horizons* (April): 16–17.

17. See also Meilach, Dona Z. 1974. *Soft Sculpture and Other Soft Art Forms with Stuffed Fabrics, Fibers and Plastics*. New York: Crown Publishers.

References

Adamson, Glenn. 2007. *Thinking Through Craft*. Oxford and New York: Berg.

Albers, Anni. 1940. "Hand Weaving Today: Textile Work at Black Mountain College". *The Weaver* 6(1): 3–7.

Albers, Anni. 1959. *Pictorial Weaves*. Cambridge, MA: MIT Press.

Andreae, Christopher. 1970. String and Rope. *The Christian Science Monitor*, January 23.

Atwater, Mary. 1941. "It's Pretty, But is it Art?" *The Weaver* 6 (3): 13–14, 26.

Battcock, Gregory. 1969. Claire Zeisler. *Arts Magazine*, 43(6): 65.

Bourgeois, Louise. 1969. The Fabric of Construction. *Craft Horizons* 29: 31–5.

Collins, James. 1973. Review. *Artforum* 11(10): 89–93.

Constantine, Mildred. 1999. Personal interview with the author, February 23.

Constantine, Mildred and Larsen, Jack Lenor. 1969. *Wall Hangings*. New York: Museum of Modern Art.

Constantine, Mildred and Larsen, Jack Lenor. 1972. *Beyond Craft: The Art Fabric*. New York: Van Nostrand.

Greenberg, Clement. "Review of Exhibitions ..." 17 November 1945. *The Nation*. Reprinted in John O'Brian, ed. 1986. *Clement Greenberg, The Collected Essays and Criticism*. Vol. 2, *Arrogant Purpose, 1945–1949*: 39–42.

Hoffman, Virginia. 1970. "When Will Weaving Be an Art Form?" *Craft Horizons* 30: 18.

Jacob, Mary Jane. 1993. "Beyond Craft: Curating for Change". *Small Works in Fiber: The Mildred Constantine Collection*. Cleveland, OH: The Cleveland Museum of Art, pp. 1–9.

Kramer, Hilton. 1966. "And Now 'Eccentric Abstraction': It's Art But Does It Matter?" *New York Times* September 25: 27.

Kuh, Katherine. 1968. "Sculpture: Woven and Knotted". *Saturday Review*. July 27: 36-7.

Lenore Tawney: A Personal World. 1978. Brookfield, CT: Brookfield Craft Center.

Lippard, Lucy. 1966. *Eccentric Abstraction*. New York: Fischbach Gallery. Reprinted in *The New Sculpture 1965-1975: Between Geometry and Gesture*. 1990. New York: Whitney Museum of American Art, pp. 54–8.

Marandel, J. Patrice. 1979. "An Interview with Claire Zeisler". *Arts Magazine* 54(1): 150–152.

O'Brien, George. 1963. "Many Materials Used in Unusual Technique". *New York Times*. April 29

Parker, Rozsika and Pollock, Griselda. 1981. *Old Mistresses: Women, Art and Ideology*. New York: Pantheon Books.

Phillips, Mary Walker. 1970. *Step-by-Step Macramé: A Complete Introduction to the Craft of Creative Knotting*. New York: Golden Press.

Rossbach, Ed. 1983. "Mary Atwater and the Revival of American Traditional Weaving". *American Craft* 43(2): 22–26.

Smith, Paul. 1963. *Woven Forms*. New York: Museum of Contemporary Craft.

Smith, Roberta. 1990. "Lenore Tawney's Work in Fiber and Beyond". *New York Times*. May 18.

String and Rope. December 1969/January 1970. New York: Sidney Janis Gallery.

30

QUEER HANDMAKING (EXCERPT) (2017)

Julia Bryan-Wilson

EDITOR'S INTRODUCTION

Julia Bryan-Wilson is the first Professor of LGBTQ Art History at Columbia University. At the time of writing *FRAY* she was Professor of Modern and Contemporary Art and Director of the University of California Berkeley Arts Research Center. Her research interests include theories of artistic labour, feminist and queer theory, critical race theory, performance and dance, production/fabrication, craft histories, photography, video, visual culture of the nuclear age and collaborative practices. Bryan-Wilson is author of *Art Workers: Radical Practice in the Vietnam War Era* (2009), *Art in the Making: Artists and Their Materials from the Studio to Crowdsourcing*, co-authored with Glenn Adamson (2016), and *FRAY: Art and Textile Politics* (2017), included as an excerpt here. Curatorial work includes *Cecilia Vicuña: About to Happen*, co-curated with Andrea Andersson which opened at the Contemporary Arts Center New Orleans (2017) before touring, and co-curation of *Women's Histories: Artists before 1900* (2019) and the online exhibition *Histórias da Dança/Histories of Dance* (2020) at the Museu de Arte de São Paulo (MASP).

FRAY spans the 1970s to 1990s. Broadly situated in the Americas, research covers gay liberation in the United States, the Pinochet dictatorship of Chile and the HIV/AIDS epidemic with particular attention to the gendered labor of textiles. The book's title term 'fray' is described in the literal sense of the textile materially wearing apart, as well as the conceptual crossing of boundaries and, finally, the textile 'in the fray' in the sense of central to debates. The research works across examples of textiles considered hobbyist and fine art, treating the costumes of the US theater troupe the Cockettes and braided rag rugs by Harmony Hammond, with equal critical attention as the sculptures of Chilean artist Cecilia Vicuña, the hand-stitched *arpilleras* announcing the 'disappeared' of Pinochet's dictatorship and the NAMES Project AIDS Memorial Quilt.

In the brief excerpt included here, Bryan-Wilson reiterates her approach apparent throughout the entire book. Focusing in this section on the United States, she addresses the place of craft, and textiles specifically, in the gay liberation movement recognizing textiles as 'the vehicles by which many queer subjects enacted their desires'. Two examples are then introduced: the 'amateur' costumes of San Francisco-based countercultural theatre troupes the Cockettes and the Angels of Light, and the lesbian artist Harmony Hammond's *Floorpieces*. When read as a glimpse of Bryan-Wilson's wide-ranging research, the writing confirms the role textiles occupy in confirming the personal as political.

Queer Handmaking

Julia Bryan-Wilson

even you, fellow creature, sister
sitting across from me, dark with love,
working like me to pick apart
working with me to remake
this trailing knitted thing, this cloth of darkness,
this woman's garment, trying to save the skein.

Adrienne Rich, "When We Dead Awaken"[1]

In a poem from Adrienne Rich's 1973 collection *Diving into the Wreck*, she metaphorizes same-sex desire as a "trailing knitted thing," a cloth that might be collectively undone and remade, a garment perpetually in process. In this Rich suggests a resonance between textile making (especially needlework) and crafting a self in relation to other selves – or what has been termed world-making. As they work to re-create themselves and actualize new forms of consciousness, the figures in Rich's poem envision themselves as fiber workers alongside mythic knitters, crocheters, and sewers like Penelope of Greek legend, who endlessly weaves and unweaves her shroud.

A more sexually explicit invocation of queer craft in the 1970s is found in Dorothy Allison's memoir *Skin: Talking about Sex, Class, and Literature*. In an essay about sex toys used by lesbians, she narrates her first experience using a dildo with a female lover. She describes the pleasure that it brought her as well as her surprise upon discovering that the toy was not a purchased object, but rather handmade by her butch lover Marty – "a large-sized glove finger stuffed with cotton." As Allison recounts, the "ingenuity impressed me but clearly embarrassed" Marty, who did not necessarily want Allison to see and hence demystify this erotically charged appendage.[2]

The year was 1973, and though commercially made dildos had been produced in the United States starting in 1966 (shaped in a factory in North Hollywood and sold by mail order),[3] this was decades before mass-manufactured sex toys would be widely available in well-lit, women-owned emporia. In the US South, where Allison was living, resources for alternative sexualities were scarce, and lesbians often had to go north to buy their sex toys or, like Marty, invent and construct their own versions. Allison goes on to describe how another lover, Carey, made her own harness in the 1970s, "stitched… up out of a couple of old belts and carpet thread."[4] Frustrated with the ill-fitting mechanism that came with her mail-order dildo, Carey had "sat down with her old belts and begun to put together the lesbian equivalent of the wheel." Notes Allison with admiration, this makeshift design "worked better than any harness I subsequently discovered."[5]

The stuffed phallus and sewn-together harness arose from a combination of need and resourcefulness – truly *crafty*, to invoke several senses of that word, both cunning (and possibly devious or deceitful) in design and crafted by hand. These objects are also *crafty*, to use the suffix in its diminutive, in that they are craftlike, or craftish, not always hewing to classic traditions of skilled manual effort but rather approaching the category of craft elliptically, or at an angle – that is, queerly. One says something is "arty" when it is not quite art and may or may not aspire to be considered such; similarly, these crafty textile-based creations take direction, but also definitively stand at some remove, from conventions of craft.

[…]

Source: Excerpt from Julia Bryan-Wilson, 'Queer Handmaking', *FRAY: Art and Textile Politics* (2017), pp. 39–41. University of Chicago Press. Reproduced with permission.

In these years around and just after the explosion of gay liberation in the United States, hybridized and unexpected techniques of fibre-based production such as stitching, sewing, and braiding (and, yes, cotton-stuffing) were the vehicles by which many queer subjects enacted their desires.[6] To say that handicraft textiles became a queer resource in this moment is not to generalize (all forms of making are resources, by definition) but rather to emphasize its urgencies – and its eccentricities – with respect to queer countercultural economies. I mean this both symbolically and materially: these techniques are used to make the tangible things that surround bodies and that organize, structure, and lend meaning to the contours of everyday life.

In what follows, I consider two formations of textile making in the early 1970s vis-à-vis the historical emergence of the queer liberation movement in the United States – first, the elaborate handmade (and not so handmade, semi-skilled, or "crafty") costumes of the Cockettes and the Angels of Light, San Francisco-based countercultural theatre troupes, and second, lesbian artist Harmony Hammond's braided rag-rug paintings (the *Floorpieces*), which she began in 1973 while living in New York City. (Though there is some overlap, I recognize that *queer* and *lesbian* are by no means interchangeable terms; I deploy *queer* to gesture to a broad spectrum of nonnormative sexualities, practices, and subject positions, while keeping alive the specificities of lesbianism.) Thus this chapter is organized around two discrete but conceptually or thematically related case studies: one that grew out of regional, hippie performance formations and one that is more firmly ensconced within fine arts discourses. At some level this distinction is based on presumed audience – the Cocketts stitched together their outfits for each other and for their initially slapdash productions, while Hammond was making her works for a gallery or museum context. Yet both fit within their respective categories uncertainly, as they consistently challenge high-low assumptions; indeed, intended venue of reception only goes so far in indicating how these crafted objects circulated differently. At the same time, both partook of larger dialogues around fabric, piecing together, and queer making in this moment.

Throughout the book, I aim to suggest that low-high divisions within textile handicraft are insufficient and faulty, as it frays these neat binaries. By juxtaposing two registers of making, I suggest that these spheres are crucially coconstitutive, feeding each other in a multitude of ways, as the perpetually intersecting realms of the amateur and the fine arts motor a greater visibility for textiles more generally. I do not mean to imply causality, or even mutual awareness, between my two case studies – rather, I hope to illuminate how different makers were working through questions of queerness *through textiles* at around the same time. On the face of it, this is a highly unlikely pairing: one, lavish but rough-hewn drag wear; the other, abstract art that is euphemistically nonrepresentational. Yet by looking first at the Cockettes and their artful self-ornamenting and then turning to Hammond's process of making the fabric-based *Floorpieces*, I emphasize that these textile-based projects both craftily comment on consumerist excess, overflow, waste, and the queer vitality of reuse. In addition, campy decoration and décor – in the sense of embellishing domestic space as well as theatrical settings – threads throughout these case studies. As theorized by Susan Sontag, camp is a conversion operation that transmutes low into high, and here I place camp's procedures alongside textile craft's related ability to transgress the line between the everyday and the refined.[7]

Notes

1. Adrienne Rich, "When We Dead Awaken," in *Diving into the Wreck: Poems 1971-1972* (New York: W. W. Norton, 1973), 5.
2. Dorothy Allison, "The Theory and Practice of the Strap-On Dildo," in *Skin: Talking about Sex, Class, and Literature* (Ithica, NY: Firebrand Books, 1994), 130.
3. John Heidenry, *What Wild Ecstasy: The Rise and Fall of the Sexual Revolution* (New York: Simon and Schuster, 1997), 75.
4. Allison, "Theory and Practice," 131.
5. Ibid.
6. Many in the queer leather community acquire textile skills to make custom pieces; see for instance the hand-knit leather penis warmer in the Peter Thomas papers,

ONE National Gay & Lesbian Archives, University of Southern California, Los Angeles.

7. Susan Sontag, "Notes on 'Camp,'" *Partisan Review* 31, no. 4 (Fall 1964): 515-30; reprinted in *Against Interpretation and Other Essays* (New York: Farrar, Straus and Giroux, 1966), 275-92.

31

THE YELLOW WALLPAPER (EXCERPT) (1892)

Charlotte Perkins Gilman

EDITOR'S INTRODUCTION

The American writer Charlotte Perkins Gilman (1860–1935) wrote poetry, short stories and non-fiction and is considered by many to be an early feminist role model. Gilman's early life was difficult. Her first marriage to Charles Walter Stetson in 1884 ended in divorce and, for several years after the birth of her daughter, Gilman suffered from what is today known as post-partum depression. Treatment involved the eradication of all activity – both mental and physical.

The experience contributed to the content of her short story 'The Yellow Wallpaper,' published in 1892, in which she explores the state of mind of a woman trapped – physically and mentally – by the repressive values of her marriage and the expectations of society. Gilman opens the short story in an American colonial mansion described as a 'hereditary estate' (feasibly wealth born of profits from enslaved labour) rented for the summer by the narrator's husband, a medical doctor who oversees his wife's 'care'.

Confiding in 'dead paper' the narrator allows herself to speculate that it may in fact be her husband who is the cause of her health problems. The narrator refers to her husband's threat of sending her to Weir Mitchell (1829–1914), a prominent doctor who treated what would now be considered psychiatric conditions with a strict system of a rest cure. In life, Gilman was treated by Mitchell, an experience she used as the basis for 'The Yellow Wallpaper'. Novelist Virginia Woolf also satirizes Mitchell's regime of treatment in her novel *Mrs. Dalloway* (1925).

The wallpaper adorning the attic-prison where Gilman's narrator 'rests' is an alternating source of comfort and torment. At night she 'lay there for hours trying to decide whether that front pattern and the back pattern really did move together or separately'. Convinced a woman is trapped behind the wallpaper's pattern, Gilman's narrator sets about trying to free her.

The Yellow Wallpaper

Charlotte Perkins Gilman

It is very seldom that mere ordinary people like John and myself secure ancestral halls for the summer.

A colonial mansion, a hereditary estate, I would say a haunted house, and reach the height of romantic felicity—but that would be asking too much of fate!

Still I will proudly declare that there is something queer about it.

Else, why should it be let so cheaply? And why have stood so long untenanted?

John laughs at me, of course, but one expects that in marriage.

John is practical in the extreme. He has no patience with faith, an intense horror of superstition, and he scoffs openly at any talk of things not to be felt and seen and put down in figures.

John is a physician, and *perhaps*—(I would not say it to a living soul, of course, but this is dead paper and a great relief to my mind)—*perhaps* that is one reason I do not get well faster.

You see he does not believe I am sick!

And what can one do?

If a physician of high standing, and one's own husband, assures friends and relatives that there is really nothing the matter with one but temporary nervous depression—a slight hysterical tendency—what is one to do?

My brother is also a physician, and also of high standing, and he says the same thing.

So I take phosphates or phosphites—whichever it is, and tonics, and journeys, and air, and exercise, and am absolutely forbidden to 'work' until I am well again.

Personally, I disagree with their ideas.

Personally, I believe that congenial work, with excitement and change, would do me good.

But what is one to do?

I did write for a while in spite of them; but it *does* exhaust me a good deal—having to be so sly about it, or else meet with heavy opposition.

I sometimes fancy that in my condition if I had less opposition and more society and stimulus—but John says the very worst thing I can do is to think about my condition, and I confess it always makes me feel bad.

So I will let it alone and talk about the house.

The most beautiful place! It is quite alone, standing well back from the road, quite three miles from the village. It makes me think of English places that you read about, for there are hedges and walls and gates that lock, and lots of separate little houses for the gardeners and people.

There is a *delicious* garden! I never saw such a garden—large and shady, full of box-bordered paths, and lined with long grape-covered arbors with seats under them.

There were greenhouses, too, but they are all broken now.

There was some legal trouble, I believe, something about the heirs and coheirs; anyhow, the place has been empty for years.

That spoils my ghostliness, I am afraid, but I don't care—there is something strange about the house—I can feel it.

I even said so to John one moonlight evening, but he said what I felt was a *draught*, and shut the window.

I get unreasonably angry with John sometimes. I'm sure I never used to be so sensitive. I think it is due to this nervous condition.

But John says if I feel so, I shall neglect proper self-control; so I take pains to control myself—before him, at least, and that makes me very tired.

I don't like our room a bit. I wanted one downstairs that opened on the piazza and had roses all over the

Source: Excerpt from Charlotte Perkins Gilman, 'The Yellow Wallpaper' (1892).

window, and such pretty old-fashioned chintz hangings! but John would not hear of it.

He said there was only one window and not room for two beds, and no near room for him if he took another.

He is very careful and loving, and hardly lets me stir without special direction.

I have a schedule prescription for each hour in the day; he takes all care from me, and so I feel basely ungrateful not to value it more.

He said we came here solely on my account, that I was to have perfect rest and all the air I could get. 'Your exercise depends on your strength, my dear,' said he, 'and your food somewhat on your appetite; but air you can absorb all the time.' So we took the nursery at the top of the house. […]

There's sister on the stairs!

Well, the Fourth of July is over! The people are all gone and I am tired out. John thought it might do me good to see a little company, so we just had mother and Nellie and the children down for a week.

Of course I didn't do a thing. Jennie sees to everything now.

But it tired me all the same.

John says if I don't pick up faster he shall send me to Weir Mitchell in the fall.

But I don't want to go there at all. I had a friend who was in his hands once, and she says he is just like John and my brother, only more so! Besides, it is such an undertaking to go so far.

I don't feel as if it was worth while to turn my hand over for anything, and I'm getting dreadfully fretful and querulous.

I cry at nothing, and cry most of the time.

Of course I don't when John is here, or anybody else, but when I am alone.

And I am alone a good deal just now. John is kept in town very often by serious cases, and Jennie is good and lets me alone when I want her to.

So I walk a little in the garden or down that lovely lane, sit on the porch under the roses, and lie down up here a good deal. […]

But the effort is getting to be greater than the relief.

Half the time now I am awfully lazy, and lie down ever so much.

John says I mustn't lose my strength, and has me take cod liver oil and lots of tonics and things, to say nothing of ale and wine and rare meat.

Dear John! He loves me very dearly, and hates to have me sick. I tried to have a real earnest reasonable talk with him the other day, and tell him how I wish he would let me go and make a visit to Cousin Henry and Julia.

But he said I wasn't able to go, nor able to stand it after I got there; and I did not make out a very good case for myself, for I was crying before I had finished.

It is getting to be a great effort for me to think straight. Just this nervous weakness I suppose.

And dear John gathered me up in his arms, and just carried me upstairs and laid me on the bed, and sat by me and read to me till it tired my head.

He said I was his darling and his comfort and all he had, and that I must take care of myself for his sake, and keep well.

He says no one but myself can help me out of it, that I must use my will and self-control and not let any silly fancies run away with me. […]

I wonder—I begin to think—I wish John would take me away from here!

It is so hard to talk with John about my case, because he is so wise, and because he loves me so.

But I tried it last night.

It was moonlight. The moon shines in all around just as the sun does.

I hate to see it sometimes, it creeps so slowly, and always comes in by one window or another.

John was asleep and I hated to waken him, so I kept still and watched the moonlight on that undulating wall-paper till I felt creepy.

The faint figure behind seemed to shake the pattern, just as if she wanted to get out.

I got up softly and went to feel and see if the paper *did* move, and when I came back John was awake.

'What is it, little girl?' he said. 'Don't go walking about like that—you'll get cold.'

I thought it was a good time to talk, so I told him that I really was not gaining here, and that I wished he would take me away.

'Why darling!' said he, 'our lease will be up in three weeks, and I can't see how to leave before.

'The repairs are not done at home, and I cannot possibly leave town just now. Of course if you were in any danger, I could and would, but you really are better, dear, whether you can see it or not. I am a doctor, dear, and I know. You are gaining flesh and color, your appetite is better, I feel really much easier about you.'

'I don't weigh a bit more,' said I, 'nor as much; and my appetite may be better in the evening when you are here, but it is worse in the morning when you are away!'

'Bless her little heart!' said he with a big hug, 'she shall be as sick as she pleases! But now let's improve the shining hours by going to sleep, and talk about it in the morning!'

'And you won't go away?' I asked gloomily.

'Why, how can I, dear? It is only three weeks more and then we will take a nice little trip of a few days while Jennie is getting the house ready. Really dear you are better!'

'Better in body perhaps—' I began, and stopped short, for he sat up straight and looked at me with such a stern, reproachful look that I could not say another word.

'My darling,' said he, 'I beg of you, for my sake and for our child's sake, as well as for your own, that you will never for one instant let that idea enter your mind! There is nothing so dangerous, so fascinating, to a temperament like yours. It is a false and foolish fancy. Can you not trust me as a physician when I tell you so?'

So of course I said no more on that score, and we went to sleep before long. He thought I was asleep first, but I wasn't, and lay there for hours trying to decide whether that front pattern and the back pattern really did move together or separately.

On a pattern like this, by daylight, there is a lack of sequence, a defiance of law, that is a constant irritant to a normal mind.

The color is hideous enough, and unreliable enough, and infuriating enough, but the pattern is torturing.

You think you have mastered it, but just as you get well underway in following, it turns a back-somersault and there you are. It slaps you in the face, knocks you down, and tramples upon you. It is like a bad dream.

The outside pattern is a florid arabesque, reminding one of a fungus. If you can imagine a toadstool in joints, an interminable string of toadstools, budding and sprouting in endless convolutions—why, that is something like it.

That is, sometimes!

There is one marked peculiarity about this paper, a thing nobody seems to notice but myself, and that is that it changes as the light changes.

When the sun shoots in through the east window—I always watch for that first long, straight ray—it changes so quickly that I never can quite believe it.

That is why I watch it always.

By moonlight—the moon shines in all night when there is a moon—I wouldn't know it was the same paper.

At night in any kind of light, in twilight, candle light, lamplight, and worst of all by moonlight, it becomes bars! The outside pattern I mean, and the woman behind it is as plain as can be.

I didn't realize for a long time what the thing was that showed behind, that dim sub-pattern, but now I am quite sure it is a woman.

By daylight she is subdued, quiet. I fancy it is the pattern that keeps her so still. It is so puzzling. It keeps me quiet by the hour.

I lie down ever so much now. John says it is good for me, and to sleep all I can.

Indeed he started the habit by making me lie down for an hour after each meal.

It is a very bad habit I am convinced, for you see I don't sleep.

And that cultivates deceit, for I don't tell them I'm awake—O no!

The fact is I am getting a little afraid of John. He seems very queer sometimes, and even Jennie has an inexplicable look.

It strikes me occasionally, just as a scientific hypothesis,—that perhaps it is the paper!

I have watched John when he did not know I was looking, and come into the room suddenly on the most innocent excuses, and I've caught him several times *looking at the paper*! And Jennie too. I caught Jennie with her hand on it once.

She didn't know I was in the room, and when I asked her in a quiet, a very quiet voice, with the most restrained manner possible, what she was doing with the paper—she turned around as if she had been caught stealing, and looked quite angry—asked me why I should frighten her so!

Then she said that the paper stained everything it touched, that she had found yellow smooches on all my clothes and John's, and she wished we would be more careful!

Did not that sound innocent? But I know she was studying that pattern, and I am determined that nobody shall find it out but myself!

Life is very much more exciting now than it used to be. You see I have something more to expect, to look forward to, to watch. I really do eat better, and am more quiet than I was.

John is so pleased to see me improve! He laughed a little the other day, and said I seemed to be flourishing in spite of my wall-paper.

I turned it off with a laugh. I had no intention of telling him it was *because* of the wall-paper—he would make fun of me. He might even want to take me away.

I don't want to leave now until I have found it out. There is a week more, and I think that will be enough.

I'm feeling ever so much better! I don't sleep much at night, for it is so interesting to watch developments; but I sleep a good deal in the daytime.

In the daytime it is tiresome and perplexing.

There are always new shoots on the fungus, and new shades of yellow all over it. I cannot keep count of them, though I have tried conscientiously.

It is the strangest yellow, that wall-paper! It makes me think of all the yellow things I ever saw—not beautiful ones like buttercups, but old foul, bad yellow things.

But there is something else about that paper—the smell! I noticed it the moment we came into the room, but with so much air and sun it was not bad. Now we have had a week of fog and rain, and whether the windows are open or not, the smell is here.

It creeps all over the house.

I find it hovering in the dining-room, skulking in the parlor, hiding in the hall, lying in wait for me on the stairs.

It gets into my hair.

Even when I go to ride, if I turn my head suddenly and surprise it—there is that smell!

Such a peculiar odor, too! I have spent hours in trying to analyze it, to find what it smelled like.

It is not bad—at first, and very gentle, but quite the subtlest, most enduring odor I ever met.

In this damp weather it is awful, I wake up in the night and find it hanging over me.

It used to disturb me at first. I thought seriously of burning the house—to reach the smell.

But now I am used to it. The only thing I can think of that it is like is the *color* of the paper! A yellow smell.

There is a very funny mark on this wall, low down, near the mopboard. A streak that runs round the room. It goes behind every piece of furniture, except the bed, a long, straight, even *smooch*, as if it had been rubbed over and over.

I wonder how it was done and who did it, and what they did it for. Round and round and round—round and round and round—it makes me dizzy!

I really have discovered something at last.

Through watching so much at night, when it changes so, I have finally found out.

The front pattern *does* move—and no wonder! The woman behind shakes it!

Sometimes I think there are a great many women behind, and sometimes only one, and she crawls around fast, and her crawling shakes it all over.

Then in the very bright spots she keeps still, and in the very shady spots she just takes hold of the bars and shakes them hard.

And she is all the time trying to climb through. But nobody could climb through that pattern—it strangles so; I think that is why it has so many heads.

They get through, and then the pattern strangles them off and turns them upside down, and makes their eyes white!

If those heads were covered or taken off it would not be half so bad.

I think that woman gets out in the daytime!

And I'll tell you why—privately—I've seen her!

I can see her out of every one of my windows!

It is the same woman, I know, for she is always creeping, and most women do not creep by daylight.

I see her on that long road under the trees, creeping along, and when a carriage comes she hides under the blackberry vines.

I don't blame her a bit. It must be very humiliating to be caught creeping by daylight!

I always lock the door when I creep by daylight. I can't do it at night, for I know John would suspect something at once.

And John is so queer now, that I don't want to irritate him. I wish he would take another room! Besides, I don't want anybody to get that woman out at night but myself.

I often wonder if I could see her out of all the windows at once.

But, turn as fast as I can, I can only see out of one at one time.

And though I always see her, she *may* be able to creep faster than I can turn!

I have watched her sometimes away off in the open country, creeping as fast as a cloud shadow in a high wind.

If only that top pattern could be gotten off from the under one! I mean to try it, little by little.

I have found out another funny thing, but I shan't tell it this time! It does not do to trust people too much.

There are only two more days to get this paper off, and I believe John is beginning to notice. I don't like the look in his eyes.

And I heard him ask Jennie a lot of professional questions about me. She had a very good report to give.

She said I slept a good deal in the daytime.

John knows I don't sleep very well at night, for all I'm so quiet!

He asked me all sorts of questions, too, and pretended to be very loving and kind.

As if I couldn't see through him!

Still, I don't wonder he acts so, sleeping under this paper for three months.

It only interests me, but I feel sure John and Jennie are secretly affected by it.

Hurrah! This is the last day, but it is enough. John is to stay in town over night, and won't be out until this evening.

Jennie wanted to sleep with me—the sly thing! but I told her I should undoubtedly rest better for a night all alone.

That was clever, for really I wasn't alone a bit! As soon as it was moonlight and that poor thing began to crawl and shake the pattern, I got up and ran to help her.

I pulled and she shook, I shook and she pulled, and before morning we had peeled off yards of that paper.

A strip about as high as my head and half around the room.

And then when the sun came and that awful pattern began to laugh at me, I declared I would finish it to-day!

We go away to-morrow, and they are moving all my furniture down again to leave things as they were before.

Jennie looked at the wall in amazement, but I told her merrily that I did it out of pure spite at the vicious thing.

She laughed and said she wouldn't mind doing it herself, but I must not get tired.

How she betrayed herself that time!

But I am here, and no person touches this paper but me,—not *alive*!

She tried to get me out of the room—it was too patent! But I said it was so quiet and empty and clean now that I believed I would lie down again and sleep all I could; and not to wake me even for dinner—I would call when I woke.

So now she is gone, and the servants are gone, and the things are gone, and there is nothing left but that great bedstead nailed down, with the canvas mattress we found on it.

We shall sleep downstairs to-night, and take the boat home to-morrow.

I quite enjoy the room, now it is bare again.

How those children did tear about here!

This bedstead is fairly gnawed!

But I must get to work.

I have locked the door and thrown the key down into the front path.

I don't want to go out, and I don't want to have anybody come in, till John comes.

I want to astonish him.

I've got a rope up here that even Jennie did not find. If that woman does get out, and tries to get away, I can tie her!

But I forgot I could not reach far without anything to stand on!

This bed will *not* move!

I tried to lift and push it until I was lame, and then I got so angry I bit off a little piece at one corner—but it hurt my teeth.

Then I peeled off all the paper I could reach standing on the floor. It sticks horribly and the pattern just enjoys it! All those strangled heads and bulbous eyes and waddling fungus growths just shriek with derision!

I am getting angry enough to do something desperate. To jump out of the window would be admirable exercise, but the bars are too strong even to try.

Besides I wouldn't do it. Of course not. I know well enough that a step like that is improper and might be misconstrued.

I don't like to *look* out of the windows even—there are so many of those creeping women, and they creep so fast.

I wonder if they all come out of that wall-paper as I did?

But I am securely fastened now by my well-hidden rope—you don't get *me* out in the road there!

I suppose I shall have to get back behind the pattern when it comes night, and that is hard!

It is so pleasant to be out in this great room and creep around as I please!

I don't want to go outside. I won't, even if Jennie asks me to.

For outside you have to creep on the ground, and everything is green instead of yellow.

But here I can creep smoothly on the floor, and my shoulder just fits in that long smooch around the wall, so I cannot lose my way.

Why there's John at the door!

It is no use, young man, you can't open it! How he does call and pound!

Now he's crying for an axe.

It would be a shame to break down that beautiful door!

'John dear!' said I in the gentlest voice, 'the key is down by the front steps, under a plantain leaf!'

That silenced him for a few moments.

Then he said—very quietly indeed, 'Open the door, my darling!'

'I can't,' said I. 'The key is down by the front door under a plantain leaf!'

And then I said it again, several times, very gently and slowly, and said it so often that he had to go and see, and he got it of course, and came in. He stopped short by the door.

'What is the matter?' he cried. 'For God's sake, what are you doing!'

I kept on creeping just the same, but I looked at him over my shoulder.

'I've got out at last,' said I, 'in spite of you and Jane. And I've pulled off most of the paper, so you can't put me back!'

Now why should that man have fainted? But he did, and right across my path by the wall, so that I had to creep over him every time!

FURTHER READING: POLITICS

Agosin, Marjorie. *Scraps of Life Chilean Arpilleras: Chilean Women and the Pinochet Dictatorship*, trans. Cola Franzen, Trenton, NJ: The Red Sea Press, 1987.

Based on oral histories collected by the author in Santiago de Chile of living under the dictatorship of General Pinochet. In text, Agosin documents the collective action of women who came together to stitch and record 'the disappeared'.

Bachmann, Ingrid and Ruth Scheuing (eds). *Material Matters: The Art and Culture of Contemporary Textiles*, Toronto: YYZ Books, 2002.

An early example of textile-specific writing that dwells in the contemporary by sixteen international contributors. Three subsections cover the themes of 'material and process', 'articulating gender and identity' and 'cloth, colonialism and resistance'.

Barber, Claire, Helen Dampier, Rebecca Gill and Bertrand Taithe (eds). *Histories of Humanitarian Handicraft: Textiles, Aid and Development*, Manchester: Manchester University Press, 2024.

A collection of essays explore how meaning has been made and communicated through humanitarian textile objects. Predominantly historical in emphasis, chapters consider a variety of textile techniques with the largest number devoted to lace making.

Barnett, Pennina. 'Afterthoughts on Curating "The Subversive Stitch"', in *New Feminist Criticism: Critical Strategies*, ed. Katy Deepwell, 76–86, Manchester and New York: Manchester University Press, 1995.

Barnett writes five years after her curation of the exhibition, reflecting on the challenges of feminist curation and criticism. Prompted by, at times hostile, feedback to the exhibition she concludes with the suggestion that the categories of 'women' and 'textiles' be considered provisional and open to change.

Chakravorty Spivak, Gayatri. *A Critique of Postcolonial Reason: Toward a History of the Vanishing Present*, Cambridge, MA: Harvard University Press, 1999, 409–21.

In 1988 Spivak wrote 'Can the Subaltern Speak', an influential text for postcolonial theory. Towards the end of this book she uses the textile to discuss multiculturalism and globalism ending the writing with her thoughts on transnational textile production.

Dillon, Lorna. *Violeta Parra's Visual Art*, London: Palgrave Macmillan, 2020.

Book about the embroideries, paintings, collage and sculptures of Chilean artist Violeta Parra (1917–67) and the crossovers between the artist's music, poetry and visual art as examples of socially engaged art.

Leeb-du Toit, Juliet. *Isishweshwe: A History of the Indigenisation of Blueprint in Southern Africa*, Pietermaritzburg: University of KwaZulu-Natal Press, 2017.

A historical account traces 500 years of printed cloth production known in English as blueprint. Worn in South Africa from the 1700s onwards, the textile's roots are traced to Europe, the United Kingdom and the United States. As a result of trade, colonization and migration the printed cloth was and continues to appear in a range of cultural and national contexts.

Robertson, Kirsty. 'Threads of Hope: The Living Healing Quilt Project', *English Studies in Canada* (Aboriginal Redress and Repatriation) 35, no. 1 (March 2009): 85–108.

Robertson discusses the Living Healing Quilt Project (LHQP), organized by Alice Williams of the Curve Lake First Nation (Curve Lake, Ontario) and sponsored by the Indian Residential Schools Truth and Reconciliation Commission. Quilts were made by survivors and intergenerational survivors of Canada's, now broadly condemned, residential school system.

Schmahmann, Brenda (ed.). *Material Matters: Appliqués by the Weya Women of Zimbabwe and Needlework by South African Collectives*, Johannesburg: Witwatersrand University Press, 2000.

Illustrated study of projects in South Africa and Zimbabwe that use embroidery and appliqué, including historical and contextual information.

Tulloch, Carol (ed.). *Black Style*, London: V&A Publications, 2004.

An early example of research into African diaspora dress traditions and styling the body from a range of disciplinary perspectives: literature, Black studies, visual culture and the histories of textiles and dress.

MacDowell, Marsha, Mary Worrall, Lynne Swanson and Beth Donaldson. *Quilts and Human Rights*, Lincoln, NE: University of Nebraska Press, 2016.

Book documents individuals as well as groups that have made use of the quilt as part of human rights awareness and activism. Examples range from suffrage and race relations to HIV/AIDS and gender discrimination.

PART FIVE

PRODUCTION

PART INTRODUCTION

This section focuses on the production – by both hand and machine – of textiles. While the production speed of textiles has increased, a number of contributors reflect on the loss of textile knowledge that has gone hand-in-hand with mechanization and then digitization of textile production. The first text in the section is a portion of the screenplay from the 1951 Ealing Studios science fiction comedy *The Man in the White Suit*. The film's use of comedy perhaps diverts attention from the seriousness of the narrative: research chemist Sidney Stratton's quest for a fiber that requires no cleaning and never wears out. Beneath the comedic portrayal of chemistry experiments gone awry, the film confronts the competing interests of Stratton's desire for innovation and the mill owner's desire to maintain the status quo and preserve their current model of production and profit.

Unanswered in the film is the question of what a society would find of greater value: the possibility of releasing women, in particular, from the labour of washing and caring for a household's clothing or the continuity of employment by the textile mills and preservation of modest, but hard won, labor rights. Maria Fusco's prose poem follows, with an evocative sense of the relentless clock time that regulates and drives factory production paid as piecework. Melanie Miller's catalogue essay about the Schiffli embroidery project in Manchester, England, then provides a focused example of the shift from mechanical to digital. Based at the Manchester School of Art in 2007, *The Schiffli Project* invited fifteen artists to create work on the last working Schiffli embroidery machine in Britain. The project was ultimately unsuccessful in saving the machine which was scrapped in 2013, but the project offers an often overlooked perspective in the creative production potential that is lost in the race towards a digital textile future.

Moving back in time, Sadie Plant's writing about Ada Lovelace and the shared history of Jacquard weaving and computing attempts to carve a place for the overlooked historical figure of Lovelace. While evoking Lovelace and her deserved place in the history of computing, Plant makes use of a writing style that is as experimental and fragmented as the history she works to reintroduce. Ele Carpenter's lecture about the curatorial project which resulted in the creation of *Open Source Embroidery* shows another route through textile and computing thinking, this time engaged with community-centred production present in open-source software and quilting. Boatema Boateng's research of intellectual property law and adinkra and kente cloth in Ghana follows. Carpenter and Boateng share in their observation that concepts of the commons deserve greater application within contexts of textile production.

Sarah Rhodes then presents an example of printed textile production in the context of southern Africa. Focusing on the San communities of Namibia, Botswana and South Africa, Rhodes introduces the Art-i-San project, an example of unusual longevity that has had success in providing long-term sales royalties to the print designers. The final text in the production section was first written in Spanish by Yosi Anaya and translated into English by the author for this publication. Anaya presents another positive example of local textile production, focusing on the plant fiber sisal, known as henequén in Mexico, and the work of designer and maker Luisa Vogel in the Yucatán. In her conclusion, Anaya sees the appropriation of Vogel's designs now found throughout the region in a positive light as evidence of increased contemporary work with the fiber traditionally used to make binder twine.

THE MAN IN THE WHITE SUIT (EXCERPT) (1951)

Roger MacDougall

EDITOR'S INTRODUCTION

In 1951 Ealing Studios released what has been described as a science fiction comedy: *The Man in the White Suit*. Directed by Alexander Mackendrick, the film was nominated for an Academy Award for Best Writing (screenplay). Ealing Studios is based in London and opened in 1902.

The Man in the White Suit begins with a scene of an automated loom weaving bright white fabric. Laboratory experiment 37825 is Sidney Stratton's quest for a fiber that never needs to be washed or replaced. Stratton, the film's protagonist, is a research chemist. In a rare moment of unity, the mill owners of England join forces to buy out Stratton's invention, supressing what they perceive has the potential to be economically destructive. By the late scenes of the film their investment in thwarting progress proves to be unnecessary when it becomes clear that Stratton's fiber is unstable, degrading before competitors' eyes.

While humorous in tone, the film exposes the conflicting perspectives of the mills' management and trade unions; the excitement Daphne (a mill owner's daughter) sees in women being released from the drudgery of washing clothes is set against concern that Stratton's invention will put mill workers out of work. In the closing scenes of the film, Stratton's great invention has a disconcerting glow because of radioactive elements. While his suit ultimately falls to pieces, the final scene suggests he is on to yet another idea.

The Man in the White Suit

Roger MacDougall

(Man) Now that calm and sanity have returned to the textile industry, I feel it my duty to reveal something of the true story behind the recent crisis, a story which we were, happily, able to keep out of the newspapers at the time.

The trouble began, not in my own mill, I'm glad to say, but during my visit to the mill owned by Michael Corland, which manufactures an artificial fibre similar to my own.

Corland is a personable young man, who seemed to have impressed my daughter.

He was also anxious to impress me with the idea that his mill was a sound financial investment.

Output is excellent. Six million yards of filament a day.

- How many?
- Six million.

That's right, isn't it, Hill?

Six million feet. Yes, Mr Corland.

- Feet, of course.
- Of course.

[…]

(Woman) Stratton! Mr Corland wants you!

No, Mr Corland, you're not firing me. I resign.

I'm not a cheat nor a swindler.

I did what I did because there was no other way.

I may have had just a menial job here, but at Cambridge they gave me a first and a fellowship.

I would be there still, if they hadn't been so short sighted.

Just as you are and all the others I've worked for.

But one day there'll be someone with real vision.

I shall have a laboratory given to me.

A proper laboratory with really modern equipment.

And assistants of my own.

No, don't interrupt me.

It's small minds like yours that stand in the way of progress.

But this is too big a thing, bigger than you...

[…]

I got the chance of working in the laboratory.

- It's a better job?
- Oh, yes, much.

- And more money?
- I shan't actually get paid for it.

What? We'll see about that!
Scab labour. Huh!

The works committee had better hear about this.

- But I don't want to get paid.
- Not want to?

I don't care whether you want to get paid or not! You've got to get paid!

Oh, you mustn't do that.
It'll ruin everything.

[…]

Look. You know about the problem of polymerising amino-acid residues?

Source: Excerpt from *The Man in the White Suit* (1951). Courtesy of STUDIOCANAL. Reproduced with permission.

What did you say?

Look, do you know what a long-chain molecule is?

A what?

Do you know what a molecule is?

No.

- Something like an atom?
- That's it!

Atoms stuck together. In this case, like a long chain.

Now, cotton and silk and every natural fibre is made up of these chains.

And recently we've learned to make artificial fibres with even longer chains such as, um... rayon and nylon.

You've heard of nylon?

Well, I think I've succeeded in the co-polymerisation of amino-acid residues and carbohydrate molecules.

Both containing ionic groups. It's really perfectly simple. I believe I've got the right catalyst to promote interaction between the reactive groups at the end of the peptide chains and the carbohydrate combination, while the charges of the ionic groups will cross-link the chains and confer valuable elastic properties. At high temperature and pressure...

[...]

- What's all this?
- I've got to see Mr Birnley.

- Mr Stratton, what's the matter?
- Mr Hoskins, it's worked!

- I've done it!
- Done what?

The radioactive groups
in the fibre-forming molecules

haven't catalysed the internal
rearrangement, not in the least.

I thought the polymerisation
would be sterically hindered.

- But it wasn't. Where are my notes?

- Mr Stratton...

Er... I'll see you later.
I've got to see Mr Birnley.

- You can't do that.
- I've done it! I've done it!

Stop him! Stop him!

(Shouting)

- Don't let him go! Don't let him go!
- (Phone rings)

Nurse Gamage.

I've got to see Mr Birnley!

You're fired. You understand? Fired!

You can't fire me! I don't work here!

- What?
- That's right. He doesn't.

- (Men arguing)
- Now, then.

(Hoskins) Ah, Sister! Come here.

- What's the trouble?
- He's mad, that's the trouble.

A strong sedative,
that's what he needs.

Fantastic.

Utterly fantastic.

- A lunatic, obviously.
- Yes, sir. Very odd, indeed.

[...]

Well, apart from costing me £8,000, what has he done?

He's made a new kind of cloth.

It never gets dirty, and it lasts forever.

Well, that's ridiculous.

Oh, it is, is it?

Do you know what a long-chain molecule is?

Do you know what happens if one makes one of infinite length, with optimum interchain attractions?

Do you know what it means?

It means that to break the fibre, you'd have to split the molecule.

It means, for all practical purposes, it would last forever.

And it has a surface charge of static electricity.

It repels dirt.

[…]

I've decided to authorise Mr Stratton
to continue his research here.

(Chuckles) I'm sure I can rely on you
to give him everything he needs.

- Yes, sir.
- Well, there you are, Sidney.

(Chuckles)
Well, you've got your contract.

And you'll get your equipment.
Now, is there anything else?

- (Coughs) There is just one thing.
- Yes, my boy?

I've been thinking about
the possibility of chain reactions,

and I think probably
we ought to clear the lab.

- Clear the lab?
- Only as a precaution.

- Secrecy, you mean?
- That... that too.

(Chuckles) You're a shrewd boy.
See about that, Hoskins.

And you'll see that not a word gets out about this, even in the mills.

Well, perhaps we shall have a little surprise to spring on our competitors.

[…]

(Gurgling stops)

It must have worked.

Were you here just now?

Yes. Why?
My dear boy, what's the matter?

Nothing. It's just that it worked.

Do you mean... just now?

Stratton, you should have...

Davidson!

Oh.

We've got it, all right. Look.

We've got the answer, Mr Birnley.
We can go ahead now.

(Chuckles)

(Ticking)

Fortunately there's a chemical change
at 300 degrees centigrade.

(Birnley) Quite remarkable.

(Sidney) We shall have to do
a little groundwork on that.

- (Man) Seven and a half.
- (Man 2) Seven and a half.

- Though as you say...
- Thirty-five.

...we only need to vary the intermediates

to make a substitute for wool,
cotton, linen, whatever you please.

- Yes, 31.
- 31.

And, of course,
there's the question of dyeing.

Excuse me. Thank you.

At the moment, the fibre's intractable.

It repels dye just as it does dirt.

But we shall have to introduce the colouring matter at an earlier stage.

Left shoulder.

While the polymer is still in the melt.

- Yes, seven.
- Seven.

There's no difficulty in stitching.

The needle will simply pass through between the weave as usual.

If he could let me have
paper patterns of the suit.

Paper patterns?

I shall have to have templates made and get the pieces cut out for you.

Well, just as you wish. I suppose you wouldn't prefer us to cut them out?

Oh, I'm afraid you wouldn't be able to.

(Laughs)

(Knock on door)

Come in.

(Daphne laughing)

- Well, what's funny about it?
- It's just the suit.

It looks as if it's wearing you.

It's still a bit luminous.

But it'll wear off.

- Oh, no.
- No?

No, it makes you look like a...

a knight in shining armour.

- That's what you are.
- Me?

Don't you understand what this means?

Millions of people all over the world, living lives of drudgery, fighting an endless losing battle against shabbiness and dirt.

You've won that battle for them. You've set them free.

The whole world's going to bless you.

Unbreakable?

That's what they're saying, Mr Corland.

Green, is... is that possible?

Well, if he's using a heavy hydrogen, he might get a more complex molecule.

In plain language, yes or no?

It's, er... possible.

[...]

Now, some fool has invented an indestructible cloth.

- Right?
- Yes.

Where is he? How much does he want?

I'm afraid we have Mr Birnley to contend with first.

As I understand it, Mr Birnley intends to manufacture and market this product.

- Certainly.
- Are you mad?

(Birnley) Well, I consider it my duty to do it.

It'll knock the bottom out of everything, right down to the primary producers.

What about the sheep farmers and the cotton growers?

- The importers and the middlemen.
- The big stores, even.

- It'll ruin all of them!

- Quite. Let us stick to the point.

What about us?

Well, I'll admit some individuals may suffer temporarily.

But I will not stand in the way of progress.

The welfare of the community must come first.

- You're not likely to suffer much.
- Michael, that's unworthy of you.

Sir John, surely you realise this is the greatest step forward.

- Step forward?
- Over a precipice.

- It means disaster.
- Disaster?

Was the spinning jenny a disaster?

Was the mechanical loom?

For those who didn't control them, yes.

Besides, they increased output.
This will finish it.

[…]

- Sid!
- Hello, Bertha. Hello.

- What have they done to you?
- Well, it's really what I've done.

We are just going
to announce it to the press.

- Announce what?
- My new fibre.

Mind!

Mr Corland. In Mr Birnley's office.

It never gets dirty?
And never wears out?

That's right.

Now what do you think of him?

- You think they'll go ahead with it?
- Certainly.

You're not even born yet.

What do you think happened
to all the other things?

The razor blade that never gets blunt.

And the car that runs on water,
with a pinch of something in it.

No. They'll never let your stuff
on the market in a million years.

He's right, you know. Vested interests.
The dead hand of monopoly.

It's not like that at all, I assure you.
Everything's organised.

We're telling the newspapers this
morning, and then going right ahead.

But if this stuff never wears out,
we'll only have one lot to make.

That's right.

I've been looking everywhere for you.
First of all, I want to apologise.

Didn't recognise a genius
when I saw one.

- Excuse me, sir. I…
- I've just come from Mr Birnley.

One or two things
he asked me to straighten out.

That's lovely. Six months' work
and that'll be the lot.

Every mill in the country
will be laid off.

It's Birnley's doing. Sidney
wouldn't invent a thing like that.

Something ought to be done about it.

Something is gonna be done about it.
Get the works committee together.

I don't want to be selfish about it.

Later on, I might be able to offer it
to other manufacturers under licence.

You want us to cut our throats,
while you build up another fortune!

(Birnley) Well, may I point out
that I control this process?

- Do you?
- Well, of course I do.

A sordid matter of details, Sir John.

Well?

Stratton's diary of his first
successful experiment.

Date, September 15th.

Stratton's contract with Mr Birnley.

Date, October 1st.

[…]

- What's this?
- A new contract.

Sign it, young man.

What was wrong with the old one?

Well, this is a big thing, Sidney.
Too big for one mill.

And so I decided it was necessary
to bring in these other gentlemen.

[…]

- You are going ahead with production?
- Well, Sidney, I…

- I'd like to think this over.
- Young man, come here.

We need control of this discovery.
Complete control.

If you want twice the amount
in that contract, we will pay it.

- A quarter of a million.

- To suppress it?

Yes.

Excuse me.

[…]

Now, we've got to get that suit to the newspapers.

Show it to them and tell them the whole story.

That will blow the lid off everything, and they'll never
get it back on.

But how?

Would you stake your life on this?

You can issue a categorical denial to the press.

The stuff does not exist.

It has never been invented.
It never could be.

There is no panic here whatsoever.

Certainly Mr Birnley will confirm that.

No, no, no. Good heavens, Davidson.

I told you to deal with them in your own way.

Yes, Mr Birnley. They've come out.

- What?
- On strike.

Strike?

(Davidson) They've got the whole mill out.

I tried to get you on the telephone, but you kept on
being engaged.

You better get them back, otherwise there'll be
a landslide.

- Landslide?
- (Davidson) Now, Mr Birnley, I…

- Good heavens!
- (Men arguing)

Then go and do something!

They want a guarantee that we're not going into production.

- But we're not intending to.
- That's what we're out to prevent.

Yes, I know. But they won't take one's word for anything.

Oh, this is insanity!

I mean, they're afraid of being out of work and so they down tools.

[...]

Here! Don't you know there's a strike on?

Now, listen, there'll only be trouble if you stay here.

It's the stability. It isn't stable.

Mrs Watson, have you got something?
My suit. They can see me.

Why can't you scientists leave things alone?

What about my bit of washing when there's no washing to do?

[...]

(Laughing)

It doesn't work! It's coming to pieces!

We're saved!

(Raucous laughter)

Look! Look!

Sir John! Sir John!

(Laughter continues)
(Man) Look! Look! Look! Look!

- (Crowd chattering)

- (Man) Look, it's rubbish. Look!

(Laughter stops)

Here, lad, wear this.

(Birnley) The crisis is over now.

The news of Sidney's failure brought relief to the world.

I see.

It had been a hard and bitter experience for all of us.

But we faced the future with confidence.

We have seen the last of Sidney Stratton.

I see.

(Birnley) At least, I hope we've seen the last of him.

(Rhythmic bubbling and gurgling)

33

MACHINE OIL SMELLS SWEET (PIECEWORK) (2018)

Maria Fusco

EDITOR'S INTRODUCTION

From 2007 to 2013, Maria Fusco was Director of Art Writing at Goldsmiths, University of London, where she founded and led the MFA Art Writing. She currently holds a Personal Chair in Interdisciplinary Writing at the University of Dundee, Scotland. Her prose poem, reprinted in full here, was first commissioned by the Paris-based magazine *Vestoj* (2014) and later included in Fusco's book *Give Up Art* (2018), a collection of her writing first published between 2002 and 2017. Fusco credits Marianne Herzog's *From Hand to Mouth: Women and Piecework* (1980), an account of the physical and emotional experience of West German factory work, as one source of inspiration for the poem. The poem features in Margaret Salmon's 2021 film *Icarus (after Amelia)*.

Fusco's writing presents an evocative description of the relentless repetition of women's textile factory work measured by clock time. The piecework named in the title refers to a system of payment based on items produced, in contrast to the amount of time worked, used to drive productivity. Sewing to the relentless expectations of the clock, workers complete no more than is visible – 'do not necessarily finish this bit'. 'Nimble eyes more washed than ours' alludes to vision damaged in poor factory working conditions. In the closing lines of the poem, Fusco suggests a factory system consuming itself, where human labour cannot keep pace with human demand.

machine oil smells sweet (piecework)

Maria Fusco

one day we will use ourselves up   the symptoms of
our speed will wear bare   parched contact between
finger and thumb   fleeting   ding ding ding ding
ding   we will not be able to   faster   we will
keep to the shade   away from reflective surfaces   clock
time   precise monsters   we will make exactly the
same movement one hundred times an hour   our
stitches converging into   even with the old machines
we could have a bit of a breather   control our   the
next break   ding ding ding ding ding   now the
machine controls the pace   owns our   the machine is
never tired   touched with tender   fitted with surprise
gifts.   the machine's future   too far   unknowable
from where we sit here   machine oil smells sweet
our end is accelerating   same time every morning
except this one   chin drops   ding ding ding ding
ding   we do not know how to   everything   we were
only shown   not necessary to see the   this bit and this

bit do not necessarily finish this bit   ding ding ding
ding ding   no women under twenty-five   nimble
eyes more washed than ours   ding ding ding ding
ding   beginning from slack scraps   started with
sun   allowed nothing with your hands   except for the
needful   death is detail   we skim shadows   arriving
early to catch the dawn   leaking gracefully   borders
are created only by the repetition of our hands   simply
binding shallow hem to hair   can almost make   out
ding ding ding ding ding   per hour   layers stacking
we are not able to move about   our necks   the window
light pumping as blood   soft motes   loose road   the
window   five red petals drop brown   ding ding ding
ding ding   we leave a small gap in the pattern   by
hand   the pattern completes itself without us   learns
more quickly than we ever will   we are no longer
needed by what we created

Source: Maria Fusco, 'machine oil smells sweet (piecework)', *Give Up Art: Collected Writings* (2005–2015), New Documents, 2018, pp. 99–100. Reproduced with permission.

34

THE ROMANCE OF MODERN MANUFACTURE
A Brief History of Embroidered Embellishment (2007)

Melanie Miller

EDITOR'S INTRODUCTION

Melanie Miller is a maker, curator, writer and editor specializing in embroidery. Research interests include traditional and digital technologies, gender stereotyping, globalization and branding. *Mechanical Drawing: The Schiffli Project* was an ambitious attempt to save Britain's last surviving Schiffli embroidery machine housed at the Manchester School of Art, Manchester Metropolitan University, England, in 2007. In the final months the Schiffli was in use, invited artists worked with the Schiffli to explore the technical potential of a machine designed to stitch in close repeat.

The accompanying exhibition catalogue, edited by Miller and June Hill, documents this work and the historical significance of the machine to Macclesfield's embroidery industry. In her catalogue essay, Miller, at the time of writing a Senior Lecturer at Manchester Metropolitan University, outlines the historical significance of the machine and considers some of the strengths that mechanical production continues to enjoy in the face of growing competition from the digital world. The text reprinted here is a revised version of the original catalogue essay.

Miller notes that in 1829 'the first hand embroidery machines in the UK were located in Manchester'. While the tools of mass-produced textiles are often associated with poor working conditions and the production of poor quality goods, this writing offers an unusual example of mechanized production treated as a creative tool. In 2013 there was a reorganization of the workshop facilities at the Manchester School of Art. Despite offers from other educational establishments to rehouse the Schiffli machine, it was scrapped.

The Romance of Modern Manufacture[1]: A Brief History of Embroidered Embellishment

Melanie Miller

THE LAST SCHIFFLI

In order to understand the significance of the Schiffli machine it is necessary to have an appreciation of the history of the commercial mass-production of embroidery. It is a surprisingly complex area. A vast range of different specialist machines have been utilised over the last 180 years to create embroidered embellishment on clothing and household textiles. These machines have ranged from individually controlled machines that stitch only one item at a time, such as the Cornely and the Irish, to the machines that employ a multitude of needles to literally mass-produce embroidery. The hand embroidery machine, the Schiffli machine, and the multi-head machine fall into this category.

Embroidered decoration has been a feature of clothing since early times – the first known examples are of Egyptian embroidery from the 6th century AD. Whilst embroidery was traditionally done by hand, a machine to replicate hand stitching was invented as early as 1828, pre-dating the lockstitch sewing machine by some 20 or so years. It is intriguing that the first machine capable of embroidering a piece of cloth was invented *before* a satisfactory method of machine stitching two fabrics together was resolved. The hand embroidery machine[2] – so-called since it replicated the way hand embroidery was done – was invented in 1828 by Josué Heilmann of Mulhouse, France. Heilmann "resolved to make something new and startling, yet at the same time useful. I thought men have woven and printed textiles by machinery but no one has ever embroidered by machinery. The very words 'machine embroidery' are never encountered in

books on textiles – all the more reason for my endeavour".[3] It seems probable that Heilmann's mission was also fuelled by the fashion for 'flowered muslin', gossamer-fine webs of cloth embroidered by hand, white on white, a key component of the long flowing empire line gowns fashionable for women at the beginning of the 19th century.

The principle on which the hand embroidery machine operated differed from that of hand embroidery: rather than moving the needles across a piece of fabric, the piece of fabric moved to create the required pattern. The fabric was held vertically in a frame, its movement controlled by a pantograph, and a long row of double pointed needles, with an eye in the middle for the thread, stitched the design into the fabric. The needles passed right through the fabric, being held by two sets of pincers, one on each side of the fabric. The design to be stitched was enlarged by a factor of six. The machine was controlled by a single operative, who had to co-ordinate all of his/her limbs in a complex and precise operation. A wheel was turned forwards and backwards with the right hand to move the pincer bars containing the needles towards and away from the fabric. The feet operated mechanisms that opened and closed the pincers, thus releasing/grasping the needles. The left hand traced the enlarged design and thus moved the frame holding the fabric. And all the time, with each stitch, the length of thread left in the needle got shorter and shorter, so the distance the right hand travelled became marginally less and less.[4]

It might be imagined that the quality of work produced on such a machine would be crude, but in

Source: Melanie Miller, 'The Romance of Modern Manufacture – A Brief History of Embroidered Embellishment', in *Mechanical Drawing: the Schiffli Project*, ed. Melanie Miller and June Hill (Righton Press, Manchester Metropolitan University, 2007). Reproduced with permission.

fact the work created was exquisite. The extensive output of the hand embroidery machines is not always acknowledged – since the method of production resulted in work that looked identical to hand embroidery some confusion can arise over the attribution of production method. Outputs included fine *broderie anglais* whitework and complex guipure fabrics, metallic threads on sheer chiffons, textured wools that mimicked woven structures, anything that was done by hand was replicated by machine.[5] Specialist embroidery designers understood perfectly the technology of production, and could thus exploit the creative potential available.

The hand embroidery machine was in widespread use throughout Europe from the 1830s–1950s, especially in Switzerland. Appropriately, given that Manchester is the location of the last Schiffli embroidery machine in the UK, the first hand embroidery machines in the UK were located in Manchester, Henry Houldsworth purchasing two machines in 1829.

After the development of the lockstitch sewing machine in the 1840s it was inevitable that the same principle – of using two continuous threads to create a line of stitching – would be applied to embroidery. The Schiffli machine was invented in Switzerland in 1863 by Isaac Groebli, and in widespread use throughout Europe and America by the 1870s. It combined the basic principles of the hand embroidery machine: long rows of needles stitching into fabric stretched over a vertical frame – with the principle of the lockstitch sewing machine, utilising a row of bobbins, or shuttle threads. The largest machines are 19 metres long, and contain 1,416 needles. Within embroidery manufacture the development of a new production method does not immediately make a previous method obsolete – use of the hand embroidery machine continued alongside the Schiffli machine – many factories utilised both production methods.

Initially a pantograph controlled the Schiffli machine, the same pattern control method as used on the hand embroidery machine. In the first decade of the 20th century, however, a punchcard system was developed so that designs could be replicated automatically, without the need for a pantograph operator. It was costly to adapt machines to this new operating system, so many Schiffli machines continued to be operated by pantograph.[6]

THE UK SCHIFFLI INDUSTRY

Used extensively in the 19th and 20th centuries in the UK for the manufacture of decorative embroidery, with a strong base in Nottingham and Macclesfield, the Schiffli industry is no longer indigenous to the UK. As recently as the 1990s there were still a significant number of Schiffli manufacturing companies operating in the UK. However, as with so many aspects of clothing and textile production, cheaper manufacturing costs in the Far East led to the closure of all the UK Schiffli companies who were unable to compete economically with offshore production. The machine at MMU is therefore the sole remnant of what was once an important industry in the UK, it is the last working Schiffli machine in the UK.

Taking up a not inconsiderable amount of workshop space, some concern has been raised in recent years as to how appropriate it is to maintain a supposedly "obsolete" machine within an art school. The Schiffli Project was developed to highlight the significance of this unique machine both within and outside MMU, and question contemporary approaches to technology, innovation and obsolescence. Using 'mechanical drawing' as the theme, since the machine can be seen as a huge drawing machine, demonstrations and workshops were offered to staff within the faculty of Art and Design. The project grew; interesting work was being produced – it should be exhibited. As the long-term future of the machine remained uncertain, it also seemed appropriate to document work as it was produced on the machine, thus recording the Schiffli process for posterity. Thanks to the dedication of support staff within MMU, the users of the machine unwittingly secured starring roles in the DVD 'Mechanical Drawing'.

Whilst the Art and Design staff came from a variety of disciplines, it also seemed appropriate to open up the use of the machine to artists from outside MMU. With the support of an Arts Council grant this became possible.[7]

THE MMU SCHIFFLI

The Schiffli machine at MMU is approximately one hundred years old. It is a Plauen machine, built by Vogtlandisher Maschinenfabrik in Plauen, Germany. As Schiffli machines go, it is relatively small, with "only" 86 needles, and a stitching area two metres wide. It was purchased in the mid 1970s from Hewetson, a large embroidery manufacturing company in Macclesfield, where it was used as a sample machine.

Augustus Hewetson established the Hewetson company in Macclesfield in 1898 with four hand embroidery machines. Over the next few years it was gradually expanded, with the purchase of further hand embroidery machines, and Schiffli machines in 1905. In 1927 'automatic machines were installed and the firm claimed to be "the largest manufacturer of all types of embroidery in the world".[8]

During the two world wars Hewetson was a major supplier of badges for the Allied armed forces, embroidering fifty million badges during the Second World War. By 1958 there were about 1,000 employees on several different sites. During all this time (1898–1958) the company was tightly controlled by one family, the Hewetsons. There was a change in ownership in 1982 when it joined the Berisford group. Following re-structuring of the company in 1993 Hewetson ceased to operate as a Schiffli manufacturing company.

While contemporary Schiffli machines are now computerised and able to offer faster production within an art school environment the pantograph Schiffli machine provides a unique opportunity to be physically involved in the creation of the embroidered image. Images are created by moving a pantograph by hand. The design has to be drawn up six times larger than the finished embroidery, the operator traces around the design, pressing a trigger to make the needles shoot forwards to create the stitches. The slightest movement by the operator is mimicked, in miniature, by the thread on the cloth.

It is a very seductive process, there is something magical seeing an image simultaneously repeated twenty, thirty or forty times or more across a piece of cloth; and the rhythmic squeak as the machine progresses is quite hypnotic, if a little noisy. The machine looks intimidating – but is surprisingly easy to operate, it is an amazing, beautifully balanced piece of engineering: a huge mechanical drawing machine.

Although the potential canvas for the artists in this exhibition is relatively large – fabric two metres wide and up to two and a half metres long can be stretched into the frame – the artists have to work within certain parameters. The needles are set a fixed distance apart, and the area visible to embroider at any one time is limited to a height of about 40 centimetres. The maximum width of an image or pattern is about 13 centimetres. Colour change can only be achieved by re-threading needles, a time-consuming, backbreaking operation. The artists represented in 'Mechanical Drawing' have each approached the machine in a very individual way, bringing something of their own practice to the machine and challenging the usual pre-conceptions of commercial embroidery.

Notes

1. Title taken from 'The Romance of Modern Manufacture: a popular account of the marvels of manufacturing' by Charles R Gibson, published in London, 1910. This book includes a chapter on embroidery mass production, 'Embroidery done by steam-power' that succinctly describes the mechanisms of both the hand embroidery machine and the Schiffli machine. It is interesting to note that the book is almost exactly contemporaneous with the MMU Schiffli machine, and thus provides an interesting contemporary account of the automation of manual labour.

2. Also known in the US as the 'handloom', and in contemporaneous sources as the 'put-through' or 'nipper'

3. Josué Heilmann, quoted by Patricia Wardle in 'Machine Embroidery' by Christine Risley, 1961

4. The Appenzeller Folkskunde Museum in Stein, Eastern Switzerland, has a hand embroidery machine on which mesmerising demonstrations are periodically given.

5. The Textile Museum in St Gallen, Switzerland, has an unparalleled collection of pattern books from Swiss embroidery companies, showing the vast range of effects possible.

6. In the 1970s the punchcard system was computerised. However some Schiffli manufacturers even in the 1990s were still utilising pantograph pattern control.

7. Fifteen artists took part in 'Mechanical Drawing – the Schiffli project': Rowena Ardern, Jill Boyes, Nigel Cheney, Isabel Dibden Wright, Stephen Dixon, Nina Edge, Kate Egan, Rozanne Hawksley, Alice Kettle, Jane McKeating, Melanie Miller, Sally Morfill, Susan Platt, Lynn Setterington, Alison Welsh.

8. Collins L and Stevenson M, 'Silk, Sarsenets, Satin, Steels and Stripes', The Macclesfield Museums Trust, 1994

ZEROES + ONES
Digital women + the new technoculture (excerpt) (1997)

Sadie Plant

EDITOR'S INTRODUCTION

Sadie Plant is a British philosopher, cultural theorist and author. Published in 1997, her book *Zeros + Ones: Digital Women + the New Technoculture* traces the shared histories of computing and the Jacquard loom via the life of Ada Lovelace. Plant has published two other books: *The Most Radical Gesture* (1992) and *Writing on Drugs* (1999).

Plant offered a prescient warning when writing a little over two decades ago: 'The sheer weight of data with which the late twentieth century finds itself awash is only the beginning of the pressures under which traditional media are buckling'. Reading from beneath that weight of data today, *Zeros + Ones* also offers an important reminder that technology can refer to the spinning of thread just as accurately as it can be used to describe digital code.

Plant's experimental writing reflects the tangled map of the networks her research also charts. Fragments of William Gibson's fiction and Lovelace's diary entries are set side-by-side in an intentionally fragmented style that is effective in revealing the shared interests of seemingly diverse sources. The excerpts printed here provide a glimpse of Plant's experimental assembly of information, from her likening of written text to a physical network of knowledge, Sigmund Freud's contentious thoughts on why women weave, to the shifting production methods of the textile industry.

Stepping outside the conventions of textual hierarchies allowed Plant to write an alternative account of both the history of weaving and computing. The unconventional format was, arguably, necessary to reconfigure histories of both people and materials. At the heart of Plant's exploration is the idea that 'Textiles themselves are very literally the software linings of all technology'.

Zeroes + Ones: Digital Women + the New Technoculture

Sadie Plant

MATRICES

Distinctions between the main bodies of texts and all their peripheral detail—indices, headings, prefaces, dedications, appendices, illustrations, references, notes, and diagrams—have long been integral to orthodox conceptions of nonfiction books and articles. Authored, authorized, and authoritative, a piece of writing is its own mainstream. Its asides are backwaters which might have been—and often are—compiled by anonymous editors, secretaries, copyists, and clerks, and while they may well be providing crucial support for a text which they also connect to other sources, resources, and leads, they are also sidelined and downplayed.

When Ada wrote her footnotes to Menabrea's text, her work was implicitly supposed to be reinforcing these hierarchical divisions between centers and margins, authors and scribes. Menabrea's memoir was the leading article; Ada's work was merely a compilation of supporting detail, secondary commentary, material intended to back the author up. But her notes made enormous leaps of both quantity and quality beyond a text which turned out merely to be providing the occasion for her work.

Only when digital networks arranged themselves in threads and links did footnotes begin to walk all over what had once been the bodies of organized texts. Hypertext programs and the Net are webs of footnotes without central points, organizing principles, hierarchies. Such networks are unprecedented in terms of their scope, complexity, and the pragmatic possibilities of their use. And yet they are also—and have always been—immanent to all and every piece of written work. "The frontiers of a book,"[1] wrote Michel Foucault long before these modes of writing hypertext or retrieving data from the Net emerged, "are never clear-cut: beyond the title, the first lines, and the last full stop, beyond its internal configuration and its autonomous form, it is caught up in a system of references to other books, other texts, other sentences: it is a node within network."

Such complex patterns of cross-referencing have become increasingly possible, and also crucial to dealing with the floods of data which have burst the banks of traditional modes of arranging and retrieving information and are now leaking through the covers of articles and books, seeping past the boundaries of the old disciplines, overflowing all the classifications and orders of libraries, schools, and universities. And the sheer weight of data with which the late twentieth century finds itself awash is only the beginning of the pressures under which traditional media are buckling. If the "treatment of an irregular and complex topic *cannot be forced in any single direction* without curtailing the potential for transfer,"[2] it has suddenly become obvious that no topic is as regular and simple as was once assumed. Reality does not run along the neat straight lines of the printed page. Only by "criss-crossing the complex topical landscape" can the "twin goals of highlighting multifacetedness and establishing multiple connections" even begin to be attained. Hypertext makes it possible for "single (or even small numbers of) connecting threads" to be assembled into a " 'woven' interconnectedness" in which "strength of connection derives from the partial overlapping of many different strands of connectedness across cases rather than from any single strand running through large numbers of cases . . . "

"It must be evident how multifarious and how mutually complicated are the considerations,"[3] wrote

Source: Excerpt from Sadie Plant, *Zeroes + Ones: Digital Women + the New Technoculture* (London: Fourth Estate, 1997). Reproduced with permission of United Agents on behalf of Sadie Plant.

Ada in her own footnotes. "There are frequently several distinct sets of effects going on simultaneously; all in a manner independent of each other, and yet to a greater or less degree exercising a mutual influence. To adjust each to every other, and indeed even to perceive and trace them out with perfect correctness and success, entails difficulties whose nature partakes to a certain extent of those involved in every question where *conditions* are very numerous and inter-complicated; such as for instance the estimation of the mutual relations amongst statistical phenomena, and of those involved in many other classes of facts."

She added, "All, and everything is naturally related and interconnected. A volume I could write on this subject."

TENSIONS

Just as individuated texts have become filaments of infinitely tangled webs, so the digital machines of the late twentieth century weave new networks from what were once isolated words, numbers, music, shapes, smells, tactile textures, architectures, and countless channels as yet unnamed. Media become interactive and hyperactive, the multiplicitous components of an immersive zone which "does *not* begin with writing; it is directly related rather to the weaving of elaborate figured silks."[4] The yarn is neither metaphorical nor literal, but quite simply material, a gathering of threads which twist and turn through the history of computing, technology, the sciences and arts. In and out of the punched holes of automated looms, up and down through the ages of spinning and weaving, back and forth through the fabrication of fabrics, shuttles and looms, cotton and silk, canvas and paper, brushes and pens, typewriters, carriages, telephone wires, synthetic fibers, electrical filaments, silicon strands, fiber-optic cables, pixeled screens, telecom lines, the World Wide Web, the Net, and matrices to come.

"Before you run out the door, consider two things:
The future is already set, only the past can be changed,
and if it was worth forgetting it's not worth
remembering."

Pat Cadigan, *Fools*

When the first of the cyberpunk novels, William Gibson's *Neuromancer* was published in 1984, the cyberspace it described was neither an actually existing plane, nor a zone plucked out of the thin airs of myth and fantasy. It was a virtual reality which was itself increasingly real. Personal computers were becoming as ubiquitous as telephones, military simulation technologies and telecommunications networks were known to be highly sophisticated, and arcade games were addictive and increasingly immersive. *Neuromancer* was a fiction, and also another piece of the jigsaw which allowed these components to converge. In the course of the next decade, computers lost their significance as isolated calculators and word processors to become nodes of the vast global network called the Net. Video, still images, sounds, voices, and texts fused into the interactive multimedia which now seemed destined to converge with virtual reality helmets and data suits, sensory feedback mechanisms and neural connections, immersive digital realities continuous with reality itself. Whatever that was now supposed to be.

At the time, it was widely assumed that machines ran on more or less straightforward lines. Fictions might be speculative and inspire particular developments, but they were not supposed to have such immediate effects. Like all varieties of cultural change, technological development was supposed to proceed step after step and one at a time. It was only logical, after all. But cyberspace changed all this. It suddenly seemed as if all the components and tendencies which were now feeding into this virtual zone had been made for it before it had even been named; as though all the ostensible reasons and motivations underlying their development had merely provided occasions for the emergence of a matrix which Gibson's novel was nudging into place; as though the present was being reeled into a future which had always been guiding the past, washing back over precedents completely unaware of its influence.

Neuromancer was neither the first nor the last of such confusions between fiction and fact, future and past. When Gibson described "bright lattices of logic unfolding across that colorless void,"[5] his cyberspace was already implementing earlier—or later—works of nonfiction: Alan Turing's universal machine had drawn the devices of his day—calculators and typewriters—into a virtual system which brought itself on-line in the Second World War; Ada's Analytical Engine, which backed the punched-card processes of the automated weaving machine; and Jacquard's loom, which gathered itself on the gathering threads of weavers who in turn were picking up on the threads of the spiders and moths and webs of bacterial activity.

ON THE CARDS

Until the early eighteenth century, when mechanisms which allowed looms to automatically select their own threads were introduced, it could take a weaver "two or three weeks to set up a draw loom for a particular pattern."[6] The new devices used punched-paper rolls, and then punched cards which, when they were strung together in the early nineteenth century, made the loom into the first piece of automated machinery. It was Joseph Marie Jacquard, a French engineer, who made this final move. "Jacquard devised the plans of connecting each group of threads that were to act together, with a distinct lever belonging exclusively to that group. All these levers terminate in rods"[7] and a "rectangular sheet of pasteboard" moves "with it all the rods of the bundle, and consequently the threads that are connected with each of them." And if this board, "instead of being plain, were pierced with holes corresponding to the extremities of the levers which meet it, then, since each of the levers would pass through the pasteboard during the motion of the latter, they would all remain in their places. We thus see that it is easy so to determine the position of the holes in the paste-board, that, at any given moment, there shall be a certain number of levers, and consequently parcels of threads, raised, while the rest remain where they were. Supposing this process is successively repeated according to a law indicated by the pattern to be executed, we perceive that this pattern may be reproduced on the stuff."

As a weaving system which "effectively withdrew control of the weaving process from human workers and transferred it to the hardware of the machine,"[8] the Jacquard loom was "bitterly opposed by workers who saw in this migration of control a piece of their bodies literally being transferred to the machine." The new frames were famously broken by Luddite rioters to whom, in his maiden speech in the House of Lords in 1812, Lord Byron offered his support. "By the adoption of one species of frame in particular,"[9] he said, "one man performed the work of many, and the superfluous laborers were thrown out of employment. Yet it is to be observed that the work thus executed was inferior in quality; not marketable at home, and merely hurried over with a view to exportation. It was called, in the cant of the trade, by the name of 'Spider-work.'"

Byron was concerned that his peers in the Lords would think him "too lenient towards these men, & *half a framebreaker* myself." But, unfortunately for both his argument and the handloom weavers who were thrown out of work, the fabrics woven on the new looms soon surpassed both the quantity and quality of those which had been made by hand. And the Spider-work did not stop here. These automated processes were only hints as to the new species Byron's daughter had in store.

> "I do *not* believe that my father was (or ever could have been)
> such a *Poet as I shall* be an *Analyst*."
> Ada Lovelace, July 1843

Babbage had a long-standing interest in the effects of automated machines on traditional forms of manufacture, publishing his research on the fate of cottage industries in the Midlands and North of England, *The Economy of Manufactures and Machinery*, in 1832. The pin factory with which Adam Smith had illustrated his descriptions of the division of labor had made a great impression on him and, like his near contemporary Marx, he could see the extent to which specialization, standardization, and systematization had made both factories and economies into enormous automated machines themselves. Babbage was later to look back on the early factories as prototype "thinking machines," and he compared the two main functions of the Analytical Engine—storage and calculation—to the basic components of a textiles plant. "The Analytical Engine consists of two parts,"[10] wrote Babbage. "1st. The store in which all the variables to be operated upon, as well as all those quantities which have arisen from the result of other operations, are placed," and "2nd. The mill into which the quantities about to be operated upon are always brought." Like the computers which were later to run, and still do, the Engine had a store and mill, memory and processing power.

It was the Jacquard loom which really excited and inspired this work. Babbage owned a portrait of Jacquard, woven on one of his looms at about 1,000 threads to the inch and its production had demanded the use of some 24,000 punched cards, each one capable of carrying over 1,000 punch-holes, and Babbage was fascinated by the fine-grained complexity of both the cloth and the machine which had woven it. "It is a known fact,"[11] he wrote, "that the Jacquard loom is capable of weaving any design which the imagination of man may conceive." The portrait was a five-feet-square "sheet of woven silk, framed and glazed, but looking so perfectly like an engraving, that it had been mistaken for such by two members of the Royal Academy."[12]

[. . .]

"Unbuttoning the coat, he thrust his hands into the trouser-pockets, the better to display the waistcoat, which was woven in a dizzy mosaic of tiny blue-and-white squares. Ada Chequers, the tailors called them, the Lady having created the pattern by programming a Jacquard loom to weave pure algebra."

William Gibson and Bruce Sterling,
The Difference Engine

ANNA 1

In 1933, Sigmund Freud made his final attempt to solve the riddle of femininity: "to those of you who are women,"[13] he wrote, "this will not apply—you are yourselves the problem." Having dealt with its wants and deficiencies and analyzed its lapses and absences, he had only a few more points to make. "It seems," he wrote, "that women have made few contributions to the inventions and discoveries of the history of civilization." They lacked both the capacity and the desire to change the world. They weren't logical, they couldn't think straight, they flitted around and couldn't concentrate.

Distracted by the rhythmic beat of a machine, Freud looked up to see his daughter at her loom. She had wandered off, she was miles away, lost in her daydreams and the shuttle's flight. But the sight of her gave him second thoughts. When he took up the thread, he had changed his mind: "There is, however, one technique which they may have invented—that of plaiting and weaving.

"If that is so, we should be tempted to guess the unconscious motive for the achievement," he writes. "Nature herself would seem to have given the model which this achievement imitates by causing the growth at maturity of the pubic hair that conceals the genitals. The step that remained to be taken lay in making the threads adhere to one another, while on the body they stick into the skin and are only matted together." Since she has only a hole where the male has his source of creativity, the folding and interlacing of threads cannot be a question of a thrusting male desire. Unless she was hiding something else, the processes which so engrossed her must, of course, be a matter of concealing the shameful "deficiency" of the female sex.

Take Anna: a weaver and a spinster too, working to cover her wounded pride, her missing sense of self, the holes in her life and the gaps in her mind. She simply doesn't have what it takes to make a difference to the civilized world. Her work is a natural compensation for a natural flaw. All she can discover is her own incompletion; all she can invent are ways and means to process and conceal her sense of shame.

If weaving was to count as an achievement, it was not even one of women's own. Their work is not original or creative: both the women and their cloths are simply copying the matted tangles of pubic hair. Should they have pretensions to authority, they would only be faking this as well. Women "can, it seems, (only) imitate nature. Duplicate what nature offers and produces. In a kind of technical assistance and substitution." Weaving is an automatic imitation of some bodily function already beyond the weaver's control. She is bound to weave a costume for the masquerade: she is an actress, a mimic, an impersonator, with no authenticity underneath it all. She has nothing to reveal, no soul to bare, not even a sex or a self to please. He pulls aside the veils, the webs of lies, the shrouds of mystery, and the layers of deception and duplicity, and finds no comfort, no there there. Only "the horror of nothing to be seen." Good of her to cover it up for him.

This tale of absence, castration, deficiency, negativity, substitution was composed by one whom Gilles Deleuze and Félix Guattari describe as "an over conscious idiot who has no understanding of multiplicities."[14] From Freud's point of view, there is one and its other, which is simply what one sees of it. And what one sees is nothing at all. "Because the path it traces is invisible and becomes visible only in reverse, to the extent that it is travelled over and covered by the phenomena it induces within the system, it has no place other than that from which it is 'missing,' no identity other than that which it lacks."[15]

Anna Freud's biographer describes her as a woman who "specialized in reversals, in making the absent present, the lost found, the past current . . . she could also make the undone done, or—even more valuable— doable. When she was tired and faced with a stack of letters to answer, for example, she would simply set her pen down on a blank page and scurry it along, making quick mountain ranges of scribble. Then she would sign her name under the rows of scribble in her characteristic way, as one flourishing word: ANNAFREUD."[16]

After that, it was downhill all the way. "Having thus written a letter in fantasy with complete ease, she wrote a real letter helped by the sense that the task was accomplished anyway." It's easy to complete a job already done. "Her lectures were composed in the same way. First she lectured in her imagination, enjoying the thunderous applause, and then she made an outline of what she had said, adjusting it if she needed to for greater simplicity and coherence. Later, with her outline in hand, she would give the lecture extempore. The method—if it can be called that—also supplemented her pleasure in sprints of thought. Intellectually she was . . . a quick sketcher."

No doubt Freud despaired at such unorthodox approaches to her work. It seemed she did everything in reverse, backward, upside down, contrary to any rational approach. But if Anna's techniques appeared to be the random tactics of a scattered brain, knowing something backward and inside out is far in advance of any straightforward procedure. And she was hardly alone in her topsy-turvy ways. This ability to win "victories *in advance*, as if acquired on credit"[17] may not figure in the history of discoveries and inventions familiar to Freud, but this is only because it underlies the entire account. According to Marshall McLuhan, "the technique of beginning at the end of any operation whatever, and of working backwards from that point to the beginning"[18] was not merely an invention or discovery to be added to the list: it was "the invention of invention" itself.

This is hysteresis, the lagging of effects behind their causes. Reverse engineering: the way hackers hack and pirates conspire to lure the future to their side. Starting at the end, and then engaging in a process which simultaneously assembles and dismantles the route back to the start, the end, the future, the past: who's counting now? As Ada said, she "did everything topsy-turvy, & certainly ought to have come into the world *feet downwards*."[19] Mere discoveries were not enough for her: "I intend to incorporate with one department of my labours a complete reduction to a system, of the principles and methods of *discovery*."[20]

The prevalence of these backward moves is not the least of the reasons why histories of technology—and indeed histories of anything at all—are always riddled with delicious gaps, mysteries, and riddles just like those perplexing Freud. No straightforward account can ever hope to deal with the tactical advantages gained by such disorderings of linear time. The names and dates and great achievements of the Read Only Memory called history may enjoy their fifteen kilobytes of digital fame on the latest encyclopedic compact disc, but what announce themselves to be founding fathers, points of origin, and defining moments only ever serve as distractions from the ongoing processes, the shifting differences that count. These are subtle and fine grained, often incognito, undercover, in disguise as mere and minor details. If, that is, they show themselves at all.

"Ada's method, as will appear, was to weave daydreams into seemingly authentic calculations."

Doris Langley Moore, *Ada, Countess of Lovelace*

[. . .]

SHUTTLE SYSTEMS

There is always a point at which, as Freud admits, "our material—for some incomprehensible reason—becomes far more obscure and full of gaps."[21] And, as it happens, Freud's weaving women had made rather more than a small and debatable contribution to his great narrative of inventions and discoveries. Far more than a big and certain one as well. It is their microprocesses which underlie it all: the spindle and the wheel used in spinning yarn are the basis of all later axles, wheels, and rotations; the interlaced threads of the loom compose the most abstract processes of fabrication. Textiles themselves are very literally the software linings of all technology.

String, which has been dated to 20,000 b.c., is thought to be the earliest manufactured thread and crucial to "taking the world to human will and ingenuity,"[22] not least because it is such multipurpose material. It can be used for carrying, holding, tying, and trapping, and has even been described as "the unseen weapon that allowed the human race to conquer the earth." Textiles underlie the great canvases of Western art, and even the materials of writing. Paper now tends to be made from wood, but it too was woven in its early form, produced from the dense interlacing of natural fibers. The Chinese, with whom the production of paper is thought to have begun some 2,000 years ago, used bamboo, rags, and old fishing nets as their basic materials; papyrus, from which the word paper is itself derived, was used in ancient Egypt, and later Arab cultures used the same flax from which linen is produced. Wood pulp gradually took over from the rags which Europe used until the nineteenth century, and most paper is now produced from fibers which are pulped and bleached, washed and dried, and then filtered onto a mesh and compressed into a fine felt.

Evidence of sophisticated textile production dates to 6,000 b.c. in the southeast regions of Europe, and in Hungary there is evidence that warp-weighted looms were producing designs of extraordinary extravagance from at least 5,000 b.c. Archaeological investigations suggest that from at least the fourth millennium b.c. Egyptian women were weaving linen on horizontal looms, sometimes with some two hundred threads per inch, and capable of producing cloths as wide as nine feet and seventy-five feet long. Circular warps, facilitating the production of seamless tubes for clothing, and tapestry looms, able to weave the dense complications of images visible in weft threads so closely woven as to completely conceal the warps, were also in use in ancient Egypt where, long before individual artisans stamped their work with their own signatures, trademarks and logos were woven in to indicate the workshop in which cloths had been produced. Cloths were used as early currency, and fine linens were as valuable as precious metals and stones. In China, where the spinning wheel is thought to have first turned, sophisticated draw-looms had woven designs which used thousands of different warps at least two and a half thousand years before such machines were developed in the West.

It may be a bare necessity of life, but textile work always goes far beyond the clothing and shelter of the family. In terms of quality, sophistication, and sheer quantity, the production of textiles always seems to put some kind of surplus in play. The production of "homespun" yarn and cloth was one of the first cottage industries; pin money was women's earliest source of independent cash, and women were selling surplus yarn and cloth and working as small-scale entrepreneurs long before the emergence of factories, organized patterns of trade, and any of the mechanisms which now define the textiles industry. Even when cloths and clothes can be bought off the rack, women continue to absorb themselves in fibrous fabrications.

There is an obsessive, addictive quality to the spinning of yarn and the weaving of cloth; a temptation to get fixated and locked into processes which run away with themselves and those drawn into them. Even in cultures assumed to be subsistence economies, women who did only as much cooking, cleaning, and childcare as was necessary tended to go into overdrive when it came to spinning and weaving cloth, producing far more than was required to clothe and furnish the family home. With time and raw materials on their hands, even "Neolithic women were investing large amounts of extra time into their textile work, far beyond pure utility,"[23] suggesting that not everything was hand to mouth. These prehistoric weavers seem to have produced cloths of extraordinary complexity, woven with ornate designs far in excess of the brute demand for simple cloth. And wherever this tendency to elaboration emerged, it fed into a continual exploration of new techniques of dyeing, color combination, combing, spinning, and all the complications of weaving itself.

Even in Europe there had been several early and sophisticated innovations. Draw looms had been developed in the Middle Ages, and while many of Leonardo da Vinci's "machines for spinning, weaving, twisting hemp, trimming felt, and making needles"[24] were never made, he certainly introduced the flyer and bobbin which brought tension control to the spinning wheel. Unlike "the spinster using the older wheel," she now "slackened her hold on the yarn to allow it to be wound on to the bobbin as it was being twisted."

It is often said that Leonardo's sixteenth-century work anticipated the industrial revolution "in the sense that his 'machines' (including tools, musical instruments, and weapons) all aspired toward systemic automation."[25] But it was his intuition that textiles machines were "more useful, profitable, and perfect than the printing press" which really placed him ahead of his time. If printing had spread across the modern world, textiles led the frantic industrialization of the late eighteenth and early nineteenth centuries. "Like the most humble cultural assets, textiles incessantly moved about, took root in new regions . . ."[26] The first manufactory was a silk mill on an island in the Derwent near Derby built early in a century which also saw the introduction of the spinning jenny, the water frame, the spinning mule, the flying shuttle, the witches' loom, and the power loom. A spiral of "inventions in both spinning and weaving (interacting and mutually stimulating) had attracted capital, concentrated labour, increased output and swollen imports and exports."[27] This was cloth capitalism, a runaway process which quite literally changed the world. In the 1850s, it was said that "if Providence had never planted the cotton shrub those majestic masses of men which stretch, like a living zone, through our central districts, would have felt no existence; and the magic impulse which has been felt . . . in every department of national energy, our literature, our laws, our social condition, our

political institutions, making us almost a new people, would never have been communicated." Textiles had not merely changed the world: they seemed to have mutated its occupants as well. "*Almost a new people . . .*" "I was surprised at the place but more so at the people,"[28] wrote one commentator of Birmingham, the site of the first cotton-spinning mill. "They were a species I had never seen."

While the industrial revolution is supposed to have made the break between handheld tools and supervised machines, the handmade and the mass-produced, the introduction of technology to more primitive textiles techniques is both a break with the old ways and a continuation of the lines on which the women were already at work. Even before its mechanization, the loom was described as the "most complex human engine of them all,"[29] not least because of the extent to which it "reduced everything to simple actions: the alternate movement of the feet worked the pedals, raising half the threads of the warp and then the other, while the hands threw the shuttle carrying the thread of the woof." When John Heathcote, who patented a lace-making machine just after Jacquard built his loom, first saw "a woman working on a pillow, with so many bobbins that it seemed altogether a maze,"[30] his impression was that lace was a "heap of chaotic material." In an attempt to unravel the mystery, he "drew a thread, which happened to draw for an inch or two longitudinally straight, then started off diagonally. The next drew out straight. Then others drew out in various directions. Out of four threads concurring to make a mesh, two passed one way, the third another and the fourth another still. But at length I found they were in fact used in an orderly manner . . ." It was then a matter of producing "a fabric which was an exact imitation of the thread movements of handmade lace."[31] This is both the ordering of chaos, and also how its networks replicate themselves.

There were other spin-offs from textiles too. The weaving of complex designs demands far more than one pair of hands, and textiles production tends to be communal, sociable work allowing plenty of occasion for gossip and chat. Weaving was already multimedia: singing, chanting, telling stories, dancing, and playing games as they work, spinsters, weavers, and needleworkers were literally networkers as well. It seems that "the women of prehistoric Europe gathered at one another's houses to spin, sew, weave, and have fellowship."[32] Spinning yarns, fabricating fictions, fashioning fashions . . . : the textures of woven cloth functioned as means of communication and information storage long before anything was written down. "How do we know this? From the cloth itself." This is not only because, like writing and other visual arts, weaving is often "used to mark or announce information"[33] and "a mnemonic device to record events and other data." Textiles do communicate in terms of the images which appear on the right side of the cloth, but this is only the most superficial sense in which they process and store data. Because there is no difference between the process of weaving and the woven design, cloths persist as records of the processes which fed into their production: how many women worked on them, the techniques they used, the skills they employed. The visible pattern is integral to the process which produced it; the program and the pattern are continuous.

Information can be stored in cloth by means of the meaningful messages and images which are later produced by the pen and the paintbrush, but data can also be woven in far more pragmatic and immediate ways. A piece of work so absorbing as a cloth is saturated with the thoughts of the people who produced it, each of whom can flash straight back to whatever they were thinking as they worked. Like Proust's madeleines, it carries memories of an intensity which completely escapes the written word. Cloths were also woven "to 'invoke magic'—to protect, to secure fertility and riches, to divine the future, perhaps even to curse," and in this sense the weaving of spells is far more than a metaphorical device. "The weaver chose warp threads of red wool for her work, 24 spun one direction, 24 spun the other way. She divided the bunch spun one way into 3 sets of 8, and the other bunch into 4 sets of 6, and alternated them. All this is perhaps perfectly innocent, but . . ."[34]

If the weaving of such magical spells gives priority to the process over the completion of a task, this tendency is implicit in the production of all textiles. Stripes and checks are among the most basic of colored and textured designs which can be woven in. Both are implicit in the grids of the woven cloth itself. Slightly more complex, but equally integral to the basic web, are the lozenges, or diamonds, still common in weaves across the world. These open diamonds are said to indicate fertility and tend to decorate the aprons, skirts, and belts which are themselves supposed to be the earliest forms of clothing. "These lozenges, usually with little curly hooks around the edge, rather graphically, if schematically, represent a woman's vulva."[35] These images are quite unlike those which are later painted on the canvas or written on the page. The lozenge is emergent from the cloth, diagonal lines implicit in the grids of the weave. And even the most ornate and complex of woven designs retains this connection to the warps and wefts. When images are later painted, or written in the form of words on a page, patterns are imposed on the passive backdrop provided by the canvas or the page. But textile images are never imposed on the surface of the cloth: their patterns are always emergent from an active matrix, implicit in a web which makes them immanent to the processes from which they emerge.

As the frantic activities of generations of spinsters and weaving women makes abundantly clear, nothing stops when a particular piece of work has been finished off. Even when magical connections are not explicitly invoked, the finished cloth, unlike the finished painting or the text, is almost incidental in relation to the processes of its production. The only incentive to cast off seems to be the chance completion provides to start again, throw another shuttle, cast another spell.

As writing and other visual arts became the privileged bearers of memory and messages, weaving withdrew into its own screens. Both canvases and paper reduce the complexities of weaving to raw materials on which images and signs are imposed: the cloths from which woven patterns once emerged now become backcloths, passive matrices on which images are imposed and interpreted as if from on high. Images are no longer carried in the weave, but imprinted on its surface by the pens and brushes with which shuttles become superficial carriers of threads. Guided by the hand–eye coordinations of what are now their male creators, patterns become as individuated and unique as their artists and authors. And whereas the weave was once both the process and the product, the woven stuff, images are now separated out from matrices to which they had been immanent. The artist sees only the surface of a web which is covered as he works; the paper on which authors now look down has no say in the writing it supports.

The processes themselves become dematerialized as myths, legends, and metaphors. Ariadne's thread, and the famous contest in which the divine Athena tore mortal Arachne's weaving into shreds, are among the many mythical associations between women and webs, spinsters and spiders, spinning yarns and storylines. For the Greeks, the Fates, the Moirai, were three spinsters—Klotho, Lachesis, and Atropos—who produced, allotted, and broke the delicate contingency of the thread of life. In the folktales of Europe, spindles become magic wands, Fates become fairies, and women are abandoned or rescued from impossible spinning and weaving tasks by supernatural entities, godmothers and crones who transform piles of flax into fine linen by means more magical than weaving itself, as in "Rumpelstiltskin," "The Three Spinsters," and "The Sleeping Beauty." "European folktales are full of references to the making of magical garments, especially girdles, in which the magic seems to be inherent in the weaving, not merely in special decoration."

As for the fabrics which persist: evaluated in these visual terms, their checks and diagonals, diamonds and stripes become insignificant matters of repeating detail. This is why Freud had gazed at work which was so literally imperceptible to him. Struggling only to interpret the surface effects of Anna's work as though he was looking at a painting or a text, the process of weaving eluded him: out of sight, out of mind, out of his world.

This was a process of disarmament which automation should have made complete. But if textiles appear to lose touch with their weaving spells and spans of time, they also continue to fabricate the very screens with which they are concealed. And because these are processes, they keep processing. "Behind the screen of representation," weaving wends its way through even the media which supplant it. While paper has lost its associations with the woven fabrics with which it began, there are remnants of weaving in all writing: yarns continue to be spun, texts are still abbreviated textiles, and even grammar—glamor—and spelling retain an occult connectivity. Silkscreens, printing presses, stencils, photographic processes, and typewriters: by the end of the nineteenth century images, texts, and patterns of all kinds were being processed by machines which still used matrices as means to their ends, but also repeated the repeating patterns downgraded by the one-off work of art. And while all these modes of printing were taking technologies of representation to new heights, they were also moving on to the matrices of times in which these imprinting procedures would reconnect with the tactile depth of woven cloth.

Notes

MATRICES
1. Michel Foucault, *The Archaeology of Knowledge*, p. 23.
2. George Landow, *Hypertext*, p. 123.
3. Ada Lovelace, Notes to *Sketch of the Analytical Engine invented by Charles Babbage Esq. By L. F. Menabrea, of Turin, Officer of the Military Engineers*, Note D.
TENSIONS
4. Philip and Emily Morrison, eds. *Charles Babbage and his Calculating Engines: Selected Writings by Charles Babbage and others*, p. xxxiii.
5. *Neuromancer*, p. 5.
ON THE CARDS
6. Philip and Emily Morrison, eds. *Charles Babbage and his Calculating Engines: Selected Writings by Charles Babbage and others*, p. xxxiv.
7. ibid., p. 233.
8. Manuel de Landa, *War in the Age of Intelligent Machines*, p. 168.
9. Humphrey Jennings, *Pandemonium The Coming of the Machine as Seen by Contemporary Observers*, p. 132.
10. Charles Babbage, *Passages from the Life of a Philosopher*, p. 89.
11. ibid., p. 88.
12. ibid., p. 127.
ANNA 1
13. Sigmund Freud, "Femininity," in Sigmund Freud, *New Introductory Lectures on Psychoanalysis*, pp. 145–69.

14. Gilles Deleuze and Félix Guattari, *A Thousand Plateaus*, p. 32.
15. Gilles Deleuze, *Difference and Repetition*, pp. 119–20.
16. Elisabeth Young-Bruehl, *Anna Freud*, p. 382.
17. Guy Debord, *Comments on the Society of the Spectacle*, p. 86.
18. Marshall McLuhan, *The Gutenberg Galaxy*, p. 276.
19. Ada Lovelace, September 1843 quoted in Betty A. Toole, *Ada, The Enchantress of Numbers*, pp. 264–65.
20. Ada Lovelace, July 1843, quoted in Dorothy Stein, *Ada, A Life and a Legacy*, p. 129.
SHUTTLE SYSTEMS
21. Sigmund Freud, *On Sexuality*, p. 320.
22. Elizabeth Wayland Barber, *Women's Work*, p. 45.
23. ibid., p. 90.
24. W. English, *The Textile Industry*, p. 6.
25. Serge Bramly, *Leonardo, the Artist and the Man*, p. 272.
26. Fernand Braudel, *Capitalism and Material Life*, p. 237.
27. Asa Briggs, *The Age of Invention*, pp. 21–22.
28. Francis D. Klingender, *Art and the Industrial Revolution*, p. 12.
29. Fernand Braudel, *Capitalism and Material Life*, p. 247.
30. W. English, *The Textile Industry*, p. 130.
31. ibid., p. 132.
32. Elizabeth Wayland Barber, *Women's Work*, p. 86.
33. ibid., p. 149.
34. ibid., pp. 159–60.
35. ibid., p. 62.

OPEN SOURCE EMBROIDERY
Curatorial Facilitation of Material Networks (2010)

Ele Carpenter

EDITOR'S INTRODUCTION

Since 2005, Ele Carpenter has developed the *Open Source Embroidery* project to investigate the relationship between craft and code. A detail image of the 'Html Patchwork' (2007–2009) project facilitated by Carpenter is on the cover of the first edition of the *Textile Reader*. The text reprinted in full here is a talk Carpenter gave at the Centre de Cultura Contemporània de Barcelona on 27 May 2010. Carpenter considers the history of open source software and the misunderstandings that have arisen around the term, before turning to the *Open Source Embroidery* project which she explains 'evolved to investigate the material and collaborative nature of computing, code and textiles through workshops, artworks and exhibitions'.

While their research contexts differ, Carpenter shares with Boatema Boatenga's research, also included in this section on production, the acknowledgement that commons and open source methods have roots in folk and craft culture based on collective rather than individual ownership. Over a decade has passed since Carpenter gave the lecture, but the topics of immaterial labour, materiality and the amateur continue to be key debates.

Professor Ele Carpenter is the Director of the UmArts Research Centre for Architecture, Art and Design at Umeå University, Sweden. Her *Embroidered Digital Commons* project was featured in the Craftspace UK touring exhibition *We Are Commoners* (2021–2). Recent curatorial work includes the exhibition *Perpetual Uncertainty* at Bildmuseet and Malmö Konstmuseum, Sweden and Z33, Belgium (touring 2016–18); *Splitting the Atom*, CAC Centre for Contemporary Art and the Energy & Technology Museum in Vilnius, Lithuania (2020).

Open Source Embroidery:
Curatorial Facilitation of Material Networks

Ele Carpenter

INTRODUCTION

The starting point for this paper is an interest in the shared language between socially engaged (relational) practices and new media art, which has led me to develop the Open Source Embroidery (OSE) project. Informed by the free and open source software movement and socially engaged arts practice, Open Source Embroidery has been developed through three key concepts:

- Investigation of (im)materiality, with a focus on the digital as material

- Facilitating amateur – professional relationships across craft + code

- Making the tension between object and process visible

- Creating an exhibition as a process, with a balance between spectator and participant

These are huge topics, and can't all be discussed in depth here. So this paper will introduce the thinking behind the project, focusing on open source, moving on to issues of materiality and the role of the amateur. But, firstly, I shall describe the curatorial landscape in which the Open Source Embroidery project is situated.

Over the last ten years the connective and collaborative characteristics of digital media have reintroduced the language of participatory production-and-distribution into the cultural sphere. New media art has contributed to the rehabilitation of discourse on the nature of the commons, materiality and open

methodologies. Although these ideas are informed by new media systems they have older histories in collectives, community organisation, folk and craft culture. Digital art and socially engaged art, along with craft, are historically on the margins of the modern 'fine' art world, also functioning within spheres of popular and folk culture.

While digital and socially engaged art has always embraced a performative and conceptual approach to immateriality, it is only recently that craft has exploded into a fashionable participatory culture. Leaving behind some of the preciousness of the hard-won fine-craft, and embracing public and activist forms of making (craftivism), the coolness of knitting is now being commodified as 'knitted cakes'. (Carpenter, 2010)

The vast amount of contemporary craft online is a perfect example of a specialist community of interest networking itself through the web. But perhaps this is only remarkable because craft, like art, has previously been thought of as an isolated if not autonomous practice.

We are now in the age of ubiquitous computing (almost). But like all art forms, net art, digital art, media art, networked and distributed creativity all have their roots in the relationship between the form and content of the medium: the live connectivity of the network, ability to upload and download, and the compatibility of digital formats across platforms.

Digital art often uses generative code and algorithmic scripts to create live interactions; exploring

Source: Eleanor Carpenter, 'Open Source Embroidery: Curatorial Facilitations of Material Networks' (2010). Presented at The Present and Future of the Exhibition Format, 'Exhibiting the Lab', Centre de Cultura Contemporània de Barcelona. Reproduced with permission.

an aesthetic or literary understanding of code, in relation to its networked functions and user input and visual outcomes. Here the artist deconstructs her/his tools to investigate the values of the media, and its relationship to the world. The website www.sketchpatch .net is a good example, where users are encouraged to patch, copy and modify processing code to create new animated sketches. Sketchpatch works well in a workshop scenario, or accessed privately at home, but is harder to present in a gallery exhibition. (Footnote: In OSE an every-day desk table was used for the Sketchpatch computer, the desktop was also projected onto the gallery wall above to create a public as well as a private viewing space for the work. The table also included Lisa Wallbank's 'Telnit Zero' Crochet computer cover.)

This is true of many online or digital works which often don't sit well within a museum exhibition. The artwork exists within the space of the computer, and the artist often forgets to think of the work in a physical space; sensitivities of light, colour balance, height, proportion, framing, seating, and contextual information are neglected in favour of the interiority of the computer screen. Formally, the work fails in sculptural terms, it is an unintentional presentation of equipment which at best distracts or, worse, hides the actual work of art. However, hiding technical equipment to create a streamlined exhibition space is equally problematic. These problems of 'display' are apparent in several of the works in the current [8 December 2009–11 April 2010] DeCode exhibition at the Victoria and Albert (V&A) museum in London, where exhibition designers have resolved the spatial requirements and created a coherent linear visitor experience flowing between works as if they were pictures inset into a wall. Interestingly the DeCode exhibition at the V&A is on show at the same time as a large quilt exhibition, but there is no curated relationship between the two exhibitions. Both exhibitions are based on the material or medium characteristics of the work as separate and distinct art forms. This is a stark reminder of early media art exhibitions which suffered from a medium-specific focus, trying to create visibility for the work, but also accused of ghetto-ising practice.

Within my curatorial practice I wanted to find a line of critical enquiry based on ideas, rather than medium, which investigated the relationship between the social functions of digital media and art practice. I was finding it hard to talk about new media art without a computer in front of me, or without being online. This was frustrating as many of the concepts I was trying to explain, such as network topologies or open source, were around long before computers and the internet. So I started to learn html, and as I typed I embroidered the code on my T-shirt making it visible and talking about it. I didn't want to instrumentalise either media. I didn't want the digital to 'document' the material, or the material to 'illustrate' the digital. So, I started stitching shared language scarves, delighted by the distinct contrast of cloth to plastic, enjoying the physicality of stitches rather than typing. Glad not to be staring at a screen.

So the OSE project developed in response to the need for a material investigation of the digital and quickly found its form through both conceptual and folk culture. At one point, it could have included other forms of open collective production informed by open source ideas. However, there is such a strong historical, material and metaphorical connection between computing and textiles (Plant, 1997; Essinger, 2004) that I decided to focus on this interdisciplinary approach.

The OSE project evolved to investigate the material and collaborative nature of computing, code and textiles through workshops, artworks and exhibitions. The workshops have taken place in media labs, conferences, exhibitions and seminars. The exhibition has been presented at the Museum of Craft and Folk Art in San Francisco, the Bildmuseet in Umeå, Sweden, and in the UK at Furtherfields' HTTP Gallery in London and Access Space in Sheffield.

The exhibition presented contemporary artwork by over 30 artists and collectives that explores how the open source software development model has been incorporated into the language of cultural participation, involving interdisciplinary approaches to skill-share and collaboration. It included material and digital works that make visible the physical characteristics of technology and social communications networks.

The project investigates the relationship between physical and virtual space, not as two opposing architectures, but as symbiotic spaces reflecting, informing and supporting the other. However, this does not mean that they lose their distinct properties, but that the boundary between virtual and real is more fluid and shifting than we might think, as we move between different modes of communication.

People create culture for social and intellectual, as well as creative, reasons. Through my experience of commissioning and facilitating socially engaged art I realise there is no such thing as the 'general public', this abstract body of people is comprised of communities of interest who have very specific social networks across amateur and professional spheres both on and offline. These groups can be mapped as network topologies through their communication patterns.

In 1964, Paul Baran illustrated the potential of a distributed communications system which we now know as the internet (Baran, 1964). The distributed network offers the potential for everyone to be connected through a net or web of interconnections. A more familiar topology is the clustering of decentralised groups, in which we recognise our professional, family, and social networks. The OSE project is a distributed project which forms a decentralised international network.

OPEN SOURCE EMBROIDERY AND OPENNESS

In many ways there is no such thing as perfect 'openness'. Open organisational methods simply invite participants to set the parameters within which they agree to work, rather than being imposed from a hierarchy or an institution. But what is open source? And what do we mean by open methodologies in relation to software? To answer these questions it is important to understand the basic principles of free and open source software, which I will outline here.

The history of free software explores software as a form of political action, referencing the Diggers and Luddites and the tensions between utopian and dystopian views of technology in early computing. The story of 'Free Libertarian Open Source Software'

(FLOSS) includes both radical (Stallman, 1985, 2007) and libertarian (Raymond, 1999) arguments for free and open source software.

The term 'open source' is used within the title Open Source Embroidery because it best describes how the open source development methodology can be used to rethink practices of participation, collaboration, socio-political functions of tools and the relationship between the value of process and a never-finished product. (Footnote: The term 'Free Embroidery' would refer to financially free work which is not the case, or free-style stitching which would be appropriate.) But there are important differences between open source and free software, which are also reflected in the political complexities behind the intentions of social engagement and digital arts.

The Free Software Foundation (FSF) was established by Richard Stallman early in 1985. The definition of open source wasn't coined by Eric Raymond until 1998, when it became known as a development methodology for popularising FLOSS within a wider social and economic context. As described on the FSF website:

> "The fundamental difference between the two movements is in their values, their ways of looking at the world. For the open source movement, the issue of whether software should be open source is a practical question, not an ethical one. As one person put it, 'Open source is a development methodology; free software is a social movement.' For the Open Source movement, non-free software is a suboptimal solution. For the Free Software movement, non-free software is a social problem and free software is the solution." (Stallman, 2005)

The Open Source Initiative (Coar, 2006) defines open source software as licensed under the General Public License (GPL) of Free Software, and freely distributed, although not always financially free. The source code is viewable and modifiable and gives credit to everyone who has contributed to it. Derived works must be distributed under the same licensing terms as the original software. Open source also has clauses to respect the 'integrity of the author's source code'. In stark contrast to proprietary software, open source must not be 'specific to a product' or 'restrict other software' and it must be technology neutral.

The FSF define their concept of freedom:

> "'Free software' is a matter of liberty, not price. To understand the concept, you should think of 'free' as in 'free speech,' not as in 'free beer.'" (Stallman, 2007b)

This much quoted and misquoted phrase emphasises the flexibility of freedom to make choices and to have your voice heard and does not advocate a financially free process of product outside of the capital economy. To remind us of the notion of 'freedom' being used here, the FSF declare:

> "Free software is a matter of the users' freedom to run, copy, distribute, study, change and improve the software." (Stallman, 2007b)

Raymond argues that the term 'free' is misleading in several ways (Raymond, 1999, p. 122). Firstly, that purchase of proprietary software is only worthwhile if the technical support is provided. This highlights the fact that the actual programs themselves are cheap and easily reproducible, whilst the investment in learning, maintenance (Raymond, 1999, p. 120) and support is where the real value lies. So the software is not 'free' but investment is directed into maintenance rather than product. This correlates to socially engaged arts practice where development and maintenance are the core focus of the social process of the work.

Of course, there are problems with the production and distribution of open source software (Brown, 2005; King, 2006), mainly due to the problems of compatibility with proprietary software and operating systems. But its emphasis on communication between producer and user has reinvigorated the debate about who owns, produces and uses culture; asking the question: *Is culture something you buy or something you do?*

The main success story of open source is Linus Torvald's development of the Linux operating system. Raymond discusses the development model of the Linux kernel:

> "Linus's cleverest and most consequential hack was not the construction of the Linux kernel itself, but rather his invention of the Linux development model." (Raymond, 1999, p. 27)

Torvald's model consisted of himself as the coordinating software developer at the centre of a core group that released their work to vast numbers of individual independent programmers who highlighted problems, fixed bugs and sent their work back to the core group. If we use Baran's centralized diagram to describe this network it's hard to describe this group as a community because they don't necessarily know or communicate with each other. As Raymond describes, their point of connection is through the centre, keeping simplicity to prevent forking or repetition of work (Raymond, 1999, p. 30).

So let's consider the analogy between the FLOSS debates and socially engaged art practices: Art can be both a utopian activity outside the traditional labour relations and ideas of what constitutes 'work', its symbolic value the perfect idea of immaterial labour. Or it can be seen as a more efficient way of making high-quality products for a select market, creating the aura of art. Socially engaged art can be seen as working towards reclaiming culture as something that everyone has, and not simply a 'culture industry'. More negatively, it can be viewed as a poor substitute for social services. Digital art can be understood as empowering people to create their own cultural content collapsing distance between communities of interest. But it can also be a form of control, creating distance between people and forcing us to travel further and further to maintain working patterns. Alex Galloway, in his book *Protocol*, examines the internet protocols that regulate the internet, not as a completely open system, but one which is heavily controlled and managed (Galloway, 2004). FLOSS attempts to keep freedom within the system so that people can develop their own tools and networks, rather than them being owned by a small handful of global corporations (Mansoux & de Valk, 2008).

So to clarify: OSE is not an 'open-exhibition' in the sense of an 'open-submission' where anyone can submit work to be shown. Instead the project is based on three distinct communities of interest: artists, crafters and programmers who are invited to come together to discuss their practice and make new work. Topics of discussion have included: creating a perfect work as a demonstration of skill and ability; translating metaphor;

use of English as the universal programming language; gendered materials; history of computing; open source software tools; utopian and dystopian approaches to open systems; attitudes to collective ownership; the cathartic nature of making; systematic creativity; software patches and fabric patches; men's embroidery; hexadecimal codes and the differences between CMYK and RGB colour sequences . . . the list goes on.

Many of the artworks in the Open Source Embroidery exhibition were produced through these workshops (Knitted Flat Screen Cover, Embroidered Digital Commons, GYRMBC Tent etc). The exhibition also presented a range of models for open production, through collectively made artworks such as: *Knitted Blog, Sampler Collective, Knitted Bench, Html Patchwork, Stitching Together* and the *Embroidered Digital Commons*.

MATERIALITY, TACTICS AND THE AMATEUR

Emerging from the discussion of open source and distributed networks is an understanding of new ways of working made possible by the internet, which have enabled new economic models. Work is no longer simply manufacturing goods, but includes the more intangible production of knowledge, ideas and services, and, crucially, the maintenance of networks. But Lazzarato's concept of 'immaterial labour' (discussed by Vishmidt, 2006; Terranova, 2006), while helpful in describing the merging of work and life through information networks and computing, can also be a confusing distraction from the material conditions of production.

This confusion can also be found in the visual arts where we often argue for the immateriality of both digital and socially engaged practices as a shift from commodifiable object to social or relational process. At the same time we recognise that an object is also a material network of relations, and that objects can be actors in the wider notion of the social network (Latour, 2005).

So, I intentionally use the word 'material' in several ways. Firstly, to acknowledge that artworks are embedded within their own material network in terms of their physical production, consumption of resources and relationship to the environment. This includes the heavy metals used in microprocessors, and the fuel for my flight to Barcelona. Secondly, 'material' is used to describe the way in which the histories of fabric and computing intertwine. From the beginning of computer history the digital is material—and it is social (Plant, 1997). Computing, far from being an ephemeral and invisible process, is produced through electronics and written instructions called code. Writers such as Alex Galloway, Matthew Fuller (2003), Josephine Berry Slater, and Tiziana Terranova have investigated the materiality of computer code.

Within OSE I use the phrase 'material network' to describe collectively made embroidery, weaving and patchwork which forms a fabric embodiment of a network of people. Fabric-metaphors are often used to describe communication networks such as weaving a web, spinning a yarn, and the thread of a story.

In the OSE exhibition, many of the works are forms of what Joseph Beuys called "social sculpture" (Beuys, 1992). Not simply that "everyone can be an artist" but in a sculptural sense, the social network can be embedded in or represented by an object. The concept lies in the action, the performativity of the work, whose primary audience is the people who participate in its production. The tension lies in how the object is viewed and mediated in a gallery exhibition, which can sometimes be experienced as an after-effect of intense engagement.

The collectively stitched *Html Patchwork* plays with these multiple senses of materiality. The work was created by artists, craftspeople, computer programmers, and html users, all contributing their work for free. But rather than simply 'immaterial labour' there are a number of different exchanges at play: skill-share, gift, individual and institutional networking, publicity, learning and social fun. We should also include the pleasure of making something by hand. But what are the material and immaterial values of this work?

Tiziana Terranova (2006) and Marina Vishmidt (2006) each investigate the concept of immaterial labour in relation to art and curating. Terranova describes how "the concept of immaterial labour challenges not only the modern emphasis on art as an autonomous sphere of existence, but also work as the only domain of economic relations and political struggle" (p. 27). It is in this in-between space of everyday creative making, art, craft and tactics that the OSE project sits.

As Terranova describes:

"Immaterial labour is a Marxist concept that aims at a redefinition of labour in the age of the general intellect—the age where the production of value is dependent on socialized labour power organized in assemblages of humans and machines exceeding the spaces and times designated as 'work'." (Terranova, 2006, p. 28)

I am certainly an amateur Marxist—but the notion of the 'general intellect', or the level of knowledge in society, is evident in user generated content online and the basis of socially engaged practices which invite people to share their skills and knowledge.

Vishmidt situates dematerialised art and curating as 'immaterial labour' within the realm of the knowledge economy as an abstract form in itself. But she takes care to argue that:

". . . the position of labour in capital remains unchanged. Just so, with 'immateriality' signaling an epochal displacement of value from object to process and symbolic analysis in art production, the position of the artist in the market remains unchanged. It is only the site of value production that shifts, not the conditions of production. Or, rather, we could contend that the sites of value production have expanded rather than shifted—the dematerialisation of the art object has not deterred the appearance of new art objects, but it has added new types of object, immaterial ones." (Vishmidt, 2006, p. 40)

OSE is certainly an investigation into the material aspects of immateriality, where informal groups work in their leisure time to create artworks which may or may not gain them cultural capital. These new objects have a precarious status somewhere between art and craft, material and process, professional and amateur.

The role of the Amateur is a significant figure in the discourse of social media and online culture, as well being the main participant of socially engaged art.

The OSE project explores the possibility of cultural value outside of economic exchange relations. Models such as the 'Gift Economy' are more commonly played out in non-professional spheres of life such as the domestic, unemployed, and un-recuperated labour such as craft. All of these roles are amateur, where the sharing of experience and transaction of knowledge is through enthusiast, hobbyist and opportunistic actions.

Lovink & Garcia's definition of *Tactical Media* (1992) situates the amateur as operating tactically within the everyday and outside long-term institutional developmental strategies. These tactical modes of behaviour lie outside the paradigm of Walter Benjamin's producer/consumer, providing a framework for rethinking the value of creativity. De Certeau's *The Practice of Everyday Life* (1984) and his definition of tactical subversive acts 'making do' within the everyday (pp. 29–44), along with Hakim Bey's 'Temporary Autonomous Zones' (1985) provide other frameworks for understanding creativity outside the Marxist production and distribution model.

However, the relationship between amateur and expert is hugely crucial, as highlighted by Critical Art Ensemble (CAE), who value the role of the amateur as a radical interventionist, respecting the relationship between amateur and expert:

"The amateur's relationship to the expert is a necessary one in many ways. For the sake of efficiency, to limit mistakes, to teach fundamental processes and protocols and to reinforce good ideas, dialogues with experts remain a key part of the amateurs' process." (CAE, 2005)

This two-way learning process is an example of strategic value of tactical knowledge, where the institution or expert can support amateur and spontaneous practices which test out ideas and (inadvertently) can contribute to institutional development, albeit incredibly slowly.

Vishmidt also introduces the amateur as a character who might circumvent the commodification of their production, but whose "parasitic" role can shift and evolve as they please (Vishmidt, 2006, pp. 52–56).

Vishmidt describes a "conservative" and "emancipatory" reading of the amateur. On the one hand the figure of a hobbyist consumer or entrepreneur, on the other hand:

> "The emancipatory aspect, however, may come to the fore whenever the amateur positions his/ her production as a challenge to the impoverishment of experience bought about by specialization, and eschews such commodification of abilities in favour of a non-specific production structured by goals other than economic, whether these be social, political or artistic." (Vishmidt, 2006, pp. 52–3)

Vishmidt also draws a correlation between the unremunerated open source programmer, the amateur and the notion of the commons (2006, pp. 53–4). She proposes that the implications of open source include "renewed attention to questions of organization, hierarchy, economies, economics and ownership and creativity" which are inherent in the amateur, "the unremunerated enthusiast, obscure or feted, that prefigures an existence beyond capital, while expressing all the contradictions that a life within capital dictates" (p. 54). So we can start to think of the amateur, not as a social figure, but an aspect of all of our knowledge. The expert brain surgeon may be an amateur gardener, the curator an amateur philosopher etc.

In relation to 'work' many artists may more accurately describe themselves as 'amateurs' rather than 'entrepreneurs' as they are mostly unsuccessful at levering the 'capital' value from their practice. Most craft practice is certainly amateur, and intends to stay that way. Curating is also a practice of being an amateur in many subjects. But this position is slowly changing due to the increase in academic-research-based curatorial and artistic practices where there is increasing demand for expert knowledge and analysis.

WHAT IS THE IMPACT OF THE NOTION OF THE AMATEUR ON CURATING CONTEMPORARY ART?

As we have seen, amateur modes of operation are complex and shifting. When they become political they become tactical, manoeuvring to create spaces for spontaneity and improvisation. Everyone is an expert in something and an amateur in other things. Embracing amateurism enables flexibility, different kinds of knowledge and storytelling, and is a prerequisite for any collaborative or interdisciplinary attitude.

Perhaps the biggest issue for the future of exhibitions is how to prevent them from becoming strategically absorbed into cultural tourism by a conglomeration of major institutions. We need to keep spaces for tactical experimentation within a range of labour relations, valuing tactical and amateur approaches to expert fields of knowledge. The mistake with the 'amateur' is to assume that the lowest common denominator will appeal to all. As we know, amateurs are specialists too.

Exhibitions need to be understood as complex poetic experience and open-ended lines of enquiry. Navigating the problems of proprietary social media, and creating spaces for rigorous approaches to amateur–professional collaboration.

Feminist writer Germaine Greer reflects on the complex nature of storytelling. Rather than focusing on the meaning and interpretation of the tale, she argues that:

> "If the child's imagination is to work, the story must not be explained away, nor should the child intuit what the grown-up's reason for telling such a tale might be." (Germaine Greer, 2010. p. 3)

Curatorial work includes the delicate art of storytelling without 'explaining away' the work, despite the driving forces of the tourism industry to create easily marketable exhibitions. Curators work with artists to communicate and disseminate their work, while identifying the complexity and intelligence of audiences who are amateurs in many things, but not necessarily experts in navigating the culture industry.

It is important that we understand the rhetoric of participation as enabling a new role for curators and artists where both individual expertise and collaborative working can co-exist within self-organised networks and horizontal teams. Here, both expert and amateur knowledge can inform each other.

References

Baran, Paul (1964). RAND memorandum, On Distributed Communications: 1. Introduction to Distributed Communications Network. (August 1964).

Brown, Andrew (2005). 'If this suite's a success, why is it so buggy?' In: *The Guardian Newspaper*. Thursday December 8, 2005. Available at: http://technology .guardian.co.uk/weekly/story/0,16376,1660763,00. html [Accessed 24.11.07]

Beuys, J. (1992). Joseph Beuys (1921–1986) I am Searching for Field Character, 1973. In: Harrison & Wood, *Art in Theory 1900–1990: An Anthology of Changing Ideas*. Oxford & Malden: Blackwell, p 903.

Bey, Hakim (1985, 1991). T.A.Z.: The Temporary Autonomous Zones. Autonomedia. Available at: http://www.t0.or.at/hakimbey/taz/taz.htm [Accessed 24.02.07]

Carpenter, Ele (2010). "Activist Tendencies in Craft." In: Concept Store #3 *Art, Activism and Recuperation*. Eds Geoff Cox, Nav Haq, Tom Trevor. Arnolfini: Bristol. May 2010. ISBN 9780 907738 97 8.

Coar, Ken (2006). *The Open Source Definition, Annotated*. Mon, 2006-07-24 19:04. Available at: http://www .opensource.org/docs/definition.php [Accessed 4.01.08]

Critical Art Ensemble (2005). The Amateur. In: Nato Thompson, *The Interventionists: User's Manual for the Creative Disruption of Everyday Life*. Massachusetts: Mass MoCA, p 147.

Essinger, James (2004). *Jacquard's Web: How a hand loom led to the birth of the information age*. Oxford University Press.

Fuller, Matthew (2003). *Beyond the Blip: Essays on the Culture of Software*. Autonomedia: New York, USA.

Galloway, Alexander R. (2004). Protocol: *how control exists after decentralisation*. Massachusetts: Massachusetts Institute of Technology.

Greer, Germaine (2010) Grandmother's Footsteps. In: Saturday *Guardian*, 15.05.2010. [newspaper] p 2–4.

Available at: http://www.guardian.co.uk/ books/2010/ may/15/germaine-greer-old-wives-tales

King, Jamie (2006). The Packet Gang. In: Marina Vishmidt. *Media Mutandis: a Node.London Reader: Surveying art, technologies and politics*. London: Node. London, p 157–170.

Latour, B. (2005). *Reassembling The Social: An Introduction to Actor Network Theory*. Oxford: Oxford University Press.

Mansoux, Aymeric,. & Marloes de Valk (2008). *FLOSS+Art*. London: Goto10 and Open Mute.

Raymond, Eric S. (1999). *The Cathedral and the Bazaar: Musings on Linux and Open Source by an Accidental Revolutionary*. O'Reilly. Available at: www.oreilly.com

Plant, Sadie (1997). *Zeros + Ones: Digital Women + the New Technoculture*. London: Fourth Estate.

Stallman, Richard (1985). The Free Software Foundation (FSF). Available at: http://www.fsf.org/ [Accessed 10.12.07]

Stallman, Richard (2005). *Why Free Software is better than Open Source*. Available at: http://www.fsf.org/licensing /essays/free-software-for-freedom.html [Accessed: 04.01.08]

Stallman, Richard (2007). *Why 'Open Source' misses the point of Free Software*. Available at: http:// www.gnu .org/philosophy/open-source-misses-the-point.html [Accessed: 24.12.07]

Stallman, Richard (2007b). *The Free Software Definition*. Available at: http://www.fsf.org/licensing/essays/free-sw .html [Accessed 2.12.07]

Terranova, Tiziana (2006). Of Sense and Sensibility: Immaterial Labour in Open Systems. In: *Curating Immateriality: The work of the curator in the age of network systems*. Edited by Joasia Krysa (2006). Databrowser03. p 27–38.

Vishmidt, Marina (2006). Twilight of the Widgets. In: *Curating Immateriality: The work of the curator in the age of network systems*. Edited by Joasia Krysa (2006). Databrowser03. p 39–62.

37

WHY *SHOULD* THE COPYRIGHT THING WORK HERE? (EXCERPT) (2011)

Boatema Boateng

EDITOR'S INTRODUCTION

Boatema Boateng is an Associate Professor at the University of California, San Diego. Her research interests include Critical Legal Studies, Critical Race Studies, Cultural Studies, Transnational Gender Studies, and African Diaspora Studies. In the book-length study *The Copyright Thing Doesn't Work Here: Adinkra and Kente Cloth and Intellectual Property in Ghana* (2011) she considers how intellectual property law converges with histories of subjugation along the lines of nation, gender and race. The personal accounts of oral histories are central to the research.

Boateng focuses on adinkra, a system of symbols printed onto textiles, and kente, a strip woven cloth – textiles associated with Asante and Ghanaian cultural nationalism. The excerpt included here is drawn from the concluding chapter of the book. In it she explains, 'The continuity of adinkra and kente producers' creative practices with those of the ancestors, as well as their insistence on locating their work within networks of kinship, ethnicity, and political power, mark that work as belonging within a distinctive mode of organizing the temporal and social contexts of cultural production.' In her conclusion, Boateng considers the concept of the commons and recommends a transnational rather than international outlook that could allow the textile makers, rather than the nation's lawmakers, greater control over design rights.

Why *Should* the Copyright Thing Work Here?

Boatema Boateng

Ghana's use of intellectual property law to protect elements of local cultural production, like adinkra and kente designs, is not simply an interesting case study of an attempt to fit non-Western cultural forms into Western legal regimes. More importantly, it has to do with the place of nations like Ghana in the current global order and the processes by which they have come to occupy that place. In 2007, Ghanaians proudly celebrated the fiftieth anniversary of their independence from Britain. This anniversary also marked fifty years of endorsing modernity as the globally sanctioned form of political and social being and modernization as the means of attaining that form. Yet by 2007, Ghana's economy had regressed to a level very similar to its state under colonization, partly the result of accepting neoliberal policies as a means of economic growth.[1] With a "hollowed-out"[2] state, weakened economy, and integration into the global economy on adverse terms, Ghanaian modernization seems permanently aspirational—a destination that is constantly elusive.

[…]

STRATEGIES OF POWER AND THE TIME OF THE ANCESTORS

The continuity of adinkra and kente producers' creative practices with those of the ancestors, as well as their insistence on locating their work within networks of kinship, ethnicity, and political power, mark that work as belonging within a distinctive mode of organizing the temporal and social contexts of cultural production. Viewing creative practices around cloth production in terms of those contexts makes it possible to understand their difference from the practices sanctioned by intellectual property law as more than a simple distinction between individual and communal creativity or between traditional and modern knowledges. Rather, the encounter between intellectual property law and indigenous and local cultural production is one between different ways of conceiving of time and society in relation to cultural production.

Intellectual property is based on understandings of the temporal and social contexts of cultural production that are bound up with modernity. These include the liberal concept of the autonomous, rational individual as the basic unit of society and the actions of that individual as distinct from the actions of all others. As a cultural producer, this individual is the essential subject of intellectual property law—the male or masculinized author or inventor whose ability and right to separate his work from all other such work and make proprietary claims over it is a function of his status as a modern subject. This separation is also temporal in demarcating the creative work of the individual from that of not only living authors but also deceased ones.

Adinkra and kente production features both individual *and* communal creativity. Individuals not only make claims over their own designs but also acknowledge the creativity of other individuals, sometimes long after the latter have died. Further, they work in communities but, far from being an ideal

Source: Boatema Boateng, 'Conclusion: Why *Should* the Copyright Thing Work Here?', *The Copyright Thing Doesn't Work Here: Adinkra and Kente Cloth and Intellectual Property in Ghana* (University of Minnesota Press, 2011), pp. 165–82. Copyright 2011 by the Regents of the University of Minnesota. Reproduced with permission.

model of cooperation, communal production features both collaboration and rivalry. At the same time, it is by appeal to the collective that craftsmen authorize their work. This is true even for cloth producers who move away from core production sites such that the social nature of their work extends across geographical space. That work also extends across time, and rather than emphasizing their individual creativity as the means of authorizing their work, it is that work's connection to deceased creators that gives it its distinctiveness.

[…]

The same distinction occurs in adinkra and kente producers' claims about the authenticity of their work—for example, when adinkra maker Kwame says, "But ours is the *cultural* one" in distinguishing between mass-produced imitations and hand-stenciled adinkra cloth. It is clear from his words that handmade cloth embodies cultural authenticity in ways that mass-produced cloth cannot. Handmade cloth, in effect, differs from mass-produced cloth in being a bearer of tradition—the source of its authenticity. However strategic Ghana's (and Ghanaians') deployment of tradition may be, it reifies the tradition-modernity divide in ways that ultimately confirm the superior status of the latter. It also reinforces the country's status as one that aspires to modernity without having fully arrived.

[…]

THE OUTSIDE OF PROPERTY?

[…]

As is evident in adinkra and kente makers' management of the boundaries of cloth production, the principle that some enclosure may be desirable holds true for forms of cultural production that take place in commons other than those of digital technology. The importance of boundaries becomes especially evident when one considers the fragility of a space like that of adinkra and kente production. Here, the challenge becomes one of ensuring cloth makers' continued ability to maintain boundaries that are robust enough to withstand destruction through rampant appropriation while retaining the permeability that ensures the continuing dynamism and viability of adinkra and kente production. The challenge is also one of resisting excessive forms of enclosure that seek to prevent the "tragedy of the commons" (that is, its overexploitation and eventual destruction) by walling it off altogether.

[…]

ECOSYSTEMS OF CULTURE

The language of environmentalism has featured in a number of analyses of intellectual property law, most notably in the work of scholar and activist Vandana Shiva. In Shiva's analyses of the threats posed by monocultural agriculture and plant patents to indigenous and local agricultural practices that sustain biodiversity, the language of environmentalism is both literal and metaphorical—the latter in her warnings of the dangers of "monocultures of the mind."[3] David Bollier has also pointed out the importance of the concept of the commons in environmental scholarship and activism.[4] Increasingly, the language and strategies of environmental activism are becoming important metaphors and models for other spheres of cultural production that have no direct links to the environment—most strikingly, in the context of networked creativity in the digital age. Some scholars have called for an environmentalist approach in protecting commons-based cultural production.[5]

[…]

In focusing on the system rather than the site and content of cultural production, such a network would also accommodate a wider range of management options than the territory-based geographical indications option. Further, it could transcend established and emerging polarities of North and South and global East in fostering multidirectional alliances. Most importantly, in offering a common basis for managing different kinds of cultural production and in linking a wide range of actors across the old divides, the network could be a basis for legitimacy that cannot be achieved through sui generis systems tailored to specific cases in isolation from each other.

ALTERNATIVE VISIONS

Against this background, an alternative starting point to that of protecting "national culture" would be to assess Ghana's intellectual property laws according to the extent to which they are compatible with the ways that folklore is produced and the spheres of its production are managed. Assessing the law would also entail critically reviewing what kinds of citizenship are possible within it and what alternative ways of conceptualizing authorship, authorization, and alienability give all cultural producers a stake in the project of managing cultural production so that it remains a viable resource for those producers and not only for the state. The networked ecosystems of commons-based cultural production and management constitute one set of alternatives that would provide more scope for cultural producers to shape the kinds of regulatory systems within which they work.

In being *trans*national rather than *inter*national, such a network would give nonstate actors greater power than they have in international regulatory systems in which states are the primary actors. They could also exert pressure on nations to be accountable to local and indigenous cultural producers. Adinkra and kente producers' presence in global circuits, however minimal, shows that the possibility exists for cloth makers to also participate in global networks of different kinds of commons. Rather than being bound by the limitations of national copyright law for both their work and subjectivity. Ghanaian adinkra and kente producers could become part of a transnational network of commons-based cultural production that, unlike intellectual property law, recognizes and supports the complex structures of authorship, authorization, and alienability within which they work.

Notes

1. Mkandawire, "The Global Economic Context."
2. Ferguson, *Global Shadows*, 10.
3. Shiva, *Monocultures of the Mind.*
4. Bollier, "The Growth of the Commons Paradigm."
5. Bollier, "Why We Must Talk about the Information Commons"; Boyle, *The Public Domain.*

38

CONTEMPORARY TEXTILE IMAGERY IN SOUTHERN AFRICA
A question of ownership (2015)

Sarah Rhodes

EDITOR'S INTRODUCTION

Sarah Rhodes is a design researcher. Completed in 2015, her PhD at Central Saint Martins, University of the Arts London, considered the role of the design process in examples of sub-Saharan African craft. The writing reprinted in full here focuses on the San communities of Namibia, Botswana and South Africa, and the textile project Art-i-San. Rhodes discusses the use of printed textile design by several San communities who have faced multiple displacements in their history, but who have also shown remarkable affinities in visual style even when separated by time and space. She considers the authenticity and ownership of work made by development initiatives, citing numerous examples of instances where the work of indigenous artists – including commissions by British Airways in the late 1990s – has received scant financial remuneration.

The Art-i-San project that makes up the core of this writing remains unusual because of its longevity. The project converts lino-cut prints into repeat patterns for screen-printed textiles sold as yardage or made into textile objects such as tablecloths or bags. Sales generate royalties that are paid back to the designer – a system that may not sound unusual, but is too infrequently seen in initiatives where grassroots indigenous groups are led by an external designer. In the conclusion, Rhodes points to the positive benefit financial renumeration through commercial relationships can provide, while acknowledging that appropriation of images made by the San, particularly for advertising purposes, unfortunately continues.

The original version of this writing included images that have not been reprinted here.

Contemporary Textile Imagery in Southern Africa:
A question of ownership

Sarah Rhodes

Utopia was the optimistically titled range of multicoloured aeroplane tail fin designs for the British Airways (BA) image rebrand in 1997. Unfortunately it was a short-lived ideal, but the airline's concept of connecting different communities in the world through symbolic imagery is reflected in the current rise of designers seeking inspiration from cultures beyond their own. Prompted by the increase in popularity of the handmade combined with a quest for authenticity in art and design, this interest in adopted cultural references can be seen as a backlash against commercial globalization. Image appropriation from indigenous artists such as Australian Aborigines has been widely documented. (Burns Coleman 2005) The most well-known case occurred in the 1970s when Aboriginal artist Wandjuk Marika asked the Australian government to investigate the use of indigenous designs on tourist art, which led to the recognition of copyright for indigenous work. (Myers 2004: 1-16) However, in relation to Southern African San groups, most intellectual property rights discussion has centred on the *hoodia* plant commercialization[1] and repatriation of San cultural objects from international museums.[2]

With the current rise of nostalgic iconography, the way indigenous San images are used in contemporary textile production should be questioned. As South African academic Marian Sauthoff explains, issues that have been stressed in many postcolonial contexts have, as yet, to receive serious consideration in South African design, including the ethics and politics of cultural appropriation, representations of previously marginalized groups and the recuperation of indigenous histories. (2004: 41) This chapter explores issues of indigenous cultural depiction and intellectual property rights within Southern African textile design. It examines the way in which Art-i-San, a textile project initiated with San communities from Namibia, began, developed and continues to run, presenting it as a positive case study.

Newell and Sorrell, the London-based graphic design agency behind the BA rebrand, were unusual at the time in their approach to the new BA livery because, not only were the selected artists and designers from diverse countries, they were also from a wide range of visual practices including painters, calligraphers, weavers, textile artists, printers, ceramicists and sculptors.[3] Newell and Sorrell sought permission to reproduce the designs, credited the artists (their signature was included on the tail fin) and bought the copyright by paying for the work. One of these was San artist Cg'ose Ntcöx'o (Cgoise) from the Kuru Art Project in Botswana, whose *Animals and Trees* design of seven jackals resting under trees around a water hole was printed on eight of the planes. This established Cgoise's reputation internationally, opening up other commissions and her participation at a printmaking workshop in the United States, as well as designs for a range of Botswana Postal Service stamps.[4] Unfortunately, BA's now infamous global scope for the designs wasn't such a success with the market, particularly with the late British Prime Minister, Margaret Thatcher, who covered up the model of Cgoise's design with her handkerchief, proclaiming 'we fly the British flag, not those awful

Source: Sarah Rhodes, 'Contemporary Textile Imagery in Southern Africa: A Question of Ownership', *Cultural Threads: Transnational Textiles Today*, ed. Jessica Hemmings (Bloomsbury Academic, London, 2014), pp. 206–23. Reproduced with permission.

things'. (Stone-Lee 2013) The Union flag was reinstated on BA planes in 2001.

In contrast to the exclusive BA tail fin design commission, the diversity of contemporary textiles produced in South Africa is vast. Embroidery, printed fabric, handmade felt and woven cloth are made by a variety of artists ranging from individual designer-makers to community-based, not-for-profit organizations. Just as the BA *Utopia* designs sought to do, the imagery on the textiles references local culture and landscape in one form or another; cultural group iconography (Afrikaner / Ndebele / San / Xhosa / Zulu), flora and fauna or narratives depicting the lives of the people who craft them. This imagery reflects South African post-apartheid nostalgia.

Under apartheid rule, South African artists were isolated in the access they had to the rest of the world, particularly in relation to culture, which was heavily censored. This has led to artists and designers post-independence questioning both personal and cultural identity. The complex nature of a country with eleven national languages and comprising many different cultural groups with images that traverse these groups was secured in national history in 1995 when Nelson Mandela wore a green Springbok rugby jersey, symbolically Afrikaner, to the rugby World Cup and the white, Afrikaner, South African team sang *Nkosi Sikelel' iAfrika*, formerly a black resistance song and now part of the national anthem. A new coat of arms was designed incorporating different cultural symbols to integrate the nation and create a sense of national identity for the future. The protea flower, secretary bird and elephant tusks were combined with two Linton stone figures of prehistoric humans (Oosthuizen 2004: 69) alongside the motto '*!Ke e: /xarra //ke*' (people who are different come together) written in !Xam, the language of a group of San who no longer exist. (Szalay 2002: 6)

In 1998 the *Proudly South African* campaign began in order to encourage the country to make and buy locally, promoting national pride, patriotism and social cohesion. Subsequently, national imagery has been explored even more through art, design and culture in many different ways, showing prominence internationally from the science fiction dystopia of

Johannesburg in the film *District 9* (Neill Blomkamp, 2009) to the controversial vandalism of Brett Murray's satirical painting of President Zuma, *The Spear* (2012).

This focus on South Africans' constant interrogation of personal, national and cultural identity is reflected in the work of textile designers Design Team from Johannesburg. Their fabric collections are titled *Homegrown, Indigenous, African Archive* and even more explicitly *Young at Heart Nostalgia*. The designs depict historical photographs from the magazine *Drum*, published in the 1950s and 1960s and the national iconography of the springbok and the protea flower.[5] Echoing this is Cape Town-based Fabricnation's work with *Veld, Old Postcards* and *African Royale* showing images that have a printed feel of the historical or antique.[6] Their *Umlungu Print* illustrates the dichotomy of white South African designers questioning their personal history in a many-layered country. The *Umlungu Print* imagery is also many-layered, depicting a blue tall sails ship with the western goddesses Artemis and Venus in the foreground, in a style referencing traditional sixteenth-century Delft blue ceramic tiles. Jane Solomon, the designer, explains that the boat and goddesses represent her European ancestors and she sees the Greek goddesses as becoming African. *Umlungu* is the isiXhosa word for 'from the sea' and is used to describe white people. As Venus was born from the sea in the myth, Solomon feels the *Umlungu* design connects European myths to an African existence, linking the complex nature of the recognition of her past history with the exploration of her identity in contemporary Southern Africa. (Soloman & Cheifitz 2010)

This postcolonial tension between social inequalities, conflicting cultural values, and negotiating identity through art are explored much less explicitly, but remain visible, in the work of San groups from both South Africa and Namibia.

Historically, the San are a marginalized group of former hunter-gatherers in Southern Africa. Their history has been widely documented and they have been extensively studied (including Bleek & Lloyd 1911, Van Der Post 1958, Winberg 1997, Skotnes 1996, 2007, 2009). Living within several countries, San is a term for different groups of people including the Naro,

!Xun, Khwe, !Kung, Khomani, Ju | 'hoansi, Hei | | omn and others, meaning 'first people' in most cases. (le Roux 2004:2) The names given to the indigenous peoples of the Kalahari by others are varied and contentious, and include Bushmen, Basarwa, First People of the Kalahari, and Khoekhoen. As Willemien le Roux, the coordinator of a San oral history testimony project in Botswana states, 'San has been accepted by a large number of representatives of several surviving groups of First People as being the least derogatory in meaning and history.' (2004: 2) In practice, most groups prefer to be known as 'Bushmen', as documented by American anthropologist Robert J. Gordon (1999: 185) and reinforced in an interview with Karin le Roux, director of the Namibian non-governmental organization (NGO), Omba Arts Trust. (2013) However, as Omba uses the name 'San' on their website and the name of their textile range is 'Art-i-San', this term is used for the purpose of this writing.

The majority of San in Southern Africa today live in Namibia, Botswana, South Africa and Angola, not through a nomadic lifestyle as might be assumed, but mainly via resettlement. The !Xun and Khwe were hunter-gatherers living in Angola before the 1960s. However like most San, their lives have changed dramatically over recent years, due in part to their involvement in the Angolan and Namibian wars. In 1974 the South African Defence Force (SADF) began to recruit and train San as trackers in the low intensity war against the South West Africa People's Organization (SWAPO) insurgents, who were fighting for the liberation of South West Africa, or Namibia as it is now known. The SADF army base in the Caprivi area grew even more the following year when San refugees fled across the border from war-torn Angola and the Omega army base was established to provide them with shelter. (Gordon 1999: 185)

When Namibia gained independence in 1990 the SADF were worried about reprisals and resettled the !Xun and Khwe to Schmidtsdrift in the Northern Cape, not far from the mining town of Kimberley. This was essentially a tented refugee camp where the San lived for over ten years while land settlement claims were disputed and eventually reconciled and the groups were moved to the town of Platfontein. This is one of the

many documented dispossessions that the San have endured over the years – all of them controversial – ending in displacement and, generally, distress for the San.

The Schmidtsdrift camp was made up of more than 4,500 !Xun and Khwe originally from Namibia and Angola, housed in 1,900 military tents. (Godwin 2000) Peter Godwin, who visited the camp for *National Geographic* magazine in 2000, reported it as 'a cheerless spot that smells of desolation'. (2000) With military pensions provided by the government, a school and health care clinic, paradoxically this was one of the most affluent San communities in Southern Africa. However, these material gains adversely affected the !Xun and Khwe. Godwin observed 'the rampant use of alcohol and marijuana is a sign of the dislocation and loss in Schmidtsdrift, palliatives against a world that has overwhelmed these people'. (2000)

It was in this environment that South African Catharina Scheepers-Meyer set up the !Xun and Khwe San Art and Culture Project in 1993. Scheepers-Meyer had successfully established the Kuru Art Project at D'Kar in the Kalahari, Botswana (from where Cgoise produced her design for the BA tail fin) in 1990. Her motivation came from first-hand experience with the D'Kar San where she observed individuals grow through art making to become respected and, in some cases, recognized internationally as artists.

Beginning with a simple textile exercise, the Kuru Art Project's remit was to provide materials and equipment for the San to express themselves through art. Typically, like many grassroots community-based organizations, the Kuru Development Trust emerged out of the missionary projects from the Dutch Reform Church in 1986. In 1989 the Trust focused its attention on strengthening its cultural identity by organizing a trip to view the San rock art paintings at the Tsodilo Hills in Northern Botswana. The success of this trip resulted in the formation of the Kuru Art Project and the first workshop was held in 1990 with the artists painting on fabric. (Scheepers 1991: 7) The results were exhibited at the Botswana National Art Gallery, who bought two of them for their permanent collection. One of these, *Playing*, was painted by one of Kuru's most well-known artists Coex'ae Qgam (Dada) who described creating it: 'They said we should just take that paint and play. It was at the beginning ... I was taking that paint and pouring it in a plate. I was not knowing what I can do, but just taking the brush there and painting whatever I can see. Yes, I like colour.' (Gollifer & Egner 2011: 84)

Scheepers-Meyer believed the San in Schmidtsdrift could also be empowered through the benefits of developing an art intervention. Backed by money from the Officers' Fund from the SADF, she instigated the project, hoping it would provide a shared social space to foster a positive sense of self and community for all members of the !Xun and Khwe at the camp, regardless of their age or sex. (Rabbethge-Schiller 2006: 18)

The themes for the artwork were generally drawn from the !Xun and Khwe's traditional knowledge and stories: bows and arrows, animals, seeds and pods, musical instruments and other cultural symbols. Unsurprisingly, many of the older men focused on animal hunting, an important traditional San activity and something that was not continued after the relocation because Schmidtsdrift and Platfontein did not have game, or veld food to forage. When documentary writer Marlene Sullivan Winberg recorded the oral stories of the !Kun and Khwe artists, she was surprised that, although the communities had suffered the most profoundly sad dispossession, their art and folk tales were full of inspirational and provocative images. (2001: 8) What she found most remarkable was the way in which the artists communicated through narrative, each choosing to answer her questions with a tale, often using animals as metaphors for human behaviour.

Scheepers-Meyers' initial aim for the !Xun and Khwe to experience the benefit of empowerment from an art project (in the same way that the Kuru Art Project achieved it) incidentally seemed to have a cathartic, almost therapeutic effect, particularly on the men involved in the war who chose to document their traumatic experiences through their art. The artist / Thaalu Bernardo Rumao explains:

The other people don't like me, they push me out because of what I draw. But I must draw what I see in my mind. I saw men kill other men – bushmen, white

and black men ... I loaded the dead men on the helicopter myself. This is why I just draw this. People don't want it and this makes my heart sore. (Sullivan Winberg 2001: 128)

A stark contrast exists between conflict-influenced titles such as *Vehicle Fright* (1995) and *Two Soldiers* (1995) and the pastoral scenes of *Giraffe and Buck* (1996) and the *Story of the Bees* (1999).

During the 1990s, South African art teacher and Kalk Bay Gallery owner, Cheryl Rumbak, developed and facilitated several art workshops for the !Xun and Khwe at Schmidtsdrift too, this time to make a textile range to sell for profit. The aim was to provide an occupation to bring an income into the camp instead of the observed pattern of the San turning to alcohol through boredom. The workshops started from basic observational drawing exercises. The San drew their hands and still-life objects collected from the bush. While it was the first time some of them had picked up a pencil, their line making was confident and the drawings led on to intricate black and white linocuts. The drawings are flat and two-dimensional, but have a graphic quality to them, making the images instantly recognizable. From the linocuts, produced mainly by the men, Rumbak translated the images into repeat designs, which were then printed onto cotton. She feels these first San workshops produced the 'most brilliant range of textiles, they were unbelievable'. (Rumbak 2013)

With the exception of one design, the textiles are no longer in production as none of the artists from the initial Schmidtsdrift workshop are living today. As Rumbak explains, it was alcohol that was partly responsible for destroying the Schmidtsdrift community; they died through neglect, starvation, tuberculosis, HIV/AIDS and alcoholism. They suffered trauma, were displaced and were bored, recurrent afflictions in displaced communities worldwide. (Rumbak 2013)

Alcohol abuse amongst San communities has been widely written about (including Guenther 1997 and Macdonald & Molamu 1999), and in 2000 Godwin documented that the army doctor at the Schmidtsdrift clinic told him that children as young as twelve were addicted to alcohol. He reported alcohol being prominently displayed in the local store and described it as 'starkly utilitarian, carrying only bottom-of-the-line, top-of-the-alcohol-content brands, such as Diamond Fields Late Harvest, a white wine that comes in a silver foil bag, stripped even of the nicety of a bottle'. (Godwin 2000) In an ironic twist, the South African Breweries funded the workshops in these communities struggling with alcoholism.

Rumbak has one textile design, *Dragonfly*, still in production from the Schmidtsdrift !Xun and Khwe artists. This was a linocut she bought from Julietta Carimbwe, originally from Angola, who was the only woman from the project to produce lino prints. Julietta was relocated from Omegain Namibia to Schmidtsdrift with her husband, Katunga. She was born in Mavinga, Angola and didn't attend formal school, however her grandmother passed on traditions and customs to her. Her two children died from illness in Angola, and the rest of her family died in the conflict in Namibia before she was relocated. *My Eland's Heart* records Julietta's words about the art project:

> I want to say that it is my work that sustains my life. When I paint I feel good. I draw just what comes into my mind. I like drawing nature, patterns, animals, trees, seeds … (Sullivan Winberg 2001: 114)

Ultimately, the textile project failed to continue mainly because of politics and infighting. Rumbak reports that she couldn't get anyone at the project to agree to release the images to allow her to transform them into designs and subsequently into royalties for the artists. There was no one in authority that understood the process of design and business development that she attempted. Today the lino prints and designs remain unused in Rumbak's archive.

Omba Arts Trust, a Southern African NGO, saw the textiles that Rumbak produced with the !Xun and Khwe at Schmidtsdrift and asked her to work with them in Namibia. This working relationship is typical of Southern African craft organizations. An NGO working at the grassroots level will bring in a consultant (sometimes from overseas) for an intervention funded by a donor, usually a development organization.

However, just as the BA tail fin design project was unusual in the way it was implemented, here the longevity of the relationship Omba and Rumbak have developed and maintain is unusual and is, in part, responsible for the Art-i-San textile project's sustained success.

Based in Windhoek, Namibia, the Omba Am Trust works with over 450 craft producers, 350 of those being Ju/'hoansi, !Kung and Khwe San. Its aim is to support the sustainable livelihoods of marginalized communities through the development, sales and marketing of quality Namibian products, generating 'sustainable income … through paintings, prints and textiles'. (Supporting the San 2013)

In the first phase of the project in 2002, instigated by UNESCO and the NGO Working Group of Indigenous Minorities in Southern Africa (WIMSA), Omba Arts Trust developed a community income project for the San in Ekoka, in the remote Ohangwena region on the Namibia-Angola border. Ekoka is a resettlement area for approximately 270 San and, typical of such resettlement areas, has a complicated structure established along linguistic lines. The Ongongolo live on one side, the Kwagga on the other and the Kwanyama, the dominant tribe of the Ohangwena region, encircle both.

Invited by Omba, Rumbak travelled to the San communities in Namibia three times in 2002 to work in collaboration with them to facilitate art workshops. As with the !Xun and Khwe in Schmidtsdrift, they began with observational and still-life drawing. The San worked with themes such as veld plants or animals and they produced lino prints, drawings and oil paintings. Rumbak identified San who had an affinity with either printing or painting and developed this further. She felt that they enjoyed the work, focussed and worked hard. Each time she returned to the community, the same artists would attend the workshops as well as others. She found this consistency from a group who usually live a subsistence lifestyle surprising, but encouraging.

Rumbak feels that it is the workshop structure that brought everyone together. She began with drawing skills, asking participants to find things in their surroundings that they found interesting and to draw them. This developed into more complex observation and life drawing and then into oil painting. She found that because the men traditionally carve wooden objects, they really enjoyed wood and lino cutting and immediately had an affinity with it. The women loved colour and tended to want to paint more, working with strong colour palettes.

However, the San artists developed their own imagery. Rumbak would offer up a theme or subject matter in a workshop and see how the San developed it. One of the most memorable was a discussion of the meanings of words and the seven cycles of life. This needs to be framed in the context of working through translators, as Rumbak's English was translated into Kwanyama, however these discussions were rich with inspiration. So, for example, they spoke about three translations of the cycle of life, from birth to adulthood, which facilitated their drawing.

For the casual viewer, the lino prints, paintings and drawings may seem overly simplistic and stylized, much as Thatcher must have thought when she put her handkerchief over the model of Cgoise's British Airways tail fin design of *Animals and Trees*. However, the most remarkable aspect of the work is that the images produced in Rumbak's Schmidtsdrift workshops in the 1990s, the artwork consistently produced by San groups at the Kuru Art Project, as well as the work from the Omba Arts Trust San, show visual affinity. This is regardless of the fact that they were made by different groups, who spoke in varying dialects and who had experienced different lives in separate countries and worked with assorted outside facilitators. Even more interesting is the fact that the images also have a resonance with the vast number of drawings and watercolours produced by six !Xam San artists recorded by early philologists Wilhelm Bleek and Lucy Lloyd between 1875 and 1881 in Cape Town. Historians assume that the drawings, watercolours and small clay figures produced by the !Xam were made at Bleek and Lloyd's instigation. (Szalay 2002: 6) Whatever their origin, it is interesting to note their resemblance to the later, contemporary San works.

These threads of a common imagery between disparate San communities who are both temporally and geographically distant can also be drawn together with narrative. *My Eland's Heart*, the title of Sullivan

Winberg's account of the !Xun and Khwe artists from Schmidtsdrift is taken from a story told to her by artist Manuel Masseka who was born in Angola in 1946. He served in the Portuguese army before working for the SADF in Namibia for twenty years and recounted an allegory to Sullivan Winberg of two friends hunting an eland and the consequences for their families and lives. The eland, an antelope from Eastern and Southern Africa and highly regarded by the San, is a recurring theme throughout their oral narrative and art traditions and, although South African archaeologist John Parkington cautions against generalities (a 'pan-San' theme) in expressive culture, he nevertheless concludes that the San cultural beliefs are widespread, long lasting and capable of being employed in a variety of contexts. (Skotnes 1996: 281-289)

Rumbak reported on the differences between the materials and equipment used by male and female San artists, and anthropologist Mathias Guenther, who lived and worked with the Kuru Development Trust for many years, notes other gendered differences amongst San contemporary art, too. He feels that the women's art (predominantly painting) tends to be more abstract and less representational in style. Resonating with the white South African female designers from Fabricnation and Design Team, he reports artworks with images that 'are themselves innocent of politics, but instead, depict nostalgic veld-set scenes of a somewhat other-worldly past, become political in an environment that draws such scenes into an identity discourse'. (2003: 95-100)

The San produce these traditional images side by side with more modern, popular cultural images such as radios, jeans, televisions and watches. Guenther feels that 'by blending in their "hybrid" pictures, old with new, the artists engage the new economic and social order, while also keeping in check its hegemonic impact. By juxtaposing elements of modernity with those of tradition they refer the former back to the latter and thereby embrace the new post-foraging order on their own terms.' (2003: 95-100) Guenther is referring to the San artists, however, this could easily be applied to other South African contemporary textile designers' interrogation of identity in today's South Africa.

The economic benefits of all the San art projects have been variable, however the Art-i-San textile project is unique because it has provided a sustained income for their artists over the last decade. The lino prints are translated into repeat patterns that can be screen-printed as textile designs, which were originally marketed as the Ekoka Textile range, but have recently been rebranded as Art-i-San Textiles.[7] The designs are flatbed screen-printed in Cape Town onto South African cotton, making them a wholly Southern African product and keeping their production local and manageable. The resulting fabrics are sold in two ways: either as finished products such as tablecloths, bags, napkins, cushions, etc. or fabric sold by the metre. This two-pronged marketing strategy also contributes to the success and longevity of the project. Local manufacturing means that production runs can be contracted and expanded quickly to meet market demand. The fact that the fabric is sold by the metre means that colourways can be easily changed to suit fluctuating fashions.

Omba works with a lawyer to set up legal contracts with Rumbak's Cape Town-based company, which markets, sells and distributes the work in conjunction with them. Each artist earns either a fee from selling their artwork or royalties when the Art-i-San textiles are sold. Omba pays the artists a lump sum once or twice a year and, for several of them, this figure is quite substantial. Omba, in turn, earns a small percentage to cover their administration and organization costs. Omba and le Roux continue to work with the Ekoka artists, introducing San from other resettlement areas in Ohangwena and Omaheke in Namibia to the textile project and Rumbak launched a new Art-i-San textile design at the annual Design Indaba in Cape Town in 2013.

One of the unexpected benefits from this profitable relationship has been to the San's way of life. With the aim of providing independent living to the San, some of whom still live in domestic servitude (a contentious practice which goes back more than 250 years), the Namibian Ministry of Lands and a local NGO have been working to provide agricultural benefits to the San, supporting them to develop fields for crop growing. Le Roux notes that the San artists who receive

Art-i-San royalties generally have much better fields and crops and puts this down to their income from art; with this they are able to hire people to work in their fields and yield better results. (2013)

By employing a lawyer to draw up a legal contract with Rumbak, Omba is securing the intellectual property rights for the Art-i-San artists. However, this is unusual in the typical development model of outside designer interventions with grassroots indigenous groups. As Sauthoff explains: 'Cultural groups, particularly developing rural communities and those with little economic or political leverage, generally have no control over the trivialization of indigenous forms or the revalorization of historically charged symbols for mainstream consumption.' (2004: 41)

Sauthoff speaks of contemporary South African design circles not questioning who holds the rights to cultural material, its appropriation and dissemination. This was made explicit in the late 1990s when a South African interior design company used a design by Kuru artist Thamae Kaashe without his permission for the carpets of the refurbished first class lounge at Johannesburg International Airport (renamed O.R. Tambo International Airport in 2006). The Kuru Art Project approached the company, who apologized and subsequently paid fees for the rights to reproduce the image. (Brown 2013)

While there are valid questions about power relations concerning the stakeholders in these projects, particularly when an outside-funded agency such as an NGO is involved, this chapter seeks to frame the positive benefits of a commercial relationship where each entity – in Art-i-San's case, the San artists, the NGO facilitator and the marketing retailer – have a vested interest and work together to ensure the success and sustainability of their partnership. This is in distinct contrast to the interior design company who used Kaashe's artwork for their own use at Johannesburg International Airport.

The image, culture and traditions of the San communities of Namibia, Botswana and South Africa continue to be appropriated by designers, particularly within graphic communication and advertising. This appropriation reinforces stereotypes, as Buntman describes, when interrogating the use of San visual imagery: 'where the "silenced" Bushman people remain subjected, being expropriated and exploited: a cultural and social "other"'. (1996: 33-34) She describes the San as epitomizing the liminal state between the old and new South Africa, echoing Monto Masako, an artist from the Schmidtsdrift art project, who describes them as 'in-between people'. (Sullivan Winberg 2001: 81)

Although the BA tail fins credited the individual artists who were commissioned for the *Utopia* designs, their financial remuneration was minimal. Cgoise was given a one-off payment, even though her design was used widely on tickets, luggage tags, upholstery and Heathrow Airport buses. (Griswold 2011) While there are further discussions needed around the complex topics of NGO interventions, hegemonic power relations and legacy, the Art-i-San project continues to supply a steady income to a group of marginalized San from Namibia through the production of art and textiles.

Notes

1. In 2001 the South African Council for Scientific and Industrial Research (CSIR) acknowledged the San's prior intellectual property rights after they patented the *hoodia* plant as a weight loss drug. A series of historic legal agreements have now been reached between the San and companies who are developing it for commercial purposes. <http://www.protimos.org/what -we-do/iprs-and biodiversity/san-ipr-project/backgr ound/> [Accessed 1 July 2013].

2. South Africa museums removed the controversial 'Bushmen' diorama displays in 2001 and the remains of Sara Baartman (referred to as 'the Hottentot Venus') were repatriated from the Musée de l'Homme in Paris to South Africa in 2002. (le Roux, 2004: 58) <http:// news.nationalgeographic.co.uk/news/2001/06/0606 _wiremuseums.html> [Accessed 1 July 2013].

3. Including Poland, South Africa, The Netherlands, Australia, Saudi Arabia, Botswana, Egypt and more.

4. Cg'ose Ntcöx'o (Cgoise) (born 1950, died 2013) <http ://www.kuruart.com/profile.php?Id=3> [Accessed 1 July 2013].

5. *Drum* Magazine was launched in the newly established Apartheid era 1950s and reflected the dynamic changes that were taking place among the new urban black and South African – African, Indian and Coloured – communities. <http://www.sahistory.org.za/topic/drum -magazine> [Accessed 1 July 2013].

6. Fabricnation was established in 2007 by designers Jane Solomon and Jann Cheifitz who are inspired by the African textile tradition, rendered in a modern urban context with its blending of diverse sources and influences to create the fabric of a nation. <www .fabricnation.co.za/about> [Accessed 1 July 2013].

7. Ekoka is the name of the village where one of the first workshops was held. In 2010 the Omba Arts Trust rebranded the textile range as Art-i-San Textiles.

Bibliography

Bleek, W. & Lloyd L. (1911), *Specimens of Bushman Folklore*, http://www.sacredtexts.com/afr/sbf/index.htm [Accessed 1 January 2014].

Blomkamp, N. (2009) *District 9*, film produced by QED International, WingNut Films, TriStar Pictures.

Brown, M. (2013), email correspondence with Kuru Art Project Coordinator.

Buntman, B. (1996), 'Selling with the San: Representations of Bushman People and Artefacts in South African Print Advertisements', *Visual Anthropology*, vol. 8: 33–54.

Burns Coleman, E. (2005), *Aboriginal Art, Identity and Appropriation*, Aldershot: Ashgate Publishing.

Godwin, P. (2000), *Bushmen*, <http://ngm .nationalgeographic.com/ngm/0 102/ feature6/fulltext .html> [Accessed 18 June 2013].

Gollifer, A. & Egner, J. (2011), *I Don't Know Why I Was Created: Dada, Coex'ae Qgam*, Gaborone, Botswana: Eggsson Books.

Gordon, R.J. (1999), *The Bushman Myth: The Making of a Namibian Underclass*, Boulder: Westview Press.

Griswold, S. (2011), *I Don't Know Why I was Created - Book Review* <http://www.mmegi.bw/indexphp?sid=7 &aid=1053&dir=2011/ October/Friday28> [Accessed 1 July 2013].

Guenther, M. (1997), 'From Lords of the Desert to Rubbish People: The Colonial and Contemporary State of the Nharo Bushmen', in P. Skotnes (ed.), *Miscast: Negotiating the Presence of the Bushmen*. Cape Town: University of Cape Town Press.

Guenther, M. (2003), 'Contemporary Bushman Art, Identity Politics and the Primitivism Discourse', Anthropologica, vol. 45, no. 1: 95–110.

le Roux, K. (2013), interview with author.

le Roux, W. (ed.) (2004), *Voices of the San: Living in Southern Africa Today*, Cape Town: Kwela Books.

Macdonald, D. & Molamu, L. (1999), 'From Pleasure to Pain: A Social History of Basarwa/San Alcohol Use in Botswana', in Peele, S. & Grant M. (eds), *Alcohol and Pleasure: A Health Perspective*. Canadian Anthropological Society: Taylor & Francis, 73–86.

Meyer, C., Mason T. & Brown, P. (1996), *Contemporary San Art of Southern Africa: KuruArt Project D'Kar, Botswana*. White River: The Artists' Press.

Myers, F. (2004), 'Ontologies of the Image and Economies of Exchange', *American Ethnologist*, vol. 31, no. 1: 1–16.

Oosthuizen, T. (2004), 'In Marketing Across Cultures: Are You Enlightening the World or Are You Speaking in Tongues?' *Design Issues*, vol. 20, no. 2 (Spring): 61–72.

Proudly South African About Us (2013), http://www.proudlysa.co.za/consumer-site [Accessed 26 July 2013].

Rabbethge-Schiller, H. (2006), *Memory and Magic: Contemporary Art of the !Xun and Khwe*. Johannesburg: Jacana.

Rumbak, Cheryl (2013), interview with author.

San Bushman Art, <http://www.kalkbaymodern.co.za/cp/10074/san-bushman-art> [Accessed 1 July 2013].

Sauthoff, M. (2004), 'Walking the Tightrope: Comments on Graphic Design in South Africa', *Design Issues*, vol. 20, no. 2 (Spring): 34–50.

Scheepers, C. (1991), *Contemporary Bushman Art of Southern Africa: Kuru Cultural Project of D'Kar*, Namibia: Die Republikein Publishers.

Skotnes, P. (2007), *Claim to the Country: The Archive of Lucy Lloyd and Wilhem Bleek*, Jacana Media (Pty) Ltd.

Skotnes, P. (ed.) (1996), *Miscast: Negotiating the Presence of the Bushmen*, Cape Town: University of Cape Town Press.

Skotnes, P. (2009), *The Unconquerable Spirit: George Stow's History Painting of the San*, Jacana Media (Pty) Ltd.

Skotnes, P. (ed.) (2010), *Rock Art Made in Translation: Framing Images From and of the Landscape*. Johannesburg & Cape Town: Jacana Media (Pty) Ltd.

Soloman, J. & Cheifitz, J. (2010), *Category Error 2*. <http://www.fabricnation.co.za/exhibitions/category-error-2/> [Accessed 18 July 2013].

Stone-Lee, O. (2013), *I Was Handbagged by Mrs Thatcher* <http://www.bbc.co.uk/news/uk-politics-11518330> [Accessed 18 July 2013].

Sullivan Winberg, M. (2001), *My Eland's Heart: A Collection of Stories and Art, !Xun and Khwe San Art and Culture Project*, Claremont, South Africa: David Phillips Publishers.

Supporting the San <www.omba.org.na/successstories/8-success-stories /22-supporting-the san> [Accessed l July 2013].

Szalay, M. (ed.) (2002), *The Moon as Shoe: Drawings of the San*, Zurich: Verlag Scheidegger & Spiess AG, 6.

Van Der Post, L. (1958), *The Lost World of the Kalahari*, London: Penguin.

Weinberg, P. (1997), *In Search of the San*, Johannesburg: The Porcupine Press.

39

HENEQUÉN, A GREEN FIBER WITH A COMPLEX HISTORY IN YUCATAN (2016/2021)

Yosi Anaya

EDITOR'S INTRODUCTION

Yosi Anaya is Professor of Visual Art at the University Veracruzana, Mexico. Her writing here draws on field research and interviews undertaken between 1997 and 2018 with designer and maker Luisa Vogel in the Yucatán region of Mexico. Sisal from Yucatán, known as henequén in Mexico, is a plant fiber harvested from agave genus *Agave fourcroydes*, one of two hundred agave species found in parts of the Americas. The plants are used for a variety of products, including the use of blue agave (*Agave tequilana*) to make the liquor tequila, as well as the sisal discussed in this article.

Sisal is a bast fiber, as is the example of braided and knitted marram grass made by Angus MacPhee included in the memory section. In this writing, Anaya outlines the history of this somewhat overlooked fiber, including the legends of its first discovery and proposes that the plant could be considered sacred to Mayan peoples, despite the plant's use on an industrial scale as twine for the McCormick reaper, a mechanical wheat harvester used throughout North America from the 1830s.

Instead of the American spelling of Louise Vogel, Luisa which is more familiar in the Spanish language, is used in the text. Earlier versions were presented at Uluslararasi Moda ve Tekstil Tasarimi Sempozyumu / 1st International Fashion and Textile Design Symposium (2012) at Akdeniz University, Antalya Turkey and the Simposio de Internacional de Diseño Sostenible (2013) at Institución Universitaria Tecnológico Pascual Bravo, Medellín Colombia. The text included here is an expanded version of the original text first published in Spanish in 2016, and translated into English for this publication by the author.

Based on extensive field work by Vogel, Anaya recounts a unique aspect of henequén production overlooked by earlier ethnographic studies but important to textile knowledge: the Mayans do not spin the fibers into thread for traditional weaving. Instead the individual fiber length dictates entirely the potential size of cloth that can be woven. In the concluding paragraphs appropriation is used in a positive and pragmatic sense – Luisa Vogel's design influence appears well beyond her own production, helping to bring innovation and contemporary relevance to traditional ways of working with the fiber.

Henequén, A Green Fiber with a Complex History in Yucatan

Yosi Anaya

If there is one plant that could stand as the symbol of the Yucatan, it would have to be the henequén plant. In tracing its story, the history of the Yucatan will be revealed in all its diverse layers. Although the peninsula is home to many fiber plants and although they have all played important roles, the henequén is the one plant that was there in the beginning – and still is.[1]

Although the name "sisal" has been applied to the various fibers produced from different agaves of Mexico, it was from the Yucatec port of Sisal (see-saul), from the 18th to the 20th Century, that "bales and crates of fiber, rope and binder twine were shipped to the rest of the world."[2] Thus henequén (known abroad by the generic term sisal) is the fiber extracted from the *Agave fourcroydes*, the most outstanding plant native to the Yucatan Peninsula. This paper explains not only the processing involved in the elaboration of henequén, but it also works through its background, context, history traditional processing and current production. I reflect on the work of a New York designer and craftswoman, Luisa Vogel, who moved to Yucatan in the late 1970's and who has remained behind the scenes all these years, promoting the usage of henequén through the different and well hand-crafted artefacts, which she develops in her small workshop.

I claim that her continued, limited-edition designs have stimulated the varied production of henequén artefacts among the Mayan craftswomen and men throughout the region, spurring tradition onto the paths of innovation. The diversity of her almost one-of-a-kind bags, purses and other utilitarian objects together with various other conjunctional factors have given henequén a renewed yet subtle prominence, to the effect that presently, practically every craft store in Yucatan offers a large variety of henequén hand-made products, off-springs of her original designs; and these, wherever presented or sold, are definitely identified as being Yucatec. Above all, I intend to underscore that despite the henequén industry's boom and fall, the cultural relevance of the fiber has continued in Mayan identity in the Yucatan Peninsula through the centuries. Thus, the current proliferation of henequén handicrafts is part of that heritage.

THE SETTING AND CONTEXT

Henequén has for millennia been a part of Mayan traditional life, integrated into Mayan thought. Because this fiber is seemingly lowly, spiny and aggressive, it was mostly overlooked by the chroniclers who came with the Conquest and subsequent colonization. There are no detailed records regarding its use, process and its importance in Mayan societies at the time of European contact, other than the minor mentions in Fernández de Oviedo[3], who recorded that hammocks

---

[1] Luisa Vogel, "Removing Fiber from Henequen Plants" http://backyardnature.net/m/crafts/fiberout.htm

[2] Sterling Evans. *The History and Ecology of the Henequen-Wheat Complex for Mexico and the American and Canadian Plains, 1880-1950* (Environmental History Series) 2007, Texas A & M University Press College Station

[3] Gonzalo Fernández de Oviedo y Valdés, mentioned in Evans, p. 37. published in 1493, *Historia General de las Indias* (Capítulo VII del libro II. "Los cuarteles de arriba son Castilla y León, las anclas como Almirante, bajo izquierda es América con islas y tierra firme") and in 1536, *Sumario de la Natural Historia de las Indias*

Source: Yosi Anaya, 'Henequén, A green fibre with a complex history in Yucatan'. 2016 Spanish version/2021 English translation by Yosi Anaya. Reproduced with permission.

were made from the strong fiber and that these could be of great use for the armies in Spain; also Fray Diego de Landa mentioned in his notable Relación de Cosas de Yucatán (1566) that there were "infinite things that could be made from henequén."[4]

But while others may have mentioned the plant in similar ways, there was no colonial effort to cultivate the plant on a plantation basis until the 19th century, when according to Sterling Evans, "It came to be one of those culturally ubiquitous and useful farm and household items that performed a million functions, perhaps as duct tape does today." (Evans 2007: 24) Henequén's ubiquity in Yucatan, manifest in the common usages among the Maya, continues today as it did five hundred or more years ago: the fiber and twisted twine serve to make ropes, cord, nets (for fishing, hunting, carrying and tying), hanging baskets, hammocks, bags, sacks and small cloths. According to Roland Chardon, the various age-old terms for the plants and their uses indicate that among the Maya, "henequen was a garden crop for family use… and that it also provided the necessary fiber for ropes and cordage in the Mayan economy."[5] This is significant because in the 19th century, the Peninsula came to experience a major transformation.

The landscape of most of the Yucatan Peninsula (currently composed of three Mexican states: Campeche, Yucatán and Quintana Roo) consists of a flat lime bedrock floor with very little earth and a varied thick, low vegetation of trees and undergrowth. It was amidst this diversity that the henequén plants grew scattered throughout the terrain and accompanying vegetation. During the colonial period, major fortune-making products had taken the forefront and were the concern of the Conquistadores and overlords throughout the New Spain – these being primarily precious metals, such as gold and silver (nonexistent in Yucatan) and secondly, precious dye-woods, which were all exploited harshly in all ways possible. Thus, from the low jungles of the Peninsula, it was logwood that was exploited and exported to Europe in large quantities for dyeing a deep black the cloths of courtly wear in Spain and elsewhere.

Deep study of pre-Columbian pictorial motifs depicting henequén as fibers, plants or objects, still has not been seriously undertaken. Although one outstanding stone carving – Lintel 24 from Yaxchilán, in southern Chiapas, depicts Lady X'oc, priestess and legendary co-ruler of that city state in the 8th century AC, in an act of self-sacrifice pulling an henequén rope with obsidian blades through her tongue. This painful bloodletting ceremony meant that she could be deemed worthy of her new position, for it provoked the visions needed for her husband's rule and she, beside him. This impressive stone lintel actually deploys the importance of henequén, here as a ritual rope, along with obsidian, alongside weavings and the regalia pertinent to ritual. The provenance of these materials and manufacturing processes were considered to be of divine origin. And for this long embedded belief, they continue to hold a place in the folklore of the Maya.

The legend of a mythological wise man, Zamná, who wanted to add the plants to his herbarium, pinpoints the discovery of the henequén fiber: Zamná and his servant were walking through the brush when he was stabbed by the spine at the tip of a henequén penca (long leaf of the agave). One of his servants then cut off the offending leaf and beat it continuously in punishment. This revealed the fibers inside. A varying version of this legend tells that Zamná tripped on a rock and his servants punished the rock by whipping it with henequén leaves, until its fibers flowed forth. Zamná is said to have seen this as an omen; he then declared, "Life was born in the company of pain; that through the wound was revealed a plant of great usefulness for the people." (Evans 2007: 34) Indeed, not only the fibers but also henequén thorns came to be involved in the daily rituals of bloodletting among the Maya, mentioned by Diego de Landa in 1536.

---

in Spain. See Juan Bautista Avalle-Arce. *Sumario de la Natural Historia de la Indias de Fernández de Oviedo*. (Biblioteca Anaya, Bilbao, 1963).

[4] Diego de Landa, Mentioned in Sterling Evans, p.37. See Tozzer, Alfred M., trans. Landa's *Relación de las Cosas de Yucatan: A Translation*. Papers of the Peabody Museum of American Archaeology and Ethnology, Vol. XVIII (Cambridge Mass: Harvard University, 1941).

[5] Roland Chardon (*cited in Evans, 24*). See Chardon, Roland. *Geographic Aspects of Plantation Agriculture in Yucatan*. (Washington, D.C.: National Academy of Science, 1961).

According to Evans, who extensively studied the mutual interdependence of the henequén and wheat industries, […] the ancient Maya rasped more fiber from local plants and discovered many uses for it. Over time they made sandals, bags and baskets, thatch for roofs, traps and bows for hunting, and nets for fishing, needles from its spines and many other household useful items. They also used henequen plants for decorative purposes. More unique uses included fashioning musical instruments from its components, fermenting its juices to make wine, and making a cloth wrap with which to bind prisoners of war. (2007: 13)

And I may add, henequén was also employed for making the cloth for the sacred bundles, which are also depicted in the stone lintels of Yaxchilán and Bonampak.

In the diverse Mesoamerican cosmologies, all things in the natural world are considered to have an owner, a guardian being, to whom permission is asked for in order to make use of the plant, animal or geological or physical entity, such as a river, land, cave, a determined space and its resources. Every plant that comes to have particular importance within a culture will certainly have beliefs and mythologies engulfing it. These are integrated into that culture's cosmology. Would it then not be valid to claim that henequén, among the Maya, is a sacred plant, in the same way that similar agaves in other parts of Mexico have been and still are considered sacred? This indeed is the reason for its perseverance on a local level, despite its industrial boom and exploitation to which it was subjected. The traditional uses continued to exist – quietly – while major industrial production surged and dominated the scene. These traditional uses continued on after henequén's industrial demise that shook the entire Yucatan Peninsula.

Henequén and Mayan daily life

At a given point with the inventions of the Industrial Revolution in the United States, henequén became the source material for a major industry. It was launched to the world as the best natural fiber for ropes and twine, not only for ships but also as the best binding twine for the large-scale mechanical wheat harvester, known as the McCormick reaper, invented in the United States and used throughout the Great Plains of the United States and Canada. Yucatec economy came to be established around henequén, which came to be known as the *Green Gold* of Yucatan, accounting for great, accrued wealth among the landowner families, who staked fortunes on this marvelous, endemic fiber grown exclusively in the Peninsula. Plantations were set up that turned the Yucatec landscape into a huge monoculture for large-scale fiber exploitation for export. Although these lands came to be owned by an elite class, henequén was harvested by hand by Mayan workers, who also worked in the processing plants. Despite industrial developments to partially process the henequén, the actual cutting of the *pencas*, once a plant is seven years old, has to be done with a hand-slung machete, cutting each *penca* one by one.

Eventually, in the 20th Century with the temporary halt in exportations due to the Mexican Revolution and other world factors, rope-making factories (formerly only in the US and Canada) were then established within Yucatan, not only to process the fiber, as had been the case earlier, but also to manufacture ropes of all sorts, floor carpets, sacks, and coarse cloth for the world.

Given henequén's world status and the temporary standstill in exportation at the beginning of the 20th century, native henequén agaves were smuggled out of Yucatan, and sold to the British, who in turn took them to their colonies to be reproduced. Kenya, Madagascar, and India were primarily allocated to grow them on a large scale, later developing and cloning their own breeds adapted to foreign soil. Thus this once endemic fiber was put on the world market at cheaper prices, which continue to reign. This, of course, eventually caused the drastic fall of the henequén industry throughout Yucatan. Nonetheless, in 1933, henequén plants were still the most outstanding feature in the Yucatec landscape, whereby a perceptive visitor, such as Sergei Eisenstein, would be impacted by the extensive fields of large henequén agaves growing out of the lime rock soil of the Peninsula, to the degree that one of the chapters of his film *Qué Viva México!* was cast in such a setting.

The commercial competition from abroad eventually brought the fall of the henequén industry throughout the Peninsula. This occurred in the latter second half of the 20th Century, causing a major crisis in the economy of Yucatan. The fields were abandoned, the major industrial weaving factories (for henequén floor carpets) such as Cordemex, started to close down. Processing plants were dismantled and the former henequén haciendas began to be sold or left derelict. Despite widespread bankruptcy of the industry and its magnates, the Mayan use of henequén pervaded in small scale, traditional hand-crafted productions, such as hammocks, Mayan carry bags known as *sabukán*, rope, twine, and netting – as had always been.

The henequén agave is an impressive plant as are other varieties of agaves, all native to the Americas. *Agave fourcroydes* of Yucatan is a particularly large one. Thus the length of the fibers running lengthwise along the interior of these pointed strong leaves is determined by the length of the *penca*. Some varieties produce henequén fibers of up to a meter and half long. For Mayans, its value lies in the length and whiteness of the fiber – white being a 'color' most appreciated in the extremely hot climate of Yucatan, where traditional dress for men and women is also, markedly, a brilliant white.

Traditional Mayan daily life in villages is centered on the *solar*, that lot of land where the house is situated with its outdoor space at the back. Very often there are several such houses in these extended family compounds. The Mayan house is traditionally a thatched, oval-shaped house with a door in the center at the front and another opposite that leads towards the back house, where usually an adjacent awning or porch is situated or a separate thatched construction that serves as the kitchen. The backspace, that could be called a patio, has trees; it can be an orchard but also the area to keep household animals such as chickens, turkeys, dogs, cats, or where larger animals such as cows, goats, donkey, horse or pigs spend the night. The interiors of homes have but a few objects. The inhabitants' clothes hang from a wooden beam or in a wardrobe, and during the day, the hammocks are rolled up and coiled into loose knots, hanging from their wall hooks at the sides of the room, so that the house space is freed up. Hammocks are also used for sitting, resting, socialising and sleeping. Thus the home in these tropics is minimalist and integrated.

Those sticks on the floor were the loom she was using

Thirty years ago after many travels to remote craft villages in Central Mexico, Luisa Vogel, who had studied textile design at Fashion Institute of Technology, a branch of the State University of New York, moved to Merida, the capital of the state of Yucatan, where she first encountered the henequén fiber. These were moments when the henequén industry had gone bankrupt; the henequén haciendas were being sold and only but a few of the processing plants were functioning. Not many henequén products were visible and those that were, were utilitarian – bags of traditional sorts made carelessly, because the Mexican Government's craft program to support craftsmen would buy up any craft production, regardless of quality, even though there was no market for them. These came to be stored indefinitely in government warehouses. Luisa recalls that at that time the government was pushing aniline colors because it was considered that the tourists were mostly looking for color in Mexican souvenirs and handicrafts.

Being highly interested in native Mexican craft traditions, Luisa began researching and visiting villages throughout. The images of henequén artefacts in the collections of the National Institute of Anthropology (INAH) and documented in a catalogue of the 1980's served as a guide. She thus began searching for the actual makers of the documented artefacts. She tells: "*When we began looking for craft, I was surprised to find no visible sign of weaving, even though we were travelling the towns pinpointed as centers for crafting henequen.*"[6]

At the time, she visited many villages from which the documented artefacts came from, yet many of them were hard to find.

As she delved deeper, a complex scene was revealed. The limited variety as well as the specialization processes pertaining to a given type of artefact in certain villages was made evident. Also was revealed the familial form of working within the compounds, so

---

[6] Vogel, Louise. "Henequen (Sisal)" http://backyardnature.net/m/crafts/henequen.htm

that the entire process was achieved with each family member contributing his or her part.

> Interestingly, like most Maya activities, producing craft in a village is a communal activity. The chores of washing, combing, carding, selecting fibers of the same length, setting up the warps, and other chores are done by different people, usually the people all coming from the same family compound. (ibid)

Thus, the men cut and extract the henequén fibers from each *penca* – pounding, then washing them, setting them out to dry, then combing them. From there, the best and longest fibers are selected.

The transcendental moment in understanding the full henequén process came when she discovered that the fibers for weaving on the backstrap loom were <u>not</u> spun into thread.[7] Rather, individual fibers are laid out on the warping board, then transferred onto the loom, where one continuous, sturdy string is used to make looped heddles that sustain the warp shed. Thus, the henequén cloths are determined by the length of the selected fibers, and hence the backstrap loom for henequén differs from the more known backstrap loom for weaving cloth panels with threads. That is, for weaving there is no continuous long thread for either warp or weft. This discovery had not been documented previously by ethnologists.

> Doña Juana Francisca invited us into the rear of her cement block, one-room house. She did her weaving on the dirt floor of a lean-to structure where she cooked over an open fire. On the ground were what appeared to be a few well-worn sticks in a pile of henequén fiber. More amazing was the realization that the warp was made of single strands of fiber rather than thread; I never heard this mentioned when I spoke with craft experts. This was a revelation, and I was definitely hooked! (idem)

Mayan henequén cloths can only measure the length of the fibers – from eighty centimeters to a meter and a half at most. This fact makes them particularly precious. A henequén cloth made of single individual fibers is a rarity, a truly very fine weaving, and is usually destined for a craft competition. Most weavers group several fibers at a time for strength, depending on the thickness of the cloth desired.

The question of width was also surprisingly peculiar given that the henequén cloths, called *sacán*, are not very wide – usually not more than forty centimeters in breadth, and sometimes even less. And although this may seem rather strange or even limited, the length is based on the shape of the *sabukán*, the shoulder bag used by workers to carry their tools and food to their fields. The weavers tend to work using the same criteria, routine and measurements. Their warping boards' longest measurement is set for a *sabukán* cloth: 40 x 80 cm. It is also a known fact that backstrap weaving is determined by the comfortable weight of the fibers and loom on the woman's waist as well as by the arm's reach of the weaver. Yet here, there is no heddle stick as in normal backstrap weaving – only the hand reaching through the fibers of the warp shed to put the weft in place. One hand puts the fibers halfway into the open shed from one side; then, the other hand enters from the other side to pull them through. When the fiber length ends there is an overlapping with the next fiber to make it almost unnoticeable on the cloth. Thicker, stronger cloths have several fibers grouped together and very fine light cloths are woven with few fibers in both warp and weft.

This particular form of weaving with this so-called 'hard' fiber still has another distinguishing factor: the blade of the beater, known as a *machete*, is different from that of other Mesoamerican looms, for it is slightly curved only on one side and is completely flat on the other. It is thus adapted to beating the henequén. Luisa considers that *"these subtleties make this hard fiber cloth something more than just another woven product."* (ibid) She thus found out that henequén cloths are made only in certain villages. Henequén hammocks are worked only in a few sites, while in other villages, the *sabukán* bag is woven. That is, a craftsman or craftswoman woman works usually in their own specialty, and does not necessarily dominate all the techniques with henequén involved in the other processes.

Luisa has delivered workshops in various Mayan communities to maintain traditions. These have entailed

---

[7] The backstrap loom has been and is used widely throughout all the Americas.

teaching techniques from other villages – not to train them in other techniques and processes, but so that knowledge of these may help them make better what they do. That is, her intention is to enrich the crafts people's knowledge of what they do, through an awareness of the other techniques carried out by Mayan artisans in other parts and the possibilities that these render. In this way, with broader knowledge, the maker excels even more in his or her own specialty, perhaps even opening up to new creativities within traditional routines.

Although in many parts of the Peninsula various crafting processes are carried out, these activities during Luisa's research seemed apparently scarce, given that the products are usually made for local use. Making henequén products, in general, has not been a *modus vivendi*, but a complement to people's lives. An artisan could not sustain himself from making henequén bags, for example, but takes them to the weekly market and offers for sale to market goers.

> And so, our education into the ways of hard fiber weaving started there. I had no knowledge of the Yucatec Maya language, and Clementina [her Mayan associate] had no experience with the specific Maya vocabulary related to sisal craft. We began to visit villages, observing, sometimes participating in the hand rasping, the washing and drying, and setting up warps and looms. (ibid)

Later, in response to the opportunity to enter a state competition, Luisa designed three bags and formed a team so that each artisan worked her own specialty:

> ...one prepared and dyed the fiber, another produced the cloth and the third made the handbag. Because we had submitted a team project we did not receive the top award but our designs were included among the most outstanding designs exhibited. We received honorable mention in the competition and pictures of the bags appeared in the local newspapers. This recognition gave our project validity among the henequen artisans. (ibid)

Luisa first posed to herself the following challenge: not to intervene in the traditional *sabukán*-making, but to reshape the actual bag in as many ways possible – such as gathering the sides, folding the bag to give it another form and so on. Eventually, she commenced working with the actual henequén cloths to explore diverse shapes. These have sprouted multifarious explorations involving, colors, shapes, folding, pleating and above all, sewing techniques which demand high quality finishes, such as braiding, cording and invisible seams; so that in every case, the henequén qualities are not disguised, but made evident. These involve the luster of the fiber, and its visibility both on the outside and within the bag. Her concern has always been that the bags as well as the other henequén products she makes have exemplary finishes.

In response to color, she commenced the exploration of vegetable dyes for new color combinations, including non-symmetrical stripes in the weavings. Using mostly bark dyes endemic to the Peninsula, diverse brown and ochres came to be her favourites. Although she and Clementina occasionally would harvest wild indigo, dying the fibers with the fresh plant is something that she considers necessary because of the nature of the Yucatec vegetation. "To the modern Maya, *'good henequen'* is *'white henequen.'* Therefore, when we dye *henequen, we're utilizing the dye stuffs the ancient Maya used, but not necessarily the way they used them.*"[8]

Luisa considers that, it is important that people in the contemporary world *desire* the henequén products. She herself hand-rolls the fibers on her thigh to make her own thread to sew up her bags and objects. Thus, the original bags, transformed *sabukanes* in diverse natural colors (almost plaids), were made over the years, each time searching for a new way to use the cloth and working in a similar way as the Mayan women. Sometimes in one-of-a-kind editions, at times several of a kind were made varying the cloth and its striped designs. The Mayan women themselves do not repeat more than once or twice a given color pattern. In laying each thread for the warp, they strive for innate symmetry. When weaving using more than one color, the weavers will do warp sequences that are balanced designs, which create a mirror image off the center of their cloth. Luisa herself has lost count of the multiple

---

[8] Louise Vogel. "Natural Dyes in Yucatan" http://backyardnature .net/m/crafts/yuc-dye.htm

designs she has executed, and although she may have made only one of a given design, that design of a bag is however found replicated many times, found in multiple craft stores with varying cloths, for that design has been taken up and appropriated by Mayan craftswomen throughout.

Currently one sees a diversity of models, some highly stylish. Although the majority are not made with the care and emphasis that Luisa puts into her bags, they are nonetheless proliferating in diverse interpretations; and some of her first designs are still currently made by the artisans. Mayan creativity too has taken traditional models of bags and integrated natural dyes to embellish them. Thus quite fashionable bags are produced as accessories, with appeal for urban dwellers. Additionally, many other objects from henequén fiber are now found in the craft boutiques of Yucatan, which Luisa originally explored as experiments, such as the coiled basket-boxes that she started, henequén place mats for table settings, henequén cushions, hardened meshed fiber boxes, and diverse accessories for the home. One can now also find earrings and toys. Clementina, her former associate, too has taken the craftmaking to her home village from where she produces substantial quantities of henequén products developed and learned during her workshop years with Luisa.

Luisa's current project involves going beyond the normal size of bags – that is going beyond the size limits of traditional henequén cloth – by joining several of the cloths for making large functional bags. And curiously enough, even Saks Fifth Avenue has ordered some samples of bags to try out. However, distinct qualities remain in the henequén – because it is, after all, completely crafted by hand: it is time consuming;

minor supposed faults in the material are sometime visible, such as its innate stiffness or flexibility which makes a machine mechanized production impossible. Because they take time to make, she produces them in very limited editions. Like the Maya, Luisa herself does not live from henequén bag-making. It is an activity that complements life. In her case, it is a creative one, and satisfaction comes in seeing that innovation regenerates and furthers the tradition.

Field Interviews

Anaya Yosi, Fieldnotes from interviews and hands-on fieldwork with Louise Vogel in Yucatán (1997, 1998, 1999, 2007, 2008, 2010, 2011, 2012, 2016, 2018).

Books

Chardon, Roland. 1961, *Geographic Aspects of Plantation Agriculture in Yuatán*. (Washington, D.C.: National Academy of Science,).

Evans, Sterling. *Bound in Twine: The History and Ecology of the Henequen-Wheat Complex for Mexico and the American and Canadian Plains, 1880–1950*. Environmental History Series. (College Station, Texas A & M University, 2007).

Internet Sources

Vogel, Louise. "Henequen (Sisal)" http://backyardnature .net/m/crafts/henequen.htm (last consulted: 28/08/2021).

——— "Removing Fiber from Henequen Plants" http:// backyardnature.net/m/crafts/fiberout.htm (last consulted: 28/08/2021).

——— "Natural Dyes in Yucatan" http://backyardnature .net/m/crafts/yuc-dye.htm (last consulted: 28/08/2021).

FURTHER READING: PRODUCTION

Bean, Susan S., Diana K. Myers and Rinzin O. Dorji, 'Modeling a Future for Handmade Textiles: Bhutan in the Twenty-First Century', *The Textile Museum Journal* (2019): 52–73, doi:10.7560/TMJ4605.

Article introduces the specific context of handweaving in Bhutan and steps taken to maintain the relevance, and ultimately survival, of contemporary handweaving. While geographically specific the writers aim to offer information applicable to other geographic contexts where handweaving continues in contemporary culture.

Beckert, Sven. *Empire of Cotton: A New History of Global Capitalism*, London: Penguin Random House, 2014.

Global history and capitalism is charted through cotton. Written from the perspective of Europe the lengthy study brings together cotton's trade, production and consumption.

Butler Greenfield, Amy. *A Perfect Red: Empire, Espionage, and the Quest for Color and Desire*, London: Harper Perennial, 2006.

Historical account of how cochineal, which is used to dye cloth red, has been traded, protected and used. Beginning with the sixteenth century the book maps the power of fashions to drive demand and production, as well as myths and misunderstandings that surround the cochineal insect.

Benjamin, Walter. 'The Work of Art in Age Mechanical Reproduction', in *Illuminations*, ed. Hannah Arendt, 217–51, New York: Schocken Books, 1968, English translation.

Benjamin's oft-cited essay was written in German in 1935. In it he observes that mechanical reproduction removes the unique aura of a work of art, resulting in debates around art's authenticity and the aesthetics of politics.

Burman, Barbara (ed.). *The Culture of Sewing: Gender, Consumption and Home Dressmaking*, Oxford and New York: Berg, 1999.

Anthology focuses on European and American home dress making with examples drawn from the past two hundred years offering a reminder that while we are now swamped with mass produced clothing, this excess remains a relatively recent phenomenon.

Dahl, Sonja. 'America's Indigo Obsession: From Colonial Plantations to Contemporary DIY Ethos', Crosscurrents: Land, Labor, and the Port: Textile Society of America's 15th Biennial Symposium Proceedings 2016, 960. http://digitalcommons.unl.edu/tsaconf/960.

Transcript of a performance-lecture based on oral histories and storytelling that opens with an account of indigo's origins in Liberia before recounting some of the changing associations of the dyestuff in the context of the United States.

Haraway, Donna, *Staying with the Trouble: Making Kin in the Chthulucene*, Durham: Duke University Press, 2016.

Haraway is a prolific writer, perhaps best known for "A Cyborg Manifesto" (1985). Credited with contributing to discourses in science and feminism, the Chthulucene of this book's title offers an alternative to the current age of the Anthropocene and advocates for "making-with" in place of "self-making" in response to the environmental crisis.

Klein, Naomi. *No Logo*, London: Harper Perennial, 2000.

Organised in four parts: No Space, No Choice, No Jobs, No Logo, Klein's best-selling book tackles topics such as American and Asian sweatshops. Global branding is often condemned and, in the final section, Klein discusses some movements aimed at ending sweat shop labour.

Livingstone, Joan and John Ploof (eds). *The Object of Labor: Art, Cloth, and Cultural Production*, Chicago: School of Art Institute of Chicago Press and Cambridge, MA and London: The MIT Press, 2007.

Extensive collection of essays and artist's projects with supporting images that address the theme of labour and the production of textiles. Approaches cover historical, economic, social as well as personal.

Miller, Daniel and Sophie Woodward (eds). *Global Denim*, Oxford: Berg, 2011.

Nine contributors by anthropologists around the world consider the ubiquity and popularity of blue jeans. Written from the social sciences the texts are informed by ethnographic research methods, rather than global history or fashion theory.

Snodgrass, Susan (ed.). *Anne Wilson: Wind/Rewind/Weave*, Knoxville: Knoxville Museum of Art & WhiteWalls, Inc., 2011.

Exhibition catalogue for Wilson's community weaving project *Local Industry*. Essays by Glenn Adamson, Jenni Sorkin, Julia Bryan-Wilson, Philis Alvic and Laura Y. Liu.

Torimaru, Sadae and Tomoko Torimaru, *Imprints on Cloth: 18 Years of Field Research among the Miao People of Guizhou, China*, trans. Yoshiko Iwamoto Wada, Fukuoka: Akishige Tada, 2004.

Bilingual Japanese and English study of indigo dye and dress traditions of the Miao peoples. Detailed oral and image accounts of production steps documenting a variety of techniques.

PART SIX

COMMUNITY

PART INTRODUCTION

Textiles can play a central role in establishing community ties. They can also be deployed for exactly the opposite: to ostracize and alienate an individual from a community. This section begins with an example of the latter. Nathaniel Hawthorne's *The Scarlet Letter* (1850) tells the story of a woman made to embroider and wear a scarlet coloured letter 'A' as the punishment for what her community assumes to be the actions of an adulteress. Here, the use of the textile is to identify and mark out an individual and ensure they remain apart from the community.

From Hawthorne's historical fiction, which is set centuries before its publication date, writing then moves to an excerpt from Joseph McBrinn's book *Queering the Subversive Stitch: Men and the Culture of Needlework* (2021). McBrinn's predominantly historical account of men's contribution to needlework makes public communities that Rozsika Parker's book *The Subversive Stitch: Embroidery and the Making of the Feminine* (1984) did not consider. Where Parker's earlier study recognized that needlework acted both as a form of oppression and a tool to act against it, McBrinn's study recognizes that periods of increased interest in needlework by men have often coincided with historical moments of renewed attention to masculinity such as war and the AIDS epidemic.

Jools Gilson reflects on her experience co-directing the *Knitting Map Project*, a year-long public art project that brought together women in the city of Cork, Ireland to knit together. The project initially faced misunderstanding from community members who thought of mapping in literal rather than abstract terms, followed by negative reception from local media who questioned the project's value, often along lines of gender, age and craft. Gilson's writing offers a poignant account of a community brought together, while also mocked. Rose Sinclair's writing then addresses the lack of diversity in both the textile hobby magazines of her local newsagent, but more broadly in the textile design profession. Her writing concludes with the warning that while the fashion industry may have shown some change in recent years, the diversity of representation in textile practices is shrinking rather than expanding.

Two pieces of fiction conclude the community section. Alice Walker's short story 'Everyday Use' is set in America. Two sisters represent two very different communities – one embodies a superficial interest in craft and handwork that could be understood as poverty tourism of her own family. The second sister has acquired the skills of quilting and sees the handmade objects of the family home as items of use rather than decoration. An excerpt from the late science fiction author Ursula K. Le Guin (1929–2018) is the concluding entry of the book. Le Guin writes of miscommunication between two trading communities: The Cloth Art and the Wine Art peoples. When the groups eventually meet and talk, the reasons for the trade disputes becomes clear. Living in a future impacted by climate change, the Cloth Art people have experienced several years of crop failure, but as a community have been too proud to divulge their troubles. After much delay, dialogue leads both communities to mutual understanding.

40

THE SCARLET LETTER (EXCERPT) (1850)

Nathaniel Hawthorne

EDITOR'S INTRODUCTION

Nathaniel Hawthorne is one of America's celebrated nineteenth-century novelists. His novel, *The Scarlet Letter* (1850) presents a criticism of the punishing religious morals that governed parts of New England in the 1600s. The novel is set, pre-American independence, in the Puritan Massachusetts Bay Colony between 1642 and 1649 and was one of the first mass-produced books sold in the country.

Hester Prynne, Hawthorne's main character, is forced to the margins of her community and required to stitch and wear an embroidered scarlet-coloured letter 'A' after giving birth to a daughter, Pearl. The letter is never explicitly defined as referring to adultery, and by the end of the story reference transfers to other possible meanings. Hawthorne's tale is a brutal example of the textile used to quite literally mark out an individual's identity and ostracize mother and daughter from the community. The father of the child, while eventually suspected by some, is not implicated in Hester Prynne's pregnancy, despite Hawthorne's narrator asking, 'Had Hester sinned alone'?

Within Hawthorne's writing the meaning and purpose of the embroidered scarlet letter is far from simple. We learn, for example, that Hester Prynne stitches the most exquisite letter, despite the punishment the embroidery is intended to be. While she and her daughter are banished to the very edges of the community, her skills as an embroiderer are in demand to stitch religious clothing worn by men, including her child's father, with far more dubious morals than her own.

Canadian author Margaret Atwood's novel *The Handmaid's Tale* (1985) and subsequent television series often draw comparisons to *The Scarlet Letter*, despite Atwood's dystopia being set after a fictitious second American Civil War where individual freedom is lost and forced surrogacy mandated. Where Hawthorne's character was first required and then elected to wear the scarlet embroidery, Atwood's handmaidens' are marked out in their society by full scarlet dress that bestows a perverse set of freedoms (nutritious food) and abuses (sanctioned rape) justified by widespread infertility in the community.

The Scarlet Letter

Nathaniel Hawthorne

When the young woman—the mother of this child—stood fully revealed before the crowd, it seemed to be her first impulse to clasp the infant closely to her bosom; not so much by an impulse of motherly affection, as that she might thereby conceal a certain token, which was wrought or fastened into her dress. In a moment, however, wisely judging that one token of her shame would but poorly serve to hide another, she took the baby on her arm, and, with a burning blush, and yet a haughty smile, and a glance that would not be abashed, looked around at her towns people and neighbors. On the breast of her gown, in fine red cloth surrounded with an elaborate embroidery and fantastic flourishes of gold thread, appeared the letter "A." It was so artistically done, and with so much fertility and gorgeous luxuriance of fancy, that it had all the effect of a last and fitting decoration to the apparel which she wore; and which was of a splendor in accordance with the taste of the age, but greatly beyond what was allowed by the sumptuary regulations of the colony.

The young woman was tall, with a figure of perfect elegance on a large scale. She had dark and abundant hair, so glossy that it threw off the sunshine with a gleam, and a face which, besides being beautiful from regularity of feature and richness of complexion, had the impressiveness belonging to a marked brow and deep black eyes. She was ladylike, too, after the manner of the feminine gentility of those days; characterized by a certain state and dignity, rather than by the delicate, evanescent, and indescribable grace, which is now recognized as its indication. And never had Hester Prynne appeared more ladylike, in the antique interpretation of the term, than as she issued from the prison. Those who had before known her and had expected to behold her dimmed and obscured by a disastrous cloud, were astonished, and even startled, to perceive how her beauty shone out and made a halo of the misfortune and ignominy in which she was enveloped. It may be true that, to a sensitive observer, there was something exquisitely painful in it. Her attire, which, indeed, she had wrought for the occasion, in prison, and had modelled much after her own fancy, seemed to express the attitude of her spirit, the desperate recklessness of her mood, by its wild and picturesque peculiarity. But the point which drew all eyes and, as it were, transfigured the wearer—so that both men and women, who had been familiarly acquainted with Hester Prynne, were now impressed as if they beheld her for the first time—was that *Scarlet Letter*, so fantastically embroidered and illuminated upon her bosom. It had the effect of a spell, taking her out of the ordinary relations with humanity and enclosing her in a sphere by herself.

"She hath good skill at her needle, that's certain," remarked one of her female spectators; "but did ever a woman, before this brazen hussy, contrive such a way of showing it! Why, gossips, what is it but to laugh in the faces of our godly magistrates, and make a pride out of what they, worthy gentlemen, meant for a punishment?"

"It were well," muttered the most iron-visaged of the old dames, "if we stripped Madam Hester's rich gown off her dainty shoulders; and as for the red letter, which she hath stitched so curiously, I'll bestow a rag of mine own rheumatic flannel, to make a fitter one!"

"O, peace, neighbors, peace!" whispered their youngest companion; "do not let her hear you! Not a stitch in that embroidered letter, but she has felt it in her heart."

The grim beadle now made a gesture with his staff.

"Make way, good people, make way, in the King's name!" cried he. "Open a passage; and, I promise ye,

Source: Excerpt from Nathaniel Hawthorne, *The Scarlet Letter* (1850).

Mistress Prynne shall be set where man, woman and child may have a fair sight of her brave apparel, from this time till an hour past meridian. A blessing on the righteous Colony of the Massachusetts, where iniquity is dragged out into the sunshine! Come along, Madam Hester, and show your scarlet letter in the market place!" [. . .]

Lonely as was Hester's situation, and without a friend on earth who dared to show himself, she, however, incurred even no risk of want. She possessed an art that sufficed, even in a land that afforded comparatively little scope for its exercise, to supply food for her thriving infant and herself. It was the art—then, as now, almost the only one within a woman's grasp—of needlework. She bore on her breast, in the curiously embroidered letter, a specimen of her delicate and imaginative skill of which the dames of a court might gladly have availed themselves, to add the richer and more spiritual adornment of human ingenuity to their fabrics of silk and gold. Here, indeed, in the sable simplicity that generally characterized the Puritanic modes of dress, there might be an infrequent call for the finer productions of her handiwork. Yet the taste of the age, demanding whatever was elaborate in compositions of this kind, did not fail to extend its influence over our stern progenitors, who had cast behind them so many fashions which it might seem harder to dispense with. Public ceremonies, such as ordinations, the installation of magistrates, and all that could give majesty to the forms in which a new government manifested itself to the people, were, as a matter of policy, marked by a stately and well-conducted ceremonial and a sombre, but yet a studied magnificence. Deep ruffs, painfully wrought bands and gorgeously embroidered gloves were all deemed necessary to the official state of men assuming the reins of power; and were readily allowed to individuals dignified by rank or wealth, even while sumptuary laws forbade these and similar extravagances to the plebeian order. In the array of funerals, too—whether for the apparel of the dead body, or to typify, by manifold emblematic devices of sable cloth and snowy lawn, the sorrow of the survivors—there was a frequent and characteristic demand for such labor as Hester Prynne could supply. Baby linen—for babies then wore robes

of state—afforded still another possibility of toil and emolument.

By degrees, nor very slowly, her handiwork became what would now be termed the fashion. Whether from commiseration for a woman of so miserable a destiny; or from the morbid curiosity that gives a fictitious value even to common or worthless things; or by whatever other intangible circumstance was then, as now, sufficient to bestow on some persons what others might seek in vain; or because Hester really filled a gap which must otherwise have remained vacant; it is certain that she had ready and fairly requited employment for as many hours as she saw fit to occupy with her needle. Vanity, it may be, chose to mortify itself by putting on, for ceremonials of pomp and state, the garments that had been wrought by her sinful hands. Her needlework was seen on the ruff of the Governor; military men wore it on their scarfs, and the minister on his band; it decked the baby's little cap; it was shut up, to be mildewed and moulder away, in the coffins of the dead. But it is not recorded that, in a single instance, her skill was called in aid to embroider the white veil which was to cover the pure blushes of a bride. The exception indicated the ever relentless vigor with which society frowned upon her sin.

Hester sought not to acquire anything beyond a subsistence, of the plainest and most ascetic description, for herself, and a simple abundance for her child. Her own dress was of the coarsest materials and the most sombre hue; with only that one ornament—the scarlet letter—which it was her doom to wear. The child's attire, on the other hand, was distinguished by a fanciful, or, we might rather say, a fantastic ingenuity, which served, indeed, to heighten the airy charm that early began to develop itself in the little girl, but which appeared to have also a deeper meaning. We may speak further of it hereafter. Except for that small expenditure in the decoration of her infant, Hester bestowed all her superfluous means in charity, on wretches less miserable than herself, and who not unfrequently insulted the hand that fed them. Much of the time which she might readily have applied to the better efforts of her art, she employed in making coarse garments for the poor. It is probable that there was an idea of penance in this mode of occupation, and that she offered up a real sacrifice of enjoyment in devoting so many hours to such rude handiwork. She had in her nature a rich, voluptuous, Oriental characteristic—a taste for the gorgeously beautiful, which, save in the exquisite productions of her needle, found nothing else in all the possibilities of her life to exercise itself upon. Women derive a pleasure, incomprehensible to the other sex, from the delicate toil of the needle. To Hester Prynne it might have been a mode of expressing, and therefore soothing, the passion of her life. Like all other joys, she rejected it as a sin. This morbid meddling of conscience with an immaterial matter betokened, it is to be feared, no genuine and steadfast penitence, but something doubtful, something that might be deeply wrong, beneath.

In this manner, Hester Prynne came to have a part to perform in the world. With her native energy of character and rare capacity, it could not entirely cast her off, although it had set a mark upon her more intolerable to a woman's heart than that which branded the brow of Cain. In all her intercourse with society, however, there was nothing that made her feel as if she belonged to it. Every gesture, every word, and even the silence of those with whom she came in contact, implied, and often expressed, that she was banished, and as much alone as if she inhabited another sphere, or communicated with the common nature by other organs and senses than the rest of humankind. She stood apart from moral interests, yet close beside them, like a ghost that revisits the familiar fireside and can no longer make itself seen or felt, no more smile with the household joy, nor mourn with the kindred sorrow; or, should it succeed in manifesting its forbidden sympathy, awakening only terror and horrible repugnance. These emotions, in fact, and its bitterest scorn besides, seemed to be the sole portion that she retained in the universal heart. It was not an age of delicacy; and her position, although she understood it well and was in little danger of forgetting it, was often brought before her vivid self-perception, like a new anguish, by the rudest touch upon the tenderest spot. The poor, as we have already said, whom she sought out to be the objects of her bounty, often reviled the hand that was stretched forth to succor them. Dames of elevated rank, likewise, whose doors she entered in the way of her occupation, were accustomed to distil drops of bitterness into her heart, sometimes through that alchemy of quiet malice, by which women can concoct a subtile poison from ordinary trifles, and sometimes, also, by a coarser expression, that fell upon the sufferer's defenceless breast like a rough blow upon air ulcerated wound. Hester had schooled herself long and well; she never responded to these attacks, save by a flush of crimson that rose irrepressibly over the pale cheek, and again subsided into the depths of her bosom. She was patient—a martyr, indeed—but she forebore to pray for her enemies, lest, in spite of her forgiving aspirations, the words of the blessing should stubbornly twist themselves into a curse.

Continually, and in a thousand other ways, did she feel the innumerable throbs of anguish that had been so cunningly contrived for her by the undying, the everactive sentence of the Puritan tribunal. Clergymen paused in the street to address words of exhortation that brought a crowd, with its mingled grin and frown, around the poor, sinful woman. If she entered a church, trusting to share the Sabbath smile of the Universal Father, it was often her mishap to find herself the text of the discourse. She grew to have a dread of children; for they had imbibed from their parents a vague idea of something horrible in this dreary woman, gliding silently through the town, with never any companion but one only child. Therefore, first allowing her to pass, they pursued her at a distance with shrill cries, and the utterance of a word that had no distinct purport to their own minds, but was none the less terrible to her, as proceeding from lips that babbled it unconsciously. It seemed to argue so wide a diffusion of her shame that all nature knew of it; it could have caused her no deeper pang had the leaves of the trees whispered the dark story among themselves, had the summer breeze murmured about it—had the wintry blast shrieked it aloud! Another peculiar torture was felt in the gaze of a new eye. When strangers looked curiously at the scarlet letter—and none ever failed to do so—they branded it afresh into Hester's soul; so that oftentimes, she could scarcely refrain, yet always did refrain, from covering the symbol with her hand. But then, again, an accustomed eye had likewise its own anguish to inflict. Its cool stare of familiarity was intolerable. From first to last, in short, Hester Prynne had always this dreadful agony in feeling a human eye upon the token; the spot never grew callous; it seemed, on the contrary, to grow more sensitive with daily torture.

But sometimes, once in many days, or perchance in many months, she felt an eye—a human eye—upon the ignominious brand, that seemed to give a momentary relief, as if half of her agony were shared. The next instant, back it all rushed again, with still a deeper throb of pain; for, in that brief interval, she had sinned anew. Had Hester sinned alone?

Her imagination was somehow affected, and, had she been of a softer moral and intellectual fibre, would have been still more so, by the strange and solitary anguish of her life. Walking to and fro with those lonely footsteps in the little world with which she was outwardly connected, it now and then appeared to Hester—if altogether fancy, it was nevertheless too potent to be resisted—she felt or fancied, then, that the scarlet letter had endowed her with a new sense. She shuddered to believe, yet could not help believing, that it gave her a sympathetic knowledge of the hidden sin in other hearts. She was terror stricken by the revelations that were thus made. What were they? Could they be other than the insidious whispers of the bad angel, who would fain have persuaded the struggling woman, as yet only half his victim, that the outward guise of purity was but a lie, and that, if truth were everywhere to be shown, a scarlet letter would blaze forth on many a bosom besides Hester Prynne's? Or, must she receive those intimations—so obscure, yet so distinct—as truth? In all her miserable experience, there was nothing else so awful and so loathsome as this sense. It perplexed as well as shocked her by the irreverent inopportuneness of the occasions that brought it into vivid action. Sometimes the red infamy upon her breast would give a sympathetic throb, as she passed near a venerable minister or magistrate, the model of piety and justice, to whom that age of antique reverence looked up as to a mortal man in fellowship with angels. "What evil thing is at hand?" would Hester say to herself. Lifting her reluctant eyes, there would be nothing human within the scope of view, save the form of this earthly saint! Again, a mystic sisterhood would contumaciously

assert itself as she met the sanctified frown of some matron, who, according to the rumor of all tongues, had kept cold snow within her bosom throughout life. That unsunned snow in the matron's bosom, and the burning shame on Hester Prynne's—what had the two in common? Or, once more, the electric thrill would give her warning—"Behold, Hester, here is a companion!"—and, looking up, she would detect the eyes of a young maiden glancing at the scarlet letter, shyly and aside, and quickly averted, with a faint, chill crimson in her cheeks as if her purity were somewhat sullied by that momentary glance. O Fiend, whose talisman was that fatal symbol, wouldst thou leave nothing, whether in youth or age, for this poor sinner to revere?—such loss of faith is ever one of the saddest results of sin. Be it accepted as a proof that all was not corrupt in this poor victim of her own frailty, and man's hard law, that Hester Prynne yet struggled to believe that no fellow-mortal was guilty like herself.

The vulgar, who, in those dreary old times, were always contributing a grotesque horror to what interested their imaginations, had a story about the scarlet letter which we might readily work up into a terrific legend. They averred that the symbol was not mere scarlet cloth tinged in an earthly dye pot, but was red hot with infernal fire, and could be seen glowing all alight whenever Hester Prynne walked abroad in the night-time. And we must needless say it seared Hester's bosom so deeply, that perhaps there was more truth in the rumor than our modern incredulity may be inclined to admit. [. . .]

It was perceived, too, that while Hester never put forward even the humblest title to share in the world's privileges—further than to breathe the common air, and earn daily bread for little Pearl and herself by the faithful labor of her hands—she was quick to acknowledge her sisterhood with the race of man, whenever benefits were to be conferred. None so ready as she to give of her little substance to every demand of poverty; even though the bitter-hearted pauper threw back a gibe in requital of the food brought regularly to his door, or the garments wrought for him by the fingers that could have embroidered a monarch's robe. None so self-devoted as Hester, when pestilence stalked through the town. In all seasons of calamity, indeed, whether general or of individuals, the outcast of society at once found her place. She came, not as a guest, but as a rightful inmate, into the household that was darkened by trouble, as if its gloomy twilight were a medium in which she was entitled to hold intercourse with her fellow-creatures. There glimmered the embroidered letter, with comfort in its unearthly ray. Elsewhere the token of sin, it was the taper of the sick-chamber. It had even thrown its gleam, in the sufferer's hard extremity, across the verge of time. It had shown him where to set his foot, while the light of earth was fast becoming dim, and ere the light of futurity could reach him. In such emergencies, Hester's nature showed itself warm and rich; a wellspring of human tenderness, unfailing to every real demand, and inexhaustible by the largest. Her breast, with its badge of shame, was but the softer pillow for the head that needed one. She was self-ordained a Sister of Mercy; or, we may rather say, the world's heavy hand had so ordained her, when neither the world nor she looked forward to this result. The letter was the symbol of her calling. Such helpfulness was found in her—so much power to do and power to sympathize—that many people refused to interpret the scarlet "A" by its original signification. They said that it meant "Able"; so strong was Hester Prynne, with a woman's strength.

41

NEEDLEWORK AND THE CREATION OF MASCULINITIES
'The prick' of patriarchy (excerpt) (2021)

Joseph McBrinn

EDITOR'S INTRODUCTION

Joseph McBrinn is an art and design historian and a Reader at the Belfast School of Art, Ulster University in Northern Ireland. His book-length study *Queering the Subversive Stitch: Men and the Culture of Needlework* (2021) provides a historical account of men's needlework based on artefacts in museum collections, artists' papers and archives, magazines, novels, photography, film and television. The book's title makes reference to Rozsika Parker's book *The Subversive Stitch: Embroidery and the Making of the Feminine* considered groundbreaking at the time of publication in 1984. Nearly forty years after Parker's publication, McBrinn's research contributes another perspective by focusing not on the overlooked contributions of women as Parker did, but instead the underacknowledged presence of men's needlework.

In the text included here, McBrinn explains that while Parker's work has more recently received critique from the perspectives of class and race, 'to query *The Subversive Stitch* from the perspective of its omission of masculinity and homosexuality has been taboo'. McBrinn notes that it is only in the eighteenth and nineteenth centuries that needlework became so connected to feminine identities, an association which rendered women's needlework feminizing and men's needlework queer. McBrinn's research also traces when moments of heightened interest in needlework by men coincide with times in history that renewed a focus on masculinity: World War I and World War II, the Cold War, as well as the AIDS epidemic and the 9/11 attacks. While it is familiar to celebrate textiles for their contribution to women's friendships and sense of community, McBrinn brings to light that the same sense of community enjoyed by women also holds the potential to ostracize men.

Needlework and the creation of masculinities:
'The prick' of patriarchy

Joseph McBrinn

Today it is widely accepted that the pervasive and oppressive ideals of femininity prevalent since Victorian times have been inculcated through everyday practices such as embroidery. The legacy of this can be traced through first-, second- and third-wave feminism which reinvested needlecrafts with a renewed sense of agency subverting their association with the tropes of abjection, amateurism and absence in canonical histories of art and design. But what can be said of the social construction of masculinity – was it in any way shaped by men's apparent exclusion from needlework's history? No matter what way it is viewed men are generally perceived as the losers in the story. What an unexpected irony within the all-pervading structures of patriarchy that otherwise privileged all men in all arenas. But what's wrong with failure? Isn't success the measuring stick of phallocentrism, anyway? While all men who take up needlework are perceived to be less masculine, they become feminized, *queer* even, in the popular imagination, there has never actually been a study of men's relation to needlework, nor a study about the relation of needlework to homosexuality. Whilst the many men who took up needle and thread since Victorian times always did so in the shadow of female archetypes, such as the 'Angel in the House', many continued undeterred. Their work may sometimes be acknowledged, but it is very rarely subject to any serious interpretation or evaluation nor is it studied in collective terms. In contrast, the study of women's needlework has gone 'where angels fear to tread', interrogating the continued contradictory role needlework holds in women's lives from its pivotal place in the global exploitation of women's labour to the private pleasures of their personal sexual liberation.[1]

As vast and diverse as scholarship on the topic of women's needlework is the omission of men remains troublesome. Men's exclusion from the culture of needlework rests on essentialist and essentializing assumptions. I realize that there could be no more phallocentric act than inserting men into the narratives of women's history (as embodied in needlework), but it remains problematic that even though feminist discourse has long exposed the relationality of hierarchical constructions of gender and cultural production, needlework is continually (mis)read in gendered terms, regulating and stabilizing the very binary identities that feminism purports to deconstruct and dismantle. It was feminism that established: 'The omission of whole categories of art and artists has resulted in an unrepresentative and distorting notion of who has contributed to "universal" ideas expressed through creativity and aesthetic effort.'[2] Elaine Showalter has suggested (taking the example of literary history) that

> feminist criticism as a process as well as a set of ideas … is not simply a mode of analysis which may be appropriated by men but a perspective on literature that comes out of the experience of marginality, negativity and exclusion, and that must begin with one's own life.[3]

This idea for this book began with this image of a young man knitting that I uncovered as part of my research into the Celtic Revival in early twentieth-century Ireland. The image, on a commercially produced postcard, shows a young man, 'John McNeil', who won first prize for the best 'hand-knitted pair of long stockings from homespun Irish wool', and then a 'Special Prize' for 'the best knitted cycling stockings', at

Source: Excerpt from Joseph McBrinn, 'Needlework and the creation of masculinities: "The prick" of patriarchy', *Queering the Subversive Stitch: Men and the Culture of Needlework*, Bloomsbury Visual Arts, 2021, pp. 40–47. Reproduced with permission.

a series of exhibitions of Irish craftwork held in 1904–5 that arose from the failed attempt to organize an Irish display the 1900 Exposition Universelle in Paris.[4] These local exhibitions are best known because Roger Casement, British diplomat and Irish revolutionary, not only attended but presented, and even sponsored, some of the prizes. When I first encountered the image, I wondered if there was any link between this young man and those Casement cruised in cities, from Belfast to London – especially given Casement's own interest in fashion and textiles. Whilst my search for the hidden history of homosexuality in the Celtic Revival proved extremely fruitful I still wondered about the image of the young male knitter.[5] The more I looked the more images like this I found. Together they suggested that there was perhaps some overlooked, hidden history of needlework by men. And further that the myth of the 'great masculine renunciation' of modern times (the historical moment when men apparently stopped having an interest in fashion and textiles) may have involved men not only ceasing to consume but also making things too.[6] I wondered if we could also rediscover the 'hidden producer' as we once did the 'hidden consumer', a concept that the design historian Christopher Breward has shown to be rich as a site for the exploration of modern masculinity.[7] I was further prompted to think of Donald E. Hall's speculation of how a 'query' can in some way 'queer' a discussion through its interjection of 'personal intrusions, theoretical provocations, and sometimes unanswerable complications'.[8]

In the early twenty-first century when gender seems less stable than ever before, is there even such a thing as masculinity as we previously understood it? In the last quarter of a century or so the study of the masculine has shifted from attempts to define it as a heuristic category to analysis of it in terms of performativity, as socially and culturally constituted and no longer authorized through essentialist notions of gender as biological destiny.[9] Even so, the discourses surrounding women's needlework, whether historic or contemporary, remain saturated with references to femininity as a binary position. By implication any study of men's needlework has been open to question as 'an act of penetration, violence, coercion, or appropriation', and further as the 'reproduction of domination'.[10] As the literary critic

Margaret Higgonet memorably put it: 'Can a man implicated in patriarchy speak for a woman constrained by it?'[11] But is there really nothing to say about men in roles traditionally seen as feminine beyond accusations of impersonation, parody and mimicry, passing, cross-dressing, drag, and as 'a way of promoting the notion of masculine power while masking it'?[12] Such approaches risk perpetuating the argument that 'all women are victims and all men are unimpeded agents of patriarchy', and they also fail to take on-board the wider shifts in thinking about gender's taxonomic instability in the wake of queer theory.[13] As Judith Butler suggested, as long ago as 1990, gender is 'neither natural or innate' and that 'gender norms' are, in fact, 'regulatory fictions'. Gender, Butler has argued, is 'the repeated stylization of the body, a set of repeated acts within a highly rigid regulatory frame that congeal over time to produce the appearance of substance, of a natural sort of being'.[14] Gender is, therefore, 'always and only an imitation of an imitation, a copy of a copy for which there is no original'.[15] This, Butler has since added, is not a self-conscious ('voluntarist') process but constructed through a nexus of social and cultural contexts.[16] Needlework can perhaps, then, be understood as a set of acts that police and enforce gendered binaries and even related facets of normativity such as compulsory heterosexuality.

If hegemonic masculinity is a socially sanctioned construct, a contingent performance of what certain cultures at certain times believe constitutes the masculine, then subordinated and marginalized masculinities are potential sites of resistance. R.W. Connell has suggested that such resistance could be 'doing something outrageously unmasculine' and gives an example of a young man, interviewed in the course of Connell's early research, 'who moved from a stifling rural background to college in the city, [and] broke out by dying his hair, wearing hipster jeans, wearing nail-polish, and taking up knitting'.[17] Needlework by men, then, as an act of performativity not only disrupts 'heteropatriarchal sexual scripts' but also visualizes and legitimizes male-femininity by upending the fixed reference points of the heteronormative.[18] It offers men a profusion of transgressive and subversive possibilities to critique the social and cultural conceptualizations that authorize the masculine ideal. This troubling of the history of needlework began as a *query* with regard to the absence of men in *The Subversive Stitch* and has evolved into a *queering* of needlework as a history.

Parker gives several instances of women using the term 'pride' to describe their investment in needlework.[19] But what of men? What do they feel when they make it? A man may find pleasure, even solace, in needlework but engaging in a form of feminized labour could be read as repudiation of all things masculine. Masculinity has often been defined through a prohibition of feeling and Parker contends in *The Subversive Stitch* that it was during the nineteenth century that feeling became aligned to the feminine, and by association needlework. Feelings associated with women's needlework, as elucidated by Parker, such as patience, selflessness, devotion and love, were compounded when men took it up by wider cultural inscriptions of 'shame, loss, melancholy, trauma, and hate'.[20] Raymond Williams defined this process as the 'social formations of a specific kind which may in turn be seen as the articulation (often the only fully available articulation) of structures of feeling which as living processes are much more widely experienced'.[21] Eve Kosofsky Sedgwick suggested there was a special queer resonance in shame as a feeling, 'the proto-form (eyes down, head averted) of this powerful affect', that links shame to performativity.[22] Ann Cvetkovich has further argued that 'affect and sexuality are not merely analogous categories but coextensive ones with shared histories'.[23] This book seeks to locate these 'structures of feeling' and in particular how men employed needlework to explore emotions such as pleasure, tenderness and mitigate against silence and shame. Throughout this book I also take up Parker's intimation that needlework can be understood through three types of emotional motivation: in the relation of artisan and activism, as self-interrogation and a return to the maternal. Even though *The Subversive Stitch* has been universally celebrated as groundbreaking, it has also raised concerns, like most other histories of needlework, for its 'transhistorical' approach to women's history, its exclusion of class-bound accounts domestic and plain sewing, its focus on 'white Western, particularly British women of the middle and upper classes', and its 'cis-gendered' delineation of femininity.[24] But, to query *The*

Subversive Stitch from the perspective of its omission of masculinity and homosexuality has been taboo.

Parker suggests in *The Subversive Stitch* women's investment in needlework correlated with moments of 'transition' in their history. Men's engagement with needlecrafts must ultimately be seen in light of this. Women in the labour market, women's political enfranchisement, women's sexual liberation, all prompted seismic shifts not just in the cultural creation of the feminine about also in the making of the masculine. Masculinity and femininity only exist in relation to one another. Throughout the twentieth century women's encroachment on the preserves of male dominance generated a perception that men were somehow slipping into a state of crisis, becoming the 'new victims'. Historians have highlighted several historical moments when masculinity seemed to become unstable.[25] John Tosh has suggested, 'The crisis over women's suffrage between 1905 and 1914 was the latest and most dramatic stage in a destabilizing of gender boundaries that had been gathering pace since the 1870s'.[26] Robert Corber has pointed to a 'masculinity crisis' in Cold War America, which was precipitated by the rise of a new consumerist domesticity, dominated by concepts of the feminine, that generated a new surveillance of homosexuality.[27] And most recently there has been discussion of a renewed 'crisis in masculinity' on a global scale in the twenty-first century.[28] However, it is hard to see where one crisis ends and another starts. John MacInnes has suggested that 'masculinity is always in one crisis or another'.[29] The twentieth century's 'crises of masculinity' all stem from the moments when women make meaningful gains in gender equality. Susan Faludi, who has documented the more recent 'chronicles of the "masculinity crisis"', has speculated that they always function as part of the 'backlash' against feminism.[30]

For the large part, however, this theory has permitted masculinity go unexamined and my desire is to delve deeper into how such apparent crises materialized the making, unmaking and remaking of the masculine. Historical moments of so-called crisis, beginning in the early twentieth century, appear to be the very instances when masculinity was under scrutiny and men turned to, and invested, in needlework: before and after the

First World War; during the Second World War and at the height of the Cold War; during and after the AIDS epidemic; and in the rise of extremism and populist politics before and after 9/11. These generally follow on from developments in first-, second- and third-wave feminism and moments of visibility and validation in the history of women's needlecrafts (the agitprop banners of the suffrage movement, the domestic craft revival of 1970s feminism and the interventions of twenty-first-century Craftivists). They also correspond to historical moments of homosexual panic as well as the ruptures of resistance and liberation. As such these periods form the organizing structure of the rest of this book. The following chapters consider: the legacies of Victorian needlework that shaped concepts of masculinity as well as homosexual panic in the early twentieth century; and the hidden history of needlepoint in the homosexual subcultures of modernism and their context in debates about popular culture in the postwar period up to the 1970s. The final chapter considers the presence of men's needlework in postmodern and post-millennial contexts and in light of the current re-investment in the politics of cloth and the continued influence of Parker's notion of the 'subversive stitch'. Historicizing men's needlework has allowed me to problematize its narrative trajectory. My periodization may seem arbitrary but it has been useful in revealing when, and how, concepts of masculinity and craft coalesce.

As Rozsika Parker and Griselda Pollock have argued, 'whilst women can justifiably take pride' in crafts such as embroidery 'it does not displace the hierarchy of values … [and] by simply celebrating a separate heritage we risk losing sight' of the base ideology that constructs and maintains systems of difference.[31] This book, then, is neither an uncritical celebration of men's needlework nor a recuperation of its notable figures and histories. Rather, it offers selective perspectives and insights into the social construction of the masculine through needlework as a paradigmatic social practice. The queering of narratives surrounding men's needlework might, I hope, stimulate further debate. This feels necessary as needle-wielding effeminate men and boys continue to face stigmatization, ostracism and even violence. The inculcation that sewing is still sissy holds

firm even today and an image of a boy sewing continues to 'play and disrupt' fixed notions of gender-appropriate behaviour, as seen in this photograph of an English schoolboy by Martin Parr.[32] The only other thing I would like to add is the case for the teaching of needlework to boys in schools. Recent research has suggested boys are engaging with the haptic pleasures, historically associated with crafts such as needlework, in the form of gaming.[33] This may be true but what better way to explain the interrelation of history and gender than through a social practice used to shape both.

Notes

1. See, for example, Maria Tamboukou, *Sewing, Fighting and Writing: Radical Practices in Work, Politics and Culture* (London and New York: Rowan & Littlefield, 2016); and Rachel P. Maines, *The Technology of Orgasm: 'Hysteria', the Vibrator, and Women's Sexual Satisfaction* (Baltimore and London: The Johns Hopkins University Press, 1998).

2. Nanette Salomon, 'The Art Historical Canon: Sins of Omission'. In Joan E. Hartman and Ellen Messer-Davidow (eds), *(En)gendering Knowledge: Feminists in Academe* (Knoxville: University of Tennessee Press, 1991), p. 222.

3. Elaine Showalter, 'Pen Men'. *London Review of Books* (20 March 1986): 8.

4. See my, 'The 1904 Feis na nGleann: Craftwork, Folk Life and National Identity'. *Folk Life: Journal of Ethnological Studies* 45(1) (2006): 24–39.

5. These ideas are explored more fully in my, 'From Parnell's Suit to Casement's Closet: Masculinity, Homosexuality and the Fashioning of the Irish Nation'. In Fintan Cullen (ed.) *The Visual Culture of Ireland and Empire* (Bern and Oxford: Peter Lang, forthcoming).

6. This term was first coined in J.C. Flugel, *The Psychology of Clothes* (London: The Hogarth Press, 1930), pp. 110–11.

7. Christopher Breward, 'Renouncing Consumption: Men, Fashion and Luxury, 1870-1914'. In Amy de la Haye and Elizabeth Wilson (eds), *Defining Dress: Dress as Object, Meaning and Identity* (Manchester and New

York: Manchester University Press, 1999), pp. 48–62; and idem, *The Hidden Consumer: Masculinities, Fashion and City Life 1860-1914* (Manchester and New York: Manchester University Press, 1999).

8. Donald E. Hall, *Queer Theories* (Basingstoke: Palgrave Macmillan, 2003), p. 7.

9. For an overview of this, see Gail Bederman, 'Why Study "Masculinity," Anyway? Perspectives from the Old Days'. *Culture, Society & Masculinities* 3(1) (2011): 13–25.

10. Paul Smith, 'Men in Feminism: Men and Feminist Theory'. In Alice Jardine and Paul Smith (eds), *Men in Feminism* (Nev, York and London: Routledge, 1987), p. 34; Stephen Heath, 'Male Feminism'. In, *Men in Feminism*, p. 4.

11. Margaret R. Higennot, 'Fictions of Feminine Voice: Antiphony and Silence in Hardy's *Tess of the d'Urbervilles*'. In Laura Claridge and Elizabeth Langland (eds), *Out of Bounds: Male Writers and Gender(ed) Criticism* (Amherst: University of Massachusetts, 1990), pp. 197–8.

12. Elaine Showalter, 'Critical Cross-Dressing; Male Feminists and Woman of the Year'. In Jardine and Smith (eds), *Men in Feminism*, p. 12.

13. Constance Penley and Sharon Willis (eds), *Male Trouble* (Minneapolis: University of Minnesota Press, 1993), xvii.

14. Judith Butler, *Gender Trouble: Feminism and the Subversion of Identity* (New York and London: Routledge, 1990), p. 30.

15. Judith Butler, 'Imitation and Gender Subordination'. In Diana Fuss (ed.), *Inside/Out: Lesbian Theories, Gay Theories* (New York and London: Routledge, 1991), p. 22.

16. Butler has stated 'performativity is neither free play nor theatrical selfpresentation; nor can it be simply equated with performance', see Judith Butler, *Bodies That Matter: On the Discursive Limits of 'Sex'* (New York & London: Routledge, 1993), p. 95.

17. R.W. Connell, 'A Very Straight Gay: Masculinity, Homosexual Experience, and the Dynamics of Gender'. *American Sociological Review* 57(6) (December 1992): 742.

18. Darryl B. Hall, '"Feminine" Heterosexual Men: Subverting Heteropatriarchal Sexual Scripts?' *The Journal of Men's Studies* 14(2) (Spring 2006): 145–59.

19. Parker, *The Subversive Stitch*, pp. 26, 58, 89, 139 and 214.

20. Ann Cvetkovich, 'Public Feelings'. *South Atlantic Quarterly* 103 (3) (Summer 2007): 453.

21. Raymond Williams, 'Structures of Feeling'. In *Marxism and Literature* (Oxford and New York: Oxford University Press, 1977), pp. 128–35 [p. 133].

22. Eve Kosofsky Sedgwick, 'Queer Performativity: Henry James's *The Art of the Novel*'. *GLQ: A Journal of Lesbian and Gay Studies* 1(1) (1993): 5.

23. Cvetkovich, 'Public Feelings': 462.

24. For these points, see Susan Frye, *Pens and Needles: Women's Textualities in Early Modern England* (Philadelphia and Oxford: University of Pennsylvania Press, 2010), p. 26; Cheryl Buckley, 'From the Margins: Theorizing the History and Significance of Making and Designing Clothes at Home'. *Journal of Design History* 11(2) (June 1998): 171; Rosemary Mitchell, 'A Stitch in Time?: Women, Needlework, and the Making of History in Victorian Britain'. *Journal of Victorian Culture* 1(2) (1996): 185–202; Rohan Amanda Maitzen, 'Stitches in Time: Needlework and Victorian Historiography'. In *Gender, Genre, and Victorian Historical Writing* (New York and London: Garland, 1998), pp. 61–102; Linda Pershing, 'Review: The Subversive Stitch: Embroidery and the Making of the Feminine by Rozsika Parker …'. *Signs* 14(2) (Winter 1989): 508; and Lisa Vinebaum, 'Carole Frances Lung's Sewing Rebellion: Resisting the Global Apparel Industry, One Stitch at a Time'. Paper delivered at 'The Subversive Stitch Revisited: The Politics of Cloth', Victoria and Albert Museum, London, 30 November 2013, https://soundcloud.com/goldsmithsuol/subversive-stitch-vinebaum?in=goldsmithsuol/sets/the-subversive-stitch (accessed 1 July 2014).

25. For conceptualizations of the various twentieth-century and twenty-first-century 'crises of masculinity', see Michael S. Kimmel, 'The Contemporary "Crisis" of Masculinity in Historical Perspective'. In Harry Brod (ed.), *The Making of Masculinities: The New Men's Studies* (Boston, MA, and London: Allen & Unwin, 1987), pp. 121–53; Roger Horrocks, *Masculinities in Crisis: Myths, Fantasies, and Realities* (Houndmills, Basingstoke:

Palgrave Macmillan, 1994); Abigail Solomon-Godeau, *Male Trouble: A Crisis in Representation* (London and New York: Thames and Hudson, 1997); Sally Robinson, *Marked Men: White Masculinity in Crisis* (New York: Columbia University Press, 2000); John MacInnes, 'The Crisis of Masculinity and the Politics of Identity'. In Stephen M. Whitehead and Frank J. Barrett (eds), *The Masculinities Reader* (Cambridge: Polity Press, 2001), pp. 311–29; and John Benyon 'Masculinities and the Notion of Crisis'. In John Benyon (ed.) *Masculinities and Culture* (Philadelphia: Open University Press, 2002), pp. 75–97.

26. John Tosh, 'The Making of Masculinities: The Middle Class in Late Nineteenth-Century Britain'. In Angela V. John and Claire Eustance (eds), *The Men's Share?: Masculinities, Male Support and Women's Suffrage in Britain, 1890-1920* (London and New York: Routledge, 1997), p. 39.

27. Robert J. Corber, *Homosexuality in Cold War America: Resistance and the Crisis of Masculinity* (Durham & London: Duke University Press, 1997).

28. Anthony Clare, *On Men: Masculinity in Crisis* (London: Chatto & Windus, 2000); for a more recent overview, see Pankaj Mishra, 'Masculinity in Crisis: Man Trouble'. *The Guardian* [Review Supplement] 9 (17 March 2018): 6–11.

29. John MacInnes, *The End of Masculinity: The Confusion of Sexual Genesis and Sexual Difference in Modern Society* (Buckingham: Open University Press, 1998), p. 11.

30. Susan Faludi *Stiffed: The Betrayal of the Modern Man* (London: Chatto & Windus, 1999), p. 6.

31. Rozsika Parker and Griselda Pollock, *Old Mistresses: Women, Art and Ideology* (London: Pandora, 1981), p. 58.

32. Images sissifying sewing for boys have been relatively commonplace in the history of children's literature. Recently the tide has started to turn. Examples include, the teenage boy, Ben Fletcher, who becomes the winner of an All-UK Knitting Competition in T.S. Easton's *Boys Don't Knit* (London: Hot Key Books, 2014) and *An English Boy in New York* (London: Hot Key Books, 2014); or Aya Kanno's Otomen manga series (2007–13) in which the lead character, Asuka Masamune, a sporty schoolboy secretly 'loves girly things - sewing, knitting, making cute animals and reading shojo comics'. Such books explore how a boy's interest and aptitude in needlework can be accepted even if it goes against prevailing social codes. The quote is Grayson Perry's from 'Martin Parr: Made in Britain'. *The Observer Magazine* (24 February 2019): 34.

33. Sandra Alfoldy has imaginatively speculated that Minecraft, as well as several games for the Sony PlayStation and Nintendo DS, employ textiles not just as visual markers but also in terms of haptic play and affect. See Sandra Alfoldy, 'Cyber Comfort: Textiles as Markers of Care in Video Games'. *Textile: Cloth and Culture* 16(1) (February 2018): 24–33.

42

NAVIGATION, NUANCE AND HALF/ANGEL'S KNITTING MAP
A series of navigational directions... (2012)

Jools Gilson

EDITOR'S INTRODUCTION

Jools Gilson is Professor of Creative Practice at University College Cork, Ireland. Her research interests cross boundaries between traditional academic scholarship, the arts and broadcast practice. From 1995 to 2006 she was Director of the performance production company *half/angel*, frequently working in collaboration with the composer and digital artist Richard Povall. More recent work has focused on choreography and performance related to the climate emergency, as well as documentary and drama for broadcast radio. Gilson's academic publications fall within the fields of Feminist Theory, Visual Culture, Gender and Sexuality, Performance Studies, Performative Writing, Somatics and Affect Studies.

The article reprinted in full here was first published in 2012, seven years after Gilson's experience of co-directing, with Richard Povall, the community-based *Knitting Map Project* in her hometown of Cork, Ireland. The original formatting of the article not only included images, but also set the voices of personal reflections and diary entries in sidebar notes, and key quotes (many from *Navigation: An RYA Manual* yachting instructions) inside grey boxes. The graphic design of the original layout signalled the article's three distinct strands of writing: the main body of Gilson's text, as well as these two further peripheral but pertinent narratives.

Central to Gilson's article is what it means to reflect upon a perceived public art failure. While the facts of the year-long *Knitting Map Project* are established, more space is given to capturing her intentions for the project, as well as the innocent and not so innocent public misunderstandings and local media reactions. The reasons the latter in particular strayed so far from the project's original intentions are explained as a combination of historical and local factors – from Ireland's colonial history to the City of Culture funding that Cork awarded the project. Gilson's writing is poetic in its intimacy, with navigation and failure both becoming literal and metaphorical devices in her reflection.

In 2019 Gilson edited, with Nicola Moffat, the book *Textiles, Community & Controversy: The Knitting Map*, a further collection of essays about the project.

Navigation, Nuance and half/angel's Knitting Map: A series of navigational directions …

Jools Gilson

This writing is a navigation of failures. The safe channels in an estuary are marked by buoys; keep the red buoy to port and the green to starboard, and you will travel safely. But I am compelled by the spaces outside of the publicly marked, and I wonder if it is possible to make it to harbour by other routes. Such heretic navigation promises possibility, but failure lurks under the surface. Such danger is profoundly part of the aspirant pedagogy I describe here, in which failure is itself a kind of buoy, one that tempts an exuberant buoyancy as much as it threatens being lost at sea. So that it makes the best sense to speak of a pedagogy of failure, rather than the failure of pedagogy.

This is a story about two publics; one involved in a vast collaborative knitting project, which used traditional as well as experimental gestures; the other a public who witnessed the same project through the media controversy that described it.

The Knitting Map (TKM) was a departure for us as a company; we had spent ten years making dance theatre and installation work. In TKM we proposed a work that we hoped could be a gift to a city that was my home and that was designated as European Capital of Culture in 2005. But by a contingent of its Irish audience (the majority of whom never visited the work), this gift was unwanted. So here is the affect of failure: It hurts. It is an injury. But being on the whole a cheerful and hardy traveller, and having made such an impossibly huge map, I'm off to chart this story with all its complexities of nationality, femininity, fury and love.[1]

We are called half/angel for a reason. The name is from a trapeze move, which I learned when studying trapeze in the early 1990s. I loved it, because one moment you are sitting prettily on the trapeze, with one hand grasping the bar, and the next you fall backwards holding on with that single grasped hand, and a flexed foot catches the place where wood and rope meet. If it works, you fly underneath the bar, and you are half an angel. I long for such falling and such flight; movements in which you have to fall in order to fly. So we are half/angels, creatures equally enamored of falls and flights, knowing in our bones and blood that there is a way to fall into flight.

But there are times when falling fails to turn into any kind of angel, even half of one. Learning this technique was a process of repeated indignity, training with a wide belt around our waist called a lunge. Should we fall, as we all do, our teacher pulls down hard on the lunge rope, so that we are caught, dangling in space. But we always try again, cajoled into ending with our (partial) angel intact. And in this way, failure is our guide. Being willing to fall is another.

And so we fall into the prosaic and everyday. We fall into our first tangle in which some contingents of the press, and many of our knitters, believe our project *The Knitting Map* to be about a literal mapping of Cork City. We are appalled, while many of our knitters think of it as a lovely idea and volunteer to knit particular parts of the city. Our understanding of processes of cartography assumed a poetic plurality. Our map wasn't literal, because such literality would not have allowed us space to be playful with how cartographic energies depict all kinds of geographies, from the tone of laughter of the cartographer, to how Mary was late on that Tuesday, to the vast impossible secrets of the complexity of knitting, to the floods in March, and the snow in November, and the heat of August, and the lull in October, to Ciara's poor tension, and Maura's cable, and nobody cleaned the toilets on Sunday so I had to

Source: Jools Gilson, 'Navigation, Nuance and Half/Angel's Knitting Map: A Series of Navigational Directions …', *Performance Research* 17:1 (2012), pp. 9–20. Reprinted by permission of the publisher (Taylor & Francis Ltd, http://www.tandfonline.com).

do it before I could change the wool for Monday, to the valuing of women's lives and community, to the ferocity of some of the press, to people crossing oceans solely to visit us, to indignant men arriving surprised at quiet industry, to the way we laughed so hard we wet our knickers at Elizabeth's leaving do, to the neighbours getting upset, to drums playing, and scones being eaten, to fury and love, and tears, and tension of all kinds, and love, and love. And women in Philadelphia weeping at the sight of it. How could we map that with something that was just a picture, that imagined streets to stay in orderly parallels, and suburbs to remain peripheral, and all of that? And while we sat appalled, we began to understand that imagination is a privilege of unparalleled proportions, far beyond the material privations that play themselves out in the lives of too many of us. To be able to be playful with imaginative possibilities is to believe in different kinds of worlds. The vision of *TKM* – the women of a city rising up and knitting the weather for a year, has a revolutionary gesture at its core. Its poetic motion sought to find a quiet but profound way to give space to the astonishing in the everyday of so much feminine activity. It sought to give space to a profound politics of care, to ask if skills normally used for gift giving and solace, could be used for something of vast collaborative gorgeousness, something whose use-value (a thing which would so often trouble our critics and collaborators alike) was both poetic and political.

> A small boat under oars need show only a lantern or
> electric torch in sufficient time to prevent collision.
> *RYA International Regulations for Preventing Collisions*
> *at Sea* (Anderson 1995: 18c)

> Reverse Stocking Stitch Check in Nutmeg.
> Quiet. Sister Susan and the girls from Knocknaheeny.
> *The Knitting Map Log* (2005: 7 June)

Holding on to my trapeze with a clasped hand and readying my flexed foot, I drop backwards. And my repeated tangling with rope and wood is still happening when I sit down and knit in this cacophony of knitting that is TKM. Here I am falling, and while failure attends my learning and my teaching, I am brave enough to carry on catching wool and knitting needles

like a trapeze move, but this time, it is the hundreds of women who visit daily who perform stunts between their dextrous arms and fingers and the twine of wool. And they come with us to risk flight.

RISKING FLIGHT

> [2]In half/angel's project *The Knitting Map*, digital codes were written to translate information about how busy Cork City was into knitting stitches, and what the weather was like into wool colour. This information was uploaded to digital screens as a simple knitting pattern (knit this stitch in this colour), and volunteer knitters sat at twenty knitting stations in a wooden amphitheatre in the crypt of St Luke's Church and knitted. And they did this every day for a year. (Barkun, Gilson-Ellis and Povall 2007: 13–14)

The technology that was part of imagining TKM had been part of half/angel's performance and installation practice for ten years prior to 2005. This work with technology allowed us to haunt performance and installation with unsettling connections between gestures and voiced text or music. In *The Lios* (2004), gallery visitors moved their hands in pools of water to trigger recordings of a community remembering the sea, as if memory itself were dissolved in water. In *The Secret Project* (1999), dancers moved and spoke poetic texts while producing another layer of the same text with their movement, so that they and the audience became unsettled by a vocal and corporeal plurality, and time itself seemed troubled. If we had not spent a decade refining this kind of work, we could not have imagined *TKM* in which a city and its weather generated knitting stitches and wool colour.

TKM, then, involved the culturally disenfranchised in the making of a vast artwork that was commissioned (and certainly perceived) as a flagship project for Cork's year as European Capital of Culture in 2005. Poetically and politically it was a work that sought to re-work the urban territory of matter and meaning: knitting was used as something monumental – an abstract cartography of Cork generated by the city itself and its weather, and knitted every day for a year. To make such a gesture using feminine and female labour aspired to re-work the relationship between femininity and power in an Irish context: it gave cartographic authority to working-class older women from Cork, for a year.

The process of conjuring the energies of a city's climate into an abstract cartography meant that in an important sense the women involved in making *TKM were knitting* the weather. Such a communal gesture brought frosts and floods and heat into the domestic and ordinary act of knitting. It opened its close, domestic and feminine associations to the literal and metaphorical sky. TKM also allowed the mathematical complexity of knitting difficult stitches to be brought into proximity to a frantic city, clogged with traffic and queues and crowded streets. In keeping track of shifting numerical combinations to produce, for example, an open honeycomb cable,[3] these women re-worked the actual digital information about busyness being sent up to them from the city, and they did so by integrating this data with their hands (their digits) in processes of communal hand-knitting. TKM allowed the prevailing cultural peripherality of middle-aged women to make a collectively original and beautiful thing, and in doing so re-mapped their own apparently tangential geography.[4]

Tidal streams flow towards a direction.
Winds flow from a direction.
Navigation: An RYA Manual (Culiffe 1994: 102)

Tw2RW: Slip next stitch onto cable needle and leave at back of work, knit one, then purl one through back of loop from cable needle.
Debbie Bliss, *How to Knit* (1999: 158)

YACHT MASTER

[5]I am a Yacht Master, but I cannot sail. I have a certificate from the Royal Yachting Association with my name on it. I have only once been in a yacht, and when we were out at sea, dolphins suddenly surrounded us – they were underneath us, and leaping beside us. They wove such playful curves again and again that I was undone with the joy of it, stumbling from one side of the small boat to the other to look at them. The old man I sailed with had sailed all his life,

and had never seen such a performance. In class I had become enchanted with extraordinary maps of the sea, called charts, and a new language – 'chart datum', 'dead reckoning', 'isolated danger mark'. We learned about meteorology, navigation and collision regulations. I took notes and drew coloured diagrams. And when it came to the exam, I got the best mark in the class. But as I say, I cannot sail, but I am a Yacht Master. And all of my hankering for navigation of one sort or another is held within this story of respected qualification and unexpected marine joy. What more could I ever master about being in a vessel in the sea than those creatures sent leaping in my heart?

So I came to *TKM* already enchanted with navigation. Making a map seemed an ordinary and straightforward thing to me. Making such a map out of wool, with the collaboration of several thousand women, and information about the weather and city busyness as its enervating cartography, seemed a sensible sort of gesture. I love maps because they purport to tell you how to get somewhere, which seems to me ridiculous. Getting somewhere is always a conundrum of analysis and surprise, rain and strange forks in the road cloud one's vision as a matter of course. We all lose our way, even when we arrive safely in good time. So it isn't that I am suspicious of maps; it's just that, for me, maps and charts are delicious in their ability to resist and recoil and affirm our ability to get to a destination. I am a Yacht Master, but I cannot sail. And when I try to learn, dolphins assault my attempt in playful cacophonies of curves. Marine joy. But I love charts, and I can plot a course for you if I have the strength of the prevailing wind, and the times of high tide, and I know who should give way if two vessels meet, but I have never done these things with real boats. So what kind of navigator does this make me? And what kind of cartographer?

Good navigation can be achieved only by experience. Imaginary passages worked on the dining room table, help to build up speed and proficiency in chart work, but they cannot be a substitute for practice at sea.... Practice does not make the waves any smaller, the driving spray less penetrating or the motion less violent. *Navigation: An RYA Manual* (Culiffe 1994: 12)

PRACTICE AT SEA

Not everyone shares my irreverence of pictorial topography and all kinds of maps that I assumed failed me as I brought my wickedry out from its poetic enclave and onto the street. Others often assume that maps will have a direct relationship to the layout of their referents. So it was that along with some of our knitters, a gleeful Irish press assumed that because *TKM* mapped the city, it would be literal: in which the shapes of streets and the actual place of the river would be reproduced, so that they could have a fine joke at our expense and conject about what would happen if someone dropped a stitch. 'What worries me is that if one of them drops a stitch, there goes Knocknaheeny' (Buckley 2004: 11). Knocknaheeny isn't a neutral suburb in this jest – it is on the north side of Cork and a byword for poverty, crime and violence.

> Yarn overs are most commonly used in lace patterns where you are creating a hole by making up stitches where some have been lost by working them together. Debbie Bliss, *How to Knit* (1999: 99)

ENCHANTMENT

[6]Knitting is an enchantment of the hands and fingers, a moving lattice work of wool and winding and tension. So that in our hands we see complexities fall away from us as something that is parochially called knitting. But in the secret glad grins we share when no one's watching and the gentleness of being guided into the mathematical intricacies of this unsettling and enchanting craft of the hands, we learn differently. Apparently, we do nothing, sitting there, chatting away, breaking for coffee and scones, but something is telling in the eagerness with which we get back to our labour of textiles and hands and fingers and wool. Tangling affect with yarn and needles, we trace and make our connection through story, gossip, argument and laughter.

And let me tell you about the densities of colour, the drench of lilac drifting up from the crypt floor. They call it Amethyst and Heather, and here it is turned into the dimensional hexagons of a honeycomb cable, or the tiny one-by-one cables running like orderly veins into basket weaves, and then shifting into the duskiness of Devon Blue, and here again drifting into the virtuosity of a moss zig-zag – seed textures jumping sideways and back again. These mauves and muted blues intensify when the weather is wet and wild, so that the finished map has swathes of such colours marking the storms of April 2005, their texture, their organization of knots made by the movement of the city itself, pedestrian and motor without distinction. So that busy Saturdays in midsummer send us cabling like nobody's business, and quiet wet Wednesdays have us mossing our single knit and single pearl, row after row, with contemplative ease. As we knit rain, lilacs attend our labour.

And what seem like a hundred tones of creams, light browns and greys; Glencoe, Ivory Cream, Naturelle, Sand, Nutmeg, Cinnamon, Biscuit, Stone, Putty, Sandstorm, Storm Cloud. They are called neutrals, but they are not. Tiny threads of grey-black in white, perfect cream, something darker; the warmth and muted pinkness of Nutmeg and Cinnamon. I turn in their heft, day after day.

And the greens, – a milky aquamarine, something grassy and another tinged with khaki.

I am ravished by colour, and I see the same happen sometimes inside visitors, the shock of moving from the damp dark entrance, into the light and labour of the work itself. It happens like a kiss, or rain. It is before language, even as I try to write it. It is colour and vastness and the shocking apprehension that it has been knitted by hundreds and soon thousands of hands.

In Philadelphia Margaret and I sit amongst it, arranging the folds and drifts and enormity of its complexity. We do so shoeless and, often choked up, crouching in the midst of it. There are drifts of it, up the walls, in pleated folds, and sometimes stretching wide and flat, and then rivulets dividing and meeting again. There is just so much of it, that it undoes people of their perception of hand-textiling. So that it is both an abundance of knitting and a cacophony of absence.[7]

> A submarine carries its steaming lights much lower than a vessel of her size is required to do ...at night this gives the impression that she is much further

away than she actually is. *Navigation: An RYA Manual* (Culiffe 1994: 5)

CABLES

[8]And here are knitting's most precocious feats – the cable! Look! Here they are tumbling; complex arrays of plaits and twists, wide and narrow beside each other, racing to the finish, their mossed foregrounds and stockinged backgrounds, blurring in the thrill of the chase. O! The twist and the turn! The leap and the dive-behind! The gymnastics of yarn, tempted into dashing frivolity by urbanity itself! And yet, and yet – the choreography of the cable is not the same kind of darling for digital technologies at all! The digerati are irritated by cabling, longing to hide it away, keep it secret or even be done with it altogether. When the President of Ireland chose to visit *TKM*, detectives came ahead of her to search our space – the crypt of St Luke's Church. They chuckled politely when I told them that we were glad they'd come because knitting can be very dangerous. But the really *funny* thing is that they thought I was joking. And then I unlocked the door that led behind the wooden amphitheatre, so that they could inspect the underside of the wooden circle where we knitted, and where Richard had hidden all the cables from the digital screens that brought the information about what knitting pattern to stitch and what colour yarn to use into the hands of our knitters. The detectives walked along the wooden curve, and stared at the cacophony of cabling, coloured leads from ten computers leading to ten screens, each computer being fed information from Richard's digital hub, which itself received information from four city-centre CCTV cameras (for the complexity of stitch) and our weather station (for the colour). Two detectives in suits stare at hundreds of cables curling into their sockets, and others leaping away irreverently to hard drives placed in an unruly line, and more-still feeding the digital screens on the amphitheatre, and others again escaping away altogether. Momentarily, two detectives with little wires behind their ears, teeter on their heels, at this sudden spectacle of convoluted complexity beneath the quiet line of women knitting above. I offer them tea, which they politely refuse,

but my question brings them to their senses, and they briskly walk along the curved space, before leaving our underworld to check for rain.

> You are a skipper of a yacht at anchor in Dover in 6.0m depth of water. It is Mean High Water Neap. A crew member drops a winch handle overboard. What will be the depth at Low Water when you send him down to get it? *RYA Coastal Skipper and Yachtmaster Offshore Exercises 1995/6* (1995: 4)

PLOT[9]

I plotted. I did plot. There was plotting, and it fell – fat plots from a grey sky, dashing us with hope. Can you hear it falling? Hope plots. Hundreds of them, thousands even, going out of focus in the movements of fingers winding wool, and shaking the balls of yarn to give them more leverage, in the counting of stitches, in the placing of wool between needles, in its being pulled back, tucked under, in its being wound around, in its being left off to pick up later, in its cabling. O how we cabled! Can you see my plot now? Can you hear the sound of plotting? What a course I navigated! What a plot! I am cabling internationally! In and out and winding behind. I haven't lost the plot. At all.

> Double moss in storm cloud (a kind of grey). Busy. Normal Monday group and school visit. *The Knitting Map Log* (2005: 18 April)

SPECULATIVE PRACTICE

Slowly, over ten years, Richard Povall and I (the directors of half/angel) learned how to do something in our art practice that was based on radical and irreverent speculation. This was a kind of improvisation with failure as a professional practice. We both needed its possibility, and like children, didn't believe in it. Developing impossibilities was the core of such work, in which we developed ways to imagine dissolving memory in water (tiny sensors in pools of water triggering recorded samples of a community remembering the ocean) or projecting poetic text onto falling rice, or haunting spaces with voice ghosts that moving figures might find

(*The Secret Project* [1999], *Spinstren* [2002] and *The Lios* [2004]). So that imagining the women of a city rising up and knitting the weather and movement of a city for a year did not seem an unusual thing, it only seemed grander in scale and time. And our project didn't stay either in the space of poetic language or in the world of conceptual art practice (as either dance theatre or installation), but instead strode boldly into the space of the actually popular, and a real community both of knitters and of Cork City. We strode blindly, because we had learned to trust such speculation as a sturdy beginning for our work. All of our work began with a poetic idea nudging technology sideways. We had always not known how our practice would 'work', but we perennially rode on the tide of its poetic core, and found a way. We were fluent at listening to our process without demanding a result too quickly.

TKM was different in this sense, because we were unable to rehearse the twin processes of collating city data / translating into a knitting pattern, and the organization of a community of knitters. We had to spend part of the year of TKM's making developing the process of its making; there was no rehearsal, or residential retreat. The idea that we might develop how the project would work technically and administratively during its year of making was enormously challenging to some of our staff and volunteers. Some of them equated not knowing exactly how everything would work from day one, with weak management. Their model of hierarchical organization was sometimes powerfully entrenched. Working with speculative technology over a decade in collaboration with Richard meant that we developed digital systems that were an idea of what might work. These were systems that might only become fully themselves through practice, through processes in which we often failed, but which used such failure as buoys; as critical markers that allowed us to navigate towards what we yearned to make. We were fortunate during the 1990s to have long-term residencies, which allowed us to develop such art and performance practice over weeks and months.[10] This was powerfully embodied work, with each performance system being 'tuned' to the movement of a particular dancer. As privileged and educated artist-scholars, our corporeal and linguistic discourse was developed in the

havens of contemporary art practice and within the theoretical playgrounds of postmodern thought. We have always been nomadic with our disciplinary boundaries, deeply interested in the ways in which form binds up meaning or sets it free, and so, transgressing another disciplinary border and venturing in such ambitious optimism out of the worlds of literature and conceptual performance practices and into the everyday, seemed another leap like so many we had taken before. But we were mistaken in this.

[11]Richard and I brought our nuanced collaborative skills to *TKM* project and watched as they slowly failed. Invisibly but palpably, more popularly accepted structures of relating made themselves felt. We began to understand that what we did was not that understandable. Bemused by the complexity of the project itself, the fact that its participants were largely middle-aged working-class women, and the several hundred thousand euros that funded it, the local and national press began to snarl, at the same time as international visitors and press were often enchanted by the scale, democracy and aspiration of the work.[12]

White over red over red over red indicates a vessel constrained by her draught and thus severely restricted in her ability to deviate from her course. *RYA International Regulations for Preventing Collisions at Sea* (Anderson 1995: 24)

While some of our staff and knitters would not or could not collaborate with us in understanding and communicating the speculative and open-ended nature of TKM, we also began to learn that this didn't matter in such a project, in the critical ways it had driven our small-scale performance and installation work. The work operated on different levels for different people. Our error, our failure, was to assume that we could collaborate with a city and a community using similar skills that we had honed in the retreats of contemporary art practice. Community is messy and disorderly, as are the cities that they compose. We came to accept that what happened during our year of knitting was the project, and eventually understand that such an audacious work could not have been completed without struggle and challenge.

Sound in fog may travel erratically causing some confusion and anxiety if the limitations in picking up fog signals are not understood. *Navigation: An RYA Manual* (Culiffe 1994: 79)

KNITTERLY KNOWLEDGE

[13]Our knowledges of playful plurality, of symbolic and literal empowerment, of making women the custodians of a wildly ambitious cartography, were not ideas that were easy to communicate, and yet many of these knitters understood their participation as a civic contribution of great material and symbolic worth.[14] For many of these women, their involvement in TKM was their first involvement in an arts project. While the context and aspiration of this work may have been difficult to grasp, these women drove the project with skills which were powerfully familiar to them – knitting and the social ability to make space warm and un-threatening. Many of them knew far more about knitting than either Richard or I. We had experienced performance and installation works that felt powerfully challenging and difficult to visit, even to the initiated. We wanted to make the space of *TKM* welcoming and inclusive, and our formidable group of knitters were as skilled at this aspect of the work as they were with knitting. This hosting of the work, this bringing of people in, showing and explaining the work, this offer to participate, to have tea, structured the form of the work as powerfully as the knitting itself.

> Loom is defined as the diffused glow observed from a light below the horizon owing to atmospheric scattering. *Navigation: An RYA Manual* (Culiffe 1994: 76)

The women who knitted *TKM* knew how to read and break code into a complexity that made singular things (sweaters, hats, blankets, scarves …). They knew about the social value of gift-giving, they knew the weight of time and care intrinsic to the knitting of garments and other textiles. They also knew its bad press, its lodgement in the public psyche as a joke about another appalling sweater made by granny as a Christmas gift. Many of them had experienced the shift of knitting from economic necessity to expensive hobby. They also knew of knitting as a solitary activity, even as they might knit while watching television with others. In their bones, they knew of knitting as profoundly feminine, as the domain of the female, so that even as boys and men might knit, they only did so with a troubling frisson.[15] They knew about the critical importance of tea breaks and lunch. They knew how to talk and laugh and sometimes guffaw. They also knew how to defend their beloved project when it was attacked, which it repeatedly was. They called up talk shows and spoke their minds, they demanded journalists and directors of festivals visit TKM for themselves (often after they had criticized the project without having done so), they wrote letters and knocked on doors. They disarmed us of intent, by acting as if they owned the project, which of course they did.

Debates about *TKM* rattled on in the Irish media for months and years (2003–6) and came quite soon to refer repeatedly to the project as 'controversial', something that floored my colleagues and me, as well as our community of knitters. TKM was blatantly not itself the site of conventional controversy; its directors had not used the public funding as security on a loan to buy land, or embezzled it to pay for holidays, cars or jewelry; the project involved no public slaughtering of chickens, child pornography or vile language. What then had failed in this process of public pedagogy?

> '… a useless monstrosity'
>
> (Mythen 2005: 10)

There are two things that are remarkable about this response to *TKM*: first that the project was not in any way conventionally controversial in *itself*, and second that this response was peculiar to Cork and Ireland.

> 'daft'
>
> Mick Hannigan, Director, Cork Film Festival (quoted in Lynch 2005: 25)

But controversy there was. This was fuelled by angry speculation about the level of *TKM*'s funding. We received €258,000 over three years to realize this project, funding which primarily paid for a staff of five, office rental and the renovation, fitting out and running of an arts centre for a year. We were forbidden by our funders to reveal the level of this funding to the media during the years of the project's development and making, a gesture that fuelled speculation and controversy.[16] But this was not the whole story.[17] The negative media on TKM so rarely referred to the actual work itself that it sometimes seemed as if it had nothing to do with it. It was as if the latticework of meanings that TKM laid down in public met with social, political and historical moment in such a way as to allow something difficult and damaged to see the light of day. And this something was about Cork and Ireland in 2005, about the powerful injuries of history, about the troubled relationship to wealth and about who has public permission to be valued and to be an artist.

'a pack of oul' biddies knitting' (Lynch 2005: 26).

The public alchemy of *TKM* within Cork and Ireland was not what I had anticipated.

What I had imagined was still within the work, available to be witnessed; gentle, slow; tangling tides and skies with yarn; marking the ebb and surge of presence with knots. But within Ireland, a different kind of alchemy attended its production. The scale, duration and femininity of *TKM* became a provocation. Metaphors are kinds of magic tricks; they work by something being able to represent something else. One of the reasons that the temporal, spatial and gendered excess of *TKM* were intolerable within an Irish context was because of the failure of metaphor. For a contingent of an Irish audience and the Irish media, women knitting cartographies couldn't mean anything else except 'a pack of oul' biddies knitting' (Lynch 2005: 26).

'If you see an old woman in a fairy tale, be very, very careful.'

Jools Gilson-Ellis, *Spinstren*, dance theatre production (1992)

I have often tried to make the invisible labour of femininity powerfully present; in 1997 I hung 10,000 sewing needles from red thread from a gallery ceiling, (*mouthplace*, Triskel Arts Centre, Cork, with Richard Povall). The response to this work was oddly gendered, many women wondered out loud about the vastness of the labour of threading so many needles, and those

men who visited wondered more quietly about what they perceived as the violence of the work.

Kieran McCarthy, a local historian, published a book in 2005 based on interviews with people who worked on or were connected with *TKM*, called *The Knitting Map Speaks*. This is an important document, and in it one of the commissioners of the work, the Irish poet Tom McCarthy, reflects on the media controversy:

Historically, *The Knitting Map* to me is also an important reminder of the importance of women's work. I remember that during Cork 800 a fantastic anthology was brought together by the Cork Women's Poetry Circle; it was called *The Box Under the Bed*. That work, which would be considered women's work, was visible to the public eye, and in many ways the story of women's action in the city was anthologized. When that small anthology was published, it was attacked in the press. It was actually mocked. *The Knitting Map*, twenty years later, has also been subject to attack. It interests me about Irish and Cork society that when women's work is made visible, it somehow attracts negativity from sources in the media. Why is it that women's activity attracts negative feeling in the media? (McCarthy, Tom 2005: 124)

[18]Stripped of nuance and bound up in the literal act of knitting, the most powerful response to TKM within Ireland was an astonishment that so much money and time had been dedicated to something that didn't matter and was such an irrelevance.

'I'm sure it's valid in its own way,' concedes Mick Hannigan with a smile.
(Lynch 2005: 26)

Because the project was a flagship one, this was also bound up with a powerful sense of not wanting to be represented internationally in this way.[19] This may seem difficult to imagine outside of Ireland, but our failure to communicate the aspiration and layered meanings of this work to an Irish, and especially to a Cork audience, meant that it remained lodged in understanding as literal knitting, and the association of homey craft with a bygone Ireland was something that was unbearable in a flagship project for Cork 2005. Historical moment did not or could not allow for such craft to be used as a way to radically re-work meaning. The historic feminization of Ireland by colonial Britain exacerbated this response.[20] Having been symbolically female as a term of abuse, being represented internationally by an excess of femininity fuelled public rage. It did not help that both directors of the project (Richard Povall and I) were English. What this work mapped, then, was not so much a year in the life of a city but its underlying injuries – symbolic, colonial and sexual. And its most powerful, cartography was its iteration of old history, not as something 'way back when' but as something stridently present in the contemporaneity of 2005.[21] *TKM*, then, was a web that made the prevailing assumptions within Ireland about value, art, women and feminine labour visible and palpable. *TKM* made a space for older, working class Irish women to make meaning, and the bad press in some sense tried to put them back in their place. But I have the knitting. Rolled up in four boxes, and hidden safely away in Cork. And I have taken it to America, where I unleashed it in a gallery. I watched as its alchemy crept up the spines of our visitors; I watched composure come undone. And it does this because it is a thing made slowly together (*thousands of us*), a feminine thing, it is time, time of seconds and days and weeks and months and now years. And it is a kind of lodestone for potential time and an assertion of unutterably powerful presence, so powerful that to bring it to the light of day, could cause a city, and sometimes a country to rise up in fury. But I have it, and even though it isn't mine, I guard it, because there will come a time, when I will unroll it again.

They didn't know that she was female, all they knew was that the young sailor had a knack for using the chip log. Casting the wooden panel, weighted on one edge, out into the dark sea, she listened for the sound of it entering the water. As it did, she turned the hour-glass, and let the line slip through her dextrous fingers. She counted knots, watched the hour-glass, and listened to the gulls. She can smell tobacco, and knows they are watching her.

And in this way, they knew how fast they travelled, and when they might arrive.

And when they did arrive just as she had quietly predicted, they were unsettled, and glanced nervously at her slight figure looking out to sea.

One knot equals one nautical mile per hour.

Notes

1. 13 October 2008 Dear Roisin, I'm writing this facing north, away from the sea, sitting in the study looking out over the spiral garden. The penstemons are still out in October, scarlet amid the grey.
2. 27 November 2008 Dear Roisin, a north wind today, fierce as a slap, whipping up clouds with brilliant sunshine, so that pushing the buggy up the boreen with my new son, I am faced with a wide sky tumbled grey and white, sun on the hay field, with its abandoned cylinders of straw, and the brilliant green of the fields around here. I am ravished by colour, and the gorgeous simplicity of pushing my child up a muddy lane, for a walk on a wild day. But as he sleeps, I slip away quietly, and write.
3. This was one of the most complex of all our knitting stitches: Open Honeycomb Cable (knitting pattern where K=knit, P=purl): The pattern begins on the wrong side, so work one row knit before starting. *Row 1*: K2, P8, K2; repeat to end. *Row 2*: P2, C4B (slip next two stitches onto cable needle and hold at back of work, K2, K2 from cable needle), C4F (slip next two stitches onto cable needle and hold at front of work, K2, K2 from cable needle), P2; repeat to end. *Row 3*: as 1st. *Row 4*: P2, K8, P2; repeat to end. *Row 5*: as 1st. *Row 6*: as 4th. *Row 7*: as 1st. *Row 8*: as 4th. These eight rows form pattern. Repeat. (Matthews 1984:63).
4. This section is adapted from Barkun and Gilson-Ellis (2007).
5. 18 January 2009 Dear Roisin, I'm writing this facing south, close to the wood burning stove in the Swallow House, on an icy day in January. Through a little window to the right of the stove, I can see the sea above a stone wall I built two summers ago. Counting summers in the frost, I navigate my writing to meet its heart.
6. 20 January 2009 Dear Roisin, today an African American man will be inaugurated as President of the

United States of America, and I am sitting in front of the warming stove in the Swallow House writing to you. There is a heavy frost, and I can still see my breath inside this little writing house. I ran in the twilight this morning. My hands moving towards the pain of cold before my beating heart warmed them again.

7. *TKM* was exhibited at The Ganser Gallery in Philadelphia in April and May 2007. Margaret Kennedy worked on this exhibition for half/angel.

8. 23 January 2009 Dear Roisin, today it is bright and still. There is a wet chill in the air, and I write this facing west. It is a little warmer than when I last wrote, so I can sit at the table in the Swallow House. Today, Vittorio came out while I dressed the children and lit the stove for me. It is burning peat, old natural peat, not the polite brickettes you can buy from supermarkets. So I sit facing west in the little writing house with a view of blue sky and an empty raised bed, a naked damson tree and a tumbled stone wall. And I burn Irish earth to keep warm. Ancient Irish earth, burning slowly.

9. 26 January 2009 Dear Roisin, the fire difficult to light this morning here in the Swallow House. Everything a bit damp. The orange peel we dried to parchment to use as firelighters in the house, have taken in moisture, and feel like peel again. I'm facing north to warm my back close to the stove. At least I can't see my breath anymore. The children have colds – chesty coughs and runny noses, so we had a broken night last night, Jacobo with me, and Vittorio sleeping downstairs near to Natalie. I had soft hair rubbed in my face at 3am, as a little boy giggled for glee that he was in bed with me. I am also full of cold, and battling it with Echinacea and blood oranges. Peter Foynes and Vittorio made marmalade yesterday, so that our kitchen was turned into a citrus sauna, as they tried to boil Seville oranges for hours on our cantankerous stove, which loses heat in the wind. Later Peter and I go down to the sea wall to see if we can see a date Toddy assures us he knows is there. But there is nothing but a wild grey sea, so that as we stand on the beach we gaze into a wall of grey amid a pinkish afternoon glow.

10. These were: STEIM Studios, Amsterdam, The Netherlands (June and September 1996); Institute for Choreography and Dance, Cork, Ireland (ICD) (October 1997, April 1998, June 1999); The Banff Centre for the Arts, Canada, Department of Media and Visual Arts (March and April 1998, August and September 1998, April 1999 and September and October 1999).

11. 28 January 2009 Dear Roisin, facing east into a misted up window. It's mild, so I sit without my coat at my desk with the lamp on, breathing into this precious space of writing and solitude. And for the first time this week, I can't see my breath. Yesterday I took the children to play group in Aghada looking out onto a glassy estuary across to Cobh. Natalie played happily with buggies and babies, and eventually accosted a real baby from a mum to sit on her lap. Jacobo drove the red car he adores and then sat and ate his snack before and after every other child.… Later Natalie is exuberant at Anna Beth's house singing out songs loudly with Fifi, as the three of them parade round the kitchen island. Anna Beth and I conspire to catch-up between bouts of nappy changing, snack fetching and refereeing.

12. Artistically, the Directors of Smartlab Digital Media Institute (London), Arts and Culture at the Council of Europe (Strasbourg), the European Cultural Foundation (Amsterdam), Dance City (Newcastle, UK) and the Chair of Visual Arts at Millersville University (Millersville, Pennsylvania) were all struck enough by their visits to *TKM* in 2005 to invite half/angel to develop further projects with them. These were, respectively, Lizbeth Goodman, Robert Palmer, Gottfried Wagner, Penny Rae and Jeri Robinson-Lawrence. Positive international media coverage of *TKM* included *Der Standard* (Austria, Alioth 2005), *Helsingen Sannomat* (Finland, Sipilä 2005), *Stavanger Aftenblad* (Norway, Andreassen 2005), *Wysokie Obcasy* (Poland, Pánków 2005), *Newzy.fr* (France, Guilcher 2005), *BBC News* (UK, Davis 2005), *The Guardian* (UK, Glancey 2005), *Vogue Knitting* (UK, Fawcett 2005) and *Simply Knitting* (UK, Bradley 2005). *TKM* was also the subject of a chapter in a PhD thesis (Sotelo 2009).

13. 30 January 2009 Dear Roisin. Rain. No writing yesterday because Vittorio had to go into work, and it was Thursday, so there was the Cuidiu (Irish Childbirth Trust) coffee morning. I've been secretly calling it Quidditch, because parenting seems just like playing hockey in three dimensions on a broom. There were fresh scones and jam and cream and tea, and the children disappeared off to play in another new play room. And lovely women, and much laughter. Somewhere in the blur of Quidditch, lunch with two toddlers in a café, shopping for supper, and all the hauling in and out of cars that that entails, I wrenched my shoulder muscles, somewhere deep inside. So I'm sitting here writing with a heat pad on my sore shoulder listening to the rain and writing to you. I've just re-lit the fire because it went out. Rain.

14. In an article written in 2006, Alan O'Riordan reports on a public forum about *TKM*, organized to coincide with the exhibition of the work in the Millennium Hall, Cork as part of the Midsummer's Festival. He wrote: 'The Knitting Map became a symbol of Cork 2005's perceived failure. By its unusual nature, it became a caricature for a grateful media to lampoon; and, in the climate of recrimination which ran through the year, it was an easy target.' But he also writes: 'From the knitters' own enthusiastic testimony, nobody could doubt that the map meant a great deal to the people who worked on it' (O'Riordan 2006).

15. Men *were* involved in knitting *TKM*, and were always welcome. But in the end, they were a tiny minority.

16. It was probably also the case that when *TKM* was commissioned in 2003, the Executive of Cork 2005 expected their budget to be far higher than it eventually was, so that funding for the project ended up as a much larger proportion of the overall budget than was intended.

17. For example, Daniel Libeskind's *Eighteen Turns* was installed as a temporary exhibit in Fota House as part of the programme for Cork's year as European Capital of Culture in 2005. This stunning architectural caprice cost almost the same as *TKM* to have as a temporary exhibit (May–December 2005) but did not attract a whisper of criticism over its funding.

18. 11 February 2009 Dear Roisin, difficult to light the fire this morning. I am out of small logs, and so have to light the stove with peat. It burns slowly, reluctantly, sending smoke billowing sleepily over the fields. Stunning day – bright, still and cold. Madge, a neighbour and dear friend, died yesterday in her ninety-eighth year. She was born in this house in 1911, and we loved her, and her gorgeous dialect from another time, her stories about dancing down at the Lios, and her twinkling smile.

19. The history of cartography in and of Ireland is closely bound up with Britain's colonial project to claim its territory as its own. See Brian Friel's play *Translations* (1981) for an exploration of the poetic and political impact of this history (Friel 1981). Sometimes this history has had violent personal consequences for the cartographer. In the early seventeenth century, Richard Bartlett, an English army officer under Charles Blount (Lord Deputy Mountjoy), depicted the taming of Ulster and the unruly O'Neill in cartographic form: 'Barlett seems to have been beheaded by Donegal militants who, in the words of one account, 'would not have their countrie discovered' (cited by Smyth 2007: 17, from Andrews 2008, then in progress).

20. For a discussion of this depiction of Ireland as feminine in relation to colonial Britain, see Tovey, Share and Corcoran (2007) and Cairns and Richards (1988).

21. 12 February 2009 Dear Roisin, there is a touch of spring in the air today. Last night we waked Madge down at her home in Ballykennealy. I am taken through to the back bedroom where Catherine, our beloved neighbour and friend and Madge's daughter, sits close to the coffin. I hold her tight and sit between her sisters and chat. I dash home for supper with the children, and then back again for the removal. The small cottage is heaving, and dozens of cars line the small road. I go inside briefly, and Richard hands me whisky. Later, sitting in the packed church, I look down the long aisle at Madge's coffin to see the photograph of her I gave to Catherine for Christmas placed on top of it. This beautiful image of this old woman with light in her eyes sitting in my kitchen briefly undoes me of my outsiderness.

References

Alioth, Martin (2005) 'Ire zu sein ist immer unbequem', Der Standard, Vienna, Austria, 9 January: 35.

Anderson, W. S. B. (1995) *RYA International Regulations for Preventing Collisions at Sea*, Shaftesbury: Blackmore Press.

Andreassen, Helene (2005) 'Folkelig Strikkeprosject Engasjerte Cork', Stavanger Aftenblad, Stavanger, Norway, 15 October: 59.

Andrews, J. H. (2008) *The Queen's Last Mapmaker: A study of Richard Bartlett*, Dublin: Geography Publications.

Barkun, Deborah and Gilson-Ellis, Jools (2007) 'Orienteering with double moss: The cartographies of half/angel's *The Knitting Map*', *International Journal of Performance Arts and Digital Media* 3(2): 183–95.

Barkun, Deborah, Gilson-Ellis, Jools and Povall, Richard (2007) *half/angel: The Knitting Map*, exhibition catalogue, Cork, Ireland and Millersville, Pennsylvania: University College Cork, The Arts Council of Ireland, Culture Ireland and Millersville University.

Bliss, Debbie (1999) *How to Knit*, London: Collins and Brown.

Bradley, Debora (2005) 'Knit One, Purl Fun!' *Simply Knitting* July: 98.

Buckley, Dan (2004) 'Cultural crown that promises us riches', *Irish Examiner*, 4 March: 11.

Cairns, David and Richards, Shaun (1988) *Writing Ireland: Colonialism, nationalism and culture*, Manchester: Manchester University Press.

Culiffe, Tom (1994) *Navigation: An RYA Manual*, London: David and Charles.

Davis, R. (2005) 'Old and new knits city together', BBC News website, 7 March, news.bbc.co.uk/2/hi/ uk_news/northern_ireland/4324955.stm, accessed 1 September 2009.

Dillon, Willie (2004) 'City of culture: It's not rubbish', *The Irish Independent*, 4 September: 4.

Gilson-Ellis, Jools (2002) *Spinstren*, half/angel performance text [unpublished].

Glancey, Jonathan (2005) 'The word made flesh', *The Guardian*, 22 August: 32, www.guardian.co.uk/ artanddesign/2005/aug/22/architecture.communities> Accessed 1 September 2009.

Guilcher, Martine (2005) 'Cork, l'Irlande en Fête', *Newzy.fr*, 1 October, www.newzy.fr/perso/un-week-end-a.../cork-l-irlande-en-fete.html, accessed 31 August 2009.

Fawcett, Sarah (2005) 'The Knitting Map', *Vogue Knitting* Fall: 65.

Friel, Brian (1981) *Translations*, London: Faber and Faber.

Lynch, Donal (2005) 'Sunk', 'Life' supplement, *Sunday Independent*, 22 May: 25–30.

Matthews, Anne (1984) *Vogue Dictionary of Knitting Stitches*, London: David and Charles.

McCarthy, Kieran ed. (2005) *Voices of Cork: The Knitting Map speaks*, Dublin: Nonsuch.

McCarthy, Tom (2005) 'The Box Over the Bed', in Kieran McCarthy (ed.) *Voices of Cork: The Knitting Map speaks*, (2005), Dublin: Nonsuch: 123–4.

Mythen, Katie (2005) 'An army of knutters!', Inside Cork, 17 March: 10.

O'Riordan, Alan (2006) 'Attempt to unravel Knitting Map', *The Irish Examiner*, 29 June: 13.

Panków, Lidia (2006) 'Miasto Według Drutów', Wysokie Obcasy, Warsaw, Poland, 10 September: 38–9.

Sipilä, Annamari (2005) 'Kaupungin Kiire Kudotaan Kartaksi', Helsingen Sannomat, Helsinki, Finland: 2 January: C3.

Smyth, William J. (2007) 'Map-making and Ireland: Presences and absences', in *[c]artography: Map-Making as Art Form*, Cork: Crawford Art Gallery: 4–27.

Sotelo, Luis C. (2009) *Participation cartography: Performance, space and subjectivity*, PhD thesis, Northampton [unpublished].

The Knitting Map Log (2005), Cork, half/angel [unpublished, various authors].

Tovey, Hilary, Share, Perry and Corcoran, Mary P. (2007) *A Sociology of Ireland*, 3rd edn, London: Gill and Macmillan.

RYA Coastal Skipper and Yachtmaster Offshore Exercises 1995/6 (1995), London: Royal Yachting Association [no author credited].

43

TRACING BACK TO TRACE FORWARDS
What does it mean/take to be a Black textile designer (2021)

Rose Sinclair

EDITOR'S INTRODUCTION

Rose Sinclair is a Lecturer in Design Education at Goldsmiths, University of London. Her two distinct research interests cover the creative potential of computer-aided design and computer-aided manufacturing as a tool in textile practice in the classroom and an ongoing investigation, started during her PhD, on the crafting practices of Black British women. The research considers the place of Dorcas Clubs attended by Caribbean women in the UK during the 1950s and 1960s, and how these Clubs were used to foreground crafting practices and create spaces for community craft.

Sinclair opens this chapter with an anecdote about her local newsagent and the numerous magazine covers that have made her alert to the invisibility of her identity as a Black British woman on magazine covers. She shares with Julia Bryan-Wilson, included in the politics section, an interest in crossing back and forth between amateur and professional textile making. Borrowing from Elaine Igoe's PhD research inspired by the psychoanalyst and painter Bracha L. Ettinger's call to follow traces—of ourselves as personal as well as professional identities—Sinclair's writing uses what she describes as a Black autoethnographic method. She traces some of her own family experience before discussion of the Black British textile designer Althea McNish (1924–2020). Sinclair's reference to Faith Ringgold can be found in the memory section of this book. In her conclusion, Sinclair observes that while the fashion industry has in recent years celebrated the increase in visibility of BAME (Black, Asian and Minority Ethnic) designers, in the field of textile design diversity of representation has continued to decrease.

The chapter included here is adapted from the original, which contained and referred to two photographs of Althea McNish from the 1960s.

Tracing Back to Trace Forwards:
What does it mean/take to be a Black textile designer

Rose Sinclair

'*The individual is both site and subject of these discursive struggles for identity and for remaking memory. Because individuals are subject to multiple and competing discourses in many realms, their subjectivity is shifting and contradictory, not stable, fixed, rigid.*' (Richardson 2000: 929)

'*On my daily walk home, I stop at a large newsagent's chain, as usual before approaching the location of the daily newspapers, I take the opportunity to browse the bulging rack of the latest crafting, knitting and sewing magazines, I regard this as my guilty pleasure. I avidly look amongst the magazines, many are wrapped in plastic covers, holding in paper patterns, fabrics, yarns, notions, free give always. I have a professional interest. This area of design is my life and at the time I am writing for the last seven years my doctoral research focus has been on the crafting practices of Black British women. I am particularly interested in the relationships between networks established in the Caribbean and re-established through migration, in textiles networks such as Dorcas clubs, on arrival in post-war England. It is these traces, exploring roots and routes through both amateur and professional practices that offer points of 'tracing'.*

What is it about these magazines? Well, they offer me, the professional, an opportunity to understand the latest consumer trends but also to continue to see if anything new has emerged as the latest 'in thing' or, just to immerse myself in the place of craft. But there is one thing, I continue to notice, one thing; just as on my numerous previous visits, there is not one person on the front cover, on closer inspection of those magazines not covered in plastic wrappers, that are no persons who are part of the editorial or contributors' team who look like me. A practitioner, designer, academic of over twenty years in the making, yet the practice space in which I

dwell, and inhabit as a person of colour, as Black woman; I am invisible in the crafting space.' A space, often liminal, (Barnes 2013) within the pages of text, allows for the reader a construction of creative methods through which they understand portrayal of self and by extension representation.

I was aware that people of colour were not visibly prominent in these liminal spaces – were not the faces on or in the magazines. However, not to see any people of colour raises unexpected concerns and responses; questions are asked of me in the spaces I inhabit within institutions, such as 'Don't Black women knit? Why would you need to knit in a hot country?' (Hamilton-Brown 2017) to 'Black women don't quilt' (Patel 2019). From this perspective the invisibility of women and people of colour in this specific space represents our real hypervisibility in the wider crafting spaces, which straddles both the spaces of the amateur and professional.

CLAIMING YOUR TRACES

Kyra Hicks (2003) in her seminal book *Black Threads: An African American Quilting Sourcebook* identifies that it is the invisibility of the Black women from the dialogue of crafting in both the profession and amateur space that leads to her highlighting the textual existence of the past, present and future legacies of quilting as a craft practice by women of colour. Black American feminist writer bell hooks (2007) highlights the absence of naming Black women in the displays of their work in museums or art gallery events, highlightings the absence and their hyperinvisibility. It is now that there needs to be a stance towards the claiming of rights to our culture through naming

Source: Rose Sinclair, 'Tracing Back to Trace Forwards: What Does It Mean/Take to be a Black Textile Designer', *Textile Design Theory in the Making* by Elaine Igoe (Bloomsbury Visual Arts, 2021), pp. 111–27. Reproduced with permission.

work of Black makers – a stance highlighted by textile artist Faith Ringgold (Ringgold and Obrist 2019) who highlights the importance of Black makers in writing their own stories. Stories written and told by others; are from their own perspectives not your own personal truth. Notably, Ringgold refashions her text as textile, a woven fabric, constructed with warp and weft threads, so providing a reading as well as creating material for a construction of identity both as tracer of her place as textile designer and her place as a Black woman telling her creative story.

What is both present in the dialogue of Hicks, hooks and Ringgold is the need to present the values, heritage and an aesthetic of Blackness, amidst a crafting dialogue that does not see Blackness. bell hooks (2007) calls into question the spaces of Black women's creativity identifying the movement between creative spaces, for example, the church space to the home space to the professional space. It is the movement between these spaces where the identity of the creative is formed and developed, but in that movement, it can become lost. While from the UK perspective there are postcolonial dialogues related to masculinity in the fashion textiles space (Checinska 2017b), the migratory factors that surround the development of the aesthetics of fashion and textiles crafts practices of a postcolonial legacy (Tulloch 2016; Sinclair 2015). The postmodern aesthetics such as Cheryl Buckley (2007, 2009) and Johnson (2018) point out failure to recognize the place of the female, the marginalized and those for whom crafting and textiles have the possibility to create new futures. Hicks (2003) believes that what fuels the practice are the networks of practice that emerge both online and in physical spaces (Gauntlett 2011; Thomas 2018). Patel (2019, 2020) explores this through the professional practice of Black, Asian & Minority Ethnic (BAME) women and their craft and textile practice in the social space.[1] All this seeks to ask – where are the places where Black women as textile designers can find spaces to connect through new geographies of space, which in turn allow them to create those 'tracers'?[2]

I wish to focus on the question of tracing practice and routes through tracing, an issue that is also discussed in Igoe (2013).

What is it therefore that fuels the tracing of crafting practice when it is invisible or when it becomes the site of 'discursive struggles for identity' (Richardson 2000: 929)? Hicks seeks to define this tracing as being fuelled by following three areas:

1. The growth of specific textile exhibitions that showcase the 'Black experience' through the textile craft.

2. The growth of online spaces that connect makers.

3. The ongoing spaces and professional bodies that facilitate face-to-face connections and exchange.

Hicks (2003: 9) and hooks (2007: 317) assert that it is essential to trace the practices of Black women, in order to do the following:

• Meet heritage and cultural needs.

• Preserve Black histories.

• Create a context for collecting and preserving the specific textiles practices of all people not just a few, thus assigning values, cultural heritage.

• It will encourage current and future cultural engagement and assist in future development and tracing of cultural capital.

Elizabeth Robinson (2012) readily acknowledges that research on women of colour in the UK concerning their crafting practices and their approaches to making is lacking; the work of Jo Turney (2009) identifies that crafts join communities of makers through process and practice but again this research has remained firmly focussed on white women and their crafting making.

The UK census (2011) identified that just over four million women identified as BAME, while just over one million identify as Black. Available industry figures currently estimate that over 4 million women in the UK knit, with 1.5 million women knitting on a regular basis; this figure however does not delineate between race and ethnicity in its figures. Recent UK Arts Council and Creative Skills research publications have highlighted that while there has been a distinct rise in the number of BAME people undertaking fashion-related practice, the figures related to BAME participation in craft, which includes the practice of textiles, are often so small that it is not actively recorded.

TRACING BACK TO LOOK FORWARDS

Tracing your own practice and how you come to dwell in the textiles space is an important dialogue that all professional designers go through. Igoe (2013) starts this process by questioning her own textiles' journey and traces her approach to practice and has an ongoing reflexive dialogue with herself about the design process and practice. This results in critical dialogues, dissecting the design and creative process in textiles practice.

Reflecting on this, questions began to emerge for me based on my own approach as a practitioner researcher and are broken down in to the following areas:

- Textiles practice as composed of traces and layers and systems – a palimpsest of interconnecting parts that have to be retraced.

- Discussion around traces; textile as traces; what can be traced can also be retraced: (Igoe 2013: 52) providing a multilayered and layered/layers/ palimpsest. The difficulties encountered in tracing (Igoe 2013: 51).

- How to trace back the possibilities attributed to tracing back (Igoe 2013: 104, 161, 185), that is, uncovering traces.

- Traces and imprints as traces (Igoe 2013: 19).

- Where our traces are painted out, what happens? Painting out traces. Painting the absences (Igoe 2013: 25).

VISIBILITY AND HYPERINVISIBILITY THROUGH A FEMINIST LENS

Both Igoe (2013: 33) and Cheryl Buckley (2009) comment on the invisible role of the designer, especially if they are female. Elinor, Richardson, Scott, Thomas and Walker (1987) in their book *Women and Craft* highlight how homeworkers act in design-as-translation (Igoe 2013) with the professional designer makers, yet are also makers at home in their own right though, but due to the prevailing social conditions

they inhabit are not duly recognized as part of a wider community of practice.

> Here I can position my own biography, my mother while training to be a nurse in the early 1970s was also an outworker for a local garment company. In this work, her professionalism as a 'dressmaker' is done through the use of her skills to further support her family. It is also the point at which as a young girl I also learnt to help my mother, I would also be sewing, adding buttons to garments, using the overlocker, I learned really quickly to make by seeing, and make by doing, knowing that every mistake would mean a reduced pay packet, the aim each week was to meet the Friday evening, Saturday morning deadline pick up, from the foreman.

The use of a Black autoethnographical perspective offers the opportunity to further provide a voice for the often multilayered complex experiences that form us as Black makers, crafters and designers. Thus, for me the fashion industry held no illusion, between who designed the clothes and who made the clothes that were sold in the shops; at this level there is no interaction with the designer, just interaction in the system of manufacture.

Through this intersectionality of fashion and dress through race, Carol Tulloch (1998: 360) reflects on the complex nature histories of fashion, that is,

> predominantly Eurocentric, with a notable concentration on Britain and Paris. Like its fellow subdiscipline, design history, published works have mainly concentrated on the 'heroes' of dress or design – again European-based and white. Race has rarely impacted on dress history.

Tulloch (2016) further highlighted this in fashion and design. Thus, the role that race plays in fashion and design can often marginalize the Black designer and maker who does not see themselves even in the histories of the subject they inhabit. Tulloch (2016) identifies the role that race plays in fashion and design, which can often marginalize the designer and maker making a clear distinction about the continuing hyperinvisibility of the Black people in the 'fashion space'.

The issue of the invisibility of black people has long been discussed in, for example, postcolonial studies. Despite their extensive range of activities in the public gaze that has snowballed over the centuries, the issue of invisibility remains a caustic point in need of address in the twenty-first century. (Tulloch 2016: 283)

TRACING SELF. TRACING OUR ROOTS

Who does what practice? How do you come to be a professional in the textiles space and do what you do? Why do we need to trace our roles, our positions and our points of professional practice at all as people of colour? hooks (2007) describes this as a form of coming out, making visible the unknown. Contemporary textile designers such as Bisa Butler draw heavily on this notion of tracing in their work, not only through the act of making but also by subverting the process through the use of 'fabulating' (Warren 2020) tales, applying an expanded Black design palette to develop new possibilities. This allows new tracers, creating new narratives of both Black textile artists and designers as well as the Black experience and placing these, as Warren states, in an 'interstitial space between fact and fiction'. Where our traces are painted out, what happens? As Black designers we find routes to re-painting in our traces, and re-painting the absences, by filling in the voids (Igoe 2013: 25).

The question I am often asked as a textiles practitioner and designer is, 'How did you get into textiles?' For me personally this was not an unusual space to be or to place myself in, as I grew up surrounded by makers. My own mother was part of the Windrush Generation arriving in the UK in 1960. My mother came from the small island of Jamaica to the much larger island of England in 1960. My mother was a professional dressmaker (Buckley 2007: 131–2) but was only able to use these skills effectively among those in her community and the local women of the church she attended. Her skills however remained in her community, as she would go on to train as a nurse and work for the National Health Service (NHS). Together with the women from her church they often used the front room (McMillan 2008) as the making space for

their local 'Dorcas Club' meetings (Sinclair 2015). Making and crafting through cloth would continue to play an important part in my mother's life, as she engaged in it through community projects. This meant that the world of making was a space that was situated for me. Growing up I was surrounded by Black women who made things, whether baked, sewed, knitted, or woven; making and crafting was a normal activity and formed an essential part of my upbringing. Making with purpose for the community was the norm, as was the exchange of knowledge within a communal setting of co-collaboration and the retention of authenticity (Twigger-Holroyd 2018).

TRACING OUR ROOTS: HOW DO I DWELL IN THIS SPACE, WHAT BROUGHT ME TO THIS POINT?

I can define I am a Black British woman who is passionate about textiles both as practice and process and everything in between.

In *Ways of Knowing, Being and Doing: A Theoretical Framework and Methods for Indigenous and Indigenist Research*, Karen Martin and Booran Mirraboopa (2003) offer a framework for this approach that I apply in the following text to define textiles practice through the tracing of (my)self and retaining ones' authenticity:

'Where I From'
I am claiming
I am declaring my genealogy, my heritage, my culture
I am positioning (because I can)
WHY?
To locate myself as a Black British woman of Caribbean heritage
As a Textile Designer/Practitioner
As researcher (in an academic space)
WHY?
This allows others to locate me
This allows others to determine the types of relations/ships that might exist.
WHY?
In providing these details I am also
Identifying
Defining

Describing
The elements of **'Where I From'**
and
Locating my research
Locating my practice
Positioning myself
Claiming my space

This reiteration of the words of bell hooks (2007), as previously discussed, calls on processes of self-identification of creative spaces for Black women. Through this dialogue, the issues of agency emerge through the textile design praxis and therefore a move towards the overlap of design discourses, which lead to a reconfiguration of the spaces occupied, and how Black women are seen and negotiate institutional spaces of praxis.

It is the movement between these liminal spaces where the identity of the creative is formed and developed, but in that movement it can become lost. It is however a contentious space, one where the designer or creative can increasingly go unrecognized as their work emerges in a 'new art' or 'professional space' and the maker or designer's identity and specificity, as hooks (2007: 327) maintains; in archives and museum spaces identities remain concealed with the title applied too often 'Maker Unknown'. In this unknown space the professional maker of colour has to negotiate vagaries of gender and race.

TRACING FURTHER: CRAFTING THE PROFESSIONAL SPACE

The complexity of the design process and the critique through feminist understandings continue to create difficulties in navigating the terrain of Black design crafting practice. In 2017, Thick/er Black Lines, a research-led art collective, presented the work *We Are Sorry for the Delay to Your Journey* which sought to clarify how the work of Black female creatives' past, present and potential futures can be explored and discussed through the linear graphics of the modern underground map (Hand, Mhondoro and Ove 2019). While this chapter focusses on predominantly female practitioners, I must acknowledge that Black male

textile designers exploring craft culture and heritage are far less reviewed or researched in either the professional or personal spaces of textile making.

TRACING BACK TO TRACE FORWARDS

Althea McNish is held up as the foremost Black textile designer of the twentieth century. She arrived in England from Trinidad in 1951 and by 1957 had graduated from the RCA as its first Black graduate of textiles. A formidable creative woman, she paved a trail in the world of textiles, art and design (Checinska 2017a, 2018; Sellers 2017) winning both national and international acclaim (Mendes and Hinchcliffe 1983 Hlaváčková 2019). She would create textile work for the leading textiles and fashion houses of the time such as Ascher, Hull Traders, Liberty's and Tootals (Jackson 2009; Walmsley 1992). Michael Webber (1968) writes, 'Textile designers are also doing well in Europe. Althea McNish regularly visits Italy, Switzerland, France and Scandinavia, and is also visited every year in her London studio by buyers from overseas manufacturers.'

McNish was also one of the leading artists of the Caribbean Artists Movement (CAM) which emerged in the 1960s to give voice to a rising Black creative aesthetic seeking to create and locate their own tradition in face of the dominant tradition (Harris, White and Beezmohun 2009; Walmsley 1992), Althea would go on to dominate this design space for over sixty years and the legacy of her research and work stills lives on.

Amongst the collection of Women Designers curated by Leah Armstrong in 2012, is an image of the textile designer Althea McNish at work reviewing wallpaper samples.

She is shown sitting at a table perusing a wallpaper book of designs, nothing extraordinary about this as an activity, except that she is also one of the designers featured in the book.

For Igoe, this is linked primarily to the issues of gendering and perceived professional status of textiles as a space of practice for females in wider society. For me, as a designer reviewing these images, and writing this text, the story extends beyond what the picture reveals; Althea had extended her design expertise beyond just fabrics and was involved in designing 'interior spaces' and by this time also designing for major wallpaper companies such as Wallpaper Manufactures Limited. By the time this image was taken, what is considered one of McNish's most successful textile designs and one of the most iconic textiles of the era 'Golden Harvest' had been printed by Hull Traders.[3]

John Berger (2013) identifies the key traits that tell us how to read photographs not only through the visual evidence they present but also in the other information they present us with about the time. Berger emphasizes that 'a photograph celebrates neither the event itself nor the faculty of sight in itself. A photograph is already a message about the events it records . . . at its simplest the message decoded means: I have decided that seeing this is worth recording' (John Berger 2013).

For McNish, her role is significant and worthy of seeing and recording not only because of her professional status and gender but also her race. In addition to the issues of gender and reading femininity, the image also presents the issue of tracing the role of race, or rather women of colour, specifically seeing Black women in the professional textiles design space. McNish was herself constantly described by her geographical origin and would often be seen in articles that referred to Althea as 'the girl from Trinidad' or as a 'West Indian' with subsequent text having connotations or perceptions of geographical imaginations, of how she is perceived to use or apply colour through the design praxis through the creation of a space the making of 'a calypso room with lazing in mind' (Hislop 1966).

A popular image of McNish is repeatedly mistaken for being taken at the Ideal Home Exhibition in 1966 but actually highlights McNish in her own design studio of the same period. What the image does show is the transition that McNish made professionally from designing fabrics to designing spaces, as well as showcasing her design space as a freelance designer, and not being shoehorned into a single design practice. What is also notable is that this was the first Ideal Home Exhibition to be filmed and featured on the BBC in colour.

The headline that accompanies the image encourages the reader to believe they are looking at the Bachelor Girl room, and not behind the scenes at a professional textile artist studio: 'My Ideal Room by a Bachelor Girl, . . . Colour, colour . . . and nothing costing more than £49.10s. Those were the principles Althea McNish worked on as she designed her strictly "66" bachelor girl's room.' The image showcases McNish in her design space, her design studio that she inhabited to make her work happen, highlighting the tools and the space where her work comes to life. What is intriguing is that this picture is often used without the adjoining article written by the author Vivien Hislop, which is used to describe McNish's ideal room and for the ideal young twenty-six-year-old 'bachelor' girl about town.

The *Daily Mail* Ideal Home Exhibition was described by Buckley (2007: 141) as the place to portray 'the ideal home, its conception and its construction . . . based on the ideas and opinions of women'. Here Althea McNish in her role as a textile designer informs these 'ideal homes'. As a Black woman, the importance lay in tracing a new space forward in identifying the needs of a wider migrant demographic that was now settling in Britain. At the same time McNish was making waves at the Ideal Home Show, she would be working on making new 'traces' with the CAM, who were seeking to establish a new 'voice' and creative agency for emerging Black artists and creatives who now found themselves needing to have a voice. And so, this image superimposes the rise of the new agency and creative voice of the Black female textile professional emerging from a post-war 'British empire'.

I argue here that traces identify pathways to which you can assign a link to a particular approach to designing and making.

I am a textile designer, and I continue to wear multiple hats as academic, practitioner and researcher; storytelling through textiles allows me to use 'tracers'. I revise 'Where our traces are painted out, what happens? Painting out traces. Painting the absences' (Ettinger cited in Igoe 2013: 25) but reframe this as 'Painting in the traces, and Painting in the absences'. My work now not only embodies textiles practice but also connects to politics such as in Windrush Arrivals 1948 (Goldsmiths Jan 2019–Feb 2019 and V&A London Design Weekend Sept 2019). I create spaces that explore the Black female creative experience through textiles, set up as immersive in person or remote experiences such as in the 'Caribbean Front Room' installation in collaboration with the Broadway Theatre, based in Catford, South East London, England.

In developing their practice, the textile designer makes decisions about their pathways of practice and this although often modelled as a cyclo-linear one, it is not. Issues of race and gender are interlinked and integral to the construct of textiles practice and its profession, yet this is an area that is not yet thoroughly explored and cannot be in such a small space as I have here.

We must shed light onto the spaces where the professional designer's roles need further unpicking. Although increased figures of BAME designers employed in the fashion sector is a point of excitement, the numbers of those participating in the crafts, including the textiles sector, are diminishing. This gives rise to concerns over the growing invisibility of BAME individuals working in textiles.

Notes

1. An Arts Council report, Creative Media Survey (2012: 38) highlighted that BAME made up 17 per cent of the fashion and textiles workforce but had limited information on further breakdown of data and clear representation across the fashion and textiles industry.

2. Between 2011 and 2014, there was a 126 per cent increase in BAME in the design industry which includes fashion, products and graphics; however, textiles is not included in this definition. Between 2011 and 2014, the number of BAME in the area of crafts was considered too small to be sampled. Taken from Creative Diversity: The State of Diversity in the UK's Creative Industries, and What We Can Do about It from the Creative Industries Federation, 2015, and Creative Industries: Focus on Employment, 30th June 2015 – a report from the Department of Culture, Media and Sport, UK Government.

3. Golden Harvest was a textile design based on a combination of English fields and flowers and sugar cane fields of Trinidad designed by Althea McNish and manufactured in 1959 by Hull Traders Ltd.

Bibliography

Arts Council report, Creative Media Survey (2012) https://www.artscouncil.org.uk/sites/default/files/download-file/Equality_and_diversity_within_the_arts_and_cultural_sector_in_England.pdf

Barnes, A. (2013) 'Geo/Graphic Design: The Liminal Space of the Page'. *Geographical Review*, 103 (2): 164–76.

Berger, J. (2013) *Understanding a Photograph*. Ed. Geoff Dyer. London: Penguin Books.

Buckley, C. (1986) 'Made in Patriarchy: Toward a Feminist Analysis of Women and Design'. *Design Issues*, 3 (2) (Autumn): 3–14. Published by: The MIT Press.

Buckley, C. (2007) *Designing Modern Britain*. London: Reaktion Books.

Buckley, C. (2009) 'Made in Patriarchy: Theories of Women and Design - A Reworking'. In D. Brody and H. Clark (eds), *Design Studies. A Reader*. Oxford: Berg.

Checinska, C. (2017a) 'Althea McNish and the British African Diaspora'. In A. Massey and A. Seago (eds), *Pop Art and Design*. London, UK: Bloomsbury Academic.

Checinska, C. (2017b) 'Re-fashioning African Diasporic Masculinities'. In E. Gaugele, and M. Titton (eds), *Fashion and Postcolonial Critique*. Vol. 22. Publication Series of the Academy of Fine Arts Vienna. Berlin: Sternberg Press, pp. 74–90.

Checinska, C. (2018) 'Christine Checinska in Conversation with Althea McNish and John Weiss'. *TEXTILE, Cloth and Culture*, 16 (2): 186–99, DOI: 10.1080/14759756.2018.1432183.

Elinor, G., Richardson, S., Scott, Thomas, A. and Walker, K. (eds) (1987) *Women and Craft*. London: Virago Press.

Gauntlett, D. (2011) *Making Is Connecting: The Social Meaning of Creativity, from DIY and Knitting to YouTube and Web 2.0*. Cambridge, Oxford, and Boston: Polity Press.

Hamilton-Brown, L. (2017) *Myth-Black People Don't Knit*. Master thesis. Royal College of Art, London, UK. Available at https://www.lornahamiltonbrown.com/about-me/. Accessed 29 September 2019.

Hand, C., Mhondoro, C. and Ove, Z. (2019) *Get Up Stand Up Now: Generations of Black Creative Pioneers* (exhibition) Somerset House Trust, UK.

Harris, R., White, S. and Beezmohun, S. (2009) *Building Britannia: Life Experience with Britain*. London, UK: George Padmore Institute Publications.

Hlaváčková, K. (2019) *Ascher: The Mad Silkman: Zika and Lida Ascher, Fashion and Textiles*. Prague: Slovart Publishing Ltd.

Hicks, K. E. (2003) *Black Threads: An African American Quilting Sourcebook*. Jefferson, NC: McFarland & Company Publishers.

Hislop, V. (1966) 'My Ideal Room by a Bachelor Girl. Daily Mail Ideal Home Exhibition'. *Daily Mail*, Tuesday March 1, p. 15.

hooks, b. (2007) 'An Aesthetic of Blackness: Strange and Oppositional'. In J. Livingstone, and J. Ploof (eds), *The Object of Labour: Art, Cloth, and Cultural Production*. Cambridge: MIT Press, pp. 315–32.

Igoe, E. (2013) In *Textasis: Matrixial Narratives of Textile Design*. PhD thesis, Royal College of Art, London.

Jackson, L. (2005) 'Caribbean Blaze'. *Crafts Magazine*, 194 (May–June): 32–7. UK.

Jackson, L. (2009) *Shirley Craven and Hull Traders: Revolutionary Fabrics and Furniture 1957–1980*. ACC Editions.

Johnson, P. (2018) 'New Caribbean Design: Revitalizing Placed-Based Products (2017)'. In S. Walker, W. Evans, *Design et al (2017) Roots, Culturally Significant Design, Products & Practices*. London: Bloomsbury.

Martin, K. and Mirraboopa, B. (2003) 'Ways of Knowing, Being and Doing: A Theoretical Framework and Methods for Indigenous and Indigenist Research'. *Journal of Australian Studies*, 27 (76): 203–14.

McMillan, M. (2008) 'The 'West Indian' Front Room: Reflections on a Diasporic Phenomenon'. *Kunapipi*, 30 (2). Available at http://ro.uow.edu.au/kunapipi/vol30/iss2/7.

Mendes, V. D. and Hinchliffe, F.M. (1983) *Ascher, Zika and Lida Ascher, Fabric, Art, Fashion*. Victoria and Albert Museum, UK.

Patel, K. (2019) 'Supporting Diversity in Craft Practice through Digital Technology Skills Development'. Crafts Council Report.

Patel, K. (2020) 'Diversity Initiatives and Addressing Inequalities in Craft'. In S. Luckman, and S. Taylor (eds), *Pathways to Creative Working Lives*. London: Palgrave Macmillan, pp. 173–95.

Richardson, L. (2000) 'Writing: A Method of Inquiry'. In N. Denzin and Y. Lincoln (eds), *Handbook of Qualitative Research* (2nd edn). Thousand Oaks, London, Delhi: Sage Publications, pp. 923–46.

Ringgold, F. and Obrist H. U. (2019) Faith Ringgold, Verlag der Buchhandlung Walther Konig.

Robinson, E. (2012) *Women and Needlework in Britain, 1920–1970*. PhD thesis, Royal Holloway, University of London.

Sellers, L. (2017) *Women Design: Pioneers in Architecture, Industrial, Graphic and Digital Design from the Twentieth Century to the Present Day*. London, UK: Quarto Publishing.

Sinclair, R. (2015) 'Dorcas Legacies, Dorcas Futures: Textile Legacies and the Formation of Identities in 'Habitus" Spaces'. *Craft Research*, 6 (2). Intellect Ltd Article.

Sinclair, R. (2019) Windrush: Arrival 1948 at the V&A Windrush by Rose Sinclair, John Price and Will Cenci. Available at https://www.gold.ac.uk/research/about/public-engagement/windrush

Sinclair, R. (2020) Caribbean Front Room (October 1–January 4). Available at HYPERLINK "https://sites.gold.ac.uk/windrush/caribbean-front-room/" https://sites.gold.ac.uk/windrush/caribbean-front-room/

Thomas, S. (2018) *Fashion Ethics*. Oxford: Routledge.

Tulloch, C. (1998) "Out of Many, One People': The Relativity of Dress, Race and Ethnicity to Jamaica, 1880–1907'. *Fashion Theory*, 2 (4): 359–82.

Tulloch, C. (2016) *The Birth of Cool: Style Narratives of the African Diaspora - Materializing Culture*. London: Bloomsbury Publishers, UK.

Turney, J. (2009) *The Culture of Knitting*. London: Bloomsbury, UK.

Twigger-Holroyd, A. (2018) 'Forging New Futures: Cultural Significance, Revitalization and Authenticity'. In S. Walker, W. Evans, T. Cassidy, A. Twigger- Holroyd and J. Jung, *Roots, Culturally Significant Design, Products & Practices*. London: Bloomsbury.

Walmsley, A. (1992) *The Caribbean Artists Movement, 1966–1972*. A Literary and Cultural History. London: New Beacon Books.

Warren, E., ed. (2020) *Bisa Butler, Portraits*. The Art Institute of Chicago, New Haven: Yale University Press.

Webb, M. (1968) 'Design as an Invisible Export'. *Design Journal*, 214: 63–5.

44

EVERYDAY USE (1973)

Alice Walker

EDITOR'S INTRODUCTION

The author and poet, Alice Walker won the Pulitzer Prize for her acclaimed novel *The Color Purple* in 1983. Her short story, 'Everyday Use' reprinted in full here, was written when Walker was in her thirties – published in the April 1973 issue of *Harper's* Magazine and included as one of thirteen stories about women in a collection of her writing titled *In Love and Trouble*. In it, Walker creates the characters Maggie and Dee – two sisters with vastly different regard for the material culture of their childhood.

Narrated by the sisters' mother, the story pokes fun at Dee's 'back to Africa' values and interest in re-appropriating craft objects made out of necessity as her souvenirs. Dee has renamed herself Wangero, explaining, 'I couldn't bear it any longer, being named after the people who oppress me' not aware that her mother felt Dee's education and literacy, 'washed us in a river of make-believe, burned us with a lot of knowledge we didn't necessarily need to know'. The family's hand stitched quilts are the point of greatest tension in the story, cherished by both sisters, but for different reasons. Dee has hopes of placing the hand stitched quilts on the walls of her home and despairs of her sister (who ironically is the one who knows how to quilt), 'She'd probably be backward enough to put them to everyday use'.

Everyday Use

Alice Walker

I will wait for her in the yard that Maggie and I made so clean and wavy yesterday afternoon. A yard like this is more comfortable than most people know. It is not just a yard. It is like an extended living room. When the hard clay is swept clean as a floor and the fine sand around the edges lined with tiny, irregular grooves, anyone can come and sit and look up into the elm tree and wait for the breezes that never come inside the house.

Maggie will be nervous until after her sister goes: she will stand hopelessly in corners, homely and ashamed of the burn scars down her arms and legs, eying her sister with a mixture of envy and awe. She thinks her sister has held life always in the palm of one hand, that "no" is a word the world never learned to say to her.

You've no doubt seen those TV shows where the child who has "made it" is confronted, as a surprise, by her own mother and father, tottering in weakly from backstage. (A pleasant surprise, of course: What would they do if parent and child came on the show only to curse out and insult each other?) On TV, mother and child embrace and smile into each other's faces. Sometimes the mother and father weep, the child wraps them in her arms and leans across the table to tell how she would not have made it without their help. I have seen these programs.

Sometimes I dream a dream in which Dee and I are suddenly brought together on a TV program of this sort. Out of a dark and soft-seated limousine I am ushered into a bright room filled with many people. There I meet a smiling, gray, sporty man like Johnny Carson who shakes my hand and tells me what a fine girl I have. Then we are on the stage and Dee is embracing me with tears in her eyes. She pins on my dress a large orchid, even though she has told me once that she thinks orchids are tacky flowers.

In real life I am a large, big-boned woman with rough, man-working hands. In the winter I wear flannel nightgowns to bed and overalls during the day. I can kill and clean a hog as mercilessly as a man. My fat keeps me hot in zero weather. I can work outside all day, breaking ice to get water for washing; I can eat pork liver cooked over the open fire minutes after it comes steaming from the hog. One winter I knocked a bull calf straight in the brain between the eyes with a sledgehammer and had the meat hung up to chill before nightfall. But of course all this does not show on television. I am the way my daughter would want me to be: a hundred pounds lighter, my skin like an uncooked barley pancake. My hair glistens in the hot bright lights. Johnny Carson has much to do to keep up with my quick and witty tongue.

But that is a mistake. I know even before I wake up. Who ever knew a Johnson with a quick tongue? Who can even imagine me looking a strange white man in the eye? It seems to me I have talked to them always with one foot raised in flight, with my head turned in whichever way is farthest from them. Dee, though. She would always look anyone in the eye. Hesitation was no part of her nature.

"How do I look, Mama?" Maggie says, showing just enough of her thin body enveloped in pink skirt and red blouse for me to know she's there, almost hidden by the door.

"Come out into the yard," I say.

Have you ever seen a lame animal, perhaps a dog run over by some careless person rich enough to own a car, sidle up to someone who is ignorant enough to be kind to him? That is the way my Maggie walks. She has been like this, chin on chest, eyes on ground, feet in shuffle, ever since the fire that burned the other house to the ground.

Dee is lighter than Maggie, with nicer hair and a fuller figure. She's a woman now, though sometimes I forget. How long ago was it that the other house burned? Ten, twelve years? Sometimes I can still hear the flames and feel Maggie's arms sticking to me, her hair smoking and her dress falling off her in little black papery flakes. Her eyes seemed stretched open, blazed open by the flames reflected in them. And Dee. I see her standing off under the sweet gum tree she used to dig gum out of; a look of concentration on her face as she watched the last dingy gray board of the house fall in toward the red-hot brick chimney. Why don't you do a dance around the ashes? I'd wanted to ask her. She had hated the house that much.

I used to think she hated Maggie, too. But that was before we raised the money, the church and me, to send her to Augusta to school. She used to read to us without pity; forcing words, lies, other folks' habits, whole lives upon us two, sitting trapped and ignorant underneath her voice. She washed us in a river of make-believe, burned us with a lot of knowledge we didn't necessarily need to know. Pressed us to her with the serious way she read, to shove us away at just the moment, like dimwits, we seemed about to understand.

Dee wanted nice things. A yellow organdy dress to wear to her graduation from high school; black pumps to match a green suit she'd made from an old suit somebody gave me. She was determined to stare down any disaster in her efforts. Her eyelids would not flicker for minutes at a time. Often I fought off the temptation to shake her. At sixteen she had a style of her own: and knew what style was.

I never had an education myself. After second grade the school was closed down. Don't ask me why: in 1927 colored asked fewer questions than they do now. Sometimes Maggie reads to me. She stumbles along good-naturedly but can't see well. She knows she is not bright. Like good looks and money, quickness passed her by. She will marry John Thomas (who has mossy teeth in an earnest face) and then I'll be free to sit here and I guess just sing church songs to myself. Although I never was a good singer. Never could carry a tune. I was always better at a man's job. I used to love to milk till I was hooked in the side in '49. Cows are soothing and slow and don't bother you, unless you try to milk them the wrong way.

I have deliberately turned my back on the house. It is three rooms, just like the one that burned, except the roof is tin; they don't make shingle roofs anymore. There are no real windows, just some holes cut in the sides, like the portholes in a ship, but not round and not square, with rawhide holding the shutters up on the outside. This house is in a pasture, too, like the other one. No doubt when Dee sees it she will want to tear it down. She wrote me once that no matter where we "choose" to live, she will manage to come see us. But she will never bring her friends. Maggie and I thought about this and Maggie asked me, "Mama, when did Dee ever have *any* friends?"

She had a few. Furtive boys in pink shirts hanging about on washday after school. Nervous girls who never laughed. Impressed with her they worshiped the well-turned phrase, the cute shape, the scalding humor that erupted like bubbles in lye. She read to them.

When she was courting Jimmy T she didn't have much time to pay to us, but turned all her faultfinding power on him. He *flew* to marry a cheap city girl from a family of ignorant flashy people. She hardly had time to recompose herself.

When she comes I will meet—but there they are!

Maggie attempts to make a dash for the house, in her shuffling way, but I stay her with my hand. "Come back here," I say. And she stops and tries to dig a well in the sand with her toe.

It is hard to see them clearly through the strong sun. But even the first glimpse of leg out of the car tells me it is Dee. Her feet were always neat-looking, as if God himself had shaped them with a certain style. From the other side of the car comes a short, stocky man. Hair is all over his head a foot long and hanging from his chin like a kinky mule tail. I hear Maggie suck in her breath. "Uhnnnh," is what it sounds like. Like when you see the wriggling end of a snake just in front of your foot on the road. "Uhnnnh."

Dee next. A dress down to the ground, in this hot weather. A dress so loud it hurts my eyes. There are yellows and oranges enough to throw back the light of the sun. I feel my whole face warming from the heat waves it throws out. Earrings gold, too, and hanging down to her shoulders. Bracelets dangling and making noises when she moves her arm up to shake the folds of the dress out of her armpits. The dress is loose and flows, and as she walks closer, I like it. I hear Maggie go "Uhnnnh" again. It is her sister's hair. It stands straight up like the wool on a sheep. It is black as night and around the edges are two long pigtails that rope about like small lizards disappearing behind her ears.

"Wa-su-zo-Tean-o!" she says, coming on in that gliding way the dress makes her move. The short stocky fellow with the hair to his navel is all grinning and he follows up with "Asalamalakim, my mother and sister!" He moves to hug Maggie but she falls back, right up against the back of my chair. I feel her trembling there and when I look up I see the perspiration falling off her chin.

"Don't get up," says Dee. Since I am stout it takes something of a push. You can see me trying to move a second or two before I make it. She turns, showing white heels through her sandals, and goes back to the car. Out she peeks next with a Polaroid. She stoops down quickly and lines up picture after picture of me sitting there in front of the house with Maggie cowering behind me. She never takes a shot without making sure the house is included. When a cow comes nibbling around the edge of the yard she snaps it and me and Maggie *and* the house. Then she puts the Polaroid in the back seat of the car, and comes up and kisses me on the forehead.

Meanwhile Asalamalakim is going through motions with Maggie's hand. Maggie's hand is as limp as a fish, and probably as cold, despite the sweat, and she keeps trying to pull it back. It looks like Asalamalakim wants to shake hands but wants to do it fancy. Or maybe he don't know how people shake hands. Anyhow, he soon gives up on Maggie.

"Well," I say. "Dee."

"No, Mama," she says. "Not 'Dee,' Wangero Leewanika Kemanjo!"

"What happened to 'Dee'?" I wanted to know.

"She's dead," Wangero said. "I couldn't bear it any longer, being named after the people who oppress me."

"You know as well as me you was named after your aunt Dicie," I said. Dicie is my sister. She named Dee. We called her "Big Dee" after Dee was born.

"But who was *she* named after?" asked Wangero. "I guess after Grandma Dee," I said.

"And who was she named after?" asked Wangero. "Her mother," I said, and saw Wangero was getting tired. "That's about as far back as I can trace it," I said. Though, in fact, I probably could have carried it back beyond the Civil War through the branches.

"Well," said Asalamalakim, "there you are."

"Uhnnnh," I heard Maggie say.

"There I was not," I said, "before 'Dicie' cropped up in our family, so why should I try to trace it that far back?"

He just stood there grinning, looking down on me like somebody inspecting a Model A car. Every once in a while he and Wangero sent eye signals over my head.

"How do you pronounce this name?" I asked.

"You don't have to call me by it if you don't want to," said Wangero.

"Why shouldn't I?" I asked. "If that's what you want us to call you, we'll call you."

"I know it might sound awkward at first," said Wangero.

"I'll get used to it," I said. "Ream it out again."

Well, soon we got the name out of the way. Asalamalakim had a name twice as long and three times as hard. After I tripped over it two or three times he told me to just call him Hakim-a-barber. I wanted to ask him was he a barber, but I didn't really think he was, so I didn't ask.

"You must belong to those beef-cattle peoples down the road," I said. They said "Asalamalakim" when they met you, too, but they didn't shake hands. Always too busy: feeding the cattle, fixing the fences, putting up salt-lick shelters, throwing down hay. When the white folks poisoned some of the herd the men stayed up all night with rifles in their hands. I walked a mile and a half just to see the sight.

Hakim-a-barber said, "I accept some of their doctrines, but farming and raising cattle is not my style." (They didn't tell me, and I didn't ask, whether Wangero (Dee) had really gone and married him.)

We sat down to eat and right away he said he didn't eat collards and pork was unclean. Wangero, though, went on through the chitlins and corn bread, the greens and everything else. She talked a blue streak over the sweet potatoes. Everything delighted her. Even the fact that we still used the benches her daddy made for the table when we couldn't afford to buy chairs.

"Oh, Mama!" she cried. Then turned to Hakim-a-barber. "I never knew how lovely these benches are. You can feel the rump prints," she said, running her hands underneath her and along the bench. Then she gave a sigh and her hand closed over Grandma Dee's butter dish. "That's it!" she said. "I knew there was something I wanted to ask you if I could have." She jumped up from the table and went over in the corner where the churn stood, the milk in it clabber by now. She looked at the churn and looked at it.

"This churn top is what I need," she said.

"Didn't Uncle Buddy whittle it out of a tree you all used to have?"

"Yes," I said.

"Uh huh," she said happily. "And I want the dasher, too."

"Uncle Buddy whittle that, too?" asked the barber.

Dee (Wangero) looked up at me.

"Aunt Dee's first husband whittled the dash," said Maggie so low you almost couldn't hear her. "His name was Henry, but they called him Stash."

"Maggie's brain is like an elephant's," Wangero said, laughing. "I can use the churn top as a centerpiece for the alcove table," she said, sliding a plate over the churn, "and I'll think of something artistic to do with the dasher."

When she finished wrapping the dasher the handle stuck out. I took it for a moment in my hands. You didn't even have to look close to see where hands pushing the dasher up and down to make butter had left a kind of sink in the wood. In fact, there were a lot of small sinks; you could see where thumbs and fingers had sunk into the wood. It was beautiful light yellow wood, from a tree that grew in the yard where Big Dee and Stash had lived.

After dinner Dee (Wangero) went to the trunk at the foot of my bed and started rifling through it. Maggie hung back in the kitchen over the dishpan. Out came Wangero with two quilts. They had been pieced by Grandma Dee and then Big Dee and me had hung them on the quilt frames on the front porch and quilted them. One was in the Lone Star pattern. The other was Walk Around the Mountain. In both of them were scraps of dresses Grandma Dee had worn fifty and more years ago. Bits and pieces of Grandpa Jarrell's Paisley shirts. And one teeny faded blue piece, about the size of a penny matchbox, that was from Great Grandpa Ezra's uniform that he wore in the Civil War.

"Mama," Wangero said sweet as a bird. "Can I have these old quilts?"

I heard something fall in the kitchen, and a minute later the kitchen door slammed.

"Why don't you take one or two of the others?" I asked. "These old things was just done by me and Big Dee from some tops your grandma pieced before she died."

"No," said Wangero. "I don't want those. They are stitched around the borders by machine."

"That'll make them last better," I said.

"That's not the point," said Wangero. "These are all pieces of dresses Grandma used to wear. She did all this stitching by hand. Imagine!" She held the quilts securely in her arms, stroking them.

"Some of the pieces, like those lavender ones, come from old clothes her mother handed down to her," I said, moving up to touch the quilts. Dee (Wangero) moved back just enough so that I couldn't reach the quilts. They already belonged to her.

"Imagine!" she breathed again, clutching them closely to her bosom.

"The truth is," I said, "I promised to give them quilts to Maggie, for when she marries John Thomas." She gasped like a bee had stung her.

"Maggie can't appreciate these quilts!" she said. "She'd probably be backward enough to put them to everyday use."

"I reckon she would," I said. "God knows I been saving 'em for long enough with nobody using 'em. I hope she will!" I didn't want to bring up how I had offered Dee (Wangero) a quilt when she went away to college. Then she had told me they were old-fashioned, out of style.

"But they're *priceless*!" she was saying now, furiously; for she has a temper. "Maggie would put them on the bed and in five years they'd be in rags. Less than that!"

"She can always make some more," I said. "Maggie knows how to quilt."

Dee (Wangero) looked at me with hatred. "You just will not understand. The point is these quilts, *these* quilts!"

"Well," I said, stumped. "What would *you* do with them?"

"Hang them," she said. As if that was the only thing you *could* do with quilts.

Maggie by now was standing in the door. I could almost hear the sound her feet made as they scraped over each other.

"She can have them, Mama," she said, like somebody used to never winning anything, or having anything reserved for her. "I can 'member Grandma Dee without the quilts."

I looked at her hard. She had filled her bottom lip with checkerberry snuff and it gave her face a kind of dopey, hangdog look. It was Grandma Dee and Big Dee who taught her how to quilt herself. She stood there with her scarred hands hidden in the folds of her skirt. She looked at her sister with something like fear but she wasn't mad at her. This was Maggie's portion. This was the way she knew God to work.

When I looked at her like that something hit me in the top of my head and ran down to the soles of my feet. Just like when I'm in church and the spirit of God touches me and I get happy and shout. I did something I had never done before; hugged Maggie to me, then dragged her into the room, snatched the quilts out of Miss Wangero's hands and dumped them into Maggie's lap. Maggie just sat there on my bed with her mouth open.

"Take one or two of the others," I said to Dee.

But she turned without a word and went out to Hakim-a-barber.

"You just don't understand," she said, as Maggie and I came out to the car.

"What don't I understand?" I wanted to know.

"Your heritage," she said. And then she turned to Maggie, kissed her, and said, "You ought to try to make something of yourself, too, Maggie. It's really a new day for us. But from the way you and Mama still live you'd never know it."

She put on some sunglasses that hid everything above the tip of her nose and her chin.

Maggie smiled; maybe at the sunglasses. But a real smile, not scared. After we watched the car dust settle I asked Maggie to bring me a dip of snuff. And then the two of us sat there just enjoying, until it was time to go into the house and go to bed.

45

THE TROUBLE WITH THE COTTON PEOPLE (EXCERPT) (1984)

Ursula K. Le Guin

EDITOR'S INTRODUCTION

Ursula K. Le Guin (1929–2018) was an American author. Over a sixty-year career, Le Guin published twenty novels and more than one hundred short stories often categorized as works of speculative fiction. Influences on her writing have been credited to cultural anthropology, Taoism and feminism – with anthropologists often cast as protagonists in her narratives. Many of the settings of her stories propose alternative political structures.

Le Guin's essay 'The Carrier Bag Theory of Fiction' (1986) has become popular in art and craft discourse for questioning if the earliest tool was really the spear with its phallic intent to dominate and kill. In place of the spear, le Guin considers a container such as a bag or gourd that allows food to be gathered. The carrier bag is collective but also potentially messy in its combination and recombination of contents – an insight not only about the nature of the artefact but also le Guin's approach to storytelling.

The excerpt included here is from Le Guin's experimental long book *Always Coming Home* (1985) about trade problems between the Cloth Art and the Wine Art peoples. At times reading like an anthropologist's record or compilation of documents, the writing describes the Kesh people, who live in present-day northern California in a future where society as it is known today has vanished.

More than forty years have passed since the Wine Art peoples had travelled south to the lands where cotton is grown. A trip south is deemed necessary to sort out why they have begun to receive poor quality cotton and sleazy (flimsy) woven textiles in exchange for their good-quality wines. After days of negotiation it becomes apparent that environmental catastrophes have plagued the recent cotton crops: a cotton leaf virus mutation, drought and earthquakes have made some of the land too saline for the cotton crop. After days of negotiation, the trip concludes with a newfound sense of understanding generated through community dialogue: 'They are not unreasonable people, except in making little paths everywhere and being ashamed to admit they have had troubles.'

The Trouble with the Cotton People

Ursula K. Le Guin

When I was a young man there was trouble with the people who send us cotton from the South in trade for our wines. We were putting good wines on the train to Sed every spring and autumn, clear Ganais and dark Berrena, Mes from Ounmalin, and the Sweet Betebbes they like down there, all good wines, selected because they travel well, and shipped in the best oak casks. But they had begun sending us short-staple, seedy cotton, full of tares, in short-weight bales. Then one year they sent half in bales and the rest stuff already woven – some of it fair sheeting weight, but some of it sleazy, or worse.

That year was the first I went to Sed, with my teacher in the Cloth Art, Soaring of the Obsidian of Kastoha-na. We went down with the wine and stayed at the inn at Sed, a wonderful place for seafood and general comfort. She and the Wine Art people had an argument with the foreigners, but it got nowhere, because the people who had brought the cotton to Sed said they were just middlemen – they hadn't sent the lousy cotton, they just loaded and unloaded it and sailed the ships that carried it and took the wine back South. The only person there, they said, who was actually from the cotton people, wasn't able to speak any language anybody else spoke. Soaring dragged him over to the Sed Exchange, but he acted as if he'd never heard of TOK; and when she tried to get a message through the Exchange to the place the cotton came from, nobody answered.

The Wine Art people were glad she was there, since they would have taken the sleazy without question and sent all the good wine they had brought in return. She advised them to send two-thirds the usual shipment, and no Sweet Betebbes in it at all, and to take the rest back home and wait to hear from the cotton people. She refused to load the sleazy stuff onto the train, so they put it back into the ships. The ship people said they didn't care, so long as they got their usual share of the wine from us for doing the shipping. Soaring wanted to cut that amount, too, to induce the ship people to pay attention to the quality of their cargo; but the other Valley traders said that was unfair, or unwise; so we gave the sailors a half-carload, as usual – all Sweet Betebbes.

When we came home there was discussion among the Cloth and Wine Arts and the Finders Lodge and the councils and the interested people of several towns, and some of us said: "Nobody from the Valley has been to that place where the cotton comes from for forty or fifty years. Maybe some people from here should go there, and talk with those people." The others agreed with that.

So after waiting awhile to see if the cotton people would send a message on the Exchange when they got their sleazy back and less wine than usual, we set out, four of us: myself, because I wanted to go, and knew something about cotton and fabrics; and three Finders Lodge people, two who had done a lot of trading and had been across the Inland Sea more than once, and one who wanted to keep up the Finders' maps of places we were going. They were named Patience, Peregrine, and Gold. We were all men and all young. I was the youngest.

[…]

The cotton people call themselves Usudegd. There are a lot of them, some thousands, living on the islands and at places on the coast where rivers come down from the mountains – they have saltwater everywhere, but not much fresh. The sea is warm there, and it's warm country, though nothing like so hot, they say, as across those desolate mountains on the shores of the Omorn Sea. There are some severely poisoned areas in their country, but since it's so dry the stuff stays put in the ground, and they know where not to go.

[…]

Their sacred places are some distance outside the towns, and are artificial mountains, hillocks with ritual paths round and round them, and beautiful small buildings or enclosures on top. We didn't mess with any of that. Patience said it was best to keep clear out of foreigners' sacred places until invited into them.

[…]

But the cotton people were already testy. Although they hadn't replied or sent any message on the Exchange, they were angry that we had sent back their woven goods and hadn't sent the usual amount of wine, and right away we were in trouble there. All we had to do was say we had come from the Valley of the Na and the hornets began to buzz.

[…]

We passed many large islands, and the cotton people kept pointing and saying, "Cotton, cotton. See the cotton? Everybody knows we grow the best cotton. People as far north as Crater Lake know it! Look at that cotton," and so on. The cotton fields were not very impressive at that time of year, but we nodded and smiled and behaved with admiration and propriety, agreeing with everything they said.

[…]

We had been travelling all that day and thirty days before it, and it was sunset by the time we landed on this island, but they hardly stopped to give us dinner before they took us straight into the town council meeting. And there they hardly said anything polite or appropriate about our having come all that way to talk with them before they started saying "Where's the Sweet Betebbes?" and "Why did you send the goods back? Do we not have an agreement, made sixty years ago? Every year since then it has been honored and renewed, until this year! Why have you of the Wally broken your word?" They spoke good TOK, but they always said Wally for Valley, and whine for wine.

Patience knew what he was doing when he took his middle name. He listened to them endlessly and remained alert, yet never frowned, or nodded, or shook his head. Peregrine, Gold, and I imitated him as well as we could.

After a great many of them had said their say, a little woman stood up, and a little man beside her. They both had twisted bodies and humped backs, and looked both young and old. One of them said, "Let our guests have a word now," and the other said, "Let the Whine People speak." They had authority, those little twins. The others all shut up like clams.

Patience let there be silence for some while before he spoke, and when he spoke his voice was grave and soft, so that they had to stay quiet to hear what he said. He was cautious and polite. He said a lot about the fitness of the agreement and its admirable age and convenience, and the unsurpassed quality of Usudegd cotton, known to be the best cotton from Crater Lake to the Omorn Break, from the Ocean Coast to the Range of Heaven – he got fairly eloquent in there – and then he quieted down again and spoke a little sadly about how Time blunts the keenest knife and changes the meaning of words and the thoughts in human minds, so that finally the firmest knot must be retied, and the sincerest word spoken once again. And then he sat down.

There was silence. I thought he had awakened reason in them and they would agree at once. I was very young. The same woman who had talked the most before, got up and said, "Why didn't you send forty barrels of Sweet Betebbes whine like always before?"

I saw that the difficult part was only beginning. Patience had to answer that question and also say why we had sent back their woven goods. For a long time he didn't. He kept talking in metaphors and images, and skirting around the issues; and after a while the little twisty twins began answering him in the same way.

[…]

It went on like that for three more days. Even Patience said he hadn't expected them to go on arguing, and that probably the reason they argued so much was that they were ashamed of something. If so, it was our part not to shame them further. So we could not say anything about the poor quality of the raw cotton for the last several years, or even about the sleazy they had tried to foist off on us. We just stayed calm and sad and said that indeed we regretted not shipping the sweet wine which we grew especially for them, but said nothing about why we had not shipped it. And sure enough, little by little it came out that they had had a lot of bad things happen in the last five years: a cotton leaf virus mutation that was hard to control, and three years of drought, and a set of unusually severe earthquakes that had drowned some of their islands and left the water on others too saline even for their hardy cotton. All these things they seemed to consider their own fault, things to be ashamed of. "We have walked in the wrong paths!" they kept saying.

[…]

When we got down to it at last, it was very simple. The terms were about the same as they had been, with more room for negotiation each year through the Exchange. Nothing was said about why they hadn't used the Exchange to explain their behavior earlier.

[…]

After speaking the contract, we stayed on nine days more, for politeness, and because Patience and the twins were drinking together.

[…]

I generally hung around with some young women who were weavers there. They had some fine mechanical looms, solar-powered, that I made notes on for my teacher Soaring, and also they were kind and friendly. Patience warned me that it's better not to have a relation of sex with people in foreign countries until you know a good deal about their customs and expectations concerning commitment, marriage, contraception, techniques, and so on. So I just flirted and did some kissing. The cotton women kissed with their mouths wide open, which is surprising if you aren't expecting it, and disagreeably wet, but very voluptuous; which was trying under the circumstances.

[…]

Since we went down there, there hasn't been any more trouble with the cotton people, and they have always sent us good, long-staple cotton. They are not unreasonable people, except in making little paths everywhere and being ashamed to admit they have had troubles.

FURTHER READING: COMMUNITY

Carden, Siún. 'Cable Crossings: The Aran Jumper as Myth and Merchandise', *Costume* 48, no. 2 (2014): 260–75.

The Aran jumper and the myths it continues to carry both within and beyond Ireland are set against an acknowledgement of the emotional role of this particular textile, particularly in the contexts of migration, the diaspora and tourism industry.

Checinska, Christine. 'Christine Checinska in Conversation with Althea McNish and John Weiss', *TEXTILE* 16, no. 2 (2018): 186–99, doi:10.1080/147597 56.2018.1432183.

Transcript of a 2015 conversation in London with the artist/writer/curator Christine Checinska, textile designer Althea McNish (1924–2020) and McNish's husband, the jewellery designer John Weiss (1933–2018).

Katz, Anna. *With Pleasure: Pattern and Decoration in American Art 1972–1985*, New Haven: Yale University Press, 2019.

Publication accompanied an exhibition of the same name charting works of painting, sculpture, collage, ceramics, installation and performance art in the United States typified by enthusiasm for aesthetics often considered and derided for being feminine, domestic, ornamental, or craft.

Kincaid, Jamaica. 'Girl', in *At the Bottom of the River*, London: Pan Books Ltd., 1978: 3–5.

Written in a three-page chain of instructions, Kincaid's voice is directed to a young woman as a list of expectations punctuated with semicolons. Each statement offers a rule of how to properly care for others, from the washing of clothes to cooking. The repeated admonishment of becoming a slut is set in the final lines against an image of a woman who knows her own allure.

Nettleton, Anitra. 'Crossing the Chest: Bandoliers with and Without Bullets in Imaging the "Zulu"', *Southern African Humanities* 30 (December 2017): 125–43.

Nettleton has undertaken extensive research into the beadwork of southern Africa. This article focuses on bandoliers worn across the torso that can be used to store and carry bullets but have become fashion. This article begins with an image dated to the Anglo-Zulu War of 1879 and ends with examples of contemporary use.

Parker, Rozsika. *The Subversive Stitch: Embroidery and the Making of the Feminine*, London: I.B. Tauris, 2010.

In the book's new introduction, Parker (1945–2010) laments the lack of progress feminism and embroidery have made since the book's first publication in 1984. The book was considered ground breaking at the time of publication and inspired Pennina Barnett's curatorial work with the theme in 1988.

Pastoureau, Michel and Jody Gladding (trans.). *The Devil's Cloth: A History of Stripes*, London: Washing Square Press and Columbia University Press, 2001.

Originally written in French, this very small book considers textiles that contain stripes and their associations. Starting with examples from the 13th century onwards examples range from coats of arms to prison uniforms, often acknowledging the pejorative associations of striped clothing.

Roberts, Lacey Jane. 'Put Your Thing Down, Flip It, and Reverse It: Reimagining Craft Identities Using Tactics of Queer Theory', in *Extra/Ordinary: Craft and Contemporary Art*, ed. Maria Elena Buszek, 243–259, Durham and London: Duke University Press, 2011.

Opening with the observation that contemporary craft is often explained as experiencing an identity crisis, Roberts argues for the usefulness of queer theory when considering contemporary craft. The writing then literally moves to consider textile practices by several American queer artists.

Scheerbart, Paul. *The Gray Cloth: A Novel on Glass Architecture*, trans. John A. Stuart, London: The MIT Press, 2003.

A novella about a newlywed Swiss couple, Edgar and Clara Krug, who travel the world in a hot air balloon to check on the progress of Edgar's glass architecture projects. Edgar stipulates his wife can only wear gray (and 10% white) for the benefit of his colourful architecture. First published in 1914 by German architect who wrote numerous texts about glass architecture.

Styles, John. *Threads of Feeling: The London Foundling Hospital's Textile Tokens 1740–1770*, Shaftesbury, Blackmore Ltd, 2010.

Illustrated exhibition catalogue reveals the textiles mothers left (cut either from their own clothes or the child's) as identification at London's Foundling Hospital which, between 1741 and 1760, received more than 4,000 babies.

Twigger-Holroyd, Amy and Emma Shercliff, 'Stitching Together: Good Practice Guidelines', https://stitchingtogether.net/good-practice-guidelines/.

How-to style booklet based on work by the Stitching Together network that offers clear steps and further resources for participatory textile projects. The publication provides advice from how to begin a participatory project, through to reflection and dissemination.

CONTRIBUTORS

Sophia Abasheva is a Russian translator and interpreter specializing in the fields of arts and humanities. She holds a master's degree in Art History from the European University at Saint Petersburg and a specialist's degree in Translation Science from Perm State University. She is a regular collaborator with the *Russian Fashion Theory* journal and book series at New Literary Observer Publishing House.

Yosi Anaya, PhD, is research-docent, based at the Instituto de Artes Plásticas of Universidad Veracruzana in Mexico, and has lectured widely on crossovers between textile traditions and the visual arts. She has curated diverse exhibitions and authored publications, including *La Magia de los Hilos: arte y tradición del textil indígena de Veracruz* (Universidad Veracruzana 1995 & Editora de Gobierno del Estado, Veracruz 2008). As a practicing artist, she produces installations, mixed-media, textiles and video works. Her main concerns center on the historic gaze toward Mesoamerican women, the effects of time and light in the land and lived experience.

American curator **Elissa Auther** is Deputy Director of Curatorial Affairs and the William and Mildred Lasden Chief Curator at the Museum of Arts and Design, New York. Her exhibitions include *Vera Paints a Scarf: The Art and Design of Vera Neumann* (2019) and *Queer Maximalism X Machine Dazzle* (2022).

Pennina Barnett is a British curator and writer. She is founding co-editor of the journal *Textile, Cloth and Culture* (Taylor & Francis). Her earlier (co)curatorial projects include: *Craft Matters: 3 attitudes to contemporary craft*, John Hansard Gallery, Southampton (1985); *The Subversive Stitch: Women and Textiles Today*, Cornerhouse, Manchester (1988); *Under Construction*, Crafts Council, London (1996); and *Textures of Memory: the poetics of cloth*, Pitzhanger Manor House and Gallery, London/Angel Row, Nottingham (1999), all UK touring exhibitions; and the international symposium 'The Subversive Stitch Revisited: The Politics of Cloth', V&A, London (2013). She was Senior Lecturer in the Department of Art, Goldsmiths, University of London (1989–2011) where she led Critical Studies on undergraduate Textiles. She has published widely on the work of artist Chohreh Feyzdjou, and her current work focuses on cloth, memory, loss and repair.

Susan S. Bean is an independent American scholar whose work focuses on the visual arts and culture of modern southern Asia. She was senior curator for South Asian and Korean art at the Peabody Essex Museum until her retirement in 2012 and previously taught anthropology at Yale University. Currently she chairs the Art & Archaeology Center of the American Institute of Indian Studies and is an associate of the Peabody Museum at Harvard University. Her explorations into cloth in southern Asia include the traveling exhibition and accompanying book, *From the Land of the Thunder Dragon: Textile Arts of Bhutan* (1994), with Diana Myers, as well as essays on the American textile trade with India, and Mahatma Gandhi's deployment of hand spinning and wearing homespun cloth as instruments to achieve Indian independence.

Philip Beesley is a multidisciplinary Canadian artist and architect. Beesley's research is recognized for its pioneering contributions to the rapidly emerging field of responsive interactive architecture. He directs the Living Architecture Systems Group (LASG) and is a professor at the School of Architecture at the University of Waterloo and the European Graduate School. His work has been featured twice at the Venice Biennale of Architecture: *Hylozoic Ground* (2010) and *Grove* (2021).

The Croatian textile artist and weaver **Otti Berger** (1898–1944) was a student and later teacher at the Bauhaus in Dessau, Germany. Along with Anni Albers and Gunta Stölzl, Berger made a significant contribution to the development of textile scholarship through her woven textile designs and writing. Her life ended in Auschwitz concentration camp.

Boatema Boateng was born in Ghana and is Associate Professor in the Department of Communication, University of California, San Diego. She has published several articles and book chapters on the political and cultural dimensions of intellectual property (IP) law, with a focus on the relation between IP and local and indigenous forms of knowledge and culture including the adinkra and kente fabrics of the Asante people of Ghana. Her book, *The Copyright Thing Doesn't Work Here: Adinkra, Kente Cloth and Intellectual Property in Ghana*, was published by the University of Minnesota Press (2011).

American art historian **Julia Bryan-Wilson**'s book, *FRAY: Art and Textile Politics* (2017), won the ASAP Book Prize, the Frank Jewett Mather Award, and the Robert Motherwell Award. Her curatorial credits include solo exhibitions of Louise Nevelson and Cecilia Vicuña, as well as group shows at the Museu de Arte de São Paulo, where she is an Adjunct Curator. In 2022 she became the first Professor of LGBTQ Art History at Columbia University.

British academic **Ele Carpenter** is a Professor and the Director of the UmArts Research Centre for Architecture, Art and Design at Umeå University, Sweden. She is convenor of the international Nuclear Culture Research Group; a member of the AHRC Research Network for Nuclear Cultural Heritage in partnership with the University of Kingston, England, and Linköping University, Sweden; and Visiting Research Fellow, Institute of the Arts, University of Cumbria, UK. She regularly advises on the inclusion of radioactive materials in contemporary artworks, and in 2019 she was awarded her Radiation Protection Supervisor Certificate.

Arthur C. Danto (1924–2013) was Johnsonian Professor Emeritus of Philosophy at Columbia University, where he worked from 1951. The American scholar authored numerous books, including *Nietzsche as Philosopher*, *Mysticism and Morality*, *The Transfiguration of the Commonplace*, *Narration and Knowledge*, *Connections to the World: The Basic Concepts of Philosophy*, *Encounters and Reflections: Art in the Historical Present*, a collection of art criticism that won the National Book Critics Circle Prize for Criticism (1990) and *Embodied Meanings: Critical Essays and Aesthetic Mediations*.

The French philosopher **Gilles Deleuze** (1925–1995) studied at the Sorbonne from 1944 to 1948. His first book, *Empiricism and Subjectivity*, was published in 1953 followed by the publication of his doctoral thesis *Différence et répétition* in 1968, which had a significant impact on the discipline of philosophy. He met Félix Guattari in the early 1970s and with him co-wrote a number of influential texts including *Capitalism and Schizophrenia*, published in two volumes as *Anti-Oedipus* (1972) and *A Thousand Plateaus* (1980).

British academic **Lorna Dillon** is a Research Fellow at the University of Cambridge. Her research is on the intersection of Latin American art history and cultural studies. Lorna has published two books on the Chilean artist Violeta Parra.

Isak Dinesen (1885–1962) is the pseudonym of the Danish author Baroness Karen von Blixen-Finecke. Blixen's well-known writings include *Out of Africa* and *Babette's Feast*, both adapted into acclaimed films, and her collection of short stories, *Seven Gothic Tales*. Blixen lived from 1914 to 1931 in Kenya, an experience that forms the basis of *Out of Africa*.

In 1951 **Ealing Studios** released what has been described as a science fiction comedy: *The Man in the White Suit*. Directed by Alexander Mackendrick, the film was nominated for an Academy Award for Best Writing (screenplay) for Roger MacDougall, John Dighton and Alexander Mackendrick. Ealing Studios is based in London and opened in 1902.

Rebecca Earley is a British design researcher and research team leader at University of the Arts London. She is based at Chelsea College of Arts where she is a Professor and Co-Director of the Centre for Circular Design (CCD). In October 2021 she co-founded *World Circular Textiles Day 2050* with a team of collaborators to create clear roadmaps for circular textiles by drawing together current academic and industry research.

American novelist **James Fenimore Cooper** (1789–1851) was born in New Jersey. The four novels that make up *The Leatherstocking Tales* include his most well-known book *The Last of the Mohicans*. While Cooper's writing continues to be enjoyed today, his depictions of American Indians are now considered highly romanticized. Cooper attended Yale University for several years before being asked to leave, it is believed, after a series of campus pranks.

Maria Fusco is a Belfast-born working class writer. She works across the registers of critical, fictional and performance writing. Her work is translated into twelve languages. She holds a personal Chair in Interdisciplinary Writing at the University of Dundee, Scotland, and was Director of Art Writing at Goldsmiths, University of London.

Born in Kent, England, **Jools Gilson** is Professor of Creative Practice at University College Cork, Ireland. Her 2005 work *The Knitting Map* is the subject of *Textiles, Community & Controversy*, published by Bloomsbury (2019). She was a 2021 Fulbright Scholar at the University of Colorado Boulder where she developed her project *Tempestries: Textiles, Tactility & the Climate Emergency*.

British researcher **Kate Goldsworthy** is a Professor and Chair of Circular Design & Innovation and Co-Director of the Centre for Circular Design, based at Chelsea College of Arts. Her core interests are designing for sustainability, the circular economy and material innovation within textile and fashion contexts.

Isabel González-Arango is a Colombian anthropologist and embroiderer. She holds a Masters in Information Sciences with an emphasis on memory and society, is a specialist in Human Rights and International Humanitarian Law and a professor and researcher at the Institute of Regional Studies of the University of Antioquia. Research interests interweave the recovery and reconstruction of memory, human rights archives and the exploration of artisanal textile practices as narrative, testimony and pedagogy.

Sabrina Gschwandtner's artwork – comprised of film, video, photography, and textiles – has been exhibited internationally at museums including the Smithsonian American Art Museum, the V&A Museum, the Museum of Arts and Design, Los Angeles County Museum of Art (LACMA) and Crystal Bridges Museum of Art, among many others. The American artist's work is held in the permanent collections of LACMA, the Smithsonian American Art Museum; Museum of Fine Arts, Boston; the RISD Museum; the Mint Museum; the Philbrook

Museum; and the Carl and Marilynn Thoma Art Foundation, among other public collections worldwide. She has lectured extensively on feminism, handcraft, film and textiles.

French philosopher and psychotherapist **Félix Guattari** (1930–1992) trained with the psychoanalyst Jacques Lacan and worked at the experimental La Borde clinic in France. He founded a number of organizations during his lifetime, including, early in his career, the Association of Institutional Psychotherapy, and later the fr:CEFRI (Centre for the Study and Research of Institutional Formation). Guattari's final collaboration with Gilles Deleuze, *What is Philosophy?*, was published in 1991. Posthumous publications include a 1996 collection of essays, *Soft Subversions*.

American author **Ursula K. Le Guin** (1929–2018) wrote over twenty novels and one hundred short stories during her prolific writing career. Often described as an author of science fiction, her writing has proved influential to the broad field of speculative fiction.

Catherine Harper, PhD, is a Professor and Deputy Vice-Chancellor at University for the Creative Arts and has held senior academic leadership positions at large multi-faculty and specialist institutions. A visual artist before turning to creative writing, she has recently returned to material as well as textual practice to examine her identity as part of the Northern Irish feminist diaspora and her creative obsession with the body's stains on cloth, land, memory and culture.

After graduation from Bowdoin College, the American author **Nathaniel Hawthorne** (1804–1864) turned his attention to writing. His early works include the short stories 'My Kinsman, Major Molineux', 'Roger Malvin's Burial' and 'Young Goodman Brown'. His most famous work, *The Scarlet Letter*, was completed in 1850. Further novels include *The House of Seven Gables*, *The Blithedale Romance* and *The Marble Faun*. He died in New Hampshire and *The Dolliver Romance*, along with a number of other works, was published posthumously.

After working as an editor in London, in 1977, **Roger Hutchinson** joined the *West Highland Free Press* in Skye. He has written for BBC Radio, the *Scotsman*, *Guardian*, *Herald* and *The Literary Review*. His numerous non-fiction books include *Polly: the True Story behind Whisky Galore*; *The Soap Man: Lewis, Harris and Lord Leverhulme* (shortlisted for the Saltire Scottish Book of the Year); *Calum's Road* (shortlisted for the Royal Society of Literature's Ondaatje Prize); and *The Butcher, the Baker, the Candlestick Maker: The story of Britain through its Census, since 1801*.

British academic **Elaine Igoe**, PhD, is a Senior Lecturer in Textile Design at Chelsea College of Arts, University of the Arts London and is Departmental Research Degree Coordinator in the School of Art, Design and Performance at the University of Portsmouth. Elaine's academic research has made a key contribution to critical thinking and design theory in the fields of textiles and materials.

Pamela Johnson is a British novelist, poet, former tutor in creative writing, Goldsmiths, University of London; she has also published critical writing on art textiles and curated UK touring exhibitions.

Galina Kareva is a Russian historian and the Head of the Ivanovo Calico Museum (Ivanovo). She is a curator and author of articles on the history of the Ivanovo industrial region and textile industry. Galina Kareva is one of the co-authors of the publication *100% Ivanovo. Agitprop Textiles of the 1920–1930s from the Collection of the Ivanovo State Museum of History and Local Lore*. She is a laureate of the Zabelin State Award for scientific research.

Sarat Maharaj was born and educated in Apartheid South Africa and in the UK. From 1980 to 2005 he was Professor of History & Theory of Art at Goldsmiths, University of London, and is currently Professor of Visual Art & Knowledge Systems, Lund University and the Malmö Art Academies, Sweden. He was the first Rudolf Arnheim Professor, Humbolt University, Berlin (2001–02) and Research Fellow at the Jan Van Eycke Akademie, Maastricht (1999–2001). His research interests include publications on a range of topics from Marcel Duchamp, James Joyce, and Richard Hamilton as well as writing on themes such as 'Visual Art as Knowledge Production & Non-Knowledge' and 'Textiles, Cultural Translation and Difference'.

Joseph McBrinn is an Irish art and design historian. He is Reader at Belfast School of Art, Ulster University in Northern Ireland and has published and lectured widely on Irish art and design history as well as on the intersecting histories of gender, sexuality and disability.

Melanie Miller is a British lecturer, curator, writer and maker: issues of gender stereotyping, globalization and branding are explored in Miller's practice. She taught at the Manchester School of Art for twenty years on the BA (Hons) Embroidery program and the MA Textiles program. Melanie's area of specialism is machine embroidery: she completed her PhD on this subject in 1997 and has co-curated exhibitions around this theme, notably *Mechanical drawing – the Schiffli project* with June Hill (2007).

Victoria Mitchell is a Research Fellow at Norwich University of the Arts, UK, where she was previously Senior Lecturer for Contextual Studies and course leader for MA Textile Culture. She has researched and published papers on various aspects of textile culture, pursuing a broad, interdisciplinary approach focusing on material, making, metaphor and meaning. She is co-editor (with Stephanie Bunn, St. Andrews) of *The Material Culture of Basketry* (Bloomsbury) and (with Sarah Horton, NUA) of *Pattern and Chaos: Making and Meaning* (Intellect).

Birgitta Nordström is a Swedish textile artist and doctoral candidate at HDK-Valand, Academy of Art and Design, University of Gothenburg, Sweden. Since 1995 she has been exhibiting nationally and internationally in Europe, Australia, Russia and the United States. Her art practice and research focus on ritual textiles and investigate the textile as an object that can help to confront, and hold, death.

Marit Paasche holds a PhD in Art History and works as an independent scholar, writer and critic. The Norwegian is author of *Hannah Ryggen: Threads of Defiance* (Thames & Hudson and University of Chicago Press, 2019), among several other books.

American **Charlotte Perkins Gilman** (1860–1935) was a lecturer, feminist and social reformer. She penned numerous works of fiction and nonfiction during her life, many focusing on the role of women in society. Gilman attended the Rhode Island School of Design and in 1884 married Charles Walter Stetson. The couple had one child. Gilman moved to California after treatment for what may today be diagnosed as postpartum depression, separating from her husband and daughter. Her 1898 book *Women and Economics: A Study of the Economic Relation Between Men and Women as a Factor in Social Relations* enjoyed critical acclaim. Alongside further books she published *The Forerunner* (1909–1916), a monthly journal.

British curator **Sue Prichard** is Head Curator at Leeds Castle, Kent, UK. From 2016 to 2021, she was Senior Curator: Arts at Royal Museums Greenwich. She was previously Curator: Modern and Contemporary Textiles at the V&A. Her recent publications include *Flagwaves: House Flags from the National Maritime Museum* and *Nelson's Trafalgar Coat: An Illustrated Guide*.

Sadie Plant is a British author and philosopher. She earned her PhD from the University of Manchester in 1989 and was later associated with the Cybernetic Culture Research Unit at the University of Warwick, UK. Her acclaimed book *Zeroes + Ones: Digital Women + The New Technoculture* was published in 1997. She now teaches at the HKB (Bern Academy of the Arts) in Switzerland.

Kay Politowicz is Professor Emeritus at the University of the Arts London. She has been engaged in practice led research since 1996, when she co-founded the Textile Environment Design (TED) research group at Chelsea College of Arts (UAL). Her focus is the design challenge of transforming material cycles into innovative, sustainable product loops.

Sarah Rhodes is a British designer and researcher with an interdisciplinary background in design for social innovation within global higher education and international development sectors. She designs participatory and co-design processes to support complex multi-partner programs leading to inclusive social and business innovation. Sarah's PhD at Central Saint Martins, University of the Arts London, interrogated the designer's role in the Global South.

The American artist **Faith Ringgold** was born in Harlem, New York, in 1930. Her career now spans more than five decades as a painter, mixed media sculptor, performance artist, writer, teacher and lecturer. She received her B.S. and M.A. degrees in visual art from the City College of New York in 1955 and 1959. Professor Emeritus of Art at the University of California San Diego, Ringgold has received twenty-three Honorary Doctorates.

American conservator **Sarah Scaturro** is the Eric and Jane Nord Chief Conservator at the Cleveland Museum of Art. She previously was the Head Conservator of the Costume Institute at the Metropolitan Museum of Art and the Textile Conservator and Assistant Fashion Curator at Cooper-Hewitt, Smithsonian Design Museum. She has an MA in Fashion and Textile Studies from the Fashion Institute of Technology and an MPhil from the Bard Graduate Center, where she is a doctoral candidate.

Gottfried Semper (1803–1879) was a German architect, art critic and professor of architecture. Between 1838 and 1841 he designed and built the Semper Opera House in Dresden. His extensive writing on architecture includes *The Four Elements of Architecture* published in 1851.

Rose Sinclair is a British Design Lecturer (Textiles) at Goldsmiths, London, teaching textiles/fashion and Design-related practice at the Postgraduate level. Her current research focuses on Black women and their crafting practices, and has included community-based textile work in museums such as V&A and Timespan. Current exhibitions include co-curator of *Althea McNish: Colour is Mine*. Rose is co-editor of the *Journal Of Textile Research and Practice*.

American **T'ai Smith** is Associate Professor in Art History, Visual Art and Theory at the University of British Columbia, Canada. Author of *Bauhaus Weaving Theory: From Feminine Craft to Mode of Design* (University of Minnesota Press, 2014), she has published and lectured internationally on textiles, contemporary art and media theory. Her articles have appeared in *Art Journal, Grey Room, Leonardo, Texte zur Kunst* and *Zeitschrift für Medien- und Kulturforschung*, and in numerous edited volumes and museum catalogues.

American **Jenni Sorkin** is Professor of the History of Art & Architecture, University of California, Santa Barbara. She writes on the intersections between gender, material culture and contemporary art, working primarily on women artists and underrepresented media. Her books include *Live Form: Women, Ceramics, and Community* (University of Chicago, 2016), *Revolution in the Making: Abstract Sculpture by Women, 1947-2016* (Skira, 2016) and *Art in California* (Thames & Hudson, 2021), as well as numerous essays in journals, museum and exhibition catalogs.

Takahashi Mizuki is a Japanese curator and the current Executive Director and Chief Curator of the Centre for Heritage, Arts and Textile in Hong Kong. After serving as a founding curatorial member at Mori Art Museum in Tokyo (1999–2003), Takahashi worked as senior curator at the Contemporary Art Center, Art Tower Mito and realized numerous transdisciplinary exhibitions addressing various artistic forms including manga, film, fashion, architecture, performance and contemporary art. She curates, writes and gives lectures extensively in Asia and Europe.

Alice Walker is an American poet, short story writer, novelist, essayist, anthologist, teacher, editor, publisher, womanist and activist. She graduated from Sarah Lawrence College in 1965. Her first novel, *The Third Life of Grange Copeland*, was published in 1970, followed by *Meridian* in 1976. She was awarded the Pulitzer Prize for Fiction for her 1983 novel *The Color Purple*, made into a film by Steven Spielberg in 1985. Her collections of short stories include *You Can't Keep a Good Woman Down* (1981), *Alice Walker: The Complete Stories* (1994) and *The Way Forward Is with a Broken Heart* (2000). She is also author of a number of works of nonfiction, including her celebrated essay 'In Search of Our Mothers' Gardens' (1983).

Catherine de Zegher is a Belgian international curator who organized many acclaimed modern and contemporary art exhibitions, such as *America: Bride of the Sun - 500 Years of Latin America and the Low Countries*; *Inside the Visible: An Elliptical Traverse of Twentieth-Century Art in, of, and from the Feminine* (ICA Boston/MIT Press); and *On Line: Drawing through the Twentieth Century* (MoMA, NY). As the author and editor of numerous books, she most recently published *Women's Work Is Never Done*, an anthology of her essays on the work of women artists.

INDEX